T0202979

Lecture Notes in Computer Science 12009

More information about this series at http://www.springer.com/series/7412

Mihaela Pop · Maxime Sermesant ·
Oscar Camara · Xiahai Zhuang · Shuo Li ·
Alistair Young · Tommaso Mansi ·
Avan Suinesiaputra (Eds.)

Statistical Atlases and Computational Models of the Heart

Multi-Sequence CMR Segmentation,
CRT-EPiggy and LV Full Quantification Challenges

10th International Workshop, STACOM 2019
Held in Conjunction with MICCAI 2019
Shenzhen, China, October 13, 2019
Revised Selected Papers

 Springer

Editors
Mihaela Pop
University of Toronto
Toronto, ON, Canada

Maxime Sermesant
Inria
Sophia Antipolis, France

Oscar Camara
Pompeu Fabra University
Barcelona, Spain

Xiahai Zhuang
Fudan University
Shanghai, China

Shuo Li
St Joseph's Health Care
London, ON, Canada

Alistair Young
King's College London
London, UK

Tommaso Mansi
Siemens Medical Solutions USA, Inc.
Princeton, NJ, USA

Avan Suinesiaputra
University of Auckland
Auckland, New Zealand

ISSN 0302-9743   ISSN 1611-3349   (electronic)
Lecture Notes in Computer Science
ISBN 978-3-030-39073-0   ISBN 978-3-030-39074-7   (eBook)
https://doi.org/10.1007/978-3-030-39074-7

LNCS Sublibrary: SL6 – Image Processing, Computer Vision, Pattern Recognition, and Graphics

This Springer imprint is published by the registered company Springer Nature Switzerland AG
The registered company address is: Gewerbestrasse 11, 6330 Cham, Switzerland

Preface

Integrative models of cardiac function are important for understanding disease, evaluating treatment, and planning intervention. In recent years, there has been considerable progress in cardiac image analysis techniques, cardiac atlases, and computational models, which can integrate data from large-scale databases of heart shape, function, and physiology. However, significant clinical translation of these tools is constrained by the lack of complete and rigorous technical and clinical validation, as well as benchmarking of the developed tools. For doing so, common and available ground-truth data capturing generic knowledge on the healthy and pathological heart is required. Several efforts have been established to provide web-accessible structural and functional atlases of the normal and pathological heart for clinical, research, and educational purposes. We believe that these approaches will only be effectively developed through collaboration across the full research scope of the cardiac imaging and modeling communities.

The 10th edition of the Statistical Atlases and Computational Modelling of the Heart workshop, STACOM 2019 (http://stacom2019.cardiacatlas.org), was held in conjunction with the MICCAI 2019 international conference (Shenzhen, China), following the past nine editions: STACOM 2010 (Beijing, China), STACOM 2011 (Toronto, Canada), STACOM 2012 (Nice, France), STACOM 2013 (Nagoya, Japan), STACOM 2014 (Boston, USA), STACOM 2015 (Munich, Germany), STACOM 2016 (Athens, Greece), STACOM 2017 (Quebec City, Canada), and STACOM 2018 (Granada, Spain). STACOM 2019 provided a forum to discuss the latest developments in various areas of computational imaging and modeling of the heart, as well as statistical cardiac atlases.

The topics of this 10th anniversary edition of the STACOM workshop included: cardiac imaging and image processing, machine learning applied to cardiac imaging and image analysis, atlas construction, statistical modeling of cardiac function across different patient populations, cardiac computational physiology, model customization, atlas based functional analysis, ontological schemata for data and results, integrated functional and structural analyzes, as well as the pre-clinical and clinical applicability of these methods. Besides regular contributing papers, additional efforts of the STACOM 2019 workshop were also focused on three challenges: Multi-Sequence Cardiac MR Segmentation Challenge; Cardiac Resynchronization Therapy CRT-EPiggy Electrophysiology Modelling Challenge; and Left Ventricle Full Quantification Challenge. These challenges are described more in detail below.

From an initial submission of 76 papers (regular and challenges), 44 papers were accepted for presentation at the workshop and 42 papers were invited for publication in this LNCS proceedings volume.

MS-CMR Seg Challenge 2019 (Multi-Sequence Cardiac MR Segmentation Challenge): Accurate computing, analysis, and modeling of the ventricle and myocardium from medical images is important, especially in the diagnosis and treatment management for patients suffering from myocardial infarction (MI). Late gadolinium enhancement cardiac magnetic resonance (LGE CMR) image is an important means to visualize MI, appearing with distinctive brightness compared with the health tissues. It is widely used to study the presence, location, and extent of MI. Before the analysis of MI, accurate segmentation of myocardium is required. However, automating this segmentation remains challenging due to the indistinguishable boundaries, heterogeneous intensity, and complex enhancement patterns of pathological myocardium from LGE CMR. Combing the complementary information of multi-sequence CMR from the same patient can assist the myocardial segmentation.

MS-CMR Seg Challenge 2019 provided an open and fair competition for various research groups to test and validate their methods, particularly for the ventricle and myocardium segmentation. The aim of the challenge was not only to benchmark various segmentation algorithms, but also to cover the topic of general cardiac image segmentation, registration, and modeling, and to raise discussions for further technical development and clinical deployment. The challenge received great interest from participants all over the world and the proposed methods have achieved substantial methodological innovations and significant performance improvement. The organizers aim at keeping the MS-CMR Seg Challenge as a long-term event for participants who were not be able to enter the competition, but are interested in further developments. Relevant information and challenge results can be found at: https://zmiclab.github.io/mscmrseg19/.

CRT-EPiggy19 Challenge: The spirit of the (not machine learning) CRT-EPiggy19 Challenge was to collectively review the current state of the art for computational cardiology models and their ability to predict pacing-based therapy outcomes, as well as the identification of the most critical phases and more promising solutions in the personalization modeling pipeline. More specifically, participants were asked to predict the electrical response of Cardiac Resynchronization Therapy (CRT) and to propose the optimal device configuration in a swine model of left bundle branch block, given fully controlled data. The unique multi-modal experimental data available in the challenge has helped to calibrate electrophysiological solvers based on different mathematical models. One key of the CRT-EPiggy19 Challenge has been to work in a collaborative way between the different participants, rather than competitively, fostering reproducible research and Open Science. Preliminary results from five international participant teams were presented during the STACOM 2019 workshop on the available data. Additionally, some lessons learned from the organization of a Biophysical Modelling Challenge and suggestions for joint initiatives between medical data science and physiological modeling communities were summarized. More information can be found here: http://crt-epiggy19.surge.sh/.

The Left Ventricle Full Quantification Challenge (LVQuan19): LVQuan19 aimed to promote effective machine learning models for efficiently assessing the heart's function. LVQuan19 provided original cardiac MRI data without preprocessing for training and testing phases, which is more clinical than the data providing by LVQuan18. In this challenge, the extraction of the LV's cavity and myocardium and subsequently the regression of regional wall thicknesses, LV dimensions and the classification of the phase of the cardiac cycle were to be performed. These are common and significant parameters to assess the LV function. However, in clinical routine, these are time consuming and prone to error and inter-observer variability. Here, the four revised full workshop papers were carefully reviewed and selected from five submissions. In these submissions, state-of-the-art technologies including transfer learning, statistical models, incorporated 2D+3D, and multi-task learning were developed, and the performance achieved to 106mm2, 0.9920mm, and 0.9185mm of mean absolute error for area, dimension, and regional wall thickness, as well as 6.7% of error rate for phase classification. More information can be found here: https://lvquan19.github.io/

We hope that the results obtained by the challenges, along with the regular paper contributions will act to accelerate progress in the important areas of heart function and structure analysis. A total of 48 papers (i.e., regular papers and from the 3 challenges) were accepted for oral or poster presentations at STACOM 2019. The selected papers are published in this Springer *Lecture Notes in Computer Science* (LNCS) proceedings volume.

October 2019

Mihaela Pop
Maxime Sermesant
Oscar Camara
Xiahai Zhuang
Shuo Li
Alistair Young
Tommaso Mansi
Avan Suinesiaputra
Kawal Rhode
Kristin McLeod

Organization

We would like to thank all organizers, reviewers, authors, and sponsors for their time, efforts, contributions, and support in making STACOM 2019 a successful event.

Chairs and Organizers

STACOM

Mihaela Pop   Sunnybrook, University of Toronto, Canada
Maxime Sermesant   Inria, Epione group, France
Oscar Camara   UPF Barcelona, Spain
Alistair Young   KCL, London, UK
Tommaso Mansi   Siemens, USA
Avan Suinesiaputra   University of Auckland, New Zealand
Kawal Rhode   KCL, London, UK
Kristin McLeod   GE, Norway

Multi-Sequence Cardiac MR Segmentation Challenge

Xiahai Zhuang   Fudan University, China
Lei Li   Shanghai Jiao Tong University, China
Jiahang Xu   Fudan University, China
Yuncheng Zhou   Fudan University, China
Xinzhe Luo   Fudan University, China

LV Full Quantification Challenge

Shuo Li   Digital Imaging Group, Canada
Guanyu Yang   Southeast University, China
Tiancong Hua   Southeast University, China
Wufeng Sue   Shenzhen University, China

CRT-EPiggy19

Oscar Camara   UPF Barcelona, Spain

Additional Reviewers

Nicolas Cedilnik   Buntheng Ly
Florian Mihai Itu   Viorel Mihalef
Shuman Jia   Boris Mailhe
Julian Krebs   Felix Meister
Lucian Itu   Matthew Ng

OCS - Springer Conference Submission/Publication System

Mihaela Pop   Medical Biophysics, University of Toronto, Canada
Maxime Sermesant   Inria, Epione group, France

Webmaster

Avan Suinesiaputra   University of Auckland, New Zealand

Workshop Website

stacom2019.cardiacatlas.org

Sponsors

We would also like to thank our industrial sponsors:

https://www.sensetime.com/
https://circlecvi.com/
https://www.tencent.com/zh-cn/index.html
http://www.scimedia.com/

Contents

Multi-Sequence Cardiac MR Segmentation Challenge

CRT-EPiggy19 Challenge

LV-Full Quantification Challenge

Regular Papers

Co-registered Cardiac *ex vivo* DT Images and Histological Images for Fibrosis Quantification

Peter Lin[1,2], Anne Martel[1,2], Susan Camilleri[3], and Mihaela Pop[1,2(✉)]

[1] Sunnybrook Research Institute, Toronto, Canada
mihaela.pop@utoronto.ca
[2] Medical Biophysics, University of Toronto, Toronto, Canada
[3] Lunenfeld Research Institute, Toronto, Canada

Abstract. Cardiac magnetic resonance (MR) imaging can detect infarct scar, a major cause of lethal arrhythmia and heart failure. Here, we describe a robust image processing pipeline developed to quantitatively analyze collagen density and features in a pig model of chronic fibrosis. Specifically, we use *ex vivo* diffusion tensor imaging (DTI) ($0.6 \times 0.6 \times 1.2$ mm resolution) to calculate fractional anisotropy maps in: healthy tissue, infarct core (IC) and gray zone (GZ) (i.e., a mixture of viable myocytes and collagen fibrils bordering IC and healthy zones). The 3 zones were validated using collagen-sensitive histological slides co-registered with MR images. Our results showed a significant ($p < 0.05$) reduction in the mean FA values of GZ (by 17%) and IC (by 44%) compared to healthy areas; however, we found that these differences do not depend on the location of occluded coronary artery (LAD vs LCX). This work validates the utility of DTI-MR imaging for fibrosis quantification, with histological validation.

Keywords: Myocardial infarct · DTI · Fibrosis · Image registration

1 Introduction

Ventricular arrhythmia and progressive heart failure associated with structural disease (e.g. chronic infarction) are major causes of death worldwide. In the clinics, the location of the fibrotic infarct is evaluated non-invasively using MR imaging [1]. In these MR images, heterogeneous fibrosis has an intermediate signal intensity between healthy (H) tissue and infarct core (IC), and is therefore named 'gray zone' (GZ) [9]. However, the clinical spatial MR resolution is often inadequate (i.e., 8–10 mm slice thickness) resulting in an overestimated GZ and IC extent due to partial volume effects [6,7]. Furthermore, in post-infarction patients, subtle fibrosis characteristics (e.g. alteration in myocardial tissue anisotropy) cannot be properly detected due to motion-related MR artifacts nor they can be histologically validated.

M. Pop et al. (Eds.): STACOM 2019, LNCS 12009, pp. 3–11, 2020.
https://doi.org/10.1007/978-3-030-39074-7_1

Fractional anisotropy (FA) is a scalar metric calculated from DTI-derived eigenvectors that describes the degree of diffusivity of water molecules in tissue. Regions with replacement fibrosis have lower FA due to increased myocardial fiber disarray resulting from local necrosis, ventricular remodeling, and infiltration of thin collagen fibrils, thus increasing the diffusivity of water molecules [8,13].

Our broad aim is to use high-resolution MR to identify subtle characteristics of heterogeneous fibrosis in a pre-clinical model of chronic infarction with histological validation, and construct 3D MRI-based models for simulations [3,10]. This type of fibrosis harbors the foci of lethal arrhythmia and is comprised of a mixture of healthy myocytes and collagen fibrils, bordering dense scar areas [4]. In this work, we aim to develop an image analysis pipeline to study myocardial anisotropy in GZ by means of high-resolution diffusion-weighted MR images acquired in explanted pig hearts. Specifically, we use DTI to calculate FA (as a measure of fiber disarray in GZ/IC), and correlate these FA maps with collagen density from co-registered histological images using affine registration.

2   Materials and Methods

2.1   Animal Model of Myocardial Infarction

Myocardial infarction was generated in Yorkshire swines (N = 10) using a 90-min occlusion-reperfusion method under x-ray fluoroscopy, as previously described in [8]. The infarctions were induced in the LAD territory of 5 pigs, and in the LCX territory of another 5 pigs. They were then allowed to heal for 5–6 weeks prior to animal sacrifice, heart explantation, and MR imaging. All animal experiments received ethical approval from Sunnybrook Research Institute, Toronto and were conducted in accordance with protocols instated by the Animal Care Committee of Sunnybrook Health Sciences Centre, Toronto.

2.2   *Ex Vivo* Diffusion-Weighted MR Imaging

All diffusion-weighted MR images were acquired using a 1.5T GE Sigma Excite scanner. The explanted hearts were fixed in 10% formalin for 3–4 days and then placed in a Plexiglas phantom box filled with Fluorinert (3M^{TM}, USA) for imaging. Each heart phantom was placed in an eight-channel head coil. The following MR parameters for diffusion-weighted imaging were used: echo time = 35 ms, repetition time = 700 ms, FOV = 160×160 mm, slice thickness = 1.2 mm, matrix = 256×256, b value = 0 s/mm^2 for unweighted images, and b = 500 s/mm^2 for diffusion-weighted images in 7 diffusion sampling gradients. The in-plane image resolution was $0.6 \times 0.6 \times 1.2$ mm and the total scan time for each heart was approximately 10 h.

2.3 Fractional Anisotropy Map Calculation

The equations describing DT imaging and eigenanalysis are described below [2]. The DWI echo signal intensity S is calculated by the following:

$$S = S_0 e^{-b \cdot D} \tag{1}$$

where S^0 is the signal of the unweighted image ($b = 0$). The b value is a diffusion weighing factor that describes the strength and timing of diffusion gradients, which is used to compute the diffusion-weighted image. D is a diffusion coefficient of water molecules and can be represented by a 3×3 tensor as shown in Eq. 2:

$$D = \begin{bmatrix} D_{xx} & D_{xy} & D_{xz} \\ D_{yx} & D_{yy} & D_{yz} \\ D_{zx} & D_{zy} & D_{zz} \end{bmatrix} = E^T \begin{bmatrix} \lambda_1 & 0 & 0 \\ 0 & \lambda_2 & 0 \\ 0 & 0 & \lambda_3 \end{bmatrix} E \tag{2}$$

This tensor is derived from directional diffusivities and is symmetric such that $D_{ij} = D_{ji}$, with $i, j = x, y, z$. Thus, there are only six independent variables in this tensor. E represents a matrix of three eigenvectors, indicating the direction of the principle axes of the tensor model. λ_1, λ_2 and λ_3 represent eigenvalues describing the size of principle axes.

Equation 3 shows the formula for FA for each voxel. For a perfect isotropic medium, $\lambda_1 = \lambda_2 = \lambda_3$ and $FA = 0$, whereas with progressive diffusion anisotropy, $FA \to 1$ (e.g. healthy myocardial muscle fibers).

$$FA = \frac{\sqrt{3}}{\sqrt{2}} \frac{\sqrt{(\lambda_1 - \lambda)^2 + (\lambda_2 - \lambda)^2 + (\lambda_3 - \lambda)^2}}{\sqrt{\lambda_1^2 + \lambda_2^2 + \lambda_3^2}} \tag{3}$$

2.4 Histopathology

From each heart, one representative 4 mm thick slab was cut in short-axis orientation (matching one DT image), sectioned to focus on the infarcted region, and then paraffin embedded. Thin slices were cut from these slabs at 4 μm thickness using a microtome, mounted on small 1×3 inch glass slides and stained. To visualize collagenous fibrosis, the slides were stained with picrosirius red and scanned at 40× magnification using a TISSUEscope TM 4000 confocal microscope (Huron Technologies International Inc.).

2.5 Fibrosis Quantification

In this work, we aimed to quantify fibrosis in FA maps (calculated from DTI) for each myocardial zone defined by the collagen density in histological images: H, GZ and IC. The pipeline for this process is briefly outlined in Fig. 1.

For each heart, FA maps were reviewed to manually select the slice corresponding to the histology image. Histology images and FA maps were then overlaid in the open source software Sedeen Viewer (Pathcore 2018)[1] for manual registration using anatomical landmarks (e.g., papillary muscles, scar morphology).

---

[1] https://pathcore.com/sedeen/.

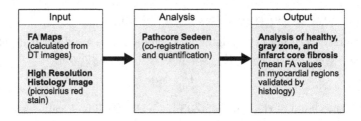

Fig. 1. Illustration of the image processing pipeline. FA maps were manually registered with histology images for collagen quantification. H, GZ and IC regions were validated with ground truth histology.

Affine registration was performed to correct non-uniform tissue shrinkage effects from tissue fixation and histology processing. This approach is more appropriate than rigid registration because it allows image scaling. Once registered, 3 × 3 MR pixel regions of interest (ROI) were selected on the histology image for stain quantification. For each heart, 2 ROIs were selected from each of H, GZ and IC zones. The stain analysis plugin [5] in Sedeen was used to quantify tissues with a positive stain for collagen and return a percent collagen composition for each ROI. Using our previous grading system, this plugin was used to classify each tissue category as either H (<20% collagen), GZ (20–70% collagen) or IC (>70% collagen) [8]. Once classified, the same ROI was imposed onto a FA map for mean FA calculations using DSI Studio (Labsolver 2018)[2].

2.6   Statistical Analysis

Mean FA values were expressed as mean ±1 SD. Tukey boxplots were used to compare mean FA values in each of the 3 cardiac zones (H, GZ and IC). Student's t-tests were performed to evaluate levels of significance between groups ($p < 0.05$). One-way analysis of variance (ANOVA) was performed to determine statistically significant differences in mean FA values in H, GZ and IC regions. All statistical tests were performed using RStudio Version 1.1.463 (RStudio Inc. 2018).

3   Results

Figure 2 shows the steps of quantitatively analyzing FA values in one heart. The bottom-right image illustrates an analyzed ROI showing pixels with a positive stain for collagen (red). The bottom-left image shows the corresponding ROI on the FA map, which is a gray-scale display of FA values across the image with brighter areas being more anisotropic than darker areas (i.e., IC).

Figure 3 shows the resulting mean FA for the 3 zones: H (0.52 ± 0.12), GZ (0.43 ± 0.13) and IC (0.29 ± 0.17). We observed a significant difference in FA

---
[2] http://dsi-studio.labsolver.org.

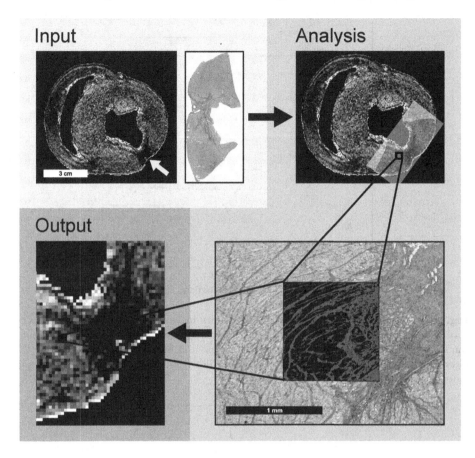

Fig. 2. Example of a co-registered histology image and FA map for quantitative collagen analysis, where the white arrow points to the infarct generated in the LCX territory. The magnified ROI in the bottom right figure shows an example of GZ classification (34% collagen) using the stain analysis plugin in Sedeen. Once the histology-based ROI was classified, a mean FA value (0.38) for its corresponding ROI in the FA map was calculated as shown in the bottom-left figure. (Color figure online)

values between all 3 zones (one way ANOVA $= 1.8 \times 10^{-5}$). Figure 4 shows the comparison of FA values between the LAD and LCX sub-groups for each region. Notably, we found no statistical difference between these 2 groups.

Figure 5 illustrates an exemplary snapshot taken from the visualization and analysis software Sedeen, in which we co-registered the FA map and the picrosirius red image at 50% opacity. Here, 2 ROIs selected from each of: H, GZ and IC regions are visible on the registered image (yellow squares).

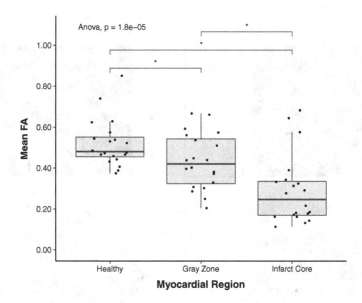

Fig. 3. Results from FA analysis. Mean FA values in healthy, gray zone and infarct core myocardium illustrated using a Tukey boxplot. Lines in the boxplots represent the statistical median. Error bars reflect the lowest and highest data point within 1.5 interquartile range of the lower and upper quartiles respectively. (* = p < 0.05 in an independent samples t-test).

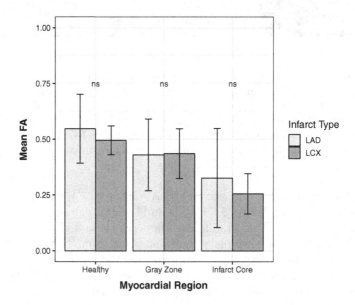

Fig. 4. Results from FA analysis. Bar graph displaying FA values in each cardiac region stratified by infarct type. Error bars reflect ±1 SD. (ns = not significant in an independent samples t-test).

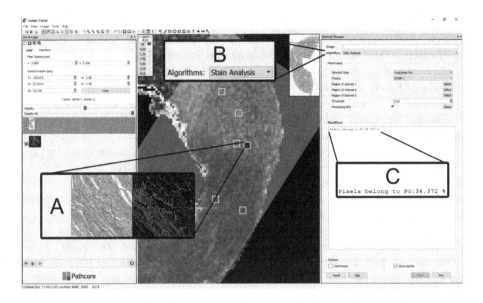

Fig. 5. Visualization of the Sedeen user interface, including its native file manager (left menu) and analysis manager (right menu). (A) shows a magnified image of one analyzed ROI. The left image is acquired from the raw histology image and the right image is the same region following analysis of the collagen stain. (B) shows the user-interface for algorithm selection. For stain quantification, we used the stain analysis plugin. (C) is a magnified image of showing the output of the stain analysis plugin. Here, we can quantitatively assess the percent collagen composition of this ROI and thus classify it as one of: H, GZ or IC. (Color figure online)

4   Discussion and Conclusion

In this work, we describe an image processing pipeline focused on co-registered histology and MR images to quantitatively assess the extent of collagenous fibrosis in H, GZ and IC myocardium using FA, a measure of the diffusivity of water molecules reflecting tissue architecture and alignment.

In histologically-classified ROIs, we found that mean FA decreases significantly in GZ (reduction of 17%, from $0.52 \pm 0.12 \rightarrow 0.43 \pm 0.13$, $p = 0.034$) and IC (reduction of 44%, from $0.52 \pm 0.12 \rightarrow 0.29 \pm 0.17$, $p = 0.00005$) myocardial zones when compared to healthy tissue. Our results are consistent with findings from Wu et al. [17], who investigated FA in porcine hearts with myocardial infarction and observed a decrease in the IC (38.4%) and GZ (6.1%). Unlike our study which performed mean FA calculations on small histologically-classified ROIs, they performed calculations on 8 large radial segments of the left ventricle which may represent a confounding mixture of both healthy and scar tissue. These FA values, in addition to the patterns of FA reduction, are similar to studies using human models of myocardial infarction, further validating our porcine model for studying myocardial infarction as seen in the clinic [14,15].

This decrease in FA is likely multifactorial, involving the loss of healthy myocyte architecture and the deposition of replacement fibrosis. Healthy myocardium is known to be highly anisotropic, reflecting its directionally organized fibers and conductive properties; however, following myocardial infarction, networks of functional myocytes are replaced by collagenous fibrosis [11,12].

Notably, we report no differences in FA between LAD and LCX sub-groups, suggesting that tissue anisotropy in H, GZ, and IC myocardial zones may not depend on infarct location. This finding is also consistent with Wu et al. [16] who compared non-reperfused occlusion-induced LAD and LCX infarctions in pig. Comparable results between two different models of infarction (our occlusion-reperfusion model vs the non-reperfusion occlusion model in [16]) indicates that patterns of tissue fibrosis, as characterized by FA measurements, are also largely independent of infarct location.

Lastly, we acknowledge limitations in our method. For the calculation of diffusion tensor, our fitting model used only 2 b-values (0 and 500) rather than 3. Our *ex vivo* high-resolution image acquisition time was roughly 10 h; thus, it was unfeasible to perform another scan for the additional fitting. Additionally, we registered *ex vivo* MR images with heart tissue using affine registration for scaling. This approach is acceptable for our work since all images (diffusion-weighted and histology) were acquired *ex vivo* following fixation; however, further investigations using *in vivo* MR images are warranted to better reflect tissue anisotropy under physiological conditions. These MR images would be subject to motion-related artifacts and differences in morphology due to *in vivo* conditions. As such, deformable image registration techniques using anisotropy scale factors may be necessary in addition to metrics for registration confidence. Notably, Sedeen can perform manual anisotropic transformations with the potential for semi-automatic registration plugins. As such, this image processing pipeline may be applied to *in vivo* studies in the future.

To conclude, this study describes a robust image processing pipeline for anisotropy characterization in myocardial infarction using high resolution DTI and histologically-classified ROIs in a chronic fibrotic scar. In doing so, we find that FA, a measure of tissue fibrosis, decreases significantly from H to GZ to IC myocardial zones. We also report that the degree of collagenous fibrosis as quantified by FA is largely independent of infarct territory (LAD or LCX). Overall, we demonstrate that DTI as a non-invasive imaging modality can identify subtle differences between H, GZ and IC tissue.

Acknowledgements. The authors would like to thank for the following financial support: CIHR Project Grant PJT 153212 (Dr. Mihaela Pop) and UROP Medical Biophysics – University of Toronto summer student award (Peter Lin).

References

1. Bello, D., et al.: Infarct morphology identifies patients with substrate for sustained ventricular tachycardia. J. Am. Coll. Cardiol. **45**(7), 1104–1108 (2005)

2. Jiang, H., van Zijl, P.C., Kim, J., Pearlson, G.D., Mori, S.: DtiStudio: resource program for diffusion tensor computation and fiber bundle tracking. Comput. Methods Programs Biomed. **81**(2), 106–116 (2006)
3. Li, M., et al.: Pipeline to build and test robust 3D T1 mapping-based heart models for EP interventions: preliminary results. In: Coudière, Y., Ozenne, V., Vigmond, E., Zemzemi, N. (eds.) FIMH 2019. LNCS, vol. 11504, pp. 64–72. Springer, Cham (2019). https://doi.org/10.1007/978-3-030-21949-9_8
4. Lin, P., et al.: High resolution imaging and histopathological characterization of myocardial infarction. Biophys. J. **116**(3), 231a (2019)
5. Martel, A.L., et al.: An image analysis resource for cancer research: PIIP— Pathology Image Informatics Platform for visualization, analysis, and management. Cancer Res. **77**(21), e83–e86 (2017)
6. Mekkaoui, C., Reese, T.G., Jackowski, M.P., Bhat, H., Sosnovik, D.E.: Diffusion MRI in the heart. NMR Biomed. **30**(3), e3426 (2017)
7. Nguyen, C., et al.: In vivo three-dimensional high resolution cardiac diffusion-weighted MRI: a motion compensated diffusion-prepared balanced steady-state free precession approach: 3D high resolution cardiac DW-MRI via diffusion-prepared bSSFP. Magn. Reson. Med. **72**(5), 1257–1267 (2014)
8. Pop, M., et al.: Quantification of fibrosis in infarcted swine hearts by ex vivo late gadolinium-enhancement and diffusion-weighted MRI methods. Phys. Med. Biol. **58**(15), 5009–5028 (2013)
9. Pop, M., et al.: High-resolution 3-D T1*-mapping and quantitative image analysis of GRAY ZONE in chronic fibrosis. IEEE Trans. Biomed. Eng. **61**(12), 2930–2938 (2014)
10. Pop, M., et al.: Construction of 3D MR image-based computer models of pathologic hearts, augmented with histology and optical fluorescence imaging to characterize action potential propagation. Med. Image Anal. **16**(2), 505–523 (2012)
11. Prabhu, S.D., Frangogiannis, N.G.: The biological basis for cardiac repair after myocardial infarction: from inflammation to fibrosis. Circ. Res. **119**(1), 91–112 (2016)
12. Valderrabano, M.: Influence of anisotropic conduction properties in the propagation of the cardiac action potential. Prog. Biophys. Mol. Biol. **94**(1–2), 144–168 (2007)
13. Whittaker, P., Boughner, D.R., Kloner, R.A.: Analysis of healing after myocardial infarction using polarized light microscopy. Am. J. Pathol. **134**(4), 15 (1989)
14. Winklhofer, S., et al.: Post-mortem cardiac diffusion tensor imaging: detection of myocardial infarction and remodeling of myofiber architecture. Eur. Radiol. **24**(11), 2810–2818 (2014)
15. Wu, E.X., et al.: MR diffusion tensor imaging study of postinfarct myocardium structural remodeling in a porcine model. Magn. Reson. Med. **58**(4), 687–695 (2007)
16. Wu, Y., Chan, C.W., Nicholls, J.M., Liao, S., Tse, H.F., Wu, E.X.: MR study of the effect of infarct size and location on left ventricular functional and microstructural alterations in porcine models. J. Magn. Reson. Imaging **29**(2), 305–312 (2009)
17. Wu, Y., Tse, H.F., Wu, E.X.: Diffusion tensor MRI study of myocardium structural remodeling after infarction in porcine model. In: 2006 International Conference of the IEEE Engineering in Medicine and Biology Society, pp. 1069–1072. IEEE (2006)

Manufacturing of Ultrasound- and MRI-Compatible Aortic Valves Using 3D Printing for Analysis and Simulation

Shu Wang[1]([✉]), Harminder Gill[1], Weifeng Wan[2], Helen Tricker[1],
Joao Filipe Fernandes[1], Yohan Noh[1], Sergio Uribe[3], Jesus Urbina[3],
Julio Sotelo[3], Ronak Rajani[1], Pablo Lamata[1], and Kawal Rhode[1]

[1] School of Biomedical Engineering and Imaging Sciences,
King's College London, London, UK
shu.l.wang@kcl.ac.uk
[2] Department of Materials, Imperial College London, London, UK
[3] Biomedical Imaging Centre, Pontificia Universidad Catolica de Chile,
Santiago, Chile

Abstract. Valve-related heart disease affects 27 million patients worldwide and is associated with inflammation, fibrosis and calcification which progressively lead to organ structure change. Aortic stenosis is the most common valve pathology with controversies regarding its optimal management, such as the timing of valve replacement. Therefore, there is emerging demand for analysis and simulation of valves to help researchers and companies to test novel approaches. This paper describes how to build ultrasound- and MRI-compatible aortic valves compliant phantoms with a two-part mold technique using 3D printing. The choice of the molding material, PVA, was based on its material properties and experimentally tested dissolving time. Different diseased valves were then manufactured with ecoflex silicone, a commonly used tissue-mimicking material. The valves were mounted with an external support and tested in physiological flow conditions. Flow images were obtained with both ultrasound and MRI, showing physiologically plausible anatomy and function of the valves. The simplicity of the manufacturing process and low cost of materials should enable an easy adoption of proposed methodology. Future research will focus on the extension of the method to cover a larger anatomical area (e.g. aortic arch) and the use of this phantom to validate the non-invasive assessment of blood pressure differences.

Keywords: Aortic stenosis · Valve fabrication · 3D printing · US-MRI compatible

1 Background and Introduction

Aortic stenosis (AS) is the most common valve-related disease, associated with inflammation, fibrosis and calcification, which can lead to progressive organ structure change [1]. AS can result from differing underlying pathologies and the macroscopic appearance is typically classified into one of the following categories: calcified valve,

© Springer Nature Switzerland AG 2020
M. Pop et al. (Eds.): STACOM 2019, LNCS 12009, pp. 12–21, 2020.
https://doi.org/10.1007/978-3-030-39074-7_2

rheumatic valve and bicuspid valve. The prevalence of aortic stenosis increases with age, and if left untreated high mortality is observed [2]. Moreover, left ventricular outflow tract obstruction increases the workload of the left ventricle ultimately leading to heart failure [3]. Treatment of the valve, by means of surgical or minimally invasive methods, is required as no pharmacological methods demonstrate efficacy at preventing progression. However, current diagnostic methods are inadequate regarding optimal management, such as the timing of valve replacement. In-vitro studies of valve disease and pre-procedural interventional planning can benefit from advances in 3D printing [4]. Due to the need of ultrasound- and MRI- compatibility, compliance, flexibility and durability when connected to a hemodynamic pump, the valve material needs to be chosen carefully while the valve shape should be realistic. Silicone is an optimal material because it is a room temperature-vulcanized material with stiffness similar to soft tissue [5]. However, the structure of the aortic valve is complicated and direct silicone printing technology is not available in the current market.

Despite the current technical limitation of rapid prototyping and 3D printing in the literature [6], it offers a significant tool for making and validating pathological valves, as well as an important education tool for trainees involved in the treatment of valvular disease. Given the difficulties of making a durable and compliant aortic valve model, several patient-specific tissue-mimicking phantoms were previously printed directly using TangoPlus and VeroBlackPlus, which can achieve a layer thickness of 30 microns. However, replication of these methods requires high printing cost even though these two materials are reported to be much stiffer than ecoflex silicone [7]. Motivated by practicing the surgical procedure, a detailed soft organ phantom was created by a technique of 3D wax printing and polymer molding [8]. The outer molds are printed with VeroClear and the inner molds are printed with wax. But the wax molding material needs to be dissolved in ethanol at 70 °C, which makes it more complicated and potentially unachievable in most labs.

Here, we present a low-cost and simple two-part mold-based technology of manufacturing a realistic aortic valve and with the use of PVA, the internal mold can be easily dissolved in water at room temperature. Besides a normal silicone valve, some typical pathological valves were also fabricated for comparison and the imaging compatibility was validated using both ultrasound and MRI. 3D-printable PVA was chosen as the molding material for its easy printability, fast water-soluble property, as well as the good performance under great external forces. The use of 3D-printed valve models and experience is expected to be broadened in the near future, with the progress in material engineering, computer aided design and diagnostic imaging systems [9]. Although it seems a far stretch of imagination, in vivo implantation of 3D-printed aortic valves may become the finale goal [10].

2 Materials and Methods

The whole procedure of making the anthropomorphic silicone valve is illustrated in Fig. 1, which contains following three main parts: suitable molding material selection, silicone perfusion and mold dissolving, final imaging validation using ultrasound and MRI.

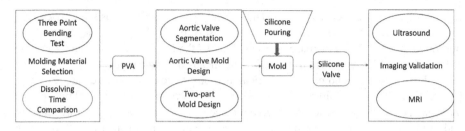

Fig. 1. Manufacturing procedure illustration & imaging compatibility validation

2.1   Molding Material Selection

Before using silicone to make the aortic valve phantom, a suitable molding material needs to be selected based on the following requirements: easy to dissolve with no additional solvents; stable when external force applied and slightly more flexible than general rigid printing materials like **Polylactic acid** (PLA). There are several water-soluble materials available on the printing market including **Polyvinyl alcohol** (PVA), High-T-Lay, Lay-PVA which fulfil these criteria [11]. In order to choose a suitable printing infill density and the best dissolving temperature, the chosen three molding materials were compared with different infills and at different water temperatures. The specimen for the infill density experiment was $3 \times 3 \times 3$ cm^3 cube with a discrete infill density range from 0% to 100%, while the specimen for the water temperature experiment was $1 \times 1 \times 1$ cm^3 cube with only 0% infill. The whole dissolving procedure was monitored by a surveillance camera (YI Dome Camera) and recorded from the starting point to fully dissolving point manually.

Meanwhile, a three-point bending test [12] was performed to compare the material flexibility and stability. The specimens for this test were $10 \times 2 \times 1$ cm^3 cuboids with infill density range from 20% to 100%. The machine used was a Zwick Roell Z010 tensile testing system and the experimental setup is shown in Fig. 2. The recorded data were analyzed in Matlab 2019. The failure force when the sample cracks is simply the maximum loading force and the flexural modulus that represents the materials' flexibility needs to be calculated using Eq. 1 [12], where E_f is flexural modulus, L is support span, b is the width and d is the depth of the specimen and m is the gradient of the initial straight-line portion of the load-deflection curve:

$$E_f = \left(L^3 m\right) / \left(4bd^3\right) \tag{1}$$

2.2   Valve Manufacturing

After performing the above experiments, it was found that the most suitable molding material to make the internal mold is PVA, while the external mold can be printed with normal PLA for reuse. The original solid valve model was segmented from a healthy human chest CT scan using ITK-SNAP (University of Pennsylvania, USA) thresholding and region growing, then smoothed using a median filter in Seg3D (The

Fig. 2. Three-point bending test setup

University of Utah, USA). Finally the hollow model was generated using the erosion-dilation method in Seg3D, the thickness of the valve being 2 mm and the whole segmentation can be viewed in Fig. 3.

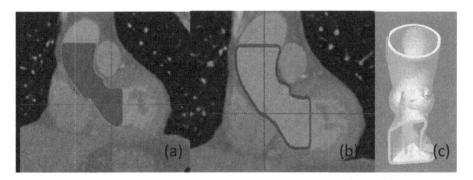

Fig. 3. Aortic valve model generation (a) Solid valve segmentation (b) Hollow valve segmentation and (c) 3D hollow valve model

After completing the valve segmentation, the 3D mold was designed using Solidworks 2018. The cavity was created based on the hollow model and the mold was then extracted as the external part (Fig. 4(a)) and the internal part (Fig. 4(b)). The external part was printed using rigid plastic PLA while the internal part was printed using PVA. With the assembled prints held with clamps Fig. 4(c), the degassed ecoflex-silicone 0030 was poured into the mold and the basic normal valve model was manufactured as depicted in Fig. 4(d). Based on the normal silicone model, some pathological valve models were created as depicted in Fig. 5, including a rheumatic one (Fig. 5(b)), a calcified one Fig. 5(c) and a bicuspid one Fig. 5(d). Each valve model started with fused valve cusps. The rheumatic valve was created by ensuring the anatomical orifice consisted of cuts made one third down each valve closure line to recreate circumferential fusion of the cusps. The calcified valve was created by paint-brushing more silicone to replicate leaflet thickening and stiffening, while the bicuspid one was created by leaving one commissure fused to mimic a raphe.

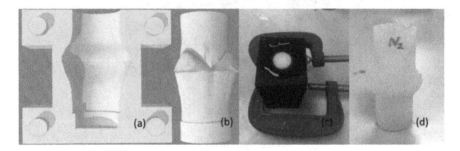

Fig. 4. Two-part mold-based silicone valve manufacturing (a) External mold (b) Internal mold (c) Two-part mold assembly and (d) Normal silicone valve

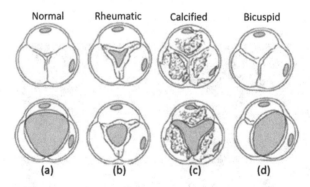

Fig. 5. [13]. Pathological valve models (a) Normal valve (b) Rheumatic valve (c) Calcified valve and (d) Bicuspid valve

2.3   US and MRI Imaging

To validate whether the valve phantoms can give the desired imaging results, the four types of silicone valves were imaged using 2D ultrasound and 3D MRI. The 2D ultrasound images were acquired on the Philips IE33 system with a S5-1 probe in water using the standard aortic valve short-axis view. For the 2D MR imaging, the silicone valves were connected to a commercial flexible silicone aorta phantom (T-S-N 005, Elastrat) and perfused by an MRI-compatible pulsatile flow pump (CardioFlow 5000

MR). This time the images were acquired in 1% Agar for optimized imaging results. Both imaging procedures are demonstrated in Fig. 6, with Fig. 6(a) showing the ultrasound imaging and Fig. 6(b) showing the MR imaging.

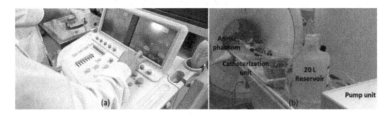

Fig. 6. Imaging validation (a) Ultrasound imaging and (b) MR imaging

3   Results and Discussions

3.1   Molding Material Selection

The mold material dissolving comparisons are presented in Tables 1 and 2. From Table 1, it is clear that PVA is the easiest to dissolve while High-T-Lay is the most difficult and the dissolving time increases non-linearly with the tested infill densities. Table 2 gives a similar result showing that PVA is the best water-soluble material at various water temperatures, while with higher temperature, all the tested materials will dissolve faster. Table 3 gives the failure force results of the materials, from which we can see Lay-PVA can withstand the highest external force and PVA can withstand the least, while with higher infill density, all the specimens' failure force increases. Regarding to the flexibility, PVA has the smallest flexural modulus and Lay-PVA has the largest, which means PVA is the best option with the requirement for flexible molding materials. With less infill density, the mold will be very fragile and the final printing option for the internal molding material was chosen to be PVA with 40% infill density (Table 4).

Table 1. Molding material dissolving time comparison with different infill densities (@ room temperature 25 °C).

Infill density (%)	Time taken to dissolve (hours)		
	PVA	High-T-Lay	Lay-PVA
0	1.62	36.08	4.75
20	10.43	163.08	58.38
40	24.43	367.50	173.42
60	116.42	656.42	284.73
80	263.33	858.25	397.57
100	377.83	1028.17	494.28

Table 2. Molding material dissolving time comparison with different temperatures (@ 0% infill density).

Temperature (°C)	Time taken to dissolve (minutes)		
	PVA	High-T-Lay	Lay-PVA
25	93	2124	311
40	72	1324	314
60	50	1293	309
80	42	1290	310
100	33	1285	306

Table 3. Molding material failure force comparison

Infill density (%)	Maximum load force (N)		
	PVA	High-T-Lay	Lay-PVA
20	134	111	216
40	163	157	497
60	165	297	546
80	326	429	737
100	435	522	1152

Table 4. Molding material flexural modulus comparison

Infill density (%)	Flexural modulus (MPa)		
	PVA	High-T-Lay	Lay-PVA
20	137	489	612
40	144	705	906
60	148	972	1276
80	276	1244	1815
100	506	1656	2454

3.2　Valve Manufacturing

Figure 7 demonstrates the final fabricated valves using ecoflex-silicone 0030. From the results we can see the normal valve can open fully under pressure, while the rheumatic one can only open partially as the leaflets stick to each other, the calcified valve can barely open due to the abnormal thickness of the leaflets and the bicuspid one opens only on one side due to the incomplete leaflets. However, there is still the need for validating the valves' performance under different imaging modalities.

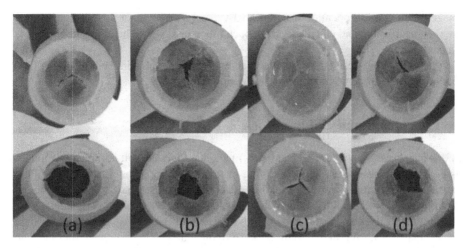

Fig. 7. Manufactured silicone valves, close on top, and open on the bottom (a) Normal valve (b) Rheumatic valve (c) Calcified valve and (d) Bicuspid valve

3.3   US and MRI Imaging

Figure 8 shows both the ultrasound and MR images of the four types of aortic valves from the short-axis view. Even though the ultrasound images are less clear and the difference is less significant, we can still see the normal valve has a perfect clear leaflet structure, while the rheumatic and calcified one have more vague anatomies and the bicuspid one demonstrates the abnormal opening from one side of the leaflets. The MR

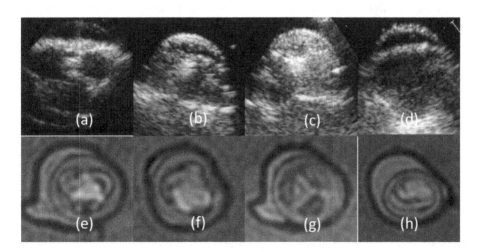

Fig. 8. 2D Ultrasound images of (a) Normal valve (b) Rheumatic valve (c) Calcified valve and (d) Bicuspid valve; MR Images of (e) Normal valve (f) Rheumatic valve (g) Calcified valve and (h) Bicuspid valve

images show the full opening of the normal valve, however, under the same pressure, the rheumatic valve and calcified valves open much less, while the bicuspid one opens eccentrically.

These imaging results qualitatively demonstrate the imaging compatibility and functionality of the artificial valves made using 3D printing.

4 Conclusion and Future Work

In this paper, we propose a novel and easy method to fabricate soft aortic valve models, using PVA, the best water-soluble printing material, to make an internal mold and PLA to make the external mold. The molding material was chosen based on its dissolving performance and flexural modulus. The fabricated silicone valves are compliant, as the human heart valves and were shown to be ultrasound- and MRI- compatible. These valves may be useful in the future for studying valve function under normal and pathological conditions.

Future work will focus on quantitative evaluation of 3D-printed valve performance and development of direct silicone printing for manufacturing these valves, thus simplifying the process further.

References

1. Hockaday, L.A., Duan, B., Kang, K.H.: 3D printed hydrogel technologies for tissue-engineered heart valves. 3D Printing Addit. Manuf. **1**(3), 122–136 (2014)
2. Everborn, G.,. Schirmer, H.: The evolving epidemiology of valvular aortic stenosis. The tromso study. Heart **99**, 396–400 (2013)
3. Donati, F., Myerson, S.: Beyond Bernoulli, improving the accuracy and precision of noninvasive estimation of peak pressure drops. Circ. Cardiovasc. Imaging **10**, 1–9 (2017)
4. Qian, Z., Wang, K., Liu, S., et al.: Quantitative prediction of paravalvular leak in transcatheter aortic valve replacement based on tissue-mimicking 3D printing. JACC Cardiovasc. Imaging **10**(7), 719–731 (2017)
5. Wang, Y., Tai, B.L., Yu, H., et al.: Silicone-based tissue-mimicking phantom for needle insertion simulation. Trans. ASME **8**, 021001-1–021001-7 (2014)
6. Byrne, N., Velasco Forte, M.: A systematic review of image segmentation methodology used in the additive manufacture of patient-specific 3D printed models of the cardiovascular system. JRSM Cardiovasc. Dis. **5**, 2048004016645467 (2016)
7. Wang, K.: Controlling the mechanical behaviour of dual-material 3D printed meta-materials for patient-specific tissue-mimicking phantoms. Mater. Des. **90**, 704–712 (2016)
8. Adams, F.: Soft 3D-printed phantom of the human kidney with collection system. Ann. Biomed. Eng. **45**(4), 963–972 (2017)
9. Bompotis, G.: Transcatheter aortic valve implantation using 3D printing modelling assistance. A single-center experience. Hellenic J. Cardiol. (2019)
10. Alkhouli, M.: 3D printed models for TAVR planning. JACC: Cardiovasc. Imaging **10**(7), 732–734 (2017)
11. https://all3dp.com/kai-parthy-shares-3d-printing-soluble-filaments-lay-away/

12. Zweben, C., Smith, W.S., Wardle, M.W.: Test methods for fibre tensile strength, composite flexural modulus, and properties of fabric-reinforced laminates. In: Composite Materials: Testing and Design (Fifth Conference), ASTM International (1979)
13. Huang, B.: Recommendations on the echocardiographic assessment of aortic valve stenosis: a focused update from the European Association of Cardiovascular Imaging and the American Society of Echocardiography. Eur. Heart J. Cardiovasc. Imaging **18**(3), 254–275 (2017)

Assessing the Impact of Blood Pressure on Cardiac Function Using Interpretable Biomarkers and Variational Autoencoders

Esther Puyol-Antón[1]([✉]), Bram Ruijsink[1,2], James R. Clough[1], Ilkay Oksuz[1], Daniel Rueckert[3], Reza Razavi[1,2], and Andrew P. King[1]

[1] School of Biomedical Engineering & Imaging Sciences, King's College London, London, UK
esther.puyol_anton@kcl.ac.uk
[2] St Thomas' Hospital NHS Foundation Trust, London, UK
[3] Biomedical Image Analysis Group, Imperial College London, London, UK

Abstract. Maintaining good cardiac function for as long as possible is a major concern for healthcare systems worldwide and there is much interest in learning more about the impact of different risk factors on cardiac health. The aim of this study is to analyze the impact of systolic blood pressure (SBP) on cardiac function while preserving the interpretability of the model using known clinical biomarkers in a large cohort of the UK Biobank population. We propose a novel framework that combines deep learning based estimation of interpretable clinical biomarkers from cardiac cine MR data with a variational autoencoder (VAE). The VAE architecture integrates a regression loss in the latent space, which enables the progression of cardiac health with SBP to be learnt. Results on 3,600 subjects from the UK Biobank show that the proposed model allows us to gain important insight into the deterioration of cardiac function with increasing SBP, identify key interpretable factors involved in this process, and lastly exploit the model to understand patterns of positive and adverse adaptation of cardiac function.

Keywords: Cardiac function · Variational autoencoder · Cardiac risk factors

1 Introduction

Preventing the development of heart disease in patients with known risk factors, such as hypertension, represents a major challenge for healthcare systems worldwide. Although much is known about how these risk factors influence development of disease, the recent availability of large scale databases such as the UK Biobank represents an excellent opportunity to extend this knowledge. Learning from a large number of highly detailed, multidimensional cardiac magnetic

---

E. Puyol-Antón and B. Ruijsink—Joint first authors.

© Springer Nature Switzerland AG 2020
M. Pop et al. (Eds.): STACOM 2019, LNCS 12009, pp. 22–30, 2020.
https://doi.org/10.1007/978-3-030-39074-7_3

resonance (CMR) datasets can help further understanding of how risk factors impact cardiac function, and tailor medical interventions to individual patients.

Traditionally, machine learning techniques have relied on the use of hand-crafted features to effectively perform a specific task without using explicit instructions. In some cases, the accuracy of these models was limited by the model being restricted to the use of these features. Recently, deep learning (DL) techniques have demonstrated a significant increase in performance over traditional machine learning methods. DL allows features to be learned from the data themselves, without preselection. One drawback of DL approaches is the lack of interpretability, as the learned relationships and features are often abstract and opaque to human users. Especially in medicine, interpretability and accountability are vital for two main reasons: (a) they can promote clinician trust in the learned models; and (b) the use of well-established, interpretable biomarkers allows the models to be used to better understand disease processes, translate the results to other populations and to interpret the newly learned information in the light of already existing clinical scientific evidence. For example, complex full 3D cardiac motion of the heart can be used to outperform current models in survival estimation for patients with pulmonary hypertension [1]. While methods like this demonstrate the power of DL, it is difficult for clinicians to understand the features underlying the predictions and to use the model to better understand the disease.

A large number of biomarkers can be calculated from CMR. These are well-understood by clinicians and provide comprehensive information about underlying physiological processes. However, estimating them all is labour-intensive. In this paper, we employ a fully automated DL-based pipeline for estimating a wide range of biomarkers of cardiac function from cine CMR data. Our main contribution is to propose a framework that enables the interpretability of these automatically computed biomarkers to be combined with the power of learned features in DL. This framework is based on the use of a variational autoencoder with a latent space regression loss (R-VAE), in which the input data are the clinical biomarkers. In addition, we use a dummy variable in the regression to differentiate between population groups. We use the proposed method to investigate the impact of systolic blood pressure (SBP: a measure of hypertension) on cardiac function in the healthy population differentiated by gender.

Related Work: In the clinical literature, many groups have investigated the relationship between SBP and ventricular structure, function and geometry [2,3]. However, most studies only investigated the influence of SBP on global parameters or only in the left ventricle. The proposed pipeline enables a more detailed investigation of the impact of SBP on cardiac function, as we demonstrate in Sect. 4. VAEs have previously been used for identification and visualization of features in medical image-based classification tasks [4–6], but the features were still learnt from the data and were not well-established clinical biomarkers as in our work. DL models have also previously been proposed for regression using interpretable features. For example, Xie *et al.* [7] proposed an autoencoder-based deep belief regression network to forecast daily particulate matter concentrations. Similarly, Bose *et al.* [8] proposed a stacked autoencoder based regression framework to optimize process control and productivity in intelligent manufacturing. Both techniques combined handcrafted features obtained from the image domain with autoencoders. In the medical field, Xie *et al.* [9] have proposed a deep autoencoder model for regression of gene expression profiles from genotype. Similar to these works we integrate a regression loss into the autoencoder to learn relationships between the latent space and another variable (SBP in our case). Our work is methodologically distinct from [7–9] as we employ a VAE, which enables us to sample from the distribution of the latent space and decode the clinical biomarkers for these samples. We also employ a dummy variable in the regression to enable the investigation to be stratified by gender. Our work also represents the first time that a regression-based autoencoder has been applied to investigate the impact of risk factors on cardiac function.

2   Materials

We evaluate our approach on subjects selected from the UK Biobank data set, which contains multiple imaging and non-imaging information from more than half a million 40–69 year-olds. We included only participants with CMR imaging data. From this group, we excluded participants with a history of cardiovascular disease, respiratory disease, renal disease, cancer, rheumatological disease, symptoms of chest pain or dyspnoea. For each subject, the following cine CMR acquisitions were used; a short-axis (SA) stack covering the full heart, and two orthogonal long-axis (LA) acquisitions (2-chamber (2Ch) and 4-chamber (4Ch) views). For each image slice 50 temporal frames were available covering a full cardiac cycle (temporal resolution ≈14–24 ms/frame). All CMR imaging was carried out on a 1.5 T scanner (Siemens Healthcare, Erlangen, Germany). Details of the image acquisition protocol can be found in [10]. Blood pressure was measured using the HEM-70151T digital blood pressure monitor (Omron, Hoofddorp, The Netherlands) [11].

3   Methods

In the following sections we first describe the automated estimation of biomarkers of cardiac function from CMR images, and secondly present the R-VAE network used to learn the relationship between cardiac function and SBP. Figure 1 summarizes these steps and how they interrelate.

3.1   Biomarker Estimation from CMR

The procedure used to extract the clinical biomarkers of cardiac function is based on the work published in [12] and is briefly summarized below.

Automatic Segmentation Network: We first used a fully-convolutional network with a 17 convolutional layer VGG-like architecture for automatic segmentation of the left ventricle (LV) blood pool, LV myocardium and right ventricle

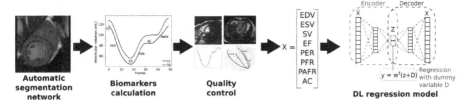

Fig. 1. Overview of the proposed framework for a VAE regression model based on automatically estimated clinical biomarkers.

(RV) blood pool from SA and LA slices in all frames through the cardiac cycle [13,14]. After this, all segmentations were aligned to correct for breath-hold induced motion artefacts using the iterative registration algorithm proposed in [14].

Biomarker Calculation: LV and RV blood volume curves were calculated from the obtained segmentations. From these curves, end-diastolic volume (EDV), end-systolic volume (ESV), stroke volume (SV), ejection fraction (EF), LVED mass (LVEDM), peak ejection rate (PER), peak early filling rate (PEFR), atrial contribution (AC) and peak atrial filling rate (PAFR) were obtained. Cardiac volumes were indexed to body surface area (BSA) using the Dubois and Dubois formula [15]. The complete list of biomarkers calculated was: iLVEDV (indexed LVEDV), iLVSV, LVEDM, LVPER, LVPFR, LVPAFR, LVAC, iRVEDV, RVPER, RVPFR, RVPAFR and RVAC.

Quality Control: Similar to [12], two quality control (QC) methods were implemented to automatically reject subjects with insufficient image quality or incorrect segmentations, ensuring the robustness of the estimated biomarkers. The first QC step (QC1) used trained DL models to reject any image with poor quality or incorrect planning, and the second QC step (QC2) detected incorrect segmentation results using an SVM model that identified physiologically unrealistic or unusual volume curves.

3.2   Deep Learning Regression Model

To combine the interpretability of handcrafted features with the power of DL we propose to use a VAE featuring a regression loss in the latent space to simultaneously learn efficient representations of cardiac function and map their change with regard to differences in SBP. As a regression model we used the multivariable regression modelling commonly used in epidemiological studies [16], where the effect of different independent variables are included as confounders on the regression model. As a result, the VAE linearizes the relationship between different clinical biomarkers and the variable of interest (SBP in this case), and these features are incorporated in a standard regression model.

Variational Autoencoder: The encoding part of a VAE allows a number of features, $\mathbf{x}$, to be mapped into a lower dimensional representation (the *latent* *space*), whilst the decoder maps this representation back to the original higher dimensional space. The proposed VAE has $N = 13$ input units representing the clinical biomarkers, two hidden layers with 8 and 4 hidden units respectively and a latent space of dimensionality 2. To avoid over-fitting we apply dropout with probability 0.3 after each hidden layer during training.

Linear Regression with Indicator (Dummy) Variable: We use a linear regression model in the latent space to estimate SBP, that incorporates a dummy variable (encoded as 0 or 1) to differentiate between population groups. In our experiments we used gender as a dummy variable, but the method is general and could be used to investigate a wide range of other factors. Mathematically, the linear regression model can be formulated as follows: $y = w^T(z + D) + \epsilon$, where z are the latent space activations, D the dummy variable, y the ground truth label (i.e. SBP) and w the regression coefficients. The regression loss is the mean squared error: $L_{\text{regression}} = \frac{1}{N} \sum_{t=1}^{N} (y_i - w_i^T(z_i + D_i))^2$.

Joint Learning for Regression: We denote the input data by $\mathbf{x} = [x_1, x_2, ...x_N]$ (i.e. a vector of $N = 13$ clinical biomarkers) and its corresponding latent space representation as $\mathbf{z} = [z_1, z_2]$. The decoded clinical biomarkers are denoted by $\hat{\mathbf{x}} = [\hat{x}_1, \hat{x}_2, ...\hat{x}_N]$, and the predicted label by $\hat{y} = \text{Regressor}(\mathbf{z})$. We combine the VAE loss and the regression loss by minimising the following joint loss function:

$$L_{\text{R}-\text{VAE}} = L_{\text{recon}} + \alpha L_{\text{KL}} + \beta L_{\text{regression}} \tag{1}$$

where α and β control the weights of the components of the loss function, L_{KL} is the Kullback-Leibler divergence between the learnt latent distribution and a unit Gaussian, and $L_{\text{regression}}$ is the Huber loss for the regression task. We first train the model only using the VAE loss, i.e. $\beta = 0$, and secondly train both the VAE and the regression together using $\beta = 2$. We set $\alpha = 0.3$ throughout.

4 Experiments and Results

Using our selection criteria, 3,781 subjects were included in our experiments. Of these, 54 subjects were rejected during QC1, and a further 127 during QC2. The remaining 3,600 cases were used to build the models. Of these cases, 1,321 had normotension (SBP < 120 mmHg), 1,697 hypertension (SBP > 140 mmHg) and 582 cases had prehypertension (a SBP between 120 and 140 mmHg).

Experiment 1 - Comparative Evaluation on Regression Task:
We compared our proposed R-VAE model with two state-of-the-art techniques for multivariate regression: (1) Lasso regression, a linear regression model with a $l1$ regularizer [17]; and (2) Random Forest regression [18], an ensemble method that has shown excellent performance in complex regression and classification tasks. For all methods, we used a five-fold cross validation to obtain the optimal model. We split the dataset into training, validation and test (60/20/20), and optimized the hyperparameters using a grid search strategy. We calculated the

root-mean-square deviation (RMSD), the normalized root-mean-square deviation (nRMSD), and the coefficient of determination (R^2) between the ground truth SBP and the predicted SBP. Table 1 shows these results. It can be seen that all methods performed similarly with regard to regression. However, note that the next two experiments are only made possible by our use of the R-VAE architecture and would not be possible with the other regression techniques.

Table 1. Comparison of R-VAE, Lasso regression and Random Forest regression.

Methods	RMSD (mmHg)	nRMSD (mmHg)	$R^2(\%)$
Lasso [17]	13.2	0.11	0.35
Random Forest [18]	12.98	0.12	0.33
R-VAE	11.36	0.10	0.69

Experiment 2 - Investigating the Effect of SBP on Cardiac Function:
We applied our R-VAE network to investigate how cardiac function changes with increasing SBP in healthy individuals, stratified by gender. We applied our R-VAE network to investigate how cardiac function changes with increasing SBP in healthy individuals, stratified by gender. We sampled the latent space of the model along the regression line for different SBP values (between 100 to 170 mmHg in steps of 10 mmHg). At each step, we took 20 random samples from a normal distribution in a perpendicular direction to the regression line and used the R-VAE to decode the clinical biomarkers. Figure 2 shows the means and standard deviations for a selection of the decoded biomarkers stratified by gender. The results show that iLVEDV (indexed LVEDV) decreases with increasing SBP, while iRVEDV (indexed RVEDV) remains constant. LVPAFR and LVPER increase with increasing SBP. For both iLVEDV and LVPER, the change seems to be larger in males compared to females. Overall, the observed changes in the models' predictions suggest that parameters associated with diastolic function of the LV are mostly affected by SBP, while the RV was less affected. These results suggest that stiffening of the LV myocardium could be an important disease process in deterioration of cardiac function in the light of increased SBP.

Experiment 3 - Identifying Abnormal Response:
In the normal population, some individuals with prehypertension might be predisposed to increased risk of cardiac disease, while others are not. We used our R-VAE model to identify subjects from the prehypertension group in whom predicted SBP was lower (i.e. predicted normotension) or higher (i.e. predicted hypertension) based on the latent space regression, assuming that being wrongly classified as normotensive or hypertensive identifies individuals with low versus increased risk of developing cardiac disease. Subsequently, we decoded the cardiac biomarkers for these cases using latent features at the regression line of

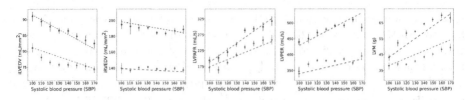

Fig. 2. SBP-related changes in iLVEDV, iRVEDV, LVPAFR and LVPER. Red represents females and blue represents males. Bars represent standard deviations. Black dotted lines represent the linear tendency curves between the cardiac biomarkers and ground-truth SBP data. (Color figure online)

their true SBP as well as using latent features at their predicted SBP. We calculated the percentage difference for each biomarker for the cases of under- and over-prediction respectively and investigated which factors contributed most to the lower or higher prediction in these subjects. Figure 3 shows the mean difference of selected biomarkers that lead to classification as normotensive (dark) and hypertensive (light). Biomarkers related to LV diastolic function (blue bars) showed the largest changes with regard to the under- and overprediction. These results show again that diastolic function of the LV was a major contributor to the model predictions of SBP. Moreover, they suggest that biomarkers related to LV diastolic function might be effective when trying to stratify cardiac risk, in particular in subjects with 'prehypertension'.

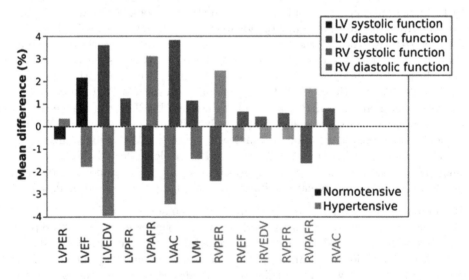

Fig. 3. Mean change (percentage) of each biomarker in prehypertension cases that were classified by the regression model as normotensive (dark) and hypertensive (light) with respect to values predicted by the model using the actual observed SBP. Values further away from zero mean a larger impact of these biomarkers. (Color figure online)

5 Discussion

In this paper, we have presented an automated DL method for analysing cardiac function and predicting cardiac risk profiles from CMR. Our framework encompasses all steps from CMR segmentation through quality control to modelling of the impact of SBP, a known cardiovascular risk factor, on cardiac function.

Instead of inputting CMR images directly into the R-VAE, we chose to first automatically estimate clinical biomarkers from the images. Combined, these biomarkers give a comprehensive description of cardiac function and are well-understood by clinicians. While some of the information of the high dimensional image data is inevitably lost by this approach, it allows the model to be interpretable by clinicians directly.

The combination of the VAE with the regression loss allowed us to decode the clinical biomarkers from the latent space, while also providing a mapping of these biomarkers to another variable, SBP. As we show in Experiment 2, this design enabled us to get a clear description of the changes in cardiac function that occur with increasing SBP. Using the trained model, we showed that increases in SBP are mainly linked to changes in diastolic LV function. This suggests that SBP results in slowly progressive changes in the myocardium that increase ventricular stiffening. As shown in Experiment 3, the model also allowed us to identify key factors separating high and low risk subjects. Again, due to the interpretability of the framework, this allowed us to identify biomarkers that could be further investigated for their utility in screening patients in clinical practice. SBP is not the only factor influencing cardiac function and that explains the relatively low R^2 of the regression models. In this paper, we used SBP as an example to illustrate the potential power of our proposed method. We aim to further extend our model in the following ways: we plan to include image and segmentation data directly into the model, in combination with the clinical biomarkers to maintain interpretability; we also plan to extend the model to investigate more risk factors. In conclusion, this work represents a novel use of DL which has produced an important contribution to furthering our understanding of the influences on cardiac function.

Acknowledgements. This work was supported by the EPSRC (grants EP/R005516/1 and EP/P001009/1) and the Wellcome EPSRC Centre for Medical Engineering at the School of Biomedical Engineering and Imaging Sciences, King's College London (WT 203148/Z/16/Z). This research has been conducted using the UK Biobank Resource under Application Number 17806.

References

1. Bello, G., Dawes, T., Duan, J., Biffi, C., et al.: Deep-learning cardiac motion analysis for human survival prediction. Nat. Mach. Intell. **1**(2), 95 (2019)
2. Bajpai, J., Sahay, A., Agarwal, A., et al.: Impact of prehypertension on left ventricular structure, function and geometry. J. Clin. Diagn. Res. **8**(4), BC07 (2014)

3. Mo, R., Nordrehaug, J.-E., Omvik, P., Lund-Johansen, P.: The bergen blood pressure study: prehypertensive changes in cardiac structure and function in offspring of hypertensive families. Blood Press. **4**(1), 16–22 (1995)
4. Biffi, C., et al.: Learning interpretable anatomical features through deep generative models: application to cardiac remodeling. In: Frangi, A.F., Schnabel, J.A., Davatzikos, C., Alberola-López, C., Fichtinger, G. (eds.) MICCAI 2018. LNCS, vol. 11071, pp. 464–471. Springer, Cham (2018). https://doi.org/10.1007/978-3-030-00934-2_52
5. Biffi, C., Cerrolaza, J., Tarroni, G., et al.: Explainable shape analysis through deep hierarchical generative models: application to cardiac remodeling. arXiv preprint arXiv:1907.00058. (2019)
6. Clough, J., Oksuz, I., Puyol-Anton, E., et al.: Global and local interpretability for cardiac MRI classification. arXiv preprint arXiv:1906.06188. (2019)
7. Xie, J., Wang, X., Liu, Y., Bai, Y.: Autoencoder-based deep belief regression network for air particulate matter concentration forecasting. J. Intell. Fuzzy Syst. **34**(6), 3475–3486 (2018)
8. Bose, T., Majumdar, A., Chattopadhyay, T.: Machine load estimation via stacked autoencoder regression. In: 2018 IEEE International Conference on Acoustics, Speech and Signal Processing (ICASSP), pp. 2126–2130. IEEE (2018)
9. Xie, R., Wen, J., Quitadamo, A., Cheng, J., Shi, X.: A deep auto-encoder model for gene expression prediction. BMC Genomics **18**(9), 845 (2017)
10. Petersen, S.E., et al.: UK Biobank's cardiovascular magnetic resonance protocol. J. Cardiovasc. Magn. Reson. **18**(1), 8 (2015)
11. Chan, M., Grossi, C., Khawaja, A., et al.: Associations with intraocular pressure in a large cohort: results from the UK biobank. Ophthalmology **123**(4), 771–782 (2016)
12. Ruijsink, B., Puyol-Antón, E., Oksuz, I., et al.: Fully automated, quality-controlled cardiac analysis from CMR: validation and large-scale application to characterize cardiac function. JACC: Cardiovasc. Imaging (2019)
13. Bai, W., Sinclair, M., Tarroni, G., et al.: Automated cardiovascular magnetic resonance image analysis with fully convolutional networks. J. Cardiovas. Magn. Reson. **20**(1), 65 (2018)
14. Sinclair, M., Bai, W., Puyol-Antón, E., Oktay, O., Rueckert, D., King, A.P.: Fully automated segmentation-based respiratory motion correction of multiplanar cardiac magnetic resonance images for large-scale datasets. In: Descoteaux, M., Maier-Hein, L., Franz, A., Jannin, P., Collins, D.L., Duchesne, S. (eds.) MICCAI 2017. LNCS, vol. 10434, pp. 332–340. Springer, Cham (2017). https://doi.org/10.1007/978-3-319-66185-8_38
15. Du Bois, D.: A formula to estimate the approximate surface area if height and weight be known. Nutrition **5**, 303–313 (1989)
16. Thompson, S., Higgins, J.: How should meta-regression analyses be undertaken and interpreted? Stat. Med. **21**(11), 1559–1573 (2002)
17. Tibshirani, R.: Regression shrinkage and selection via the lasso. J. Roy. Stat. Soc.: Ser. B (Methodol.) **58**(1), 267–288 (1996)
18. Lin, Y., Jeon, Y.: Random forests and adaptive nearest neighbors. J. Am. Stat. Assoc. **101**(474), 578–590 (2006)

Ultra-DenseNet for Low-Dose X-Ray Image Denoising in Cardiac Catheter-Based Procedures

Yimin Luo[1(✉)], Daniel Toth[1,2], Kui Jiang[3], Kuberan Pushparajah[1], and Kawal Rhode[1]

[1] School of Biomedical Engineering and Imaging Sciences,
King's College London, London, UK
yimin.luo@kcl.ac.uk
[2] Siemens Healthineers, Frimley, UK
[3] School of Computer Science, Wuhan University, Wuhan, China

Abstract. The continuous development and prolonged use of X-ray fluoroscopic imaging in cardiac catheter-based procedures is associated with increasing radiation dose to both patients and clinicians. Reducing the radiation dose leads to increased image noise and artifacts, which may reduce discernable image information. Therefore, advanced denoising methods for low-dose X-ray images are needed to improve safety and reliability. Previous X-ray imaging denoising methods mainly rely on domain filtration and iterative reconstruction algorithms and some remaining artifacts still appear in the denoised X-ray images. Inspired by recent achievements of convolutional neural networks (CNNs) on feature representation in the medical image analysis field, this paper introduces an ultra-dense denoising network (UDDN) within the CNN framework for X-ray image denoising in cardiac catheter-based procedures. After patch-based iterative training, the proposed UDDN achieves a competitive performance in both simulated and clinical cases by achieving higher peak signal-to-noise ratio (PSNR) and signal-to-noise ratio (SNR) when compared to previous CNN architectures.

1 Introduction

Image-guided interventions which require navigating medical therapeutic devices through a patient's cardiovascular system using X-ray imaging have seen growing use [1]. Such procedures play an important role in cardiac catheter-based intervention, a type of minimally invasive surgery for treating cardiovascular diseases, such as arrhythmias and stenoses. Despite a much quicker recovery and less postoperative discomfort for the patient, these procedures can result in significant X-ray exposure to the patient as well as to the medical staff, which is a major concern especially in paediatric patients. Given the potential risk of X-ray radiation, low-dose X-ray fluoroscopic imaging is of great value. The most common way to lower the radiation dose is to reduce the X-ray flux by decreasing the tube operating current, shortening the exposure time and decreasing the frame rate. However, this increases the noise and artifacts in the obtained images, which can reduce discernible information during the

© Springer Nature Switzerland AG 2020
M. Pop et al. (Eds.): STACOM 2019, LNCS 12009, pp. 31–42, 2020.
https://doi.org/10.1007/978-3-030-39074-7_4

procedures. Therefore, it is worthwhile to develop new efficient denoising method-ologies that allow significant X-ray dose reduction without loss of discernible information.

Traditional image denoising approaches mainly utilise non-local statistics and image self-similarity [4–6], and they usually suffer from complex parameter selection. To overcome this drawback, some discriminative learning methods have been developed to learn image prior models in the context of truncated inference [7]. However, they train a specific model for a certain noise level, which results in poor performance when facing complex noise. Inspired by recent success of deep convolutional neural networks (CNNs) on feature representation, several CNN-based denoising methods in various fields [3, 4, 7–12] have been proposed to achieve a better image restoration through a deep end-to-end mapping between low- and high-quality images. Unlike general images, low-dose X-ray images used in cardiac catheter-based procedures suffer from quantum noise which is often modelled by a Poisson law according to the physics of X-ray generation and imaging. This that means homogeneous regions can appear highly noisy and the contrast of heterogenous regions can be extremely low, which results in complexity of denoising. Considering the strengths of CNN frameworks in recovering high-frequency details caused by complex noise, this paper develops this framework for cardiac catheter-based procedures as an X-ray image denoiser. Recently, to improve the efficiency and effectiveness of feature extraction, CNN frameworks witnessed a rapid development on their architecture [13, 14]. However, deeper architectures are particular demanding especially in the case of X-ray images which typically have a large matrix size and frame rate. To improve feature propagation and reuse in classification tasks, Huang et al. [16] connected each layer to every other layer in a feed-forward manner and proposed dense convolutional network (DenseNet). As this new architecture provides a more tenacious way to combine the low- and high-level features, it visibly outperforms other CNN-based methods. In addition, dense skip connection can also alleviate the vanishing-gradient problem in training, as it enables short paths linking directly to every layer output. Despite the increasing utilization of information, this all-round connection increases computation burden and memory consumption to a large degree.

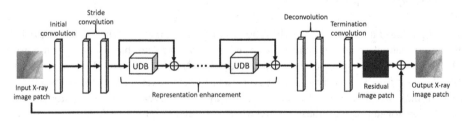

Fig. 1. Outline of the proposed ultra-dense denoising network (UDDN).

In this study, based on dense skip connection, a novel ultra-dense denoising network is proposed to achieve X-ray image denoising in cardiac catheter-based procedures with less memory consumption. This network effectively improves feature extraction by establishing rich correlation between multiple-path neural units in each residual block and a better mapping between low-dose X-ray images and their full-dose ground truth can be searched. As illustrated in Fig. 1, this network contains several ultra-dense blocks (UDBs). As each UDB has three conventional dense blocks given the same convolution layers, it can greatly enhance the representational power of the network. Since the parameters between UDBs are shared with each other, this network can also release the memory burden to a large degree. Trained with high- and low-dose X-ray image pairs, a model specified in X-ray image denoising can be obtained. Experiments on both the simulated and clinical datasets validate the effectiveness of this network.

2   Methodology

As illustrated in Fig. 2, the ultimate goal is to learn a non-linear mapping function which can reconstruct the corresponding high-dose X-ray image from the given low-dose input. Therefore, to obtain a robust model specified in X-ray image denoising, low-dose X-ray images and their high-dose counterparts are required as samples and labels for training respectively. Firstly, to implement the training process, noise must be added to original high-dose X-ray images artificially to simulate the low-dose X-ray samples. Trained with those image pairs, a robust CNN model specified in X-ray image denoising can be obtained by iteratively minimizing the difference between the predicted high-dose X-ray image and the ground truth. Finally, with a low-dose X-ray image and the obtained network, its high-lose denoising result can be directly predicted.

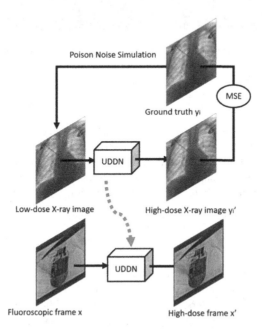

Fig. 2. Flowchart for X-ray image denoising via the proposed UDDN. The flowchart can be divided into two parts: training (upper) and denoising (lower).

2.1 Poison Noise Simulation

For X-ray imaging, quantum noise is the most dominant source of noise and is usually modelled by a Poisson law, hence, a Poisson model for the noise measurement is calculated by (1) and (2)

$$\textbf{Noise} = \textbf{Poisson}(\lambda) + \lambda \tag{1}$$

$$\lambda = \sigma\mu \tag{2}$$

Where σ denotes the noise level in the X-ray image and μ denotes the mean image intensity. The network is trained from normal-dose X-ray images and their corresponding low-dose images which were generated by adding Poisson noise according to this physical model. Figure 3 makes a comparison of a high-dose X-ray image and its simulated noisy counterpart with 60% poison noise which is approximately equivalent to quarter-dose acquisition.

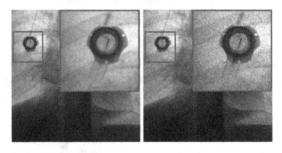

Fig. 3. An example of adding simulated noise to an X-ray image (Left: Image acquired at a high dose. Right: Image with 60% simulated added noise)

2.2 Network Architecture

In this section, we present the design of each key module under the UDDN framework in detail. As illustrated in Fig. 1, the first convolution layer is an initial layer for shallow feature extraction of the input X-ray image patches. Then, two stride convolution layers are added to map the extracted features to low-dimensional domain and this operation aims at reducing the amount of calculation. The main part of our network is stacked with multiple residual blocks and this design enhances the representation of the obtained low-dimensional features to a large degree. As shown in Fig. 4, on the basis of the dense connection, we propose a triple-path residual block called UDB, the black lines in it represent flat and common used skip connections and the blue lines represent cross connections between paths which enable sharing of information. Compared to previous dense networks, UDB contains three times as many richer paths with the same convolution layers. For the sake of these triple-path units and transition layer, the feature channels become shallower and the parameters become less, which visibly decreases the computational burden and memory consumption. In particular, the

UDBs in our network interact with each other by skip connection, so they can utilize the feature information of their predecessor, which facilitates the reuse of features. Subsequently, two deconvolution layers are added to map the obtained features back to high-dimensional domain. Finally, other convolution layers are added in our network as a termination layer to output a residual noisy image which is as the same size as the input one.

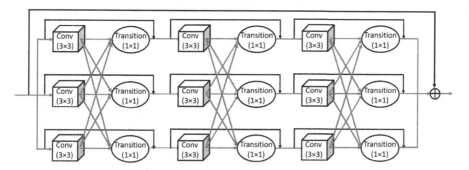

Fig. 4. Outline of the proposed ultra-dense blocks (UDBs) in UDDN. (Color figure online)

2.3 Loss Function

According to various CNN-based image processing methods [6, 7, 9–14], the loss function is commonly used to fit the target image by minimizing the distance between the output image and the ground truth based on feature level and Euclidean distance and cosine distance are the most commonly used similarity measurements. In terms of denoising, to obtain a substantially improved CNN architecture, as most of the previous methods [13–15] constrain output by iteratively minimizing the mean squared error (MSE), we use this measurement during our network training. As shown in Fig. 2, for a certain low-dose X-ray image, the MSE of its real high-dose X-ray image y_i and predicted high-dose X-ray y_i' is calculated by (3)

$$\text{MSE}_i = \frac{1}{\textbf{width} \times \textbf{height}} ||\mathbf{y_i} - \mathbf{y_i'}||^2 \tag{3}$$

For the whole training datasets, the loss function of our network can be calculated by (4)

$$\textbf{Loss} = \frac{1}{2\mathbf{N}} \sum\nolimits_{i=1}^{\mathbf{N}} \text{MSE}_i \tag{4}$$

Where N represents the number of X-ray image samples for training.

2.4 Quantitative Indicators

Besides visual perception, peak-to-signal-noise ratio (PSNR) and structural similarity (SSIM) are usually used as evaluation metrics to assess the model performance in previous image denoising methods [5–9]. PSNR is a widely used metric in image reconstruction tasks and it is calculated based on MSE by (5)

$$PSNR = 10\log_{10}\frac{(2^n - 1)}{MSE} \qquad (5)$$

Both of these two metrics need reference images for comparison, hence, they are suitable to assess the denoising results of the simulated X-ray images. However, in clinical images, we have only low-dose X-ray images with uncertain noise level to be denoised, as there is no corresponding high-dose reference image. Therefore, for clinical images, we need an effective non-reference image quality assessment method. We utilize signal-to-noise ratio (SNR) to assess the denoising performance of our models on clinical datasets, and the SNR of a single image is the average of all patches in it. In the experiment, the patch size of sub-image is usually set to 16. Since the indicator used only stands for a ratio of average pixel value and standard deviation, there are no units for it.

3 Experiments

In our experiments, we used a desktop computer with an NVIDIA GTX1060Ti GPU with 6.0 Gb RAM, an Intel I7-8700K CPU @ 3.20 GHz with 16.0 Gb RAM for training and testing. Our model was implemented on TensorFlow with Python3.6 under Windows10, CUDA9.0 and CUDNN5.1.

3.1 Datasets

Table 1 shows a summary of all data used for experiments. Data sources were a publically available data of plain chest X-ray images [18] and clinical catheter laboratory images acquired at St. Thomas' hospital during cardiac catheter procedures.

Table 1. Summary of all data used in experiments

Dataset	Source	Training	Testing
Chest X-ray (CXR) [18]	Standard plain chest X-rays 108,948 frontal view X-ray images from 32,717 patients	5,000 X-rays images (1024 × 1024 pixels) 30,443 patches (96 × 96 pixels) + synthetic noise	300 images, 300 central patches 576 × 576 pixels + synthetic noise

(*continued*)

Table 1. (*continued*)

Dataset	Source	Training	Testing
Catheter Laboratory Data 1 (CL1)	1,080 X-rays images (96 × 96 pixels) Procedures at St. Thomas' Hospital, London	800 X-rays images (512 × 512 pixels) 10,554 patches (96 × 96 pixels) + synthetic noise	
Catheter Laboratory Data 2 (CL2)	623 X-ray sequences from 20 patients Procedures at St. Thomas' Hospital, London		100 low-dose X-ray sequences with 3,262 images (400 × 400 pixels) 72 high-dose X-ray sequences with 2,166 images (400 × 400 pixels)

3.2 Training

The training data were created by adding 60% Poisson noise to the original training images. This represents a significant simulated reduction in radiation dose as mentioned previously and is comparative to what can be achieved on a clinical X-ray system. Based on the settings presented in [18], we inputted one batch consisting of 16 patches with the size of 96 × 96 from the training datasets (CXR & CL1) to our network each time. The learning rate was initialized to 10^{-3} for all layers and halved for every 10^4 steps up to 10^{-5} and we selected PReLU as our activation following each convolution layer which contains 8 × 8 filters. The depth of UDB in our network was 6 and training a denoising model took approximately 20 h. We compared our method with other image denoising methods, including DnCNN [7] and DenseNet [15] (8 dense blocks) and trained these networks with the same training data.

3.3 Validation

We firstly examined the effectiveness of the proposed UDDN on both training and testing datasets to check whether the obtained model was overfitting or not. Figure 5 displays the comparison denoising results according to the iterations of UDDN on these two datasets. For the training dataset we used 10% of the complete training data (CXR & CL1) and for the testing data set we used all the data (CXR). Comparatively, the denoising results of training dataset exhibit faster convergence and visibly higher PSNR and SSIM than that of the testing dataset, and this superiority shows that the obtained denoising model performs better on training dataset than testing dataset. Accordingly, there is no overfitting for the proposed method and our UDDN is reliable for X-ray image denoising.

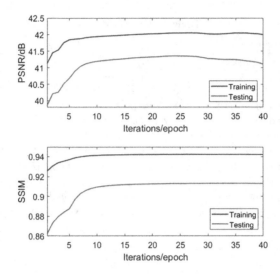

Fig. 5. Training process for UDDN with the noise level of 60%. The blue lines denote the convergence process of the training dataset and the red lines at the bottom refer to that of the testing dataset. (Color figure online)

3.4   Testing on CXR Dataset

The denoising results on the test CXR data with the noise level of 60% for the proposed approach and the comparison methods are shown in Fig. 6. We selected several but representative images with different contained structures (i.e., rib, spine, electrode and catheter). Subjectively it can be seen that our UDDN outperforms the other methods by visual inspection. In terms of the evaluation results, UDDN achieves a better PSNR and SSIM (41.4 dB and 0.914), which are about 0.4 dB and 0.015 higher than those of DenseNet and 4 dB and 0.12 higher than those of DnCNN, respectively.

Furthermore, to validate the more general ability of the CNN-based algorithms, we tested them with a range of noise levels from 0% to 100%. Figure 7 tabulates the results in terms of PSNR and SSIM. From these results, we can see that both the DenseNet and DnCNN denoising methods exhibit lower scores than our new network. DenseNet and UDDN are less sensitive to changes in noise level than DnCNN and UDDN shows better denoising capability when facing higher noise levels. Amongst the methods, UDDN shows the best performance because of its ultra-dense-connection-based effective framework for local spatial information extraction.

3.5   Testing on Clinical Data

Testing was also carried out using the CL2 clinical dataset. For these data there was no ground truth and so we used SNR as a measure of denoising performance. The CL2 dataset had both low-dose fluoroscopic images and high-dose acquisition images as detailed in Table 1. The results are shown in Table 2. In terms of fluoroscopic sequences, the proposed UDDN achieves the highest SNR (25.8), which is about

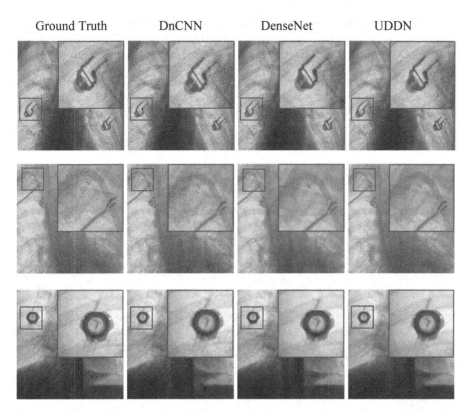

Fig. 6. Examples of the denoising results on the CXR test data using the noise level of 60%.

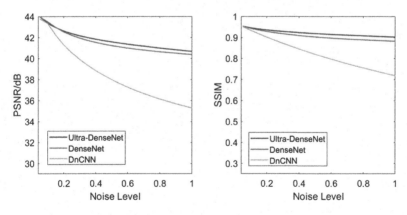

Fig. 7. A comparison of denoising results on the CXR test data for carrying noise levels using three CNN-based methods: DnCNN, DenseNet and our UDDN.

1.5 dB higher than that of DenseNet and 6.5 dB higher than that of DnCNN, respectively. However, both DenseNet and UDDN show less effectiveness on acquiration X-ray images than DnCNN, this may because they are insensitive to high-dose X-ray images.

Table 2. Average denoising results on the clinical dataset CL2

	Fluoroscopic	Acquisition
UDDN	25.8	25.7
DenseNet	24.3	25.4
DnCNN	19.4	27.6
Input	11.5	19.0

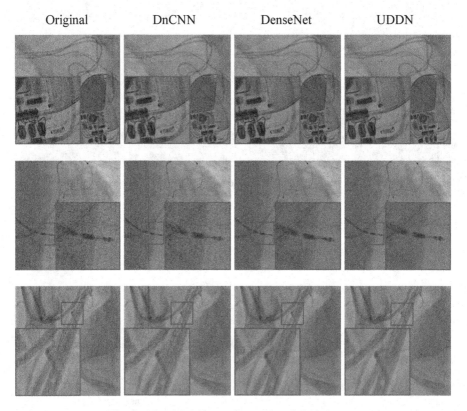

Fig. 8. The denoising results on the clinical dataset.

In terms of visual perception, we selected several different but representative structures from fluoroscopic images, i.e. vessels, electrodes and catheters to make comparisons. Notably, the proposed UDDN and previous DenseNet surpass DnCNN significantly and UDDN is subjectively best under visual inspection. As illustrated in Fig. 8, compared to UDDN, the other two CNN-based methods produce more noticeable artifacts. These observations remained to be proved by future observational study using clinical experts as observers.

Both DenseNet and the proposed UDDN show effectiveness on low-dose X-ray image denoising, which validates the advantages of dense connection on network design. And UDDN slightly outperforms previous DenseNet by achieving higher quantitative Indicators but limited improvements on visual perception.

4   Conclusions and Future Works

In this study, we propose a simple but effective technique for X-ray image denoising in cardiac catheter-based procedures. In particular, we present a multiple-path UDB for local feature extraction. Unlike the previous DenseNet, more flexible dense connections between layers and units in our network promote information interaction and improve reutilization. Extensive experiments on both the simulated and clinical datasets indicate that UDDN outperforms existing CNN-based denoising techniques. This technique may prove valuable in dose reduction in the setting of real-time X-ray imaging for guiding interventions, especially paediatric interventions. Future work will focus on more extensive clinical testing (especially visual scoring of denoised imaged by expert clinicians), real-time implementation (current frame rate is 4 frames per second on the mentioned hardware) and real-time testing in the clinical setting. Moreover, the noise level of X-ray images obtained in actual clinical cases is uncertain and unpredictable. Therefore, a more flexible training method instead of using a fixed noise level should be proposed to promote network effectiveness.

Acknowledgements. This work was funded by the KCL NIHR Healthcare Technology Centre and KCL-China Scholarship Scheme. This research was also supported by the National Institute for Health Research (NIHR) Biomedical Research Centre at Guy's and St. Thomas' NHS Foundation Trust and King's College London. The views expressed are those of the authors and not necessarily those of the NHS, the NIHR or the Department of Health.

References

1. Cleary, K., Peters, T.M.: Image-guided interventions: technology review and clinical applications. Ann. Rev. Biomed. Eng. **12**, 119–142 (2010)
2. Wang, S., Housden, J., Zar, A., Gandecha, R., Singh, D., Rhode, K.: Strategy for monitoring cardiac interventions with an intelligent robotic ultrasound device. Micromachines **9**(2), 65 (2018)
3. Chen, H., et al.: Low-dose CT with a residual encoder-decoder convolutional neural network. IEEE Trans. Med. Imaging **36**(12), 2524–2535 (2017)
4. Kang, E., Min, J., Ye, J.C.: A deep convolutional neural network using directional wavelets for low-dose X-ray CT reconstruction. Med. Phys. **44**(10), 360–375 (2017)
5. Crouse, M.S., Nowak, R.D., Baraniuk, R.G.: Wavelet-based statistical signal processing using hidden Markov models. IEEE Trans. Sig. Process. **46**(4), 886–902 (1998)

6. Dabov, K., Foi, A., Katkovnik, V., Egiazarian, K.: Image denoising by sparse 3-D transform-domain collaborative filtering. IEEE Trans. Image Process. **16**(8), 2080–2095 (2007)
7. Zhang, K., Zuo, W., Chen, Y., Meng, D., Zhang, L.: Beyond a Gaussian denoiser: residual learning of deep CNN for image denoising. IEEE Trans. Image Process. **26**(7), 3142–3155 (2017)
8. Wang, R., Tao, D.: Non-local auto-encoder with collaborative stabilization for image restoration. IEEE Trans. Image Process. **25**(5), 2117–2129 (2016)
9. Zhang, K., Zuo, W., Zhang, L.: FFDNet: toward a fast and flexible solution for CNN-based image denoising. IEEE Trans. Image Process. **27**(9), 4608–4622 (2018)
10. Kang, E., Chang, W., Yoo, J., Ye, J.C.: Deep convolutional framelet denosing for low-dose CT via wavelet residual network. IEEE Trans. Med. Imaging **37**(6), 1358–1369 (2018)
11. Cho, S.I., Kang, S.: Gradient prior-aided CNN denoiser with separable convolution-based optimization of feature dimension. IEEE Trans. Multimedia **21**(2), 484–493 (2019)
12. Yuan, Q., Zhang, Q., Li, J., Shen, H., Zhang, L.: Hyperspectral image denoising employing a spatial-spectral deep residual convolutional neural network. IEEE Trans. Geosci. Remote Sens. **57**(2), 1205–1218 (2019)
13. Kim, J., Lee, J.K., Mu Lee, K.: Accurate image super-resolution using very deep convolutional networks. In: IEEE Conference on Computer Vision and Pattern Recognition, pp. 1646–1654 (2016)
14. Lai, W., Huang, J., Ahuja, N., Yang, M.: Deep Laplacian pyramid networks for fast and accurate super-resolution. In: IEEE Conference on Computer Vision and Pattern Recognition, pp. 5835–5843 (2017)
15. Tong, T., Li, G., Liu, X., Gao, Q.: Image super-resolution using dense skip connections. In: IEEE Conference on International Conference on Computer Vision, pp. 4809–4817 (2017)
16. Huang, G., Liu, Z., Maaten, L., Weinberger, K.Q.: Densely connected convolutional networks. In: IEEE Conference on Computer Vision and Pattern Recognition, pp. 2261–2269 (2017)
17. Tao, X., et al.: Detail-revealing deep video super-resolution. In: IEEE International Conference on Computer Vision, pp. 4482–4490 (2017)
18. Wang, X., et al.: ChestX-ray8: hospital-scale chest X-ray database and benchmarks on weakly-supervised classification and localization of common thorax diseases. In: IEEE Conference on Computer Vision and Pattern Recognition, pp. 2097–2106 (2017)

A Cascade Regression Model
for Anatomical Landmark Detection

Zimeng Tan[1,2,3], Yongjie Duan[1,2,3], Ziyi Wu[1,2,3], Jianjiang Feng[1,2,3(✉)],
and Jie Zhou[1,2,3]

[1] Department of Automation, Tsinghua University, Beijing, China
jfeng@tsinghua.edu.cn
[2] State Key Lab of Intelligent Technologies and Systems,
Tsinghua University, Beijing, China
[3] Beijing National Research Center for Information Science and Technology,
Beijing, China

Abstract. Automatic anatomical landmark detection is beneficial to many other medical image analysis tasks. In this paper, we propose a two-stage cascade regression model to make coarse-to-fine landmark detection. Specifically, in the first stage, a Gaussian heatmap regression model customized from U-Net is exploited to make primary prediction, which takes the downsampled entire image as input. In the second stage, we develop a CNN to regress displacements from the primary prediction to the landmarks, using patches in original resolution centered at the previous localization as input. Owing to the different sizes and resolutions of inputs in two stages, the global context information and local appearance can be integrated by our algorithm. The spacial relationships among landmarks can also be exploited by predicting all the landmarks simultaneously. In evaluation on the coronary and aorta CTA images, we show that our proposed method is widely applicable and delivers state-of-the-art performance even with limited training data.

Keywords: Anatomical landmark detection · Heatmap regression · Cascade model

1 Introduction

Anatomical landmark detection plays an important assisted role in many medical image analysis tasks, such as organ segmentation, registration and vessel extraction [1]. However, for accurate landmark detection, there still remain many challenges: (a) anatomical differences between patients are widespread, (b) while detecting multiple landmarks simultaneously, spatial constrains among landmarks should be taken into account, (c) detection of 3D anatomical landmarks aggravates the computational cost intensively, making real-time application challenging, (d) limited annotated training data available restricts algorithmic design typically. Although many methods have been proposed [2–5], there is still room for improvement. Among these methods, our method is more related to [3,4].

© Springer Nature Switzerland AG 2020
M. Pop et al. (Eds.): STACOM 2019, LNCS 12009, pp. 43–51, 2020.
https://doi.org/10.1007/978-3-030-39074-7_5

For landmark detection, an intuitive patch-based approach is to regress displacements from patches center to the target landmark [3]. Then the landmark position is calculated by these displacements following a majority/average voting strategy. Trained by numerous patches, it is possible to design deep networks which can capture discriminative information and perform better than the shallow ones. Nonetheless, these methods always focus on local appearance merely and global information is not well utilized. The large number of patches also leads to a heavy computational burden. For improvement, Noothout et al. [6] proposed a model performing classification and regression jointly, in which only displacements of patches classified as containing landmarks contributed to the final result.

Another interesting method is based on regressing heatmaps [4]. With entire image as input, these models are supposed to output synthetic heatmap, denoting the probability of each voxel belonging to the target landmark. The prediction position is simply chosen to be the output voxel with the maximum temperature. Apparently, they can utilize global context information and have good spatial generalization. However, the input volume shrinks in methods using FCN [7], which causes theoretical lower bound of prediction error. For instance, output heatmap of size 128 with input of size 512 leads to 3 voxels error at most. Furthermore, the total number of network weights for 3D medical images increases intensively, making the training difficult with limited training data at hand.

Combining the advantages of the two methods above, we propose a cascade regression model combining heatmap regression and displacement regression. The proposed method makes coarse-to-fine prediction, taking entire image in lower resolution and patches in higher resolution as input respectively, which combines global information and local appearance. The spatial relationships among landmarks are also taken into account by learning long-range context, which improves overall performance. The cascade structure is similar to the method of He et al. [9], in which the facial landmark localizations were refined via finer and finer modeling. In contrast, instead of the deep CNN, a carefully designed heatmap regression model is exploited to make initial prediction in our method. Besides, the local patches are extracted as input in the subsequent stage [10], rather than entire image in [9].

We evaluated our method on the coronary and aorta CTA images by detecting 5 and 9 anatomical landmarks respectively. These landmarks are of great clinical significance: cardiac landmarks contribute to diagnosis, prognosis, and therapy of cardiovascular diseases [1]; detection of aortic landmarks is an effective assistant tool in aortic vascular modeling [6]. The results demonstrate our method is competent for the cardiac and aortic landmark detection task and achieves performance comparable to the state-of-the-art approach [6].

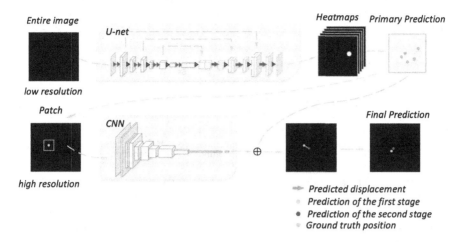

Fig. 1. The overview of our cascade regression model.

2 Proposed Method

Figure 1 illustrates the overall cascade regression model framework for single landmark detection. We show the 2D case for clarity but the model works similarly in 3D. In the first stage, a modified U-Net is employed to get a relatively accurate initial localization, taking the entire image in lower resolution as input and heatmaps as output. Owing to the skip architecture, this module can capture multi-scale knowledge. Aiming to learn more precise context information, in the second stage, the patch centered at initial localization in higher resolution is extracted and fed to the displacement regression model. The CNN adjusts the initial localization by moving it toward ground truth position. The different sizes and resolutions of two stages emphasize that they focus on long-range context and local appearance, respectively.

2.1 Primary Prediction

We exploit heatmap regression to make the first stage prediction. In this scheme, each landmark has a separate output channel where a Gaussian heat spot is centered at its location. During inference, the predicted position is simply determined by the maximum response. Following the principle of classification, for N_l landmarks, the model is trained for $N_l + 1$ channels, where the first N_l channels describe the probability belonging to the corresponding landmark and the last channel belonging to background. Particularly, considering that softmax operation may influence the status of landmark positions in heatmap ground truth (e.g. for 5 landmarks, the values of 1th landmark in 6 channels are changed from $(1, 0, ..., 0)$ to $(0.35, 0.13, ..., 0.13)$ after softmax, which can be smaller than its neighbors), we adjust the sum of all channels to 1 by fixing the background channel and scaling the others.

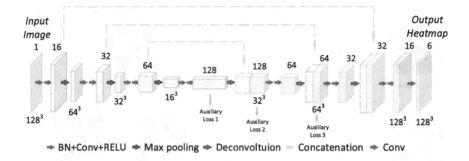

Fig. 2. The architecture of the proposed model in the first stage.

The temperature t_i for ith landmark (i.e. ith channel) can be defined as:

$$f(x) = \begin{cases} k\exp(\frac{-(v-p_i)^2}{2\sigma^2}), & i = 1,2,3,...,N_l, \\ 1 - k\exp(\frac{-(v-p_{closest})^2}{2\sigma^2}), & i = N_l + 1. \end{cases} \quad (1)$$

The heatmaps of first N_l channels are determined by the distance from the voxel v to the landmark position p_i, while the heatmap of background channel is according to the closest landmark position $p_{closest}$. σ is standard deviation and k is Gaussian height.

As shown in Fig. 2, our model realizes this scheme by customizing the original 3D U-Net [8]. Similar to its standard version, the network is comprised of 3D convolution, max-pooling, deconvolution (up sampling) and short-cut connections from layers in contracting path to the ones in expansive path with equal resolution. Each convolution layer follows 'same mode' (i.e. ouput has the same size as input) and uses RELU activation function. The model takes entire downsampled image as input and outputs heatmap volumes. Benefiting from the natural superiority of U-Net, the model can capture long-range context information, where the spatial relationships among landmarks can also be taken into account, increasing overall accuracy.

Aiming to tackle the problem of class imbalance, namely heat spot only occupies a small proportion of volume, we employ a weighted mean squared error (MSE) loss function between the predicted and ground truth heatmaps. The weights are chosen to be the exponential powers of the predicted values in the output. On the other hand, to deal with gradient vanishing problem, we shorten the backpropagation path of gradient flow signals by incorporating three side-paths auxiliary loss. The final formulation of loss function is expressed as:

$$\mathcal{L}(P; H^{GT}) = \mathcal{L}_{mse}(P; H^{GT}) + \sum_{s=1,2,3} \beta_s \mathcal{L}^s_{mse}(p^s; H^{GT}) \quad (2)$$

where H^{GT} is the ground truth heatmap, P is the final output, β_s is the weight of different side-path p^s and set as 0.3, 0.6, 0.9 corresponding s as 1, 2, 3.

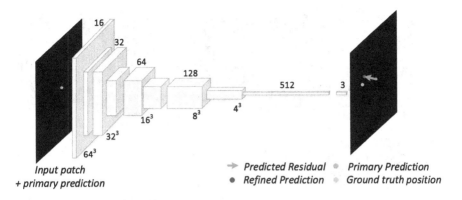

Fig. 3. The architecture of the displacement regression module in the second stage.

2.2 Refinement Strategy

In the second stage, we propose a CNN model to refine the primary prediction. Given the first stage model taking the entire image as input, we assume that landmarks should be distributed around the initial prediction. The CNN takes patches in original resolution centered at the inital prediction to capture more precise local information. Considering that local appearance of certain landmarks may be ambiguous (e.g. locally similar vascular structures), we restrict this stage model to change the initial prediction in a small range.

The CNN is trained to predict the displacement vector $\triangle S$ from the primary prediction S_0 to the true landmark position S^{GT}. Given a volume V, a training sample is represented by $(\Gamma(V, q), \triangle S^{GT})$ where q is a point randomly sampled around S_0 in a small range from V and $\Gamma(V, q)$ is its associated patch. The ground truth displace vector $\triangle S^{GT}$ is given by $\triangle S^{GT} = S^{GT} - S_0$. During inference, patch $\Gamma(V, S_0)$ is fed to the model and the final prediction is obtained by $S = S_0 + \triangle S$. The CNN is trained by minimising Euclidean loss between the predicted and the true displacement vector.

As shown in Fig. 3, the CNN model contains 4 convolutional layers followed by max-pooling layers, and 2 fully-connected layers. Each layer except the last one employs RELU activation function. Considering that certain landmarks may have distinct appearance than the others (e.g. the apex cordis), we refine them separately. That is, we train a refinement network per landmark. Since the CNN is trained by patches, a small number of training data is sufficient in this stage.

3 Experiments and Results

3.1 Data and Experiment Settings

We evaluated the proposed method on the two datasets of coronary and aorta CTA images. As shown in Figs. 4 and 5 cardiac landmarks and 9 aortic landmarks

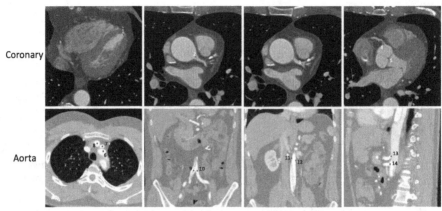

Cardiac: 1. apex cordis   2. left coronary ostium   3. LM Bifurcation
4. right coronary ostium   5. origin of the non-coronary aortic valve commissure
Aorta: 6. Left subclavian artery   7. Left common carotid artery   8. brachiocephalic trunk
9. left Iliac artery   10. right Iliac artery   11/12. left/right renal artery
13/14. superior/inferior mesenteric artery

Fig. 4. Landmarks defined on the coronary and aorta CTA images.

are annotated manually by a expert. For both datasets, we do not apply data augmentation such as scaling and rotation, which may increase the complexity of landmark distribution.

Coronary dataset is randomly divided into training data with 75 scans and test data with 40 scans. All volumes were zero-padded to $512 \times 512 \times 512$ voxels with isotropic voxel size 0.4 mm. Then they were downsampled 4 times and fed into the model in the first stage. In the second stage, patches size 64 in the original resolution were extracted and the batch size was set to 4. The model was trained using Adam with a learning rate of 0.001 for 11,250 and 45,000 iterations in the two stages, respectively.

Aorta dataset consists of training data with 25 scans and test data with 23 scans. which has an average size of $512 \times 512 \times 777$ voxels, with a voxel size of $0.71 \times 0.71 \times 0.81$ mm^3. The annotated landmarks are located at the bifurcation of the aorta and its main branches. Considering that aortic landmark detection is more challenging due to its low resolution and complex organ distribution, the volumes were manually cropped first and downsampled 2 times to fed into the first stage model. The rest of the training process is similar.

3.2   Results

Summary metrics obtained by different networks on the coronary dataset are listed in Table 1. We use average Euclidean distance between ground truth and estimated landmark positions as evaluation measure. We first compared two-stage cascade model and only the first stage model. After refinement, the detection accuracy improves significantly, demonstrating the benefit of our cascade architecture.

Table 1. Average Euclidean distance errors expressed in mm, for the detection of 5 cardiac landmarks on the coronary dataset. The results are obtained by the two-stage model and the first stage model only, which takes either patches or entire image as input, comparing with the algorithms of Noothout et al. [6].

	1	2	3	4	5	Mean
First Stage						
Patch-based	3.14	1.45	8.43	17.12	1.12	6.25
Entire image	3.18	4.79	3.23	6.17	2.60	3.99
Two-stage model						
Our proposed	**2.58**	**1.48**	**1.37**	**3.51**	**1.46**	**2.08**
Noothout et al. [6]	-	2.88	2.19	3.78	2.10	-

Table 2. Average with standard deviation Euclidean distance errors in mm for the detection of 14 landmarks on the two datasets by the proposed algorithm.

Landmarks	1	2	3	4	5					Overall
Cardiac	2.58±1.33	1.48±1.87	1.37±0.84	3.51 ±2.1	1.46±0.86					2.08±1.71
Landmarks	6	7	8	9	10	11	12	13	14	Overall
Aortic	5.62±3.53	7.43±4.72	6.38±4.34	5.60±4.71	7.38±4.17	6.22±3.68	7.82±5.99	4.40±3.35	4.39±1.57	6.14±4.33

To demonstrate that integrating spatial relationships among landmarks can improve overall performance, we adjusted the model in the first stage to take patches size of 48 as input instead of entire image. In this way, the network can only utilize the context information around one landmark at a time. It was trained to predict heatmap patch according to the input. The predicted position was determined by the maximum response in the volume composed of predicted patches. The experiment results show our method in the first stage performs better overall. Specifically, the patch-based network is superior in detecting the left coronary ostium and the origin of the non-coronary aortic valve commissure, which may be more dependent on precise context information. On the other hand, our proposed model performs much better in detecting the right coronary ostium and the bifurcation of the LM, where the relationships among landmarks are probably necessary for accurate detection (e.g. the position of the left coronary ostium is important for localizing the bifurcation of the LM).

Furthermore, we compared our model with the method of Noothout et al. [6], which detected 6 anatomical landmarks in cardiac CT scans (4 of them are the same as us). The metrics are quoted directly from [6] since that dataset is not publicly available. Although our dataset is different from that in [6], we can conclude that the performance of the proposed algorithm is at least comparable to [6].

Table 2 lists more detailed metrics of detection for each landmark on the two datasets using our algorithm. The high detection error of aortic landmarks is due to the low resolution of aortic images. In the model design, we do not utilize unique atlas information related to coronary or aorta, which guarantees the method capable for the anatomical landmark detection tasks in different regions of the human body. Some visual results are shown in Fig. 5.

Coronary

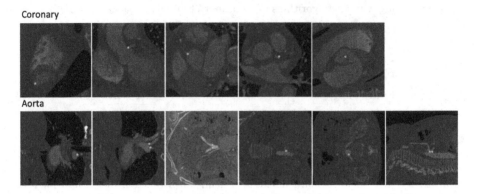

Aorta

Fig. 5. Visualisation of landmark detection in coronary and aorta images by the cascade regression model. The ground truth and predictions are indicated by green and red dots, respectively. (Color figure online)

4   Conclusion

We have proposed a two-stage cascade regression model for detecting anatomical landmarks in coronary and aorta CTA images. Owing to different sizes and resolutions of input in two stages, the model combines the global information and local appearance. By learning long-range context, the spatial relationships among landmarks are also taken into account, increasing overall performance. The experiment results demonstrate that our method achieved performance comparable to the state-of-the-art algorithm [6]. Limited by memory and computation time, we used downsampled image in the first stage. It is foreseeable that the model would gain better performance with images of higher resolution as input. Another limitation is we only have one annotator, which makes it impossible to assess inter-observer error for landmarks. It is also worthwhile to apply multistage refinement to capture more precise information. The experiment results have demonstrated that our method is generic for anatomical landmarks detection and the next step is to extend it to other medical images.

References

1. Zhou, S.K.: Discriminative anatomy detection: classification vs regression. Pattern Recogn. Lett. **43**, 25–38 (2014)
2. Yang, D., et al.: Automated anatomical landmark detection ondistal femur surface using convolutional neural network. In: IEEE ISBI (2015)
3. Gao, Y., Shen, D.: Context-aware anatomical landmark detection: application to deformable model initialization in prostate CT images. In: Wu, G., Zhang, D., Zhou, L. (eds.) MLMI 2014. LNCS, vol. 8679, pp. 165–173. Springer, Cham (2014). https://doi.org/10.1007/978-3-319-10581-9_21

4. Payer, C., Štern, D., Bischof, H., Urschler, M.: Regressing heatmaps for multiple landmark localization using CNNs. In: Ourselin, S., Joskowicz, L., Sabuncu, M.R., Unal, G., Wells, W. (eds.) MICCAI 2016. LNCS, vol. 9901, pp. 230–238. Springer, Cham (2016). https://doi.org/10.1007/978-3-319-46723-8_27

5. Ghesu, F.C., Georgescu, B., Mansi, T., Neumann, D., Hornegger, J., Comaniciu, D.: An artificial agent for anatomical landmark detection in medical images. In: Ourselin, S., Joskowicz, L., Sabuncu, M.R., Unal, G., Wells, W. (eds.) MICCAI 2016. LNCS, vol. 9902, pp. 229–237. Springer, Cham (2016). https://doi.org/10.1007/978-3-319-46726-9_27

6. Noothout, J.M.H., de Vos, B.D., Wolterink, J.M., Leiner, T., Isgum, I.: CNN-based landmark detection in cardiac CTA scans. In: MIDL (2018)

7. O'Neil, A.Q., et al.: Attaining human-level performance with atlas location auto-context for anatomical landmark detection in 3D CT data. In: Leal-Taixé, L., Roth, S. (eds.) ECCV 2018. LNCS, vol. 11131, pp. 470–484. Springer, Cham (2019). https://doi.org/10.1007/978-3-030-11015-4_34

8. Ronneberger, O., Fischer, P., Brox, T.: U-net: convolutional networks for biomedical image segmentation. In: Navab, N., Hornegger, J., Wells, W.M., Frangi, A.F. (eds.) MICCAI 2015. LNCS, vol. 9351, pp. 234–241. Springer, Cham (2015). https://doi.org/10.1007/978-3-319-24574-4_28

9. He, Z., Kan, M., Zhang, J., Chen, X., Shan, S.: A fully end-to-end cascaded CNN for facial landmark detection. In: IEEE FG (2017)

10. Sun, Y., Wang, X., Tang, X.: Deep convolutional network cascade for facial point detection. In: CVPR (2013)

Comparison of 2D Echocardiography and Cardiac Cine MRI in the Assessment of Regional Left Ventricular Wall Thickness

Vera H. J. van Hal[1,4], Debbie Zhao[1], Kathleen Gilbert[1(✉)],
Thiranja P. Babarenda Gamage[1], Charlene Mauger[1], Robert N. Doughty[2,5],
Malcolm E. Legget[2], Jichao Zhao[1], Aaqel Nalar[1], Oscar Camara[7],
Alistair A. Young[6], Vicky Y. Wang[1], and Martyn P. Nash[1,3]

[1] Auckland Bioengineering Institute, University of Auckland, Auckland, New Zealand
kat.gilbert@auckland.ac.nz
[2] School of Medicine, University of Auckland, Auckland, New Zealand
[3] Department of Engineering Science, University of Auckland,
Auckland, New Zealand
[4] Department of Biomedical Engineering, Eindhoven University of Technology,
Eindhoven, The Netherlands
[5] Greenlane Cardiovascular Service, Auckland District Health Board,
Auckland, New Zealand
[6] Department of Biomedical Engineering, King's College London, London, UK
[7] Physense, Department of Information and Communication Technologies,
Universitat Pompeu Fabra, Barcelona, Spain

Abstract. The generation of kinematic models of the heart using 3D echocardiography (echo) can be difficult due to poor image contrast and signal dropout, particularly at the epicardial surface. 2D echo images generally have a better contrast-to-noise ratio compared to 3D echo images, thus wall thickness (WT) estimates from 2D echo may provide a reliable means to constrain model fits to 3D echo images. WT estimates were calculated by solving a pair of differential equations guided by a vector field, which is constructed from the solution of Laplace's equation on binary segmentations of the left ventricular myocardium. We compared 2D echo derived WT estimates against values calculated using gold-standard cardiac cine magnetic resonance imaging (MRI) to assess reliability. We found that 2D echo WT estimates were higher compared to WT values from MRI at end-diastole with a mean difference of 1.3 mm (95% CI: 0.74–1.8 mm), 1.5 mm (95% CI: 0.91–2.1 mm) and 2.1 mm (95% CI: 1.6–2.6 mm) for basal, mid-ventricular and apical segments respectively. At end-systole, the WT estimates from MRI were higher compared to those derived from 2D echo with a mean difference of 2.6 mm (95% CI: 2.0–3.1 mm), 2.1 mm (95% CI: 1.5–2.7 mm) and 1.1 mm (95% CI: 0.49–1.7 mm) for basal, mid-ventricular and apical segments, respectively. The

The authors gratefully acknowledge the Health Research Council of NZ for funding this project (17/608). This would not have been possible without the dedicated work of our research support staff, Craig McDougal, and the MRI technologists at Center of Advanced MRI, University of Auckland.

M. Pop et al. (Eds.): STACOM 2019, LNCS 12009, pp. 52–62, 2020.
https://doi.org/10.1007/978-3-030-39074-7_6

quantitative WT comparison in this study will contribute to the ongoing efforts to better translate kinematic modelling analyses from gold-standard cardiac MRI to the more widely accessible echocardiography.

Keywords: Wall thickness · Echocardiography · Cardiac MRI

1 Introduction

Kinematic modelling of the heart is important to the understanding of the underlying mechanisms of heart failure, which is a complex, multifactorial disease with divergent characteristics [1]. Cardiovascular disease is the world's leading cause of mortality and morbidity. It is estimated that 23 million people worldwide are suffering from heart failure, which has a mortality rate of 50% within five years [1]. Recent advances in pharmacologic therapy and implantable cardiac devices have improved survival, however continued advancements in diagnostics and therapeutics are needed to further reduce the economic burden of heart failure as the current therapies rarely prove curative [1]. The new knowledge that can be gathered from kinematic modelling can be key for the development of novel treatments that are patient specific [12].

In order to create a model of the heart, an accurate representation of its geometry is needed from cardiac imaging techniques. Magnetic resonance imaging (MRI) is the gold standard imaging technique for assessing cardiac function, due to its high contrast-to-noise ratio, resolution and reproducibility compared to other imaging techniques [4]. However MRI is expensive, time consuming and often not suitable for patients with implantable devices [9]. Echocardiography (echo) remains the work-horse for diagnostic imaging in hospitals, due to its portability and relative low cost. It is also widely available and deeply embedded in clinical decision making for patients with heart disease [9].

3D echo evaluations of left ventricular (LV) mass and volume are known to be systematically different to those acquired from MRI, due to shadowing artefacts in patients with poor acoustic windows and a lower contrast-to-noise ratio, which makes the quantification of LV shapes from 3D echo images difficult [14]. Previous research has shown the feasibility of building cardiac statistical shape atlases using MRI and 3D echo, but also using 3D echo alone by applying a multi-view subspace learning algorithm to establish the discrepancy between the image modalities [11].

In this study, both 2D and 3D echo images, as well as MRI acquisitions from the same person were gathered. 3D echo images have poor epicardial surface definition which increases difficulty in accurately defining wall thickness from these images. 2D echo images generally have a better image quality compared to 3D echo images, thus 2D echo may be used to constrain kinematic model generation from 3D echo. This can be done using wall thickness (WT) estimates from 2D echo to obtain a more accurate geometry as well as wall mass.

We quantified regional WT from 2D echo data by solving a pair of differential equations guided by a vector field, constructed from the solution of Laplace's equation on binary segmentation's of the LV myocardium. These WT measurements were compared against values calculated using gold-standard cardiac cine MRI taken from the same participants to assess the reliability of WT estimates from 2D echo.

2   Methods

2.1   Data Collection

18 participants underwent cardiac MRI and echocardiographic examinations within 1 h of each other. Ethical approval for this study was obtained from the health and disability ethics committee of New Zealand (17/CEN/226). All participants gave written informed consent to participate in the study. The MRI was performed on a 1.5T Siemens AvantoFit. All cine images were acquired in long and short axis orientations with a steady-state free precession (SSFP) sequence with the following standard imaging parameters: echo time (TE) of 1.6 ms, repetition time (TR) of 3.7 ms, flip angle of 45°, field of view of 360 cm × 360 cm, temporal resolution of 48 ms, voxel size of 1.5 mm × 1.5 mm, and slice thickness of 6 mm. The echocardiographic examination was performed using a Siemens Acuson SC2000 ultrasound system. A standard 2D echo examination was performed in line with guidelines [6], and the cardiac cycle was captured three times for each acquisition. Four 3D echo datasets were acquired using a 4Z1c 3D transducer which captures the cardiac geometry in one heart beat. The field of view and frame rate were varied to fit the patient geometry, and optimise image quality. All apical two chamber (A2C), apical four chamber (A4C) and apical long axis (ALX) views with the best image quality were chosen for the WT measurements.

2.2   Segmentation of the LV Myocardium from 2D Echo Images and Cardiac Cine MRI

Segmentation of the LV myocardium in 2D echo images was performed manually in ITK-SNAP 3.8.0[1] [18]. Both end-diastolic (ED) and end-systolic (ES) frames in each of the three views were manually segmented, resulting in six annotated images for each of the 18 participants. Each of the manual contours were free drawn by hand, with no image processing techniques utilized. The ED and ES frames were selected according to the recommendation of the American Society of Echocardiography and the European Association of Cardiovascular Imaging [6]. The segmentations of the endocardial and epicardial borders were closed at the level of the mitral valve. Trabeculae and papillary muscles were excluded from the LV wall mass. 3D geometric models of the LV were made for all points in the cardiac cycle using CIM (v8.1.7), and the protocol defined in [17]. An example pair of contours on a 2D echo image and a 3D model overlayed on a MR image of the same patient is shown in Fig. 1. The triangular mesh defining

---

[1] www.itksnap.org.

the endo- and epicardial surfaces was converted into a mask of the myocardium using a voxelization methodology based on a ray intersection method similar to that described by [8]. The voxel size in the resulting mask was set to 0.75 mm × 0.75 mm × 0.75 mm.

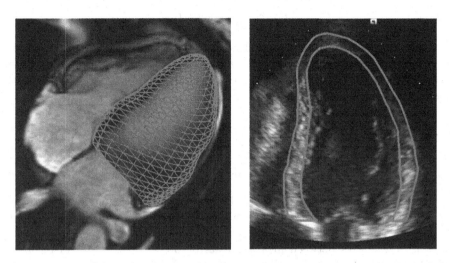

Fig. 1. Segmentation of a MR image and echo image of the same patient. Left: 3D geometric model overlayed on an A4C MRI view. Right: endo- and epicardial contours overlayed on an A4C echo view.

2.3   Estimation of Regional Wall Thickness

The LV WT estimates from 2D echo and MRI were calculated using Laplace's equation. This is an established method to calculate regional WT, for example, to identify cortical thickness [5]. It has also been used to calculate regional WT of the myocardium from MRI [10]. Solving Laplace's equation over the myocardial domain provided a gradient field indicating the correspondence trajectories between the endocardial and epicardial surfaces of the domain. These correspondence trajectories have desirable properties as they are orthogonal to each surface, do not intersect, and are nominally parallel. The WT is then defined as the arc length of these correspondence trajectories, and is defined at each point (pixel) [16]. For the numerical implementation of Laplace's equation ($\Delta\phi = 0$), Dirichlet boundary conditions with values of 300 and 100 were applied on the endocardial (Γ_{endo}) and epicardial (Γ_{epi}) borders of the domain, respectively. The Laplace solver was implemented in MATLAB (R2018a) and adjusted from [15]. Solving for ϕ by a finite difference scheme, the gradient field T is calculated according to Eq. 1.

$$T = \frac{\nabla\phi}{||\nabla\phi||} \tag{1}$$

Regional WT was calculated by solving two partial differential equations (PDEs) that determine two length functions: $L_0(x)$ and $L_1(x)$ (see Eqs. 2 and 3).

$$\nabla L_1(x) \cdot \boldsymbol{T} = 1 \qquad \text{with } L_1|\Gamma_{epi} = 0 \qquad (2)$$
$$-\nabla L_0(x) \cdot \boldsymbol{T} = 1 \qquad \text{with } L_0|\Gamma_{endo} = 0 \qquad (3)$$

Given a point x on the correspondence trajectory, $L_0(x)$ gives the arc length between the endocardial border and x and $L_1(x)$ returns the arc length of the correspondence trajectory between the epicardial border and x. The WT is then defined by Eq. 4 [16].

$$WT(x) = L_0(x) + L_1(x) \qquad (4)$$

2.4 Intra- and Inter-observer Variability Analyses

To assess the reproducibility of cardiac labelling on 2D echo images, both intra- and inter-observer variability analyses were performed on a randomly generated 10% sample (12 images) of the dataset. Each of the images was segmented three times with 2–3 days between measurements by an observer that had received some basic training in echo image segmentation. Furthermore, the most recent segmentations were chosen for evaluation against an independent segmentation provided by an observer with one year experience in image analysis. The intra- and inter-observer variabilities were evaluated using the Dice score (DSC) and Hausdorff distance (HD) and were also assessed on the derived WT estimates, after which paired t-tests were performed to test for significant differences.

2.5 Comparison of Regional WT Estimates

The WT was compared for each region in the American Heart Association (AHA) 17-segment model [6] using the clinical guidelines described in [2] for 2D echo. For cardiac cine MRI, the same guidelines were used to divide the 3D participant specific model derived from the cines at ED and ES into regions so that regional comparison of WT estimates could be performed. The AHA regions are shown in Fig. 2.

The mean of all the pixels/voxels in each surface region for 2D echo and each volume region for MRI were taken for comparison. First, WT estimates were compared using a correlation and an unpaired t-test at the levels of base, mid-ventricular and apex at ED and ES separately. Then, a two-way ANOVA was performed to assess the dependency of the WT estimates on the imaging modality and the different regions from the AHA 17-segment model. If significant terms were found in the ANOVA model, a Tukey multiple comparison of means (Tukey HSD) was performed to investigate the importance of each of the individual terms. The ANOVA model was analysed for the basal, mid-ventricular

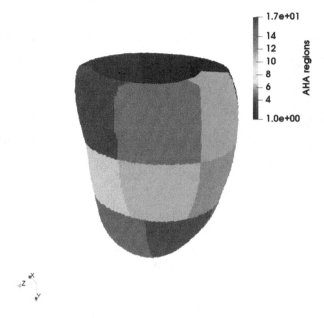

Fig. 2. AHA regions overlayed on a 3D mask of the myocardium generated from cardiac cine MRI.

and apical segments at ED and ES separately, to be able to examine the differences between the individual segments at each level. All analyses were performed with R 3.4.3 and R Commander 2.4-4 [3].

3   Results

Results from the Laplace solver for the calculation of the WT are displayed on a model fitted to cardiac cine MRI in Fig. 3.

The intra- and inter-observer variability analyses is shown in Table 1. The intra-observer differences in WT were not significant when assessed using a paired t-test, while the inter-observer differences were found to be significant.

Results for the regional comparison of WT estimates from 2D echo to cardiac cine MRI are shown in Table 2. At ED, the WT was found significantly higher for 2D echo compared to cardiac cine MRI. At ES, this relationship is reversed. There was no correlation between the WT estimates from the two modalities.

Two-way ANOVA showed significant terms for the main effects, which were the imaging modality and the AHA region. Furthermore, there was a significant interaction term between the AHA region and the modality. The only exception was encountered for the two-way ANOVA model at the basal level at ES. The mean WT derived from 2D echo and cardiac cine MRI are shown in Figs. 4 and 5. Post-hoc analysis (Tukey multiple comparison of means) showed significant differences for regions 4, 5, 10, 11, 13, 15 and 16 at ED and regions 2, 3, 6, 8, 9 and 14 at ES.

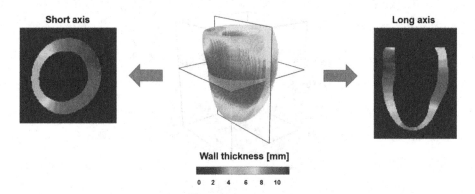

Fig. 3. Wall thickness (mm) computed from a 3D model based on MRI data. Short and long axis sections through the 3D model are shown.

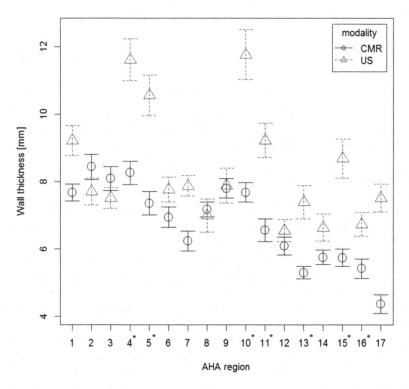

Fig. 4. Mean ED values of WT estimates calculated in each region of the AHA 17-segment model in both 2D echo (red) and cardiac cine MRI (black) for the 18 participants. The bars on each point display the standard errors on the means.The asterisks indicate the regions that were found to be significantly different in WT estimates using Tukey multiple comparison of means. (Color figure online)

Table 1. Intra- and inter-observer variability analyses on manual contours from 2D echo. The intra-observer comparisons were done for the three different days (t1, t2 and t3) separately. The Dice score (DSC), Hausdorff distance (HD) and relative difference in WT is reported as mean values from the 12 images.

	t1 - t2	t1 - t3	t2 - t3	Inter-observer
DSC (mean ± std)	0.84 ± 0.058	0.83 ± 0.059	0.82 ± 0.059	0.68 ± 0.16
HD (mean ± std)	5.6 ± 2.9 mm	5.3 ± 2.1 mm	6.2 ± 2.5 mm	6.7 ± 3.5 mm
Mean diff. WT base	0.23 mm (2.3%)	0.55 mm (6.7%)	0.79 mm (8.1%)	1.9 mm (24%)
Mean diff. WT mid	1.1 mm (11.5%)	0.97 mm (10.3%)	0.11 mm (1.2%)	2.6 mm (34%)
Mean diff. WT apex	0.25 mm (3.3%)	0.063 mm (0.8%)	0.32 mm (4.2%)	2.8 mm (42%)

Table 2. Regional comparison of WT estimates from 2D echo and cardiac cine MRI at the basal, mid-ventricular and apical levels at ED and ES separately. Mean values for the relative difference in WT between the two modalities in all 18 participants and 95% confidence intervals (CI) are shown. The relative difference is reported as the difference between the WT from 2D echo minus the WT from cardiac cine MRI.

	Base	mid-ventricular	Apex
Mean relative difference at ED	1.3 mm (15%)	1.5 mm (19%)	2.1 mm (37%)
95% CI (ED)	[0.74, 1.8] mm	[0.91, 2.1] mm	[1.6, 2.6] mm
Mean relative difference at ES	−2.6 mm (24%)	−2.1 mm (21%)	−1.1 mm (13%)
95% CI (ES)	[−3.1, −2.0] mm	[−2.7, −1.5] mm	[−1.7, −0.49] mm

4 Discussion

From the regional comparison of WT estimates, there was a clear difference in WT estimations for segmentations of ED and ES. At ED, the estimated WT from 2D echo is larger than when derived from cardiac MRI. At ES, this relationship is reversed. In cardiac MRI during systole, the trabeculae appear to combine with the compact myocardium, making the boundary between these structures difficult to distinguish, whereas in 2D echo this boundary is well defined [7].

Tukey HSD indicated that several segments differed significantly in WT derived from 2D echo and MRI at ED and ES. At ED, the segments with the largest differences in WT between the modalities were located in the inferior and inferolateral side of the heart. At ES, significant differences in WT were found on the septal side of the heart. Also within each modality, variations in WT across the different AHA regions were found. Whether these differences are consistent needs to be evaluated on a larger dataset and could be used to provide better translation in clinical indices between echo and MRI.

WT estimates were calculated using Laplace's equation and PDE constraints. There are alternative techniques for calculating regional WT, such as the centerline method [13]. It has been reported that the use of the Laplace solver is more accurate than the centerline method because the latter carries the implicit assumption that the myocardial wall is always perpendicular to the acquisition

Wall thickness at end-systole

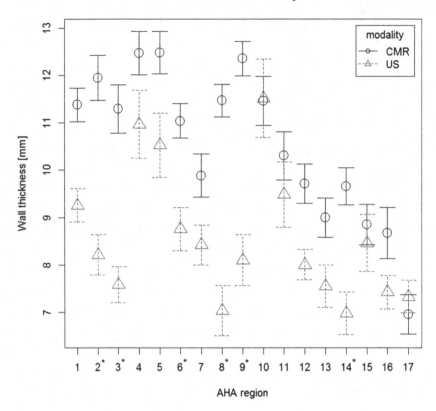

Fig. 5. Mean ES values of WT estimates calculated in each region of the AHA 17-segment model in both 2D echo (red) and cardiac cine MRI (black) for the 18 participants. The bars on each point display the standard errors on the means. The asterisks indicate the regions that were found to be significantly different in WT estimates using Tukey multiple comparison of means. (Color figure online)

plane [10]. Some limitations in the WT estimation include the fact that part of the basal myocardium needed to be excluded from the solution analysis. This was because an edge artefact occurred here due to the way the boundary conditions were defined. This could have been solved by adjusting the geometry only for the computation, although it would have required more computation time.

While the accuracy of the Laplace solver is good (in the order of 1 pixel), the use of manual segmentations for the delineation of the myocardial domain reduces the accuracy of the WT estimates on 2D echo, as there are inter- and intra-observer errors. The intra-observer error was relatively small (about 5%), which indicates a good consistency. The inter-observer error was much larger at about 35%. However, with a more detailed protocol for the segmentations and more training of the observers, the error is expected to decrease. It is important to investigate how these uncertainties in the 2D echo WT estimates can influence kinematic model predictions.

The comparison of regional WT estimates was performed based on the mean values found across one AHA region. These mean values come from a distribution of WT values and could be considered for future research.

5 Conclusions

This study has shown that WT estimates derived from 2D echo images of the heart are significantly different to WT estimates derived from 3D geometric models of the LV fitted to cardiac cine MRI using Laplace's equation. As a next step, the WT estimates from 2D echo will be used to constrain model fits to 3D echo images. This knowledge contributes towards ongoing efforts to better translate kinematic modelling analyses from gold-standard cardiac MRI to the more widely accessible echocardiography.

References

1. Alpert, C., et al.: Symptom burden in heart failure: assessment, impact on outcomes, and management. Heart Fail. Rev. **22**(1), 25–39 (2017)
2. Badano, L.P., Picano, E.: Standardized myocardial segmentation of the left ventricle. Stress Echocardiography, pp. 105–119. Springer, Cham (2015). https://doi.org/10.1007/978-3-319-20958-6_7
3. Fox, J.: The R commander: a basic-statistics graphical user interface to RJ Stat. Software **14**, 42 (2005)
4. Gonzalez, J.A., Kramer, C.M.: Role of imaging techniques for diagnosis, prognosis and management of heart failure patients: cardiac magnetic resonance. Curr. Hear. Fail. Rep. **12**(4), 276–283 (2015)
5. Jones, S.E., et al.: Three-dimensional mapping of cortical thickness using Laplace's equation. Hum. Brain Mapp. **11**(1), 12–32 (2000)
6. Lang, R.M., et al.: Recommendations for cardiac chamber quantification by echocardiography in adults: an update from the American society of echocardiography and the European association of cardiovascular imaging. Eur. Hear. J.-Cardiovasc. Imaging **16**(3), 233–271 (2015)
7. Park, E.A., et al.: Effect of papillary muscles and trabeculae on left ventricular measurement using cardiovascular magnetic resonance imaging in patients with hypertrophic cardiomyopathy. Korean J. Radiol. **16**(1), 4–12 (2015)
8. Patil, S., Ravi, B.: Voxel-based representation, display and thickness analysis of intricate shapes. In: Ninth International Conference on Computer Aided Design and Computer Graphics (CAD-CG 2005) (2005)
9. Ponikowski, P., et al.: 2016 ESC guidelines for the diagnosis and treatment of acute and chronic heart failure: the task force for the diagnosis and treatment of acute and chronic heart failure of the European Society of Cardiology (ESC). Developed with the special contribution of the heart failure association (HFA) of the ESC. Eur. J. Hear. Fail. **18**(8), 891–975 (2016)
10. Prasad, M., et al.: Quantification of 3D regional myocardial wall thickening from gated magnetic resonance images. J. Magn. Reson. Imaging **31**(2), 317–327 (2010)

11. Puyol-Antón, E., et al.: A multimodal spatiotemporal cardiac motion atlas from MR and ultrasound data. Med. Image Anal. **40**, 96–110 (2017)
12. Sengupta, P.P., et al.: The new wave of cardiovascular biomechanics. JACC: Cardiovasc. Imaging **12**(7), 1297–1299 (2019)
13. Sheehan, F.H., Bolson, E.L., Dodge, H.T., Mathey, D.G., Schofer, J., Woo, H.: Advantages and applications of the centerline method for characterizing regional ventricular function. Circulation **74**(2), 293–305 (1986)
14. Shimada, Y.J., Shiota, T.: A meta-analysis and investigation for the source of bias of left ventricular volumes and function by three-dimensional echocardiography in comparison with magnetic resonance imaging. Am. J. Cardiol. **107**(1), 126–138 (2011)
15. Wang, Y., et al.: A robust computational framework for estimating 3D bi-atrial chamber wall thickness. Trans. Biomed. Eng. (2019, under Revision)
16. Yezzi, A.J., Prince, J.L.: An eulerian PDE approach for computing tissue thickness. IEEE Trans. Med. Imaging **22**(10), 1332–1339 (2003)
17. Young, A.A., et al.: Left ventricular mass and volume: fast calculation with guide-point modeling on MR images. Radiology **216**(2), 597–602 (2000)
18. Yushkevich, P.A., et al.: User-guided 3D active contour segmentation of anatomical structures: significantly improved efficiency and reliability. Neuroimage **31**(3), 1116–1128 (2006)

Fully Automatic 3D Bi-Atria Segmentation from Late Gadolinium-Enhanced MRIs Using Double Convolutional Neural Networks

Zhaohan Xiong[1]([✉]), Aaqel Nalar[1], Kevin Jamart[1], Martin K. Stiles[2],
Vadim V. Fedorov[3], and Jichao Zhao[1]

[1] Auckland Bioengineering Institute, University of Auckland,
Auckland, New Zealand
zxio506@aucklanduni.ac.nz
[2] Waikato Clinical School, Faculty of Medical and Health Sciences,
University of Auckland, Auckland, New Zealand
[3] Department of Physiology and Cell Biology,
The Ohio State University Wexner Medical Center, Columbus, USA

Abstract. Segmentation of the 3D human atria from late gadolinium-enhanced (LGE)-MRIs is crucial for understanding and analyzing the underlying atrial structures that sustain atrial fibrillation (AF), the most common cardiac arrhythmia. However, due to the lack of a large labeled dataset, current automated methods have only been developed for left atrium (LA) segmentation. Since AF is sustained across both the LA and right atrium (RA), an automatic bi-atria segmentation method is of high interest. We have therefore created a 3D LGE-MRI database from AF patients with both LA and RA labels to train a double, sequentially used convolutional neural network (CNN) for automatic LA and RA epicardium and endocardium segmentation. To mitigate issues regarding the severe class imbalance and the complex geometry of the atria, the first CNN accurately detects the region of interest (ROI) containing the atria and the second CNN performs targeted regional segmentation of the ROI. The CNN comprises of a U-Net backbone enhanced with residual blocks, pre-activation normalization, and a Dice loss to improve accuracy and convergence. The receptive field of the CNN was increased by using 5×5 kernels to capture large variations in the atrial geometry. Our algorithm segments and reconstructs the LA and RA within 2 s, achieving a Dice accuracy of 94% and a surface-to-surface distance error of approximately 1 pixel. To our knowledge, the proposed approach is the first of its kind, and is currently the most robust automatic bi-atria segmentation method, creating a solid benchmark for future studies.

Keywords: Atrial segmentation · Convolutional neural network · MRI

1 Introduction

Atrial fibrillation (AF) is the most common form of cardiac arrhythmia and is associated with substantial morbidity and mortality [1]. Current clinical treatments for AF perform poorly due to a lack of basic understanding of the underlying atrial anatomical

© Springer Nature Switzerland AG 2020
M. Pop et al. (Eds.): STACOM 2019, LNCS 12009, pp. 63–71, 2020.
https://doi.org/10.1007/978-3-030-39074-7_7

structure which directly sustains AF in the human atria [2]. In recent years, gadolinium-based contrast agents are utilized in a third of all MRI scans to improve the clarity of a patient's internal structures such as the atria by enhancing the visibility of disease-associated structures such as fibrosis/scarring, inflammation, tumors, and blood vessels [3]. Late gadolinium-enhanced MRI (LGE-MRI) is widely used to study fibrosis/scarring [4], and clinical studies on AF patients using LGE-MRIs have shown that the extent and distribution of atrial fibrosis can be used to reliably predict ablation success rates [5]. As a result, direct analysis of the atrial structure in patients with AF is vital to improving the understanding and patient-specific treatment of AF.

Segmentation of both the left atrial (LA) and right atrial (RA) chambers is a crucial task for aiding medical management for AF patients based on structural analysis of the segmented 3D geometry. Due to the rising popularity of convolutional neural networks (CNN) in the field of medical imaging, many algorithms have been developed utilizing CNNs, particularly for the segmentation of the LA directly from LGE-MRIs [6]. These methods have drastically improved on the previous traditional atlas-based or shape-based approaches [7] in terms of both performance and adaptability due to their fully data-driven nature. In 2018, numerous CNN methods were submitted to the STACOM 2018 Left Atrial Segmentation Challenge [8] aiming at optimizing LA segmentation performance from LGE-MRIs. Through the challenge, the U-Net was shown to be the most widely used and most easily adaptable architecture for the task [9]. In particular, pipelines with enhancements to the U-Net baseline such as the addition of residual connections, dilated convolutions, and custom loss functions achieved far superior segmentation accuracies.

Despite the extensive research in LA segmentation, no established study has been conducted for the fully automatic segmentation of the RA directly from LGE-MRIs. A 2017 benchmarking study investigated methods of segmenting the LA, RA, left ventricle (LV), and right ventricle (RV) from non-contrast MRIs [10]. However, segmentation from LGE-MRIs compared to non-contrast MRIs is much more challenging due to the attenuation caused by the contrast agent resulting in a lack of distinguishable features between the atrial tissue and background. Thus, there is still an urgent need of an intelligent algorithm capable of automatically segmenting both the LA and the RA simultaneously from LGE-MRIs.

In this paper, we propose and evaluate a robust approach for fully automatic segmentation of the atria, particularly the RA, from 3D LGE-MRIs. In order to effectively learn the complex geometry of the atrial chambers, we designed a double CNN pipeline for targeted segmentation and reconstruction of the LA and RA without human intervention. This exciting study is the first of its kind to present a method of segmenting both atrial chambers simultaneously, and is a very important step towards more effective and efficient patient specific diagnostics and treatment.

2 Methods

2.1 Data and Pre-processing

20 3D LGE-MRIs from patients with AF were provided by the University of Utah [4]. The *in vivo* patient images were acquired at a spatial resolution of 0.625 mm 0.625 mm × 1.25 mm using either a 1.5T Avanto or 3.0T Verio clinical whole-body scanner. All 3D LGE-MRI scans contained 44 slices along the Z direction, each with an *XY* spatial size of 640 × 640 pixels or 576 × 576 pixels. The LA segmentations were provided by the University of Utah alongside the LGE-MRIs [4]. The RA segmentations were manually performed by our team based on the protocols used for LA segmentation to achieve consistency across both atrial chambers (Fig. 1c). Firstly, the RA endocardium was defined by manually tracing the RA blood pool in each slice of the LGE-MRI. The tricuspid valve connecting the RA and RV was defined by a 3D plane to create a smooth linear surface. The RA endocardium was then morphologically dilated and manually adjusted according to the RA geometry to obtain the boundary of the epicardium. Next, the septum, the region of tissue connecting the RA and LA, was manually traced such that the epicardial surfaces of the LA and RA joined together. Finally, the dilated tricuspid valve was manually removed from the RA epicardium. Overall, the three labels for the dataset were the background, the endocardium of the RA and LA, and the epicardium of the RA and LA.

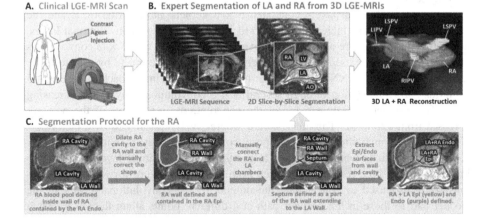

Fig. 1. Data acquisition and the protocol for labelling the left atrial (LA) and right atrial (RA) epicardium (Epi) and endocardium (Endo) from late gadolinium-enhanced magnetic resonance imaging (LGE-MRI). (A) Clinical MRI scanners were used to acquire LGE-MRIs. (B) The LGE-MRIs were manually segmented in a slice-by-slice manner by experts to obtain labels of the LA/RA epicardium and LA/RA endocardium. (C) RA manual annotation based on the LA annotation protocol provided by University of Utah [4]. AO, aorta; LV, left ventricle; PV, pulmonary vein; LS/LIPV, left superior/inferior PV; RS/RIPV, right superior/inferior PV.

The 20 3D LGE-MRI data were randomly split for performing 4-fold cross validation such that in each fold, 15 data was used for training and 5 data was used for validation. All data and labels were uniformly center cropped to a size of $576 \times 576 \times 44$ pixels, and mean and standard deviation normalization were performed. Contrast limited adaptive histogram equalization (CLAHE), a type of color intensity normalization, was also performed on the dataset during pre-processing.

2.2   Convolutional Neural Network Architecture

Our pipeline consisted of two 2D CNNs used in a sequential manner (Fig. 2a). The first CNN performed coarse segmentation on a down-sampled version of the entire 3D LGE-MRI ($144 \times 144 \times 44$) in a slice-by-slice manner to construct an approximate segmentation of the atria. The center of mass of the atria was calculated from the coarse segmentation in each slice of the LGE-MRI, and a 240×240 patch was cropped around this point, leaving out the majority of background pixels which significantly decreased computational costs. 240×240 was chosen it could contain the entire atria which had a maximum size of 200×200 from measurements on the entire dataset. The second CNN then performed slice-by-slice regional segmentation on the ROIs cropped from the 3D LGE-MRI. Finally, the individual slice-by-slice segmentations were stacked together and zero-padded to a size of $576 \times 576 \times 44$ to obtain the final segmentation.

The same CNN was used for both stages of our pipeline and consisted of an enhanced U-Net architecture (Fig. 2b). The first half of the CNN was an encoder to learn dense features from the input through several convolutional layers of increasing depth. The convolutional layers contained 5×5 kernels and a stride of 1, and the number of feature maps increased from 16 to 256. At every 1–3 convolutional layers, residual connections were added to improve feature learning and 2×2 convolutions with a stride of 2 were used to progressively down sample the image by a factor of 2. The second half of the CNN was a decoder to reconstruct the image back to the original resolution for segmentation through several 5×5 convolutional layers of decreasing depth. The number of feature maps of the convolutions in this part of the network increased from 128 to 32. The images were progressively up-sampled by a factor of 2 with 2×2 deconvolutional, or transpose convolutional, layers with stride of 2. Residual connections were also added at every 1–3 convolutional layers. In order to directly preserve high-resolution features from the input, feature forwarding connections were also used to concatenate the outputs of the convolutional layers in the encoder part to those in the decoder path at 4 different points along the CNN. Batch normalization (BN) and parametric rectified linear units (PReLU) were used after every convolutional layer along the entire CNN for improving convergence, and 50% dropout was used at every layer for regularization. The final output layer of the CNN contained a 1×1 convolution with a stride of 1, 3 feature maps, and a softmax activation function to predict for the 3 classes in the data (LA/RA epicardium, LA/RA endocardium, background). All hyper-parameters were selected as a result of extensive experimentation under controlled settings to derive the optimal parameter combinations.

The CNN was trained with the 2D Dice loss function (Eq. 2) to prioritize the segmentation of the foreground pixels over the background. At each epoch, online augmentation was used to randomly augment each data with a probability of 50% and included translation, scaling, rotation and flipping. The adaptive moment estimation gradient descent optimizer was used with a learning rate of 0.0001 and the exponential decay rate of 0.9. After training, the CNN with the highest cross-validation accuracy was selected as the final model. The network was developed in TensorFlow and was trained on an Nvidia Titan V GPU with 5120 CUDA cores and 12 GB RAM. Training took 2 h and predictions on each 3D LGE-MRI took 2 s.

2.3 Evaluation

To measure the accuracy of the first CNN in detecting of the center of mass of the atria when extracting the ROI, the mean squared error (MSE) was defined as

$$MSE = \sqrt{(x - x')^2 + (y - y')^2} \tag{1}$$

for the ground truth co-ordinates (x, y) and the predicted coordinates (x', y') of the center of mass in each 2D slice of the 3D LGE-MRIs.

To measure the accuracy of the second CNN for segmentation, the Dice score, surface-to-surface distance (STSD), sensitivity, and specificity were used. The DICE score was calculated as

$$Dice = \frac{2N_{true\,positive}}{2N_{true\,positive} + N_{false\,positive} + N_{false\,negative}} \tag{2}$$

for the atrial epicardium and endocardium predictions and ground truths. The STSD measured the average distance error between the surfaces of the predicted LA volume, A, and the ground truth, B, and was calculated as

$$STSD(A, B) = \frac{1}{n_A + n_B} \left(\sum_{p=1}^{n_A} \sqrt{p^2 - B^2} + \sum_{p'=1}^{n_B} \sqrt{p'^2 - A^2} \right) \tag{3}$$

where n_A is the number of pixels in A, n_B is the number of pixels in B, and p and p' describes all points in A and B. The sensitivity and specificity were calculated and reflected the success for segmenting the foreground and the background respectively.

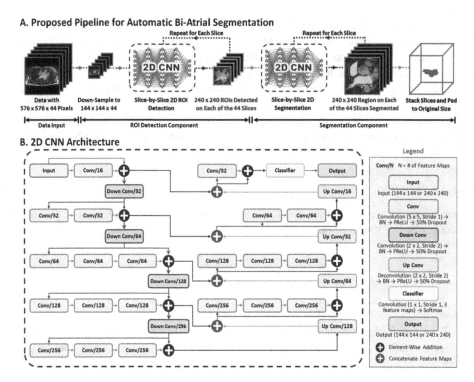

Fig. 2. The proposed double 2D convolutional neural network (CNN) pipeline for fully automatic segmentation of the left atrium (LA) and right atrium (RA) from late gadolinium-enhanced magnetic resonance imaging (LGE-MRI). (A) Overall workflow in which the first CNN detected the region of interest (ROI) containing the LA/RA and the second CNN performed regional segmentation of the ROI. (B) The architecture of the proposed 2D CNN. BN, batch normalization; PReLU, parametric rectified linear unit.

3   Results and Discussion

Table 1 summarizes the final evaluation metrics for the best performing CNN used in our proposed double CNN pipeline. Evaluation shows that the ROI containing the atria for each slice of could be calculated within 5 mm, or 8 pixels, of the ground truth through the coarsely segmented atria provided by the first CNN. Individually for each co-ordinate, the CNN had an error of 2.3 mm, or approximately 3 pixels, in the x axis and an error of 3.8 mm, or approximately 6 pixels, in the y axis. The second CNN was evaluated on the entire final 3D segmentations produced for each test data. The LA and RA endocardium were segmented with a Dice score of 92.9% and a STSD of 0.63 mm. The LA and RA epicardium were segmented with a Dice score 94.0% and a STSD of 0.68 mm. Overall, the STSD showed that the predictions were approximately within 1 pixel of the ground on average for both the endocardium and epicardium.

3D visualization of the ground truth and the predictions for the test set in one cross-validation fold shows that the proposed CNN pipeline successfully captured the overall

Table 1. Overall evaluation results of the proposed double CNN pipeline. The first CNN was evaluated on the accuracy of the region of interest detected and the second CNN was evaluated on the accuracy of the final segmentation in 3D.

First CNN		Second CNN				
	Distance (mm)		Dice (%)	STSD (mm)	Sensitivity	Specificity
Error in (x, y)	(2.27 ± 2.78, 3.77 ± 4.67)	LA + RA Endocardium	92.9 ± 1.4	0.63 ± 0.11	92.9 ± 1.6	99.9 ± 0.01
MSE	4.79 ± 5.09	LA + RA Epicardium	94.0 ± 1.4	0.68 ± 0.15	93.7 ± 2.0	99.9 ± 0.01

MSE, mean squared error; STSD, surface-to-surface distance; LA/RA, left/right atrium.

geometry of the LA and RA endocardium with a high degree of precision (Fig. 3). 3D visualization of the STSD errors of the predictions shows the most erroneous regions to be the LA pulmonary veins which some parts containing an error of up to 10 mm from the ground truth. However, minimal error can be seen on the RA in general, showing that the RA may potentially be easier to segment considering there are no complex and small structures such as the pulmonary veins present. Visualizations of the LA and RA epicardium were not shown, however, had comparable accuracies as the endocardium as seen from the higher Dice score and similar STSD.

To further analyze the regions of the predictions containing the most errors, 2D slice-by-slice visualizations and comparisons were performed for each test LGE-MRI. Figure 4 illustrates the segmentation results for the LA and RA endocardium and epicardium by our proposed pipeline compared with the ground truth for selective slices at the same depth for a test 3D LGE-MRI. The results shown are representative of the errors seen in other test LGE-MRIs. The relative depth of each slice from the bottom of the LGE-MRI scan is provided in millimeters. At the bottom slices of the LGE-MRIs (12–18 mm), it can be seen that the network was not able to reproduce the linear plane used to define the tricuspid valve, but instead, produced a more rounded prediction at this region, potentially due to the fact that there is no anatomically visible border between the RA and the RV. The segmentation at the middle slices (18–31 mm) successfully captured the geometry of the RA and LA in detail, while also showing a clear gap between the epicardium and endocardium which denotes the atrial walls. At this region, the main source of error was also at the tricuspid and mitral valve as the CNNs produced segmentations which were smooth and rounded. The septum, on the other hand, was precisely captured despite the decreased contrast in this region, showing the network was able to successfully learn the shape of the epicardium in its entirety. At the top slices of the LGE-MRIs (31–38 mm), the pulmonary vein regions were the main sources of error, consistent with previous the 3D error visualizations. The predictions show that the pulmonary veins predicted by the CNN are smaller and thinner than that of the ground truth labels, further reflecting the difficulty of segmenting this structure. However, the epicardium segmentation is shown to be fairly consistent and effectively accounts for the gaps in its morphology caused by the pulmonary veins and valves across all slices of the LGE-MRI, which was also reflected in the higher Dice score.

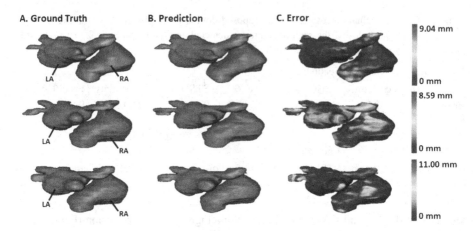

Fig. 3. 3D visualizations of the left atrial (LA) and right atrial (RA) chambers for 3 representative test late gadolinium-enhanced magnetic resonance imaging (LGE-MRI). (A) Ground truth provided. (B) Predictions segmented by the convolutional neural network (CNN). (C) Surface-to-surface error of the predictions from the ground truth in millimeters (mm).

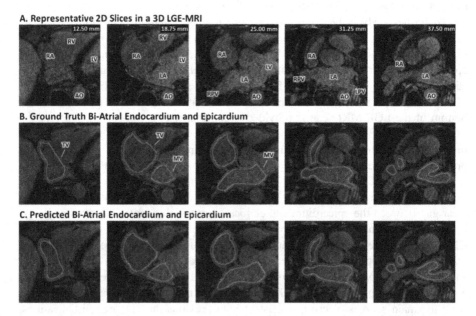

Fig. 4. The left atrial (LA) and right atrial (RA) endocardium (orange) and epicardium (blue) results from the proposed convolutional neural network (CNN) pipeline compared to the ground truth for representative slices on the same 3D late gadolinium-enhanced magnetic resonance imaging (LGE-MRI) for a test patient. (A) LGE-MRI scans. (B) Ground truths. (C) Predictions by the CNN. AO, aorta; LV, left ventricle; RV, right ventricle; LPV, left pulmonary veins; RPV, right pulmonary veins; TV, tricuspid valve; MV, mitral valve. (Color figure online)

4   Conclusion

We have developed and evaluated a double convolutional neural network for robust automatic bi-atria segmentation from LGE-MRIs. Our algorithm enables the reconstruction of both the LA and RA chambers in 3D with a Dice accuracy of 94% and a surface-to-surface distance error of approximately 1 pixel from the ground truth. Our study is the first automated method to segment both atrial chambers, particularly the RA, creating a solid benchmark for future studies. The exciting findings from this study may lead to the development of a more accurate and efficient atrial reconstruction and analysis approach, which can potentially be used for improved clinical diagnosis, patient stratification, and clinical guidance during treatment for AF patients.

Acknowledgements. This work was funded by the Health Research Council of New Zealand (16/385) and the National Institutes of Health (HL135109). We would like to acknowledge The NIH/NIGMS Center for Integrative Biomedical Computing (CIBC) at The University of Utah for providing the LGE-MRIs and LA labels. We also thank Nvidia for donating a Titan V GPU to accelerate our research.

References

1. Narayan, S.M., et al.: Ablation of focal impulses and rotational sources: what can be learned from differing procedural outcomes? Curr. Cardiovasc. Risk Rep. **11**(9), 27 (2017)
2. Zhao, J., et al.: Three dimensional integrated functional, structural, and computational mapping to define the structural "fingerprints" of heart specific atrial fibrillation drivers in human heart Ex Vivo. J. Am. Hear. Assoc. **6**(8), e005922 (2017)
3. Hansen, B.J., Zhao, J., Fedorov, V.V.: Fibrosis and atrial fibrillation: computerized and optical mapping: a view into the human atria at submillimeter resolution. JACC: Clin. Electrophysiol. **3**(6), 531–546 (2017)
4. McGann, C., et al.: Atrial fibrillation ablation outcome is predicted by left atrial remodeling on MRI. Circ. Arrhythmia Electrophysiol. **7**(1), 23–30 (2014)
5. Oakes, R., et al.: Detection and quantification of left atrial structural remodeling with delayed-enhancement magnetic resonance imaging in patients with atrial fibrillation. Circulation **119**, 1758, 1767 (2009)
6. Xiong, Z., Fedorov, V.V., Fu, X., Cheng, E., Macleod, R., Zhao, J.: Fully automatic left atrium segmentation from late gadolinium enhanced magnetic resonance imaging using a dual fully convolutional neural network. IEEE Trans. Med. Imaging **38**(2), 515–524 (2019)
7. Tobon-Gomez, C., et al.: Benchmark for algorithms segmenting the left atrium from 3D CT and MRI datasets. IEEE Trans. Med. Imaging **34**(7), 1460–1473 (2015)
8. Pop, M.: Statistical Atlases and Computational Models of the Heart. Atrial Segmentation and LV Quantification Challenges. Springer, Heidelberg (2019)
9. Ronneberger, O., Fischer, P., Brox, T.: U-Net: convolutional networks for biomedical image segmentation. In: Navab, N., Hornegger, J., Wells, W.M., Frangi, A.F. (eds.) MICCAI 2015. LNCS, vol. 9351, pp. 234–241. Springer, Cham (2015). https://doi.org/10.1007/978-3-319-24574-4_28
10. Zhuang, X., et al.: Evaluation of algorithms for multi-modality whole heart segmentation: an open-access grand challenge. arXiv preprint arXiv:1902.07880 (2019)

4D CNN for Semantic Segmentation of Cardiac Volumetric Sequences

Andriy Myronenko[1(✉)], Dong Yang[1], Varun Buch[2], Daguang Xu[1],
Alvin Ihsani[1], Sean Doyle[2], Mark Michalski[2], Neil Tenenholtz[2],
and Holger Roth[1]

[1] NVIDIA, Santa Clara, USA
{amyronenko,dongy,daguangx,aihsani,hroth}@nvidia.com
[2] MGH and BWH Center for Clinical Data Science, Boston, USA
{varun.buch,sdoyle}@mgh.harvard.edu
{mmichalski1,ntenenholtz}@partners.org

Abstract. We propose a 4D convolutional neural network (CNN) for the segmentation of retrospective ECG-gated cardiac CT, a series of single-channel volumetric data over time. While only a small subset of volumes in the temporal sequence is annotated, we define a sparse loss function on available labels to allow the network to leverage unlabeled images during training and generate a fully segmented sequence. We investigate the accuracy of the proposed 4D network to predict temporally consistent segmentations and compare with traditional 3D segmentation approaches. We demonstrate the feasibility of the 4D CNN and establish its performance on cardiac 4D CCTA (video: https://drive.google.com/uc?id=1n-GJX5nviVs8R7tque2zy2uHFcN_Ogn1.).

1 Introduction

Cardiovascular disease is responsible for 18 million deaths annually, making it one of the leading causes of mortality globally [13]. Coronary computed tomography angiography (CCTA) uses contrast-enhanced CT to evaluate cardiac muscle morphology, function, and vascular patency. Two measurements derived from CCTA with significant diagnostic and prognostic importance are the Left Ventricular Ejection Fraction (LVEF) and Left Ventricular Wall Thickness. Both measurements require the segmentation of the left ventricular muscle, with the former requiring temporal segmentation over the cardiac cycle. The American College of Radiology (ACR) has highlighted the importance of these measurements by listing them among the most important initial 'use cases' of artificial intelligence as applied to radiology [1]. A segmentation model of the left ventricular muscle and cavity over the cardiac cycle, especially the end-systole and end-diastole time points, would allow for automated determination of both measurements from 4D CCTA studies. The clinical utility of such a model is highly relevant as it reduces study reading time and improves the consistency of measurements, thereby potentially preventing missed pathology in cases where the measurements may not have otherwise been performed.

© Springer Nature Switzerland AG 2020
M. Pop et al. (Eds.): STACOM 2019, LNCS 12009, pp. 72–80, 2020.
https://doi.org/10.1007/978-3-030-39074-7_8

Modern 4D CCTA images are acquired over the entire cardiac cycle, including end-systole and end-diastole. A typical 4D scan includes 20 3D volumes reflecting the cardiac anatomy at equally-spaced time points within a 240 ms time interval. This allows for enough temporal resolution to study the heart's function. In order to limit the amount of effort required to annotate these images, we restrict the annotation to only certain frames, an example of which is shown in Fig. 2.

While convolutional neural networks (CNNs) have demonstrated state-of-the-art performance across a variety of segmentation tasks [8], the adoption of 4D CNNs for 4D medical imaging (3D + time – e.g., CT or ultrasound) has been limited due to the high computational complexity and lack of manually segmented data. The cost of annotating volumetric imaging is significant, making 4D labeling prohibitively expensive. Nevertheless, the temporal dimension offers valuable information that is otherwise lost when treating each volume independently.

In this work, we propose a 4D CNN for the segmentation of the left ventricle (LV) and left ventricular myocardium (LVM) from 4D CCTA images, enabling the computation of the aforementioned cardiac measurements. To reduce annotation costs, our 4D dataset is sparsely labeled across the temporal dimension – only a fraction of volumes in the sequence are labeled. This enables us to leverage a 4D CNN with a sparse loss function, allowing our algorithm to take advantage of unlabeled images which would otherwise be discarded in a 3D model. The network jointly segments the sequence of volumes, implicitly learning temporal correlations and imposing a soft temporal smoothness constraint. We describe the 4D convolution layer generalization in Sect. 3.1 and introduce a sparse Dice loss function as well as a temporal consistency regularization in Sect. 3.2. We demonstrate the feasibility of a 4D CNN and compare its performance to a traditional 3D CNN in Sect. 4.

2   Related Work

Deep learning has achieved state-of-the-art segmentation performance in 2D natural images [2] and 2D [8] & 3D medical images [6,7]. To leverage the temporal dependency and account for segmentation continuity, recurrent neural networks (RNNs) have been adopted for videos [11] and 2D + T cardiac MRI datasets [16]. 3D CNNs have also been applied spatio-temporally and proven effective in segmentation of videos [9,10] and 2D + T cardiac MRIs [15].

For sequences of volumetric imaging, such as 3D + T CT or ultrasound, 4D CNNs are a natural extension. Wang et al. [12] proposed a CNN for 4D light-field material recognition incorporating separable 4D convolutions to reduce computational complexity. Clark et al. [3] adopted a 4D CNN for the de-noising of low-dose CT, where three independent 3D convolutions (with fixed cyclic time delay) were used to simulate 4D convolutions.

To date, 4D CNNs for semantic segmentation have not been explored in similar depth to 2D and 3D CNNs, in part due to their high computational requirements and lack of available annotations. In this work, we demonstrate the feasibility and advantageousness of a true 4D CNN.

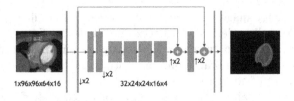

Fig. 1. 4D network architecture: input is a single channel (grayscale) 4D CT crop, followed by initial $3 \times 3 \times 3 \times 3$ 4D convolution with 8 filters. Each green building block is a ResNet-like block with GroupNorm normalization. The output has three channels followed by a softmax: background, left ventricle, and myocardium. For a detailed description of the building blocks see Table 1. (Color figure online)

3 Methods

Our 4D segmentation network architecture follows an encoder-decoder semantic segmentation strategy, typical for 2D and 3D images. Throughout the network, we use 4D convolutions with a kernel size of $3 \times 3 \times 3 \times 3$, where the last dimension corresponds to time. The network architecture follows the one proposed in [7], where only the main decoder branch is used and modified to fit 4D images within GPU memory limits. The input size of the network is $1 \times 1 \times 96 \times 96 \times 64 \times 16$ (corresponding to a batch size of 1, input channel 1, and a spatial crop of $96 \times 96 \times 64$ with 16 frames). We randomly crop this 4D array from the input data during training. No other form of augmentation is employed in this study.

Each building block of the network consists of two convolutions with group normalization [14] and ReLU, followed by identity skip-connections similar to ResNet [5] blocks. A sequence of the building blocks is applied sequentially at different spatial levels. In the encoder part of the network, we downscale the spatial dimension after each level and double the feature dimension. We use strided convolutions (stride of 2) for downsizing, and all convolutions are $3 \times 3 \times 3 \times 3$. We use one block at level 0 (initial size), two blocks at level 1, and four blocks at level 2. At the smallest scale, the input image crop is downsized by a factor of 4 (to $24 \times 24 \times 16 \times 4$), which provides a balance between network depth and GPU memory limits. For the encoder branch, we leverage a similar structure with a single block per each spatial level. To upsample, we use 4D nearest-neighbor interpolation after $1 \times 1 \times 1 \times 1$ convolution. Finally, we use additive skip-connections between the corresponding levels. The details of network structure are shown in Table 1 and in Fig. 1.

3.1 4D Convolutions

While 4D convolutional layers are not available in common deep-learning frameworks (such as TensorFlow[1] of PyTorch[2]), they can be represented as a sum

---

[1] https://www.tensorflow.org.
[2] https://pytorch.org.

Table 1. Network structure, where GN stands for group normalization (with group size of 8), Conv - $3 \times 3 \times 3 \times 3$ convolution, AddId - addition of identity/skip connection. Repeat column shows the number of repetitions of the block. The output, after softmax, has 3 channels (background and 2 foreground classes)

Name	Ops	Repeat	Output size
Input			$1 \times 96 \times 96 \times 64 \times 16$
InitConv	Conv $3 \times 3 \times 3 \times 3$		$8 \times 96 \times 96 \times 64 \times 16$
EncoderBlock0	GN,ReLU,Conv,GN,ReLU,Conv, AddId		$8 \times 96 \times 96 \times 64 \times 16$
EncoderDown1	Conv $3 \times 3 \times 3 \times 3$ stride 2		$16 \times 48 \times 48 \times 32 \times 8$
EncoderBlock1	GN,ReLU,Conv,GN,ReLU,Conv, AddId	$\times 2$	$16 \times 48 \times 48 \times 32 \times 8$
EncoderDown2	Conv $3 \times 3 \times 3 \times 3$ stride 2		$32 \times 24 \times 24 \times 16 \times 4$
EncoderBlock2	GN,ReLU,Conv,GN,ReLU,Conv, AddId	$\times 4$	$32 \times 24 \times 24 \times 16 \times 4$
DecoderUp1	Conv1, UpNearest, +EncoderBlock1		$16 \times 48 \times 48 \times 32 \times 8$
DecoderBlock1	GN,ReLU,Conv,GN,ReLU,Conv, AddId		$16 \times 48 \times 48 \times 32 \times 8$
DecoderUp0	Conv1, UpNearest, +EncoderBlock0		$8 \times 96 \times 96 \times 64 \times 16$
DecoderBlock0	GN,ReLU,Conv,GN,ReLU,Conv, AddId		$8 \times 96 \times 96 \times 64 \times 16$
DecoderEnd	Conv $1 \times 1 \times 1 \times 1$, Softmax		$3 \times 96 \times 96 \times 64 \times 16$

over a sequence of 3D convolutions along the fourth (temporal) dimension. For efficiency, we rearranged the loop to avoid repeated 3D convolutions by implementing 4D convolution as a custom TensorFlow layer. This strategy allows for a true (non-separable) 4D convolution. A common approach to maintain the same image dimension is to zero-pad prior to a convolution. We were concerned that such an approach may introduce boundary effect for the very first and last frames (when padding with zeros). We have experimented with several padding strategies for the 4th dimension only, including zero padding, mirror reflection, and replication but did not observe any noticeable performance differences, thus we decided to use conventional zero padding.

3.2 Loss

Our training dataset is sparsely labeled along the temporal dimension since labeling medical images in 4D (and even in 3D) is complex and time-consuming. Therefore, we have defined a sparse loss function that is applied only to the labeled time-frames and includes a regularization term to ensure temporal consistency between frames.

The proposed loss function is therefore composed of two terms,

$$\mathbf{L} = \sum_{i \in \text{labeled}} D(p_{\text{true}}^i, p_{\text{pred}}^i) + \sum_{i=0}^{K-2} ||p_{\text{pred}}^{i+1} - p_{\text{pred}}^i||^2 \tag{1}$$

where D is a soft dice loss [6] applied only to labeled time points (3D images) p_{true} to match the corresponding outputs p_{pred}:

$$D(p_{\text{true}}, p_{\text{pred}}) = 1 - \frac{2 * \sum p_{\text{true}} * p_{\text{pred}}}{\sum p_{\text{true}}^2 + \sum p_{\text{pred}}^2 + \varepsilon} \qquad (2)$$

K is the number of frames (K=16 in our case, since we use the $96 \times 96 \times 64 \times 16$ crop size). The second term in (1) is a first-order derivative over time to enforce similarity between frames. Re-weighting the contributions between the loss terms did not show consistent difference, so we kept the equal contributions.

3.3   Optimization

Similar to [7], we apply the Adam optimizer with an initial learning rate of $\alpha_0 = 1\text{e}{-}3$ and progressively decrease it according to the following schedule $\alpha = \alpha_0 \left(1 - \eta/N_\eta\right)^{0.9}$, where η is an epoch counter, and N_η is the total number of training epochs.

We use a batch size of 1 and sample input sequences randomly (ensuring that each training sequence is drawn once per epoch). From each 4D sequence, we apply a random crop of size $96 \times 96 \times 64 \times 16$ centered on a foreground (with a probability of 0.6), otherwise centered on a background voxel. Thus, at each iteration, a different number of ground truth labels is available, depending on the location of the crop window (16) of the time dimension.

3.4   Dataset

Our dataset consists of 61 4D CCTA sequences, each of $512 \times 512 \times (40\text{--}108) \times 20$ size (512×512 axial size, with 40–108 slices of variable thickness and 20 time points). The spatial image resolution is $(0.24\text{--}0.46) \times (0.24\text{--}0.46) \times 2\,\text{mm}$. All images were acquired at Massachusetts General Hospital, Boston, USA, using a 128-slice dual-source multi-detector CT with retrospective ECG gating and tube current modulation. Sequences were reconstructed from multiple R-R[3] intervals, measured via electrocardiogram.

All images were resampled to an isotropic spatial resolution of $1 \times 1 \times 1\,\text{mm}$, retaining the temporal resolution. After re-sampling, the 4D image sizes vary between $112 \times 122 \times 80 \times 20$ and $238 \times 238 \times 158 \times 20$ voxels. We apply a random data split, with 49 4D images used for training and 12 4D images for validation.

The number of annotated frames in each sequence varies widely, ranging from only 2 out 20 (i.e. end-systole and end-diastole) to 9 (every second time point). Overall, 247 time-points have been annotated throughout the dataset, which represents approximately 20% of all frames. We include studies with differing numbers of annotated frames in both training and validation splits to maximize temporal coverage during both training and validation.

As a second form of validation, we compare our model's segmentation results with clinical findings. One such clinical finding is the ejection fraction measure which typically is being judged as reduced when less than 55% [4].

---

[3] R corresponds to the peak of the QRS complex in the ECG wave.

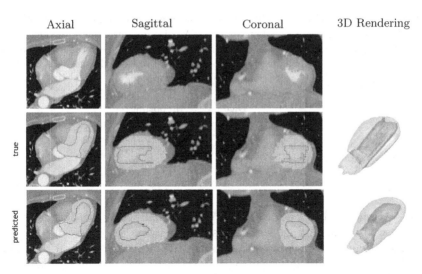

Fig. 2. A typical segmentation example of our 4D network in axial, sagittal and coronal views of a single 3D frame. Notice that the predicted results look better and much smoother than manual annotations in sagittal and coronal cross sections. Manual labeling was done by a trained clinician slice-by-slice, which results in noisy out-of-plane ground-truth labels. The 4D segmentation network is able to average out these errors when learning such noisy data examples.

4 Results

We implemented our 4D network in Tensorflow and trained it on an NVIDIA Tesla P100 SXM2 GPU with 16 GB memory based on the *NVIDIA Clara Train SDK*[4]. Data is normalized to $[-1, 1]$ using a fixed scaling from input CT range $[-1024, 1024]$. We train for 500 epochs and use the model at the end of training for evaluations.

For comparison, we also implemented a 3D network largely following the same architecture as in Fig. 1, except that all convolutions are 3D and include a greater number of layers with one additional down-sampling level (the end of the encoder being of size $12 \times 12 \times 8$) as GPU memory requirements permit deeper architecture in the 3D case. For the 3D network, we use a crop of size $96 \times 96 \times 64$ and train it only on labeled 3D frames. The 3D network learns to predict segmentation without any temporal constraint considerations. We acknowledge that such a 3D network is trained on less number of images (only the annotate frames), and weakly-supervised 3D segmentation might be a candidate for better comparison.

Segmentation performance: We evaluate both networks on the validation set, using only the labeled frames, in terms of average Dice score. In addition, we assess the temporal continuity of the produced results. A temporal smoothness

---

[4] https://devblogs.nvidia.com/annotate-adapt-model-medical-imaging-clara-train-sdk.

Table 2. Performance evaluation of the 4D semantic segmentation network. LVM - left ventricular myocardium and LV - left ventricle. We also measure temporal smoothness in the result using the L2 norm of temporal derivative of the predictions and average surface distance between the consecutive frames. The proposed 4D network produces temporally smoother results with comparable dice scores.

Arch	Dice		Smoothness	
	LVM	LV	L2	Surf
3D network	0.85	0.91	1.28	0.74
4D network	0.85	0.90	1.05	0.59

metric, we compute the L2 norm of the first-order time derivative of segmentation labels, as well as the average surface distance between the consecutive frames. Intuitively, accurate segmentation results must respect the temporal continuity of the heart motion, and are expected to be smoother in the time domain.

The evaluation results are shown in Table 2. In terms of the dice score alone, the proposed 4D network demonstrated only comparable results, with one of the structures (LV cavity) 1% better dice of the 3D network. One reason for this might be that 4D network is not as deep as its 3D counterpart and the dice score is estimated frame by frame; frame-by-frame Dice score may not be the most representative accuracy measure of temporal sequence segmentations as it does not account for consistency across frames.

Visually, the 4D CNN segmentation results have superior temporal consistency, where the label changes more "fluidly" between time-frames. Our smoothness metric confirms this observation, with the proposed 4D network achieving lower smoothness loss than its 3D counterpart (see Table 2). We also observe that in many cases, 4D CNN results look better than the ground truth (See Fig. 2). The manual annotations are done slice-by-slice, which results in jittery out-of-plane annotation profiles; this especially visible in sagittal and coronal views. The proposed 4D segmentation network is able to average out these errors while learning from the overall dataset and produce coherent results both spatially and temporally. In future work, manual relabeling of some cases in all 2D planes consistently (in spatial and time dimensions) could result in a clearer advantage of our 4D approach.

Ejection Fraction: We computed the ejection fraction for 12 cases (10 with normal and 2 with reduced ejection fraction) based on the ratio of minimum and maximum LV cavity volume throughout the cardiac cycle as predicted by our models. For both, 3D and 4D models, we achieve a 100% sensitivity and specificity in detecting reduced ejection fraction when compared to the findings reported in the clinical reports (provided by radiologists).

5 Conclusion

We proposed a 4D convolutional neural network for semantic segmentation of the left ventricle (LV) and left ventricular myocardium (LVM) from 4D CCTA studies. The network is fully convolutional and jointly segments a temporal sequence of volumetric images from CCTA.

We utilize a sparse Dice loss function and a temporal consistency regularization to handle the problem of sparse temporal annotation. We have demonstrated the feasibility and advantageousness of a true 4D CNN compared to 3D CNNs, where the first shows improvement in segmentation temporal consistency. The model's result showed promise in being useful for automatically quantifying clinically measures, such as ejection fraction.

References

1. American College of Radiology: Touch-AI Directory (2019). https://www.acrdsi.org/DSI-Services/TOUCH-AI
2. Chen, L.C., Zhu, Y., Papandreou, G., Schroff, F., Adam, H.: Encoder-decoder with atrous separable convolution for semantic image segmentation. arXiv:1802.02611 (2018)
3. Clark, D., Badea, C.: Convolutional regularization methods for 4D, x-ray CT reconstruction. In: Medical Imaging: PMI, vol. 10948 (2019)
4. Curtis, J.P., et al.: The association of left ventricular ejection fraction, mortality, and cause of death in stable outpatients with heart failure. ACC **42**(4), 736–742 (2003)
5. He, K., Zhang, X., Ren, S., Sun, J.: Identity mappings in deep residual networks. In: Leibe, B., Matas, J., Sebe, N., Welling, M. (eds.) ECCV 2016. LNCS, vol. 9908, pp. 630–645. Springer, Cham (2016). https://doi.org/10.1007/978-3-319-46493-0_38
6. Milletari, F., Navab, N., Ahmadi, S.A.: V-net: fully convolutional neural networks for volumetric medical image segmentation. In: Fourth International Conference on 3D Vision (3DV) (2016)
7. Myronenko, A.: 3D MRI brain tumor segmentation using autoencoder regularization. In: Crimi, A., Bakas, S., Kuijf, H., Keyvan, F., Reyes, M., van Walsum, T. (eds.) BrainLes 2018. LNCS, vol. 11384, pp. 311–320. Springer, Cham (2019). https://doi.org/10.1007/978-3-030-11726-9_28. https://arxiv.org/abs/1810.11654
8. Ronneberger, O., Fischer, P., Brox, T.: U-Net: convolutional networks for biomedical image segmentation. In: Navab, N., Hornegger, J., Wells, W.M., Frangi, A.F. (eds.) MICCAI 2015. LNCS, vol. 9351, pp. 234–241. Springer, Cham (2015). https://doi.org/10.1007/978-3-319-24574-4_28
9. Tran, D., Bourdev, L., Fergus, R., Torresani, L., Paluri, M.: Learning spatiotemporal features with 3D convolutional networks. In: Proceedings of the IEEE International Conference on Computer Vision, pp. 4489–4497 (2015)
10. Tran, D., Bourdev, L., Fergus, R., Torresani, L., Paluri, M.: Deep end2end voxel2voxel prediction. In: Proceedings of the IEEE Conference on Computer Vision and Pattern Recognition Workshops, pp. 17–24 (2016)
11. Valipour, S., Siam, M., Jagersand, M., Ray, N.: Recurrent fully convolutional networks for video segmentation. In: 2017 IEEE Winter Conference on Applications of Computer Vision (WACV), pp. 29–36. IEEE (2017)

12. Wang, T.-C., Zhu, J.-Y., Hiroaki, E., Chandraker, M., Efros, A.A., Ramamoorthi, R.: A 4D light-field dataset and CNN architectures for material recognition. In: Leibe, B., Matas, J., Sebe, N., Welling, M. (eds.) ECCV 2016. LNCS, vol. 9907, pp. 121–138. Springer, Cham (2016). https://doi.org/10.1007/978-3-319-46487-9_8
13. World Health Organization: Cardiovascular Diseases (CVDs) (May 2017). https://www.who.int/en/news-room/fact-sheets/detail/cardiovascular-diseases-(cvds)
14. Wu, Y., He, K.: Group normalization. In: European Conference on Computer Vision (ECCV) (2018)
15. Yang, D., Huang, Q., Axel, L., Metaxas, D.: Multi-component deformable models coupled with 2D–3D U-Net for automated probabilistic segmentation of cardiac walls and blood. In: ISBI, pp. 479–483 (2018)
16. Zhang, D., et al.: Segmentation of left ventricle myocardium in porcine cardiac cine MR images using a hybrid of fully convolutional neural networks and convolutional LSTM. In: Medical Imaging 2018: Image Processing, vol. 10574, p. 105740A. International Society for Optics and Photonics (2018)

Two-Stage 2D CNN for Automatic Atrial Segmentation from LGE-MRIs

Kevin Jamart[1]([⊠]), Zhaohan Xiong[1], Gonzalo Maso Talou[1], Martin K. Stiles[2], and Jichao Zhao[1]

[1] Auckland Bioengineering Institute, Auckland, New Zealand
kjam268@aucklanduni.ac.nz
[2] Waikato Clinical School, Faculty of Medical and Health Sciences, University of Auckland, Auckland, New Zealand

Abstract. Atrial fibrillation (AF) is the most common sustained heart rhythm disturbance and a leading cause of hospitalization, heart failure and stroke. In the current medical practice, atrial segmentation from medical images for clinical diagnosis and treatment, is a labor-intensive and error-prone manual process. The atrial segmentation challenge held in conjunction with the 2018 the Medical Image Computing and Computer Assisted Intervention Society (MICCAI) conference and Statistical Atlases and Computational Modelling of the Heart (STACOM), offered the opportunity to develop reliable approaches to automatically annotate and perform segmentation of the left atrial (LA) chamber using the largest available 3D late gadolinium-enhanced MRI (LGE-MRI) dataset with 154 3D LGE-MRIs and labels. For this challenge, 11 out the 27 contestants achieved more than 90% Dice score accuracy, however, a critical question remains as which is the optimal approach for LA segmentation. In this paper, we propose a two-stage 2D fully convolutional neural network with extensive data augmentation and achieves a superior segmentation accuracy with a Dice score of 93.7% using the same dataset and conditions as for the atrial segmentation challenge. Thus, our approach outperforms the methods proposed in the atrial segmentation challenge while employing less computational resources than the challenge winning method.

Keywords: Automatic cardiac segmentation · LGE-MRI · Atrial fibrillation

1 Introduction

Atrial fibrillation (AF), is the most common sustained heart rhythm disturbance, with nearly 33 millions of people affected worldwide. The current overall prevalence of AF is 2% to 5% of the general population worldwide and is projected to more than double in the following couple of decades, becoming a global epidemic [1]. Currents treatments remain sub-optimal [2] and recent clinical studies, using late gadolinium enhancement MRI (LGE-MRI), suggest that this is probably due to the lack of understanding of the underlying left atrial (LA) structures which sustain AF. Unfortunately, most studies that use LGE-MRIs have relied on labor-intensive and error-prone manual segmentation methods [3], and therefore cannot reach beyond research

M. Pop et al. (Eds.): STACOM 2019, LNCS 12009, pp. 81–89, 2020.
https://doi.org/10.1007/978-3-030-39074-7_9

studies to be implemented in clinical practice. Alas, initial attempts for automatic segmentation using conventional approaches or some early machine learning strategies have also achieved limited efficacy [5, 6].

However, in 2018, new approaches were proposed for the atrial segmentation challenge held by the Statistical Atlases and Computational Modeling of the Heart (STACOM) workshop [7], during the 2018 edition of the Medical Image Computing and Computer-Assisted Intervention (MICCAI) conference. The challenge was a success with 18 teams attending the conference and proposing diverse approaches, with the winning team, Xia et al. [8], reaching 93.2% Dice score with a fully convolutional neural network (CNN). Nevertheless, the best score of the challenge was obtained using a 3D approach to render accurately the volume of the LA, we argue that such a small 3D dataset (100 3D LGE-MRIs) might not provide enough learning material for the CNN to reach the maximum score possible. Moreover, 3D segmentation approaches usually require more computational resources and are less efficient than CNN using 2D images. Furthermore, data augmentation, proven to be an effective method to extend and enrich the dataset, would remain of limited efficacy for 3D images, as the dataset can only be so much extended, and therefore we argue that a 2D approach is more appropriate to exploit the full potential of the dataset.

Our study addresses these problems. Firstly, we built a two-stage 2D convolutional neural network using extensive data augmentation to fully exploit the dataset potential. Secondly, we investigated the impact of the main transformations employed for data augmentation in medical segmentation tasks. Finally, we analyzed the volumetric prediction yielded from the aggregated 2D predictions.

2 Methods

2.1 Dataset

For this study, we employed the 3D LGE-MRI dataset used in the 2018 atrial segmentation challenge in conjunction with the 2018 MICCAI and STACOM workshop. The dataset was acquired and labeled by experts' consensus at the University of Utah and consists of 154 original 3D LGE-MRIs with a spatial resolution of $0.625 \times 0.625 \times 0.625$ mm^3 and dimensions of $640 \times 640 \times 88$ and $576 \times 576 \times 88$ assorted with their respective manual segmentation of the LA cavity and used as *ground truth* (labels).

For the challenge, the dataset was divided into a training set (100 3D LGE-MRIs) and a testing set (54 3D LGE-MRIs) yielding a grand total of 8800 2D images MRIs and labels for training and 4752 MRIs and labels for testing, respectively. For our approach development, and fair comparison with other approaches published in the 2018 STACOM proceedings [7], we split the original training dataset into 80 3D LGE-MRIs for training and 20 3D LGE-MRIs for validation. Finally, our approach was evaluated using the other 54 3D LGE-MRIs kept unseen during training and fine-tuning of the network hyper-parameters, to replicate the challenge testing conditions.

2.2   Network Architectures

For each 3D LGE-MRI, the atrial cavity represents only a small fraction of the image volume, therefore creates a severe class imbalance ($\sim 0.7\%$ cavity pixels versus $\sim 99.3\%$ of background). As class imbalance is a recurrent and serious problem in segmentation tasks [9] the first stage of our two-stage 2D CNN approach was dedicated to reduce the background predominance by extracting the region of interest (ROI). To this end, the first network (*Vnet 1*), using an image-based regression approach, was employed to precisely locate the LA by determining the coordinate of the LA cavity center of mass on each 2D image. Once the LA was localized, the images were cropped to an optimized size (240 × 240 pixels), increasing speed and accuracy of the training process. The second network (*Vnet 2*) was dedicated to accurately segment the LA from the cropped image. The final prediction image was reconstructed to the original image input size as illustrated in Fig. 1.

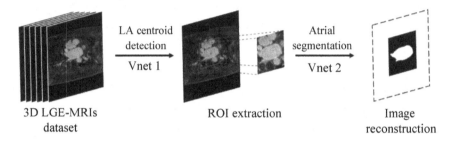

Fig. 1. Framework of our proposed two-stage 2D convolutional neural network (CNN) approach. The first network (Vnet 1) was used to determinate the center of the region of interest (ROI), i.e., left atrium (LA) cavity, on each MRI, then the images were cropped to an optimized region with a dimension of 240 × 240 pixels. The second network (Vnet 2) was used to accurately segment LA cavity.

For this study, both of the CNNs we used were based on the V-net [10] architecture as depicted in Fig. 2. In order to make the best of the dataset, we implemented a 2D version of V-net which allowed us to process 8800 2D LGE-MRIs. Our approach used a fully convolutional neural network in which the convolution operations were used to extract information, reduce the image resolution and reconstruct the image for the final output (prediction). The architecture of our V-net can be described in two parts: an initial encoder part in which the image information is extracted in a local-to-global manner, and a subsequent decoder part mirroring the encoding part and used to reconstruct the predicted segmentation. In our approach, we used 5 encoding and 5 decoding blocks where each block consisted of a batch normalization [11] followed by a succession of 5 × 5 of padded 2D convolutions keeping constant image size, and an increasing number of feature maps as the network goes deeper (respectively 8/16/32/64/128 features maps). Each block was followed by a strided 2D convolution layer for the encoding part allowing image down-sampling and global features extraction, and a strided 2D deconvolution layer for the decoding part permitting image up-sampling and prediction reconstruction. Each convolution or deconvolution layer was followed by a leaky rectifier linear unit (Leaky ReLU) activation function (using $\alpha = 0.1$) to ensure non-linearity while limiting vanishing gradient problems. In addition, we applied 25% dropout on every layer to prevent overfitting. Moreover, we used skip connections to keep proper information forwarding as usually used in residual block architectures [12], by merging (element-wise sum) the first layer input and the final layer output of a residual block before each strided convolution or deconvolution layer. Furthermore, our network utilized horizontal features map forwarding between same level residual blocks from the encoding path, to the decoding path to avoid network singularities [13].

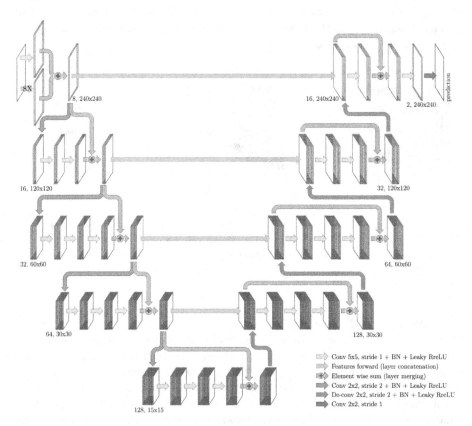

Fig. 2. Our proposed 2D V-net architecture consists of an encoder part extracting features and a decoder part reconstructing the predicted image.

The two networks differ in the loss function that we used and the activation function for the final layer of the network. For the first network (*Vnet 1*) we used mean squared error loss function and sigmoid activation function in the regression approach to determine the coordinates of the centroid of the LA. Whereas for the segmentation task of the second network (*Vnet 2*), we used Dice loss as loss function and softmax activation function to distinguish background information from LA cavity information.

2.3 Data Augmentation

Data augmentation is a worthy tool for many application in machine learning and image processing, but every dataset presents their specificities and therefore requires tailored data augmentation. As the utilized dataset was of limited size, we applied online data augmentation, a more efficient approach than the alternative offline strategy, to train the network over a wider range of biological variations to obtain the best coverage of the human heart shape variability. To this end, we investigated the impact of four different image augmentation, two transformations – rotation and left/right flip, and two shape deformation– scaling and perspective alteration. Rotation and left/right flip addressed the relative position of the heart within the image, whereas scaling and perspective alteration varied the cavity volume and the contours of the LA, respectively. For our approach we used a rotation angle randomly selected between $-25°$ and $25°$, a scaling coefficient randomly selected between 0.5 and 1.5 for x and y, and a perspective factor ranging from 0.05 and 0.1. Moreover, we also investigated the effects of two image histogram augmentations, "add" and "gamma" addressing the contrast and brightness variations generally encountered in LGE-MRIs. Add consisted of adding selected values to each pixel values on the image (between -40 and 40), and gamma adjusted the contrast of the image by scaling each pixel value using $255 \times (I_{ij}/255)^{\gamma}$ (with γ between 0.3 and 1.7).

As image transformation can generate artifacts on the LGE-MRIs, it is important to control the emergence of these aberrant features, in order to prevent the network to learn them. Moreover, using multiple image augmentation at the same time amplifies the risk of artifacts appearance and therefore can impair the learning process. To avoid these effects, we only applied data augmentation on 50% of the dataset and only one type of image transformation and one type of image histogram augmentation to each image.

2.4 Metrics

In order to evaluate our results, several commonly used metrics were utilized to represent different aspects of the predictions. We used Dice score to evaluate the similarity between the ground truth and the predictions. We also employed Jacquard index (intersection over union) more sensible and severe upon small variation than Dice score. Moreover, we also included surface distance metrics, such as mean symmetric surface distance and Hausdorff distance, which are more representative of shape and contour accuracy of the LA than the Dice score. Finally, we added antero-posterior diameter error and volume error calculations used clinically to assess the medical relevance of the predicted reconstructed LA volumes.

3 Results

We implemented our approach using TFLearn, a high-level API of TensorFlow, and ran all experiments on Nvidia Tesla V100-PCIe with cuDNN. Our final results were obtained after training our network for 300 epochs with a learning rate of 0.001 using Adam optimizer and a maximum batch size up to 44 for speed and performance. Weights were initialized once using He normalization [14], saved, and re-employed for each experiments in order to avoid weights bias from initialization.

Performance of the Two-Stage 2D CNN Approach. Our two-stage 2D CNN achieved 93.72% Dice score accuracy, outperforming the proposed approaches for the 2018 atrial segmentation challenge. Moreover, our framework also obtained better accuracy for most of the other metrics (Jacquard index, Mean surface distance, LA diameter error and volume error) as shown in Table 1, only, the Hausdorff distance appeared larger than for the other approaches compared. We believe that the superiority of our approach relies on its two-stage architecture, the total exploitation of the dataset using 2D images and the optimized data augmentation employed. Furthermore, our approach alleviated the class imbalance issue by using small patch size images centered on the ROI, and improved the ROI learning process, providing by centering the image on the centroid of the LA cavity allowing to obtain a better Dice score. Finally, we employed carefully selected image augmentation to improve the learning process and provide an enlarged shape variability database increasing the segmentation accuracy further.

Table 1. Comparison between our approach (2D V-net), the top participants [7] of the 2018 atrial segmentation challenge and Unet 2D [15] using various metrics (Dice score, Jacquard index, Mean square distance (MSD), Hausdorff distance, Diameter error and Volume error).

Metrics						
Network	Dice score (%)	Jacquard (%)	MSD (mm)	Hausdorff (mm)	Diam. Err (%)	Volume Err (%)
Xia et al.	93.2	87.4	0.748	8.892	4.0	4.9
Huang et al.	93.1	87.2	0.754	**8.495**	3.6	4.9
Bian et al.	92.6	86.9	0.759	9.213	3.9	4.4
Yang et al.	92.5	86.1	0.850	9.759	3.6	6.1
Unet 2D	92.5	86.2	0.842	15.88	3.1	4.9
2D V-net	**93.7**	**88.2**	**0.614**	10.60	**2.7**	**4.2**

Patch Size and Centroid Cropping. As the LA on a 3D LGE-MRI represented only a fraction of the image to segment, we first investigated the effects of cropping the image to different patch size on the Dice score with decreasing patch sizes (from 512 × 512 to 240 ×240 Fig. 3A). Using image centered cropping (blue bars Fig. 3A) we observed a minor increase on the Dice score using small patches (240 × 240 to

320×320) rather than large patches (400×400 to 512×512). Secondly, we evaluated the importance of the location of the LA within the selected region using LA centroid cropping (red bars Fig. 3A). To this end, the first network of our approach, dedicated to locate the centroid of the LA, was able to precisely determine the coordinates of the LA centroid with a 15 pixels mean precision (mean square error = 0.35). Applying LA centroid cropping, we observed a significant Dice score increase compared to image centered cropping (form 92% to 92.56%, *p-value* > 0.01) for all patch size (Fig. 3A). Moreover, applying LA centroid cropping we noticed a significant accuracy increase using small patches (92.86% versus 92.26% for large patches, *p*-value < 0.01). These results show the importance of controlling the background, by, for example removing irrelevant background (appropriate patch size) associated with pertinent centering (LA centroid cropping), to improve the learning process, and obtain a better prediction.

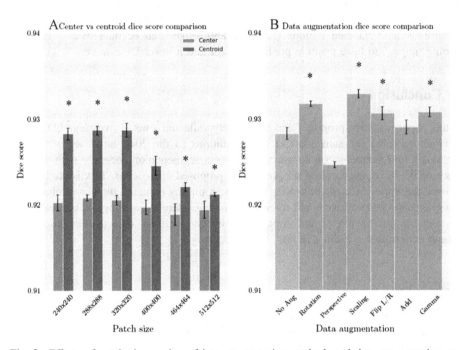

Fig. 3. Effects of patch size, region of interest extraction method, and data augmentation on Dice score. A: Comparison between the different patch size and cropping method. Using small patch size and LA centroid cropping yields better accuracy. B: Comparison of the effect on the Dice score of various data augmentation on 240×240 images using atrial centroid cropping.

Data Augmentation. Then, we investigated individually the effect of various online data augmentation usually employed for segmentation tasks (Fig. 3B). We showed that 4 out of the 6 image modifications employed (rotation, scaling, left/right flip, and gamma) yielded significant Dice score improvement compared with no data augmentation. However, perspective alteration worsened the results (*p*-value < 0.01), and "add" didn't improve the Dice score significantly. This shows that whole shape alterations (rotation, scale, left/right flip) can be beneficial for the learning process while local contours modification (perspective alteration) using Dice loss can impair the learning process. Moreover, gamma also improved the Dice score, this can indicate the importance of considering the contrast as part of the data augmentation. Thus, combined inline data augmentation (rotation, scale, left/right flip and gamma) with 240x240 centroid cropped images allowed us to rise the Dice score to 93.72% (Table 1).

Segmentation Error Analysis. By examining 3D predictions, we observed that the best segmentation results were obtained at the center of the atrial volume reaching a Dice score 98.6% and a lower accuracy, mostly due to over-prediction (false positive), on the atrial regions presenting the smallest surface area, corresponding to the upper region of the LA (LA roof, Dice score 28.2%), and LA lower region (mitral valve opening, Dice score 66.9%). This can be explained by the use of the Dice loss function which weighs more towards the volume rather than the boundary of the atrium, therefore smaller labeled regions (LA roof and valve) can become over-weighted, leading, *in fine*, to false positive prediction error and a lower Dice score.

4   Conclusion

In this paper, we have proposed and extensively validated a novel two-stage 2D CNN architecture using the same dataset and conditions as the 2018 atrial segmentation challenge. Our segmentation approach achieves a segmentation accuracy with a Dice score of 93.7% outperforming all previously proposed approaches. In this study, we showed the importance of controlling the background by reducing the class imbalance using appropriate patch size and relevant region of interest centering for the learning process, we also displayed the impact of selecting pertinent data augmentation for dataset enrichment, yielding, *in fine*, better accuracy.

References

1. Krijthe, B.P., Kunst, A., Benjamin, E.J., Lip, G.Y., Franco, O.H., Hofman, A., et al.: Projections on the number of individuals with atrial fibrillation in the European Union, from 2000 to 2060. Eur. Heart J. **34**(35), 2746–2751 (2013)
2. Brooks, A.G., Stiles, M.K., Laborderie, J., Lau, D.H., Kuklik, P., Shipp, N.J., et al.: Outcomes of long-standing persistent atrial fibrillation ablation: a systematic review. Heart Rhythm **7**(6), 835–846 (2010)
3. Oakes, R.S., Badger, T.J., Kholmovski, E.G., Akoum, N., Burgon, N.S., et al.: Detection and quantification of left atrial structural remodeling with delayed-enhancement magnetic resonance imaging in patients with atrial fibrillation. Circulation **119**(13), 1758–1767 (2009)
4. Mortazi, A., Karim, R., Kawal, R., Burt, J., Bagci, U.: CardiacNET: segmentation of left atrium and proximal pulmonary veins from MRI using multi-view CNN. arXiv:170506333 (2017)

5. Tobon-Gomez, C., Geers, A.J., Peters, J., Weese, J., Pinto, K., Karim, R., et al.: Benchmark for algorithms segmenting the left atrium from 3D CT and MRI datasets. IEEE Trans. Med. Imaging **34**(7), 1460–1473 (2015)
6. Xiong, Z., Zhao, J., Stiles, M.: Machine learning for fully automatic 3D atria segmentation and reconstruction from gadolinium enhanced MRIs. Heart Lung Circ. **26**, S33 (2017)
7. Pop, M., et al. (eds.): Statistical Atlases and Computational Models of the Heart: Atrial Segmentation and LV Quantification Challenges: 9th International Workshop, STACOM 2018, Held in Conjunction with MICCAI 2018, Granada, Spain, September 16, 2018, Revised Selected Papers. Springer, Heidelberg (2019). https://doi.org/10.1007/978-3-030-12029-0
8. Xia, Q., Yao, Y., Hu, Z., Hao, A.: Automatic 3D atrial segmentation from GE-MRIs using volumetric fully convolutional networks. In: Pop, M., et al. (eds.) STACOM 2018. LNCS, vol. 11395, pp. 211–220. Springer, Cham (2019). https://doi.org/10.1007/978-3-030-12029-0_23
9. Buda, M., Maki, A., Mazurowski, M.: A systematic study of the class imbalance problem in convolutional neural networks. Neural Netw. **106**, 249–259 (2018)
10. Milletari, F., Navab, N., Ahmadi, S.A.: V-net: fully convolutional neural networks for volumetric medical image segmentation. In: 2016 Fourth International Conference on 3D Vision (3DV). IEEE (2016)
11. Ioffe, S., Szegedy, C.: Batch normalization: accelerating deep network training by reducing internal covariate shift. arXiv:1502.03167 (2015)
12. He, K., Zhang, X., Ren, S., Sun, J.: Deep residual learning for image recognition. In: Proceedings of the IEEE Conference on Computer Vision and Pattern Recognition, pp. 770–778 (2016)
13. Orhan, E., Pitkow, X.: Skip connections eliminate singularities. arXiv:1701.09175 (2017)
14. He, K., Zhang, X., Ren, S., Sun, J.: Delving deep into rectifiers: surpassing human-level performance on ImageNet classification. In: Proceedings of the IEEE International Conference on Computer Vision, pp. 1026–1034 (2015)
15. Ronneberger, O., Fischer, P., Brox, T.: U-Net: convolutional networks for biomedical image segmentation. In: Navab, N., Hornegger, J., Wells, W.M., Frangi, A.F. (eds.) MICCAI 2015. LNCS, vol. 9351, pp. 234–241. Springer, Cham (2015). https://doi.org/10.1007/978-3-319-24574-4_28

3D Left Ventricular Segmentation from 2D Cardiac MR Images Using Spatial Context

Sofie Tilborghs[1,4]($\boxtimes$), Tom Dresselears[2,4], Piet Claus[3,4], Jan Bogaert[2,4], and Frederik Maes[1,4]

[1] Department of Electrical Engineering, ESAT/PSI, KU Leuven, Leuven, Belgium
sofie.tilborghs@kuleuven.be
[2] Department of Imaging and Pathology, Radiology, KU Leuven, Leuven, Belgium
[3] Department of Cardiovascular Sciences, KU Leuven, Leuven, Belgium
[4] Medical Imaging Research Center, UZ Leuven, Leuven, Belgium

Abstract. Accurate left ventricular (LV) segmentation in cardiac MRI facilitates quantification of clinical parameters such as LV volume and ejection fraction (EF). We present a CNN-based method to obtain a 3D representation of LV by integrating information from 2D short-axis and horizontal and vertical long-axis images. Our CNN is flexible to the number of input slices and uses an additional input of image coordinates as spatial context. This concept is validated on variations of two well-known CNN architectures for medical image segmentation: U-Net and DeepMedic. Five-fold cross validation on a dataset of 20 patients achieved a correlation of 95.0/93.1% for quantification of end-diastolic volume, 91.6/90.8% for end-systolic volume and 80.5/84.5% for EF for the two architectures respectively. We show that (1) incorporating long-axis data improves segmentation performance and (2) providing spatial context by adding image coordinates as input to the CNN yields similar performance with a smaller receptive field.

Keywords: 3D cardiac MRI segmentation · Integration of short and long axis views · 3D CNN with spatial context

1 Introduction

Accurate left ventricular (LV) segmentation in cardiac MRI facilitates quantification of clinical parameters such as LV volume and ejection fraction (EF). To this end, numerous convolutional neural network (CNN) approaches have been published in the past years, for example in the STACOM 2017 ACDC challenge [1]. In clinical practice, generally a stack of thick (8–10 mm) short-axis (SA) 2D slices instead of a 3D volume is acquired, since acquiring a 2D slice is faster and requires consequently a shorter breath hold. Due to the low through-plane resolution of this SA stack, the extent of the heart in longitudinal direction (from apex to base) is difficult to perceive accurately, especially at the apex, such that

M. Pop et al. (Eds.): STACOM 2019, LNCS 12009, pp. 90–99, 2020.
https://doi.org/10.1007/978-3-030-39074-7_10

two long-axis (LA) 2D cine images are generally additionally acquired to obtain information on cardiac geometry in longitudinal direction.

State-of-the-art methods for LV segmentation are mainly using 2D SA images, occasionally integrating information of adjacent SA images to improve robustness [2,3]. To cope with incomplete information from 2D slices instead of 3D volumes, two approaches can be taken: (1) introduce a shape prior or (2) use additional images of complementary views i.e. LA images. Since CNNs make a voxelwise prediction of the probability of being part of LV, they are missing explicit shape constraints. In this respect, several authors have proposed to integrate a shape prior in their CNN. Examples are use of an atlas [4], the average of aligned training ground truths [5], a hidden representation of anatomy [6], or a statistical shape model fitted to a prior segmentation [7]. Combining information of both SA and LA images in a CNN is done by [8] to generate a super resolution 3D cardiac image from 2D SA and LA image stacks. Furthermore, SA and LA images are also used by [9] and in [10] to estimate end-diastolic (ED) and end-systolic (ES) volume. While [9] uses three views, mid-cavity SA, basal SA and two chamber LA, as input to a regression CNN, in [10], an ensemble of volume predictions obtained from 2D segmentations of different views is used. However, both approaches do not calculate a 3D segmentation and thus do not provide visual feedback on the performance of the CNN.

In this paper, we present a CNN-based method to obtain a 3D representation of LV from 2D SA and LA images. To ensure spatial consistency between the slices, every slice is transformed to the 3D world coordinate system (WCS) before being used as CNN input. Furthermore, we augment our network with image coordinates [11] to automatically learn spatial constraints as a weak shape prior during training.

2   Methods

2.1   From 2D to 3D: Transformation to Spatially Consistent Volumes

For each patient, a set of cine SA and LA slices, which can vary in number between patients, is available to predict the 3D LV. These 2D images are each transformed to a separate 3D volume in a common reference space. Before transforming the slices to volumes, we first correct for respiratory motion between them. This is performed jointly for all time points in a cine scan using a two step approach: first, large motion is corrected based on ground truth ED endo- and epicardial contours and second, motion correction is refined with the algorithm of [12] which uses the image content of the full cine scan. During contour-based initialization, motion of SA images is restricted to an in-plane translation and motion of LA images to a 3D translation. In the final breath hold correction [12], 3D translation and rotation parameters are obtained for every slice. The same correction parameters are applied to every time point in the cine scan. After breath hold correction, every 2D slice is transformed to a 3D volume with an isotropic resolution of 1 mm in scanner world coordinates using position and orientation parameters of the DICOM header. The transformation is performed with linear interpolation and voxels outside the respective slices are set to zero. To adjust for varying position of the subjects in the scanner, the middle point of LV in the central slice of the SA image stack is defined to be the center of the WCS. This results in a separate, sparse, 3D volume for every slice spanning each the same field of view (FOV) (Fig. 1).

Since our dataset lacks a true 3D ground truth, we artificially create a 3D LV model for each patient from breath hold corrected 2D expert contours for training and validation. The contours of every 2D SA image are first converted to 2D distance images which contain in every pixel the distance to the contour. Pixels in- and outside the contour are given respectively negative and positive values. Every distance image is then transformed to a 3D volume in SA orientation using linear interpolation and the breath hold correction parameters calculated before. Voxels outside the respective slices are set to "not a number" (nan). Since the slices are not inherently parallel anymore after breath hold correction, we use a heuristic approach to obtain the breath hold corrected SA contours: for every SA slice position, the contour is calculated from the distance volume with the least nan's at that specific slice position. The final model is created in SA image space: all breath-hold corrected SA contours are sampled every 5° and intermediate contours are calculated by linearly interpolating corresponding SA points of adjacent slices to obtain an interslice distance of 1 mm. The LA contours are transformed to SA orientation and used to extend the 3D model towards apex and base. This 3D model in SA orientation is then transformed to the WCS, identically as the MR images, to obtain the final 3D high resolution model.

2.2   CNN with Arbitrary Number of Inputs and Spatial Context

Since the number of SA slices in a clinical exam varies among subjects, we propose a CNN architecture where an undetermined number of 3D volumes, each containing information of one slice, can be imported. The concept is illustrated in Fig. 2: a first subnetwork (CNN1) extracts relevant features at different resolutions for every volume separately by running each volume through the same CNN. The features of all volumes are then combined by averaging and a second subnetwork (CNN2) processes this combined information and outputs the probability map for LV. Second, we also use additional spatial information by importing volumes of WCS x, y, z image coordinates in the CNN (Fig. 2) and hypothesize that this allows to decrease the receptive field (RF) of the CNN while preserving similar segmentation performance. To validate the concepts introduced above, we use variations on two established CNN architectures for medical image segmentation. Our first network (A1) is inspired by U-Net [13] and the second (A2) has two pathways of different resolution as in DeepMedic [14] (Fig. 3). Both A1 and A2 have a limited receptive field (A1: RF = 25 × 25 × 25, A2: RF = 21 × 21 × 21) and are thus only capable of using intensity information of a small part of the heart for voxelwise predictions. We also use a baseline architecture (A3) with a substantially larger receptive field

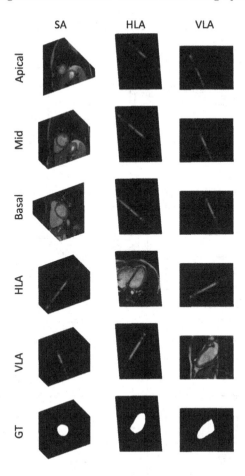

Fig. 1. SA, HLA and VLA (left to right) cross sections of 3D volumes of apical, mid and basal SA slices, HLA and VLA slices and 3D GT (top to bottom). The SA cross sections for HLA, VLA and GT are taken at mid-cavity position.

(RF = 69 × 69 × 69) but without a coordinate input to test our hypothesis on the benefit of incorporation of image coordinates in CNNs with limited RF. Like A2, A3 is inspired by DeepMedic but has three pathways of different resolutions. Details on the different architectures can be found in Fig. 3.

2.3   Training

We use a patch based training approach and extract every epoch 2000 samples of 3D patches from the training set. The training samples are chosen to have an equal class distribution of center voxels: half of the patches have a LV center voxel and the other half has a background center voxel. For every subject in the training set, an equal number of patches is randomly chosen from the two

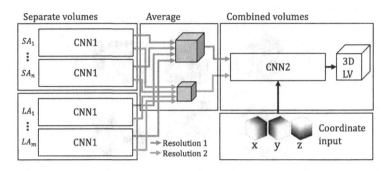

Fig. 2. Concept of proposed network architecture. Besides a variable number of SA views, also LA views and image coordinates are used as input.

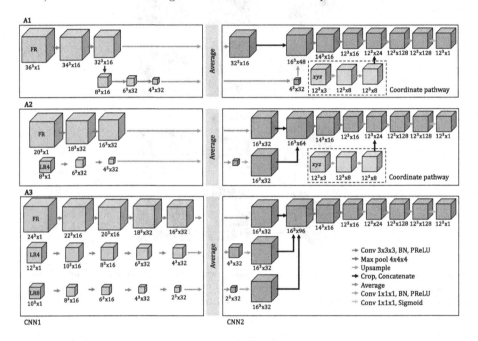

Fig. 3. Implementation details of architectures used for CNN1 (left) and CNN2 (right) in Fig. 3. The shape of the feature maps (FMs) in every step is given as (patch size) × (number of FMs). Besides full resolution (FR) input patches, A2 and A3 have also low resolution (LR) input patches with downsampling factors of 4 and 8. Each convolutional layer (Conv) is followed by batch normalization (BN) [15] and a parametric rectified linear unit (PReLU) activation function [16].

classes. The network is trained end-to-end over 200 epochs with stochastic gradient descent (SGD) optimizer with Nestrov momentum of 0.99 and an adaptive learning rate (lr) which is halved every 25 epochs (max lr = 0.016, min lr = 1e-5) to minimize the binary cross entropy. The network weights are initialized according to [17].

3   Experiments

We use clinical datasets of 20 subjects with variable pathology, acquired with a 1.5T MR scanner (Ingenia, Philips Healthcare, Best, the Netherlands), and a 32-channel cardiac phased array receiver coil setup. For each patient, 10 to 14 SA images (interslice distance = 8 mm), covering the heart from apex to base, and one horizontal (HLA) and one vertical (VLA) LA view are available. The endo- and epicardium in ED and the endocardium in end-systole (ES) were manually delineated by a clinical expert. The 2D images have a FOV of 350 × 350 mm^2 and an in-plane voxelsize of 0.99 mm which is transformed to a volume with FOV 201 × 201 × 201 mm^3 and an isotropic voxelsize of 1 mm. Before transformation, all images are intensity normalized to have zero mean and unit variance. After CNN prediction, we use simple postprocessing consisting of binarization, maintaining the largest connected component and hole filling.

We explore the effect of introducing additional spatial context by incorporating LA images and image coordinates with three variations on A1 and A2: (1) only SA images without image coordinates are used for CNN training and validation, (2) both SA and LA images but no image coordinates are used, (3) SA, LA and image coordinates are used. This last variation is compared to A3, which has a larger RF and uses both SA and LA images but no image coordinates. These experiments are performed for ED phase only. Additionally, we also test the performance of our approach on ES images and investigate the effect of training two CNNs for ED and ES phase separately or training one CNN for both cardiac phases. For all experiments, we use a five-fold cross validation and calculate Dice similarity coefficient (DSC), precision, sensitivity and average symmetric surface distance (ASSD) with respect to the created 3D ground truths. Furthermore, the correlation coefficients (ρ) for LV volume at ED and ES (EDV, ESV), and EF are calculated. Statistical significance of the results is assessed using the two-sided Wilcoxon signed rank test with a significance level of 5%.

4   Results

Figure 4 shows an example of the impact of breath hold correction. Before correction, the myocardium in SA stack appears to be discontinuous along the LA orientation, which is resolved after breath hold correction. Proper 3D consistency after breath hold correction was visually verified for every dataset.

The impact of incorporating LA images and image coordinates is presented in Table 1. All measures show improvement after introduction of LA data but not all differences are statistically significant. For both A1 and A2, incorporating spatial context significantly improves DSC, sensitivity and ASSD. The comparison of CNNs with small receptive field and spatial context (A1 and A2) and a CNN with larger receptive field (A3) does not show a statistically significant difference in DSC and ASSD, but A3 is significantly better in precision and significantly worse in sensitivity. A1 achieved the highest correlation for EDV. Figure 5 visualizes LV

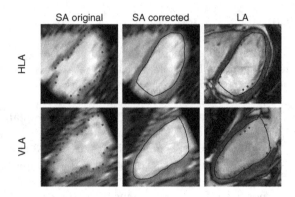

Fig. 4. Left to right: SA stack reformatted to LA orientation before breath hold correction, after correction and LA image. Red are the intersection points of the SA expert segmentation before correction and green is our 3D LV model in LA orientation. (Color figure online)

as predicted with the different CNNs, together with the distance to the ground truth, for one subject. Without additional spatial information, CNNs with small receptive field are prone to oversegmentation by not distinguishing between left and right ventricle. A3 tends to undersegment LV.

Table 2 presents the segmentation results in ED and ES for the two proposed architectures and two training strategies. While no obvious conclusions can be drawn about which training strategy is to be preferred based on the measures calculated for ED or ES separately, the correlation of EF increases respectively with 19.2% and 31.0% for A1 and A2 when training on ED and ES together.

Table 1. DSC, precision, sensitivity and ASSD (mean (std)) and ρEDV. Significant improvement of including LA (*) or coordinates ($^+$) is assessed for A1 and A2 separately. Significant differences between A3 and A1 (SA+LA+c)(*) or A2 (SA+LA+c)($^+$) are indicated on A3 results. Best results are shown in bold.

ED	DSC [%]	Precision [%]	Sensitivity [%]	ASSD [mm]	ρEDV [%]
A1: SA	76.3 (19.1)	84.1 (19.7)	79.3 (24.9)	4.93 (3.23)	20.7
A1: SA+LA	86.0 (7.4)	91.9 (8.3)	82.7 (12.9)	3.41 (2.15)*	60.0
A1: SA+LA+c	**91.7 (2.3)**$^+$	88.3 (4.9)$^+$	**95.6 (2.6)**$^+$	1.84 (0.53)$^+$	**95.3**
A2: SA	80.0 (9.1)	75.6 (16.8)	88.9 (10.0)	5.77 (2.99)	46.0
A2: SA+LA	85.5 (7.6)*	84.0 (13.8)*	89.1 (7.7)	4.02 (2.99)	53.4
A2: SA+LA+c	91.1 (3.7)$^+$	88.5 (7.5)	94.5 (3.8)$^+$	1.96 (0.96)$^+$	88.5
A3: SA+LA	91.5 (2.6)	**93.3 (3.9)**$^{*+}$	90.2 (5.7)$^{*+}$	**1.68 (0.45)**	92.8

GT   A1: SA   A1: SA+LA   A1: SA+LA+c   A2: SA   A2: SA+LA   A2: SA+LA+c   A3: SA+LA

Fig. 5. 3D representation of LV ground truth and CNN predictions. The distance of predicted LV to ground truth LV is color coded. Blue and red represents respectively undersegmentation and oversegmentation. (Color figure online)

Table 2. DSC, precision, sensitivity and ASSD (mean (std)) and correlation coefficient for volumes and EF. Significant difference between training on ED and ES separately (S) or together (T) is indicated with $^{\#}$. Best results are shown in bold.

			DSC [%]	Precision [%]	Sensitivity [%]	ASSD [mm]	ρV [%]	ρEF [%]
ED	A1	S	91.7 (2.3)	88.3 (4.9)	**95.6 (2.6)**	1.84 (0.53)	**95.3**	
		T	**93.0 (2.4)$^{\#}$**	**92.9 (4.9)$^{\#}$**	93.5 (3.1)$^{\#}$	**1.47 (0.61)$^{\#}$**	95.0	
	A2	S	91.1 (3.7)	88.5 (7.5)	94.5 (3.8)	1.96 (0.96)	88.5	
		T	92.3 (2.3)$^{\#}$	91.4 (4.9)$^{\#}$	93.4 (4.1)	1.60 (0.47)$^{\#}$	93.1	
ES	A1	S	**88.0 (7.0)**	**85.9 (10.9)**	91.3 (5.4)	**1.86 (1.41)**	93.3	61.3
		T	86.3 (8.6)	82.1 (12.2)$^{\#}$	**92.5 (5.2)**	2.30 (1.78)$^{\#}$	91.6	80.5
	A2	S	86.2 (6.0)	82.7 (11.1)	91.3 (5.4)	2.15 (0.92)	91.3	53.5
		T	81.1 (9.4)$^{\#}$	72.6 (13.0)$^{\#}$	93.5 (5.9)	3.39 (1.64)$^{\#}$	90.8	**84.5**

5 Discussion

We presented an approach to obtain a 3D segmentation of LV from 2D SA and LA images. In our experiments, we show that introducing additional information by incorporating LA images and image coordinates improves the segmentation results. Another advantage of our network architecture is that it allows to input an arbitrary number of 3D volumes. If, for example, a SA image set with more slices is available than the network was trained on, no retraining is needed since every volume uses the same filter weights in the first subnetwork (CNN1). This network configuration allows in principle also to readily input other modalities such as late gadolinium enhanced (LGE) images, provided that images of similar contrast and resolution are used during training. Additionally, we also show that augmenting a CNN with image coordinates allows to substantially decrease the required receptive field while maintaining similar segmentation results. It is argued that the RF of A1 and A2 is on itself too small for this segmentation task such that information about the position of each voxel in the image largely improves the segmentation. Once the CNN has a sufficiently large RF, we don't expect that the inclusion of additional spatial context will further improve the results which we noticed with initial experiments on A3 with image coordinate input. A1 and A2 have respectively a 64% and 70% smaller receptive field compared to A3 and have 55% and 47% less parameters to train (97,705 and 114,225 vs 216,849). The image coordinates were introduced towards the end of the network to not unnecessarily complicate the network and to avoid loss of coordinate information due to premature mixing of coordinate data with the more complex image data. Although a first experiment where the coordinates were introduced at the start of the network confirms this hypothesis, finding the undeniably best point for the introduction of image coordinates is a heuristic process and is out of the scoop of this paper. In this study, we showed the feasibility of our 3D segmentation approach on a clinical dataset of 20 patients using five-fold cross validation. The results in Table 1 were thus obtained by training from scratch on only 16 LV volumes, which is rather limited. To thoroughly compare the presented method in terms of segmentation accuracy or EDV, ESV and EF correlation with literature, evaluation on a public dataset would be beneficial. Furthermore, the 3D ground truth LV used for training and validation of the CNNs, was constructed from 2D contours. For a true 3D ground truth, a full 3D scan will be needed. However, we put great effort in making our 3D model as accurate as possible and visually verified model correspondence with SA and LA images. The main limitation of our presented approach is that CNN training and validation are performed on motion corrected datasets, while manual contours are used for this motion correction itself. Future work is thus to fully automate 3D LV prediction without contours as input for breath hold correction. Possible solutions are: (1) adapt breath hold correction initialization, (2) use a 2D CNN for rough initial segmentation in every slice or (3) train the 3D CNN with motion corrupted input data and a motion free output segmentation.

6   Conclusion

We presented an approach to obtain a 3D segmentation of LV from 2D SA and LA images and showed that introducing additional information by incorporating LA images and image coordinates improves the results.

Acknowledgement. Sofie Tilborghs is supported by a Ph.D. fellowship of the Research Foundation - Flanders (FWO).

References

1. Bernard, O., et al.: Deep learning techniques for automatic MRI cardiac multi-structures segmentation and diagnosis: is the problem solved? IEEE Trans. Med. Imaging **37**(11), 2514–2525 (2018)
2. Zheng, Q., et al.: 3D consistent & robust segmentation of cardiac images by deep learning with spatial propagation. IEEE Trans. Med. Imaging **37**(9), 2137–2148 (2018)
3. Poudel, R.P.K., Lamata, P., Montana, G.: Recurrent fully convolutional neural networks for multi-slice MRI cardiac segmentation. In: Zuluaga, M.A., Bhatia, K., Kainz, B., Moghari, M.H., Pace, D.F. (eds.) RAMBO/HVSMR -2016. LNCS, vol. 10129, pp. 83–94. Springer, Cham (2017). https://doi.org/10.1007/978-3-319-52280-7_8

4. Duan, J., et al.: Automatic 3D bi-ventricular segmentation of cardiac images by a shape-refined multi-task deep learning approach. IEEE Trans. Med. Imaging **38**(9), 2151–2164 (2019)
5. Zotti, C., et al.: Convolutional neural network with shape prior applied to cardiac MRI segmentation. IEEE J. Biomed. Health Inform. **23**(3), 1119–1128 (2019)
6. Oktay, O., et al.: Anatomically constrained neural networks (ACNNs): application to cardiac image enhancement and segmentation. IEEE Trans. Med. Imaging **37**(2), 384–395 (2018)
7. Wang, C., Smedby, Ö.: Automatic whole heart segmentation using deep learning and shape context. In: Pop, M., et al. (eds.) STACOM 2017. LNCS, vol. 10663, pp. 242–249. Springer, Cham (2018). https://doi.org/10.1007/978-3-319-75541-0_26
8. Oktay, O., et al.: Multi-input cardiac image super-resolution using convolutional neural networks. In: Ourselin, S., Joskowicz, L., Sabuncu, M.R., Unal, G., Wells, W. (eds.) MICCAI 2016. LNCS, vol. 9902, pp. 246–254. Springer, Cham (2016). https://doi.org/10.1007/978-3-319-46726-9_29
9. Luo, G., et al.: Multi-views fusion CNN for left ventricular volumes estimation on cardiac MR images. IEEE Trans. Biomed. Eng. **65**(9), 1924–1934 (2018)
10. Kaggle, Booz Allen Hamilton Inc.: Second Annual Data Science Bowl Kaggle (2015). https://www.kaggle.com/c/second-annual-data-science-bowl
11. Wachinger, C., et al.: DeepNAT: deep convolutional neural network for segmenting neuroanatomy. NeuroImage **170**, 434–445 (2018)
12. Elen, A., Hermans, J., Ganame, J., et al.: Automatic 3-D breath-hold related motion correction of dynamic multisclice MRI. IEEE Trans. Med. Imaging **29**(3), 868–878 (2010)
13. Ronneberger, O., Fischer, P., Brox, T.: U-net: convolutional networks for biomedical image segmentation. In: Navab, N., Hornegger, J., Wells, W.M., Frangi, A.F. (eds.) MICCAI 2015. LNCS, vol. 9351, pp. 234–241. Springer, Cham (2015). https://doi.org/10.1007/978-3-319-24574-4_28
14. Kamnitsas, K., et al.: Efficient multi-scale 3D CNN with fully connected CRF for accurate brain lesion segmentation. Med. Image Anal. **36**, 61–78 (2017)
15. Ioffe, S., Szegedy, C.: Batch normalization: accelerating deep network training by reducing internal covariate shift. In: ICML (2015)
16. Maas, A.L., et al.: Rectifier nonlinearities improve neural network acoustic models. In: ICML (2013)
17. He, K., et al.: Delving deep into rectifiers: surpassing human-level performance on ImageNet classification. In: ICCV 2015, pp. 1026–1034 (2015)

Towards Hyper-Reduction of Cardiac Models Using Poly-affine Transformations

Gaëtan Desrues[✉], Hervé Delingette, and Maxime Sermesant

Inria, Universit Cte d'Azur, Sophia Antipolis, France
gaetan.desrues@inria.fr

Abstract. This paper presents a method for frame-based finite element models in order to develop fast personalised cardiac electromechanical models. Its originality comes from the choice of the deformation model: it relies on a reduced number of degrees of freedom represented by affine transformations located at arbitrary control nodes over a tetrahedral mesh. This is motivated by the fact that cardiac motion can be well represented by such poly-affine transformations. The shape functions use then a geodesic distance over arbitrary Voronoï-like regions containing the control nodes. The high order integration of elastic energy density over the domain is performed at arbitrary integration points. This integration, which is associated to affine degrees of freedom, allows a lower computational cost while preserving a good accuracy for simple geometries. The method is validated on a cube under simple compression and preliminary results on simplified cardiac geometries are presented, reducing by a factor 100 the number of degrees of freedom.

Keywords: Model reduction · Finite elements method · Affine transformation

1 Introduction

Patient specific cardiac modelling is important for understanding pathologies, planning therapy or rehearsing a surgery. In order to be used in routine by clinicians, models have to be fast enough while providing an accurate solution to given boundary and initial conditions. The finite element method is a classical approach to solve physics-based deformation problems where the computational domain depends on an underlying mesh, implying that the computation time and the accuracy will depend on the mesh discretisation. Particle-based meshless frameworks have recently been proposed [2,3] and have the advantage of being less dependent from the topology. Particles, called control nodes, can be placed arbitrarily. It has also been shown in the literature [5,7] that cardiac motion can be well represented by mixing affine transformations located at the centre of sub-regions of the American Heart Association (AHA) segments, see Fig. 1. Furthermore, the decomposition into a mixture of affine transformations provides clinically meaningful parameters related to cardiac regional strain.

© Springer Nature Switzerland AG 2020
M. Pop et al. (Eds.): STACOM 2019, LNCS 12009, pp. 100–108, 2020.
https://doi.org/10.1007/978-3-030-39074-7_11

The key idea of this paper is to combine these approaches to propose an efficient reduced model. Compared to other reduction approaches using statistical learning of a reduced basis, this approach builds upon prior physiological knowledge of the cardiac function.

2   Frame-Based Deformation

We first define the degrees of freedom (DOFs), regions and integration points. The internal forces resulting from the deformation of the solid are computed based on the minimisation of an elastic energy density, itself resulting from the relation between strain and stress.

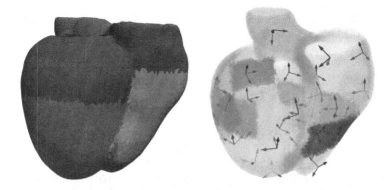

Fig. 1. 29 AHA regions (left) and oriented control nodes (right)

Figure 2 presents the framework used in our simulation of elastic solids. The different elements and the link between them through mappings will be described in further sections.

Our scheme relies on a reduced number of affine frames as degrees of freedom acting on a tetrahedral mesh $\mathcal{V}$. If N is the number of vertices of $\mathcal{V}$, the classical approach is to define a displacement field based on the displacement of each vertex, which makes this field of dimension $3N$. Yet the cardiac motion usually does not require such a high number of DOFs since the motion of neighbouring vertices is highly correlated. This is why we propose to discretise the displacement field as a combination of n affine frame motions which makes it a $12n$ dimensional space. Instead of the 3-coordinate vector displacement field classically used, we propose to use a poly-affine displacement field for which at each control node $\mathbf{q}_i$, $1 \leq i \leq n$, the 12 DOFs are the 12 coefficients of the affine transformation $\mathbf{T}(\mathbf{q}_i) = \mathbf{T}_i \in \mathcal{M}_{3 \times 4}$ (3 coefficients for the 3D translation and 9 for the linear transformation combining rotation, scaling and shearing).

The whole computational domain Ω is partitioned into n non overlapping regions Ω_i, centred on $\mathbf{q}_i$, each region being defined as a set of tetrahedra.

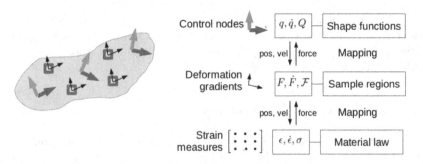

Fig. 2. Three levels continuum mechanics. The shape functions map the degrees of freedom, supported by the control nodes, to the deformation gradients located in the sample regions (grey square). Then, the material law computes the internal forces from the stress and strain. These forces are finally mapped back to the degrees of freedom. This process is repeated at each simulation step. Source: Flexible plugin documentation (Sofa-framework).

At a point x in the domain, the local affine transformation $\mathbf{T}(x)$ is defined as a weighted sum of DOFs $\mathbf{T}_i$:

$$\forall x \in \Omega, \ \mathbf{T}(x) = \sum_{i=1}^{n} \phi_i(x)\mathbf{T}_i$$

The weights $\phi(x)$ are the shape functions and represent the influence of the control frames over the domain. Their definition depends on the mesh geodesic signed distance $\mathcal{D}_i(x)$ of a point x with respect to region i:

$$\forall x \in \Omega, \ \forall i \in [\![1, n]\!], \ \mathcal{D}_i(x) \begin{cases} = 0 & \text{on the border of } \Omega_i \\ < 0 & \text{inside } \Omega_i \\ > 0 & \text{outside } \Omega_i \end{cases}$$

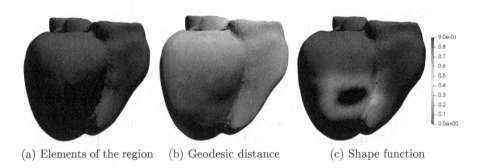

(a) Elements of the region   (b) Geodesic distance   (c) Shape function

Fig. 3. Example on a cardiac topology

This distance is computed after solving an Eikonal problem with the fast marching method [6]. It is normalised as $\bar{\mathcal{D}}_i(x)$ such that its minimum value is -1 at its centre $\mathbf{q}_i$.

If σ_a is the sigmoid function, the shape function ϕ_i is defined as:

$$\phi_i(x) = \sigma_a\left[\bar{\mathcal{D}}_i(x)\right], \quad \sigma_a(x) = \frac{1}{1 + e^{ax}}$$

The parameter a controls the overlap of the kernel function over neighbouring regions. We observed better results with $a = 2.25$, thus $\phi_i(\mathbf{q}_i) = 0.90$. It has been noticed that a big overlap (a small) leads to a smooth solution while a small one leads to more independent regions, in both cases introducing unrealistic values in the solution. An example with $a = 2.25$ is presented in Fig. 3(c).

3   Numerical Integration Method

The elastic energy of a deformable solid is the work done by the elastic forces between the undeformed and deformed positions, integrated across the whole domain. The numerical integration of the elastic forces is classically performed at the tetrahedron level in regular finite element methods. In our approach, we partition the domain Ω into M integration regions V^m consisting of a set of tetrahedra. In the spirit of our affine frame control nodes, we use a high order integration rule called elastons introduced in [4] and generalised in [2]. The classical integration approach assumes a constant force within each integration region V^m. The elaston framework relies on a first order Taylor expansion of the field to be integrated in order to reach a higher level of accuracy. More precisely, a field $f(x)$ is locally approximated as $f(x) \approx \mathbf{F}\,\tilde{p}$ where $\mathbf{F}$ is a vector containing the value of the field and its derivatives at the centre of V^m, and $\tilde{p}$ is the polynomial basis of order α in dimension d, for example $[1, x, y, z]$ at order 1, in 3D. Finally, the integration is performed as:

$$\int_\Omega f(x)\,dx = \sum_m \int_{V^m} f(x_m)\,dx = \sum_m \mathbf{F}_m \int_{V^m} \tilde{p}\,dx$$

In our approach, the strain and stress are approximated by a first order polynomial function in the vicinity of each integration sample which is estimated thanks to a Generalised Moving Least Square (GMLS) interpolation scheme [4].

4   Kinematic Mappings

The mappings are templated functions allowing to project forces, displacement and their derivatives between the affine frame DOFs and the tetrahedral mesh. We present the well known linear blend skinning and the GMLS mapping, very suitable with our first order framework.

4.1   Position and Force Mappings

The mesh vertices are displaced based on a linear blending of the affine frame DOFs using the shape functions defined in Sect. 2.

Let $\bar{x}_j$ be the rest position of the jth mesh vertex. Its deformed position x_j is computed as a function of the affine transformations $\mathbf{T}_i$:

$$\forall j \in [\![1, N]\!],\ x_j = \sum_{i=1}^{n} \phi_i(\bar{x}_j)\mathbf{T}_i \begin{bmatrix} \bar{x}_j \\ 1 \end{bmatrix}$$

Conversely, to compute the resulting force F_i applied to the ith frame DOF, we gather all the forces f_j applied to the vertices with the weighted sum:

$$\forall i \in [\![1, n]\!],\ F_i = \sum_{j=1}^{N} \phi_i(\bar{x}_j)\, f_j$$

4.2   GMLS Mapping

The GMLS method was shown [1,4] to be an efficient method to approximate globally a function from sparse discrete values with a minimisation problem. This problem seeks new shape functions $N_i(x)$ representing accurately the function over the whole domain.

$$\mathbf{T}(x) = \sum_{i=1}^{n} \mathbf{T}_i N_i(x)$$

In our framework, this mapping is used to compute the deformation gradients from vertices position at integration points. See [4] for an analytical formulation of $N_i(x)$.

5   Results

The proposed method was tested on different geometries, increasing in complexity. The simulation was performed on an Intel(R) Core(TM) i7-8650U CPU @ 1.90 GHz laptop, using the SOFA framework. The method widely uses the Flexible plugin approach of Fig. 2.

5.1   Cube Under Simple Compression

First, we simulate the compression of a cube $[0, 1]^3\, m^3$ discretised with 420 points and 1402 tetrahedra. Forces of $2000N$ are applied to the bottom and upper faces while other faces are free. The Young modulus is $E = 15MPa$ and the Poisson ratio is $\nu = 0.49$.

At each simulation, regions are randomly generated by picking seeds among the tetrahedra, then extended according to a classic Voronoï sampling followed by a Lloyd relaxation.

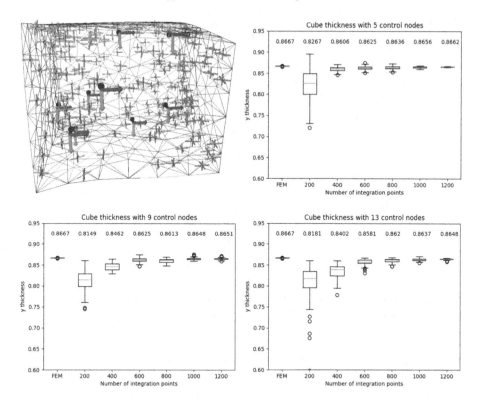

Fig. 4. Thickness of the cube under compression. Top left figure corresponds to the deformed cube with 9 regions and 200 integration points. The yellow crosses represent the deformation gradients at these points. Frames indicate the position of the control nodes. (Color figure online)

The integration samples are generated with the same process within the regions. Their number is proportional to the volume of the zone. To evaluate the simulation results, we use a full order finite element model referred as FEM in which the control nodes are placed at the mesh vertices and the DOFs are the 3 components of the displacement vector. Barycentric shape functions are used within the elements and the integration is performed within the tetrahedra.

Table 1 shows the computation time increasing accordingly to the number of affine control nodes and integration points (from 0.088 to 2.669 s). Choosing suitable numbers of DOFs and integration points will consist in a trade off between speed and accuracy, depending on the complexity of the deformation to approximate. When selecting as many integration points as the number of tetrahedra, the simulation time of the proposed method is similar to the FEM.

The thickness of the cube under compression is studied for one, five and nine control nodes. The relative error compared to FEM is listed in Table 1. The compression, consisting in a simple scaling, is exactly represented by one affine transformation. In this case, one integration sample is sufficient to represent

Table 1. Cube computation time and relative error comparison. The error uncertainty represents the tilting of the upper and bottom faces. FEM computation time is 2.41 s.

Gauss Points \Zones		1	5	9
200	Time (s)	0.088	0.575	1.157
	Error (%)	0.0	3.796 ± 9.864	4.511 ± 4.469
500	Time (s)	0.116	0.891	1.823
	Error (%)	0.0	1.142 ± 1.297	2.192 ± 3.987
800	Time (s)	0.144	1.125	2.263
	Error (%)	0.0	0.312 ± 1.228	0.646 ± 1.608
1100	Time (s)	0.173	1.409	2.669
	Error (%)	0.0	0.104 ± 1.203	0.115 ± 1.064
1400	Time (s)	0.204	1.293	2.402
	Error (%)	0.0	0.081 ± 0.272	0.081 ± 0.380

the deformation. The results for one region validate the simulation in this sense but are not physically interesting. The other experiments show that a denser sampling will lead to a more accurate solution. This is expected since the deformations are captured in more local areas.

Since the regions are randomly generated, their size and position can vary, leading to areas less represented in integration points. We observed that the stiffness is higher in the well sampled areas. Such a heterogeneity causes the upper and bottom faces to tilt. This phenomena can be observed for a high number of regions and low number of integration points, corresponding to a high uncertainty in Table 1. For example, the top left figure in Fig. 4 shows the random sampling of integration points. At the bottom of the cube, the lack in integration points introduces errors in the deformations leading to the bending of the cube edge.

5.2 Inflation of a Truncated Ellipsoid

The second experiment deals with Dirichlet boundary conditions on an axially symmetric shape. We studied the deformations of a truncated ellipsoid discretised with 1801 points and 6181 tetrahedra. The regions are linearly generated. One fixed-size region is placed at the apex. A pressure force of 1000 N is applied on the interior triangles along the normal surface. The following results are obtained with 4000 integration points, $E = 1GPa$ and $\nu = 0.49$.

The top mesh vertices are fixed with a projective constraint. To do so, we modify the control node location and shape function of all regions sharing at least one mesh vertex with the boundary. For these regions, the affine control node is arbitrary placed on the boundary. The shape function is equal to 1 on the boundary vertices and then classically decreases on the remaining vertices. We finally project the constraint on the previously selected DOFs, thus constraining the mesh vertices on the boundary.

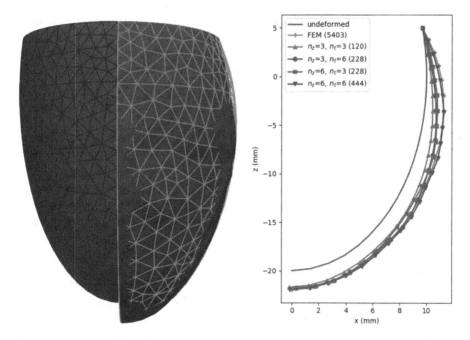

Fig. 5. Left: ellipsoid at rest (blue with edges) and deformed with full (orange wireframe) and reduced (plain brown) models. Right: position of the points on the external surface in the plane $(x^+, 0, z)$. n_z corresponds to the number of zones on the vertical axis and n_t along the circumference of the ellipsoid (plus one zone for the apex). The number of DOFs of each model is indicated in parenthesis. (Color figure online)

The orange curve on Fig. 5 represents the converged FEM deformation. Our method tends to converge toward the FEM one when increasing the number of control nodes. These results are two to three times faster than the full order method.

6   Discussion

On the ellipsoid case, we can notice that the external surface position is directly dependent on the number of regions.

Furthermore, it is good to notice that with the projective constraint, the slope of the curve near the Dirichlet boundary condition is well approximated. Another solution is to apply very stiff forces on the top nodes as boundary condition. However, this leads to stiffer top regions. In this case, the forces are mapped to the control nodes, thus influencing other vertices contained in these regions. This problem does not appear in the classical FEM since the shape functions are defined at the element level. With the projective constraint applied to the control nodes on the boundary and smoothly decreasing shape functions, this problem is tackled.

Finally, we observed small bumps on the deformed mesh, more visible for a large number of regions and probably due to the shape functions definition. The inflation seems more pronounced at the center of the regions than the reference one as it is visible on the ellipsoid Fig. 5. This phenomenon is reduced when a, the parameter of the sigmoid shape function, is high but leads to a smaller deformation.

7   Conclusion

The method presented in this paper shows promising advances in reducing the degrees of freedom for cardiac models, with an impact on computation time. Deformations on simple geometries are well approached with suitable parameters and validate the method. More complex geometries, such as the truncated ellipsoid, which is a simplified model of a ventricle, are also well approached by poly-affine deformations providing a sufficient number of DOFs. To be efficient, this hybrid method still requires a fine mesh for the offline computation of the geodesic distance as well as the regions volume. With circular shapes, the required number of control nodes to obtain an accurate solution is still high to efficiently use the large regions defined by the AHA segments. Finally, simple boundary conditions are well handled providing an extra care on the control nodes location and the mapping between the mesh vertices and the basis of affine degrees of freedom.

References

1. Fries, T.P., Matthies, H.G.: Classification and overview of meshfree methods. Informatik-Berichte der Technischen Universität Braunschweig **2003–03** (2004)
2. Gilles, B., Faure, F., Bousquet, G., Pai, D.K.: Frame-based interactive simulation of complex deformable objects. In: Deformation Models. LNCVB. Springer (2013). https://doi.org/10.1007/978-94-007-5446-1_6
3. Lluch, E., et al.: Breaking the state of the heart: meshless model for cardiac mechanics. Biomech. Model. Mechanobiol. 1–13 (2019)
4. Martin, S., Kaufmann, P., Botsch, M., Grinspun, E., Gross, M.: Unified simulation of elastic rods, shells, and solids. ACM Trans. Graph. (Proc. SIGGRAPH) **29**(3), 39:1–39:10 (2010)
5. Mcleod, K., Sermesant, M., Beerbaum, P., Pennec, X.: Spatio-temporal tensor decomposition of a polyaffine motion model for a better analysis of pathological left ventricular dynamics. IEEE Trans. Med. Imaging **34**(7), 1562–1675 (2015)
6. Pernod, E., Sermesant, M., Konukoglu, E., Relan, J., Delingette, H., Ayache, N.: A multi-front Eikonal model of cardiac electrophysiology for interactive simulation of radio-frequency ablation. Comput. Graph. **35**, 431–440 (2011)
7. Zhou, Y., et al.: 3D harmonic phase tracking with anatomical regularization. Med. Image Anal. **26**(1), 70–81 (2015)

Conditional Generative Adversarial Networks for the Prediction of Cardiac Contraction from Individual Frames

Julius Ossenberg-Engels$^{(\boxtimes)}$ and Vicente Grau

Institute of Biomedical Engineering, University of Oxford, Oxford, UK
julius.ossenberg-engels@dtc.ox.ac.uk

Abstract. Cardiac anatomy and function are interrelated in many ways, and these relations can be affected by multiple pathologies. In particular, this applies to ventricular shape and mechanical deformation. We propose a machine learning approach to capture these interactions by using a conditional Generative Adversarial Network (cGAN) to predict cardiac deformation from individual Cardiac Magnetic Resonance (CMR) frames, learning a deterministic mapping between end-diastolic (ED) to end-systolic (ES) CMR short-axis frames. We validate the predicted images by quantifying the difference with real images using mean squared error (MSE) and structural similarity index (SSIM), as well as the Dice coefficient between their respective endo- and epicardial segmentations, obtained with an additional U-Net. We evaluate the ability of the network to learn "healthy" deformations by training it on $\sim$33,500 image pairs from $\sim$12,000 subjects, and testing on a separate test set of $\sim$4,500 image pairs from the UK Biobank study. Mean MSE, SSIM and Dice scores were 0.0026 ± 0.0013, 0.89 ± 0.032 and 0.89 ± 0.059 respectively. We subsequently re-trained the network on specific patient group data, showing that the network is capable of extracting physiologically meaningful differences between patient populations suggesting promising applications on pathological data.

Keywords: cGANs · Image transformation · Cardiac contraction · UK Biobank

1 Introduction

Cardiovascular diseases account for 31% of annual fatalities worldwide [5], making them the most common cause of death. Reasons for this include the poor understanding of many such diseases, which frequently results in the ineffective treatment of patients and sub-optimal clinical outcomes. In particular, the relationship between disease phenotype and clinical outcome is often poorly understood. This is a particular challenge for pathologies such as hypertrophic cardiomyopathy, which present with high phenotype heterogeneity, with a wide range of structural cardiac abnormalities such as myocardial wall thickening

© Springer Nature Switzerland AG 2020
M. Pop et al. (Eds.): STACOM 2019, LNCS 12009, pp. 109–118, 2020.
https://doi.org/10.1007/978-3-030-39074-7_12

or aortic outflow obstructions. Structural changes such as these can affect the mechanical function of the heart, i.e. cardiac contraction, in a variety of ways. However, the exact relationships are not well understood. Since it is largely cardiac function that determines clinical outcomes, a better understanding of the relationship between cardiac structure and function could lead to more effective risk estimation, diagnosis and treatment.

Whilst structure-function relationships have been studied, this has mostly occurred in isolated approaches typically examining specific global parameters and clinical biomarkers (e.g. cardiac wall thickness/ventricular volumes vs ejection fraction (EF)). Although such biomarkers are clinically established, there is agreement that they are often too coarse for accurate clinical prognosis.

To better understand these relationships and to subsequently improve outcome predictions and treatments, we believe that a more comprehensive approach is necessary which could be achieved using generative methods. We have developed an approach based on conditional Generative Adversarial Networks (cGANs). cGANs, as shown by Isola et al. [6], can be used for image transformation and are therefore suitable for transforming one frame of the cardiac sequence into another, thereby modelling the cardiac sequence and the functional behaviour of the heart. Here, we are primarily interested in the transformation of end-diastolic (ED) to end-systolic (ES) frames, which represent the two extreme states in the cardiac cycle and contain a large part of the functional information.

It is therefore the hypothesis of this paper that by training a cGAN to transform ED to ES frames we can model healthy cardiac motion. Moreover, we hypothesise that our network is capable of capturing cardiac motion that is specific to individual patient groups. In order to validate these hypotheses we conduct two stages of experiments. Firstly, the network is trained on a data set of healthy volunteers representative of a heterogeneous population as given in the UKBiobank study (https://www.ukbiobank.ac.uk/). The network is evaluated based on how accurately the ES frame predictions match the acquired images for a test set using image and segmentation similarity metrics (MSE, SSIM & Dice). Our assumption is that an accurate prediction of ES frames indicates that the cGAN has captured healthy cardiac motion. Secondly, the network is re-trained on data from specific patient groups and tested on separate test sets from the same and different groups. The assumption is that the cGAN will perform sub-optimally when tested on the latter groups, thereby indicating that it has captured features of the cardiac structure-function relationships that are specific to certain patient groups.

2   Related Work

cGANs form an extension to the original GAN network as proposed by Goodfellow et al. [4] in 2014, which functions on the principle of adversarial learning whereby two networks compete in a minimax two-player game. In [10] this principle has been extended by adding conditional inputs to the GAN structure, allowing for outputs to be generated which are conditioned on input labels.

This has been taken further in a method proposed in [2], which allows for progressively increased information capacity of the latent space and more distinct modes of data variation. Isola et al. [6] have shown that cGANs can be adapted for multi-modal image transformation tasks whereby the input condition is the image itself. This paper is primarily based on their method. Further generative methods include Variational Autoencoders (VAEs) [7] and their conditional extension (cVAE) [12]. These, however, have been shown to struggle with image blurriness, due to injected noise in the re-sampling process and the fact that cVAE loss, in contrast to adversarial GAN loss, does not penalise unrealistic images. GANs/cGANs have been used in medical image analysis for a variety of tasks including reconstruction and registration. Specifically in cardiac imaging, GANs have been used for tasks such as image synthesis, for example CMR image synthesis using a Cycle-GAN based on CT scans [3]. Work on image segmentation in cardiology using GANs include quantification of myocardial infarction by Xu et al. [13]. GANs have also been used in identifying cardiac images with incomplete information using SCGANs by Zhang et al. [14]. Generative models for modelling cardiac motion have been proposed by Krebs et al. [8,9] who have investigated probabilistic approaches of modelling cardiac deformation using generative methods including cVAEs.

3 Methods

3.1 Conditional GANs

The cGAN used in this paper is based on the method proposed by Isola et al. [6] Two networks, namely a generator G and a discriminator D, compete in a minimax two-player game, causing them to learn in an adversarial fashion. The generator, a U-Net (Fig. 1), takes a grayscale ED image as an input and generates a "fake" transformed ES image as its output. The discriminator, which is a PatchGAN with the same structure as the encoder part of G with an additional softmax layer at the end, takes both fake and real ES images and learns to discriminate between them in a supervised manner. The discriminator loss given in Eq. 1 is used to train both D and G using mini-batch gradient descent and the Adam optimizer.

$$G = \arg \min_{G} \max_{D} \mathcal{L}_{cGAN}(G, D) + \lambda \mathcal{L}_{L1}(G), \tag{1}$$

where

$$\mathcal{L}_{cGAN}(G, D) = \mathbb{E}_{x,y}[\log D(x, y)] + \mathbb{E}_{x,z}[\log(1 - D(x, G(x, z)))] \tag{2}$$

In addition to the $\mathcal{L}_{cGAN}$, which is a conditioned version of the GAN loss, Eq. 1 also incorporates an $L1$ reconstruction loss which forces the transformed image to be close to the ground truth in an $L1$ sense. Hyperparameters and general methodology are based on the Isola method. However, we have adapted the number of layers and filters in G and D following empirical cross-validation.

We validate the performance of the cGAN at accurately predicting ES frames by computing the Mean Squared Error (MSE) and Structural Similarity Index (SSIM) between ES predictions and ground truth images. These metrics are computed over the entire image.

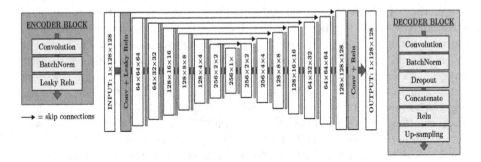

Fig. 1. cGAN U-Net generator architecture; numbers indicate number of filters × image dimensions for each layer. The discriminator architecture is equivalent to the encoding part of the generator, followed by a softmax layer at the end.

3.2 Segmentation U-Net

As seen in the workflow diagram of Fig. 2, following the ED to ES image transformation, the ES prediction and ground truth images are fed into the U-Net segmentation network created by Bai et al. [1], who trained it on data from the UKBiobank to segment short-axis frames into a four-label segmentation output, namely left ventricle (LV) cavity, LV myocardium, right ventricle (RV) and background. ED frames are pre-processed in order to fit the orientation and size of the segmentation network input. The binary LV cavity segmentations from predicted and ground truth ES images are compared using Dice coefficients.

4 Experiments

4.1 Healthy Cardiac Motion Prediction

The data for all experiments was obtained from the UK Biobank study. The initial experiment was conducted using the data of a heterogeneous group of healthy volunteers. Short-axis mid-axial cardiac sequences were selected from ~12,000 patients from which ED and ES frames were extracted. The images were subsequently cropped with a 128 × 128 pixel window centred on the LV endocardium, using as guidance rough LV automated segmentations included in UKBiobank. Images intensities were normalised to [0–1]. The image pairs were split into independent training and test sets, with no inter-subject overlap, with ~33,500 ED-ES image pairs for training and a further ~4,500 for testing. No image augmentation was applied, given the size of the training set. The cGAN was trained on a 5 GB 1060 Nvidia GPU for 200 epochs (~8 h training time).

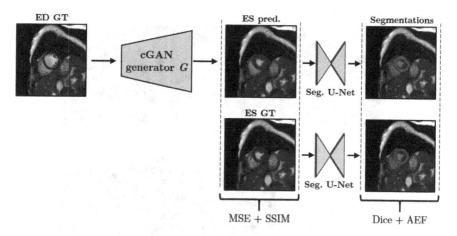

Fig. 2. Workflow diagram: ED ground truth (GT) frames are fed into cGAN generator to produce ES predictions from which MSE and SSIM are computed; predictions and ES GTs are segmented by U-Net from which Dice and AEF are computed.

4.2 Subject Group Re-training

Following the evaluation of the ES frame prediction for a general population of healthy volunteers, the network was re-trained with data from specific subject groups, differentiated by gender, age and Body Mass Index (BMI), also drawn from the UK Biobank study. For gender, the cGAN was separately re-trained on ~27,500 ED-ES image pairs from female healthy volunteers and tested on separate data sets of female and male healthy volunteers with ~4,500 image pairs each. For age, the network was re-trained on ~5,300 ED-ES image pairs from "young" healthy volunteers (ages 40–45) and tested on separate data sets of young and old (ages 65–70) healthy volunteers with ~700 image pairs each. Lastly, the network was trained on ~6,000 ED-ES image pairs from volunteers with low BMIs (BMI < 22) and tested on separate sets of subjects with low and high BMIs (BMI > 38) with ~800 image pairs each.

5 Results

5.1 cGAN ES Frame Predictions

Example results of cGAN ES frame predictions when trained on a general healthy population can be seen in Fig. 4. Mean MSE and SSIM scores between the ES ground truth and ES prediction were 0.0026 ± 0.0013 and 0.89 ± 0.032 respectively. The mean Dice score between the LV myocardial segmentations of ES ground truth and predictions for the general population was 0.89 ± 0.059 (Fig. 3).

5.2 Subject Group Differences

The analysed subject groups were: female/male, young/old and low/high BMI. For each pair the network has been trained on the former group and tested

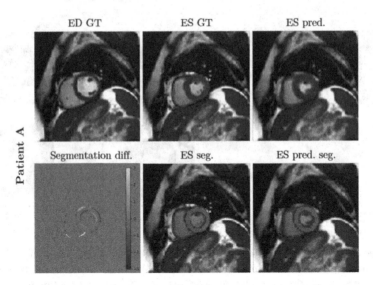

Fig. 3. cGAN prediction of ES frame for Patient A, including segmentations and difference between ES seg and ES pred.seg.; MSE, SSIM and Dice scores of [0.0035, 0.89 & 0.91] respectively.

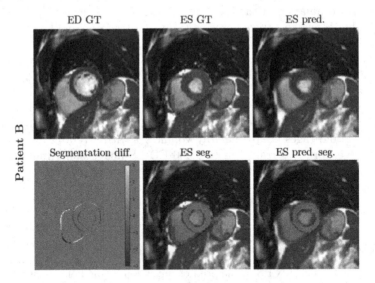

Fig. 4. cGAN prediction of ES frame for Patient B, including segmentations and difference between ES seg and ES pred.seg.; MSE, SSIM and Dice scores of [0.0047, 0.85 & 0.94] respectively.

on separate validation sets from both groups. MSE and SSIM values have been computed using the ES gold standard images and ES predictions for each patient group. Subsequently, all images have been segmented and Dice coefficients of the segmentations have been computed. Using the LV cavity segmentations, area ejection fractions (AEF) were computed according to $AEF = (EDA - ESA)/EDA$, where EDA is the end-diastolic area and ESA the end-systolic area. The mean percentage differences between the AEF of ground truth images and predictions were computed, as seen in Table 1. The SSIM and Dice scores of the individual patient groups have been plotted on normalised histograms to display frequency distributions, as seen in Fig. 5, which also shows p-values between the distributions calculated using the Kolmogorov-Smirnov test.

Table 1. MSE (in 10^{-3}s), SSIM, Dice scores and AEF differences for patient groups. Note that lower MSE and AEF, and higher SSIM and Dice, indicate better predictions.

Subject group	MSE score	SSIM score	Dice score	AEF diff.
A: Female	2.4 ± 1.2	0.90 ± 0.027	0.88 ± 0.058	14.9 ± 12.7
B: Male	3.2 ± 1.6	0.87 ± 0.038	0.87 ± 0.056	17.1 ± 20.3
A: Young	2.8 ± 1.2	0.88 ± 0.033	0.89 ± 0.048	14.8 ± 12.9
B: Old	3.3 ± 1.6	0.88 ± 0.037	0.87 ± 0.072	18.7 ± 19.0
A: Low BMI	2.7 ± 1.4	0.90 ± 0.032	0.88 ± 0.071	15.1 ± 13.7
B: High BMI	3.8 ± 1.8	0.86 ± 0.039	0.85 ± 0.092	22.6 ± 18.5

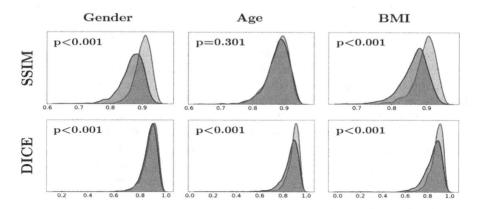

Fig. 5. Subject group histograms; Y-axis = frequency; X-axis = Metric; Group A in green, Group B in blue (Color figure online)

6   Discussion

The prediction of ES frames, shown in Fig. 4, can be evaluated qualitatively and quantitatively. Visual inspection shows that the cGAN is capable of predicting

ES frames with a high degree of accuracy resulting in remarkably realistic predictions. The cGAN can accurately predict LV myocardial wall movements and ES shapes, showing clear delineations of myocardial contours. RV contraction is also captured. It needs to be emphasised, however, that the cGAN does not explicitly capture motion in the sense of predicting motion vector fields, but rather predicts cardiac states as a result of cardiac motion. Quantitative evaluation confirms the quality of cGAN performance with low MSE scores and SSIM scores close to 1. Yet, since these metrics take into account differences across the entire image, local myocardial deformations might be masked by larger feature changes located outside the heart. Hence Dice coefficients based on LV cavity segmentations were used to compare LV shapes. The segmentations showed high agreement between the ground truth and predicted ES frames, which confirms that the cGAN has captured the structure-function interactions in a diverse population of healthy volunteers, thereby validating our first hypothesis.

Nevertheless some limitations can be appreciated, particularly on the RV shape which occasionally lacks crisp delineation of its contours. The edges of the LV myocardium also experience occasional blurriness. The intensities of pixels within the myocardium are sometimes not as homogeneous as in the ground truth. Furthermore, some images display difficulties with capturing papillary muscles or valve movements. Figure 5 and Table 1, together with their p-values, show that when trained on a specific sub-group, the cGAN performs significantly better when tested on separate subjects from that group, as compared to subjects not from that group. Whilst MSE/SSIM/Dice/AEF difference scores are significantly better for trained populations across all tested groups, the level of difference varies between patient group categories. For gender, statistically significant differences can predominately be observed in MSE/SSIM values. This could potentially indicate that image differences other than heart deformation between male and female subjects are responsible for the performance difference. For age groups, the opposite is true. Whilst MSE/SSIM values are more similar, Dice scores differ significantly, indicating significant differences in mechanical function between volunteers of different age groups. In the case of BMI, significant differences can be observed in both Dice and MSE/SSIM scores.

The difference in the metrics clearly suggests that the network has learned what "normal deformation" during the cardiac cycle looks like, because when subjected to a different population, where a physiological difference might be expected [11], the ES predictions are not as accurate. Whilst this performance may be expected, it has to be emphasised that both test groups were drawn from the same study and only varied in the test variable (age, gender and BMI respectively) whilst the distribution of the all other variables was consistent across the groups. Hence a difference in performance could potentially not be present and there requires experimental evaluation. The positive outcome of this experiment validates the hypothesis that cGANs can be used to learn structure-function interactions unique to specific subject groups, and suggests that when using this method for pathological data, we might be able to detect differences due to pathological cardiac function. Furthermore, by analysing the regions with greatest differences between prediction and ground truth, further anatomical and physiological understanding of structure-function interactions and clinical outcomes might be derived. The technique could potentially be improved by training the cGAN directly on segmented ED-ES image pairs. Advantages of this approach include the focus on the relevant area around the heart and the reduction of ambiguity in fuzzy areas, however, disadvantages are that the segmentations themselves have to be very precise to begin with and that organ texture for example in the form of intensity variations within the myocardium are not taken into account.

Acknowledgements. This research has been conducted using the UK Biobank Resource under Application Number 40161. This work was supported by funding from the Engineering and Physical Sciences Research Council (EPSRC) and Medical Research Council (MRC) [grant number EP/L016052/1].

References

1. Bai, W., et al.: Automated cardiovascular magnetic resonance image analysis with fully convolutional networks. J. Cardiovasc. Magn. Reson. **20**(1), 65 (2018)
2. Burgess, C.P., et al.: Understanding disentangling in β-vae. arXiv preprint. arXiv:1804.03599 (2018)
3. Chartsias, A., Joyce, T., Dharmakumar, R., Tsaftaris, S.A.: Adversarial image synthesis for unpaired multi-modal cardiac data. In: Tsaftaris, S.A., Gooya, A., Frangi, A.F., Prince, J.L. (eds.) SASHIMI 2017. LNCS, vol. 10557, pp. 3–13. Springer, Cham (2017). https://doi.org/10.1007/978-3-319-68127-6_1
4. Goodfellow, I., et L.: Generative adversarial nets. In: Advances in Neural Information Processing Systems, vol. 27, pp. 2672–2680. Curran Associates, Inc. (2014)
5. Institute for Health Metrics and Evaluation (IHME): Global burden of disease collaborative network. Global Burden of Disease Study 2017 (GBD 2017) Results (2018)
6. Isola, P., Zhu, J.Y., Zhou, T., Efros, A.A.: Image-to-image translation with conditional adversarial networks. In: The IEEE Conference on Computer Vision and Pattern Recognition (CVPR) (July 2017)
7. Kingma, D.P., Welling, M.: Auto-encoding variational bayes. arXiv preprint. arXiv:1312.6114 (2013)
8. Krebs, J., Mansi, T., Ayache, N., Delingette, H.: Probabilistic motion modeling from medical image sequences: application to cardiac cine-MRI. arXiv preprint. arXiv:1907.13524 (2019)
9. Krebs, J., Mansi, T., Mailhé, B., Ayache, N., Delingette, H.: Unsupervised probabilistic deformation modeling for robust diffeomorphic registration. In: Stoyanov, D., et al. (eds.) DLMIA/ML-CDS -2018. LNCS, vol. 11045, pp. 101–109. Springer, Cham (2018). https://doi.org/10.1007/978-3-030-00889-5_12
10. Mirza, M., Osindero, S.: Conditional generative adversarial nets. arXiv preprint. arXiv:1411.1784 (2014)
11. Petersen, S.E., et al.: Reference ranges for cardiac structure and function using cardiovascular magnetic resonance (CMR) in caucasians from the UK biobank population cohort. J. Cardiovasc. Magn. Reson. **19**(1), 18 (2017)

12. Sohn, K., Lee, H., Yan, X.: Learning structured output representation using deep conditional generative models. In: Advances in Neural Information Processing Systems, pp. 3483–3491 (2015)
13. Xu, C., Xu, L., Brahm, G., Zhang, H., Li, S.: MuTGAN: simultaneous segmentation and quantification of myocardial infarction without contrast agents via joint adversarial learning. In: Frangi, A.F., Schnabel, J.A., Davatzikos, C., Alberola-López, C., Fichtinger, G. (eds.) MICCAI 2018. LNCS, vol. 11071, pp. 525–534. Springer, Cham (2018). https://doi.org/10.1007/978-3-030-00934-2_59
14. Zhang, L., Gooya, A., Frangi, A.F.: Semi-supervised assessment of incomplete LV coverage in cardiac MRI using generative adversarial nets. In: Tsaftaris, S.A., Gooya, A., Frangi, A.F., Prince, J.L. (eds.) SASHIMI 2017. LNCS, vol. 10557, pp. 61–68. Springer, Cham (2017). https://doi.org/10.1007/978-3-319-68127-6_7

Learning Interactions Between Cardiac Shape and Deformation: Application to Pulmonary Hypertension

Maxime Di Folco[1]($\boxtimes$), Patrick Clarysse[1], Pamela Moceri[2,3], and Nicolas Duchateau[1]

[1] Creatis, CNRS UMR5220, INSERM U1206, Université Lyon 1, INSA Lyon, Villeurbanne, France
`difolco@creatis.insa-lyon.fr`
[2] Centre Hospitalier Universitaire de Nice, Service de Cardiologie, Nice, France
[3] Université Côte d'Azur, Faculté de médecine, Nice, France

Abstract. Cardiac shape and deformation are two relevant descriptors for the characterization of cardiovascular diseases. It is also known that strong interactions exist between them depending on the disease. In clinical routine, these high dimensional descriptors are reduced to scalar values (ventricular ejection fraction, volumes, global strains...), leading to a substantial loss of information. Methods exist to better integrate these high-dimensional data by reducing the dimension and mixing heterogeneous descriptors. Nevertheless, they usually do not consider the interactions between the descriptors. In this paper, we propose to apply dimensionality reduction on high dimensional cardiac shape and deformation descriptors and take into account their interactions. We investigated two unsupervised linear approaches, an individual analysis of each feature (Principal Component Analysis), and a joint analysis of both features (Partial Least Squares) and related their output to the main characteristics of the studied pathology. We experimented both methods on right ventricular meshes from a population of 254 cases tracked along the cycle (154 with pulmonary hypertension, 100 controls). Despite similarities in the output space obtained by the two methods, substantial differences are observed in the reconstructed shape and deformation patterns along the principal modes of variation, in particular in regions of interest for the studied disease.

1 Introduction

Clinical routine mainly uses simplified measurements of the cardiac function to characterize cardiovascular diseases, among which scalars such as ejection fraction or volumes, and myocardial strain. These scalars summarize high dimensional information about the cardiac shape and its deformation, and may therefore represent a substantial loss of information for complex pathologies.

Dimensionality Reduction Methods (DRM) have been used in cardiac imaging applications to better consider high-dimensional descriptors encoding shape

© Springer Nature Switzerland AG 2020
M. Pop et al. (Eds.): STACOM 2019, LNCS 12009, pp. 119–127, 2020.
https://doi.org/10.1007/978-3-030-39074-7_13

and deformation, either individually [1–4] or jointly [5]. Very recently, [6] went beyond these techniques and used auto-encoders on dynamic cardiac shapes to compute a latent low-dimensional space optimized for survival prediction.

However, cardiac shape and deformation undergo strong interactions depending on the disease. For example, in the case of pulmonary hypertension, a pressure overload forces the Right Ventricle (RV) to adapt by increasing its contractility to maintain a normal RV function. After a certain amount of time, the contractility can no longer increase and a progressive RV shape dilation and motion abnormalities may appear [7].

Methods that mix several high-dimensional heterogeneous descriptors all at once do not take into account their interactions and redundancy, which may limit the analysis. In methods reported in [8–10], an affinity matrix is established as composed of blocks that represent either the affinity between samples according to a single descriptor (diagonal blocks), or the interactions between two descriptors (extra diagonal blocks). Because of the nonlinearity of the methods and the unique output space returned, the reconstruction to the input space is not obvious. Other works proposed to link two learnt representations using additional constraints that express the hypothesized interactions between descriptors [11,12]. These methods first determine the low-dimensional representations independently and then consider interactions, which can substantially alter the initially learnt representations. In [13], linear techniques consider interactions while learning the low-dimensional representation, demonstrated for linking two different imaging modalities from the same heart. Nonetheless, this application concerned two descriptors that theoretically represent very similar information, while we target the study of shape and deformation descriptors, with known but only partial interactions.

In this paper, we explore the interactions between two partially interacting high-dimensional descriptors (cardiac shape and deformation), with unsupervised linear DRM either applied to descriptors independently or to both descriptors jointly. In the perspective of risk stratification from the low-dimensional output space, we notably evaluate how critical DRM can be for the assessment of the main local characteristics of a given disease: pulmonary hypertension, looked at through 3D RV echocardiographic data. In particular, we consider deformation patterns or shape as whole entities and not at each location independently from the others [14–16].

2   Methods

2.1   Data and Pre-processing

We processed a database of right ventricular meshes tracked on 3D echocardiographic images along the cardiac cycle, obtained from the commercial software 4D-RV Function 2.0 (TomTec Imaging Systems GmbH, Unterschleißheim, Germany). The meshes have 822 cells and 1587 points. The database is composed of 254 cases with 100 controls and 154 patients with pulmonary hypertension.

Point-to-point correspondences already exist between the meshes from different subjects, which allows straightforward comparisons within a population. Nonetheless, to reduce the bias due to different spatial heart positions, we realigned the meshes rigidly with Procrustes alignment (limited to global translations and rotations) [17]. This also provides an average shape for the controls population, used as template for display and analysis.

Then, two descriptors representing shape and deformation respectively were computed. The first one, called area strain (Fig. 1a), is the relative area change (in %) of each mesh cell between End-Diastole (ED) and End-Systole (ES). It summarizes the deformation of the RV over the systole. The second one characterizes shape at ED, through a distance vector (Fig. 1b) computed at each mesh point between a given case and the average shape of the controls, used as reference for normality.

These two features are high-dimensional: 822×1 for area strain (a scalar at each mesh point) and 822×3 for the distance vector (a 3D vector at each mesh point).

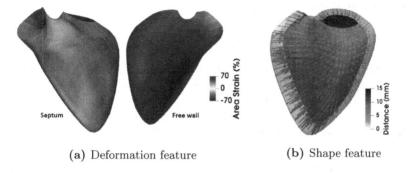

(a) Deformation feature   (b) Shape feature

Fig. 1. (a) Area strain pattern at end-systole for a healthy case expressed in % (b) Distance vector (mm) colored by magnitude for the same healthy case. The blue mesh stands for the reference mesh used for the computations. (Color figure online)

2.2   Dimensionality Reduction

DRM take as input high-dimensional data and return a low-dimensional space encoding the main characteristics of the input space. Here, we focus on the following two linear approaches. Principal Component Analysis (PCA) looks for the main directions of variance in the data. This can be written as the following eigenvalues problem, for a single descriptor $\mathbf{x}$:

$$\mathbf{C_x w} = \lambda \mathbf{w}, \tag{1}$$

where $\mathbf{C_x}$ is the covariance matrix of the studied descriptor, $\mathbf{w}$ and λ are the eigenvectors and the eigenvalues of $\mathbf{C_x}$, respectively.

The second considered method is the two-block Partial Least Square (PLS) regression [18], which mutually maximizes the covariance between the set of projections for two features, which amounts at solving the following eigenvalues problem:

$$\mathbf{C_{xy}}\mathbf{C_{yx}}\mathbf{w_x} = \lambda_{PLS}^2\mathbf{w_x}, \tag{2a}$$

$$\mathbf{w_y} = \frac{1}{\lambda_{PLS}}\mathbf{w_y}, \tag{2b}$$

where $\mathbf{C_{xy}}$ and $\mathbf{C_{yx}}$ are the cross-covariance matrices of the descriptors $\mathbf{x}$ and $\mathbf{y}$, and $\mathbf{w_x}$ and λ_{PLS} are the eigenvectors and eigenvalues of the matrix $\mathbf{C_{xy}}\mathbf{C_{yx}}$. Note that with PLS, we obtain at once two output spaces, one for each descriptor.

Due to the linearity of both methods, the inverse transformation (from the output space to the input space) is known. Therefore, the reconstruction of meaningful points from the output space is straightforward in particular along the first components. Note that for the shape descriptors, the reconstruction from the output space provides a vector field encoding distances from the template shape: a final step is needed for visualization and analysis purposes, which consists in reconstructing the corresponding shape by applying this vector field to the template shape.

3   Experiments and Results

The following section reports on the application of the DRM to the entire population (patients and controls). Considering patients and controls at the same time allows to study the continuum that exists from normality to the most severe grades of pulmonary hypertension, in line with what has recently been recommended for cardiac applications [19].

3.1   Output Spaces

We first compare the two methodologies (individual analysis of each features using PCA and joint analysis using PLS) based on their output spaces. Each analysis returns two output spaces (one per descriptor, Fig. 2).

A comparison between the obtained components by each strategy reveals that the first and second components are highly correlated (shape: $r^2 = 0.99$ first component, $r^2 = -0.59$ second component; deformation: $r^2 = 0.98$ first component, $r^2 = -0.69$ second component).

Nevertheless, another way of comparing the output spaces reveals differences unseen with the previous assessment. We evaluated the correlation between the components of the two output spaces, for each strategy (Table 1). With PCA, the first components of a given descriptor are linked with all the other components of the other descriptor. This is different with PLS, where each component of a given descriptor is only linked to the corresponding component of the other descriptor (low extra-diagonal coefficients in the table). This comes from the fact that PLS maximizes the covariance of both spaces at the same time, so the corresponding components are linked together but not with the others. This link is the main difference between the output spaces of both analysis.

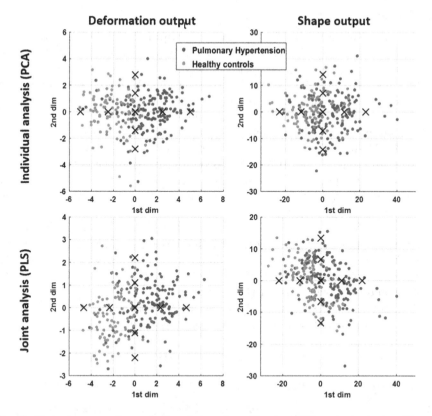

Fig. 2. Output spaces for each descriptor, from the two different strategies. Crosses indicate the samples at $[-2, -1, 0, +1, +2]\,\sigma$ used to reconstruct the modes of variations examined in Sect. 3.2.

Table 1. Correlation coefficient (r^2) between the components of the two output spaces.

(a) Individual analysis (PCA)

		Deformation		
		1st	2nd	3rd
Shape	1st	**−0.39**	0.19	−0.28
	2nd	−0.27	**0.023**	−0.13
	3rd	−5e−3	4e−3	**−0.065**

(b) Joint analysis (PLS)

		Deformation		
		1st	2nd	3rd
Shape	1st	**0.51**	1e−17	1.5e−16
	2nd	−4.3e−18	**0.48**	3.8e−16
	3rd	1e−17	2.4e−16	**0.37**

3.2   Principal Modes of Variations

The first mode of variations for the shape descriptor quantifies the size of the right ventricle (Fig. 3). The differences plotted on the right side of the figure correspond to the point-to-point distance between the PCA and PLS shapes at $+2\sigma$. Samples around $+2\sigma$ ($+2$ standard deviations) lie in the side of the output space where pulmonary hypertension patients predominate, and have bigger shapes (characteristic RV dilatation in pulmonary hypertension). The second mode of variations encodes the intra-valve distance. The meshes obtained from the two DRM substantially differ close to the apex (near 10 mm for a ventricle around 80 mm long). The third mode encodes changes in the curvature of the septum, and corresponds to reported changes in this zone for severe pulmonary hypertension cases ("septal bowing", which means that the septum bows itself and becomes almost straight [20]).

Note that the differences between meshes at -2σ is equal to the differences at $+2\sigma$ due to the linear dimensionality reduction and reconstruction methods, if the differences are unsigned (absolute differences). If signed, differences at -2σ are the exact opposite of differences at $+2\sigma$.

We should also keep in mind that the commercial software that tracks the RV along the cycle uses a surface model adjusted to the image data [21], which may reduce the amount of modes of variation in the mesh data we study.

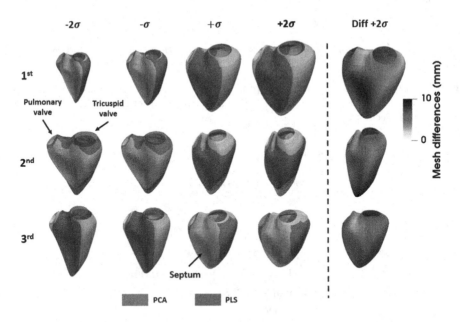

Fig. 3. Comparison of the first three modes of variations for the shape descriptor for both dimensionality reduction strategies.

The first mode of variations for area strain mostly quantifies the global amplitude of deformation (increase of the absolute strain values along the component).

Lower strain is observed for samples at $+2\sigma$, which corresponds to the lower deformation observed in pulmonary hypertension cases [14] (Fig. 4). Differences between the two DRM (difference between the two area strain pattern at $+2\sigma$) stay under 10% except close to the pulmonary valve (top left when facing the septum). The second mode encodes more local information and in particular the location of the maximal strain on the free wall (moving from left to right) and on the septum (close to the valve, positive to negative strain). Up to 30% differences are observed in some zones of the ventricle, although these do not correspond to characteristics zones reported for this disease.

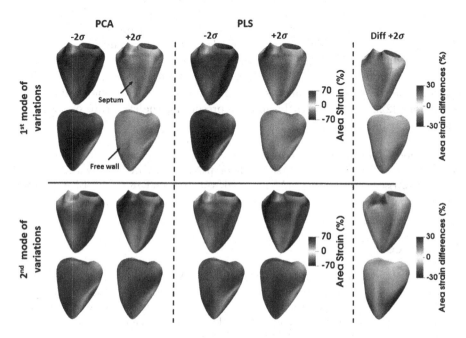

Fig. 4. Comparison of the first three modes of variations for the strain descriptor for both dimensionality reduction strategies. We show both septal and free wall views for better visualization.

4   Conclusion

In this paper, we explored ways to analyse cardiac shape and deformation, which are two high-dimensional descriptors partially interacting. We aimed at obtaining a relevant low-dimensional space that can be used later on for risk stratification. To take into account the interaction between both descriptors, we assessed two unsupervised linear dimensionality reduction strategies that consider the descriptors either independently or jointly. Similarities exist between the outputs of the two strategies (correlated first dimensions, similar patterns encoded along the first dimensions). Nevertheless, some substantial differences have been identified on zones of the right ventricle that convey relevant information for the study of pulmonary hypertension.

Recent work explored supervised techniques to represent shape data against survival in the context of pulmonary hypertension [6]. We preferred unsupervised learning for our analysis, as it allows identifying hidden data structures that can be used for risk stratification (for example, identifying clusters of patients at higher risk, or situating a new patient's risk against known cases) without being conditioned by clinical labels, which may be arguable in some cases [5].

Nonetheless, PLS may be restrictive in the sense that it does not allow controlling the weight given to the interactions between descriptors, which may limit the analysis on partially interacting heterogeneous descriptors such as cardiac shape and deformation. Further work will also extend the analysis to non-linear methods, which may better preserve the structure of the data spaces associated to each descriptor. It may also include recent developments for transporting spatiotemporal shape data among a population through diffeomorphic transformations [22], which explicitly aims at preserving the structure of the space encoding cardiac meshes.

Acknowledgements. The authors acknowledge the partial support from the French ANR (LABEX PRIMES of Université de Lyon [ANR-11-LABX-0063], within the program Investissements d'Avenir [ANR-11-IDEX-0007]), and from the EEA doctoral school.

References

1. Zhang, X., Cowan, B.R., Bluemke, D.A., et al.: Atlas-based quantification of cardiac remodeling due to myocardial infarction. PLoS ONE **9**, e110243 (2014)
2. Bai, W., Shi, W., de Marvao, A., et al.: A bi-ventricular cardiac atlas built from 1000+ high resolution MR images of healthy subjects and an analysis of shape and motion. Med. Image Anal. **26**, 133–145 (2015)
3. McLeod, K., Sermesant, M., Beerbaum, P., et al.: Spatio-temporal tensor decomposition of a polyaffine motion model for a better analysis of pathological left ventricular dynamics. IEEE Trans. Med. Imaging **34**, 1562–1575 (2015)
4. Duchateau, N., De Craene, M., Piella, G., et al.: Constrained manifold learning for the characterization of pathological deviations from normality. Med. Image Anal. **16**, 1532–1549 (2012)
5. Sanchez-Martinez, S., Duchateau, N., Erdei, T., et al.: Characterization of myocardial motion patterns by unsupervised multiple kernel learning. Med. Image Anal. **35**, 70–82 (2017)
6. Bello, G.A., Dawes, T.J.W., Duan, J., et al.: Deep-learning cardiac motion analysis for human survival prediction. Nat. Mach. Intell. **1**, 95–104 (2019)
7. Sanz, J., Sánchez-Quintana, D., Bossone, E., et al.: Anatomy, function, and dysfunction of the right ventricle: JACC state-of-the-art review. J. Am. Coll. Cardiol. **73**, 1463–1482 (2019)

8. Valencia-Aguirre, J., Álvarez Meza, A., Daza-Santacoloma, G., Acosta-Medina, C., Castellanos-Domínguez, C.G.: Multiple manifold learning by nonlinear dimensionality reduction. In: San Martin, C., Kim, S.W. (eds.) CIARP 2011. LNCS, vol. 7042, pp. 206–213. Springer, Heidelberg (2011). https://doi.org/10.1007/978-3-642-25085-9_24

9. Lee, C.S., Elgammal, A., Torki, M.: Learning representations from multiple manifolds. Pattern Recogn. **50**, 74–87 (2016)

10. Benkarim, O.M., et al.: Revealing regional associations of cortical folding alterations with in utero ventricular dilation using joint spectral embedding. In: Frangi, A., Schnabel, J., Davatzikos, C., Alberola-López, C., Fichtinger, G. (eds.) MICCAI 2018. LNCS, vol. 11072, pp. 620–627. Springer, Cham (2018). https://doi.org/10.1007/978-3-030-00931-1_71

11. Ham, J., Lee, D.D., Saul, L.K., et al.: Semisupervised alignment of manifolds. In: Proceedings of the AISTATS, vol. 10 (2005)

12. Xiong, L., Wang, F., Zhang, C.: Semi-definite manifold alignment. In: Kok, J.N., Koronacki, J., Mantaras, R.L., Matwin, S., Mladenič, D., Skowron, A. (eds.) ECML 2007. LNCS, vol. 4701, pp. 773–781. Springer, Heidelberg (2007). https://doi.org/10.1007/978-3-540-74958-5_79

13. Puyol-Antón, E., Sinclair, M., Gerber, B., et al.: A multimodal spatiotemporal cardiac motion atlas from MR and ultrasound data. Med. Image Anal. **40**, 96–110 (2017)

14. Moceri, P., Duchateau, N., Baudouy, D., et al.: Three-dimensional right-ventricular regional deformation and survival in pulmonary hypertension. Eur. Heart J. Cardiovasc. Imaging **19**, 450–458 (2018)

15. López-Candales, A., Rajagopalan, N., Gulyasy, B., et al.: Differential strain and velocity generation along the right ventricular free wall in pulmonary hypertension. Can. J. Cardiol. **25**, 73–77 (2009)

16. Seo, H.S., Lee, H.: Assessment of right ventricular function in pulmonary hypertension with multimodality imaging. J. Cardiovasc. Imaging **26**, 189 (2018)

17. Gower, J.C.: Generalized Procrustes analysis. Psychometrika **40**, 33–51 (1975)

18. Wegelin, A.: A survey of partial least squares (PLS) methods, with emphasis on the two-block case (2000)

19. Triposkiadis, F., Butler, J., Abboud, F.M., et al.: The continuous heart failure spectrum: moving beyond an ejection fraction classification. Eur. Heart J. **40**, 2155–2163 (2019)

20. Kind, T., Mauritz, G.-J., Marcus, J.T., et al.: Right ventricular ejection fraction is better reflected by transverse rather than longitudinal wall motion in pulmonary hypertension. J. Cardiovasc. Magn. Reson. **12**, 35 (2010)

21. Schreckenberg, M.: Adaptation of a 3D-surface model to boundaries of an anatomical structure in a 3D-image data set. US Patent, US9280816B2 (2013)

22. Guigui, N., Jia, S., Sermesant, M., Pennec, X.: Symmetric algorithmic components for shape analysis with diffeomorphisms. In: Nielsen, F., Barbaresco, F. (eds.) GSI 2019. LNCS, vol. 11712, pp. 759–768. Springer, Cham (2019). https://doi.org/10.1007/978-3-030-26980-7_79

Multimodal Cardiac Segmentation Using Disentangled Representation Learning

Agisilaos Chartsias[1(✉)], Giorgos Papanastasiou[2,3], Chengjia Wang[2,3],
Colin Stirrat[2,3], Scott Semple[2,3], David Newby[2,3], Rohan Dharmakumar[5],
and Sotirios A. Tsaftaris[1,4]

[1] School of Engineering, University of Edinburgh, Edinburgh EH9 3FB, UK
agis.chartsias@ed.ac.uk
[2] Edinburgh Imaging Facility QMRI, Edinburgh EH16 4TJ, UK
[3] Centre for Cardiovascular Science, Edinburgh EH16 4TJ, UK
[4] The Alan Turing Institute, London, UK
[5] Cedars Sinai Medical Center, Los Angeles, CA, USA

Abstract. Magnetic Resonance (MR) protocols use several sequences
to evaluate pathology and organ status. Yet, despite recent advances,
the analysis of each sequence's images (modality hereafter) is treated in
isolation. We propose a method suitable for multimodal and multi-input
learning and analysis, that disentangles anatomical and imaging factors,
and *combines* anatomical content across the modalities to extract more
accurate segmentation masks. Mis-registrations between the inputs are
handled with a Spatial Transformer Network, which non-linearly aligns
the (now intensity-invariant) anatomical factors. We demonstrate applications in Late Gadolinium Enhanced (LGE) and cine MRI segmentation. We show that multi-input outperforms single-input models, and
that we can train a (semi-supervised) model with few (or no) annotations for one of the modalities. Code is available at https://github.com/
agis85/multimodal_segmentation.

Keywords: Multimodal segmentation · Disentanglement ·
Representation learning · Cardiac MR

1 Introduction

MR is non-invasive and offers high soft-tissue contrast suitable for numerous
applications. Multiple sequences are used in a single MR session, producing
images of different contrast (modalities), that are characterised by disparities
in overall image quality and signal-to-noise ratio, but also provide complementary information of anatomy and function. Developing methods to automatically
segment tissue from such multimodal data remains important: for example in
cardiac MR, cine and LGE needs to be jointly assessed to characterise myocardial infarction [11], since cine contains high anatomical information, whereas
LGE focuses on nulling myocardial signal to detect hyper-intense infarct zones.

© Springer Nature Switzerland AG 2020
M. Pop et al. (Eds.): STACOM 2019, LNCS 12009, pp. 128–137, 2020.
https://doi.org/10.1007/978-3-030-39074-7_14

To this date, processing of such multimodal data treats each modality in isolation. Yet, jointly considering different modalities should be beneficial to obtain information from another modality that better captures anatomy (see Fig. 1 for a motivating example). Herein, we offer a step change: we propose a model designed to overcome challenges presented by multimodal analysis in cardiac MR solving the core problems of representation learning, cross-modal registration, information fusion and segmentation all in a joint end-to-end fashion in a semi-supervised setting, without requiring exhaustive annotations.

Deep learning has been successfully used for automating segmentation, however, most methods in the heart focus on single modalities. This is mainly because of the high variability observed in signal intensity patterns across different MR modality data and organ characteristics. While, in the brain, multimodal images are commonly used together [6], in the heart, multi-input processing and multimodal learning are substantially *challenging* due to inherent spatiotemporal and signal intensity differences (between modalities). These compromise learning direct pixel-to-pixel correspondences.

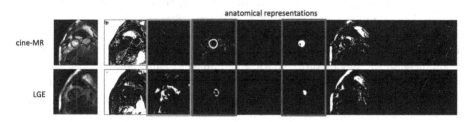

Fig. 1. Cine-MR and LGE images with corresponding anatomical factors. Common and unique information is marked with green and red boxes. Low tissue contrast (myocardial nulling) in LGE leads to poor separation in distinct channels between myocardium and surrounding tissues (e.g. ventricle). This can be corrected using the cine anatomy. (Color figure online)

We address the above difficulties, for the first time, with disentangled representations, i.e. mappings from multimodal images to corresponding anatomical and imaging factors. Anatomical factors contain structure (multi-channel binary maps); imaging factors contain input signal intensity characteristics. A Spatial Transformer Network (STN) [9] co-registers the corresponding (intensity-invariant) anatomical factors, avoiding the co-registration in image space (difficult in cardiac and other soft-tissue organs). We then combine (fuse) the aligned anatomical factors to find complementary features useful for segmentation.

Contributions: (1) Multimodal learning based on disentangled representations, that combines information present in different modalities without the explicit requirement for registered image pairs. **(2)** An application in cardiac segmentation, in which we improve on the segmentation accuracy of single-input (unimodal) models. **(3)** Semi-supervised learning: when few (or no) labels are

130 A. Chartsias et al.

available, we transfer information from the other modality and use reconstruction costs.

2 Related Work

Disentangled Representations: Decomposing the feature space into spatial and style-like factors has shown success in computer vision [7,13], and recently in semi-supervised cardiac segmentation [2] and multimodal registration [17]. In medical imaging, disentangled representations have more stringent requirements, since the anatomical factors must have semantic and quantifiable meaning (e.g. be useful for segmentation). Our proposed method thus differs significantly from related multimodal methods; it strives for anatomical factors to be semantic and geometrically consistent across modalities, as well as maintain the image dimensions to allow a direct mapping to segmentations. These properties are essential for anatomical registration and fusion, as well as semi-supervised learning.

Multiple Inputs in Cardiac: Level sets have been applied for cine-MR and LGE segmentation given shape constraints, generated by convolutional networks [14]. In [8], unannotated data were translated into a modality with annotations using "style transfer". However, this relies on learning good pixel-wise transformations, which is not always possible [23]. Also the lack of an explicit fusion mechanism may be problematic when images exhibit low contrast-to-noise between different organs. Non-deep learning approaches include multimodal atlases [25], whereas simultaneous segmentation and registration of multimodal cardiac MR images has been proposed with Multivariate Mixture Models [24].

Multimodal Learning: In medical imaging, e.g. brain MRI, most multimodal approaches assume perfect alignment between the inputs. Many methods have been proposed for synthesis [10], and segmentation, for example with concatenated multi-channel inputs [5,6]. To aid the learning process, in [20] they use cross-modal convolutions and convolutional LSTMs, whereas in [4] they propose densely connected streams (one per modality) to fuse high and low level features.

One approach to handle unregistered multimodal data is to treat them separately and share parts of single-input models. An empirical study of different sharing options [22] concluded that a common feature space connected with individual encoders and decoders has the best performance. Small mis-registrations have been previously handled with an affine STN [10]. Our method is able to fuse multimodal information, and differently from [10], uses a non-linear STN.

3 Proposed Approach

Multimodal Spatial Decomposition Network (MMSDNet) consists of multiple components (see Fig. 2), described in Sects. 3.1 and 3.2. At inference time, MMSDNet can take as input a 2D image (of either modality) or two images (of different modalities) simultaneously. One encoder per modality extracts anatomical factors, which are used for segmentation or input reconstruction. If multimodal image pairs are available, anatomical factors are aligned by a STN, and combined to produce a fused anatomy, which is used for the final segmentation mask.

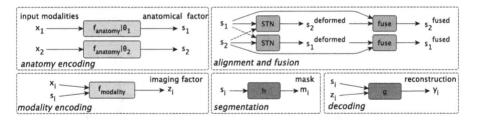

Fig. 2. MMSDNet components. Top left: anatomy encoders (one per modality) extract anatomical factors from images. Top right: misalignments are corrected with a STN; aligned factors are then fused to produce one factor. Bottom left: imaging factors are extracted by a modality encoder. Bottom right: the anatomical factor produces a segmentation; anatomical and imaging factors together reconstruct an image.

3.1   Model

Encoding: Assuming two input modalities, and image samples x_i (of height H and width W), where $i \in \{1,2\}$, the anatomy factor is derived from an encoder $f_{anatomy}$ with parameters θ_i: $s_i = f_{anatomy}(x_i|\theta_i)$. Anatomy encoders are fully convolutional networks (architecture is shown in Fig. 3), which output $s_i \in \{0,1\}^{H \times W \times 8}$, a one-hot encoding (in the channel dimension), 8-channel binary feature map of the same spatial dimension as the input (each channel represents a different anatomical area). These two restrictions encourage a semantic representation, since each tissue will be present only in one channel. They also disentangle anatomy from imaging, since a binary image does not encode any modality information in gray levels.

Alignment: The two anatomical factors are aligned using a Spatial Transformer Network (STN) [9] (architecture is shown in Fig. 3), which, through non-rigid registration, generates two deformed anatomies $s_1^{deformed} = stn(s_1, s_2)$ and $s_2^{deformed} = stn(s_2, s_1)$. The STN learns a matrix of 5×5 control points that define the displacement field, which registers the second to the first anatomical factor. Thin plate spline [1] is applied to interpolate the surface that passes through each control point.

Fusion: The deformed anatomy $s_1^{deformed}$ is an approximation of the anatomy s_2 corresponding to image x_2. Thus, it can be fused with s_2 to produce a single representation of x_2 that preserves the encoded multimodal anatomical features. We require the union of the aligned features, and thus use the pixel-wise max: $s_1^{fused} = \max(s_1^{deformed}, s_2)$. Accordingly, s_2^{fused} is also generated.

Segmentation: The previous steps produce six anatomical factors, namely s_1, s_2, $s_1^{deformed}$, $s_2^{deformed}$, s_1^{fused} and s_2^{fused}, which are used as input (one at a time) to a convolutional network $h(.)$ (architecture is shown in Fig. 3) to obtain the final segmentation masks. Depending on the inference task, we can get a

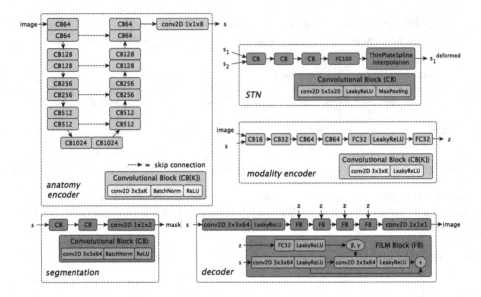

Fig. 3. Architectures of the MMSDNet components. Top left: the anatomy encoder follows a U-Net [18] architecture and maps an image to an anatomical factor s. Downsampling and upsampling are performed with max pooling and nearest neighbour interpolation respectively. Bottom left: the segmentation network is a small fully convolutional network that given s, produces a segmentation mask. Top right: the spatial transformer network consists of three convolutional and one fully connected layers and predicts the interpolation parameters used to register s_1 to s_2. Middle right: the modality encoder is a convolutional network that predicts the modality factor z. Bottom right: the decoder is a convolutional network that modulates an anatomy factor s with a modality factor z to generate an image.

segmentation using the appropriate anatomy, as also demonstrated in Sect. 4. If only x_i is available, the segmentation is obtained from s_i, whereas if both x_1, x_2 are available the fused anatomy s_i^{fused} produces the most accurate result.

3.2   Additional Networks and Losses

Our end-to-end strategy enables the model to learn from multimodal data to separate anatomy from imaging characteristics, whilst doing good segmentation, registration and reconstruction. Critically, reconstruction enables semi-supervised learning, aided via adversarial objectives on segmentation masks. Below we detail the breakdown of the overall training loss, $L = \lambda_1 L_{KL} + \lambda_2 L_{seg} + \lambda_3 L_{adv} + \lambda_4 L_{rec} + \lambda_5 L_{z_{rec}}$. (The λ's are set to 0.1, 10, 1, 10, 1 respectively.)

L_{KL} and $L_{z_{rec}}$: Given an image x_i, from modality i, then a corresponding anatomy s can either be the encoded $s_i = f_{anatomy}(x_i|\theta_i)$, or the deformed $s_j^{deformed}$ and fused anatomies s_j^{fused} if x_i has a paired slice x_j in modality j. Key is the disentanglement of the latent space into anatomical factors s_i and imaging factors z_i (8-dimensional vector), which requires a **modality encoder**,

$z_i = f_{modality}(x_i, s_i)$, and a **decoder**. The decoder reconstructs the input, $\hat{x}_i = g(s, z_i)$, using FiLM [16], by modulating s with scaling and offset parameters β and γ, that are learned from z_i. The network architectures of both the modality encoder and the decoder are shown in Fig. 3. The posterior distribution given the inputs $q(z|x, s)$ is modelled after the Variational Autoencoder [12] to follow a Gaussian prior $p(z) = \mathcal{N}(0, 1)$, by minimising the KL-divergence between q and p: $L_{KL} = D_{KL}(q(z|x, s)\|p(z))$. The representation disentanglement is further encouraged by a $z-$reconstruction cost using the ℓ_1 loss: $L_{z_{rec}} = \|z - f_{modality}(\hat{x}_i, f_{anatomy}(\hat{x}_i|\theta_i))\|_1$, where $\hat{x}_i$ is produced by a z that is sampled from the Gaussian prior.

$\mathbf{L_{rec}}$: Image reconstruction between the input and synthetic image is trained with $L_{rec} = \sum_{s \in \{s_i, s_j^{deformed}, s_j^{fused}\}} \|x_i - g(s, z_i)\|_1$. Essential for disentanglement is the cross-reconstruction between modalities by properly mixing the anatomical and modality factors. In addition, the reconstruction error is back-propagated to the STN and provides the learning signal for aligning anatomical factors.

$\mathbf{L_{seg}}$: When segmentation masks m_i, corresponding to the input x_i, are available, then a supervised cost is defined using differentiable Dice between real and predicted masks: $L_{seg} = \sum_{s \in \{s_i, s_j^{deformed}, s_j^{fused}\}} Dice(m_i, h(s))$.

$\mathbf{L_{adv}}$: Finally, an unsupervised cost with least-squares adversarial loss [15] is defined, $L_{adv} = \sum_{s \in \{s_i, s_j^{deformed}, s_j^{fused}\}} [D_M(h(s))^2 + (D_M(m) - 1)^2]$, using a discriminator over masks D_M. Here, the encoder $f_{anatomy}$ and segmentor h are trained to minimise L_{adv} adversarially against D_M which maximises it.

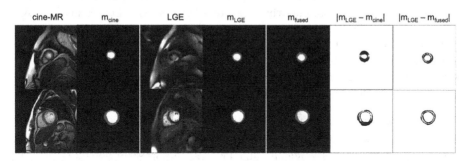

Fig. 4. Two segmentation examples from LGE+cine dataset. Each row shows a paired cine-MR and LGE with their respective ground truth masks (m_{cine} and m_{LGE}); the MMSDNet predicted mask (m_{fused}); and finally, the absolute difference of m_{LGE} with m_{cine} and m_{fused} respectively. Row-wise: $Dice(m_{cine}, m_{LGE}) = 0.51$, $Dice(m_{fused}, m_{LGE}) = 0.81$, $Dice(m_{cine}, m_{LGE}) = 0.77$, $Dice(m_{fused}, m_{LGE}) = 0.89$.

4   Experiments and Discussion

Data: We evaluate MMSDNet in LGE segmentation using a private dataset acquired at Edinburgh Imaging Facility QMRI with image pairs of 28 patients from cine-MR and LGE [19]. Myocardial contours are provided for the end diastolic frame of the cine-MR and the LGE data. The spatial resolution is 1.562 mm^2 per pixel, and the slice thickness is 9 mm. The dataset contains 358 expertly paired cine-MR and LGE images and their corresponding segmentation masks. The image resolution is 208 × 208 pixels.

Baselines: A lower-bound is obtained from the Dice between the real masks of both modalities, referred as "copy masks". This is repeated after affine image registration using mutual information, followed by symmetric diffeomorphic using cross-correlation [21]. We also consider uni- and multi-modal single-input U-Nets by mixing training data. The uni-modal UNet is trained only with the LGE images (UNet-single), whereas the multi-modal UNet is trained with both LGE and cine images (UNet-both). Finally, we compare with DualStream [22] setup of two encoders and decoders, the most recent deep learning method for unpaired multimodal segmentation.

Training and Evaluation: We train, using data augmentations of rotation, translation and scaling in Keras [3], with the Adam optimiser and a learning rate of 0.0001. Results are produced by held-out test sets on 3-fold cross-validation, where the training, validation and test sets are split using 70%, 15% and 15% of the dataset subjects, respectively.

4.1 Multi-input vs. Single-input Segmentation

Initially, we test whether multiple inputs benefit LGE segmentation, compared to single-input models. Two experimental scenarios are considered: LGE masks are available during training or not. Table 1 compares the performance of MMSDNet with the baselines and presents the mean test Dice score of Left Ventricle (LV) and myocardium (MYO) segmentation, as well as their average.

Given fully annotated LGE data (100% column of Table 1), the highest Dice is achieved when using multiple inputs at inference time (MMSDNet-multi), confirming knowledge transfer from source to target modality. The effect of multimodal registration is qualitatively demonstrated in Fig. 4, which shows the improvement achieved by MMSDNet compared with the cine segmentation. MMSDNet, which is trained with multiple inputs, outperforms a single-input U-Net, even when at inference time the paired cine-MR image is not available (referred to as MMSDNet-single in Table 1). Most importantly, when LGE masks are not available during training, but only images (0% column of Table 1), the U-Net and DualStream baselines fail to achieve accurate LGE segmentation since they are only trained on cine-MR data. MMSDNet, with the use of its unsupervised objectives, can still learn multimodal features and outperforms the registration baseline. The achieved Dice scores are comparable with the ones reported in related works [14, 24].

4.2 Segmentation with a Varying Number of Annotations

Here we vary the amount of LGE annotations during training to demonstrate the unique capabilities of semi-supervised learning in our approach. In this experiment a fixed number of annotated cine-MR images is used, that is equal

Table 1. Average myocardium and left ventricle test Dice results when training with a varying amount of masks. Best results are underlined; * denotes statistical significance at 0.05 compared to the best baseline. Number of cine-MR masks is always at 100%.

LGE masks:	100%			50%			25%			0%		
	MYO	LV	avg	MYO	LV	avg	MYO	LV	avg	MYO	LV	avg
Copy masks	50_{05}	81_{06}	67_6	50_{05}	81_{06}	67_{06}	50_{05}	81_{06}	67_6	50_{05}	81_{06}	67_{06}
Registration	51_{08}	80_{07}	68_{07}	51_{08}	80_{07}	68_{07}	51_{08}	80_{07}	68_{07}	51_{08}	80_{07}	68_{07}
UNet-single	66_{07}	87_{03}	78_{04}	64_{11}	83_{13}	76_{12}	51_{10}	75_{15}	66_{14}	-	-	-
UNet-both	$\underline{69}_{02}$	$\underline{89}_{02}$	$\underline{81}_{03}$	64_{10}	84_{08}	76_{08}	56_{09}	79_{12}	71_{10}	27_{17}	44_{27}	38_{23}
DualStream	65_{01}	86_{03}	80_{06}	64_{05}	84_{04}	76_{03}	48_{08}	69_{17}	61_{13}	27_{17}	44_{27}	38_{23}
MMSDNet-single	$\underline{69}_{02}$	86_{04}	80_{04}	64_{08}	81_{10}	75_{08}	61_{07}	84_{06}	75_{06}	56_{07}	83_{04}	72_{06}
MMSDNet-multi	$\underline{69}_{03}$	$\underline{89}_{02}$	$\underline{81}_{02}$	$\underline{65}_{04}$	$\underline{85}_{04}$	$\underline{77}_{04}$	$\underline{63}^{*}_{03}$	$\underline{87}^{*}_{04}$	$\underline{77}^{*}_{03}$	$\underline{59}^{*}_{05}$	$\underline{84}^{*}_{03}$	$\underline{74}^{*}_{04}$

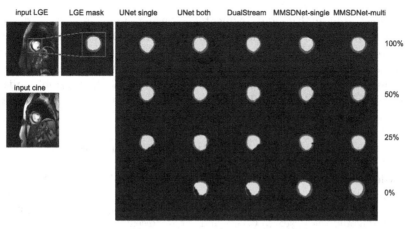

Fig. 5. LGE segmentations when training with varying amounts of LGE annotations.

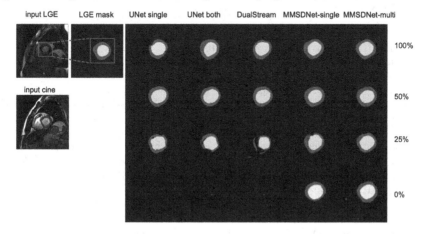

Fig. 6. LGE segmentations when training with varying amounts of LGE annotations. Observe that the baselines did not produce any segmentation mask when trained only with cine-MR data, i.e. for the 0% case.

to the number of LGE images at 100%. Qualitative testing set examples in Fig. 5 and Fig. 6, show the predictions of baseline and MMSDNet models with varying amount of training data. Observe how our approach offers more consistency.

Table 1 reinforces these observations quantitatively on segmentation accuracy for MMSDNet and various baselines. When the number of images is high (above 50%), all methods perform on par. However, as they decrease, the performance of the baselines also decreases. MMSDNet though is consistent and maintains a good performance even when training with no LGE masks. The performance of MMSDNet-multi is always higher than MMSDNet-single, suggesting that our method can leverage information from cine-MR to improve segmentation.

5   Conclusion

We demonstrated multimodal segmentation using input images of different modalities. We devise representation disentanglement to extract the individual anatomical factors, and then use these factors to fuse common and unique information. Our results show that accurate segmentation can be achieved when combining multimodal images, even when no annotations of the target modality are available (during training). We used two MR modalities with expert pairing of the inputs. Our methodology can be extended for additional modalities, by adding new encoders and by accordingly learning a pairing mechanism. Both are under investigation, along with further applications in other organs.

Acknowledgements. This work was supported by UK EPSRC (EP/P022928/1) and US National Institutes of Health (1R01HL136578-01), and used resources from the Edinburgh Compute and Data Facility. S.A. Tsaftaris acknowledges the Royal Academy of Engineering and the Research Chairs and Senior Research Fellowships scheme.

References

1. Bookstein, F.L.: Principal warps: thin-plate splines and the decomposition of deformations. IEEE PAMI **11**(6), 567–585 (1989)
2. Chartsias, A., et al.: Disentangled representation learning in cardiac image analysis. Med. Image Anal. **58**, 101535 (2019)
3. Chollet, F.: Keras (2015). https://keras.io
4. Dolz, J., Gopinath, K., Yuan, J., Lombaert, H., Desrosiers, C., Ayed, I.B.: HyperDense-Net: a hyper-densely connected CNN for multi-modal image segmentation. In: IEEE TMI (2018)
5. Fidon, L., et al.: Scalable multimodal convolutional networks for brain tumour segmentation. In: Descoteaux, M., Maier-Hein, L., Franz, A., Jannin, P., Collins, D.L., Duchesne, S. (eds.) MICCAI 2017. LNCS, vol. 10435, pp. 285–293. Springer, Cham (2017). https://doi.org/10.1007/978-3-319-66179-7_33
6. Havaei, M., et al.: Brain tumor segmentation with deep neural networks. Med. Image Anal. **35**, 18–31 (2017)
7. Huang, X., Liu, M.-Y., Belongie, S., Kautz, J.: Multimodal unsupervised image-to-image translation. In: Ferrari, V., Hebert, M., Sminchisescu, C., Weiss, Y. (eds.) ECCV 2018. LNCS, vol. 11207, pp. 179–196. Springer, Cham (2018). https://doi.org/10.1007/978-3-030-01219-9_11

8. Huo, Y., et al.: SynSeg-Net: synthetic segmentation without target modality ground truth. In: IEEE TMI (2018)
9. Jaderberg, M., Simonyan, K., Zisserman, A., Kavukcuoglu, K.: Spatial transformer networks. In: NIPS, pp. 2017–2025 (2015)
10. Joyce, T., Chartsias, A., Tsaftaris, S.A.: Robust multi-modal MR image synthesis. In: Descoteaux, M., Maier-Hein, L., Franz, A., Jannin, P., Collins, D.L., Duchesne, S. (eds.) MICCAI 2017. LNCS, vol. 10435, pp. 347–355. Springer, Cham (2017). https://doi.org/10.1007/978-3-319-66179-7_40
11. Kim, H.W., Farzaneh-Far, A., Kim, R.J.: Cardiovascular magnetic resonance in patients with myocardial infarction: current and emerging applications. JACC **55**(1), 1–16 (2009)
12. Kingma, D.P., Welling, M.: Auto-encoding variational Bayes. In: ICLR (2014)
13. Lee, H.-Y., Tseng, H.-Y., Huang, J.-B., Singh, M., Yang, M.-H.: Diverse image-to-image translation via disentangled representations. In: Ferrari, V., Hebert, M., Sminchisescu, C., Weiss, Y. (eds.) ECCV 2018. LNCS, vol. 11205, pp. 36–52. Springer, Cham (2018). https://doi.org/10.1007/978-3-030-01246-5_3
14. Liu, J., Xie, H., Zhang, S., Gu, L.: Multi-sequence myocardium segmentation with cross-constrained shape and neural network-based initialization. CMIG **71**, 49–57 (2019)
15. Mao, X., Li, Q., Xie, H., Lau, R.Y.K., Wang, Z., Smolley, S.P.: On the effectiveness of least squares generative adversarial networks. In: IEEE PAMI (2019)
16. Perez, E., Strub, F., De Vries, H., Dumoulin, V., Courville, A.: Film: visual reasoning with a general conditioning layer. In: Thirty-Second AAAI Conference on Artificial Intelligence (2018)
17. Qin, C., Shi, B., Liao, R., Mansi, T., Rueckert, D., Kamen, A.: Unsupervised deformable registration for multi-modal images via disentangled representations. In: Chung, A.C.S., Gee, J.C., Yushkevich, P.A., Bao, S. (eds.) IPMI 2019. LNCS, vol. 11492, pp. 249–261. Springer, Cham (2019). https://doi.org/10.1007/978-3-030-20351-1_19
18. Ronneberger, O., Fischer, P., Brox, T.: U-Net: convolutional networks for biomedical image segmentation. In: Navab, N., Hornegger, J., Wells, W.M., Frangi, A.F. (eds.) MICCAI 2015. LNCS, vol. 9351, pp. 234–241. Springer, Cham (2015). https://doi.org/10.1007/978-3-319-24574-4_28
19. Stirrat, C.G., et al.: Ferumoxytol-enhanced magnetic resonance imaging assessing inflammation after myocardial infarction. Heart **103**(19), 1528–1535 (2017)
20. Tseng, K.-L., Lin, Y.-L., Hsu, W., Huang, C.-Y.: Joint sequence learning and cross-modality convolution for 3D biomedical segmentation. In: CVPR, pp. 6393–6400 (2017)
21. Tustison, N.J., Yang, Y., Salerno, M.: Advanced normalization tools for cardiac motion correction. In: Camara, O., Mansi, T., Pop, M., Rhode, K., Sermesant, M., Young, A. (eds.) STACOM 2014. LNCS, vol. 8896, pp. 3–12. Springer, Cham (2015). https://doi.org/10.1007/978-3-319-14678-2_1
22. Valindria, V., et al.: Multi-modal learning from unpaired images: application to multi-organ segmentation in CT and MRI. In: WACV (2018)
23. Zhang, Z., Yang, L., Zheng, Y.: Translating and segmenting multimodal medical volumes with cycle-and shape-consistency generative adversarial network. In: CVPR, pp. 9242–9251 (2018)
24. Zhuang, X.: Multivariate mixture model for myocardial segmentation combining multi-source images. In: IEEE PAMI (2019)
25. Zhuang, X., Shen, J.: Multi-scale patch and multi-modality atlases for whole heart segmentation of MRI. Med. Image Anal. **31**, 77–87 (2016)

DeepLA: Automated Segmentation of Left Atrium from Interventional 3D Rotational Angiography Using CNN

Kobe Bamps[1(✉)], Stijn De Buck[2,3,4(✉)], Jeroen Bertels[4(✉)], Rik Willems[3(✉)], Christophe Garweg[3(✉)], Peter Haemers[3(✉)], and Joris Ector[1,3(✉)]

[1] Department of Cardiovascular Sciences, KU Leuven, Leuven, Belgium
kobe.bamps@kuleuven.be
[2] Radiology UZ Leuven, Leuven, Belgium
stijn.debuck@uzleuven.be
[3] Cardiology UZ Leuven, Leuven, Belgium
{rik.willems,christophe.garweg,peter.haeners,joris.ector}@uzleuven.be
[4] Department of Electrical Engineering, KU Leuven, Leuven, Belgium
jeroen.bertels@kuleuven.be

Abstract. Accurate segmentation of the shape of the left atrium (LA) is important for treatment of atrial fibrillation (AF) by catheter ablation. Interventional 3D rotational angiography (3DRA) can be used to obtain 3D images during the intervention. Low dose 3DRA poses segmentation challenges due to high image noise. There is a significant amount of research focusing on the automatic segmentation from 3DRA images, all based on an active shape or atlas-based approaches.

We present an algorithm based on a 3D deep convolutional neural network (CNN) for automated segmentation of 3DRA images to predict the shape of the LA. The CNN is based on the U-Net architecture and consists of an encoder and a decoder part. It is designed to be trained end-to-end from scratch on interactive semi-automated 3DRA images, which include the body of the LA and the proximal pulmonary veins up to the first branching vessel.

The CNN is trained and validated using 5-fold cross-validation on 20 3DRA images by computing the Dice score (0.959 ± 0.015), recall (0.962 ± 0.026), precision (0.957 ± 0.021) and mean surface distance (0.716 ± 0.276 mm). We further validated the algorithm on an additional data set of 5 images. The algorithm achieved a Dice score and mean surface distance of 0.937 ± 0.016 and 1.500 ± 0.368 respectively.

Keywords: Segmentation · Atrial fibrillation · Left atrium · CNNs

1 Introduction

Atrial fibrillation (AF) is one of the most common cardiac arrhythmias [13]. The irregular heart beats originate from abnormal electrical discharges in the

© Springer Nature Switzerland AG 2020
M. Pop et al. (Eds.): STACOM 2019, LNCS 12009, pp. 138–146, 2020.
https://doi.org/10.1007/978-3-030-39074-7_15

LA. AF is treated by performing catheter ablation to isolate the pulmonary veins from the atrial body [1]. The ablation procedure is typically guided by X-ray fluoroscopy and electroanatomical mapping (EAM). Although a 3D surface of the LA can be generated by a roving catheter. A lot of centers use an image-based anatomical representation because of its superior anatomical detail. This image-based representation can be obtained from CT, MRI or interventional 3DRA and can be integrated in the EAM system. Furthermore, it improves patient outcome and reduces radiation dose from fluoroscopy [8]. Thus, a correct segmentation of the LA is important for the success of the ablation procedure.

The use of preoperative CT or MRI has already been proven useful to facilitate the guidance during interventions [4]. However, preoperative CT and MRI imaging is often performed days or weeks before the actual intervention and possibly under different cardiac loading conditions. As a consequence, the anatomical structures of the patient can differ between the preoperative acquisition and the intervention. Besides resulting in a more complicated workflow, CT or MRI may be contra-indicated and often associated with an additional financial cost [12]. Interventional 3DRA can address some of these shortcomings.

Previously, automated LA segmentation methods were primarily based on model-based approaches. These approaches make use of a prior shape of the LA and intensity values of a stack of known LA 3DRA images. Model-based methods have been implemented for CT and MR [2,11]. The success of these methods relies on both the excellent image quality of CT and MRI acquisitions and sufficiently large data sets. However, model-based methods can be less robust on low dose 3DRA due to the limited image quality in combination with a rather small data set [11]. The limited image quality is caused by the variable contrast density, catheter streak artefacts, low X-ray dose and possibly a reduced frame rate [3]. Recently, CNNs were used to segment the LA from MRI [7]. They proposed a multi-view 2D CNN with an adaptive fusion strategy to segment the pulmonary veins (PVs) and LA. However, automated LA segmentation based on CNN is nonexistent for 3DRA.

In this paper, we present DeepLA, an automated LA segmentation method for low dose 3DRA. Our method is based on a modified version of the U-Net architecture [10]. In order to train the CNN, 3D patches were sampled from low dose 3DRA images. Furthermore, we implemented a preprocessing step. It reduces redundant information to improve the learning process. The overall segmentation process for a given 3DRA takes on average 19.6 ± 5.2 s on a GPU (Geforce GTX 1080 Ti) at test time.

2   Method

The method is composed of two parts: preprocessing and training. First, we discuss the preprocessing step. This is important to optimize the training process. Then, we elucidate the architecture and training process.

2.1 Preprocessing

Preprocessing aims at making the data more meaningful to the CNN. This is accomplished by removing redundant information and ensuring that the intensity value range matches across images of the entire data set. The latter avoids an initial bias in the CNN at test time. The preprocessing is realized in two steps. First, we construct a LA region that consists of all voxels with an intensity value higher than zero. The region outside the LA is set to zero. In addition, the gaps in the LA region are filled with morphological closing operations. Secondly, we normalize every patient's image by subtracting its mean and dividing by its standard deviation.

2.2 Network Architecture

In this paper, we propose a modified 3D U-Net architecture. The network consists of a contracting path and an expanding path. The contracting path contains successive convolutions and pooling layers to extract semantic features at the expense of spatial information. Two max pooling layers are used to reduce the dimensions of the image, first by $3 \times 3 \times 3$ and then by $3 \times 3 \times 1$. Before every max-pooling layer, we find two successive convolutional layers with a filter size of $3 \times 3 \times 3$ and $3 \times 3 \times 1$, respectively. In addition, we used batch normalization and a Parametric Rectified Linear Unit (PReLU) activation after every convolution. The PReLU activation function is a function with a learnable parameter. It follows: $f(x) = \alpha * x$ for $x < 0$, $f(x) = x$ for $x >= 0$, where α is learned [5].

However, in order to perform a correct segmentation, both spatial and semantic information is needed. The U-Net recovers the spatial information by shortcut connections from the feature maps in the contracting path of the same resolution. First the feature maps of the expanding path are cropped and then concatenated with the feature maps in the expanding path of the same resolution. Furthermore, the semantic information is passed on from bottom to top by up-sampling. The convolutional layers in the expanding path have the same configurations as in the contracting path. Due to the valid padding of the CNNs, the output size ($38 \times 38 \times 13$) of the U-Net is smaller than the input. In order to allow for sharper boundaries between voxels, the output of the U-Net is connected to two successive convolutional layers with 32 filters of size $1 \times 1 \times 1$. In front of each of the final convolutional layers, we added dropout with a probability of 0.25 to improve the generalization of the network. The final layer of the network includes a convolution with a filter size of 1 and a sigmoid activation function for generating a probability score for each voxel. Eventually, the LA shapes are produced by thresholding the probabilities of the output at 0.5. The algorithm is implemented in Keras (Python). A summary of the CNN is presented in Fig. 1.

2.3 Training Procedure

The training procedure is an important step to learn the right features in order to perform a correct segmentation of the LA. The whole training procedure was

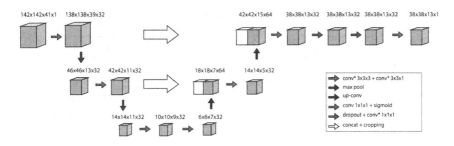

Fig. 1. Details of the U-Net architecture. Conv* refers to a convolutional, a batch normalization and PReLU activation layer.

designed using the DeepVoxNet [9]. This is a framework that enables a fast implementation of neural networks on medical images. DeepVoxNet provides components to handle the memory requirements, the various image modalities and data augmentation. The proposed network architecture is trained with input-patches of size $142 \times 142 \times 41$ and corresponding output-patches of size $38 \times 38 \times 13$. These patches are sampled via a class weighted sampler to compensate the class imbalance between the background and foreground. We define one epoch as 128 batches, with one batch consisting of 8 samples. The training is terminated early if there is no improvement during 70 epochs in the validation Dice coefficient. The weights of the network are optimized by the ADAM optimizer with an initial learning rate of 10^{-3}. The learning rate is divided by a factor of 2 when the validation Dice coefficient did not improved over the last 20 epochs. Furthermore, the network is regularized by L1 and L2 weight delay, both with a weight of 10^{-5}. Lastly, we use the binary cross-entropy loss function to train our network.

3   Validation

The 3DRA images were obtained through a floor-mounted Siemens Axiom Artis dBC biplane fluoroscopy system (Siemens). During joint rapid atrial and ventricular pacing at 250 ms, contrast was injected directly into the left atrium. Iomeron 350 contrast (Bracco) was diluted up to 50% using normal saline. Ninety millilitres of diluted contrast was injected at a rate of 20 mL/s, starting 4 s before the actual start of the C-arm rotation. The X-ray tube rotates around the patient over a course of 200°. During the rotation, fluoroscopic images were sequentially acquired with target detector entrance doses of 0.24 µGy/frame. In total, 62 frames were acquired. These 62 frames were used to reconstruct a 3D volume. This 3D volume is also called a 3DRA image. Further information about the image acquisition can be found in [3].

Twenty subjects were interactively semi-automated annotated by an expert. The annotated images include the body of the LA and the proximal pulmonary veins up to the first branching vessel. The 20 3DRA images were randomly divided into 5 subsets of 4 images. The learning process was repeated for 5 times while each time a different validation set of 4 images was used. In addition,

Table 1. Mean, median and standard deviation of the metrics for LA segmentation

	Mean	STD			Mean	STD
DICE	0.959	0.015		DICE	0.937	0.016
sDICE	0.932	0.020		sDICE	0.915	0.024
PRE	0.957	0.021		PRE	0.961	0.035
REC	0.962	0.026		REC	0.917	0.038
MSD	0.716	0.276		MSD	1.500	0.368
HD	11.088	4.770		HD	32.390	13.390
HD95	2.451	1.686		HD95	6.888	2.749

(a) Validation set   (b) Test set

(a)   (b)

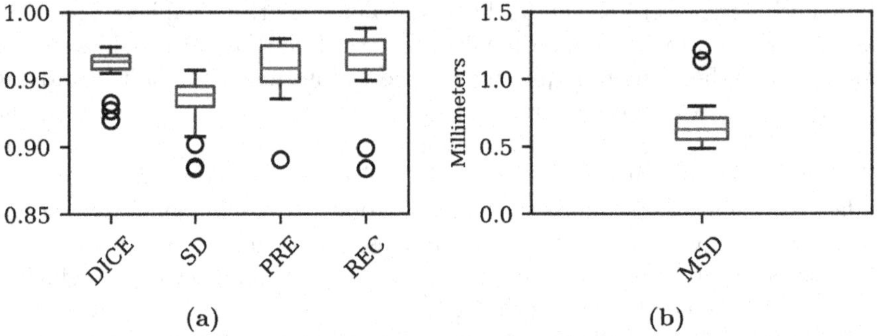

Fig. 2. Box plots for Dice, soft Dice, precision, recall and mean-surface-distance in the validation set

Table 2. Clinical usefulness

Case	1	2	3	4	5	Mean
Overall segmentation of the LA and PVs	4	4	4	4	4	**4.0**
Ridge between the LPVs and LAA	3	3	4	4	5	**3.8**
Position of the Mitral valve	4	3	4	4	5	**4.0**
Number of PVs correctly segmented	4	3	4	4	4	**3.8**

5 unseen 3DRA images were independently collected. These 5 3DRA images were semi-automated annotated by a different reviewer. This resulted in slightly different ground truth masks compared to the other 20 3DRA images. The automatic LA segmentation on the test data were generated by the model that yielded the highest Dice score on the validation set. For evaluation of the proposed method, we computed the Dice coefficient (DICE), soft Dice coefficient (sDICE), recall (REC) and precision (PRE) for both validation and test set. In addition, we assessed the mean-surface-distance (MSD) maximal Hausdorff distance (HD) and 95 percentile Hausdorff distance (HD95).

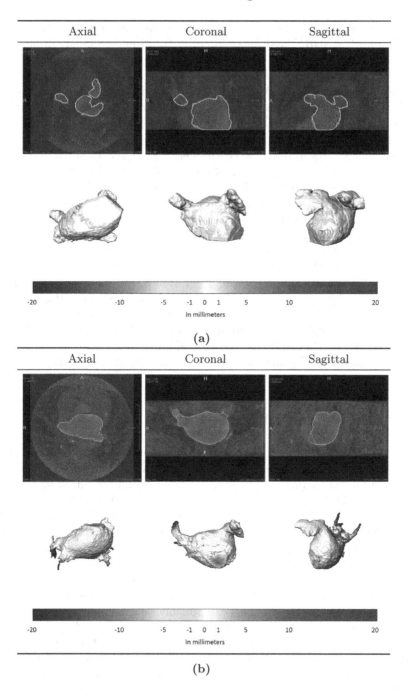

Fig. 3. Visualization of segmentation in validation (a) and test set (b). The first row of each table presents 3DRA slices from axial, coronal and sagittal views. The white contour is the ground truth. The red contour was generated by the proposed method. The second row visualizes the difference between surface of the ground truth and the surface of the output. (Color figure online)

Using 5-fold cross-validation on the training and validation set, we obtained a DICE (0.959 ± 0.015) and MSD (0.716 ± 0.276 mm). Similar, in almost all evaluation metrics in the test set, the algorithm achieved promising performance (DICE 0.937 ± 0.016 and MSD 1.500 ± 0.368 mm). More details about the performance and the distributions of the evaluation metrics are presented in Table 1 and Fig. 2. Furthermore, an additional test is performed to assess the clinical usefulness. The generated shapes in the test set were reviewed by a physician. Every shape is scored on the base of three criteria, namely the overall segmentation of the LA and PVs, the ridge between the Left PVs (LPVs) and the Left Atrial Appendage (LAA) and the position of the Mitral valve. The score per criterion ranges from 0 (very poor) to 5 (excellent). Moreover, the number of correctly segmented PV ostia were counted. The results of the review are presented in Table 2. It can be noticed that on average the proposed method scored a 3.9 out of 5 on the three criteria. In order to perform this qualitative evaluation, we used surface rendering of the predictions in the test set and compared them with the ground truth (Fig. 3).

Figure 3 shows an example of a segmentation in the validation and test set. The first row of the figure shows 3DRA slices from axial, coronal and sagittal views. The white contour represents the contour of the ground truth and the red contour was generated by the proposed method. The second row visualizes the difference between the surface of the ground truth and the surface of the predicted segmentation. The differences between the ground truth and the predicted segmentation of the proposed method is around 1.00 mm.

4   Conclusion and Discussion

Accurate knowledge of the shape of the LA is important for treatment of AF by cardiac ablation. In this paper we present DeepLA, an automated LA segmentation tool for 3DRA images. DeepLA was trained and optimized on 20 3DRA images by 5-fold cross-validation. Additionally, DeepLA is tested on 5 3DRA images and assessed by a physician. To the best of our knowledge, we are first to present results of a CNN based approach to segment the LA from 3DRA images.

We were able to achieve promising performance in Dice coefficient and MSD on the training and test set through a deep learning algorithm. Despite overall promising results on the validation and test sets, some local discrepancies between the ground truth and predictions can be found in the test set as reflected by the MSD values (Table 1b). This can possibly be explained by the differences in annotations of the ground truth in the training and test set (Fig. 3b). In terms of clinical usefulness, the segmentation of the LA scores well (Table 2).

We cannot directly compare our approach with those reported in the literature due to the difference in imaging modalities used and datasets. In [7], the LA is segmented from cardiac MRI data sets provided by the STACOM 2013 challenge through a 2D multi-view CNN. Their method achieved a Dice score of 0.905. Furthermore, Zheng et. al [14] and Manzke et. al [6] proposed a model-based method to segment LA from 3DRA images and obtained a mean segmentation error of 1.30 and 1.50 mm respectively. Even though they obtained a slightly smaller mean segmentation error than our method, DeepLA is trained with 3DRA images which were acquired with a lower radiation dose and consequently higher image noise.

We can conclude that we are able to *successfully* segment the LA and PVs as a whole. Our method achieves a mean accuracy of 1.5 ± 0.368 mm with a mean processing time of 19.6 ± 5.2 s. Hence, it may be easily implemented for online use during PVI, given an ablation lesion size ≥ 5 mm.

References

1. Bajpai, A., Savelieva, I., Camm, A.J.: Treatment of atrial fibrillation. Br. Med. Bull. **88**(1), 75–94 (2008)
2. von Berg, J., Lorenz, C.: Accurate left atrium segmentation in multislice CT images using a shape model. In: Fitzpatrick, J.M., Reinhardt, J.M. (eds.) Medical Imaging 2005: Image Processing, vol. 5747, p. 351. International Society for Optics and Photonics (2005)
3. De Buck, S., et al.: Cardiac three-dimensional rotational angiography can be performed with low radiation dose while preserving image quality. Europace **15**(12), 1718–1724 (2013)
4. De Buck, S., et al.: An augmented reality system for patient-specific guidance of cardiac catheter ablation procedures. IEEE Trans. Med. Imaging **24**(11), 1512–1524 (2005)
5. He, K., Zhang, X., Ren, S., Sun, J.: Delving deep into rectifiers: surpassing human-level performance on ImageNet classification. In: Proceedings of the IEEE International Conference on Computer Vision 2015 International Conference on Computer Vision, ICCV 2015, pp. 1026–1034 (2015)
6. Manzke, R., et al.: Automatic segmentation of rotational X-ray images for anatomic intra-procedural surface generation in atrial fibrillation ablation procedures. IEEE Trans. Med. Imaging **29**(2), 260–272 (2010)
7. Mortazi, A., Karim, R., Rhode, K., Burt, J., Bagci, U.: *CardiacNET*: segmentation of left atrium and proximal pulmonary veins from MRI using multi-view CNN. In: Descoteaux, M., Maier-Hein, L., Franz, A., Jannin, P., Collins, D.L., Duchesne, S. (eds.) MICCAI 2017. LNCS, vol. 10434, pp. 377–385. Springer, Cham (2017). https://doi.org/10.1007/978-3-319-66185-8_43
8. Nakagawa, H., et al.: 2017 HRS/EHRA/ECAS/APHRS/SOLAECE expert consensus statement on catheter and surgical ablation of atrial fibrillation. Heart Rhythm **14**(10), e275–e444 (2017)
9. Robben, D., Bertels, J., Willems, S., Vandermeulen, D., Maes, F., Paul, S.: DeepVoxNet: voxel-wise prediction for 3D images (2018)
10. Ronneberger, O., Fischer, P., Brox, T.: U-Net: convolutional networks for biomedical image segmentation. In: Navab, N., Hornegger, J., Wells, W.M., Frangi, A.F. (eds.) MICCAI 2015. LNCS, vol. 9351, pp. 234–241. Springer, Cham (2015). https://doi.org/10.1007/978-3-319-24574-4_28
11. Stender, B., Blanck, O., Wang, B., Schlaefer, A.: Model-based segmentation of the left atrium in CT and MRI scans. In: Camara, O., Mansi, T., Pop, M., Rhode, K., Sermesant, M., Young, A. (eds.) STACOM 201. LNCS, vol. 8330, pp. 31–41. Springer, Heidelberg (2014). https://doi.org/10.1007/978-3-642-54268-8_4

12. Thiagalingam, A., et al.: Intraprocedural volume imaging of the left atrium and pulmonary veins with rotational X-ray angiography: implications for catheter ablation of atrial fibrillation. J. Cardiovasc. Electrophysiol. **19**(3), 293–300 (2008)
13. Wyndham, C.R.: Atrial fibrillation: the most common arrhythmia. Texas Heart Inst. J. **27**(3), 257–67 (2000)
14. Zheng, Y., Wang, T., John, M., Zhou, S.K., Boese, J., Comaniciu, D.: Multi-part left atrium modeling and segmentation in C-Arm CT volumes for atrial fibrillation ablation. In: Fichtinger, G., Martel, A., Peters, T. (eds.) MICCAI 2011. LNCS, vol. 6893, pp. 487–495. Springer, Heidelberg (2011). https://doi.org/10.1007/978-3-642-23626-6_60

Non-invasive Pressure Estimation in Patients with Pulmonary Arterial Hypertension: Data-Driven or Model-Based?

Yingyu Yang[1(✉)], Stephane Gillon[2], Jaume Banus[1], Pamela Moceri[2], and Maxime Sermesant[1]

[1] Inria, Université Côte d'Azur, Sophia Antipolis, France
yingyu.yang@inria.fr
[2] Nice University Hospital, Université Côte d'Azur, Nice, France

Abstract. Right heart catheterisation is considered as the gold standard for the assessment of patients with suspected pulmonary hypertension. It provides clinicians with meaningful data, such as pulmonary capillary wedge pressure and pulmonary vascular resistance, however its usage is limited due to its invasive nature. Non-invasive alternatives, like Doppler echocardiography could present insightful measurements of right heart but lack detailed information related to pulmonary vasculature. In order to explore non-invasive means, we studied a dataset of 95 pulmonary hypertension patients, which includes measurements from echocardiography and from right-heart catheterisation. We used data extracted from echocardiography to conduct cardiac circulation model personalisation and tested its prediction power of catheter data. Standard machine learning methods were also investigated for pulmonary artery pressure prediction. Our preliminary results demonstrated the potential prediction power of both data-driven and model-based approaches.

Keywords: Cardiac modelling · Machine learning · Pulmonary hypertension

1 Introduction

Pulmonary arterial hypertension (PAH) is a pathological hemodynamic condition defined as mean pulmonary arterial pressure (mPAP) at rest >25 mmHg, measured by gold standard - right heart catheterisation (RHC) [12]. Pulmonary arterial hypertension can originate in lungs, heart, pulmonary artery and blood, and eventually leads to right heart failure or death. Standard diagnostic procedure requires clinical evaluation, non-invasive imaging and right heart catheterisation [8].

However, some patients do not receive RHC as part of their diagnostic routine and this may be related to lack of training or the potential perception of

M. Pop et al. (Eds.): STACOM 2019, LNCS 12009, pp. 147–156, 2020.
https://doi.org/10.1007/978-3-030-39074-7_16

RHC invasive risk, especially in the pediatric population [13]. This phenomenon increases the possibility of incomplete diagnosis, which diminishes the effect of targeted therapies [4]. In reality, echocardiography and catheterisation are usually conducted in separated labs. In order to combine the hemodynamic information provided by RHC and echocardiography, in our work, we explored the possibility of incorporating catheter-based data prediction, specifically, mean pulmonary artery pressure (mPAP) and pulmonary vascular resistance (PVR), into routine echocardiography diagnosis.

There exists very simple ways to estimate PVR [11] and mPAP [3] but most of them only rely on one or two echocardiographic measurements, which largely propagates measurement uncertainty to prediction and constrains their usage under different physiological conditions. Recently, with the advance of machine learning techniques, data-driven algorithms demonstrated good performance in cardiac tasks [5]. Besides, numerical modeling of pulmonary circulation also showed the ability to assess hemodynamic values non-invasively [9]. In our work, we used a simplified cardiac lumped model which can be easily personalised from clinical data in order to simulate cardiac indicators. In addition, machine-learning based regression methods were also tested for their prediction power.

2   Methods

2.1   Data Presentation

Our retrospective dataset was collected from the records of Nice University Hospital in 123 patients with known or suspected pulmonary hypertension. Echocardiography-based cardiac indicators, such as ejection fraction, end-diastolic left and right ventricular volumes, were extracted by an experienced cardiologist. Complete or incomplete catheterisation measurement records (44% received both echocardiography and catheterisation within 48 h) are available for all the patients (see detailed data description in Table 1*). Specifically, RAP in echocardiography data is estimated from inferior vena cava (IVC) diameter and its respirophasic variations, which leads to an ordinal value with possible values from {5,10,15,20}. sPAP is then calculated by $sPAP = 4 * TRV_{max}^2 + RAP$,

---

*Abbreviations: Body Surface Area (BSA), Pulmonary Artery HyperTension (PAHT), Heart Rate (HR), Brain Natriuretic Peptide (BNP), Blood Pressure (BP), Left Ventricle Ejection Fraction (LVEF), Left Ventricle Outflow Track Diameter (D_{LVOT}), Velocity Time Integral of Left Ventricle Outflow Tract (VTI_{LVOT}), Left Ventricle End-Diastolic Diameter (LVEDD), Left Ventricle End-Systolic Diameter (LVESD), Left Ventricle End-Diastolic volume (LVEDV), Right Ventricle Ejection Fraction 3D (RVEF 3D), Right Ventricle Outflow Tract Diameter (D_{RVOT}), Velocity Time Integral of Right Ventricle Outflow Tract (VTI_{RVOT}), Right Ventricle End-Systolic Diameter (RVESD), Right Ventricle End-Diastolic Volume (RVEDV), Systolic Pulmonary Artery Pressure (sPAP), Tricuspid Annular Plane Systolic Excursion (TAPSE), Right Atrium Pressure (RAP), Mean Pulmonary Artery Pressure (mPAP), Pulmonary Capillary Wedge Pressure (Pcap), Pulmonary Vascular Resistance (PVR), Cardiac Output (CO), Cardiac Index (CI)

Table 1. Detailed description of patient data

Feature	Missing	Statistics	Feature	Missing	Statistics
Clinical information					
Age	0	62 ± 18	Sex	0	50.5% female
Height (cm)	1	166.2 ± 9.5	Weight (kg)	1	68.2 ± 16.6
BSA	5	1.75 ± 0.23	BNP (ng/L)	7	275.4 ± 508.6
HR	24	76 ± 13	BP (mmHg)	72	132 ± 22 & 81 ± 16
		61.0% (1), 22.1% (3)			36.8%, (2), 46.3% (3)
PAHT group	1	13.6% (4), 2.1% (5)	NYHA	3	13.6% (4)
		1.2% (NAN)			3.3% (NAN)
Echocardiography data					
LVEF (%)	2	67.5 ± 8.9	RVEF 3D (%)	8	35.0 ± 9.8
D_{LVOT} (mm)	59	18.9 ± 4.6	D_{RVOT} (mm)	85	26.3 ± 5.2
VTI_{LVOT} (cm)	59	19.4 ± 5.7	VTI_{RVOT} (cm)	3	14.6 ± 4.5
LVEDD (mm)	18	43.7 ± 6.7	RVEDD (mm)	21	46.2 ± 6.4
LVESD (mm)	42	26.1 ± 6.3	RVEDV (mL)	8	98.1 ± 39.7
sPAP (mmHg)	1	73.5 ± 23.5	RAP (mmHg)	0	10.6 ± 4.6
TAPSE (mm)	1	19.9 ± 5.5	S'Wave (cm/s)	1	11.3 ± 3.0
Catheter data					
mPAP (mmHg)	0	43.5 ± 13.0	Pcap (mmHg)	1	11.4 ± 4.0
RAP (mmHg)	0	8.9 ± 4.3	PVR (UW)	4	7.5 ± 4.0
CO (L/min)	4	4.7 ± 1.4	CI (L/min/m^2)	6	2.7 ± 0.7

where TRV_{max} refers to tricuspid regurgitation maximum velocity. In our analysis, records of 95 patients were included. The other 28 records were discarded because of lack of catheter measurement.

2.2 Modeling-Based Prediction

Cardiovascular 0D Model. To incorporate cardiovascular dynamics into the prediction model, we consider a 0D model of the whole cardiovascular circulation system [2]. Derived from a 3D cardiac electromechanical model, the 0D model not only consists of less ordinary differential equation but also preserves the capacity to describe the important properties of the heart. Under the assumption of the spherical ventricle symmetry in 0D model, the inner radius (R_0) is directly related to the myocardial size. Reduced deformation and stress tensors demonstrate good representation of important cardiac characteristics, such as heart contractility (σ_0) and stiffness (C_1).

This 0D model has manifested its modeling potential in solving personalisation problems [10]. Consider a 0D model M, with a set of parameters P_M and model states O_M. We take a subset $\theta \subseteq P_M$, which contains parameters such as heart contractility (σ_0) and myocardial stiffness (C_1), and fix all the other parameters with default values. Interesting model states $O \subseteq O_M$, such as pulmonary artery pressure and ejection fraction, present cardiac indicators of the heart model. Given a set of clinical observations $\hat{O}$, the aim of personalisation is to find suitable varying parameters $\hat{\theta}$ so that the corresponding output of the fitted 0D model is as close as possible to clinical references, i.e. $O(\hat{\theta}) \approx \hat{O}$ (Fig. 1).

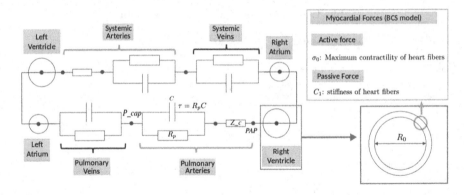

Fig. 1. Schema of used cardiac 0D model (Adapted from [1]).

We assume Gaussian distribution priors for both interested parameters θ and model states O, i.e. $\theta \sim \mathcal{N}(\mu, \Sigma)$ and $O|\theta \sim \mathcal{N}(\hat{O}(\theta), \Delta)$. Essentially, the personalisation problem equals to Maximum A Posterior. With Gaussian distribution, the objective function is derived as:

$$min\{(O(\theta) - \hat{O})^T \Delta^{-1}(O(\theta) - \hat{O}) + \gamma(\theta - \mu)^T \Sigma^{-1}(\theta - \mu)\}$$

where $\hat{O}$ refers to observed model states and Δ, a diagonal covariance matrix, represents the tolerance interval for each dimension of model states. The second term is regarded as a regulariser. γ controls to what extent we forces the parameter θ to follow the prior distribution, which helps to attenuate the non-unique solution effect of this ill-posed inverse problem.

We solve this high-dimensional and non-convex problem by applying a non-parametric evolutionary strategy CMA-ES [6]. Iteratively Updated Prior (IUP) method, as defined in [10], is deployed to iteratively update the prior distribution based on former population personalisation results.

Experiments. We first investigate the intrinsic prediction power of the 0D cardiovascular model. Based on the available clinical data, we chose the following 5 features extracted from echocardiography for personalisation: systolic pulmonary artery pressure (sPAP), right ventricle ejection fraction (RVEF), right ventricle end-diastolic volume (RVEDV), left ventricle ejection fraction (LVEF). In order to assure equal stroke volume of left and right heart, the left ventricle end-diastolic volume (LVEDV) is calculated from available data: $LVEDV = \frac{RVEDV*RVEF}{LVEF}$. Considering the uncertainty of measurement, we assign a tolerance interval for every selected feature: 200 Pa for sPAP, 5% for LVEF and RVEF and 10 mL for RVEDV and LVEDV. Available RAP values are not included in our setting. Finally, parameters of both left heart and right heart are selected for personalisation: left and right heart contractility (σ_0), left and right myocardial stiffness (c_1), right ventricle inner radius (R_0), pulmonary proximal resistance (Z_c) and pulmonary distal resistance(R_p). Left ventricle radius is set by $(LVEDD + LVESD)/4$ if both LVEDD and LVESD are available. Or else it is set to 18 mm, the mean value in the population. Since every patient possesses at least one target feature, we fit the model on the whole dataset of 95 patients. We assume the covariance Σ of varying parameters is a full matrix and γ is selected from $\{0.1, 0.5, 1, 2\}$.

We follow the same protocol as the cardiologist to extract mPAP and PVR from model output curves: mPAP is calculated as the mean value of pulmonary pressure-time integral during one cardiac cycle, and PVR is calculated as PVR (UW) = (mPAP − Pcap)/CO, where CO comes from flow-time integral and heart rate and Pcap is fixed at 10 mmHg.

A supervised method is also proposed based on personalisation. We split our dataset into training data and test data with a configuration of 5-fold cross-validation. In the training phase, echocardiography and catheter features are fitted iteratively with $\gamma = 0.5$ for 10 iterations. Then the fitted parameter distribution of the 10th iteration of training data is used as test prior. We then perform one iteration of personalisation to fit only echocardiography features for test data with $\gamma \in \{0.5, 1, 2\}$.

The optimisation of 0D model personalisation is performed over the logarithm of the parameter values (Table 2).

Table 2. Selected features and parameters for 0D model personalisation

Echo	Catheter	Varying parameters
spAP	mPAP	Left heart contractility σ_0
RVEF	CO	Left heart stiffness c_1
LVEF	Pcap	Right heart contractility σ_0
RVEDV	PVR	Right heart stiffness c_1
LVEDV		Right ventricular radius R_0
		Pulmonary proximal resistance Z_p
		Pulmonary distal resistance R_p

Model Implementation. Our cardiac 0D model is originally implemented in CellML language. It was exported into C language and incorporated into a Python program which enables flexible experiments. The 0D model is very fast and it takes less than 1 s to output cardiac curves. CMA package implemented by Hansen et al. [7] is used in our optimisation. With parallel computation, optimal parameters for one patient can be found in 3 min on a computer with 8 cores (Intel i7-8650U CPU 1.90 GHz).

2.3   Learning-Based Prediction

5 regression methods implemented in $scikit - learn\,0.21.2$ were tested using echocardiographic cardiac features to predict catheter data: lasso regression, ridge regression (RR), k-nearest neighbour regression (KNN), partial least-square regression (PLR) and ada-boosting decision tree regression

(ADAT). Optimal hyper-parameters of different estimators were determined through nested 10-fold cross-validation grid search. Specifically, we search $\alpha \in \{10^{-3}, 10^{-2}, ...10^{2}\}$ for Lasso and Ridge, number of neighbors $N \in \{2, 3, ...10\}$ for KNN , number of components $N \in \{1, 2, ...15\}$ for PLR and number of estimators $N \in \{2, 4, 8, 16, 50, 100, 200\}$ for ADAT.

We use all the data except catheter data to perform regression analysis. Category data, such as NYHA, Group PAH, and columns with more than 40% missing values (VTI_{LVOT}, D_{RVOT}, D_{LVOT}, LVESD and BP) were eliminated. From available data, we are able to calculate TRV_{max} and $\frac{TRV_{max}}{VTI_{RVOT}}$, the later of which is reported correlated with PVR [11]. A correlation analysis on the 18 predictors shows linearity between some predictors (correlation coefficient larger than 0.6) and finally we have 11 predictors left for regression analysis: age, BSA, LVEF, RVEF, HR, RAP, sPAP, LVEDD, RVEDV,VTI_{RVOT}, TAPSE. Considering the missing value problem of our dataset, simple and multiple imputation methods implemented in $scikit - learn$ 0.21.2 are also conducted before every regression learning: mean imputation, median imputation, Bayesian ridge regression iterative imputation, k-nearest neighbour iterative imputation, decision tree regression iterative imputation and extra-tree iterative imputation. We report R^2 score (coefficient of determination) and root mean squared error (RMSE) for each regression method based on a 5-fold cross validation.

We also test simple estimation (SIMPLE) methods for mPAP and PVR based on formulas $mPAP = 0.61 * PAPs + 2(mmHg)$ following the work of [3] and $PVR = 29.7 * (TRV_{max}/VTI_{RVOT}) - 0.29$ following the work of [11].

3 Results

Modelling-Based Prediction. With only echocardiography-based indicators, our result of 0D model personalisation indicate that a reasonable γ improves prediction accuracy. A large γ will nominate objective function and forces varying parameter to follow prior distribution, while a small γ enables more accurate feature fitting. In our case, with $\gamma = 0.5$, estimated mPAP correlates modestly with ground truth ($r = 0.65, p < 0.0001$) and demonstrates a reasonable error (shown in Table 3: MF0.5). With $\gamma = 1$, estimated PVR has the lowest error and correlates slightly with ground truth ($r = 0.40, p < 0.001$).

Table 3. 0D cardiac model based prediction results

State	Metrics	MF0.1	MF0.5	MF1	MF2	MF-CV0.5	MF-CV1	MF-CV2
mPAP	$RMSE$	11.08	10.61	10.83	11.44	13.01	12.76	12.92
	R^2	0.26	0.32	0.30	0.21	-0.05	-0.01	-0.05
PVR	$RMSE$	6.17	5.72	4.84	5.00	10.55	9.44	9.34
	R^2	-1.36	-1.04	-0.45	-0.55	-7.33	-6.30	-5.53

However, in modelling-based supervised method (MF-CV), when echocardiography and catheter data are mixed for personalistion, the discrepancy between ECHO and CAT data mislead parameter prior direction. After training phase, we obtain prior distribution from last iteration of group personalisation. When new test data comes, personalisation is moving to a biased direction.

Learning-Based Prediction. In Fig. 2, we observe that LASSO and PLR estimators not only demonstrate less prediction error, but also are more stable to various imputed data. Lasso coefficients show that both sPAP and TAPSE are significant factors for mPAP and PVR regression. This is consistent with the fact that mPAP and PVR are highly correlated ($r = 0.81, p < 0.01$).

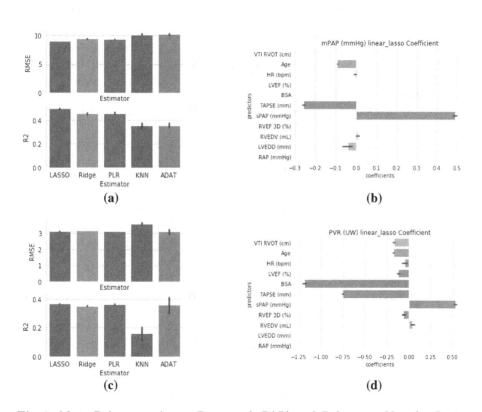

Fig. 2. Mean Pulmonary Artery Pressure (mPAP) and Pulmonary Vascular Resistance (PVR) prediction results (Data-driven methods). Results of models with different imputation methods are averaged to distinguish the performance of estimators. Results shown in mean ± std. (a) RMSE and R2 metric of different estimator for mPAP. (b) Lasso regression coefficient (alpha = 0.1) for mPAP prediction. (c) RMSE and R2 metric of different estimator for PVR. (d) Lasso regression coefficient (alpha = 0.01) for PVR prediction.

Prediction Summary. We present the averaged metric value (based on different imputation methods) and involved features for all estimators. With lasso regression result, we exclude the features with normalized coefficient smaller than 0.01 for mPAP and 0.2 for PVR, e.t. we have sPAP, TAPSE, LVEDD and age for mPAP and BSA, sPAP, TAPSE for PVR. We then redo LASSO RIDGE and PLR with those selected features. Here mPAP's best prediction is with tuned hyperparameter: $\alpha = 0.01$ for Lasso, $\alpha = 0.1$ for RR, $N = 8$ for KNN, $N = 2$ for PLR and $N = 500$ for ADAT. PVR best result is with hyperparameters: $\alpha = 0.01$ for Lasso, $\alpha = 0.5$ for RR, $N = 7$ for KNN, $N = 2$ for PLR and $N = 500$ for ADAT (Table 4).

Table 4. Best regression results of different estimators for mPAP and PVR

State	Metrics	LASSO	RR	PLR	KNN	ADAT	SIMPLE	MF-CV1	MF1
mPAP	$RMSE$	8.75	8.72	8.76	10.12	10.18	11.52	12.76	10.83
	R^2	0.52	0.53	0.52	0.35	0.36	0.20	-0.01	0.30
	Features	TAPSE sPAP Age LVEDD			All 11 Features		sPAP	sPAP LVEF LVEDV RVEF RVEDV	
PVR	$RMSE$	2.99	2.98	2.94	3.56	3.09	3.96	9.44	4.84
	R^2	0.41	0.41	0.42	0.16	0.35	0.04	-6.30	-0.45
	Features	TAPSE sPAP BSA			All 11 Features		$\frac{TRV_{max}}{VTI_{RVOT}}$	sPAP LVEF LVEDV RVEF RVEDV	

Using LASSO regression, we average the coefficient from different imputation methods and get the following estimation formula:

$$mPAP = 0.32*sPAP - 0.65*TAPSE - 0.12*Age - 0.12*LVEDD + 45.83 \quad (1)$$

$$PVR = 0.05 * sPAP - 0.33 * TAPSE - 4.94 * BSA + 18.83 \quad (2)$$

Supervised 0D model prediction (MD-CV1) fails to retain a good parameter prior for prediction however, echocardiography-based group optimisation demonstrates a prediction potential, which reveals the regularizing effect of population-based prior distribution. Here, best result is reached at $\gamma = 1$.

SIMPLE methods provide simple approximation of mPAP and PVR but their validity is restricted due to their dependence on one single measurement. Besides, regression methods surpass model-based estimation approaches. There may be two main reasons for their difference. First, we are not using all the available information for 0D model personalisation. For example, TAPSE, who is of significance in regression, are difficult to incorporate into 0D personalisation system.

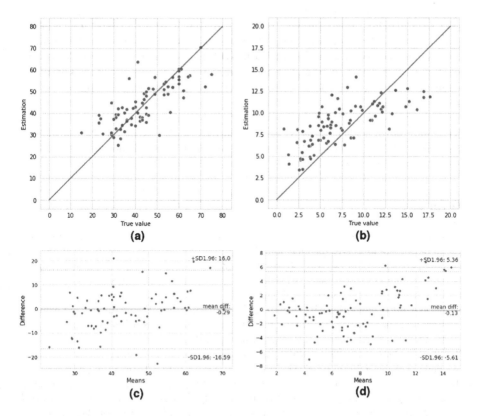

Fig. 3. Estimated value and ground truth comparison (lasso formulas). (a) The plot of mPAP ground truth and its estimated value using Eq. 1. (b) The plot of PVR ground truth and its estimated value using Eq. 2. (c) Bland-Altman analysis demonstrating the limits of agreement between invasive mPAP and mPAP determined via echocardiography, using Eq. 1. (d) Bland-Altman analysis demonstrating the limits of agreement between invasive PVR and PVR determined via echocardiography, using Eq. 2.

Secondly, our 0D model is highly reduced, some important measurements like VTI_{RVOT} and TR_{max} which exhibit important hemodynamic characteristics, is not compatible. Whereas, unlike the imperative demand of complete data for regression methods, 0D model personalisation can deal with missing data issue naturally [10] (Table 4).

4 Conclusion

Our preliminary results show a good potential of using data-driven methods and model-based approaches for estimating pulmonary pressure in pulmonary hypertension patients. Data-driven method is fast, simple and give good approximation of pulmonary pressure, but it strongly demands complete observation. Model-based approach captures complex hemodynamics from observed data and deals with missing data issue naturally. Compared with data-driven methods, it exhibits a slightly poorer prediction accuracy. Based on current exploration, there are two directions of future work. One is to extend 0D model personalisation method so as to integrate more observed data into system. The other is adopting data-driven methods to predict accurate parameter distribution for personalisation.

Acknowledgements. This work was supported by the Inria Sophia Antipolis - Mediterranée, 'NEF' computation cluster. The authors would like thank the work of relevant engineers and scholars.

References

1. Banus, J., Lorenzi, M., Camara, O., Sermesant, M.: Large scale cardiovascular model personalisation for mechanistic analysis of heart and brain interactions. In: Coudière, Y., Ozenne, V., Vigmond, E., Zemzemi, N. (eds.) Functional Imaging and Modeling of the Heart, FIMH 2019. Lecture Notes in Computer Science, vol. 11504, pp. 285–293. Springer, Cham (2019)
2. Caruel, M., Chabiniok, R., Moireau, P., Lecarpentier, Y., Chapelle, D.: Dimensional reductions of a cardiac model for effective validation and calibration. Biomech. Model. Mechanobiology **13**(4), 897–914 (2014)
3. Chemla, D., et al.: New formula for predicting mean pulmonary artery pressure using systolic pulmonary artery pressure. Chest **126**(4), 1313–1317 (2004)
4. Deaño, R.C., et al.: Referral of patients with pulmonary hypertension diagnoses to tertiary pulmonary hypertension centers. JAMA Intern. Med. **173**(10), 887 (2013)
5. Gudigar, A., et al.: Global weighted LBP based entropy features for the assessment of pulmonary hypertension. Pattern Recogn. Lett. **125**, 35–41 (2019)
6. Hansen, N.: The CMA evolution strategy: a comparing review. Towards New Evol. Comput. **102**(2006), 75–102 (2016)
7. Hansen, N., Akimoto, Y., Baudis, P.: CMA-ES/pycma on Github, February 2019
8. Howard, L.S., et al.: Echocardiographic assessment of pulmonary hypertension: standard operating procedure. Eur. Respir. Rev. **21**(125), 239–248 (2012)
9. Kheyfets, V.O., O'Dell, W., Smith, T., Reilly, J.J., Finol, E.A.: Considerations for numerical modeling of the pulmonary circulation-a review with a focus on pulmonary hypertension. J. Biomech. Eng. **135**(6), 061011 (2013)
10. Molléro, R., Pennec, X., Delingette, H., Ayache, N., Sermesant, M.: Population-based priors in cardiac model personalisation for consistent parameter estimation in heterogeneous databases. Int. J. Numer. Methods Biomed. Eng. **35**, e3158 (2018)
11. Rajagopalan, N., et al.: Noninvasive estimation of pulmonary vascular resistance in pulmonary hypertension. Echocardiography **26**(5), 489–494 (2009)
12. Rosenkranz, S., Preston, I.R.: Right heart catheterisation: best practice and pitfalls in pulmonary hypertension. Eur. Respir. Rev. **24**(138), 642–652 (2015)
13. Zuckerman, W.A.: Safety of cardiac catheterization at a center specializing in the care of patients with pulmonary arterial hypertension. Pulm. Circul. **3**(4), 831–839 (2013)

Deep Learning Surrogate of Computational Fluid Dynamics for Thrombus Formation Risk in the Left Atrial Appendage

Xabier Morales[1]([✉]), Jordi Mill[1], Kristine A. Juhl[2], Andy Olivares[1], Guillermo Jimenez-Perez[1], Rasmus R. Paulsen[2], and Oscar Camara[1]

[1] Physense, Department of Information and Communication Technologies, Universitat Pompeu Fabra, Barcelona, Spain
xtaltec@gmail.com
[2] DTU Compute, Technical University of Denmark, Kongens Lyngby, Denmark

Abstract. Recently, the risk of thrombus formation in the left atrium (LA) has been assessed through patient-specific computational fluid dynamic (CFD) simulations, characterizing the complex 4D nature of blood flow in the left atrial appendage (LAA). Nevertheless, the vast computational resources and long computing times required by traditional CFD methods prevents its embedding in the clinical workflow of time-sensitive applications. In this study, two distinct deep learning (DL) architectures have been developed to receive the patient-specific LAA geometry as an input and predict the endothelial cell activation potential (ECAP), which is linked to the risk of thrombosis. The first network is based on a simple fully-connected network, while the latter also performs a dimensionality reduction of the variables. Both models have been trained with a synthetic dataset of 210 LAA geometries being able to accurately predict the ECAP distributions with an average error of 4.72% for the fully-connected approach and 5.75% for its counterpart. Most importantly, the obtention of the ECAP predictions was quasi-instantaneous, orders of magnitude faster than conventional CFD.

Keywords: Deep learning · Computational Fluid Dynamics · Thrombus formation · Hemodynamics · Left Atrial Appendage

1 Introduction

Atrial fibrillation (AF) is the most common arrhythmia of clinical significance, often leading to wall rigidity of the left atrium (LA), which severely disrupts local hemodynamics [4]. This may lead to blood stagnation increasing the risk of thrombosis. In fact, around 90% of such intracardiac thrombus formation in AF patients takes place in the left atrial appendage (LAA) [10]. At the moment,

M. Pop et al. (Eds.): STACOM 2019, LNCS 12009, pp. 157–166, 2020.
https://doi.org/10.1007/978-3-030-39074-7_17

blood flow velocity can only be assessed through noisy imaging data from trans-esophageal echocardiography (TEE) at one single point in space and time, vastly oversimplifying the characterization of the 4D nature of cardiac hemodynamics.

Recently, computational fluid dynamics (CFD) have been applied to image-based LA geometries seeking to assess the risk of thrombogenesis more quantitatively [6]. CFD has proven to be an invaluable tool in establishing a mechanistic relation between patient-specific organ morphology and its characteristic hemodynamics. Nevertheless, traditional CFD methods are renowned for their large memory requirements and long computing times [5], which severely hinders its suitability for time-sensitive clinical applications. Moreover, the studies available on the LAA are few and with very limited number of real or synthetic cases.

Hence, this study seeks to harness the immense potential of deep learning (DL) with the objective of generating a fast and accurate surrogate of CFD analysis on the LAA. For this purpose, two distinct deep neural networks (DNN) have been developed, which receive the specific LAA geometry as an input, and accurately predict its corresponding endothelial cell activation potential (ECAP) map, parameter linked to the risk of thrombosis. To the best of our knowledge, this study represents the first successful implementation of a DL surrogate of finite element analysis in a biological structure as complex and heterogeneous as the LAA, which had only been previously attempted in the aorta [5].

2   Methods

The general pipeline of the study is shown in Fig. 1. Initially, the virtual LAA geometries are created, assembled to the oval LA and aligned (steps 1–3 in the figure, respectively). Afterwards, the 3D volumetric mesh is generated (4) to carry out the CFD simulations (5) before calculating the ECAP maps (6). Once the training data has been generated, the DNNs are trained (in red). As the final step, the performance of the networks is evaluated through Monte Carlo cross-validation (in green).

2.1   Geometry

Due to the high anatomical complexity and variability of both the LA and the LAA, several assumptions had to be made to keep the model simple. Based on the work by García-Isla et al. [3], the LA cavity was approximated to an ovoid structure, aiming to disregard the effect of LA heterogeneity on atrial hemodynamics and focus on the LAA.

The spatial (x, y, z) coordinates of the nodes conforming the LAA surface mesh were chosen as the input to the DNNs. Therefore, correspondence between LAA geometries was set as a requirement, that is, each geometry had to share the same number of nodes and maintain inter-nodal connectivity. In addition, training of DNNs requires huge datasets, which can rarely be achieved with real patient geometries. To fulfill such demands, a virtual dataset of 300 LAAs was generated from a statistical shape model (SSM) based on principal component

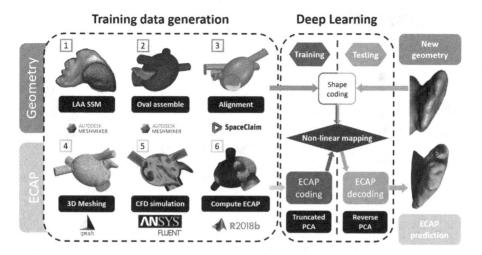

Fig. 1. General pipeline of the project. LAA: Left Atrial Appendage, SSM: Statistical Shape Model, CFD: Computational Fluid Dynamics, ECAP: Endothelial Cell Activation Potential. (Color figure online)

analysis (PCA) [8], by varying the 10 most meaningful eigenvalues according to a normal distribution $N(0,1)$. Each virtual LAA consists on a triangular mesh of 2536 nodes and 5000 elements.

The assembly to the ovoid structure was done on Meshmixer[1]. Afterwards, the mitral valve of the geometries were longitudinally aligned on the z-axis on Space Claim[2]. Finally, the tetrahedral volumetric mesh was generated on gmsh[3], composed of approximately 350,000 elements each. It should be noted that while correspondence was imposed on the LAA surface mesh, being the input to the DNN, the same does not apply to the volumetric and LA surface meshes.

2.2 Generation of Risk Indices for Thrombus Formation - ECAP

The ECAP, defined by Di Achille et al. [1], was the parameter chosen to evaluate the risk of thrombus formation. High values are linked with high endothelial susceptibility and thrombogenesis risk. The ECAP is defined as the oscillatory shear index (OSI) divided by the time averaged wall shear stress (TAWSS).

The in silico ECAP distributions for the training of the DNNs were obtained through CFD simulations performed on Ansys Fluent 19.2[4]. They were completed automatically by leveraging the MATLAB AAS toolbox (R2018b Academic license)[5]. Each simulation encompasses a whole cardiac cycle with a systole and diastole lasting 0.4 s and 0.65 s respectively. An input blood flow was

---

[1] http://www.meshmixer.com/.
[2] https://www.ansys.com/academic/free-student-products.
[3] http://gmsh.info/.
[4] https://www.ansys.com/products/fluids/ansys-fluent.
[5] https://es.mathworks.com/products/matlab.html.

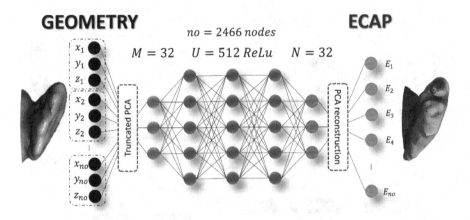

Fig. 2. Architecture of the dimensionality reduction network. no = Number of mesh nodes, U = Number of activation units, LAA: Left Atrial Appendage, ECAP: Endothelial Cell Activation Potential, $M - N$: Number of retained principal components. Figure adapted from Liang et al. [5].

imposed on the PVs obtained from clinical observations made by Fernandez-Perez et al. [2]. In addition, the mitral valve was considered as a wall boundary during diastole, while an outlet pressure of 1067 Pa was set through the systole. The rest of the setup of the CFD simulations was implemented similarly to García-Isla et al. [3] Moreover, to simulate the LA motion and preventing mass-imbalance during the cardiac cycle, a diffusion-based smoothing dynamic mesh was applied in the longitudinal direction (z-axis) of the mitral valve annulus [7] with data from real-time 3D echocardiography measurements by Veronesi et al. [9]. After a qualitative visual quality control of fluid simulation results, seeking to discard unrealistic flow patterns or exceedingly high or low ECAP values (by several orders of magnitude), the final training dataset was comprised by 210 LAA geometries and its corresponding ECAP maps.

2.3 Deep Learning Model

Keras 2.2.4[6], with TensorFlow 1.13.1[7] backend, was chosen as the high-level neural network API. Two distinct DNN architectures were developed.

First and simplest, a fully-connected feed-forward (SFC) network was implemented to perform a non-linear regression between the space coordinate triplets and their corresponding ECAP values. The final layout was comprised of two equally sized hidden layers, counting a total of 5000 nodes each.

Alternatively, another network was developed which performed dimensionality reduction of the variables as a first step. The spatial coordinates and the ECAP maps were reduced to a small set of scalar values through truncated PCA,

---

[6] https://keras.io/.
[7] https://www.tensorflow.org/.

aiming to simplify the non-linear mapping between the input and the output. Each node can be expressed as follows:

$$X = \overline{X} + \sum_{i=1}^{M} \alpha_i \sqrt{\lambda_i} W_i, \tag{1}$$

where $\overline{X}$ is the mean shape and W_i and λ_i is the set of eigenvectors and eigenvalues of the covariance matrix for the retained number, i, of principal components (PC). If the variability of the dataset is explained by a small set of PCs, the data can be accurately represented by a small set of scalar values as:

$$\beta_m = \frac{W_m^T(X - \overline{X})}{\sqrt{\lambda_m}}, \qquad \epsilon_n = \frac{W_n^T(Y - \overline{Y})}{\sqrt{\lambda_n}}, \tag{2}$$

β_m and ϵ_n being the low-dimensional representation of the geometry and the ECAP respectively. A total of $m = n = 32$ PCs were kept retaining 97.6% of variability for the shape and 90.3% for the ECAP. Afterwards, non-linear mapping between the low dimensional scalars was completed through a fully-connected feed-forward neural network composed of 3 hidden layers of 512 units, as shown on Fig. 2. Once successfully trained, predicted ECAP values were reconstructed from its low-dimensional representations reversing Eq. 2:

$$Y = \overline{Y} + \sum_{n=1}^{N} \left(\epsilon_n \cdot \sqrt{\lambda_n} \right) W_n \tag{3}$$

Adam was chosen as a compiler and the mean square error (MSE) was selected as the loss function. A batch size of 20 was employed on both networks. Likewise, ReLU units were chosen over other non-linear units, such as Leaky ReLU or Softplus, due to superior performance. The predictive capabilities of both DL models were evaluated through a 10-fold Monte Carlo cross-validation with 100 repetitions, randomly selecting 90% of the dataset for each training round. The mean absolute error (MAE) on ECAP values and its normalized counterpart (NMAE) were chosen as metrics, following Liang et al. [5].

$$MAE = \frac{1}{n} \sum_{j=1}^{n} \mid y_j - \overline{y}_j \mid \qquad NMAE = \frac{MAE}{max(\mid y_j \mid)} \cdot 100 \tag{4}$$

3   Results

The training of the PCA network was quick, requiring just 30 s to complete each cross-validation round, while it took almost 25 min for the SFC model. However, considering that each CFD simulation required up to 2 h to complete

162   X. Morales et al.

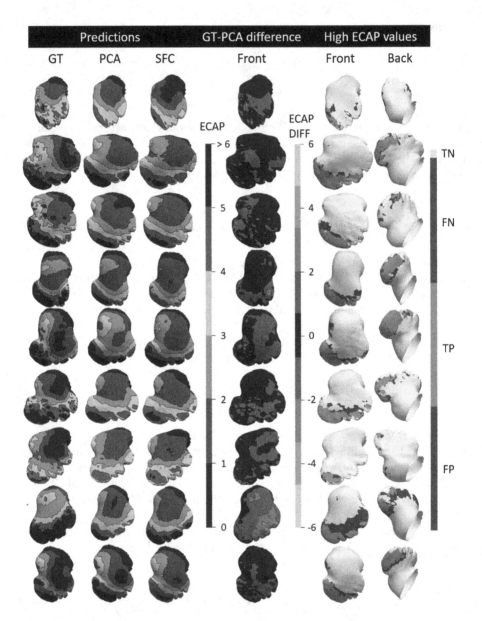

Fig. 3. Set of ECAP values on a random test dataset of 21 shapes from a single iteration of the Monte Carlo cross-validation, 9 of which are shown in here. Each row corresponds to a given geometry while the columns from left to right represent: (1) Ground truth (GT) obtained from CFD simulations, (2) Prediction of the dimensionality reduction PCA network, (3) Predicted ECAP from the simple fully-connected (SFC) network, (4) Difference between GT and PCA prediction, (5–6) Binary classification with positive condition ECAP > 4. (5) Front face and (6) Posterior face. TN: True negative, FN: False negative, TP: True positive, FP: False positive.

the improvement is substantial. Especially, if we consider that once trained, the ECAP predictions were obtained almost instantaneously.

The accuracy achieved by each of the networks is shown on Table 1. Both our DL models achieve very similar accuracy, attaining an average MAE ~0.64 and a NMAE ~5%. Furthermore, the predicted ECAP maps alongside with its ground truth, can be visualized for 9 representative LAA shapes in Fig. 3. These specific set of LAA shapes, belong to one single iteration of the Monte Carlo cross-validation.

Table 1. Performance of DL models on a 10-fold Monte Carlo cross-validation. MAE: Mean Absolute Error, NMAE: Normalized Mean Absolute Error.

Network	MAE	NMAE
PCA	0.6457 ± 0.0493	4.7197 ± 1.4625%
SFC	0.6486 ± 0.0462	5.7558 ± 1.523%

Additionally, the predictive capability of the DL networks to detect the areas with the highest thrombi formation risk was assessed. Following the study by Di Achille et al. [1] on thrombotic abdominal aortic aneurysms, a value of 4, corresponding to the upper 99th percentile, was chosen as the lower bound of thrombosis risk, being more robust than only considering isolated peak values. Consequently, a binary classification was performed with the positive condition being ECAP > 4. The results are shown on column (5) and (6) of Fig. 3. In addition, pursuing a more quantitative assessment, a couple of confusion matrices were constructed for each network which are reported on Table 2.

Table 2. Confusion matrices for both PCA and SFC predicted ECAP values

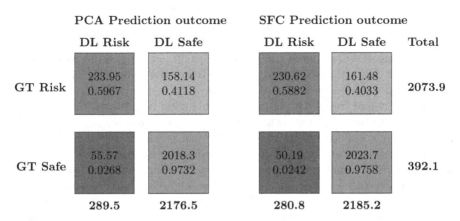

4 Discussion

Upon close inspection of Fig. 3, the developed DNNs seem to successfully grasp the non-linear function relating the LAA geometry and its ECAP maps. Nevertheless, interpreting the results is highly challenging due to the "black box" nature of DNN methods. Interestingly, there are no striking visual or quantitative differences between the accuracy achieved by each of the DL models. This was unexpected, since the non-linear mapping relating the LAA shape and the ECAP is far more simple in the dimensionality reduction PCA network.

Afterwards, the accuracy attained by both developed networks was benchmarked against that achieved by Liang et al. [5], which attained an NMAE of 0.492%. While it may look like a huge drop in accuracy, there are a number of reasons that explain such a disparity with the obtained results. Firstly, compared to the LAA, the aorta is a very simple geometry with mainly laminar flow, making DNN-based surrogate estimation easier. Secondly, this very complexity of LAA morphology, severely restricted the possibility of applying structured grids. This entails that potentially more successful DL methods such as convolutional neural networks could not be employed.

Regarding the detection of high ECAP values, both networks exhibit an almost identical number of correctly classified nodes. On the other hand, it seems that the developed DL networks are not capable of properly adjusting to the most extreme ECAP values, as false negative (FN) nodes are 3-fold more numerous than false positives (FP). This is probably due to the lower frequency of occurrence of ECAP values far from the mean in the training dataset. Nonetheless, although the true positive rate is rather low at $\sim$0.6, it must be stated that almost all significantly large FP and FN areas on Fig. 3 are found surrounding the edges of true positive patches. This means that the developed DL architectures managed to grasp the overall layout of the areas in high risk of thrombus formation with few misclassifications outside of these regions.

Finally, it is worth mentioning the limitations and assumptions faced by this study due to the complexity of the task in hand. First and foremost, the network has been trained exclusively with synthetic populations of both, the LA and the LAA. Therefore, the developed DL models would most certainly be unable to successfully predict the ECAP maps on patient-specific geometries at the moment. Nevertheless, this could be overcome if a sufficiently big dataset of real LA and LAA geometries is obtained, so that it does fully capture the real heterogeneity and complexity of their morphologies. Afterwards, the geometries would have to be registered to a template to share the same number of nodes and preserve connectivity similarly to Slipsager et al. [8]. On the other hand, solely geometric parameters (3D spatial coordinates) have been fed to the neural networks during training, including no flow-specific parameters since all the CFD simulations have been carried out with the same boundary conditions. This implies that the networks would fail on patients with different systolic pressure or inlet velocity profile. Finally, the CFD and DL based ECAP values could not be properly validated as it is currently impossible to measure the ECAP on the LAA until technologies such as 4D-Flow MRI are further developed.

5   Conclusion

To the best of our knowledge, this study represents the first successful implementation of a DL surrogate of CFD in a biological structure as complex and heterogeneous as the LAA, which had only been previously attempted in the aorta [5]. The developed DNNs managed to capture the non-linear function relating the geometry of the LAA and its ECAP distributions, which resulted in accurate predictions consistent with the ground truth. Moreover, the overall layout of the LAA regions with higher risk of thrombosis were also successfully detected by the networks. Most importantly, the task was completed order of magnitudes faster than any conventional CFD approach.

Funding. This work was supported by the Spanish Ministry of Economy and Competitiveness under the Maria de Maeztu Units of Excellence Programme (MDM-2015-0502), the Retos I+D project (DPI2015-71640-R) and the Retos investigación project (RTI2018-101193-B-I00).

Data Availability. The files containing the code to reproduce this study can be downloaded from github.com/Xtaltec/DL-surrogate-CFD-LAA.

Conflicts of Interest Statement. The authors declare that the research was conducted in the absence of any commercial or financial relationships that could be construed as a potential conflict of interest.

References

1. Di Achille, P., Tellides, G., Figueroa, C.A., Humphrey, J.D.: A haemodynamic predictor of intraluminal thrombus formation in abdominal aortic aneurysms. Proc. R. Soc. A: Math. Phys. Eng. Sci. **470**(2172), 20140163–20140163 (2014)
2. Fernández-Pérez, G., Duarte, R., de la Calle, M.C., Calatayud, J., Sánchez González, J.: Analysis of left ventricular diastolic function using magnetic resonance imaging. Radiología (Engl. Ed.) **54**(4), 295–305 (2012)
3. García-Isla, G., et al.: Sensitivity analysis of geometrical parameters to study haemodynamics and thrombus formation in the left atrial appendage. Int. J. Numer. Methods Biomed. Eng. **34**(8), e3100 (2018)
4. Hirose, T., et al.: Left atrial function assessed by speckle tracking echocardiography as a predictor of new-onset non-valvular atrial fibrillation: results from a prospective study in 580 adults. Eur. Heart J. - Cardiovasc. Imaging **13**(3), 243–250 (2011)
5. Liang, L., Liu, M., Martin, C., Sun, W.: A deep learning approach to estimate stress distribution: a fast and accurate surrogate of finite-element analysis. J. R. Soc. Interface **15**(138), 20170844 (2018)
6. Masci, A., et al.: The impact of left atrium appendage morphology on stroke risk assessment in atrial fibrillation: a computational fluid dynamics study. Front. Physiol. **9**, 1938 (2019)
7. Mill, J., et al.: Optimal boundary conditions in fluid simulations for predicting occlude related thrombus formation in the left atria. In: Computational and Mathematical Biomedical Engineering, Sixth International Conference (2019)

8. Slipsager, J.M., et al.: Statistical shape clustering of left atrial appendages. In: Pop, M., et al. (eds.) STACOM 2018. LNCS, vol. 11395, pp. 32–39. Springer, Cham (2019). https://doi.org/10.1007/978-3-030-12029-0_4
9. Veronesi, F., et al.: Quantification of mitral apparatus dynamics in functional and ischemic mitral regurgitation using real-time 3-dimensional echocardiography. J. Am. Soc. Echocardiogr. **21**(4), 347–354 (2008)
10. Wunderlich, N.C., Beigel, R., Swaans, M.J., Ho, S.Y., Siegel, R.J.: Percutaneous interventions for left atrial appendage exclusion: options, assessment, and imaging using 2D and 3D echocardiography. JACC: Cardiovasc. Imaging **8**(4), 472–488 (2015)

End-to-end Cardiac Ultrasound Simulation for a Better Understanding of Image Quality

Alexandre Legay[1], Thomas Tiennot[2], Jean-François Gelly[1],
Maxime Sermesant[2(✉)], and Jean Bulté[1(✉)]

[1] GE Parallel Design SAS, Sophia-Antipolis, France
jean.bulte@ge.com
[2] Inria, Université Côte d'Azur, Sophia-Antipolis, France
maxime.sermesant@inria.fr

Abstract. Ultrasound imaging is a very versatile and fast medical imaging modality, however it can suffer from serious image quality degradation. The origin of such loss of image quality is often difficult to identify in detail, therefore it makes it difficult to design probes and tools that are less impacted. The objective of this manuscript is to present an end-to-end simulation pipeline that makes it possible to generate synthetic ultrasound images while controlling every step of the pipeline, from the simulated cardiac function, to the torso anatomy, probe parameters, and reconstruction process. Such a pipeline enables to vary every parameter in order to quantitatively evaluate its impact on the final image quality. We present here first results on classical ultrasound phantoms and a digital heart. The utility of this pipeline is exemplified with the impact of ribs on the resulting cardiac ultrasound image.

Keywords: Ultrasound · Cardiac modelling · Probe design · Image quality

1 Introduction

Simulation of medical images has been an active research area for several years. Synthetic images are often associated with ground-truth information on the underlying anatomy and function used to generate the images [2].

Therefore, it enables to evaluate image processing algorithms [4] as well as generating data for machine learning. Approaches vary from simulating the whole physics of medical image acquisition to warping an existing image, including all the intermediate combinations.

In this work, we developed an original approach integrating a full simulation pipeline in order to leverage image simulation for image quality understanding

---

A. Legay and T. Tiennot—Co-first authors, they contributed equally to this work.

© Springer Nature Switzerland AG 2020
M. Pop et al. (Eds.): STACOM 2019, LNCS 12009, pp. 167–175, 2020.
https://doi.org/10.1007/978-3-030-39074-7_18

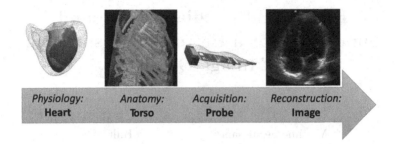

Fig. 1. End-to-end modelling pipeline for echocardiography simulation.

(see Fig. 1). It includes detailed modelling of both human anatomy and ultrasound probe. This is the first time that such simulations are directly linked to probe parameters in order to understand better the relationship between these parameters and image quality. Moreover, some modifications of our anatomy numerical model such as addition, removal and resizing of organs, tissues and bones can be easily done and their impacts studied.

2   Cardiac Model

Modelling cardiac electromechanical activity has been an active research area for the last decades, as can be seen in references from recent reviews like [3]. Simulating 3D cardiac function enables to completely control the multi-physics phenomena including electrophysiology, biomechanics and blood flows. In the context of simulating ultrasound images, cardiac modelling enables to generate ground-truth data on position, motion, strain, velocities, etc. for the subsequently generated images.

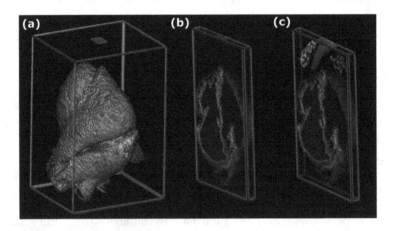

Fig. 2. (a) 3D cardiac model and probe location. Corresponding 2D imaging slice without (b) and with the rib cage (c).

In this work, we used a detailed segmentation of the heart available from the Visible Human Project [1]. We only simulated a static ultrasound image as a proof-of-concept of the whole pipeline. See Fig. 2 for the anatomy of the heart and the imaging slice used in this manuscript.

3   Torso Model

Once cardiac activity has been simulated, it is necessary to include it within a digital representation of the human torso, as the heterogeneities within the thorax are responsible for an important part of artifacts and echogenicity problems. We used a detailed segmentation of the human torso from the Visible Human project. It enables to introduce various structures of the human body and to see their influence on the simulated images (Fig. 3).

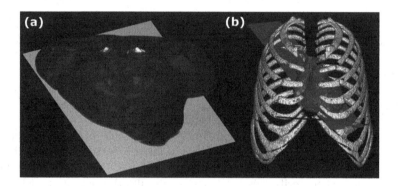

Fig. 3. 3D torso model (a) and imaging plan (b).

4   Probe Model

Numerical simulations were performed using k-Wave, a k-space pseudospectral method-based solver [8]. The k-Wave toolbox solves coupled first-order acoustic equations. An ultrasonic source, a medium (heterogeneous or not) and a sensor should be defined within these equations. In our case, the ultrasonic source and the sensor are modeled by the 3Sc-RS sector probe designed for cardiac applications (General Electric Healthcare, Illinois, USA.) The k-Wave solution enables the definition of every physical property of the probe: the number of piezoelectric elements and their width, height and spatial positioning. It also allows the complete tuning of the emission and reception beam-forming with the definition of the focal distance in azimuth, the focal distance in elevation as well as transmitted and received apodizations.

We could have chosen Field II [5,6] but k-Wave was selected for two main reasons. Firstly, it defines the medium of propagation as a grid where the physical parameters influencing the propagation of the ultrasonic wave (speed of sound, density, absorption, acoustic non-linearity parameter B/A) can be defined inhomogeneously. In contrast, Field II defines it as a collection of scatterers defined by their positions and amplitudes. The final objective of this project was to study the anatomical causes of the image degradation so we decided to keep a simulation tool that allowed us to model these physical parameters precisely. Secondly, k-Wave offers a free parallel version on GPU whereas the parallel version of Field II is not open-source. Considering that we can use a GPU cluster for the project, k-Wave was chosen.

The input signal used to drive the piezoelectric elements was made of n sinusoidal periods ($0.5 < n < 3$) at a central frequency $f_0 = 1.7$ MHz. Results are presented with harmonic imaging (reception at $2f_0 = 3.4$ MHz).

5   Reconstruction

B-mode imaging consists in a gray-scaled representation of the echogenicity of the tissue. A mechanical wave is sent in the body and is back-scattered because of the speed of sound and density heterogeneities. k-Wave models the medium of propagation as a speed of sound and a density distribution mapped on a Cartesian grid. Other parameters like absorption or the non-linearity coefficient B/A can also be defined on this grid. This medium of propagation can be defined in 2D or 3D. The choice made should be studied case by case.

To do 2D modeling is equivalent to ignore the influence of the planes parallel to the imaging plane. Clearly, this hypothesis is directly satisfied if the medium of propagation is invariant along the elevation direction of the probe. The 3D case can be considered to verify this hypothesis or in all other situations where the parallel planes are important. 3D simulations can be made using an optimized version of k-Wave running on Graphics Processing Unit (GPU) which drastically reduces the computation time (up to 10 times faster than the original code on Matlab). This version is currently unavailable in 2D and 2D simulations can only be run in Matlab (The MathWorks Inc., Massachusetts, USA.) Nonetheless, the memory available on current GPU limits the size of the Cartesian grid that has to be modeled. This essential drawback will be discussed in Sect. 7.

6   Results

6.1   Theoretical Validation of the Point Spread Function (PSF)

The Point Spread Function (PSF) of any imaging system is its response to a point source. For B-mode imaging, such a source consists in an infinitesimally small region where the speed of sound and the density distributions slightly differ from the rest of the medium. Recovering the physical PSF of the 3Sc sector probe within our pipeline is a key step towards its validation.

We here present this validation for the 2D case (see the Discussion section for its extension in 3D). Nonetheless, the spatial steps and the number of points used for the simulation grid have a direct impact on the quality of the PSF recovering. In fact, the maximum frequency that can propagate and be solved in the numerical simulations is inversely proportional to the smallest spatial step used. Here we chose a 2008×2008 2D grid with respectively $90\,\mu m$ and $75\,\mu m$ spatial steps. The corresponding dimensions of the modeled medium are $180\,mm$ (depth) and $150\,mm$ (width). Thus the maximum frequency respecting the Nyquist theorem of two points-per-wavelength is $f_{max} = 8.6\,MHz$.

The emitted signal is made of 2.56 sinusoidal cycles at $f_0 = 1.7\,MHz$. No apodization or filtering is applied to this signal. The imaging sequence is composed of 120 angles between $-30°$ and $30°$. The modeled medium consists in an homogeneous speed of sound of $c_0 = 1540\,m.s^{-1}$ and an homogeneous density of $d_0 = 1035\,kg.m^{-3}$, apart from the point source where $c_1 = 1600\,m.s^{-1}$ and $d_1 = 1040\,kg.m^{-3}$. This point source is made of one single point of the simulation grid aligned with the middle of the simulated probe and placed at $100\,mm$.

An intensity profile is extracted from the $100\,mm$-radius circle centered in the middle of the 1D-transducer. A log compression is applied and relative intensities are displayed with respect to the orientation of the point with the probe (Fig. 4). Both profiles are normalized to the maximum intensity obtained in the simulation. The simulated profile is in excellent agreement with the theoretical expectation. The agreement (in particular for the five main lobes) is nonetheless sufficient to validate the PSF recovery within our simulations. This result also confirms the relevance of the spatial steps chosen in our study.

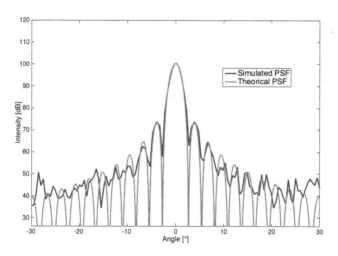

Fig. 4. Simulated (blue line) and theoretical (red line) PSF. (Color figure online)

6.2   Experimental Validation on an Acoustic Phantom

The theoretical validation of the PSF has been completed by an experimental validation of the simulations. B-mode images of an acoustic phantom 403GS LE

(Gammex Inc., Middleton, Wisconsin, USA.) have been acquired with the 3Sc
probe connected to a commercial console Vivid S70 (General Electric Healthcare,
Illinois, USA.) Contrary to more complex modeling (like in Sect. 6.3), simulating
the phantom in 2D is still relevant since it is invariant in one direction (height
direction). Elevation imaging plane is thus not impacted by structural heterogeneities. The grid parameters used for the theoretical validation are conserved
($90\,\mu m$ and $75\,\mu m$ spatial steps, 2008×2008 points, $180 \times 150\,mm$ dimensions).
Here we chose to use an emission frequency at $2.3\,MHz$ and to focus on harmonic
imaging (reception at $4.6\,MHz$). The spatial steps upper defined guarantee 3
points-per-wavelength at $4.6\,MHz$.

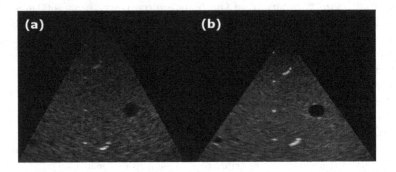

Fig. 5. (a) Simulated B-mode image of the Gammex phantom. (b) Corresponding
experimental B-mode image of the Gammex phantom acquired with the 3Sc probe on
the Vivid S70 console.

Figure 5 provides both the experimental and simulated B-mode images. The
agreement between the two images is fairly good. Both pin targets and anechoic
cysts' acoustic behaviours are caught up within our simulation (respectively
higher and lower reflection than the background). Speckle pattern of the phantom
background is also well recovered.

6.3   Numerical Simulation of a Cardiac Image in Apical View

An echographic image of the numeric heart phantom described in Sect. 2 has
been simulated. In that case, the elevation dimension has to be modeled leading
to the realization of simulations in 3D. The imaging slice used here is shown in
Fig. 2(b). The grid dimensions are $1024 \times 512 \times 64$ (depth $\times$ width $\times$ height) with
respectively $189\,\mu m$, $219\,\mu m$ and $200\,\mu m$ spatial steps. These grid dimensions
correspond to the largest grid that can fit the memory of GPU currently available
and used in this study. The corresponding dimensions of the modeled medium
are $193\,mm$ (depth), $112\,mm$ (width) and $15\,mm$ (height). Thus, the maximum frequency respecting the Nyquist theorem of two points-per-wavelength
is $f_{max} = 4.1\,MHz$ in depth, $f_{max} = 3.4\,MHz$ in width and $f_{max} = 2.3\,MHz$ in

height. In that case we study fundamental imaging at $f_0 = 2.8$ MHz. The simulated image is provided in Fig. 6(a). Myocardium as well as both ventricles and atria are well recovered. Speckle pattern is coherent near the probe but spatial resolution is slightly too high further away from it (see Discussion). Such an image can be obtained in about 30 min.

Finally we provide preliminary results showing how our pipeline can be used to study the impact of anatomical structures on image quality. We have added a modelling of the rib cage on our previous imaging slice (see Fig. 2(c)). The corresponding simulated image is provided in Fig. 6(b). One can see that the rib cage causes a shadowing of the right ventricle that makes disappear its walls. Ribs also cause a blurring of left atrium and left ventricle. This leads to an apparent thickening of the mitral valve as well as a distortion of the atria's shape. These results are coherent with physicians experience during clinical exams.

Nonetheless both images of Fig. 6 display a numerical artefact because of the limited number of points along the height direction. As mentioned above the maximum frequency that satisfies the Nyquist theorem in that direction is $f_{max} = 2.3$ MHz which is lower than our fundamental frequency at emission ($f_0 = 2.8$ MHz). Thus a bright point can be seen around the coordinate (100,60) on both images. This is due to aliasing and the non-propagation of frequencies above $f_{max} = 2.3$ MHz.

7 Discussion

The accuracy of our simulations has been demonstrated both theoretically and experimentally in the 2D case where smaller spatial steps can be used with reasonable computational costs. The extension to 3D simulations is still limited by the memory size currently available on GPU. Video cards used in this study (GeForce GTX 1080 Ti, NVIDIA Corporation, California, USA) have a memory of 11 GB which can contain a grid made of 2^{25} points. Cardiac simulations presented in this study are designed to meet the best trade-off between this memory constraint, the spatial steps needed to propagate relevant frequencies and the actual size of the medium to simulate. To do so, we had to increase the step size in the height direction leading to aliasing and poor spatial resolution far from the probe.

Nonetheless we believe these limitations will soon disappear. First, the memory available on GPU is rapidly increasing. Second, a discussion with the creators of k-Wave lets us think that a new version of the optimized code, distributed over several GPUs, will soon be available. This will lead to smaller computation times and will also allow running simulations on a far larger grid than today, therefore improving precision and complexity.

For now, absorption and non-linearity are not taken into account. These two features can directly be set in k-Wave when defining the medium of propagation. Their addition will increase the accuracy of our pipeline.

Moreover, the propagation of shear-waves in bony structures like ribs would also have to be studied. The k-Wave toolbox provides a wave-equation solver

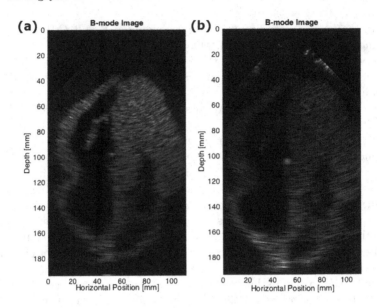

Fig. 6. Simulated B-mode image of the heart model without (a) and with (b) ribs within the imaging field.

based on a visco-elastic definition of the medium of propagation [7]. This solver has not been used in this study but its implementation should be straightforward.

Finally, the cardiac modeling could benefit from many add-ons related to many anatomic or functional diseases that have to be studied. Important computational improvements can even lead to a 4D (3 spatial dimensions and time) modeling of the heart. In such a case, complex dysfunctions like arrhythmia and their translation into an echographic image could be developed.

8   Conclusion

An end-to-end simulation pipeline including realistic cardiac, torso and ultrasonic probe modelling has been presented. The control over every simulation steps offers a great freedom for investigating the echographic image quality. The simulations' accuracy has been confirmed by recovering a theoretical PSF and the comparison of 2D simulations with experimental B-mode images of an acoustic phantom. Finally, simulated B-mode images of the heart model with and without the rib cage have been created to investigate its impact on the image quality. The inclusion of more advanced anatomical and physiological features together with current computational improvements, making this simulation pipeline a useful tool to investigate the key aspects of image quality.

References

1. Ackerman, M.J.: The visible human project. In: 1998 IEEE International Ultrasonics Symposium, vol. 86, pp. 504–511 (1998)
2. Alessandrini, M., et al.: A pipeline for the generation of realistic 3D synthetic echocardiographic sequences: methodology and open-access database. IEEE Trans. Med. Imaging **34**(7), 1436–1451 (2015)
3. Chabiniok, R., et al.: Multiphysics and multiscale modelling, data-model fusion and integration of organ physiology in the clinic: ventricular cardiac mechanics. Interface Focus **6**(2), 20150083 (2016)
4. De Craene, M., et al.: 3D strain assessment in ultrasound (straus): a synthetic comparison of five tracking methodologies. IEEE Trans. Med. Imaging **32**(9), 1632–1646 (2013)
5. Jensen, J.: Field: a program for simulating ultrasound systems. Med. Biol. Eng. Comput. **4**, 351–353 (1996)
6. Jensen, J., Svendsen, N.B.: Calculation of pressure fields from arbitrarily shaped, apodized, and excited ultrasound transducers. IEEE Trans. Ultrason. Ferroelectr. Freq. Control **39**, 262–267 (1992)
7. Treeby, B.E., Jaros, J., Rohrbach, D., Cox, B.T.: Modelling elastic wave propagation using the k-Wave Matlab toolbox. In: 2014 IEEE International Ultrasonics Symposium, pp. 146–149 (2014)
8. Treeby, B.E., Jaros, J., Rendell, A.P., Cox, B.T.: Modeling nonlinear ultrasound propagation in heterogeneous media with power law absorption using a k-space pseudospectral method. J. Acoust. Soc. Am. **131**(6), 4324–4336 (2012)

Probabilistic Motion Modeling from Medical Image Sequences: Application to Cardiac Cine-MRI

Julian Krebs[1,2]([✉]), Tommaso Mansi[1], Nicholas Ayache[2], and Hervé Delingette[2]

[1] Siemens Healthineers, Digital Services, Digital Technology and Innovation,
Princeton, NJ 08540, USA
julian.krebs@inria.fr
[2] Université Côte d'Azur, Inria, Epione Team, 06902 Sophia Antipolis, France

Abstract. We propose to learn a probabilistic motion model from a sequence of images. Besides spatio-temporal registration, our method offers to predict motion from a limited number of frames, useful for temporal super-resolution. The model is based on a probabilistic latent space and a novel temporal dropout training scheme. This enables simulation and interpolation of realistic motion patterns given only one or any subset of frames of a sequence. The encoded motion also allows to be transported from one subject to another without the need of inter-subject registration. An unsupervised generative deformation model is applied within a temporal convolutional network which leads to a diffeomorphic motion model – encoded as a low-dimensional motion matrix. Applied to cardiac cine-MRI sequences, we show improved registration accuracy and spatio-temporally smoother deformations compared to three state-of-the-art registration algorithms. Besides, we demonstrate the model's applicability to motion transport by simulating a pathology in a healthy case. Furthermore, we show an improved motion reconstruction from incomplete sequences compared to linear and cubic interpolation.

1 Introduction

In medical imaging, an important task is to analyze temporal image sequences to understand physiological processes of the human body. Dynamic organs, such as the heart or lungs, are of particular interest to study as detected motion patterns are helpful for the diagnosis and treatment of diseases. Moreover, recovering the motion pattern allows to track anatomical structures, to compensate for motion, to do temporal super-resolution and motion simulation.

Motion is typically studied by computing pairwise deformations – the registration of each of the images in a sequence with a target image. The resulting dense deformation fields track moving structures from the beginning to the end of the sequence. Providing an invertible and smooth transformation, diffeomorphic registration algorithms such as the SyN algorithm [2], the LCC-demons [11] or recent learning-based algorithms [6,10] are especially suited for the registration

© Springer Nature Switzerland AG 2020
M. Pop et al. (Eds.): STACOM 2019, LNCS 12009, pp. 176–185, 2020.
https://doi.org/10.1007/978-3-030-39074-7_19

of sequential images. One difficulty is to acquire temporally smooth deformations that are fundamental for tracking. That is why registration algorithms with a temporal regularizer have been proposed [7,12,13,15]. In the computer vision community, temporal video super-resolution and motion compensation are of related interest [5].

However, while these methods produce accurate dense deformations, they do not aim to extract intrinsic motion parameters crucial for building a comprehensive motion model useful for analysis tasks such as motion classification or simulation. Rohé et al. [14] proposed a parameterization, the Barycentric Subspaces, as a regularizer for cardiac motion tracking. Yang et al. [16] generated a motion prior using manifold learning from low-dimensional shapes.

We propose to learn a probabilistic motion model from image sequences directly. Instead of defining a parameterization explicitly or learning from pre-processed shapes, our model captures relevant motion features in a low-dimensional motion matrix in a generic but data-driven way. This learned latent space can be used to fill gaps of missing frames (motion reconstruction), to predict the next frames in the sequence or to generate an infinite number of new motion patterns given only one image (motion simulation). Motion can be also transported by applying the motion matrix on an image of another subject.

The probabilistic motion encoding is learned by generalizing a pair-wise registration method [10] based on Bayesian inference [9] using a temporal regularizer with explicit time dependence. Furthermore, to enforce temporal consistency, we introduce a novel self-supervised training scheme called temporal dropout sampling. The framework is learned in an unsupervised fashion from image sequences of varying lengths. Smooth, diffeomorphic and symmetric deformations are ensured by applying an exponentiation layer, spatio-temporal regularization and a symmetric local cross-correlation metric. Besides motion simulation, the model demonstrates state-of-the-art registration results for diffeomorphic tracking of cardiac cine-MRI. The main contributions are as follows:

- An unsupervised probabilistic motion model learned from image sequences
- A generative model using explicit time-dependent temporal convolutional networks trained with self-supervised temporal dropout sampling
- Demonstration of cardiac motion tracking, simulation, transport and temporal super-resolution.

2   Methods

The motion observed in an image sequence with $T + 1$ frames is typically described by deformation fields ϕ_t between a moving image I_0 and the fixed images I_t with $t \in [1, T]$. Inspired by the probabilistic deformation model of [10] based on conditional variational autoencoder (CVAE) [9], we define a motion model for temporal sequences. The model is conditioned on the moving image and parameterizes the set of diffeomorphisms ϕ_t in a low-dimensional probabilistic space, the motion matrix $z \in \mathbb{R}^{d \times T}$, where d is the size of the deformation

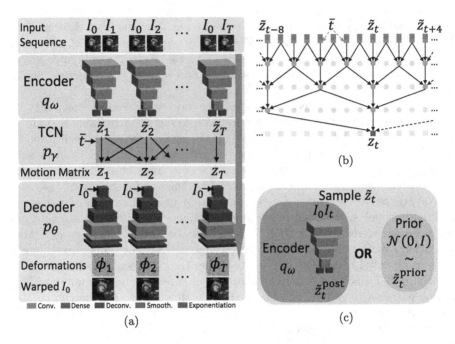

Fig. 1. Probabilistic motion model (a): The encoder q_ω projects the image pair (I_0, I_t) to a low-dimensional deformation encoding $\tilde{z}_t$ from which the temporal convolutional network p_γ (b) constructs the motion matrix $z \in \mathbb{R}^{d \times T}$ conditioned on the normalized time $\bar{t}$. The decoder p_θ maps the motion matrix to the deformations ϕ_t. The temporal dropout sampling procedure (c) randomly chooses to sample $\tilde{z}_t$ either from the encoder q_ω or the prior distribution.

encoding per image pair. Each column's z_t-code corresponds to the deformation ϕ_t. To take temporal dependencies into account, z_t is conditioned on all past and future time steps. To learn this temporal regularization directly from data, we apply Temporal Convolutional Networks [3] with explicit time dependence and temporal dropout sampling enforcing the network to fill time steps by looking at given past and future deformations. An illustration of the model is shown in Fig. 1a.

Probabilistic Motion Model. Our motion model consists of three distributions. First, the encoder $q_\omega(\tilde{z}_t | I_0, I_t)$ maps each of the image pairs (I_0, I_t) independently to a latent space denoted by $\tilde{z}_t \in \mathbb{R}^d$. Second, as the key component of temporal modeling, these latent vectors $\tilde{z}_t$ are jointly mapped to the motion matrix z by conditioning them in all past and future time steps and on the normalized time $\bar{t}$: $p_\gamma(z | \tilde{z}_{1:T}, \bar{t}_{1:T})$. Finally, the decoder $p_\theta(I_t | z_t, I_0)$ aims to reconstruct the fixed image I_t by warping the moving image I_0 with the deformation ϕ_t. This deformation ϕ_t is extracted from the temporally regularized z_t-codes. The decoder is conditioned on the moving image by concatenating the features at each scale with down-sampled versions of I_0.

The distributions q_ω, p_γ, p_θ are approximated by three neural networks with trainable parameters ω, γ, θ. During training, a lower bound on the data likelihood is maximized with respect to a prior distribution $p(\tilde{z}_t)$ of the latent space $\tilde{z}_t$ (cf. CVAE [9]). The prior $p(\tilde{z}_t)$ is assumed to follow a multivariate unit Gaussian distribution with spherical covariance I: $p(\tilde{z}_t) \sim \mathcal{N}(0, I)$. The objective function results in optimizing the expected log-likelihood p_θ and the Kullback-Leibler (KL) divergence enforcing the posterior distribution q_ω to be close to the prior $p(\tilde{z}_t)$ for all time steps:

$$\sum_{t=1}^{T} \mathbb{E}_{z_t \sim p_\gamma(\cdot|\tilde{z}_{1:T}, \bar{t}_{1:T})} \left[\log p_\theta(I_t|z_t, I_0) \right] - \mathrm{KL}\left[q_\omega(\tilde{z}_t|I_0, I_t) \| p(\tilde{z}) \right]. \tag{1}$$

Unlike the traditional CVAE model, the temporal regularized z_t-code is used in the log-likelihood term p_θ instead of the $\tilde{z}_t$. We model p_θ as a symmetric local cross-correlation Boltzmann distribution with the weighting factor λ. Encoder and decoder weights are independent of the time t. Their network architecture consists of convolutional and deconvolutional layers with fully-connected layers for mean and variance predictions in the encoder part [9]. We use an exponentiation layer for the stationary velocity field parameterization of diffeomorphisms [10], a linear warping layer and diffusion-like regularization with smoothing parameters σ_G in spatial and σ_T in temporal dimension.

Temporal Convolutional Networks with Explicit Time Dependence. Since the parameters of encoder q_ω and decoder p_θ are independent of time, the temporal conditioning p_γ plays an important role in merging information across different time steps. In our work, this regularization is learned by Temporal Convolutional Networks (TCN). Consisting of multiple 1-D convolutional layers with increasing dilation, TCN can handle input sequences of different lengths. TCN have several advantages compared to recurrent neural networks such as a flexible receptive field and more stable gradient computations [3].

The input of the TCN is the sequence of $\tilde{z}$ concatenated with the normalized time $\bar{t} = t/T$. Providing the normalized time explicitly, provides the network with information on where each $\tilde{z}$ is located in the sequence. This supports the learning of a motion model from data representing the same type of motion with varying sequence lengths. The output of the TCN is the regularized motion matrix z. We use non-causal instead of causal convolutional layers to also take future time steps into account. We follow the standard implementation using zero-padding and skip connections. Each layer contains d filters. A schematic representation of our TCN is shown in Fig. 1b. For cyclic sequences, one could use a cyclic padding instead of zero-padding, for example by linking $\tilde{z}_T$ to $\tilde{z}_0$. However, in case of cardiac cine-MRI, one can not assume the end of a sequence coincides with the beginning as 5–10% of the cardiac cycle are often omitted [4].

Training with Temporal Dropout Sampling. Using Eq. 1 for training could lead to learning the identity transform $z \approx \tilde{z}$ in the TCN p_γ such that deformations of the current time step are independent of past and future time steps.

To avoid this and enforce the model to search for temporal dependencies during the training, we introduce the concept of temporal dropout sampling (TDS). In TDS, some of the $\tilde{z}_t$ are sampled from the prior distribution $p(\tilde{z})$ instead of only sampling from the posterior distribution $q_\omega(\tilde{z}_t|I_0, I_t)$ as typical for CVAE. At the time steps the prior has been used for sampling, the model has no knowledge of the target image I_t and is forced to use the temporal connections within the TCN in order to minimize the objective.

More precisely, at each time step t, a sample from the prior distribution $\tilde{z}_t^{\mathrm{prior}} \sim p(\tilde{z}_t)$ is selected instead of a posterior sample $\tilde{z}_t^{\mathrm{post}} \sim q_\omega(\tilde{z}_t|I_0, I_t)$ using a binary Bernoulli random variable r_t. All independent Bernoulli random variables $r \in \mathbb{R}^T$ have the success probability δ. The latent vector $\tilde{z}_t$ can be defined as:

$$\tilde{z}_t = r_t * \tilde{z}_t^{\mathrm{prior}} + (1 - r_t) * \tilde{z}_t^{\mathrm{post}}. \tag{2}$$

Figure 1c illustrates the TDS procedure. At test time, for each time step independently, one can either draw $\tilde{z}_t$ from the prior or take the encoder's prediction.

3   Experiments

We evaluate our motion model on 2-D cardiac MRI-cine data. First, we demonstrate accurate temporal registration by evaluating motion tracking and compensation of the cardiac sequence, taking the end-diastolic (ED) frame as the moving image I_0. Stabilization, is accomplished by warping all frames I_t to the ED frame. Pair-wise registration results are presented for ED-ES (end-systolic) frame pairs. Second, we present motion transport, motion sampling and reconstruction with a limited number of frames.

Data. We used 334 short-axis sequences acquired from different hospitals including 150 sequences from the Automatic Cardiac Diagnosis Challenge 2017 (ACDC [4]). The remaining cases were obtained from the EU FP7-funded project MD-Paedigree (Grant Agreement 600932), mixing congenital heart diseases with healthy and pathological images from adults. The cine images were acquired in breath hold using 1R-R or 2R-R intervals with a retrospective or prospective gating. The sequence length T varied from 13 to 35 frames. We used the 100 cases from ACDC that contain ED-ES segmentation information for testing while the remaining sequences were used for training. All slices were resampled with a spacing of $1.5 \times 1.5\,\mathrm{mm}$ and cropped to a size of 128×128 pixels.

Implementation Details. The encoder q_ω consisted of 4 convolutional layers with strides $(2, 2, 2, 1)$ and dense layers of size d for mean and variance estimation of the VAE. The TCN consisted of four 1-D convolutional layers with dilations $(1, 2, 4, 8)$, *same* padding, a kernel size of 3 and skip connections (cf. Fig. 1b). The decoder p_θ had 3 deconvolutional and 1 convolutional layer before the exponentiation and warping layers (Fig. 1a). The regularization parameters σ_G and σ_T were set to $3\,\mathrm{mm}$ respectively 1.5. The loss weighting factor λ was chosen

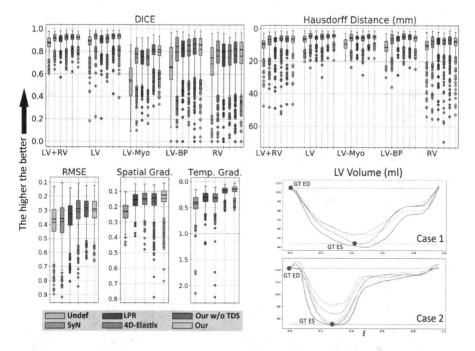

Fig. 2. Tracking results showing RMSE, spatial and temporal gradient of the displacement fields, DICE scores and Hausdorff distances. LV volumes in ml are shown for two test sequences (ground truth ED/ES volumes marked with points). The proposed algorithms (Our and Our w/o TDS) show slightly higher registration accuracy and temporally smoother deformations than the state-of-the-art algorithms: SyN [2], LPR [10] and 4D-Elastix [12].

empirically as $6 \cdot 10^4$. The deformation encoding size d was set to 32. The dropout sampling probability δ was 0.5. We applied a first-order gradient-based method for stochastic optimization (Adam [8]) with a learning rate of 0.00015 and a batch size of one. We performed data augmentation on-the-fly by randomly shifting, rotating, scaling and mirroring images. We implemented the model in Tensorflow [1] with Keras[1]. The training time was 15 h on a NVIDIA GTX TITAN X GPU.

3.1 Registration: Tracking and Motion Compensation

We compare our model with and without the temporal dropout sampling (Our w/o TDS) with three state-of-the-art methods: SyN [2], the learning-based probabilistic registration (LPR, 2-D single-scale version [10]) and the b-spline-based 4D algorithm in elastix [12]. In contrast to the results in [10], in this work, LPR was trained in 2-D taking all images from a sequence into account, not only ED/ES pairs. The following results are reported for full sequences, except the

---

[1] https://github.com/fchollet/keras.

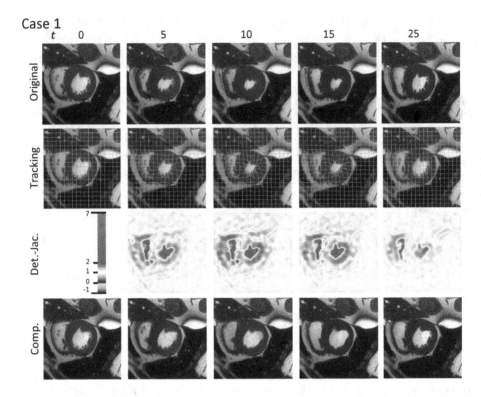

Fig. 3. Visual results of one test sequence, showing tracking, the Jacobian determinant (Det.-Jac.) and motion compensation (Comp.).

metrics based on segmentations which are only reported on frame pairs with provided ground truth information (ED/ES pairs).

In Fig. 2, tracking results are visualized for the test data taking sequences of all slices where segmentation in ED and ES frames are available, resulting in 677 sequences. We report the root mean square error (RMSE), the spatial (Spatial Grad.) and temporal gradient (Temp. Grad.) of the displacement fields for evaluating the smoothness of the resulting deformations. Our model shows spatially and temporally smoother deformations. We also report DICE scores and 95%-tile Hausdorff distances (HD in mm) on five anatomical structures: myocardium (LV-Myo) and epicardium (LV) of the left ventricle, left bloodpool (LV-BP), right ventricle (RV) and LV+RV. Note, that DICE scores and HD were evaluated on ED-ES frame pairs only. The proposed method showed improved mean DICE scores and smaller mean HD of 84.6%, 6.2 mm (w/o TDS: 84.7%, 6.1 mm) compared to SyN, LPR, 4D-Elastix with (82.7%, 7.0 mm), (82.1%, 6.6 mm) respectively (83.7%, 6.3 mm%). Compared to training without temporal dropout sampling, HD and DICE scores show minimal differences, indicating that using TDS does not degrade registration accuracy while improving deformation regularity.

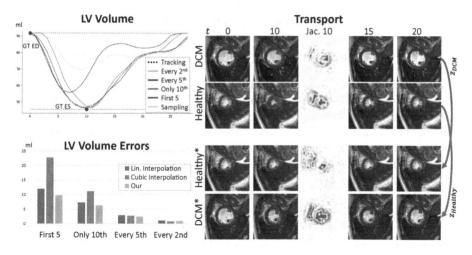

Fig. 4. Left Top: LV volume curves from simulated and reconstructed motion by providing only a subset of frames and predicting the complete motion sequence from them. We provided only the first frame I_0 (sampling), every second, every fifth, the first five frames or only the tenths frame of the same sequence. Left Bottom: Mean volume errors with respect to the tracking volumes of all 677 testing cases comparing our sampling procedure with linear interpolation between velocity fields of the given frames. Right: The motion matrix z from a pathological (first row: dilated myopathy DCM) and a healthy subject (second row) are transported from one to the other (bottom rows).

Furthermore, only TDS offers consistent motion simulation and temporal interpolation.

In the bottom right of Fig. 2, LV volume curves computed by warping the ED mask are plotted. One can see that the SyN algorithm underestimates big deformations. Both, the volume and the gradient metrics show smoother deformations for both versions of our motion model compared to the SyN, LPR and 4D-Elastix algorithms. Visual results for one case including tracking, determinant of Jacobians and compensated motion are shown in Fig. 3. Motion compensation was done by warping the I_t's frame with inverted diffeomorphisms.

3.2 Sampling, Sequence Reconstruction and Motion Transport

We then evaluate motion sampling, reconstruction and transport. We extract simulated reconstructed motion patterns if we provide our model with different subsets of images from the original sequence. In the time steps without frames, the motion matrix z is created by randomly sampling $\tilde{z}_t$ from the prior distribution as depicted in Fig. 1c (take same $\tilde{z}_t$ for all slices of one volume). Here, we choose sampling over interpolation in $\tilde{z}$-space to remain an uncertain, a probabilistic, estimation of the interpolated deformations. The left side of Fig. 4 shows LV volume curves and reconstruction errors if every second, every fifth, only the 10th, no frame (sampling) or the first 5 frames are provided besides the moving frame (ED). The LV volume errors are computed on all test sequences by taking the mean absolute differences between sampled and tracking volumes. We compare with linear and cubic interpolation of velocities (extracted from tracking) between given times. One can see that our model performs better in recovering the LV volume, compared to linear and cubic interpolation when fewer frames are provided. Given the first five frames or only one additional frame (10th frame), the model estimates the motion consistently with plausible cardiac motion patterns for the missing time steps. In the cases of providing every second and every fifth frame, our method performs equally good or marginally better. Note, the motion simulation given only the ED frame (sampling) does not overlap with the original motion, which is not intended. Nevertheless, one can see cardiac specific motion patterns such as the plateau phase before the atrial systole.

Motion can be transported by taking the motion matrix z from one sequence and apply it on the ED frame I_0 of another sequence. The right side of Fig. 4 shows the transport of a pathological motion to a healthy subject and vice versa. The resulting simulated motion shows similar heart contractions and motion characteristics as the originating motion while the transported deformations are adapted to the target image without requiring explicit inter-subject registration.

4 Conclusions

In this paper, we presented an unsupervised approach for learning a motion model from image sequences. Underlying motion factors are encoded in a low-dimensional probabilistic space, the motion matrix, in which each column represents the deformation between two frames of the sequence. Our model demonstrated accurate motion tracking and motion reconstruction from missing frames, which can be useful for shorter acquisition times and temporal super-resolution. We also showed motion transport and simulation by using only one frame. Limitations of the presented approach include the support for 3-D image sequences and the generalization to other use cases such as respiratory motion.

For future work, we aim to explore these points and especially the spatial coherence between slices for 3-D applications and the influence of using different training datasets (pathological and non-pathological) on the learned motion matrix.

Disclaimer: The concepts and information presented in this paper are based on research results that are not commercially available.

References

1. Abadi, M., et al.: Tensorflow: large-scale machine learning on heterogeneous distributed systems. arXiv preprint arXiv:1603.04467 (2016)
2. Avants, B.B., Epstein, C.L., Grossman, M., Gee, J.C.: Symmetric diffeomorphic image registration with cross-correlation: evaluating automated labeling of elderly and neurodegenerative brain. Med. Image Anal. **12**(1), 26–41 (2008)

3. Bai, S., Kolter, J.Z., Koltun, V.: An empirical evaluation of generic convolutional and recurrent networks for sequence modeling. arXiv preprint arXiv:1803.01271 (2018)
4. Bernard, O., et al.: Deep learning techniques for automatic MRI cardiac multi-structures segmentation and diagnosis: is the problem solved? IEEE Trans. Med. Imaging 37(11), 2514–2525 (2018)
5. Caballero, J., et al.: Real-time video super-resolution with spatio-temporal networks and motion compensation. In: Proceedings of the IEEE Conference on Computer Vision and Pattern Recognition, pp. 4778–4787 (2017)
6. Dalca, A.V., Balakrishnan, G., Guttag, J., Sabuncu, M.R.: Unsupervised learning for fast probabilistic diffeomorphic registration. In: Frangi, A.F., Schnabel, J.A., Davatzikos, C., Alberola-López, C., Fichtinger, G. (eds.) MICCAI 2018. LNCS, vol. 11070, pp. 729–738. Springer, Cham (2018). https://doi.org/10.1007/978-3-030-00928-1_82
7. De Craene, M., et al.: Temporal diffeomorphic free-form deformation: application to motion and strain estimation from 3D echocardiography. Med. Image Anal. 16(2), 427–450 (2012)
8. Kingma, D.P., Ba, J.: Adam: a method for stochastic optimization. arXiv preprint arXiv:1412.6980 (2014)
9. Kingma, D.P., Mohamed, S., Rezende, D.J., Welling, M.: Semi-supervised learning with deep generative models. In: Advances in Neural Information Processing Systems, pp. 3581–3589 (2014)
10. Krebs, J., Delingette, H., Mailhé, B., Ayache, N., Mansi, T.: Learning a probabilistic model for diffeomorphic registration. IEEE Trans. Med. Imaging 38(9), 2165–2176 (2019)
11. Lorenzi, M., Ayache, N., Frisoni, G.B., Pennec, X., et al.: LCC-Demons: a robust and accurate symmetric diffeomorphic registration algorithm. NeuroImage 81, 470–483 (2013)
12. Metz, C., Klein, S., Schaap, M., van Walsum, T., Niessen, W.J.: Nonrigid registration of dynamic medical imaging data using nD + t B-splines and a groupwise optimization approach. Med. Image Anal. 15(2), 238–249 (2011)
13. Qin, C., et al.: Joint learning of motion estimation and segmentation for cardiac MR image sequences. In: Frangi, A.F., Schnabel, J.A., Davatzikos, C., Alberola-López, C., Fichtinger, G. (eds.) MICCAI 2018. LNCS, vol. 11071, pp. 472–480. Springer, Cham (2018). https://doi.org/10.1007/978-3-030-00934-2_53
14. Rohé, M.M., Sermesant, M., Pennec, X.: Low-dimensional representation of cardiac motion using barycentric subspaces: a new group-wise paradigm for estimation, analysis, and reconstruction. Med. Image Anal. 45, 1–12 (2018)
15. Shi, W., et al.: Temporal sparse free-form deformations. Med. Image Anal. 17(7), 779–789 (2013)
16. Yang, L., Georgescu, B., Zheng, Y., Wang, Y., Meer, P., Comaniciu, D.: Prediction based collaborative trackers (PCT): a robust and accurate approach toward 3D medical object tracking. IEEE Trans. Med. Imaging 30(11), 1921–1932 (2011)

Deep Learning for Cardiac Motion Estimation: Supervised vs. Unsupervised Training

Huaqi Qiu$^{(\boxtimes)}$, Chen Qin, Loic Le Folgoc, Benjamin Hou, Jo Schlemper, and Daniel Rueckert

Biomedical Image Analysis Group, Imperial College London, London, UK
huaqi.qiu15@imperial.ac.uk

Abstract. Deep learning based registration methods have emerged as alternatives to traditional registration methods, with competitive accuracy and significantly less runtime. Two different strategies have been proposed to train such deep learning registration networks: *supervised* training strategy where the model is trained to regress to generated ground truth deformation; and *unsupervised* training strategy where the model directly optimises the similarity between the registered images. In this work, we directly compare the performance of these two training strategies for cardiac motion estimation on cardiac cine MR sequences. Testing on real cardiac MRI data shows that while the *supervised* training yields more regular deformation, the *unsupervised* more accurately captures the deformation of anatomical structures in cardiac motion.

1 Introduction

Cardiac motion analysis assesses regional deformation parameters such as volume output, strain and torsion, which are indicative for the diagnosis and treatment for patients with cardiovascular diseases [8,9]. The deformation parameters can be derived from displacement field estimated from cardiac magnetic resonance (MR) images. Traditionally cardiac motion estimation is cast as a series of pairwise registration tasks. Shen et al. [8] extended a hierarchical attribute-matching based registration method to simultaneously estimate cardiac motion of all frames in a sequence by formulating cardiac motion as spatial-temporal 4D registration. Shi et al. [9] applied B-spline free-form deformation (FFD) registration [7] on both cine and tagged cardiac MR images by spatially weighting the complementary information from the two modalities.

Deep learning methods have been successfully applied to deformable registration, demonstrating competitive performances with significantly superior speed. Several methods that train deep convolutional neural networks (ConvNets) to perform one-shot prediction of the deformation between two images have been proposed. A critical difference in the proposed methods is the supervision signal used during training. On the one hand, networks are trained to perform a regression task using ground truth deformation that are acquired either via random

© Springer Nature Switzerland AG 2020
M. Pop et al. (Eds.): STACOM 2019, LNCS 12009, pp. 186–194, 2020.
https://doi.org/10.1007/978-3-030-39074-7_20

simulation [3,10] or traditional registration algorithms [2,12]. These methods are termed *supervised* methods since the ground truth of the deformation is used in training. On the other hand, several recent *unsupervised* methods opt to directly optimise the parameters of the network to maximise intensity-based similarity for all image pairs in a training dataset [1,11]. Most related to this work, [6] incorporated unsupervised registration method to provide complementary motion information for cardiac segmentation. Despite the advances of both *supervised* and *unsupervised* methods, it remains unclear which training strategy is more suitable for cardiac motion estimation.

In this work, we trained a deep learning registration network to perform cardiac motion estimation using both *supervised* and *unsupervised* training strategy, and compared the performances on both the accuracy and the regularity of the estimated motion. We show that the *unsupervised* model was able to extract motion that describes the deformation of anatomical structure more accurately, while the *supervised* model produced spatially smoother and more topology-preserving deformation.

2   Background

The objective of cardiac motion estimation is to determine the spatial transformation of cardiac structures over time. Let $\{I_t\}_{t=0,1,2,...,N_T}$ represent a sequence of cardiac cine MR images where N_T is the total number of frames and let $\mathbf{p}_0 \in \mathbb{R}^2$ denotes the position of a point on the first frame ($t = 0$). We can determine the spatial transformation $\mathcal{T}(\cdot)$ using image registration such that $I_0(\mathbf{p}_0)$ and $I_t(\mathcal{T}_t(\mathbf{p}_0))$ represent the same anatomical structure. The transformation can be described by a dense displacement field (DDF), denoted by $\mathbf{u}_t$ where $\mathbf{u}_t(\mathbf{p}_0) = \mathbf{p}_t - \mathbf{p}_0$.

Deep learning has been used to perform the registration with one-step prediction by modelling a complex function $f_\theta(I_0, I_t) = \mathbf{u}_t$ that maps a pair of images to the optimal displacement field using convolutional neural network (ConvNet), where θ is the parameters of the network. The parameters θ in the registration network can be trained using two different supervision signals: ground truth DDF $\mathbf{u}_{GT}$ (*supervised*), or the similarity between the pairs of images after registration (*unsupervised*).

3   Method

This paper adapts and compares two training strategies, *supervised* and *unsupervised*, for a deep learning based cardiac motion estimation in cine MR image sequences. The registration networks and the training strategies were set up in a comparable manner for a fair comparison. An overview of both the *supervised* and *unsupervised* registration frameworks is illustrated in Fig. 1.

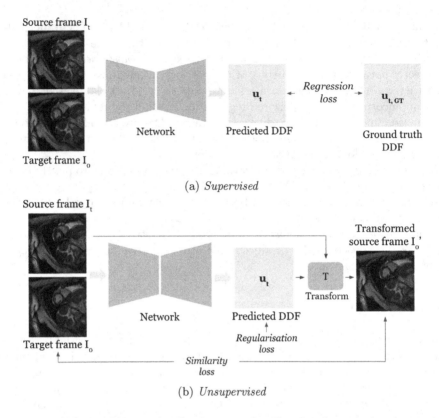

(a) *Supervised*

(b) *Unsupervised*

Fig. 1. *Supervised* and *unsupervised* registration framework

3.1 Supervised Training

Ground Truth Deformation. The ground truth deformation is required for *supervised* training of the registration network. Existing deep learning methods for deformable registration usually generate the ground truth displacement u_{GT} using traditional registration methods [2], and use the original image pair $\{(I_0, I_t)\}$ as input to the network. The network sees the real image pairs during training but the ground truth deformation does not completely capture the transformation due to residual errors from the traditional registration methods used to estimate the ground truth deformation. Alternatively, the deformation field acquired from traditional registration can be used to deform image I_t to generate a pseudo-target image $I_0' = I_t \circ \mathcal{T}_{u_t}$. We then use the image pairs $\{(I_0', I_t)\}$ as input to the network. The ground truth in this setting fully captures the deformation between the input image pair (I_0', I_t) and thus is not limited by residual registration errors. These two variants of supervised training are compared in Sect. 4.2. B-spline FFD [7] is used for traditional registration.

Training. As shown in Fig. 1(a), the network predicts the DDF u_t from each pair of input images. For cardiac motion estimation, a sequence of image pairs

$\{(I_0, I_t)\}_{t=1,2,3,\dots,N_T}$ is given as input to the network in one batch such that each training iteration optimises the group registration of the sequence [6,8]. The end-diastolic (ED) frame is used as the first frame (or the *target* frame) and is repeated in each pair in the batch. To train the model, we use Mean Square Error (MSE) between the predicted and ground truth DDF as the regression loss:

$$\mathcal{L}_{supervised} = \frac{1}{N_T} \sum_{t=1}^{N_T} \left(\frac{1}{|\Omega|} \sum_{\mathbf{p} \in \Omega} (\mathbf{u}_t(\mathbf{p}) - \mathbf{u}_{GT}(\mathbf{p}))^2 \right) \tag{1}$$

where N_T is the number of frames in one batch/sequence and Ω is the spatial domain of the images.

3.2 Unsupervised Training

As illustrated in Fig. 1(b), we use image intensity-based similarity as loss function with an additional regularisation on the predicted displacements. The loss function that the training minimises at each iteration is:

$$\mathcal{L} = \mathcal{L}_{MSE} + \lambda \mathcal{L}_{smooth} \tag{2}$$

The first term in the loss function measures the pixel-wise difference between the target image and the registered source image:

$$\mathcal{L}_{MSE} = \frac{1}{N_T} \sum_{t=1}^{N_T} \left(\frac{1}{|\Omega|} \sum_{\mathbf{p} \in \Omega} (I_0'(\mathbf{p}) - I_0(\mathbf{p}))^2 \right) \tag{3}$$

Here I_t is transformed to I_0' using differentiable bi-linear sampling in the spatial transformation network [4], enabling backpropagation for training. The second term in the loss function encourages spatially smooth deformation by minimising the variation of displacements using approximated Huber loss [6] on first-order spatial derivatives of $\mathbf{u}_t$,

$$\mathcal{L}_{smooth} = \frac{1}{N_T} \sum_{t=1}^{N_T} \left(\frac{1}{|\Omega|} \sum_{\mathbf{p} \in \Omega} \sqrt{\left| \frac{\partial \mathbf{u}_t(\mathbf{p})}{\partial x} \right|^2 + \left| \frac{\partial \mathbf{u}_t(\mathbf{p})}{\partial y} \right|^2} \right) \tag{4}$$

Similar to the *supervised* training, one sequence of image pairs from one cardiac sequence is used in each input batch. The weight λ of the smoothness regularisation loss is set to 10^{-4} which is selected based on the performance on the validation dataset.

3.3 Network Architecture

A schematic of the network is shown in Fig. 2. The same network architecture is used in both training strategies and is adapted from the motion estimation branch of the joint segmentation and motion estimation framework proposed in [6]. The network employs two encoder branches with 3 × 3 convolutional kernels to extract features from the images. A stride of 2 is used every two convolutional layers to reduce the resolution of feature maps by 2 and increase the size of receptive field [1]. The features from all levels of the two encoders are concatenated before a convolution layer and upsampling to full resolution. Further convolutional layers are applied to fuse information from different scales before making the final prediction.

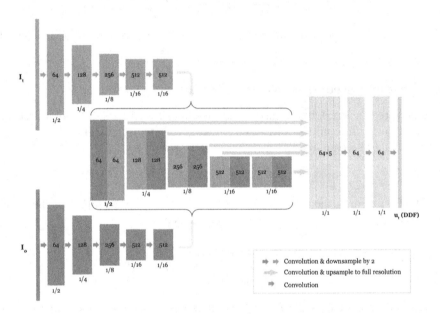

Fig. 2. Architecture of the registration network. The coloured blocks represent images or feature maps with the number of channels written inside. The resolution of the feature maps with respect to the input is written underneath the blocks. The final output has 2 channels encoding the displacement in 2 directions. (Color figure online)

4   Experiments

4.1   Set up

Data. The two training strategies are evaluated using short-axis view cardiac MR images of healthy subjects from the UK BioBank study[1]. Randomly selected image sequences of 120 subjects were used for training and validation with another 100 subjects used for testing. Each sequence contains temporally prealigned 2D stacks of images of 50 consecutive time points in a complete cardiac cycle. In-plane resolution of the images is 1.8 × 1.8 mm per pixel while through-plane resolution is 10 mm per pixel. The low resolution between planes could

---

[1] UK Biobank Imaging Study. http://imaging.ukbiobank.ac.uk.

lead to physically implausible displacements of anatomical structure in 3D registration, which is the reason that our motion estimation is performed in 2D plane. The segmentation of the left-ventricular cavity (LV), myocardium wall (MYO) and right-ventricular cavity (RV) on the ED frame and the end-systolic (ES) frame is used to evaluate the accuracy of the estimated motion.

Metrics. The estimated cardiac motion is evaluated on both accuracy and smoothness. To evaluate the accuracy, we first estimate the motion between the ED frame and the ES frame. Then we apply the estimated motion to deform the segmentation mask of the ES frame towards the ED frame, and measure its overlap with the ground true ED frame segmentation using the Dice score and Hausdorff Distance (HD). HD is measured on the outer contours of the anatomical structures. To evaluate regularity of deformation, we calculate the determinant of the Jacobian matrix $J_\phi(\mathbf{p}) = \nabla \phi(\mathbf{p})$, or simply *the Jacobian*, where ϕ denotes the transformation. We compute the percentage of points that exhibit non-diffeomorphic deformation, indicated by $|J_\phi(\mathbf{p})| \leq 0$. We also calculate magnitudes of the gradient of *the Jacobian*, i.e. $|\nabla|J_\phi||$ which is a second-order metric measuring the spatial smoothness of deformation [5].

Comparison. To ensure fairness of the comparison, the *supervised* and *unsupervised* model use exactly the same network architecture described in Sect. 3.3. Both models are trained using the same amount of data for the same number of iterations and tested on data of the same testing subjects. As a reference of performance, the traditional B-spline FFD registration algorithm is also evaluated on the same testing data. The FFD algorithm is set to use the sum squared difference (SSD) as dissimilarity measure and Bending Energy (BE) as regularisation [7]. A 3-level hierarchical multi-resolution approach is used where the spacing of B-spline control points on the highest resolution is set to 8 mm. The same setting of FFD was used to generate the ground truth deformation for *supervised* training. The regularisation weights in the unsupervised method and FFD introduce a trade-off between accuracy and deformation regularity, making the selection of these parameters for fair comparison non-trivial. In this paper, both regularisation weights were selected to maximise the accuracy performance on the validation dataset.

Implementation Details. Input images are pre-processed by cropping to the size of 160×160 so that the registration is focused on the region of interest. The intensity value of input images is normalised to $[0, 1]$. The deep learning registration networks were implemented in Pytorch and trained for 500 epochs on NVIDIA® GeForce® Titan Xp GPUs. The B-spline FFD registration was performed using the implementation in MIRTK[2]. The runtime of FFD is measured on an Intel® Core™ i7-8700 CPU.

---

[2] https://mirtk.github.io/.

4.2 Results

Table 1 shows the results of the accuracy and regularity of different methods. When comparing the results of different methods, the Wilcoxon signed-rank test is performed to assess the statistical significance. It can be observed that the *unsupervised* training outperforms ($p \ll 0.001$) *supervised* training in terms of accuracy especially on left ventricle and right ventricle, and on-par with B-spline FFD on most metrics. Between *supervised* models, the one trained using the $\{(I_0', I_t)\}$ image pair ("sup+warp.") performs similar to the one trained using the $\{(I_0, I_t)\}$ image pair ("sup+orig.") except better on myocardium measurements. In terms of regularity, the supervised methods produce deformations that are spatially smoother (lower $|\nabla|J_\phi||$) and significantly less topology-altering (lower $\%|J| \leq 0$).

Table 1. Accuracy and regularity of cardiac motion estimated by different methods. The accuracy metrics are also evaluated on unregistered input images ("Unreg") as a reference. The mean and standard deviation over 100 testing subjects are presented. The best results with statistical significant advantage ($p \ll 0.001$) are highlighted in bold.

Method	Dice			HD			$|\nabla|J_\phi||$	$\%|J| \leq 0$
	LV	Myo	RV	LV	Myo	RV		
Unreg	0.641(0.058)	0.322(0.086)	0.551(0.077)	11.40(1.40)	8.90(2.00)	11.50(1.90)	-	-
FFD	**0.941(0.049)**	**0.754(0.084)**	0.671(0.109)	4.52(2.33)	**4.73(1.44)**	8.93(2.16)	0.021(0.023)	0.081(0.119)
DL(unsup)	**0.943(0.046)**	0.740(0.077)	**0.709(0.087)**	**4.05(1.47)**	4.62(1.25)	9.34(2.13)	0.047(0.014)	0.375(0.162)
DL(sup+warp.)	0.920(0.049)	0.735(0.080)	0.668(0.101)	4.61(1.11)	**4.84(1.48)**	9.06(1.91)	0.040(0.007)	**0.025(0.038)**
DL(sup+orig.)	0.926(0.048)	0.702(0.0801)	0.657(0.089)	4.41(1.35)	5.29(1.22)	9.22(1.88)	**0.019(0.004)**	0.030(0.040)

Figure 3 visually demonstrates the difference amongst different motion estimation methods on one exemplar subject. The deep learning model trained using *supervised* strategy performs inferior to its *unsupervised* counterpart. It can be observed, from the ED frame image reconstructed by deforming the ES frame image, that the supervised method significantly underestimates the deformation and produces some artefacts in the middle of the LV blood pool. The unsupervised method captures the deformation better but violates some topological structure especially around epicardial contour, as illustrated by the folding that can be observed on the deformed meshgrid.

Runtime Advantage. Despite not achieving significant performance advantage over the traditional method, the deep learning models are able to register a sequence of 50 2D frames in 80.05 ms whereas FFD takes 23.18 s. The runtimes are measured and averaged over 100 test subjects.

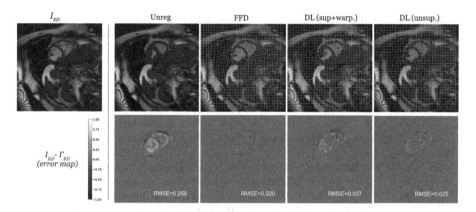

Fig. 3. Visualisation of motion estimation results. The target ED frame image I_{ED} is shown on the top left. The rest of the first row shows the ED frame reconstructed by deforming the ES frame image using deformation estimated by the various methods (I'_{ED}), overlaid by the meshgrid deformed using the same estimated deformation. The second row shows the error maps (with RMSE values) between the reconstructed image and the ED frame.

5   Conclusion and Discussion

In this work, we evaluated and compared the effect of different training strategy on the performance of deep learning registration network on the task of cardiac motion estimation. In terms of accuracy, we found that *unsupervised* training, which uses only image similarity, outperforms the *supervised* training strategies. This could be attributed to the fact that the unsupervised learning optimise directly on the image intensity difference, while the *supervised* training is either restricted by the registration error from FFD ("sup+orig.") or the difference between the testing target images and training target images ("sup+warp"). Although performing inferior on accuracy, the *supervised* methods produce spatially smoother and more topology-preserving deformation.

The superior regularity of the supervised methods could be a result of inheriting spatial smoothness property from the B-spline basis functions in FFD and further regularisation in the regression. It is also possible that the better regularity can only be achieved while under-estimating deformation. This will be further investigated in the future. Future studies should also include a supervised model trained using randomly generated or permuted deformation ground truth in the comparison. This will help to understand the need for realistic ground truth deformation for the supervised method. Another limitation of the paper is that only two representative *supervised* and *unsupervised* designs are experimented whereas a study of more existing methods under the same experimental setting would be able to draw a more general conclusion.

Acknowledgements. This work was supported by the EPSRC Programme Grant EP/P001009/1 and EP/R005982/1. The cardiac image dataset has been provided under UK Biobank Access Application 40119.

References

1. Balakrishnan, G., Zhao, A., Sabuncu, M.R., et al.: VoxelMorph: a learning framework for deformable medical image registration. IEEE Trans. Med. Imaging **38**, 1788–1800 (2019)
2. Cao, X., et al.: Deformable image registration based on similarity-steered CNN regression. In: Descoteaux, M., Maier-Hein, L., Franz, A., Jannin, P., Collins, D.L., Duchesne, S. (eds.) MICCAI 2017. LNCS, vol. 10433, pp. 300–308. Springer, Cham (2017). https://doi.org/10.1007/978-3-319-66182-7_35
3. Eppenhof, K.A., Lafarge, M.W., Moeskops, P., et al.: Deformable image registration using convolutional neural networks. In: Medical Imaging 2018: Image Processing, vol. 10574, p. 105740S (2018)
4. Jaderberg, M., Simonyan, K., Zisserman, A., et al.: Spatial transformer networks. In: Advances in Neural Information Processing Systems, pp. 2017–2025 (2015)
5. Krebs, J., e Delingette, H., Mailhé, B., et al.: Learning a probabilistic model for diffeomorphic registration. IEEE Trans. Med. Imaging **38**, 2165–2176 (2019)
6. Qin, C., et al.: Joint learning of motion estimation and segmentation for cardiac MR image sequences. In: Frangi, A.F., Schnabel, J.A., Davatzikos, C., Alberola-López, C., Fichtinger, G. (eds.) MICCAI 2018. LNCS, vol. 11071, pp. 472–480. Springer, Cham (2018). https://doi.org/10.1007/978-3-030-00934-2_53
7. Rueckert, D., Sonoda, L.I., Hayes, C., et al.: Nonrigid registration using free-form deformations: application to breast MR images. IEEE Trans. Med. Imaging **18**(8), 712–721 (1999)
8. Shen, D., Sundar, H., Xue, Z., Fan, Y., Litt, H.: Consistent estimation of cardiac motions by 4D image registration. In: Duncan, J.S., Gerig, G. (eds.) MICCAI 2005. LNCS, vol. 3750, pp. 902–910. Springer, Heidelberg (2005). https://doi.org/10.1007/11566489_111
9. Shi, W., Zhuang, X., Wang, H., et al.: A comprehensive cardiac motion estimation framework using both untagged and 3-d tagged mr images based on nonrigid registration. IEEE Trans. Med. Imaging **31**(6), 1263–1275 (2012)
10. Sokooti, H., de Vos, B., Berendsen, F., Lelieveldt, B.P.F., Išgum, I., Staring, M.: Nonrigid image registration using multi-scale 3D convolutional neural networks. In: Descoteaux, M., Maier-Hein, L., Franz, A., Jannin, P., Collins, D.L., Duchesne, S. (eds.) MICCAI 2017. LNCS, vol. 10433, pp. 232–239. Springer, Cham (2017). https://doi.org/10.1007/978-3-319-66182-7_27
11. de Vos, B.D., Berendsen, F.F., Viergever, M.A., et al.: A deep learning framework for unsupervised affine and deformable image registration. Med. Image Anal. **52**, 128–143 (2019)
12. Yang, X., Kwitt, R., Styner, M., Niethammer, M.: Quicksilver: fast predictive image registration-a deep learning approach. NeuroImage **158**, 378–396 (2017)

Multi-Sequence Cardiac MR Segmentation Challenge

Style Data Augmentation for Robust Segmentation of Multi-modality Cardiac MRI

Buntheng Ly[1]([✉]), Hubert Cochet[2], and Maxime Sermesant[1]

[1] Inria, Université Côte d'Azur, Sophia Antipolis, France
buntheng.ly@inria.fr
[2] IHU Liryc, University of Bordeaux, Pessac, France

Abstract. We propose a data augmentation method to improve the segmentation accuracy of the convolutional neural network on multi-modality cardiac magnetic resonance (CMR) dataset. The strategy aims to reduce over-fitting of the network toward any specific intensity or contrast of the training images by introducing diversity in these two aspects. The style data augmentation (SDA) strategy increases the size of the training dataset by using multiple image processing functions including adaptive histogram equalisation, Laplacian transformation, Sobel edge detection, intensity inversion and histogram matching. For the segmentation task, we developed the thresholded connection layer network (TCL-Net), a minimalist rendition of the U-Net architecture, which is designed to reduce convergence and computation time. We integrate the dual U-Net strategy to increase the resolution of the 3D segmentation target. Utilising these approaches on a multi-modality dataset, with SSFP and T2 weighted images as training and LGE as validation, we achieve 90% and 96% validation Dice coefficient for endocardium and epicardium segmentations. This result can be interpreted as a proof of concept for a generalised segmentation network that is robust to the quality or modality of the input images. When testing with our mono-centric LGE image dataset, the SDA method also improves the performance of the epicardium segmentation, with an increase from 87% to 90% for the single network segmentation.

Keywords: Image segmentation · Multi-modality · Cardiac magnetic resonance imaging · Late Gadolinium enhanced · Deep learning

1 Introduction

The combination of different MRI sequences, signal weighting techniques and contrast agents that are currently used for MRI gives rise to diverse modalities and qualities of the output image. Although each technique yields exploitable results, the variation in the image contrast can be detrimental for the development of automatic analysis tools in medical imaging.

© Springer Nature Switzerland AG 2020
M. Pop et al. (Eds.): STACOM 2019, LNCS 12009, pp. 197–208, 2020.
https://doi.org/10.1007/978-3-030-39074-7_21

To answer to the input diversity problem in machine learning segmentation, Seeböck et al. used an unpaired modality transfer generator network to reduce the variability between multi-centric datasets [12]. On the other hand, Isensee et al. proposed the nnU-Net (no-new U-Net), which automatically generates a CNN pipeline that is optimised for each specific dataset [5]. However, these methods require a sufficient mono-modality dataset, as they were built to be used for mono-modality segmentation.

In this study, we propose an alternative approach to this problem. We design a data augmentation method to train a single Deep Learning model to be robust to multi-modality input, including the modality that was not used for optimisation, thus the trained model can be used as a generalised segmentation tool. The style data augmentation introduces diversity of image contrast into the training dataset, with the goal to prevent the model from over-fitting toward the training image modality and to focus the network attention to the fundamental geometry features of the target. We base this method on the idea that despite having different contrasts, the organ geometry features are consistent between MRI modalities.

In this study, we use a 3D convolutional neural network for the segmentation [1]. Nonetheless, this method can be costly in term of memory usage and computation time. We have devised two strategies to combat these issues. Firstly, we proposed a minimalist U-Net inspired network, tailored to accelerate the convergence speed and to decrease memory usage. Secondly, we adopt the dual network strategy [6], which allows for the segmentation of high resolution targets.

2 Method

2.1 Thresholded Connection Layer Network

We propose a segmentation convolutional neural network called thresholded connection layer or TCL-Net. The network architecture is shown in Fig. 1. This architecture is an iteration of the U-Net architecture, originally proposed by Ronneberger et al. [11]. As such, the network follows the same U-shape design and is made up of an encoder and a decoder.

The architecture of TCL-Net exploits the segmentation network ultimate objective, which is to eliminate non-target pixels and to highlight the target pixels of the input image. TCL-Net uses, as the building unit, two consecutive, padded, $3 \times 3 \times 3$ convolutional layers, each followed by a normalisation and a non-linear activation layer. At the end of each encoder unit, a $2 \times 2 \times 2$ max pooling is applied. Correspondingly, a $2 \times 2 \times 2$ upsampling is applied to the output of the decoder unit.

For the normalisation layer, we use the instance normalisation function [13], since the training is done with a single-input batch. We used the LeakyReLU [9] as the activation function of both convolutional layers of the encoder unit. For the decoder units, the LeakyReLU layer is used after the first convolutional and the ThresholdedReLU [7] is used after the second convolutional layer, before the

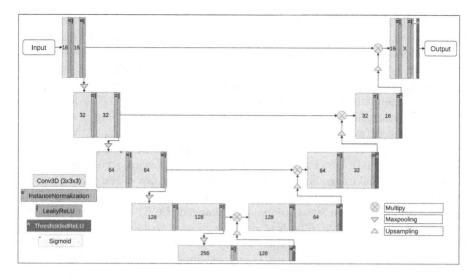

Fig. 1. Thresholded connection layer network. Noted that the ThresholdedReLU layers (red boxes) are only used at the end of each decoder unit. *The number indicates the filter of each convolutional layer. X is set according to the segmentation label (1 for single label segmentation).* (Color figure online)

upsampling layer. We used 0.3 as the coefficient of the LeakyReLU layer and 0.5 as the threshold value of the ThresholdedReLU layer.

The LeakyReLU layer would allow the negative pixels of the feature matrices to pass through, while the ThresholdedReLU would reduce pixels smaller than the threshold to zero. The goal is to let the features to be liberally processed through each level of the encoder and to only apply thresholding at the very end of each resolution level. In order for the network to preserve the elimination progress from the thresholding, we used multiplication to connect the output of the encoder with the decoder, instead of concatenation. Additionally, the multiplication operation could greatly amplify or reduce the value of the output features, which influences the elimination likelihood of each pixel in the next thresholded layer.

Toward the end of TCL-Net, the sigmoid activation layer is added to scale each pixel's value down to between 0 and 1. The output of the sigmoid function can be used to gauge the certainty of the segmentation at the pixel level. The final ThresholdedReLU layer is used as the final processing function to eliminate the pixels less than 0.5 from the output segmentation. The last two activation layers would facilitate the integration of the Dice loss function detailed in Subsect. 2.4.

2.2 Dual U-Net Strategy

In this study, we implement the dual U-Net strategy [6], where two networks are trained independently but can be used consecutively in the segmentation pipeline. The first network is trained to segment the target from the low resolution inputs, as the original image has to be shrunk down to reduce memory consumption. The segmented results of the first network are used to crop the original images, which will be used as input for the second network.

To crop the output of the first network, we round up all the nonzero pixel values to 1, then only one biggest region of connected positive pixels is kept. Note that we integrate this strategy with TCL-Net, where thresholding is applied at the end of the network. Additional thresholding might be necessary with other architecture. To take into account the segmentation error, we apply the binary dilation transformation on the cluster using a 5×5×5 spherical structure element. Finally, the original image is cropped using the bonding box of the dilated region.

For this study, we are interested in left ventricular segmentation from CMR images, specifically from late Gadolinium enhanced (LGE) images, in which the myocardial scar is visible. The first network is used to locate the epicardium, and then second network can either be used to refine the segmentation of the same target or smaller targets such as endocardium and myocardial scar.

2.3 Style Data Augmentation

The style data augmentation strategy focuses on introducing contrast diversity in the training dataset, via different image processing algorithms. The aim is to prevent the model from over-fitting to any specific contrast and to focus the optimisation toward the fundamental geometry features of target.

The image transformation algorithms were selected arbitrarily, as the goal is to simply increase the variety of the training images. For this study, we selected 5 transformation functions, including adaptive histogram equalisation [3], Laplacian transformation, Sobel edge detection, intensity inversion and histogram matching [10], as shown in Fig. 2.

The histogram matching method can be used to convert the histogram of the original training images (C0 and T2) toward the histogram of the validation images (LGE) without the ground truth mask. More details on the dataset used for this study is described in Subsect. 3.1. These functions were applied to the normalized original image using the functions provided by SimpleITK's python package [8,14].

Our goal is to pre-train a segmentation model that is robust to any unknown-to-the-model modality. As the method focuses on the geometry features, it is only suited to be used for the image modalities where the target shape is consistent.

2.4 Experimental Setting

To validate the effectiveness of TCL-Net, we compare the validation result of the new architecture with a baseline network proposed by Isensee et al. [4]. Both networks were trained using a single 3D input per batch. The 3D images are interpolated to equalise the spacing of each dimension, thus the extracted data would closely correspond to the physical size. We use linear and nearest neighbour interpolation methods on the greyscale and mask images, respectively. The interpolated images are then resized to 128 × 128 × 128. Finally, the

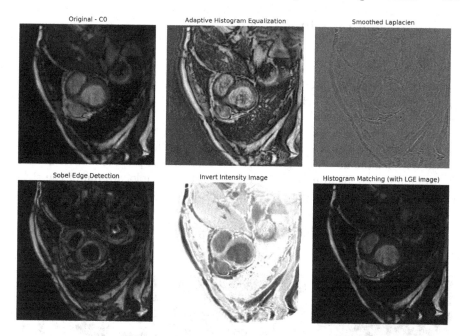

Fig. 2. Different variations of input training images and the image processing methods. *C0 denotes the steady-state free precession CMR modality image.*

images are normalised using linear normalisation function to bring the greyscale value between [0–255]. To test the validity of our method, we do not apply any shape transformation for additional augmentation or any complex pre-processing method on the validation or training images.

We use an initial learning rate of $1e - 4$, which decays by half each 5 epochs with no validation improvement. An early stop is also programmed after 20 epochs of no increase in validation performance. At each epoch, 100 images will be chosen randomly from the training dataset to be used to train the network. The network is updated using Adam optimisation and Dice loss, calculated using Eq. 1, where $\hat{Y}$ is the prediction mask, and Y is the manual labelled mask. During the training, we also measure the original Dice coefficient [2] between the prediction and the manual mask, by applying the "half to even" round function to binarise the output segmentation, Eq. 2. The round function breaks the gradient chain, which prevents Dice coefficient from being used for backpropagation.

$$Dice_{Loss} = 1 - 2 * \frac{\sum(\hat{Y} * Y)}{\sum \hat{Y} + \sum Y} \tag{1}$$

$$Dice_{Coeff} = 2 * \frac{\sum(round(\hat{Y}) * Y)}{\sum round(\hat{Y}) + \sum Y} \tag{2}$$

3   Evaluation on Clinical Data

3.1   Materials

For the multi-modal dataset, we use the dataset provided in MS-CMRSeg 2019 segmentation challenge [15,16]. The challenge dataset consists of 135 3D CMR images of 45 patients taken under three modalities: T2-Weighted (T2), balanced-Steady State Free Precession (C0) and late Gadolinium enhanced (LGE), Fig. 3. The manually labelled masks were provided for the first 35 images of T2 and C0 but only for the first 5 images of LGE modality. The provided labels include epicardium and endocardium of the left ventricle and endocardium of the right ventricle. By applying our data augmentation method, we trained the network with 420 images of different variations of the original C0 and T2 images and validated the network with the 5 LGE images.

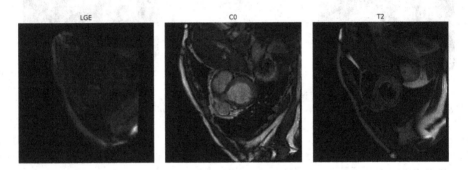

Fig. 3. Short-axis view of original LGE, C0 and T2 CMR images. Note that despite having different contrasts, all these images show the same anatomical structure.

While the SDA method was not designed to be used with mono-modal datasets, we still wish to study the effectiveness of the training input's contrast diversity under this context. We used our local dataset, which consists of 119 mono-centric LGE-CMR images provided by IHU Lyric. Since the dataset is mono-modal, we remove histogram matching from the SDA algorithms. The original dataset was first split in 9:1 ratio for training and validation, before the augmentation method was applied to the training images. We then compare the mean of best validation scores from 5 different sets of validation images of the model trained with and without SDA method.

3.2   Results

Multi-modality. The Table 1 shows the validation results of TCL-Net and Isensee on the multi-modal dataset. Using the TCL-Net with dual network and SDA method, the validation scores reach 0.967 and 0.904 for the epicardium and endocardium segmentations. This is a considerable improvement from 0.833 and

Table 1. The validation Dice coefficient on multi-modality dataset. *: *the best results;* w/o HM: *without Histogram Matching.*

	Single Network		Dual Network	
	TCL-Net	Isensee's	TCL-Net	Isensee's
Epi				
Original(C0&T2)	0.833 ± 0.020	0.791 ± 0.015	0.878 ± 0.006	0.787 ± 0.007
+SDA	$*0.915 \pm 0.006$	0.845 ± 0.013	$*0.9677 \pm 0.012$	0.866 ± 0.011
+SDA(w/o HM)	0.908 ± 0.007	0.854 ± 0.129	0.9671 ± 0.004	0.874 ± 0.007
Endo				
Original(C0&T2)	0.692 ± 0.041	0.651 ± 0.008	0.767 ± 0.008	0.787 ± 0.005
+SDA	$*0.865 \pm 0.021$	0.805 ± 0.038	$*0.904 \pm 0.003$	0.836 ± 0.006
+SDA(w/o HM)	0.857 ± 0.011	0.780 ± 0.019	0.900 ± 0.007	0.839 ± 0.010

0.692 without these two improvements. There is a slight decrease in performance when histogram matching is removed from the SDA algorithms. Nonetheless, the network still performs better compared to training with only original images.

As shown in Fig. 4, TCL-Net performance is enhanced considerably with multi-modality training set (SDA and C0&T2) compared with mono-modality. We can observe in Fig. 4b that the model would quickly overfit to the training modality, as the gap between training and validation scores get higher each epoch. On the contrary, the over-fitting becomes less severe when there is diversity in the training input, as shown in Fig. 4c. The validation also appears more stable at the end of the training with SDA compared with the training with only original C0&T2.

The Fig. 5 shows the validation output of epicardium and endocardium segmentations using the dual TCL-Net models trained with SDA method. Both models perform well and produce accurate segmentation in the region where there is no myocardial scar. Yet, the models struggle at the scar regions, as pointed by the arrows in the Fig. 5b and c.

Mono-modality. When testing on the mono-centric and mono-modal dataset the SDA method does show improvement in validation Dice coefficients from 0.874 to 0.905 for the epicardium segmentation in the first TCL-Net, Table 2. However, the method has an adverse effect on the myocardial scar segmentation in the second TCL-Net. Figure 6 shows the validation segmentation output of the myocardial scar using the TCL-Net models trained with and without SDA method. Despite the poor Dice scores, both models can adequately detect the scar regions, Fig. 6c and b.

TCL-Net. As shown in Tables 1 and 2, TCL-Net achieves better final validation score than the baseline model, both in multi- and mono-modal datasets with or without SDA. Figure 7 shows the validation Dice coefficient of both networks during the first network training. Figure 7a shows that TCL-Net required less

204   B. Ly et al.

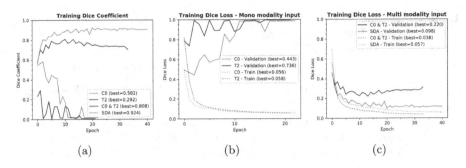

(a)   (b)   (c)

Fig. 4. Validation results of epicardium segmentation of the first TCL-Net on multi-modal dataset.

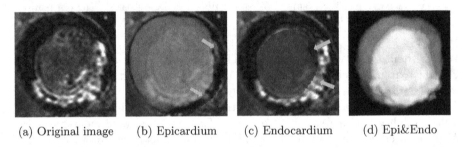

(a) Original image   (b) Epicardium   (c) Endocardium   (d) Epi&Endo

Fig. 5. Epicardium and endocardium segmentation from LGE image using models trained with original and augmented C0 & T2 images (multi-modality dataset, dual TCL-Net with SDA). *Blue: Ground Truth; Orange, Green: Predicted Segmentations.* (Color figure online)

Table 2. The validation Dice coefficient on mono-modality dataset. *: best results.

	Single Network	Dual Network
	Epicardium	Scar
TCL-Net		
Original(LGE)	0.874 ± 0.002	$*0.462 \pm 0.070$
+SDA	$*0.905 \pm 0.011$	0.444 ± 0.061
Isensee's		
Original(LGE)	0.853 ± 0.012	0.439 ± 0.042
+SDA	0.851 ± 0.012	0.348 ± 0.040

epochs for the optimisation. When factoring the training time in Fig. 7b, TCL-Net has faster training speed than the baseline network, with the validation Dice coefficient reaching 85% in less than 5 min.

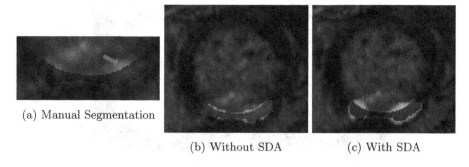

(a) Manual Segmentation

(b) Without SDA   (c) With SDA

Fig. 6. Myocardial scar segmentation using dual U-Net strategy. *Blue: manual segmentation* (Color figure online)

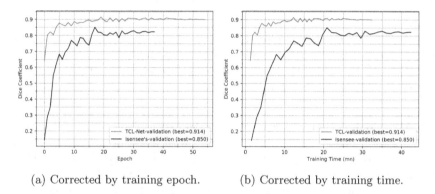

(a) Corrected by training epoch.   (b) Corrected by training time.

Fig. 7. Training and validation results of TCL-Net vs. Isensee's (multi-modality dataset, first network with SDA).

Dual Network Segmentation. The results from Tables 1 and 2 show that the dual network strategy increases significantly the segmentation accuracy. On top of that, compared with the single network, the dual network also produces higher resolution segmentation output, Fig. 8.

4 Discussion

SDA-Epicardium and Endocardium. The image processing functions implemented in SDA create images of different contrasts with defined border and geometric features, thus making the method applicable to the target regular structure such as the epicardium and endocardium. The results in Sect. 3.2 show the increase in performance in both mono- and multi-modal datasets for the segmentation of the epicardium. As shown in multi-modal experiments, the SDA improves segmentation validation score of the LGE images, without any optimisation with the actual LGE data.

The slight decrease in performance when histogram matching was not included in SDA further proves that the strategy does not overly depend on this

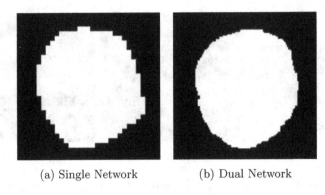

(a) Single Network   (b) Dual Network

Fig. 8. Segmentation output of single vs. dual network.

particular transformation. It also validates that the increase in contrast diversity in augmentation algorithms leads to the increase in performance, rather than over-fitting. Nevertheless, the trained model still reaches a limit, as observed in dual network segmentation in Table 1.

SDA-Myocardial Scar. Because the model can no longer depend on image contrast for the segmentation when training with SDA method, it has to rely on the patterns of the target, such as the traces of the myocardium wall and the homogeneity of the intensity of each structure. Therefore, the method might not be suitable for the targets without uniform structure, such as the myocardial scar. For instance, when training on C0 and T2 images of MS-CMRSeg challenge, the model is only familiar with homogeneous myocardium. Thus, it does not perform well when scar is present on the myocardium of LGE images, Fig. 5.

The inconsistency in contrast of the myocardial scar may explain why the network achieves better result without SDA for the scar segmentation on the mono-modal dataset. As shown in Fig. 6a by the red arrow, the scar region does not include the entire area of the same intensity, since the upper area belongs to the cavity of the ventricle. Because the scar does not have specific geometric shape like the epicardium or endocardium, the model trained with only the original image would perform better, since it can depend more on the specific contrast of the LGE modality during optimisation than the model trained with SDA.

TCL vs. Isensee. In their original paper [4], Isensee et al. integrate a more elaborate preprocessing technique on the input image than what is done in this experiment. Therefore, our experiment might not present the optimal condition for the baseline network. Our goal is to simply compare the performance of the larger network with our new architecture on the minimal processing datasets. The TCL-Net architecture used in the experiment is considerably smaller with only 3,529,635 trainable parameters, than Isensee's model, which has 8,294,659.

The experiment shows that compared to Isensee's, our architecture achieves faster convergence and better validation performance.

5 Conclusion

We proposed a data augmentation strategy that increases the accuracy of the segmentation and is invariant to the modality of the validation image. The SDA strategy forces the network to be independent from the input image modality and prevents it from over-fitting to any specific contrast. This validates our theory that the diversity in training input increases the neural network performance.

The image transformation algorithms in SDA can also be seen as placeholders and be easily replaced by the real world MR modalities. Our current experiment uses the validation result of LGE images to terminate the training, thus making the trained coefficients bias toward the LGE modality. A more diverse real-world multi-modality dataset is needed to improve the universality of the trained network.

The efficiency of SDA method also challenges the traditional concept of complex normalisation or equalisation of the dataset in medical image segmentation. It pushes the boundary of the convolutional neural network in term of its flexibility and adaptability toward the input quality in semantic segmentation task.

Acknowledgement. This research is a collaboration between Inria Sophia Antipolis - Méditerrané and IHU Lyric. This work is possible due to the datasets provided by MICCAI's MS-CMRSeg 2019 challenge and IHU Lyric and the NEF computational cluster provided by Inria. The author would like to thank the work of relevant engineers and scholars.

References

1. Çiçek, Ö., Abdulkadir, A., Lienkamp, S.S., Brox, T., Ronneberger, O.: 3D U-Net: learning dense volumetric segmentation from sparse annotation. In: Ourselin, S., Joskowicz, L., Sabuncu, M.R., Unal, G., Wells, W. (eds.) MICCAI 2016. LNCS, vol. 9901, pp. 424–432. Springer, Cham (2016). https://doi.org/10.1007/978-3-319-46723-8_49
2. Dice, L.R.: Measures of the amount of ecologic association between species. Ecology **26**(3), 297–302 (1945)
3. Hummel, R.: Image enhancement by histogram transformation. Comput. Graph. Image Process. **6**(2), 184–195 (2008)
4. Isensee, F., Kickingereder, P., Wick, W., Bendszus, M., Maier-Hein, K.H.: Brain tumor segmentation and radiomics survival prediction: contribution to the BRATS 2017 challenge. In: Crimi, A., Bakas, S., Kuijf, H., Menze, B., Reyes, M. (eds.) BrainLes 2017. LNCS, vol. 10670, pp. 287–297. Springer, Cham (2018). https://doi.org/10.1007/978-3-319-75238-9_25
5. Isensee, F., Petersen, J., Kohl, S.A.A., Jäger, P.F., Maier-Hein, K.H.: nnU-Net: breaking the spell on successful medical image segmentation 1, 1–8 (2019)

6. Jia, S., et al.: Automatically segmenting the left atrium from cardiac images using successive 3D U-nets and a contour loss. In: Pop, M., et al. (eds.) STACOM 2018. LNCS, vol. 11395, pp. 221–229. Springer, Cham (2019). https://doi.org/10.1007/978-3-030-12029-0_24

7. Konda, K., Memisevic, R., Krueger, D.: Zero-bias autoencoders and the benefits of co-adapting features. ICLR **2015**, 1–11 (2014)

8. Lowekamp, B.C., Chen, D.T., Ibáñez, L., Blezek, D.: The design of SimpleITK. Front. Neuroinformatics **7**, 45 (2013)

9. Maas, A.L., Hannun, A.Y., Ng, A.Y.: Rectifier nonlinearities improve neural network acoustic models. ICML **28**, 6 (2013)

10. Nyúl, L.G., Udupa, J.K., Zhang, X.: New variants of a method of MRI scale standardization. IEEE Trans. Med. Imaging **19**(2), 143–150 (2000)

11. Ronneberger, O., Fischer, P., Brox, T.: U-Net: convolutional networks for biomedical image segmentation. In: Navab, N., Hornegger, J., Wells, W.M., Frangi, A.F. (eds.) MICCAI 2015. LNCS, vol. 9351, pp. 234–241. Springer, Cham (2015). https://doi.org/10.1007/978-3-319-24574-4_28

12. Seeböck, P., et al.: Using CycleGANs for effectively reducing image variability across OCT devices and improving retinal fluid segmentation (2019)

13. Ulyanov, D., Vedaldi, A., Lempitsky, V.: Instance Normalization: The Missing Ingredient for Fast Stylization (2016)

14. Yaniv, Z., Lowekamp, B.C., Johnson, H.J., Beare, R.: Simpleitk image-analysis notebooks: a collaborative environment for education and reproducible research. J. Digit. Imaging **31**(3), 290–303 (2018)

15. Zhuang, X.: Multivariate mixture model for cardiac segmentation from multi-sequence MRI. In: Ourselin, S., Joskowicz, L., Sabuncu, M.R., Unal, G., Wells, W. (eds.) MICCAI 2016. LNCS, vol. 9901, pp. 581–588. Springer, Cham (2016). https://doi.org/10.1007/978-3-319-46723-8_67

16. Zhuang, X.: Multivariate mixture model for myocardial segmentation combining multi-source images. IEEE Trans. Pattern Anal. Mach. Intell. **41**, 2933–2946 (2018)

Unsupervised Multi-modal Style Transfer for Cardiac MR Segmentation

Chen Chen[1]([✉]), Cheng Ouyang[1]([✉]), Giacomo Tarroni[1], Jo Schlemper[1],
Huaqi Qiu[1], Wenjia Bai[2,3], and Daniel Rueckert[1]

[1] Biomedical Image Analysis Group, Imperial College London, London, UK
{chen.chen15,c.ouyang}@imperial.ac.uk
[2] Data Science Institute, Imperial College London, London, UK
[3] Department of Medicine, Imperial College London, London, UK

Abstract. In this work, we present a fully automatic method to segment cardiac structures from late-gadolinium enhanced (LGE) images without using labelled LGE data for training, but instead by transferring the anatomical knowledge and features learned on annotated balanced steady-state free precession (bSSFP) images, which are easier to acquire. Our framework mainly consists of two neural networks: a multi-modal image translation network for style transfer and a cascaded segmentation network for image segmentation. The multi-modal image translation network generates realistic and diverse synthetic LGE images conditioned on a single annotated bSSFP image, forming a synthetic LGE training set. This set is then utilized to fine-tune the segmentation network pre-trained on labelled bSSFP images, achieving the goal of unsupervised LGE image segmentation. In particular, the proposed cascaded segmentation network is able to produce accurate segmentation by taking both shape prior and image appearance into account, achieving an average Dice score of 0.92 for the left ventricle, 0.83 for the myocardium, and 0.88 for the right ventricle on the test set.

1 Introduction

Cardiac segmentation from late-gadolinium enhanced (LGE) cardiac magnetic resonance (CMR) which highlights myocardial infarcted tissue is of great clinical importance, enabling quantitative measurements useful for treatment planning and patient management. To this end, the segmentation of the myocardium is an important first step for myocardial infarction analysis.

Since manual segmentation is tedious and likely to suffer from inter-observer variability, it is of great interest to develop an accurate automated segmentation method. However, this is a challenging task due to the fact that (1) the infarcted myocardium presents an enhanced and heterogeneous intensity distribution different from the normal myocardium region and (2) the border between infarcted myocardium and blood pool appears blurry and ambiguous [1]. While

C. Chen and C. Ouyang—Equal contribution.

M. Pop et al. (Eds.): STACOM 2019, LNCS 12009, pp. 209–219, 2020.
https://doi.org/10.1007/978-3-030-39074-7_22

210   C. Chen et al.

the borders of the myocardium can be difficult to delineate on LGE images, they are clear and easy to identify on the balanced steady-state free precession (bSSFP) CMR images, which have high signal-to-noise ratio and whose contrast is less sensitive to pathology (see red arrows in Fig. 1(a)). Conventional methods [2,3] use the segmentation result from the bSSFP CMR of the same patient as prior knowledge to assist the segmentation on LGE CMR images. These methods generally require accurate registration between the bSSFP and LGE images, which can be challenging as the imaging field-of-view (FOV), image contrast and resolution between the two acquisitions can vary significantly [1,4]. Figure 1(b) visualizes the discrepancy between the intensity distributions of the two imaging modalities in the cardiac structures (specifically, left ventricle (LV), myocardium (MYO), and right ventricle (RV)).

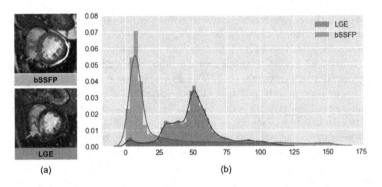

(a)   (b)

Fig. 1. The differences of image appearance (a) and intensity distributions (b) in the cardiac region (the union of LV, MYO, RV) between LGE images and bSSFP images (Color figure online)

Most recently, a deep neural network-based method has been proposed to segment the three cardiac structures directly from LGE images [5], reporting superior performance. However, this supervised segmentation method requires a large amount of labelled LGE data. Because of the heterogeneous intensity distribution of the myocardium in LGE images and the scarcity of experienced image analysts, it is difficult to perform accurate manual segmentations on LGE images and collect a large training set, compared to that on bSSFP images.

In this paper, we present a fully automatic framework that addresses the above mentioned issues by training a segmentation model without using manual annotations on LGE images. This is achieved by transferring the anatomical knowledge and features learned on annotated bSSFP images, which are easier to acquire. Our framework mainly consists of two neural networks:

– A multi-modal image translation network: this network is used for translating annotated bSSFP images into LGE images through style transfer. Of note, the network is trained in an unsupervised fashion where the training bSSFP

images and LGE images are **unpaired**. In addition, unlike common one-to-one translation networks, this network allows the generation of **multiple** synthetic LGE images conditioned on a single bSSFP image;
- A cascaded segmentation network for LGE images consisting of two U-net [6] models (Cascaded U-net): this network is first trained using the labelled bSSFP images and then fine-tuned using the synthetic LGE data generated by the image translation network.

The main contributions of our work are the following: (1) we employ a translation network that can generate **realistic** and **diverse** synthetic LGE images given a single bSSFP image. This network enables generative model-based data augmentation for unsupervised domain adaptation, which not only closes the domain gap between the two modalities, but also improves the generalization properties of the following segmentation network by increasing data variety; (2) we demonstrate that the proposed two-stage cascaded network, which takes both anatomical **shape** information and image **appearance** information into account, produces accurate segmentation on LGE images, greatly outperforming baseline methods; (3) the proposed framework can be easily extended to other unsupervised cross-modality domain adaptation applications where labels of one modality are not available.

2   Methodology

The proposed method aims at learning an LGE image segmentation model using labelled bSSFP $\{(x_b, y_b)\}$ and unlabelled LGE $\{x_l\}$ only. Specifically, the proposed method is a two-stage framework. In the first stage, an unsupervised **image translation** network is trained to translate each bSSFP image x_b into multiple instances of LGE-like images, noted as $\{x_{bl}\}$. In the second stage, these LGE-stylized bSSFP images are used together with their original labels $\{(x_{bl}, y_b)\}$ to adapt an **image segmentation** network pre-trained on labelled bSSFP images to segment LGE images.

2.1   Image Translation

We employ the state-of-the-art multi-modal unsupervised image-to-image translation network (MUNIT) [7] as our multi-modal image translator. Let $\{x_l\}$ and $\{x_b\}$ denote unpaired images from the two different imaging modalities (domains): LGE and bSSFP, given an image drawn from one domain as input, the network is able to change the appearance (i.e. image style) of the image to that of the other domain while preserving the underlying anatomical structure [8]. This is achieved by learning disentangled image representations.

As shown in Fig. 2, each image x is disentangled into (a) a domain-invariant content code c: $c = E^c(x)$ and (b) a domain-specific style code s: $s = E^s(x)$ using the content encoder E^c and the style encoder E^s relative to its domain where the content code captures the anatomical structure and the style code

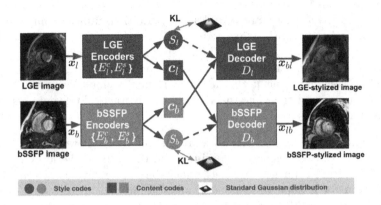

Fig. 2. Overview of the multi-modal image translation network. The network employs the structure of MUNIT [7], which consists of two encoder-decoder pairs for the two domains: bSSFP and LGE, respectively.

carries the information for rendering the structure which is determined by the imaging modality. The image-to-image translation from one domain to the other is achieved by swapping latent codes in two domains. For example, translating a bSSFP image x_b to be stylized as LGE, is achieved by feeding the content code c_b for the bSSFP image and the style code s_l into the LGE decoder D_l: $x_{bl} = D_l(c_b, s_l)$.

Of note, during training, each style encoder is trained to embed images into a latent space that matches the standard Gaussian distribution $\mathcal{N}(0, I)$, minimizing the Kullback-Leibler (KL) divergence between the two. This allows to generate an arbitrary number of synthetic LGE images given a single bSSFP image during inference, by repeatedly sampling the style code from the prior distribution $\mathcal{N}(0, I)$. Of note, although this prior distribution is unimodal, the distribution of translated images in the output space is multi-modal thanks to the nonlinearity of the decoder [7]. We apply this translation network to translate annotated bSSFP images, resulting in a synthetic labelled LGE dataset, which will then be used to finetune a segmentation network. For more details about training the translation network, readers are referred to the original work by Huang *et al.* [7].

2.2   Image Segmentation

Let x_l be an observed LGE image, the aim of the segmentation task is to estimate label maps y_l having observed x_l by modeling the posterior $p(y_l|x_l)$. Inspired by curriculum learning [9] and transfer learning, we first train a segmentation network using annotated bSSFP images (source domain; easy examples) and then fine-tune it to segment LGE images (target domain; hard examples). Since labelled LGE images $\{(x_l, y_l)\}$ are not available for finetuning, we use a synthetic dataset $\mathcal{X}_{bl} : \{(x_{bl}, y_b)\}_{1..N}$ generated by the aforementioned multi-modal image

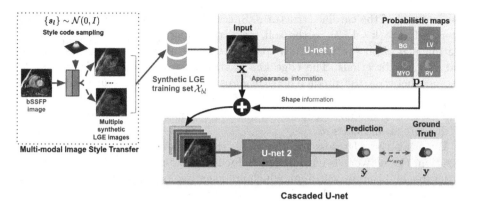

Fig. 3. Overview of the two-stage cascaded segmentation network. The architecture of each U-net is the same as the one of the vanilla U-net, except for two main differences: (1) batch normalization is applied after each convolutional layer; (2) a dropout layer (dropout rate $= 0.1$) is applied after each concatenation operation in the network's expanding path to encourage model generalizability. Of note, in this diagram, we simplify the training procedure by omitting the pre-training procedure using labelled bSSFP images.

translator. Ideally, the posterior modelled by the network $p(y_b|x_{bl})$ matches $p(y_l|x_l)$ when image space and label space are shared. For simplicity, we use x and y to denote an image and its corresponding label map from the synthetic dataset in the following paragraphs.

The segmentation network is a two-stage cascaded network which consists of two U-nets [6], see Fig. 3. Specifically, given an image x as input, the first U-net (U-net 1) aims at predicting four-class pixel-wise probabilistic maps $p_1 = f^1_{\text{U-net}}(x; \theta)$ for the three cardiac structures (i.e. LV, MYO, RV) and the background class (BG). Inspired by the auto-context architecture [10], we combine these learned probabilistic maps p_1 from the first network with the raw image x to form a 5-channel input to train the second U-net (U-net 2) for fine-grained segmentation: $p_2 = f^2_{\text{U-net}}(x, p_1; \phi)$. By combining the appearance information from the image x with the shape prior information from the initial segmentation p_1 as input, the cascaded network has the potential to produce more precise and robust segmentations even in the presence of unclear boundaries for the different cardiac structures.

To train the network, we use a **composite segmentation loss** function $\mathcal{L}_{seg}$ which consists of two loss terms: $\mathcal{L}_{seg} = \mathcal{L}_{wce} + \lambda \mathcal{L}_{edge}$. The first term $\mathcal{L}_{wce}$ is a weighted cross entropy loss: $\mathcal{L}_{wce} = -\sum_m w^m y^m \log(p^m)$ where w^m denotes the weight for class m and p^m is the corresponding predicted probability map. We set the weight for myocardium w^{MYO} to be higher than the weights for the other three classes to address class imbalance problem since there is a lower percentage of pixels that corresponds to the myocardium class in CMR images. The second term $\mathcal{L}_{edge}$ is an edge-based loss which penalizes the disagreement on the contours of the cardiac structures. Specifically, we apply two 2D 3×3 Sobel filters [11] S_k (k $= 1$, 2) to the soft prediction maps $\boldsymbol{p}$ as well as the one-hot heatmaps $\boldsymbol{y}$ of the ground truth to extract edge information along horizontal and vertical directions. The edge loss is then computed by calculating the l_2 distance between the predicted edge maps and the ground truth edge maps: $\mathcal{L}_{edge} = \sum_{m, m \neq BG} \sum_{k=1,2} \| f_{S_k}(\boldsymbol{p}^m) - f_{S_k}(\boldsymbol{y}^m) \|_2$, where $f_{S_k}(\boldsymbol{p}^m)$ is the edge map extracted by applying the sobel filter S_k to the predicted probabilistic map $\boldsymbol{p}^m$ for foreground class m.

By using the edge loss together with the weighted cross entropy for optimization, the network is encouraged to focus more on the contours of the three structures and the myocardium, which are usually more difficult to delineate. In our experiments, we set $\lambda = 0.5$ to balance the contribution of the two losses.

2.3   Post-processing

At inference time, each slice from a previously unseen LGE stack is fed to the cascaded network to get the probabilistic maps for the four classes. Dense conditional random field (CRF) [12] is then applied to refine the 2D predicted segmentation mask slice by slice. After that, 3D morphological dilation and erosion operations are applied to the whole segmentation stack to further improve the global smoothness. In particular, we perform the operations in a hierarchical order: first we apply them to the binary map covering all the three structures, then to the MYO and the LV labels, separately.

3   Experiments and Results

3.1   Data

The framework was trained and evaluated on the Multi-sequence Cardiac MR Segmentation Challenge (MS-CMRSeg 2019) dataset[1]. We used a subset of 40 bSSFP and 40 LGE images to train the image translation network. Then, we created a synthetic dataset by applying the learned translation network to 30 labelled bSSFP images. Specifically, for each bSSFP image, we randomly sampled the style code from $\mathcal{N}(0, I)$ five times, resulting in a set of 150 synthetic LGE images in total. This synthetic dataset and the original 30 bSSFP images with corresponding labels formed the training set for the segmentation network. Exemplar results of these synthetic LGE images are provided in the supplemental material. For validation, we used a subset of 5 annotated LGE images provided by the challenge organizers.

3.2   Implementation Details

Image Preprocessing. To deal with the different image size and heterogeneous pixel spacing between different imaging modalities, all images were resampled to

---

[1] https://zmiclab.github.io/mscmrseg19/.

a pixel spacing of $1.25\,\mathrm{mm} \times 1.25\,\mathrm{mm}$ and then cropped to 192×192 pixels, with the heart roughly at the center of each image. This spatial normalization would reduce the computational cost and task complexity in the following training procedure of image translation and segmentation, making the networks focus on the relevant regions. To identify the heart, we trained a localization network based on U-net using the 30 annotated bSSFP images in the training set to produce rough segmentations for the three structures. The localization network employs instance normalization layers which perform style normalization [13], encouraging the network invariance to image style changes (e.g. image contrast). As a result, the network is able to produce coarse masks localizing the heart on all bSSFP images and most LGE images even though it was trained on bSSFP images only. In case that this network might fail to locate the heart on certain LGE slices, we summed the segmentation masks across slices in each volume and then cropped them according to the center of the aggregated mask. After cropping, each image was intensity normalized.

Network Training. (1) For the image translation network, we used the official implementation[2] of [7]. Network configuration and hyper-parameters were kept the same as in [7] except the input and output images are 2D, single-channel. It was trained for 20k iterations with a batch size of 1. (2) For the segmentation network, we first trained the first U-net with the labelled bSSFP images and then fine-tuned it with synthetic LGE images. This procedure was replicated to train the second U-net with the parameters of the first U-net being fixed. Both networks were optimized using the composite loss $\mathcal{L}_{seg}$ where adam was used for stochastic gradient descent. The learning rate was initially set to 0.001 and was then decreased to 1×10^{-5} for fine-tuning. The weights for BG, LV, MYO, and RV in $\mathcal{L}_{wce}$ were empirically set to $0.2 : 0.25 : 0.3 : 0.25$. During training, we applied data augmentation on the fly. Specifically, elastic deformations, random scaling and random rotations as well as gamma augmentation [14] were used. The algorithm was implemented using python and PyTorch and was trained for 1000 epochs in total on an NVIDIA Tesla P40 GPU.

3.3 Results

To evaluate the accuracy of segmentation results, the Dice metric and the average surface distance (ASD) between the automatic segmentation and the corresponding manual segmentation for each volume were calculated.

We compare the proposed method with two baseline methods: (1) a registration-based method and (2) a single U-net. Specifically, for the registration-based method, each LGE segmentation result was obtained by directly registering the corresponding bSSFP labels to the LGE image using MIRTK toolkit[3] for ease of comparison. The transformation matrix was learned by applying mutual information-based registration (Rigid+Affine+FFD)

---

[2] https://github.com/NVlabs/MUNIT.
[3] https://mirtk.github.io/.

between the two images. For U-net, we trained it with two settings: (a) **U-net**: trained on labelled bSSFP images only; (b) **U-net with fine-tuning (FT)**: trained on labelled bSSFP images and then fine-tuned using the synthetic LGE data, which is the same training procedure of the proposed method. Quantitative and qualitative results are shown in Table 1 and Fig. 4.

While the registration-based method (MIRTK) outperforms the U-net (see row 1 and row 2 in Table 1), it still fails to produce accurate segmentation on the myocardium (see the italic number in row 1), indicating the limitation of this registration-based method. However, by contrast, neural network-based methods (row 3–5) fine-tuned using the *synthetic LGE dataset* significantly improves the segmentation accuracy, increasing the Dice score for MYO by ∼15%. This improvement demonstrates the learned translation network is capable of generating realistic LGE images while preserving the domain-invariant structural information that is informative to optimize the segmentation network. In particular, compared to U-net (FT), the proposed **Cascaded U-net** (FT) achieves more accurate segmentation performance with improvement in terms of both Dice and ASD (see bold numbers). The model even produces robust segmentation results on the challenging apical and basal slices (please see the last column in Fig. 4). This demonstrates the benefit of integrating the high-level shape knowledge and low-level image appearance to guide the segmentation procedure. In addition, the proposed post-processing further refines the segmentation results through smoothing, reducing the average ASD from 1.37 to 1.26 (see the last row in Table 1).

Table 1. Dice scores and ASD (mm) of the proposed segmentation method (Cascaded U-net) and baseline methods on the validation set. Bold numbers indicate the best scores among the results obtained by those methods before post-processing (PP) whereas italic numbers are those mean Dice scores under 0.700. FT: fine-tuning using the synthetic LGE dataset. N/A means that the ASD value cannot be calculated due to missing predictions for that cardiac structure.

Method	Dice				ASD			
	LV	MYO	RV	AVG[a]	LV	MYO	RV	AVG[a]
MIRTK	0.819	*0.665*	0.831	0.772	2.56	1.65	2.11	2.11
U-net	*0.624*	*0.441*	*0.577*	*0.547*	10.03	6.07	N/A	N/A
U-net (FT)	0.874	0.781	0.896	0.850	1.78	1.50	1.28	1.52
Cascaded U-net (FT)	**0.895**	**0.812**	**0.898**	**0.868**	**1.41**	1.46	**1.23**	**1.37**
Cascaded U-net (FT) + PP	0.897	0.816	0.895	0.869	1.17	1.42	1.18	1.26

[a]For ease of comparison, we calculate the average (AVG) Dice score and the average ASD score over the three structures for each method.

Finally, we applied ensemble learning to improve our model's performance in the test phase. Specifically, we trained the proposed segmentation network for multiple times, each time regenerating a new synthetic LGE dataset for fine-tuning. We trained four models in total. Our final submission result for each test image was obtained by averaging the probabilistic maps from these models

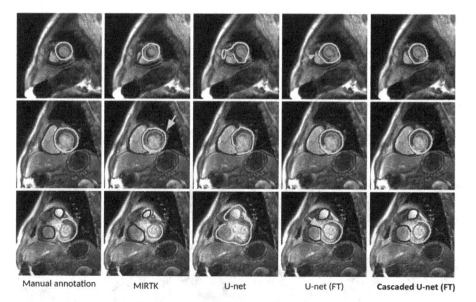

Manual annotation   MIRTK   U-net   U-net (FT)   Cascaded U-net (FT)

Fig. 4. Segmentation results for the proposed Cascaded U-net and the baseline approaches. Our proposed method (the right-most column) produces more anatomically plausible segmentation results on the images, greatly outperforming the baseline methods, especially in the challenging cases: the apical (the top row) and the basal slices (the bottom row).

and then assigning to each pixel the class with the highest score. In the testing stage of the competition, the method achieves very promising segmentation performance on a relative large test set (40 subjects), with an average Dice score of 0.92 for LV, 0.83 for MYO, and 0.88 for RV; an ASD of 1.66 for LV, 1.76 for MYO, and 2.16 for RV.

4   Conclusion

In this paper, we showed that synthesizing multi-modal LGE images from labelled bSSFP images to finetune a pre-trained segmentation network shows impressive segmentation performance on LGE images even though the network has not seen *real* labelled LGE images before. We also demonstrated that the proposed segmentation network (Cascaded U-net) outperformed the baseline methods by a significant margin, suggesting the benefit of integrating the high-level shape knowledge and low-level image appearance to guide the segmentation procedure. More importantly, our cascaded segmentation network is independent of the particular architecture of underlying convolutional neural networks. In other words, the basic neural network (U-net) in our work can be replaced with any of the state-of-the-art segmentation network to potentially improve the prediction accuracy and robustness. Moreover, the proposed solution based on unsupervised multi-modal style transfer is not only limited to the cardiac image segmentation but can be extended to other multi-modal image analysis tasks where the manual annotations of one modality are not available. Future work will focus on the application of the method to the problems such as domain adaptation for multi-modality brain segmentation.

Supplemental Material

See Fig. 5.

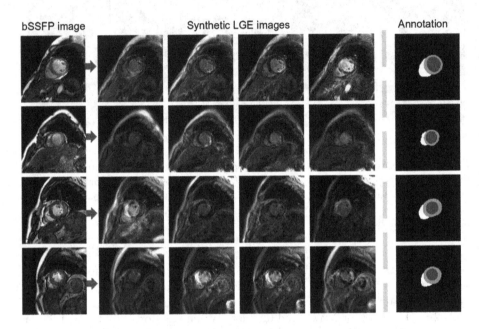

Fig. 5. Exemplar synthetic LGE images generated from bSSFP images using the multi-modal image translation network. Given **one** bSSFP image (column 1), the translation network translates the image into **multi-modal** LGE-like images (column 2 to 4). These translated images differ in image brightness and contrast as well as the intensity distribution in the cardiac region, while preserving the same cardiac anatomy. These synthetic images, in together with the annotations on the original bSSFP images (the last column) contribute to the synthetic dataset which is used to fine-tune the proposed segmentation network.

References

1. Zhuang, X.: Multivariate mixture model for cardiac segmentation from multi-sequence MRI. In: Ourselin, S., Joskowicz, L., Sabuncu, M.R., Unal, G., Wells, W. (eds.) MICCAI 2016. LNCS, vol. 9901, pp. 581–588. Springer, Cham (2016). https://doi.org/10.1007/978-3-319-46723-8_67

2. YingLi, L., et al.: Automatic myocardium segmentation of LGE MRI by deformable models with prior shape data. JCMR **15**(1), P14 (2013)
3. Tao, Q., et al.: Automated left ventricle segmentation in late gadolinium-enhanced MRI for objective myocardial scar assessment. JMRI **42**(2), 390–399 (2015)
4. Zhuang, X.: Multivariate mixture model for myocardium segmentation combining multi-source images. PAMI **41**(12), 2933–2946 (2018). https://ieeexplore.ieee.org/document/8458220
5. Yue, Q., Luo, X., Ye, Q., Xu, L., Zhuang, X.: Cardiac segmentation from LGE MRI using deep neural network incorporating shape and spatial priors. In: Shen, D., et al. (eds.) MICCAI 2019. LNCS, vol. 11765, pp. 559–567. Springer, Cham (2019). https://doi.org/10.1007/978-3-030-32245-8_62
6. Ronneberger, O., Fischer, P., Brox, T.: U-Net: convolutional networks for biomedical image segmentation. In: Navab, N., Hornegger, J., Wells, W.M., Frangi, A.F. (eds.) MICCAI 2015. LNCS, vol. 9351, pp. 234–241. Springer, Cham (2015). https://doi.org/10.1007/978-3-319-24574-4_28
7. Huang, X., Liu, M.-Y., Belongie, S., Kautz, J.: Multimodal unsupervised image-to-image translation. In: Ferrari, V., Hebert, M., Sminchisescu, C., Weiss, Y. (eds.) ECCV 2018. LNCS, vol. 11207, pp. 179–196. Springer, Cham (2018). https://doi.org/10.1007/978-3-030-01219-9_11
8. Qin, C., Shi, B., Liao, R., Mansi, T., Rueckert, D., Kamen, A.: Unsupervised deformable registration for multi-modal images via disentangled representations. In: Chung, A.C.S., Gee, J.C., Yushkevich, P.A., Bao, S. (eds.) IPMI 2019. LNCS, vol. 11492, pp. 249–261. Springer, Cham (2019). https://doi.org/10.1007/978-3-030-20351-1_19
9. Bengio, Y., Louradour, J., Collobert, R., Weston, J.: Curriculum learning. In: Proceedings of the 26th Annual International Conference on Machine Learning, ICML 09, New York, NY, USA, pp. 41–48. ACM (2009)
10. Tu, Z., Bai, X.: Auto-context and its application to high-level vision tasks and 3D brain image segmentation. PAMI **32**, 1744–1757 (2010)
11. Sobel, I., Feldman, G.: A 3x3 isotropic gradient operator for image processing. Pattern Classif. Scene Anal. 271–272, January 1973. https://www.scirp.org/(S(351jmbntvnsjt1aadkozje))/reference/ReferencesPapers.aspx?ReferenceID=83629
12. Krähenbühl, P., et al.: Efficient inference in fully connected CRFs with Gaussian edge potentials. In: NeuralIPS (2011)
13. Huang, X, et al.: Arbitrary style transfer in real-time with adaptive instance normalization. In: ICCV (2017)
14. Chen, C., Bai, W., Rueckert, D.: Multi-task Learning for left atrial segmentation on GE-MRI. In: Pop, M., et al. (eds.) STACOM 2018. LNCS, vol. 11395, pp. 292–301. Springer, Cham (2019). https://doi.org/10.1007/978-3-030-12029-0_32

An Automatic Cardiac Segmentation Framework Based on Multi-sequence MR Image

Yashu Liu, Wei Wang, Kuanquan Wang$^{(\boxtimes)}$, Chengqin Ye,
and Gongning Luo

Harbin Institute of Technology, Harbin 150001, China
wangkq@hit.edu.cn

Abstract. LGE CMR is an efficient technology for detecting infarcted myocardium. An efficient and objective ventricle segmentation method in LGE can benefit the location of the infarcted myocardium. In this paper, we proposed an automatic framework for LGE image segmentation. There are just 5 labeled LGE volumes with about 15 slices of each volume. We adopted histogram match, an invariant of rotation registration method, on the other labeled modalities to achieve effective augmentation of the training data. A CNN segmentation model was trained based on the augmented training data by leave-one-out strategy. The predicted result of the model followed a connected component analysis for each class to remain the largest connected component as the final segmentation result. Our model was evaluated by the 2019 Multi-sequence Cardiac MR Segmentation Challenge. The mean testing result of 40 testing volumes on Dice score, Jaccard score, Surface distance, and Hausdorff distance is 0.8087, 0.6976, 2.8727 mm, and 15.6387 mm, respectively. The experiment result shows a satisfying performance of the proposed framework. Code is available at https://github.com/Suiiyu/MS-CMR2019.

Keywords: Ventricle segmentation · Histogram match · LGE-CMR · Data augmentation

1 Introduction

Cardiac MRI is a significant technology for cardiac function analysis. Benefiting from this technology, the doctor can evaluate the heart function noninvasively. There are many kinds of Cardiac MRI modalities, such as balanced-Steady State Free Precession (b-SFFP) and LGE. b-SSFP can learn the cardiac motions and obtain a clear boundary of cardiac. LGE CMR can enhance the infarcted myocardium, appearing with distinctive brightness compared with the healthy tissues. LGE CMR is widely used to study the presence, location, and extent of myocardium infarction (MI) in clinical studies [1, 2]. Exactly extracting the ventricles and myocardium from LGE is crucial for MI therapy. However, the infarcted myocardium is enhanced, meanwhile, the healthy myocardium is suppressed. Hence, the boundaries of the ventricles and myocardium are bedimmed on the LGE CMR.

© Springer Nature Switzerland AG 2020
M. Pop et al. (Eds.): STACOM 2019, LNCS 12009, pp. 220–227, 2020.
https://doi.org/10.1007/978-3-030-39074-7_23

In the clinical application, ventricle segmentation on LGE CMR image still relies on manual segmentation. However, manual segmentation is tedious and subjective. The automatic segmentation method is more efficient and objective. Kurzendorfer et al. [3] proposed an automatic framework to segment left ventricle (LV). They firstly initialized the LV by a two-step registration method and then adopted principal components to estimate the LV. At last, the myocardium was refined on the poly space. Oktay et al. [4] incorporated global shape information into CNN. They utilized auto-encoder to estimate the global shape information of LV and then it was adopted to constrain the segmentation model. Duan et al. [5] proposed a combined CNN and level set model to segment ventricles. The probability maps of ventricles and myocardium are estimated by CNN. Then they initialized the energy function of the level set by the probability maps. Khened et al. [6] adopted a densely connected CNN model with inception block to segment 2D cardiac MRI. There are also other researchers interesting on the ventricles, myocardium and other tissues MR segmentation [7–13]. Their methods are mostly based on CNN. Besides, these methods rely on a large number of training data. However, in our situation, there are just 5 labeled and 40 unlabeled LGE CMR with about 15 slices of each volume. The rare data cannot guarantee training an efficient cardiac segmentation model from scratch. Although the registration method, such as atlas, is often utilized on the rare data segmentation, it has some shortages. In order to obtain the label for the unlabeled data, the atlas set must be labeled data. Moreover, it will deform the original data and decreases the data diversity. Hence, we utilize histogram match technology to achieve effective augmentation based on b-SSFP modality CMR data, which has 35 labeled volumes, to solve the lack of data problem. Histogram matching [14] technology is efficient and does not deform the shape of the original data. Hence, we can adopt other modalities data while the data diversity is maintained. Then, we adopt this augmented dataset to train a cardiac segmentation model. At last, we utilize a label-vote strategy and connected component analysis to get the final segmentation.

The rest of this manuscript is organized as follows: we introduce our method in Sect. 2. Results are analyzed in Sect. 3. Finally, we conclude this manuscript in Sect. 4.

2 Method

The whole structure of the proposed framework is shown in Fig. 1. There are three steps. Firstly, we pre-process the volumes into images and then we map the b-SSFP images on the LGE images to generate fake LGE images. Secondly, the fake images are fed into the Res-UNet [15, 16] model. Our model is trained based on the leave-one-out strategy. The final prediction is determined by all models. Thirdly, the predicted results are reconstructed to the original shape and a connected component analysis is adopted to keep the maximum component for each class as the final segmentation result.

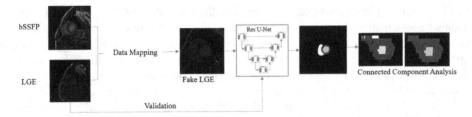

Fig. 1. The proposed framework for ventricles and myocardium segmentation on LGE CMR image. The white, light gray and dark gray correspond to represent right ventricle, left ventricle and left ventricle myocardium.

2.1 Data Processing

The dataset is coming from the 2019 Multi-sequence Cardiac MR Segmentation Challenge (MS-CMR2019)[1]. It published 45 patients CMR data with three modalities, T2, b-SSFP, and LGE. There are 35 labeled T2 CMR data with about 3 slices of each patient, and 35 labeled b-SSFP CMR data with about 11 slices of each patient, and just 5 labeled LGE CMR data with about 15 slices of each patient. The rest volumes are unlabeled data. The main purpose of this challenge is segmenting left ventricle (LV), right ventricle (RV) and left ventricle myocardium (LVM) from LGE CMR data. The rarely labeled target data increases the challenge sharply. To enlarge the number of labeled LGE CMR data, we utilize histogram match on the other labeled modalities.

According to the data analysis, the b-SSFP data has the similarity slices with LGE data of each patient and it has a clearer boundary than T2 modality data. Considering the data-matching problem and data quality, we just utilize b-SFFP data to assist the cardiac segmentation on LGE data. We find that the main difference between LGE image and b-SSFP image is the appearance. The shape of the heart among the same patient is similar. Hence, we utilize histogram match to generate the fake LGE data. Histogram match is an easy and efficient data pre-process for this challenge. It matches the histogram of the source image to the target histogram by establishing the relationship between the source image and the target image. Moreover, the shape of the source image is still maintained. That is mean that the label of fake LGE CMR images is still consistent with the original b-SSFP CMR images.

In order to retain the data diversity, each b-SSFP image has its own target LGE image histogram. Because of the original b-SSFP data and LGE data have different data scope. The scope of the short axis of LGE data is about twice larger than b-SSFP's. Hence, we resize the LGE data into the shape of b-SSFP data. Then, we obtain 2D images of the short axis from the resized data. So far, we have got the consistent image size and number of b-SSFP and LGE. The target histogram for each b-SSFP image is calculating from the corresponding LGE image. Figure 2 presents an example of a resized LGE image, b-SSFP image, and fake LGE image. a, b are corresponding to the short axis of LGE and b-SSFP; d, e are corresponding to the long axis of LGE and b-

---

[1] https://zmiclab.github.io/mscmrseg19/.

SSFP; c, f are the short axis and long axis of fake LGE which are generating from real LGE and b-SSFP. Image c and f owns the shape information of b-SSFP image and the appearance information of LGE image.

Our model is trained on 2D images, which are extracting from fake LGE data and real original labeled LGE data. In order to keep the same input to the model, we resize all images into (256, 256). After data analysis, we center crop the resized images into (144, 144) to filter the unrelated background. The output of the model will do the inverse operation to keep the data consistency. Moreover, the evaluation is performed on the 3D volumes.

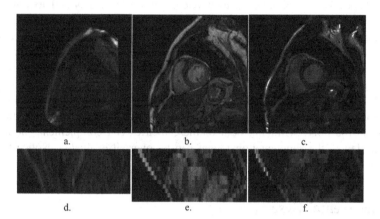

Fig. 2. The example of LGE, b-SSFP, and fake LGE. a–c: Corresponding to the short axis LGE, b-SSFP, and fake LGE generating from a and b; d–f: Corresponding to the long axis LGE, b-SSFP, and fake LGE.

2.2 Implementation

The segmentation model is a Res-UNet, which utilizes residual connection on the convolutional block. Each convolutional block contains two 3*3 convolutional layers with ReLU activation function and batch normalization. We adopt 4 down-sampling blocks as the encoder and corresponding up-sampling blocks as the decoder. The last block utilizes a dropout layer with 0.5 drop rate to overcome the over-fitting problem. The output layer is a 1*1 convolutional layer with a Softmax activate function. The model is implemented using Keras based on NVIDIA 2080 Ti GPU.

In order to maximize the data utilization, we divide the 5 labeled LGE volumes into 5 groups by the leave-one-out strategy. At last, we have trained 5 models, and the training data of each model consists of 35 fake LGE volumes and 4 real LGE volumes. The rest one real LGE volume is utilized to evaluate the model. The final prediction is determined by the average of these models. Each model has trained 300 epochs with 0.001 learning rate and 8 batch size. The training time is about 1 h for each model. Moreover, we utilize a weighted cross entropy loss function to solve the class imbalance problem. The loss function is shown in Eq. 1:

$$wCE = -\sum_{c=0}^{4} w_c (\sum_{i=1}^{N} g_{c_i} \log p_{c_i}),$$

$$w_c = \frac{\sum g_c}{\sum g}$$

(1)

where c is the class index; i is the pixel index; g_{c_i} and p_{c_i} represent the ground truth class and prediction class of pixel i. The weight w_c is calculated by the ratio of each class in the all labeled set. And g is the all labeled pixels set.

After training the segmentation model, we reconstruct the prediction results in the original shape. Then, a connected component analysis is performed to remain the largest connected region for each class as the final segmentation result. Our segmentation model is evaluated by the official evaluation metrics, which are Dice score, Jaccard score, Surface distance, and Hausdorff distance. Dice score and Jaccard score are overlapped metrics. They evaluate the overlap ratio between the ground truth and predicted result. However, they have a shortage on the boundary details of the subject. Although similarity metrics, Surface distance and Hausdorff distance, are mainly focused on the similarity between the ground truth and predicted result, they are sensitive on the noisy. Utilizing both of these metrics can complement one another perfectly. Hence, the segmentation model can be over-all evaluated. Notice that the Dice score is the main metric.

3   Experimental Results

The score of metrics during the validation stage is shown in Table 1. These scores are the mean value of the three classes, which are calculated by average operation without weighted. The segmentation model has a satisfying performance on the overlap metrics. Due to the model is trained on the short axis, the performance on the similarity metrics are worse than overlap metrics. Figure 3 represents the segmentation results and corresponding ground truths of patient 1 and patient 2. The green and red contours represent ground truth and segmentation result, respectively. We select three representative slices to show the result. The result shows that our prediction contours can perfectly fit the ground truth.

Table 1. Segmentation results of the validation stage. SD and HD correspond to the abbreviation of Surface distance and Hausdorff distance.

Patient	Dice score	Jaccard score	SD (mm)	HD (mm)
#1	0.9289	0.8685	0.3873	6.6570
#2	0.9461	0.8997	0.3012	14.2289
#3	0.9277	0.8665	0.3761	5.8568
#4	0.9416	0.8899	0.2801	4.8050
#5	0.9128	0.8439	0.4608	5.7329
Mean	0.9315	0.8737	0.3611	7.4561

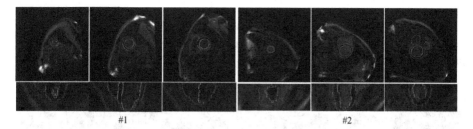

Fig. 3. Segmentation result and ground truth of patient 1 and patient 2. The first row is the short axis view; the second row is the long axis view. Color representation: green-ground truth; red-segmentation result. (Color figure online)

Figure 4 exhibits the metrics of 40 patients during the testing stage. The testing segmentation result is evaluated by the organizer. The patient IDs are anonymous, but their orders are consistent across the four metrics. We obtain a satisfying result on the testing set except for three worse results, 5th, 19th, and 39th. From these sub-pictures, we can find that the LV cavity has the regular shape and largest area in the three classes. It gets the highest scores across all metrics. On the opposite, the model performs worse on the irregular RV.

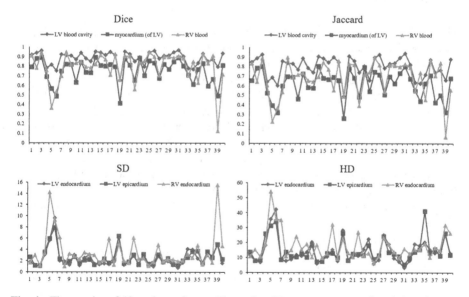

Fig. 4. The metrics of 40 testing volumes. The patient IDs are anonymous, but their orders are consistent across the four metrics. SD and HD correspond to the abbreviation of Surface distance and Hausdorff distance.

Figure 5 exhibits the segmentation results of patient 6 and patient 24, which are randomly chosen from the testing dataset. The green, red and yellow contours represent LVM, RV and LV, respectively. The three columns of each patient are from three different slices in order to demonstrate a comprehensive result of the proposed model. The model obtains a perfect performance on the short axis, especially the LV. However, there still some shortages on the long axis view due to our segmentation model is processed on the short axis.

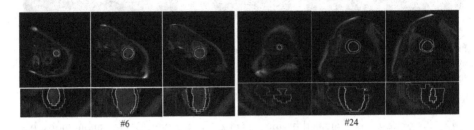

Fig. 5. Segmentation result of patient 6 and patient 24. The first row is the short axis view; the second row is the long axis view. The three columns of each patient are from three different slices according to the long axis. Color representation: green-left ventricle myocardium; yellow-left ventricle; red-right ventricle. (Color figure online)

4   Conclusion

LGE CMR is an efficient technology to identify infarcted myocardium. In this paper, we proposed an automatic framework for LGE CMR segmentation. This framework contains three steps. Firstly, we adopted a histogram match process on the b-SSFP images to generate fake LGE images. Secondly, we divided the labeled LGE images into 5 groups through the leave-one-out strategy. Our segmentation model, Res-UNet, was trained based on the fake LGE images and labeled LGE images. Thirdly, the final prediction of the model was reconstructed and a connected component analysis process was done on these data to keep the maximum connected component for each class as the final segmentation. The final segmentation is evaluated by the organizer, and the mean metrics score of Dice score, Jaccard score, Surface distance, and Hausdorff distance are corresponding to 0.8087, 0.6976, 2.8727 mm, and 15.6387 mm. There are three worse volumes out of 40 testing volumes. The performance on the most volumes are satisfied.

Acknowledgment. This work was supported by the National Key R&D Program of China under Grant 2017YFC0113000.

References

1. Kim, R., et al.: Relationship of MRI delayed contrast enhancement to irreversible injury, infarct age, and contractile function. Circulation **100**(19), 1992–2002 (1999)
2. Dastidar, A., et al.: Coronary artery disease imaging: what is the role of magnetic resonance imaging. Dialogues Cardiovasc. Med. **21**, 267–276 (2016)

3. Kurzendorfer, T., et al.: Fully automatic segmentation of left ventricular anatomy in 3-D LGE-MRI. Comput. Med. Imaging Graph. **59**, 13–27 (2017)
4. Oktay, O., et al.: Anatomically constrained neural networks (ACNNs): application to cardiac image enhancement and segmentation. IEEE Trans. Med. Imaging **37**(2), 384–395 (2017)
5. Duan, J., et al.: Deep nested level sets: fully automated segmentation of cardiac MR images in patients with pulmonary hypertension. In: Frangi, A.F., Schnabel, J.A., Davatzikos, C., Alberola-López, C., Fichtinger, G. (eds.) MICCAI 2018. LNCS, vol. 11073, pp. 595–603. Springer, Cham (2018). https://doi.org/10.1007/978-3-030-00937-3_68
6. Khened, M., Alex, V., Krishnamurthi, G.: Densely connected fully convolutional network for short-axis cardiac cine MR image segmentation and heart diagnosis using random forest. In: Pop, M., et al. (eds.) STACOM 2017. LNCS, vol. 10663, pp. 140–151. Springer, Cham (2018). https://doi.org/10.1007/978-3-319-75541-0_15
7. Duan, J., et al.: Automatic 3D bi-ventricular segmentation of cardiac images by a shape-constrained multi-task deep learning approach. arXiv preprint. arXiv:1808.08578 (2018)
8. Zhuang, X.: Multivariate mixture model for cardiac segmentation from multi-sequence MRI. In: Ourselin, S., Joskowicz, L., Sabuncu, M.R., Unal, G., Wells, W. (eds.) MICCAI 2016. LNCS, vol. 9901, pp. 581–588. Springer, Cham (2016). https://doi.org/10.1007/978-3-319-46723-8_67
9. Zhuang, X.: Multivariate mixture model for myocardial segmentation combining multi-source images. IEEE Trans. Pattern Anal. Mach. Intell. (TPAMI) **41**, 2933–2946 (2018). https://doi.org/10.1109/tpami.2018.2869576
10. Ma, C., et al.: Concatenated and connected random forests with multiscale patch driven active contour model for automated brain tumor segmentation of MR images. IEEE Trans. Med. Imaging **37**(8), 1943–1954 (2018)
11. Kayalibay, B., et al.: CNN-based segmentation of medical imaging data. arXiv:1701.03056 (2017)
12. Dong, S., et al.: VoxelAtlasGAN: 3D left ventricle segmentation on echocardiography with atlas guided generation and voxel-to-voxel discrimination. In: Frangi, A.F., Schnabel, J.A., Davatzikos, C., Alberola-López, C., Fichtinger, G. (eds.) MICCAI 2018. LNCS, vol. 11073, pp. 622–629. Springer, Cham (2018). https://doi.org/10.1007/978-3-030-00937-3_71
13. Luo, G., et al.: Multi-views fusion CNN for left ventricular volumes estimation on cardiac MR images. IEEE Trans. Biomed. Eng. **65**(9), 1924–1934 (2017)
14. Wang, L., et al.: Correction for variations in MRI scanner sensitivity in brain studies with histogram matching. Magn. Reson. Med. **39**, 322–327 (1998)
15. He, K., et al.: Deep residual learning for image recognition. In: Proceedings of the IEEE Conference on Computer Vision and Pattern Recognition (CVPR), pp. 770–778 (2016)
16. Ronneberger, O., Fischer, P., Brox, T.: U-Net: convolutional networks for biomedical image segmentation. In: Navab, N., Hornegger, J., Wells, W.M., Frangi, A.F. (eds.) MICCAI 2015. LNCS, vol. 9351, pp. 234–241. Springer, Cham (2015). https://doi.org/10.1007/978-3-319-24574-4_28

Cardiac Segmentation of LGE MRI with Noisy Labels

Holger Roth[(✉)], Wentao Zhu, Dong Yang, Ziyue Xu, and Daguang Xu

NVIDIA, Bethesda, USA
{hroth,wentaoz,dongy,ziyuex,daguangx}@nvidia.com

Abstract. In this work, we attempt the segmentation of cardiac structures in late gadolinium-enhanced (LGE) magnetic resonance images (MRI) using only minimal supervision in a two-step approach. In the first step, we register a small set of five LGE cardiac magnetic resonance (CMR) images with ground truth labels to a set of 40 target LGE CMR images without annotation. Each manually annotated ground truth provides labels of the myocardium and the left ventricle (LV) and right ventricle (RV) cavities, which are used as atlases. After multi-atlas label fusion by majority voting, we possess noisy labels for each of the targeted LGE images. A second set of manual labels exists for 30 patients of the target LGE CMR images, but are annotated on different MRI sequences (bSSFP and T2-weighted). Again, we use multi-atlas label fusion with a consistency constraint to further refine our noisy labels if additional annotations in other modalities are available for a given patient. In the second step, we train a deep convolutional network for semantic segmentation on the target data while using data augmentation techniques to avoid over-fitting to the noisy labels. After inference and simple post-processing, we achieve our final segmentation for the targeted LGE CMR images, resulting in an average Dice of 0.890, 0.780, and 0.844 for LV cavity, LV myocardium, and RV cavity, respectively.

Keywords: LGE MRI · CMR · Cardiac segmentation · Deep learning · Multi-atlas label fusion · Noisy labels

1 Introduction

Segmentation of cardiac structures in magnetic resonance images (MRI) has potential uses for many clinical applications. In particular for cardiac magnetic resonance (CMR) images, late gadolinium-enhanced (LGE) imaging is useful to visualize and detect myocardial infarction (MI). Another common CMR sequence is T2-weighted imaging which highlights acute injury and ischemic regions. Additionally, balanced-steady state free precession (bSSFP) cine sequences can be utilized to analyze the cardiac motion of the heart [1,2]. Each CMR sequence is typically acquired independently, and they can exhibit significant spatial deformations among each other even when stemming from the

© Springer Nature Switzerland AG 2020
M. Pop et al. (Eds.): STACOM 2019, LNCS 12009, pp. 228–236, 2020.
https://doi.org/10.1007/978-3-030-39074-7_24

same patient. Nevertheless, segmentation of different anatomies from LGE could still benefit from the combination with the other two sequences (T2 and bSSFP) and their annotations. An example of different CMR sequences utilized in this work can be seen in Fig. 1. LGE enhances infarcted tissues in the myocardium and therefore is an important sequence to focus on for the detection and quantification of myocardial infarction. The infarcted myocardium tissue appears with a distinctively brighter intensity than the surrounding healthy regions. In particular, LGE images are important to estimate the extent of the infarct in comparison to the myocardium [1]. However, manual delineation of the myocardium is time-consuming and error-prone. Therefore, automated and robust methods for providing a segmentation of the cardiac anatomy around the left ventricle (LV) are needed to support the analysis of myocardial infarction. Modern semantic segmentation methods utilizing deep learning have significantly improved the performance in various medical imaging applications [3–6]. At the same time, deep learning methods typically require large amounts of annotated data in order to train sufficiently robust and accurate models depending on the difficulty of the task. However, in many use cases, the availability of such annotated cases may be limited for a specific targeted image modality or sequence. For CMR applications containing multiple sequences, annotations for the same anatomy of interest might be available for sequences other than the target one of the same patient. In this work, we attempt the segmentation of cardiac structures in LGE cardiac magnetic resonance (CMR) images utilizing classical methods from multi-atlas label fusion in order to provide "noisy" pseudo labels to be used for training deep convolutional neural network segmentation models.

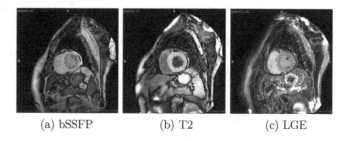

(a) bSSFP   (b) T2   (c) LGE

Fig. 1. Sagittal view of different cardiac magnetic resonance (CMR) image sequences of the same patient's heart. Images (a–c) show balanced-steady state free precession (bSSFP), T2-weighted, and late gadolinium-enhanced (LGE) images with overlays of the corresponding manual ground truth (g.t.) annotations [patient 2 of the challenge dataset].

2   Method

Our method can be described in two steps. In the first step, we register a small set, e.g. 5, LGE CMR with ground truth labels ("atlases") to a set of target LGE

CMR images without annotation. Each ground truth atlas provides manually annotated labels of the myocardium, and the left and right ventricle cavities. After multi-atlas label fusion by majority voting, we possess noisy labels for each of the targeted LGE images. A second set of manual labels exists for some of the patients of the targeted LGE CMR images, but are annotated on different MRI sequences (bSSFP and T2-weighted). Again, we use multi-atlas label fusion with a consistency constraint to further refine our noisy labels if additional annotations in other sequences are available for that patient. In the second step, we train a deep convolutional network for semantic segmentation on the target data while using data augmentation techniques to avoid over-fitting to the noisy labels. After inference and simple post-processing, we arrive at our final label for the targeted LGE CMR images.

2.1   Multi-atlas Label Fusion of CMR

Many methods of multi-atlas label fusion exist [7]. In this work, we use a well-established non-rigid registration framework based on a B-spline deformation model [8] using the implementation provided by [9]. The registration is driven by a similarity measurement S based on intensities from LGE, T2, and bSSFP images. We perform two sets of registrations

1. Inter-patient and intra-modality registration, i.e. the registration of LGE with annotations to the targeted LGE images of different patients.
2. Intra-patient and inter-modality registration, i.e. the registration of bSSFP/T2 with annotations to the targeted LGE images of the same patient.

In both cases, an initial affine registration is performed followed by non-rigid registration between the source image F (providing annotation, i.e. the "atlas") and the targeted reference image R. A coarse-to-fine registration scheme is used in order to first capture large deformations between the images, followed by more detailed refinements. The deformation is modeled with a 3D cubic B-spline model using a lattice of control points $\{\phi\}$ and spacings between the control points of δ_x, δ_y, and δ_z along the x-, y-, and z-axis of the image, respectively. Hence, the deformation $\mathbf{T}(x)$ of a voxel $x = (x, y, z)$ to the domain Ω of the target image can be formulated as

$$\mathbf{T}(x) = \sum_{i,j,k} \beta^3(\frac{x}{\delta_x} - i) \times \beta^3(\frac{y}{\delta_y} - j) \times \beta^3(\frac{y}{\delta_z} - k) \times \phi_{ijk}. \tag{1}$$

Here, β^3 represents the cubic B-Spline function. By maximizing an overall objective function

$$\mathcal{O}\left(I_\mathrm{p}, I_\mathrm{s}\left(\mathbf{T}\right); \{\phi\}\right) = (1 - \alpha - \beta) \times \mathcal{S} - \alpha \times \mathcal{C}_\mathrm{smooth}(\mathbf{T}) - \beta \times \mathcal{C}_\mathrm{inconsistency}(\mathbf{T}), \tag{2}$$

we can find the optimal deformation field between source and targeted images. Here, the similarity measure $\mathcal{S}$ is constrained by two penalties $\mathcal{C}_\mathrm{smooth}$ and $\mathcal{C}_\mathrm{inconsistency}$ which aim to enforce physically plausible deformations. The contribution of each penalty term can be controlled with the weights α and β, respectively. We use normalized mutual information (NMI) [10] which is commonly used in inter-modality registrations [7] as our driving similarity measure

$$S = \frac{H(R) + H(F(\mathbf{T}))}{H(R, F(\mathbf{T}))}. \tag{3}$$

Here, $H(R)$ and $H(F(\mathbf{T}))$ are the two marginal entropies, and $H(R, F(\mathbf{T}))$ is the joint entropy. In [9], a Parzen Window (PW) approach [11] is utilized to fill the joint histogram necessary in order to compute the NMI between the images efficiently. To encourage realistic deformations, we utilize bending energy which controls the "smoothness" of the deformation field across the image domain Ω:

$$C_{smooth} = \frac{1}{N} \sum_{x \in \Omega} \left(\left| \frac{\partial^2 \mathbf{T}(x)}{\partial x^2} \right|^2 + \left| \frac{\partial^2 \mathbf{T}(x)}{\partial y^2} \right|^2 + \left| \frac{\partial^2 \mathbf{T}(x)}{\partial z^2} \right|^2 \right. \tag{4}$$

$$\left. + 2 \times \left[\left| \frac{\partial^2 \mathbf{T}(x)}{\partial xy} \right|^2 + \left| \frac{\partial^2 \mathbf{T}(x)}{\partial yz} \right|^2 + \left| \frac{\partial^2 \mathbf{T}(x)}{\partial xz} \right|^2 \right] \right).$$

In an ideal registration, the optimized transformations from F to R (forward) and R to F (backward) are the inverse of each other. i.e. $\mathbf{T}_{forward} = \mathbf{T}_{backward}^{-1}$ and $\mathbf{T}_{backward} = \mathbf{T}_{forward}^{-1}$ [12]. The used implementation by [13] follows the approach by [12] using compositions of $\mathbf{T}_{forward}$ and $\mathbf{T}_{backward}$ in order to include a penalty term that encourages inverse consistency of both transformations:

$$C_{inconsistency} = \sum_{x \in \Omega} \| \mathbf{T}_{forward}(\mathbf{T}_{backward}(x)) \|^2 + \sum_{x \in \Omega} \| \mathbf{T}_{backward}(\mathbf{T}_{forward}(x)) \|^2 \tag{5}$$

At each level of the registration, both the image and control point grid resolutions are doubled compared to the previous level. We find suitable registration parameters for both type (1) and type (2) registrations using visual inspection of the transformed image and ground truth atlases. For type (1) registrations, multiple atlases are available to be registered with each target image. We perform a simple majority voting in order to generate our "noisy" segmentation label $\hat{Y}$ for each target image X.

2.2   Label Consistency with Same Patient Atlases

Because of anatomical consistency between different sequences of the same patient, we employ inter-modality registration to obtain noisy labels for LGE images in type (2) registrations. Two sets of segmentations, denoted by $\hat{Y}_{bSSFP}^{LGE}$ and $\hat{Y}_{T2}^{LGE}$, can be obtained from the registrations: bSSFP to LGE, and T2 to LGE. In order to make sure our noisy labels are accurate enough, we only employ the consistent region $\hat{Y}_{bSSFP}^{LGE} \cap \hat{Y}_{T2}^{LGE}$ where both segmentations agree. In the non-consistent regions, we still use the noisy label from type (1) registrations. In type (1) registrations, we use symmetric registration with bending energy factor $\alpha = 0.001$ and inconsistency factor $\beta = 0.001$. We use five resolution levels and the maximal number of iteration per level is 300. The final grid spacing along x,

y and z are the same with five voxels. In type (2) registrations, we use six levels and the maximal number of iteration per level is 4000. The final grid spacing along x, y and z are the same with one voxel.

2.3   Deep Learning Based Segmentation with Noisy Labels

In the second step, we train different deep convolutional networks for semantic segmentation on the target data while using data augmentation techniques (rotation, scaling, adding noise, etc.) to avoid over-fitting to the noisy labels.

Given all pairs of images X and pseudo labels $\hat{Y}$, we re-sample them to 1 mm^3 isotropic resolution and train an ensemble $\mathcal{E}$ of n fully convolutional neural networks to segment the given foreground classes, with $P(X) = \mathcal{E}(X)$ standing for the *softmax* output probability maps for the different classes in the image. Our network architectures follow the encoder-decoder network proposed in [14], named *AH-Net*, and [5] based on the popular 3D U-Net architecture [3] with residual connections [15], named *SegResNet*. For training and implementing these neural networks, we used the *NVIDIA Clara Train SDK*[1] and NVIDIA Tesla V100 GPU with 16 GB memory. As in [14], we initialize *AH-Net* from *ImageNet* pretrained weights using a ResNet-18 encoder branch, utilizing anisotropic ($3 \times 3 \times 1$) kernels in the encoder path in order to make use of pretrained weights from 2D computer vision tasks. While the initial weights are learned from 2D, all convolutions are still applied in a full 3D fashion throughout the network, allowing it to efficiently learn 3D features from the image. In order to encourage view differences in our ensemble models, we initialize the weights in all three major 3D image planes, i.e. $3 \times 3 \times 1$, $3 \times 1 \times 3$, and $1 \times 3 \times 3$, corresponding to axial, sagittal, and coronal planes of the images. This approach results in three distinct *AH-Net* models to be used in our ensemble $\mathcal{E}$. The Dice loss [4] has been established as the objective function of choice for medical image segmentation tasks. Its properties make it suitable for the unbalanced class labels common in 3D medical images:

$$\mathcal{L}_{Dice} = 1 - \frac{2 \sum_{i=1}^{N} y_i \hat{y}_i}{\sum_{i=1}^{N} y_i^2 + \sum_{i=1}^{N} \hat{y}_i^2} \qquad (6)$$

Here, y_i is the predicted probability from our network f and $\hat{y}_i$ is the label from our "noisy" label map $\hat{Y}$ at voxel i. For simplicity we show the Dice loss for one foreground class in Eq. 6. In practice, we minimize the average Dice loss across the different foreground classes. After inference and simple post-processing, we arrive at our final label set for the targeted LGE CMR images. We resize the ensemble models' prediction maps to the original image resolution using trilinear interpolation, fuse each probability map using an *median* operator in order to reduce outliers. Then, the label index is assigned using the *argmax* operator:

$$Y(X) = \text{argmax} \left(\text{median} \left(\{ \mathcal{E}_0(X), \ldots, \mathcal{E}_n(X) \} \right) \right) \qquad (7)$$

---

[1] https://devblogs.nvidia.com/annotate-adapt-model-medical-imaging-clara-train-sdk.

Finally, we apply 3D largest connected component analysis on the foreground in order to remove isolated outliers.

3 Experiments and Results

3.1 Challenge Data

The challenge organizers provided the anonymized imaging data of 45 patients with cardiomyopathy who underwent CMR imaging at the Shanghai Renji hospital, China, with institutional ethics approval. For each patient, three CMR sequences (LGE, T2, and bSSF) are provided as multi-slice images in the ventricular short-axis views acquired at breath-hold. Slice-by-slice manual annotations of the right and left ventricular, and ventricular myocardium have been generated as gold-standard using ITK-SNAP[2] for training of the mdoels and for evaluation the segmentation results. The manual segmentation took about 20 min/case as stated by the challenge organizers. We also use ITK-SNAP for all the visualizations shown in this paper. For more details, see the challenge website[3]. The available training and test data have the following characteristics:

Training data:
- Patient 1-5:
  - LGE CMR (image + manual label) for validation
  - T2-weighted CMR (image + manual label)
  - bSSFP CMR (image + manual label)
- Patient 6-35:
  - T2-weighted CMR (image + manual label)
  - bSSFP CMR (image + manual label)
- Patient 36-45:
  - T2-weighted CMR (only image)
  - bSSFP CMR (only image)

Test data:
- Patient 6-45:
  - LGE CMR (only image)

As one can see, only five ground truth annotations are available in the targeted LGE images. However, 30 images have gold standard annotations available in different image modalities, i.e. bSSFP and T2. We use all available annotations for type (1) and type (2) multi-atlas label fusion approaches described in Sect. 2. After "noisy" label generation for all testing LGE images, we train our deep neural network ensemble to produce the final prediction labels for 40 LGE images in the test set. The five manually annotated LGE cases are used as the validation set during deep neural network training in order to find the best model

---

[2] http://www.itksnap.org.
[3] https://zmiclab.github.io/mscmrseg19/data.html.

Table 1. Evaluation scores on 40 LGE test images as provided by the challenge organizers. Both overlap and surface distance-based metrics are shown. LV and RV denote the left and right ventricle, respectively.

Metric	LV cavity	LV myocardium	RV cavity	Average
Dice	0.890	0.780	0.844	0.838
Jaccard	0.805	0.642	0.735	0.727
Surface distance [mm]	2.13	2.32	2.80	2.41
Hausdorff distance [mm]	11.6	16.3	18.1	15.3

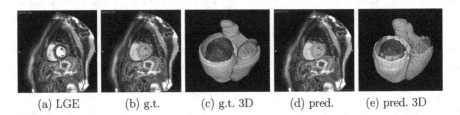

(a) LGE   (b) g.t.   (c) g.t. 3D   (d) pred.   (e) pred. 3D

Fig. 2. Comparison of the available ground truth annotation (b) and (c) in a validation LGE dataset and our model's prediction (d) and (e) [patient 2 of the challenge dataset].

parameters and avoid overfitting completely to the noisy labels. Throughout the challenge, the authors are blinded to the ground truth of the test set during model development and evaluation. Our evaluation scores on the test set are summarized in Table 1. A comparison of the available ground truth annotation in a validation LGE dataset and our model's prediction is shown in Fig. 2.

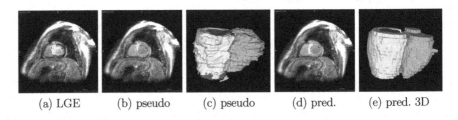

(a) LGE   (b) pseudo   (c) pseudo   (d) pred.   (e) pred. 3D

Fig. 3. Comparison of the result after multi-atlas label fusion (b) and (c) in a testing LGE dataset (a) and our model's prediction (d) and (e) [patient 45 of the challenge dataset].

4   Discussion and Conclusion

In this work, we combined classical methods of multi-atlas label fusion with deep learning. We utilized the ability of multi-atlas label fusion to generate labels for new images using only a small set of labeled images of the targeted image modality as atlases, although resulting in less accurate (or "noisy") labels when compared to manual segmentation. Furthermore, we enhanced the noisy labels by merging more atlas-based label fusion results if annotations of the same patient's anatomy are available in different image modalities. Here, they came from different MRI sequences, but they could potentially stem from even more different modalities like CT, using multi-modality similarity measures to drive the registrations. After training a round of deep convolutional neural networks on the "noisy" labels, we can see a clear visual improvement over multi-atlas label fusion result. This points to the fact that neural networks can still learn correlations of the data and the desired labels even when training labels are not as accurate as ground truth supervision labels [16]. The networks are able to compensate for some of the non-systematic errors in the "noisy" labels and hence improve the overall segmentation. We are blinded to the test set ground truth annotations and cannot quantify these improvements but visually, the improvements are noticeable as shown in Fig. 3. In conclusion, we achieved the automatic segmentation of cardiac structures in LGE magnetic resonance images by combing classical methods from multi-atlas label fusion and modern deep learning-based segmentation, resulting in visually compelling segmentation results.

References

1. Zhuang, X.: Multivariate mixture model for myocardial segmentation combining multi-source images. IEEE Trans. Pattern Anal. Mach. Intell. **41**, 2933–2946 (2019)
2. Zhuang, X.: Multivariate mixture model for cardiac segmentation from multi-sequence MRI. In: Ourselin, S., Joskowicz, L., Sabuncu, M.R., Unal, G., Wells, W. (eds.) MICCAI 2016. LNCS, vol. 9901, pp. 581–588. Springer, Cham (2016). https://doi.org/10.1007/978-3-319-46723-8_67
3. Çiçek, Ö., Abdulkadir, A., Lienkamp, S.S., Brox, T., Ronneberger, O.: 3D U-Net: learning dense volumetric segmentation from sparse annotation. In: Ourselin, S., Joskowicz, L., Sabuncu, M.R., Unal, G., Wells, W. (eds.) MICCAI 2016. LNCS, vol. 9901, pp. 424–432. Springer, Cham (2016). https://doi.org/10.1007/978-3-319-46723-8_49
4. Milletari, F., Navab, N., Ahmadi, S.A.: V-Net: fully convolutional neural networks for volumetric medical image segmentation. In: 2016 Fourth International Conference on 3D Vision (3DV), pp. 565–571. IEEE (2016)
5. Myronenko, A.: 3D MRI brain tumor segmentation using autoencoder regularization. In: Crimi, A., Bakas, S., Kuijf, H., Keyvan, F., Reyes, M., van Walsum, T. (eds.) BrainLes 2018. LNCS, vol. 11384, pp. 311–320. Springer, Cham (2019). https://doi.org/10.1007/978-3-030-11726-9_28
6. Zhu, W., et al.: AnatomyNet: deep learning for fast and fully automated whole-volume segmentation of head and neck anatomy. Med. Phys. **46**(2), 576–589 (2019)
7. Iglesias, J.E., Sabuncu, M.R.: Multi-atlas segmentation of biomedical images: a survey. Med. Image Anal. **24**(1), 205–219 (2015)
8. Rueckert, D., Sonoda, L., Hayes, C., Hill, D., Leach, M., Hawkes, D.: Nonrigid registration using free-form deformations: application to breast MR images. IEEE Trans. Med. Imaging **18**(8), 712–721 (1999)

9. Modat, M., et al.: Fast free-form deformation using graphics processing units. Comput. Methods Programs Biomed. **98**(3), 278–284 (2010)
10. Studholme, C., Hill, D.L., Hawkes, D.J.: An overlap invariant entropy measure of 3D medical image alignment. Pattern Recogn. **32**(1), 71–86 (1999)
11. Mattes, D., Haynor, D.R., Vesselle, H., Lewellen, T.K., Eubank, W.: PET-CT image registration in the chest using free-form deformations. IEEE Trans. Med. Imaging **22**(1), 120–128 (2003)
12. Feng, W., Reeves, S., Denney, T., Lloyd, S., Dell'Italia, L., Gupta, H.: A new consistent image registration formulation with a B-spline deformation model. In: ISBI, pp. 979–982 (2009)
13. Modat, M., Cardoso, M.J., Daga, P., Cash, D., Fox, N.C., Ourselin, S.: Inverse-consistent symmetric free form deformation. In: Dawant, B.M., Christensen, G.E., Fitzpatrick, J.M., Rueckert, D. (eds.) WBIR 2012. LNCS, vol. 7359, pp. 79–88. Springer, Heidelberg (2012). https://doi.org/10.1007/978-3-642-31340-0_9
14. Liu, S., et al.: 3D anisotropic hybrid network: transferring convolutional features from 2D images to 3D anisotropic volumes. In: Frangi, A.F., Schnabel, J.A., Davatzikos, C., Alberola-López, C., Fichtinger, G. (eds.) MICCAI 2018. LNCS, vol. 11071, pp. 851–858. Springer, Cham (2018). https://doi.org/10.1007/978-3-030-00934-2_94
15. He, K., Zhang, X., Ren, S., Sun, J.: Deep residual learning for image recognition. In: CVPR, pp. 770–778 (2016)
16. Heller, N., Dean, J., Papanikolopoulos, N.: Imperfect segmentation labels: how much do they matter? In: Stoyanov, D. (ed.) LABELS/CVII/STENT -2018. LNCS, vol. 11043, pp. 112–120. Springer, Cham (2018). https://doi.org/10.1007/978-3-030-01364-6_13

Pseudo-3D Network for Multi-sequence Cardiac MR Segmentation

Tao Liu[1]●, Yun Tian[1(✉)]●, Shifeng Zhao[1], XiaoYing Huang[1], Yang Xu[1],
Gaoyuan Jiang[1], and Qingjun Wang[2]

[1] Beijing Normal University, Beijing 100875, China
liutao@mail.bnu.edu.cn, tianyun@bnu.edu.cn
[2] Sixth Medical Center of PLA General Hospital, Beijing 100048, China

Abstract. Deep learning approaches have been regarded as a powerful
model for cardiac magnetic resonance (CMR) image segmentation. However, most current deep learning approaches do not fully utilize the information from multi-sequence (MS) cardiac magnetic resonance. In this
work, the deep learning method is used to fully-automatic segment the
MS CMR data. The balanced-Steady State Free Precession (bSSFP) cine
sequence is used to perform left ventricular positioning as a priori knowledge, and then the Late Gadolinium Enhancement (LGE) cine sequence
is used for precise segmentation. This segmentation strategy makes full
use of the complementary information from the MS CMR data. Moreover, to solve the anisotropy of volumetric medical images, we employ
the Pseudo-3D convolution neural network structure to segment the LGE
CMR data, which combines the advantage of 2D networks and preserving
the spatial structure information in 3D data without compromising segmentation accuracy. Experimental results of the Multi-sequence Cardiac
MR Segmentation Challenge (MS-CMRSeg 2019) show that our approach has achieved gratifying results even with limited GPU computing
resources and small amounts of annotated data. The full implementation
and configuration files in this article are available at https://github.com/
liut969/Multi-sequence-Cardiac-MR-Segmentation.

Keywords: Multi-sequence · Pseudo-3D network · Segmentation

1 Introduction

Heart disease is the leading cause of death globally, cardiac magnetic resonance
(CMR) imaging is the gold-standard for assessment and diagnosis of a wide range
of heart diseases. Usually, the ventricle and myocardium need to be manually
segmented from the CMR data by clinicians, and then ventricle volume, mass
and ejection fraction can be calculated from the segmentation results to diagnose the heart disease. With the increasing medical image data, time-consuming,
laborious and tedious manual segmentation methods are considered to be inefficient. Therefore, it is imperative to develop computer-aided techniques to analyze
medical images automatically [6].

© Springer Nature Switzerland AG 2020
M. Pop et al. (Eds.): STACOM 2019, LNCS 12009, pp. 237–245, 2020.
https://doi.org/10.1007/978-3-030-39074-7_25

Multi-sequence (MS) CMR usually include three-sequence CMR images: the Late Gadolinium Enhancement (LGE) cine sequence, the T2-weighted (T2) and the balanced-Steady State Free Precession (bSSFP) cine sequence. The difficulties of MS CMR segmentation have been mainly composed of the following points [12,13]: (i) CMR image presence poor contrast between the myocardium and the surrounding structure, for example, in LGE CMR, the infarcted myocardium is similar to the blood pools, and the healthy myocardium is similar to the adjacent liver or lung; (ii) the location, size and shape of the heart are different in different people, and the lesions exacerbate this difference; (iii) efficient fusion strategies are lacking to take fully utilize the information from MS CMR data; (iv) some other factors, such as the inherent noise caused by motion artifacts and cardiac dynamics. Therefore, ventricular segmentation based on MS CMR data is still a challenging task.

Automatic heart segmentation and diagnosis has become more and more necessary. In the last decade, the international challenge has released a large number of CMR datasets and brought together the state-of-the-art methods. The automatic CMR data segmentation method based on deep learning has achieved gratifying results. For example, in the Automated Cardiac Diagnosis Challenge - MICCAI 2017[1], the 8 highest-ranked segmentation methods were all neural network-based methods, so deep learning approaches have been regarded as a powerful model for CMR image segmentation.

In this work, we employed the deep learning method to fully-automatic segment the MS CMR data. The main contributions of this study consist of the following:

- We segment the ventricles combining the complementary information from two-sequence CMR data. The bSSFP cine sequence is used to perform left ventricular positioning as a priori knowledge, and then the LGE cine sequence is used for precise segmentation. Our segmentation strategy makes full use of the complementary information in the MS CMR data.
- In order to solve the anisotropy of volumetric medical images [1], the Pseudo-3D [8] convolution neural network structure is used to segment the LGE CMR data. Compared to 2D convolution and 3D convolution, the Pseudo-3D convolution neural network structure combining the advantage of 2D networks and preserving the spatial structure information in 3D data without compromising segmentation accuracy.

2   Related Work

Typically for MS CMR data, two-sequence CMR is widely used for automated myocardial segmentation. For example, Rajchl et al. [9] used the segmentation results of the bSSFP cine CMR as a priori knowledge, and then performed ventricular segmentation on the LGE CMR, which compensates for differences between slices of different sequences. In [13], a unified framework combining

---

[1]   https://www.creatis.insa-lyon.fr/Challenge/acdc/databases.html.

three-sequence CMR (bSSFP, T2 and LGE) was proposed to align the MS CMR data from the same patient into a common space for segmentation.

Present, MS CMR data segmentation based on deep learning also has a good performance. In [4], a multi-task deep learning network for automatic 3D bi-ventricular segmentation of CMR was proposed, this network combines high-resolution and low-resolution CMR volume. However, it should be noted that this network requires additional landmark localization information, which undoubtedly increased the requirements for data. Also, Tseng et al. [11] proposed a deep encoder-decoder structure with cross-modality convolution layers to incorporate different modalities of MRI data. However, this multi-modal encoder method does not apply to MS CMR data due to misalignment between image slices, the resolution is not uniform, the difference in slice thickness between the short-axis.

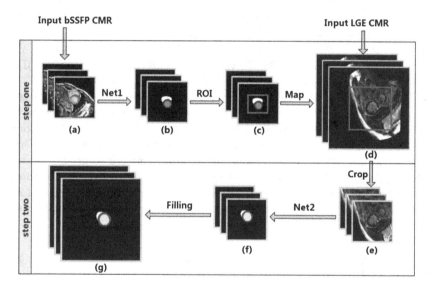

Fig. 1. Proposed pipeline for multi-sequence cardiac MR segmentation. (a) Input bSSFP CMR; (b) ventricular segmentation from bSSFP CMR; (c) the ROI (marked with a red square) obtained after positioning; (d) the ROI on the bSSFP CMR is mapped onto the input LGE CMR; (e) cropped LGE CMR; (f) segmentation result; (g) final output. Different sized rectangles represent different resolutions, smaller rectangular represents low-resolution CMR volume, and conversely, larger rectangular represents high-resolution CMR volume. (Color figure online)

For the segmentation of volumetric medical image data, a slice-by-slice learning strategy is frequently used. This method processed the 3D volumetric medical image data into multiple 2D slices and then performed semantic segmentation on each 2D slice. However, simply connecting 2D segmentations into 3D will lose spatial correlation between the $z-$direction. A straightforward way to learn spatial structure information in volumetric medical image data is to extend the

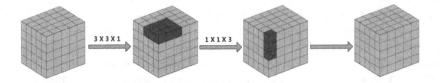

Fig. 2. The Pseudo-3D convolution.

2D convolution kernel to 3D convolution kernel, such as 3D U-Net [3] or V-Net [7]. Although 3D convolutional networks can learn more information, 3D convolutional networks require more computing resources (high memory consumption and more learning parameters) than 2D convolutional networks. Furthermore, volumetric medical image data are usually anisotropic [1]. For example, the Multi-sequence Cardiac MR Segmentation Challenge (MS-CMRSeg 2019[2]) data used in this work, the LGE CMR consisting of 10 to 18 slices, typically, the voxel scale in depth (the z−direction, 5 mm) is much larger than that in the xy plane (0.75 mm). To solve the above problems we employ the Pseudo-3D [8] convolution neural network structure to segment the LGE CMR data.

In [8], the Pseudo-3D network was first proposed and applied to learn spatio-temporal video representation. The Pseudo-3D convolution factorizes a standard $3 \times 3 \times 3$ convolution into two successive convolutional layers: $3 \times 3 \times 1$ convolutional filter to learn spatial features and $1 \times 1 \times 3$ convolutional filter to learn temporal features. This spatio-temporal separation network structure has been widely applied for video processing. Chen et al. [2] extended the Pseudo-3D network structure to the medical image field and segmented the small cell lung cancer, inspired by this, our study used this lightweight network structure to segment the ventricles in LGE CMR data.

3   Methods

Figure 1 illustrates the framework for multi-sequence cardiac MR segmentation, which can be roughly divided into two steps: (i) left ventricular positioning. First, the bSSFP CMR is taken as input, the left ventricle is obtained by segmentation network, and then the center position and radius of the left ventricle are obtained by Gaussian kernel-based circular Hough transform approach. Finally, the left ventricle position in the bSSFP CMR is mapped into the LGE CMR, and the region of interest (ROI) is obtained by the cropping operation. (ii) ventricle and myocardium segmentation. First, the ROI of the LGE CMR is taken as input, and the ventricular and myocardial segmentation results are obtained through a customized Pseudo-3D network structure. Finally, the filled image is used as the final output result.

---

[2] https://zmiclab.github.io/mscmrseg19/data.html.

3.1   Left Ventricular Positioning

In this work, we choose to use bSSFP CMR for left ventricular positioning for the following reasons: (i) compared with other modal CMRs, the bSSFP CMR captures cardiac motions and presents clear boundaries; (ii) compared to LGE CMR, the bSSFP CMR has more manual labels; (iii) each set of bSSFP CMR has more slices than the T2 CMR. Typically, the T2 CMR slice has a thickness of 20 mm, and a set of data usually consists of 3 to 5 slices, but the bSSFP CMR slice has a thickness of 8–13 mm and a set of data consists of 8 to 12 slices, more slices help the left ventricle to locate.

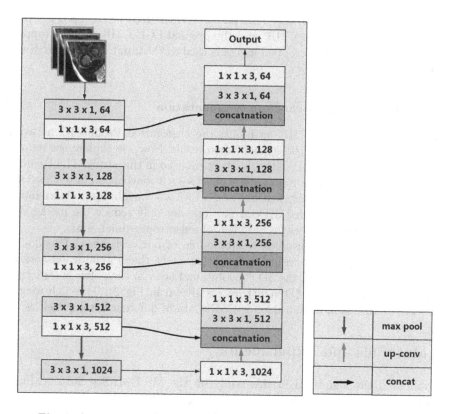

Fig. 3. An overview of the customized Pseudo-3D network framework.

First, the ventricle is segmented from the bSSFP CMR through a segmentation network. U-Net [10] only needs a small number of annotations to get better results, and is widely used in medical image segmentation, so U-Net is selected as our first segmentation network.

Next, the left ventricle is positioned on the segmented result to obtain a ROI. There are many interfering tissues around the ventricle. By locating the position of the left ventricle center point and extracting a ROI with a size of 256 × 256 centered around it, the interference tissue can be effectively reduced. At the same time, ROI operations can reduce computing resources and normalize data sizes. In this study, the left ventricular center point is extracted by Gaussian kernel-based circular Hough transform approach. The main idea of the algorithm we implemented is from [5], a little different from [5] is that this study calculates the left ventricular center point directly from the 3D data. In addition, it is difficult to calculate the left ventricular center point directly from the original data. Therefore, we first segment the original data and then perform ventricular positioning. Our left ventricle position method greatly improves the calculation accuracy of the center point.

Finally, the LGE CMR is used as the input, because each set of MS CMR is from the same location of the same patient, so the ROI of the bSSFP CMR can be mapped to the LGE CMR, and the original LGE CMR can be cropped according to the ROI. The cropped image is used as the input for the next stage (Sect. 3.2).

3.2 Ventricle and Myocardium Segmentation

Using the cropped LGE CMR as input, the customized Pseudo-3D network structure is used to obtain the segmentation result. Now, we explain the details of the customized Pseudo-3D network structure used in this study. The Pseudo-3D convolution, as shown in Fig. 2, splits one $3 \times 3 \times 3$ convolution into a $3 \times 3 \times 1$ convolution to learn intra-slice features and a $1 \times 1 \times 3$ convolution to learn inter-slice features. Such decoupled 3D convolutions not only reduce the model size significantly, but also address the problem of anisotropic dimensions.

Here, 3D U-Net [3] is used as a submodule of our customized Pseudo-3D network framework. As shown in Fig. 3, in this study, the original framework of 3D U-Net is preserved, and the 3D convolutional layer in the network structure is replaced by the Pseudo-3D structure (as shown in Fig. 2). This lightweight network structure is more suitable for CMR data of different heterogeneities.

4   Materials and Experiments

We validated the algorithm in this study on the MS CMRSeg 2019[3] (Multi-sequence Cardiac MR Segmentation Challenge). MS CMRSeg 2019 not only provides a multi-sequence ventricle and myocardium dataset with manual labels, but also provides an open and fair competitive platform to validate the ventricular segmentation algorithm. We implemented our framework using Keras with cuDNN, and ran all experiments on a personal computer with NVIDIA-GeForce-GTX-1080-Ti GPU, Intel Core i7–4790 CPU @ 3.60 GHz and 32 GB RAM.

The MS CMRSeg 2019 consisted of 45 patients with cardiomyopathy, and each set of patient data consists of three CMR sequences (the LGE, T2, and bSSFP), all of which were breath-hold, multi-slice, acquired in the ventricular

---

[3] https://zmiclab.github.io/mscmrseg19/.

short-axis views. In this study, our use of data is roughly divided into two steps. In the first step, 45 sets of bSSFP CMR were used for left ventricular positioning, 35 of which had manually labeled data as training sets, and the remaining 10 sets contained only image data as test sets. In the second step, 45 sets of LGE CMRs were used for fine segmentation, of which 5 sets of data containing tags were used as training sets, and the remaining 40 sets of unlabeled data were used as test sets. Finally, we send the segmentation results of the test set to the organizer of MS CMRSeg 2019. The test performance of the organizer feedback is shown in Table 1.

Table 1. Segmentation accuracy. Note: LV: Left ventricle; RV: Right ventricle; Myo: Myocardium.

Segmentation accuracy	LV blood cavity	Myo of LV	RV blood cavity
Dice	0.807 ($\pm$0.074)	0.617 ($\pm$0.086)	0.680 ($\pm$0.118)
Jaccard	0.683 ($\pm$0.103)	0.452 ($\pm$0.090)	0.526 ($\pm$0.129)
Surface distance (mm)	4.094 ($\pm$1.493)	5.687 ($\pm$1.794)	8.730 ($\pm$3.437)
Hausdorff distance (mm)	40.773 ($\pm$11.361)	43.351 ($\pm$7.186)	56.379 ($\pm$15.505)

From the Table 1 we can see that our method left ventricular Dice score is 0.807. Here, the Dice score, Jaccard, average surface distance and Hausdorff distance will be used as evaluation metrics, the Dice score and Jaccard can be computed as:

$$Dice(V_{manual}, V_{auto}) = \frac{2\,|V_{manual} \cap V_{auto}|}{|V_{manual}| + |V_{auto}|} \tag{1}$$

$$Jaccard(V_{manual}, V_{auto}) = \frac{|V_{manual} \cap V_{auto}|}{|V_{manual}| + |V_{auto}| - |V_{manual} \cap V_{auto}|} \tag{2}$$

where, V_{auto} is the segmented volume and the V_{manual} is the manual marker result. The scores of Dice and Jaccard represent the amount of overlap between the automatic segmentation results and the manually labeled results, which give a measurement value between 0 and 1. The average surface distance and the Hausdorff distance measure the distance between the automatic segmentation result and the manual marker result, and the smaller distance value represents a better segmentation result. It should be noted here that the LGE CMR data only provides 5 sets of training sets with labels, such a small amount of training data is also one of the challenges of this segmentation task.

5 Conclusions

This study detailed a simple but effective approach for automatic ventricle and myocardium segmentation from MS CMR, which uses the bSSFP CMR to perform left ventricular positioning, and use the LGE CMR to precise segmentation.

This segmentation method combines multiple sequences of CMR information. In addition, for the segmentation of LGE CMR, we used a customized Pseudo-3D convolution neural network, this framework not only reduces the size of the network, but also learns spatial structure information. In future work, we will continue to challenge the issue of multi-sequence CMR segmentation.

Acknowledgments. This work is supported by National Natural Science Foundation of China (Grant Nos. 61472042 and 61802020), and by Beijing Natural Science Foundation (Grant No. 4174094), and by the Fundamental Research Funds for the Central Universities (Grant No. 2015KJJCB25).

References

1. Chen, J., Yang, L., Zhang, Y., Alber, M., Chen, D.Z.: Combining fully convolutional and recurrent neural networks for 3D biomedical image segmentation. In: Advances in Neural Information Processing Systems, pp. 3036–3044 (2016)
2. Chen, W., Wei, H., Peng, S., Sun, J., Qiao, X., Liu, B.: HSN: hybrid segmentation network for small cell lung cancer segmentation. IEEE Access **7**, 75591–75603 (2019)
3. Çiçek, Ö., Abdulkadir, A., Lienkamp, S.S., Brox, T., Ronneberger, O.: 3D U-Net: learning dense volumetric segmentation from sparse annotation. In: Ourselin, S., Joskowicz, L., Sabuncu, M.R., Unal, G., Wells, W. (eds.) MICCAI 2016. LNCS, vol. 9901, pp. 424–432. Springer, Cham (2016). https://doi.org/10.1007/978-3-319-46723-8_49
4. Duan, J., et al.: Automatic 3D bi-ventricular segmentation of cardiac images by a shape-constrained multi-task deep learning approach. arXiv preprint (2018)
5. Khened, M., Kollerathu, V.A., Krishnamurthi, G.: Fully convolutional multi-scale residual densenets for cardiac segmentation and automated cardiac diagnosis using ensemble of classifiers. Med. Image Anal. **51**, 21–45 (2019)
6. Liu, T., Tian, Y., Zhao, S., Huang, X., Wang, Q.: Automatic whole heart segmentation using a two-stage u-net framework and an adaptive threshold window. IEEE Access **7**, 83628–83636 (2019). https://doi.org/10.1109/ACCESS.2019.2923318
7. Milletari, F., Navab, N., Ahmadi, S.A.: V-net: fully convolutional neural networks for volumetric medical image segmentation. In: 2016 Fourth International Conference on 3D Vision (3DV), pp. 565–571. IEEE (2016)
8. Qiu, Z., Yao, T., Mei, T.: Learning spatio-temporal representation with pseudo-3D residual networks. In: proceedings of the IEEE International Conference on Computer Vision, pp. 5533–5541 (2017)
9. Rajchl, M., et al.: Interactive hierarchical-flow segmentation of scar tissue from late-enhancement cardiac MR images. IEEE Trans. Med. Imaging **33**(1), 159–172 (2013)
10. Ronneberger, O., Fischer, P., Brox, T.: U-Net: convolutional networks for biomedical image segmentation. In: Navab, N., Hornegger, J., Wells, W.M., Frangi, A.F. (eds.) MICCAI 2015. LNCS, vol. 9351, pp. 234–241. Springer, Cham (2015). https://doi.org/10.1007/978-3-319-24574-4_28
11. Tseng, K.L., Lin, Y.L., Hsu, W., Huang, C.Y.: Joint sequence learning and cross-modality convolution for 3D biomedical segmentation. In: Proceedings of the IEEE Conference on Computer Vision and Pattern Recognition, pp. 6393–6400 (2017)

12. Zhuang, X.: Multivariate mixture model for cardiac segmentation from multi-sequence MRI. In: Ourselin, S., Joskowicz, L., Sabuncu, M.R., Unal, G., Wells, W. (eds.) MICCAI 2016. LNCS, vol. 9901, pp. 581–588. Springer, Cham (2016). https://doi.org/10.1007/978-3-319-46723-8_67
13. Zhuang, X.: Multivariate mixture model for myocardial segmentation combining multi-source images. In: Proceedings of IEEE Transactions on Pattern Analysis and Machine Intelligence (2018)

SK-Unet: An Improved U-Net Model with Selective Kernel for the Segmentation of Multi-sequence Cardiac MR

Xiyue Wang[1], Sen Yang[1,4], Mingxuan Tang[2], Yunpeng Wei[3],
Xiao Han[4], Ling He[1(✉)], and Jing Zhang[1(✉)]

[1] College of Electrical Engineering, Sichuan University, Chengdu, China
{ling.he,jing_zhang}@scu.edu.cn
[2] The School of Computer Science, Chengdu University of Information
Technology, Chengdu, China
[3] Chinese Academy of Medical Sciences and Peking Union Medical College,
Beijing, China
[4] Tencent AI Lab, Shenzhen, China

Abstract. In the clinical environment, myocardial infarction (MI) as one common cardiovascular disease is mainly evaluated based on the late gadolinium enhancement (LGE) cardiac magnetic resonance images (CMRIs). The automatic segmentations of left ventricle (LV), right ventricle (RV), and left ventricular myocardium (LVM) in the LGE CMRIs are desired for the aided diagnosis in clinic. To accomplish this segmentation task, this paper proposes a modified U-net architecture by combining multi-sequence CMRIs, including the cine, LGE, and T2-weighted CMRIs. The cine and T2-weighted CMRIs are used to assist the segmentation in the LGE CMRIs. In this segmentation network, the squeeze-and-excitation residual (SE-Res) and selective kernel (SK) modules are inserted in the down-sampling and up-sampling stages, respectively. The SK module makes the obtained feature maps more informative in both spatial and channel-wise space, and attains more precise segmentation result. The utilized dataset is from the MICCAI challenge (MS-CMRSeg 2019), which is acquired from 45 patients including three CMR sequences. The cine and T2-weighted CMRIs acquired from 35 patients and the LGE CMRIs acquired from 5 patients are labeled. Our method achieves the mean dice score of 0.922 (LV), 0.827 (LVM), and 0.874 (RV) in the LGE CMRIs.

Keywords: Cardiac magnetic resonance · Late gadolinium enhancement · Multi-Sequence Image · SK-Unet framework

1 Introduction

Cardiac magnetic resonance images (CMRIs) with the capacity of discriminating various types of tissues are primarily used in the diagnosis and treatment of cardiovascular diseases, such as the myocardial infarction (MI). Late gadolinium

---

X. Wang and S. Yang—Co-first authors.

© Springer Nature Switzerland AG 2020
M. Pop et al. (Eds.): STACOM 2019, LNCS 12009, pp. 246–253, 2020.
https://doi.org/10.1007/978-3-030-39074-7_26

enhancement (LGE) cardiac magnetic resonance (CMR) sequence has the capacity to visualize the infarcted myocardium that has the enhanced brightness compared with the healthy myocardium [1, 2]. Thus, accurate delineation of the left ventricle (LV), right ventricle (RV), and left ventricular myocardium (LVM) in the LGE CMRIs is important in the clinical diagnosis. The manual delineation by a clinical radiologist for these three parts is time-consuming, tedious, and rater-dependent [1, 3]. Hence, an automatic segmentation method for this task is desirable in clinical setups.

Currently, a majority of studies for the automatic cardiac segmentation are based on the cine CMR sequence [3–8], since the cine CMR sequence has the ability to capture the cardiac motions during the whole cardiac cycle and can present clear boundary [1]. The LGE CMR sequence enhances the representation of the infarcted myocardium and is routinely used in the clinical diagnosis of MI. However, there is few research on automatic cardiac segmentation directly in the LGE CMR sequence, since the CMRIs with poor image quality have heterogenetic intensity distribution. The current LGE CMR based cardiac segmentation research mainly targets to delineate the contour of LVM [1, 9–14]. They accomplish the segmentation task utilizing a semi-automated approach [12] or combining the prior segmentation contour in the corresponding cine CMR sequence from the same patient with the same phase [9–11, 13, 14]. The prior knowledge based methods usually require the assistance of various image registration algorithms. The result of image registration may produce errors due to the varied slice thickness and spatial resolution in different patients.

To the best of our knowledge, there is almost no research focusing on the simultaneously automatic segmentation of the LV, RV, and LVM in the LGE CMRIs. Manual delineation in the LGE CMRIs is particularly arduous. This paper proposes an automatic segmentation algorithm for these three parts in the LGE CMRIs. The utilized dataset is from the MICCAI challenge (MS-CMRSeg 2019), which is collected from 45 patients. Only 5 of 45 patients have their LGE CMRIs labeled, and 35 of 45 patients have their cine and T2-weighted CMRIs labelled. In this paper, the LGE CMRIs with a small amount of manual delineations are segmented by combing anther two CMR sequences (cine and T2-weighted CMRIs) acquired from the same patient. This paper achieves this segmentation based on a modified U-net architecture. The squeeze-and-excitation residual (SE-Res) [15] and selective kernel (SK) modules [16] are respectively inserted in the down-sampling and up-sampling stages of the conventional U-net architecture. The SE-Res module considers more channel dependencies and lacks the spatial information of feature maps. The spatial information is important for the pixel-level localization in the image segmentation task. The SK module is utilized to relieve this problem, which adaptively adjusts the size of local respective field in the convolutional operation to collect multi-scale spatial information [16]. The proposed SK-Unet framework has achieved robust segmentation performance in the LGE CMR sequences.

2 Methodology

The modified architecture used for this cardiac segmentation task is based on the classical U-net architecture. The proposed LV, RV, and LVM segmentation algorithm includes three parts: image preprocessing, SK-Unet model based image segmentation, and image postprocessing.

2.1 Image Preprocessing

In order to remove the influence of the surrounding organ of heart in the CMRIs, region of interest (ROI) extraction is a crucial step in the prepossessing stage. The distribution range of intensity, image contrast, and image size are different in these three CMR sequences. It is difficult to develop a robust ROI detection method. Since the three CMR sequences of each patient are acquired in same session and with the same cardiac phase, the anatomical structure is consistent in the three CMR sequences. Thus, this paper performs a statistical work to roughly locate the position of the heart.

The second step in the preprocessing process is to normalize the input images as the distribution of zero mean and variance of 1. Then, due to the limited training images, the data augmentation is applied to create an expanded dataset from the original dataset. The adopted data augmentation methods include image transpose, flipping, cropping, and rotation. Finally, to fully utilize the dependences between slices, the neighbored three slices are stacked as the new three-channel image that has the same mechanism as the RGB channel in the color image.

2.2 SK-Unet Based Image Segmentation Model

The proposed SK-Unet based CMR segmentation model consists of the encoding and decoding stages. The skip connections exist between encoder and decoder blocks with the same image spatial resolution. Figure 1 illustrates the overall structure of the proposed SK-Unet based CMR segmentation model.

As shown in Fig. 1(a), the input is the neighbored three slices in one CMRI, and the output is the probability that each pixel in the CMRI is classified as the background, LV, RV, and LVM. The left part performs the encoding operation with pooling layer, convolution layers, and SE-Res module, and the decoding operation with up-sampling unit, convolution layers, and SK module is performed in the right part. The horizontal connections mean that the extracted features in the encoding stage are forwarded to the corresponding decoding stage.

The pooling layers reduce the spatial resolution of feature maps to attain high-level feature representation. As shown in Fig. 1(a), the stride in pooling layers is adopted as 2. The up-sampling unit has the inverse operation as the pooling layer.

The convolution operation at each convolution layer applies filters to learn informative features by combining the spatial and channel-wise information within the local receptive fields. In order to attain global feature fusion, the SE-Res and SK modules are inserted in the conventional U-net architecture. The SE-Res module factors out the spatial correlations among features and captures the relationships among channels, which is effective in the classification task. In this CMR image segmentation task, the

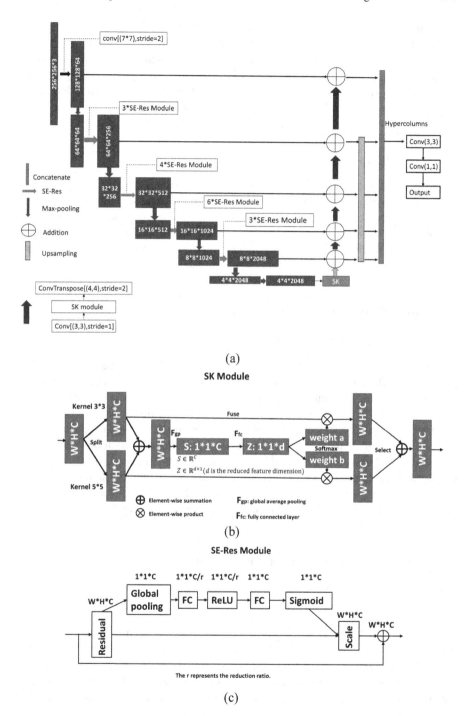

Fig. 1. The overall structure of the proposed SK-Unet based CMR segmentation model. The SK and SE-Res modules are shown in (b) and (c).

spatial information with the representation of texture, boundary, and gray-level, is also important. The SK module can adaptively adjust the size of local respective field in the procedure of the CNN operation, which helps capture multi-scale spatial correlations among features. Thus, the SK module makes the obtained feature maps more informative in both spatial and channel-wise space. The proposed architecture has robustness for the classification between the target region and background, and for the precise localization of the target region in the CMR image segmentation task.

2.3 Image Postprocessing

The image postprocessing process aims to refine the result of the cardiac segmentation. First, the hole filling technique is applied to attain more complete segmentation. Then, a connected component analysis for all the obtained segmentation is performed. The largest connected component of all slices in each patient is found, which is set as the constraint for modifying the segmentation of the remaining slices in each patient. Segmentations that exceed the largest connected range will be removed.

3   Experimental and Results

3.1   Dataset: MS-CMRSeg 2019

Our algorithm is evaluated on the Multi-sequence Cardiac MR Segmentation Challenge MICCAI 2019 (MS-CMRSeg 2019) dataset [1, 2]. This dataset covers 45 patients with cardiomyopathy, and each patient has been scanned by the cine, T2-weighted, and LGE CMR sequences from the short-axis orientation. The cine CMRIs acquired with the balanced-steady state free precession (bSSPF) sequence covers the full ventricles, which are selected in the same cardiac phase as the following LGE and T2-weighted CMRIs. The LGE and T2-weighted CMRIs cover the main body of the ventricles, which are collected at the end-diastolic phase. Since the number of labelled samples is limited, the cine and the T2-weighted CMRIs collected from 35 patients, and the LGE CMRIs collected from 5 patients are used as the training data. The testing data adopts the LGE CMRIs collected from 40 patients.

3.2   The Overall Performance of the Proposed Approach

Four commonly used indicators in medical image segmentation are used to evaluate the performance of the model. These four indicators include dice score, Hausdorff distance, average surface distance, and Jaccard index, which are listed in Table 1.

As shown in Table 1, the segmentation for the LV cavity reaches the highest performance in term of dice score, Jaccard index, Hausdorff distance, and surface distance. The segmentation of LV myocardium is relatively difficult since the existence of the invalid tissue. The invalid tissue, for instance the MI, has the same appearance as the blood pool, which results in the difficulty in the localization of the LV myocardium.

Table 1. The mean and standard deviation of the dice score, Hausdorff distance, surface distance, and Jaccard index in the cardiac segmentation task.

	Mean ± standard deviation		
	LV blood cavity	LV myocardium	RV blood
Dice score (%)	0.922 ± 0.036	0.827 ± 0.060	0.874 ± 0.058
Jaccard index (%)	0.857 ± 0.059	0.709 ± 0.084	0.781 ± 0.089
	LV endocardium	LV epicardium	RV endocardium
Hausdorff distance (mm)	10.058 ± 3.820	11.426 ± 3.574	16.721 ± 7.509
Surface distance (mm)	1.589 ± 0.637	1.696 ± 0.585	2.208 ± 1.016

3.3   Comparison with Various Image Segmentation Architectures

In order to intuitively represent the segmentation performance of the proposed algorithm, the visual segmentation results for the LV, LVM, and RV are compared with various architectures including DenseUnet [17], Linknet [18], and U-net [19], which are represented in Fig. 2.

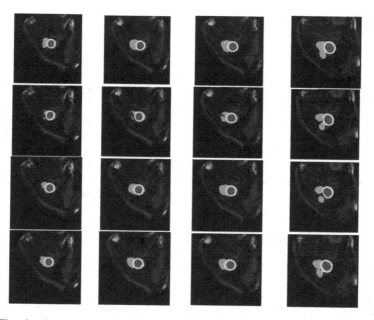

Fig. 2. The visual segmentation results for the LV, LVM, and RV of the same slices from one specific patient using various architectures. The results from the first to the last columns are obtained using SK-Unet, DenseUnet, Linknet, and U-net, respectively.

As shown in Fig. 2, the SK-Unet based algorithm achieves the best segmentation result. The Linknet and U-net based methods produce unsmooth segmentation in the boundary. The DenseUnet has difficulty in segmenting the RV part.

The SK-Unet module fully utilizes the information of channels in the feature maps through the inserted SE-Res module. Meanwhile, the adaptive adjust of the receptive field size helps capture multi-scale spatial information. The combination of the channel and spatial information could learn more inter-slices and intra-slice features, and then produce more precise segmentation result.

4   Conclusion

This paper proposes an approach for the multi-sequence ventricle and myocardium segmentation using deep learning technique. We employ a modified U-net architecture with SE-Res and SK model. The SK model with concurrent spatial and channel information is beneficial for the target localization and pixel-level based classification in this segmentation task. These results suggest that our approach has the potential to provide aided diagnoses for clinical cardiac surgeon.

References

1. Zhuang, X.: Multivariate mixture model for myocardial segmentation combining multi-source images. IEEE Trans. Pattern Anal. Mach. Intell. (2018). https://doi.org/10.1109/TPAMI.2018.2869576
2. Zhuang, X.: Multivariate mixture model for cardiac segmentation from multi-sequence MRI. In: Ourselin, S., Joskowicz, L., Sabuncu, M.R., Unal, G., Wells, W. (eds.) MICCAI 2016. LNCS, vol. 9901, pp. 581–588. Springer, Cham (2016). https://doi.org/10.1007/978-3-319-46723-8_67
3. Khened, M., Kollerathu, V.A., Krishnamurthi, G.: Fully convolutional multi-scale residual DenseNets for cardiac segmentation and automated cardiac diagnosis using ensemble of classifiers. Med. Image Anal. 51, 21–45 (2019)
4. Guo, F., Ng, M., Wright, G.: Cardiac MRI left ventricle segmentation and quantification: a framework combining U-Net and continuous max-flow. In: Pop, M., et al. (eds.) STACOM 2018. LNCS, vol. 11395, pp. 450–458. Springer, Cham (2019). https://doi.org/10.1007/978-3-030-12029-0_48
5. Isensee, F., Jaeger, P.F., Full, P.M., Wolf, I., Engelhardt, S., Maier-Hein, K.H.: Automatic cardiac disease assessment on cine-MRI via time-series segmentation and domain specific features. In: Pop, M., et al. (eds.) STACOM 2017. LNCS, vol. 10663, pp. 120–129. Springer, Cham (2018). https://doi.org/10.1007/978-3-319-75541-0_13
6. Kerfoot, E., Clough, J., Oksuz, I., Lee, J., King, A.P., Schnabel, J.A.: Left-ventricle quantification using residual U-Net. In: Pop, M., et al. (eds.) STACOM 2018. LNCS, vol. 11395, pp. 371–380. Springer, Cham (2019). https://doi.org/10.1007/978-3-030-12029-0_40
7. Li, J., Hu, Z.: Left ventricle full quantification using deep layer aggregation based multitask relationship learning. In: Pop, M., et al. (eds.) STACOM 2018. LNCS, vol. 11395, pp. 381–388. Springer, Cham (2019). https://doi.org/10.1007/978-3-030-12029-0_41
8. Zheng, Q., Delingette, H., Duchateau, N., Ayache, N.: 3-D consistent and robust segmentation of cardiac images by deep learning with spatial propagation. IEEE Trans. Med. Imaging 37(9), 2137–2148 (2018)

9. Ciofolo, C., Fradkin, M., Mory, B., Hautvast, G., Breeuwer, M.: Automatic myocardium segmentation in late-enhancement MRI. In: 5th IEEE International Symposium on Biomedical Imaging: From Nano to Macro, pp. 225–228. IEEE, Piscataway (2008)

10. Dikici, E., O'Donnell, T., Setser, R., White, R.D.: Quantification of delayed enhancement MR images. In: Barillot, C., Haynor, D.R., Hellier, P. (eds.) MICCAI 2004. LNCS, vol. 3216, pp. 250–257. Springer, Heidelberg (2004). https://doi.org/10.1007/978-3-540-30135-6_31

11. El Berbari, R., Kachenoura, N., Frouin, F., Herment, A., Mousseaux, E., Bloch, I.: An automated quantification of the transmural myocardial infarct extent using cardiac DE-MR images. In: Annual International Conference of the IEEE Engineering in Medicine and Biology Society, pp. 4403–4406. IEEE, Piscataway (2009)

12. Rajchl, M., Jing, Y., White, J.A., Ukwatta, E., Stirrat, J., Nambakhsh, C.M.S., et al.: Interactive hierarchical-flow segmentation of scar tissue from late-enhancement cardiac MR images. IEEE Trans. Med. Imaging 33(1), 159–172 (2014)

13. Wei, D., Sun, Y., Ong, S.H., Chai, P., Teo, L.L., Low, A.F.: Three-dimensional segmentation of the left ventricle in late gadolinium enhanced MR images of chronic infarction combining long-and short-axis information. Med. Image Anal. 17(6), 685–697 (2013)

14. Xu, R.S., Athavale, P., Lu, Y., Radau, P., Wright, G.A.: Myocardial segmentation in late-enhancement MR images via registration and propagation of cine contours. In: 10th International Symposium on Biomedical Imaging, pp. 844–847. IEEE, Piscataway (2013)

15. Hu, J., Shen, L., Sun, G.: Squeeze-and-excitation networks. In: 2018 IEEE Conference on CVPR, pp. 7132–7141, IEEE, Piscataway (2018)

16. Li, X., Wang, W., Hu, X., Yang, J.: Selective kernel networks. arXiv:1903.06586 (2019)

17. Li, X., Chen, H., Qi, X., Dou, Q., Fu, C.W., Heng, P.A.: H-DenseUNet: hybrid densely connected UNet for liver and tumor segmentation from CT volumes. IEEE Trans. Med. Imaging 37(12), 2663–2674 (2018)

18. Chaurasia, A., Culurciello, E.: Linknet: exploiting encoder representations for efficient semantic segmentation. In: 2017 IEEE Visual Communications and Image Processing, pp. 1–4, IEEE, Piscataway (2017)

19. Ronneberger, O., Fischer, P., Brox, T.: U-Net: convolutional networks for biomedical image segmentation. In: Navab, N., Hornegger, J., Wells, W.M., Frangi, A.F. (eds.) MICCAI 2015. LNCS, vol. 9351, pp. 234–241. Springer, Cham (2015). https://doi.org/10.1007/978-3-319-24574-4_28

Multi-sequence Cardiac MR Segmentation with Adversarial Domain Adaptation Network

Jiexiang Wang, Hongyu Huang, Chaoqi Chen, Wenao Ma, Yue Huang, and Xinghao Ding$^{(\boxtimes)}$

School of Information Science and Engineering, Xiamen University, Xiamen, China
{wangjx,huanghy,cqchen94,wenaoma}@stu.xmu.edu.cn,
{yhuang2010,dxh}@xmu.edu.cn

Abstract. Automatic and accurate segmentation of the ventricles and myocardium from multi-sequence cardiac MRI (CMR) is crucial for the diagnosis and treatment management for patients suffering from myocardial infarction (MI). However, due to the existence of domain shift among different modalities of datasets, the performance of deep neural networks drops significantly when the training and testing datasets are distinct. In this paper, we propose an unsupervised domain alignment method to explicitly alleviate the domain shifts among different modalities of CMR sequences, *e.g.*, bSSFP, LGE, and T2-weighted. Our segmentation network is attention U-Net with pyramid pooling module, where multi-level feature space and output space adversarial learning are proposed to transfer discriminative domain knowledge across different datasets. Moreover, we further introduce a group-wise feature recalibration module to enforce the fine-grained semantic-level feature alignment that matching features from different networks but with the same class label. We evaluate our method on the multi-sequence cardiac MR Segmentation Challenge 2019 datasets, which contain three different modalities of MRI sequences. Extensive experimental results show that the proposed methods can obtain significant segmentation improvements compared with the baseline models.

1 Introduction

Accurate segmentation of the ventricles and myocardium is fundamental to the diagnosis and treatment of myocardial infarction (MI) [17]. Cardiac MRI sequences are usually used for the MI diagnosis, in particular the T2-weighted MRI detect damaged and ischemic areas, the balanced-Steady State Free Precession (bSSFP) MRI clearly shows the heart structure boundary, and the late gadolinium enhancement (LGE) MRI can enhance infarcted myocardium with distinctive brightness compared to healthy structure [16]. Manual segmentation is time-consuming, so automatic segmentation is significant in the clinic.

J. Wang and H. Huang—Indicates equal contributions.

M. Pop et al. (Eds.): STACOM 2019, LNCS 12009, pp. 254–262, 2020.
https://doi.org/10.1007/978-3-030-39074-7_27

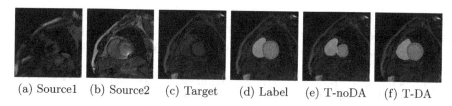

(a) Source1   (b) Source2   (c) Target   (d) Label   (e) T-noDA   (f) T-DA

Fig. 1. Performance drops due to domain shift. (a) Original T2-weighted MRI (Source1). (b) Original bSSFP MRI (Source2). (c) Original LGE MRI (Target). (d) LGE MRI annotation (Label). (e) The segmentation results of LGE MRI using an established model trained on T2-weighted and bSSFP MRI data (T-noDA). (f) The segmentation results of an LGE MRI using our model trained on T2-weighted and bSSFP MRI data (T-DA). The yellow region denotes the right ventricle, the green region denotes the left ventricle, and the blue region denotes the myocardium. (Color figure online)

Recently, deep learning network has become a powerful tool for semantic segmentation on heart structures [12,13]. Obviously, the ventricles and myocardium segmentation results can be improved combining the complimentary information from T2-weighted and bSSFP MRI sequences [16]. To save labeling time, sometimes only the T2-weighted and bSSFP MRI sequences and corresponding labels are available. However, a well-trained segmentation model may underperform when being tested on data from different modalities, which is caused by the domain shift (as shown in Fig. 1). Fine-tuning on the target domain data is a simple but efficient method to alleviate the performance drop. But it still requires massive data collection and enormous annotation workload which are impossible for many real-world medical scenarios. For this reason, constructing a general segmentation model suitable for various modalities is promising yet still challenging.

Unsupervised Domain Adaptation (UDA) methods have shown compelling results on reducing the dataset shift across distinct domains. Prior efforts on this problem intended to match the source and target data distributions to learn a domain-invariant representation. For example, Maximum Mean Discrepancy (MMD) was introduced to minimize the distance of source and target feature distributions in Reproducing Kernel Hilbert Space (RKHS) [11]. CycleGAN [15] tackled the image-to-image translation task in a fully unsupervised manner, and thus is capable of reducing the domain shift in the pixel-level. AdaptSegNet [10] solved the unsupervised cross domain segmentation problem by leveraging the domain adversarial training approach. In the context of medical imaging, [3] developed an UDA framework based on adversarial networks for lung segmentation on chest X-rays. [8] improved the UDA framework with Siamese architecture for Gleason grading of histopathology tissue. [5] proposed a domain critic module and a domain adaptation module for the unsupervised cross-modality adaptation problem. These approaches, which based on the domain adversarial training, required empirical feature selection. [2] proposed the synergistic fusion of adaptations from both image and feature perspectives for heart structures segmentation. However, this approach, which based on image-to-image adaptation, cannot be directly introduced to the multiple source domain adaptation problems due to the presence of multiple domain shifts between different source domains.

In this paper, we propose a domain alignment method for the UDA problem, which helps the established model segment the ventricles and myocardium accurately in the target domain without requiring target labels. Firstly, in order to reduce the domain shift with respect to the image appearance, we propose a histogram match operation for all the data. Secondly, we introduce the domain adversarial training in the output space, which can directly align the predicted segmentation results across different domains. Finally, we further propose a group-wise feature recalibration module (GFRM) to improve the domain adversarial training by integrating multi-level features without requiring manual selection to progressively align the source and target feature distributions. The proposed method is extensively evaluated on the multi-sequence cardiac MR Segmentation (MS-CMRSeg) Challenge 2019 datasets, including bSSFP, LGE and T2-weighted MRI sequences.

2   Method

Figure 2 overviews our segmentation method for ventricles and myocardium in MRI sequences. We use modified 2D attention U-Net with pyramid pooling module as our segmentation backbone architecture [7,14]. To align the distance over feature and output spaces across different domain, feature-level and mask-level discriminator are adopted. Moreover, the group-wise feature recalibration module (GFRM) is introduced to transfer multi-level feature information. The details of the above modules are shown in Fig. 3.

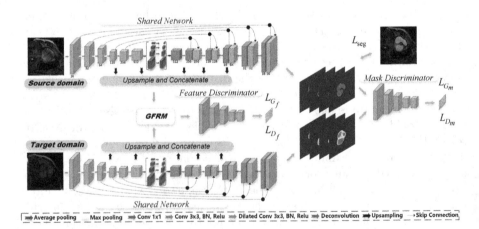

Fig. 2. Schematic view of our proposed framework.

2.1   Network Architecture

Segmentation Network. It is essential to build upon a good baseline model to achieve high-quality segmentation results. Our segmentation network follows the spirit of attention U-Net architecture [7]. In encoder network, we keep the convolution layer as the initial setting. We perform three maxpool operations totally. Dilated convolution is adopted after third maxpool operation to capture large receptive field to alleviate loss of structural information. Inspired by [14], pyramid pooling module is introduced to generate multi-scale features to alleviate the variance of heart size over each patient. In decoder network, we perform three deconvolution operations totally. For further accurate segmentation results, attention gate (as the black dot shown in Fig. 3(a)) is utilized to learn to focus on ventricles and myocardium structures. In attention gate, the features in the encoder part (as the blue rectangle shown in Fig. 3(a)) and decoder part (as the gray rectangle shown in Fig. 3(a)) are first squeezed with 3 × 3 convolution layer along the channel direction respectively and then added together. After that, we squeeze the features to single channel feature map to form structure attention with 1 × 1 convolution layer and generate final feature maps by dot product. Finally, we use 1 × 1 convolution layer with four output channels followed by the *sigmoid* activation function to generate the probability maps. To save computational resources, we share the network with the same parameters between source and target domain.

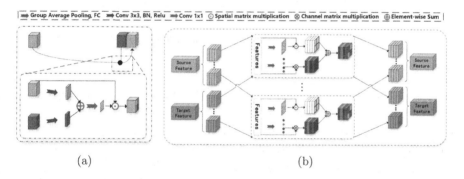

(a)   (b)

Fig. 3. Architecture of the sub-networks in our framework. (Color figure online)

Group-wise Feature Recalibration Module. Before we perform group-wise feature recalibration operation, different size features from segmentation network above are expanded and concatenated via upsampling and concatenating operations. The features are send to GFRM. Our GFRM follows the spirit of [9]. Different from the above method, we divide features into four groups corresponding to the segmentation categories to focus on specific heart structures and we recalibrate features in each group (as shown in Fig. 3(b)). GFRM consists of two parts: channel attention part and spatial attention part. In channel attention part, we first squeeze global spatial information with global average pooling and fully connection layer. Then, we can generate the channel-wise attention features by simple dot product. In the spatial attention part, we first squeeze channel information with 1×1 convolution layer. Then, we can obtain the spatial-wise attention features by simple dot product. The features from channel attention part are added with the features from spatial attention part to generate group-wise recalibrated features. Finally, the features from each group are concatenated to generate final recalibrated features.

Discriminator. The feature-level and mask-level discriminator are based on the multi-level features from GFRM and predicted mask results. We use Patch-GAN as our discriminator [6]. The network consists of 3 convolution layers with stride of 2 and 2 convolution layers with stride of 1. The kernel size of all convolution layers is 4×4 and the corresponding channel number is $64, 128, 256, 256, 1$. Except for the last layer, each convolution layer is followed by a leaky ReLU parameterized by 0.2.

2.2 Hybrid Loss Function for Source Data

Since the labels for source domain are available, we train the segmentation network with a hybrid loss. The vanilla cross-entropy loss with our unbalanced training data leads to low accuracy. We add the Jaccard loss [1] into our loss function. The training objective for source data is

$$\mathcal{L}_{ce}^s = -\mathbb{E}_{x_s \sim S}(\sum_{i=1}^{N_s}\sum_{c=1}^{C} y_{s,i,c} \log G(x_{s,i}; \Theta_g)) \tag{1}$$

$$\mathcal{L}_{jac}^s = -\mathbb{E}_{x_s \sim S}(\sum_{i=1}^{N_s}\sum_{c=1}^{C} \frac{y_{s,i,c}G(x_{s,i}; \Theta_g)}{y_{s,i,c} + G(x_{s,i}; \Theta_g) - y_{s,i,c}G(x_{s,i}; \Theta_g)}) \tag{2}$$

S represents source domain; For each source image x_s, there is one corresponding annotation y_s; N_s is the number of all source images; $\mathbb{E}_{x_s \sim S}$ means that all x_s are from S; C is the number of all categories; G is segmentation network; Θ_g is the parameters of G; $y_{s,i,c}$ and $G(x_{s,i}; \Theta_g)$ mean the annotation and prediction vectors, respectively. For cross entropy loss, the imbalance of training data leads to a local optimum with inappropriate direction of gradient decreasing, especially in the early stage. The Jaccard loss effectively helps to avoid the local optimum due to its better perceptual quality and scale invariance [1].

2.3 Adversarial Learning for Target Data

In the target domain, due to the lack of annotations, we leverage the adversarial learning to train the segmentation network by minimizing the discrepancy across the source and target domain. Domain adaptation based on both feature and output space is proved to be effective for heart structure segmentation [4].

In our framework, we employ two discriminators. The features input to feature domain discriminator are selected empirically in [4]. To overcome this problem, we propose the GFRM to leverage the full feature spectrum and automatically select prominent features in the feature space. In the segmentation network, each feature scale generates one output feature map in the same dimension via convolution and upsampling operations. The feature maps are further processed by the GFRM to highlight the prominent features and suppress the irrelevant ones. The combined feature maps are then fed to the feature discriminator network for the adversarial learning, where the losses are defined as

$$
\begin{aligned}
\mathcal{L}_{adv_{D_f}} = &- \mathbb{E}_{x_s \sim S} \log D_f(R(G(x_s; \Theta_g); \Theta_r); \Theta_{d_f}) \\
&- \mathbb{E}_{x_t \sim T}(1 - \log D_f(R(G(x_t; \Theta_g); \Theta_r); \Theta_{d_f}))
\end{aligned}
\tag{3}
$$

$$
\mathcal{L}_{adv_{G_f}} = -\mathbb{E}_{x_t \sim T} \log D_f(R(G(x_t; \Theta_g); \Theta_r); \Theta_{d_f})
\tag{4}
$$

T represents target domain; where x_t is target data; $\mathbb{E}_{x_t \sim T}$ means that all x_t are from T; R is the GFRM; Θ_r is the parameters of R; D_f is the feature discriminator; Θ_{d_f} is the parameters of D_f.

In the output space, the segmentation results of target domain should be similar to the ones of source domain. To achieve this, we employ the adversarial learning technique in the output space, where the losses are defined as

$$
\begin{aligned}
\mathcal{L}_{adv_{D_m}} = &- \mathbb{E}_{x_s \sim S} \log D_m(G(x_s; \Theta_g); \Theta_{d_m}) \\
&- \mathbb{E}_{x_t \sim T}(1 - \log D_m(G(x_t; \Theta_g); \Theta_{d_m}))
\end{aligned}
\tag{5}
$$

$$
\mathcal{L}_{adv_{G_m}} = -\mathbb{E}_{x_t \sim T} \log D_f(G(x_t; \Theta_g); \Theta_{d_m})
\tag{6}
$$

where D_m is the mask discriminator; Θ_{d_m} is the parameters of D_m.
Combined with the aforementioned loss, the full objective function

$$
\begin{aligned}
\mathcal{L}_{FULL} = &\lambda_{ce}\mathcal{L}_{ce} + \lambda_{jac}\mathcal{L}_{jac} + \lambda_{D_f}\mathcal{L}_{adv_{D_f}} \\
&+ \lambda_{G_f}\mathcal{L}_{adv_{g_f}} + \lambda_{D_m}\mathcal{L}_{adv_{D_m}} + \lambda_{G_m}\mathcal{L}_{adv_{g_m}}
\end{aligned}
\tag{7}
$$

3   Experiment

Dataset. The validation of the proposed method is performed in the MS-CMRSeg Challenge 2019 dataset covering 45 patients. There are bSSFP, T2-weighted and LGE MRI sequences in each patient data. In one patient data, the slice number and annotation of three MRI modalities are different. We combine labeled bSSFP and T2-weighted MRI sequences as source data, and unlabeled LGE MRI sequences as target data. Experienced experts manually annotated the left ventricle (LV), right ventricle(RV) and myocardium (Myo) as ground truth. We pre-processing the data for domain adaptation. The data is resized and cropped to 400×400 in the center of each slice. In order to eliminate the inconsistency in appearance, we perform histogram match operation on both source and target data, as shown in Fig. 4.

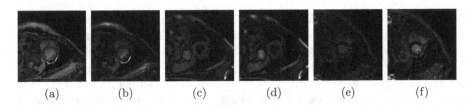

(a)   (b)   (c)   (d)   (e)   (f)

Fig. 4. Visual comparison for histogram match operation: (a) T2-weighted MRI. (b) T2-weighted MRI after histogram match. (c) bSSFP MRI. (d) bSSFP MRI after histogram match. (e) LGE MRI. (f) LGE MRI after histogram match.

Implementation Details. In our experiments, we implement our whole network with PyTorch, using a standard PC with a single NVIDIA 1080Ti. To train the segmentation network, we use the Stochastic Gradient Descent (SGD) optimizer with Nesterov acceleration where the momentum is 0.9 and the weight decay is $1e^-4$. The initial learning rate is set as 0.01 and is decreased to 0.001 after 80 epochs. For training the both feature and mask discriminator, we use Adam optimizer with the fixed learning rate as 0.0002. The weight decay is set as $5e^-5$. We totally trained 150 epochs with a mini-batch size of 8. We set λ_{ce}, λ_{jac}, λ_{G_f}, λ_{D_f}, λ_{G_m} and λ_{D_m} to $0.5, 0.5, 0.05, 1.0, 0.005$ and 1.0. The training time cost only 5 h to converge.

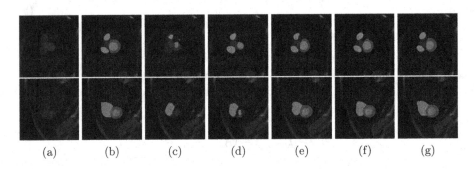

(a)   (b)   (c)   (d)   (e)   (f)   (g)

Fig. 5. Visual comparison for the LV, RV, and Myo segmentation results from ablation setting. (a) Original image from source domain. (b) Annotation. (c) S2T. (d) S2T+HM. (e) S2T+HM+MDA. (f) S2T+HM+MDA+FDA. (g) S2T+HM+MDA+FDA+GFRM.

Quantitative and Qualitative Analysis. In order to verify the effectiveness of the proposed method, we adopt Dice coefficient (DSC), Jaccard coefficient (Jac) for further evaluation. We first trained segmentation network on the source data and then test on the target data (S2T). The results in Table 1 shows that the mean Dice in S2T is too slow. As we can see, our method can promote about 36.09% in DSC and 38.38% in Jac than S2T, which indicates that our method can alleviate dataset shift across different domains.

In addition, we examine the effect of the histogram match operation (HM), mask-level adversarial learning (MDA), feature-level adversarial learning (FDA) and GFRM on the performance in the target domain. The result of the ablation study in Table 1 shows that our proposed modules can achieve a better performance than S2T. Figure 5 demonstrates that each proposed module can contribute to alleviate the domain misalignment.

Table 1. Quantitative evaluation of our proposed methods

Method	LV		RV		Myo		Mean	
	DSC [%]	Jac [%]	DSC [%]	Jac [%]	DSC [%]	Jac [%]	DSC [%]	Jac [%]
S2T	50.01	37.41	66.72	51.03	31.69	21.88	49.47	36.78
S2T+HM	59.80	47.66	76.02	62.98	38.13	26.73	57.98	45.79
S2T+HM+MDA	85.67	75.48	86.19	75.89	75.35	60.70	82.40	70.69
S2T+HM+MDA+FDA	88.43	79.68	85.70	75.14	78.43	64.57	84.19	73.13
S2T+HM+MDA+FDA+GFRM	89.33	81.15	87.17	77.29	80.17	67.04	85.56	75.16

4 Conclusion

In this paper, we proposed an unsupervised domain alignment method for left ventricle (LV), right ventricle (RV) and myocardium (Myo) segmentation from different cardiac MR sequences. We first introduced a segmentation network with hybrid segmentation loss to generate accurate prediction. We alleviate the dataset shift across different domains by leveraging the adversarial learning in both feature and output spaces. The proposed GFRM can enforce the fine-grained semantic-level feature alignment that matching features from different networks but with the same class label. Experiments show that the proposed method can achieve competitive results.

Acknowledgments. This work was supported in part by the National Natural Science Foundation of China under Grants 61571382, 81671766, 61571005, 81671674, 61671309 and U1605252, in part by the Fundamental Research Funds for the Central Universities under Grants 20720160075 and 20720180059, in part by the CCF-Tencent open fund, and the Natural Science Foundation of Fujian Province of China (No. 2017J01126).

References

1. Berman, M., Rannen Triki, A., Blaschko, M.B.: The lovász-softmax loss: a tractable surrogate for the optimization of the intersection-over-union measure in neural networks. In: Proceedings of the IEEE Conference on Computer Vision and Pattern Recognition, pp. 4413–4421 (2018)
2. Chen, C., Dou, Q., Chen, H., Qin, J., Heng, P.A.: Synergistic image and feature adaptation: towards cross-modality domain adaptation for medical image segmentation. arXiv preprint arXiv:1901.08211 (2019)

3. Dong, N., Kampffmeyer, M., Liang, X., Wang, Z., Dai, W., Xing, E.: Unsupervised domain adaptation for automatic estimation of cardiothoracic ratio. In: Frangi, A., Schnabel, J., Davatzikos, C., Alberola-López, C., Fichtinger, G. (eds.) MICCAI 2018. LNCS, vol. 11071, pp. 544–552. Springer, Cham (2018). https://doi.org/10.1007/978-3-030-00934-2_61

4. Dou, Q., et al.: PnP-AdaNet: plug-and-play adversarial domain adaptation network with a benchmark at cross-modality cardiac segmentation. arXiv preprint arXiv:1812.07907 (2018)

5. Dou, Q., Ouyang, C., Chen, C., Chen, H., Heng, P.A.: Unsupervised cross-modality domain adaptation of convnets for biomedical image segmentations with adversarial loss. In: Proceedings of the 27th International Joint Conference on Artificial Intelligence, pp. 691–697. AAAI Press (2018)

6. Isola, P., Zhu, J.Y., Zhou, T., Efros, A.A.: Image-to-image translation with conditional adversarial networks. In: Proceedings of the IEEE Conference on Computer Vision and Pattern Recognition, pp. 1125–1134 (2017)

7. Oktay, O., et al.: Attention u-net: learning where to look for the pancreas. arXiv preprint arXiv:1804.03999 (2018)

8. Ren, J., Hacihaliloglu, I., Singer, E.A., Foran, D.J., Qi, X.: Adversarial domain adaptation for classification of prostate histopathology whole-slide images. In: Frangi, A., Schnabel, J., Davatzikos, C., Alberola-López, C., Fichtinger, G. (eds.) MICCAI 2018. LNCS, vol. 11071, pp. 201–209. Springer, Cham (2018). https://doi.org/10.1007/978-3-030-00934-2_23

9. Roy, A.G., Navab, N., Wachinger, C.: Concurrent spatial and channel 'squeeze & excitation' in fully convolutional networks. In: Frangi, A., Schnabel, J., Davatzikos, C., Alberola-López, C., Fichtinger, G. (eds.) MICCAI 2018. LNCS, vol. 11070, pp. 421–429. Springer, Cham (2018). https://doi.org/10.1007/978-3-030-00928-1_48

10. Tsai, Y.H., Hung, W.C., Schulter, S., Sohn, K., Yang, M.H., Chandraker, M.: Learning to adapt structured output space for semantic segmentation. In: Proceedings of the IEEE Conference on Computer Vision and Pattern Recognition, pp. 7472–7481 (2018)

11. Tzeng, E., Hoffman, J., Zhang, N., Saenko, K., Darrell, T.: Deep domain confusion: maximizing for domain invariance. arXiv preprint arXiv:1412.3474 (2014)

12. Yang, X., et al.: Combating uncertainty with novel losses for automatic left atrium segmentation. In: Pop, M., et al. (eds.) STACOM 2018. LNCS, vol. 11395, pp. 246–254. Springer, Cham (2018). https://doi.org/10.1007/978-3-030-12029-0_27

13. Yue, Q., Luo, X., Ye, Q., Xu, L., Zhuang, X.: Cardiac segmentation from LGE MRI using deep neural network incorporating shape and spatial priors. arXiv preprint arXiv:1906.07347 (2019)

14. Zhao, H., Shi, J., Qi, X., Wang, X., Jia, J.: Pyramid scene parsing network. In: Proceedings of the IEEE Conference on Computer Vision and Pattern Recognition, pp. 2881–2890 (2017)

15. Zhu, J.Y., Park, T., Isola, P., Efros, A.A.: Unpaired image-to-image translation using cycle-consistent adversarial networks. In: Proceedings of the IEEE International Conference on Computer Vision, pp. 2223–2232 (2017)

16. Zhuang, X.: Multivariate mixture model for cardiac segmentation from multi-sequence MRI. In: Ourselin, S., Joskowicz, L., Sabuncu, M., Unal, G., Wells, W. (eds.) MICCAI 2016. LNCS, vol. 9901, pp. 581–588. Springer, Cham (2016). https://doi.org/10.1007/978-3-319-46723-8_67

17. Zhuang, X.: Multivariate mixture model for myocardial segmentation combining multi-source images. IEEE Trans. Pattern Anal. Mach. Intell. (2018)

Deep Learning Based Multi-modal Cardiac MR Image Segmentation

Rencheng Zheng[1,3], Xingzhong Zhao[1,2(✉)], Xingming Zhao[1,2], and He Wang[1,3]

[1] Institute of Science and Technology for Brain-inspired Intelligence,
Fudan University, Shanghai, China
18210850006@fudan.edu.cn
[2] Key Laboratory of Computational Neuroscience and Brain-inspired
Intelligence, Fudan University, Ministry of Education, Shanghai, China
[3] Zhangjiang International Brain Imaging Centre (ZIC), Fudan University,
Shanghai, China

Abstract. Accurate modelling and segmentation of the ventricles and myocardium in cardiac MR (CMR) image is crucial for diagnosis and treatment management for patients suffering from myocardial infarction (MI). As the infarcted myocardium can be enhanced in LGE CMR through appearing with distinctive brightness compared with the healthy tissues, it can help doctors better study the presence, location, and extent of MI in clinical diagnosis. Hence it is of great significance to delineate ventricles and myocardium from LGE CMR images. In this study, we proposed a multi-modal cardiac MR image segmentation strategy via combining the T2-weighted CMR and the balanced-Steady State Free Precession (bSSFP) CMR sequence. Specifically, the T2-weighted CMR and bSSFP are co-registered and set as the input of the convolution neural network to do the first stage segmentation in bSSFP space. By predicting all the labels, we further registered T2-weighted CMR, bSSFP and the corresponding labels into LGE space, and as an input to the convolution neural network to do the second stage segmentation. In the end, we post-processed the output masks to further ensure the accuracy of the segmentation results. The dice score of the proposed method in test set of Multi-sequence Cardiac MR (MS-CMR) Challenge 2019 achievers 0.8541, 0.7131 and 0.7924 for left ventricular (LV), left ventricular myocardium (LV myo), and right ventricular (RV).

Keywords: Myocardial infarction · Multi-modal · Cardiac MR · Image segmentation · Convolution neural network

1 Introduction

Cardiovascular diseases (CVDs) consistently rank among the top major causes of morbidity and mortality [1], and early detection and prevention of cardiovascular disease is a hot topic of research in recent years. Cardiac magnetic resonance imaging has many different sequences which can reveals observe structural information as well as respond to certain functional information, e.g., myocardial infarction (MI) can be

© Springer Nature Switzerland AG 2020
M. Pop et al. (Eds.): STACOM 2019, LNCS 12009, pp. 263–270, 2020.
https://doi.org/10.1007/978-3-030-39074-7_28

observed clearly in late sputum enhancement (LGE) cardiac magnetic resonance (CMR) sequences, while local area acute injury is shown apparently in T2-weighted CMR images, and the cardiac motions and clear boundaries can be delineated through the balanced-Steady State Free Precession (bSSFP) cine sequence [2]. Meanwhile, CMR has great potential to be used in structural (e.g. volume) and functional (e.g. ejection fraction) cardiac parameters estimation, which is helpful in clinical diagnosis and disease management. However, it's extremely time consuming to manually identify and delineate the corresponding structure in cardiac, and the result depends on the professional ability of doctors and varies from person to person. Automatic cardiac segmentation algorithm is far more efficient and robust and commonly has higher accuracy than human. Many studies have been proposed for right and left ventricular, and ventricular myocardium segmentation in cardiac segmentation field [3–5]. For example, Gaussian mixture model (GMM)-based segmentation, which depended on the different intensity distributions in different issues [3], atlas-based segmentation based on large samples and EM algorithm [6]. Otherwise, some deep learning model based on various neural network structure have been also described in literature, e.g. the Fully Convolutional Neural Network [7], and the U-net [8]. However, most of the mentioned studies were based on a specific CMR imaging sequence, which may encounter the problem of valuable information missing and lead to a not good result. Differently, Zhuang proposed the multivariate mixture model (MvMM) segmentation model based multi-sequence CMR [9], and Liu developed a new segmentation framework based on conditional generative adversarial network (cGAN) technique, which integrated the LGE and T2-weight sequence information for accuracy improvement in cardiac segmentation [10]. In general, accurate cardiac MR segmentation is still facing challenges due to the high heterogeneity in cardiac MR imaging.

In this work, we proposed a deep learning based cardiac registration and segmentation model for RV, LV and LV myo segmentation in LGE space. The model combined valuable information in T2-weighted CMR, bSSFP CMR and LGE CMR for more accurate and robust cardiac segmentation.

2   Method

Our cardiac MR image segmentation framework comprised several stages. The cardiac segmentation was firstly performed in C0 (bSSFP cine sequence is referred as C0) space combining C0 images and the registered T2 images, followed by registered C0 images, T2 images and the corresponding segmented labels into LGE space. After that, we performed segmentation processing combining three series (C0, T2, and LGE) in LGE space, followed by neural network fine tune with the provided ground truth labels for LGE images. Finally, some post processing methods were applied for further segmentation accuracy improvement. The entire framework is shown in Fig. 1.

2.1   Stage1: Automatic Cardiac Segmentation in T2 and C0

As the final purpose of our work was to combine T2, C0 assisting cardiac segmentation in LGE images, the first stage of our work was the achievement of fully automatic cardiac segmentation in T2 and C0. It is believed that images of T2-weighted CMR has the better contrast to show acute injury and ischemic regions, and the C0 CMR is superior in cardiac motions capture and presents clear boundaries. Here we proposed deep learning based segmentation scenario which used T2 and C0 images as two-channel input. Co-registration was performed between T2 and C0, specifically, we registered the T2 CMR images into C0 space based on Normalized Mutual Information criterion [11] Eq. 1:

$$NMI(A, B) = \frac{H(A) + H(B)}{H(A, B)} \tag{1}$$

where $H(A)$ and $H(B)$ is the Shannon entropy of image A and image B, and $H(A, B)$ represents the joint entropy.

The registration processing can be built as Eq. 2:

$$rI_{T2} = y_{T2\_bSSFP} I_{T2} \tag{2}$$

where y_{T2_bSSFP} is the estimated transformation matrix from T2 to C0, I_{T2} represents for the original T2 images, and rI_{T2} stands for the registered T2 images. The interpolation method is using 4th degree B-spline.

After co-registration, C0 images and T2 images were used as two-channel input of the U-net based neural network [12], and the ground truth was the provided C0 labels. The reason for directly choosing C0 labels as the ground truth is the spatial resolution of C0 and LGE was closer compared to T2, as we further registered these two sequences into LGE space in the next step, the registration error of C0 label was relatively small. In addition, label fusion did not seem to be helpful for our segmentation.

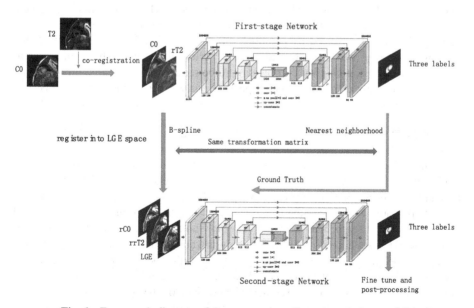

Fig. 1. Framework diagram of the proposed cardiac segmentation model

2.2   Stage2: Automatic Cardiac Segmentation in LGE

Here we performed the segmentation processing based on three sequence (C0, T2, LGE) in LGE space. C0, registered T2 images and the corresponding segmented labels in stage1 were registered into LGE space firstly. It should be mentioned that the image and label were using the same transformation matrix, however, 4th degree B-spline interpolation method was applied for image data and nearest neighborhood interpolation algorithm was used for label(performed in SPM12), which can ensure the registered labels would not generate new values. Furthermore, rather than directly registered T2 data into LGE space, we firstly registered C0 image into LGE space and obtained the transformation matrix, followed by applied the estimated transformation matrix on the registered T2 data in C0 space performed in stage1. As the difference of Inter-layer resolution between T2 and LGE data is relatively large, the strategy of using C0 image as a transition can improve the registration accuracy of T2 in LGE space.

The registration processing can be expressed as Eqs. 3, 4, 5:

$$rI_{C0} = y_{C0\_LGE}I_{C0} \qquad (3)$$

$$rrI_{T2} = y_{C0\_LGE}rI_{T2} \qquad (4)$$

$$rL_{C0T2} = y_{C0\_LGE}L_{C0T2} \qquad (5)$$

where y_{C0_LGE} is the estimated transformation matrix from C0 to LGE, I_{C0} stands for original C0 images, rI_{C0} refers to registered C0 images in LGE space, rI_{T2} represents the registered T2 image in C0 space performed in stage1, L_{C0T2} is the segmented labels in stage1 and rL_{C0T2} means the corresponding registered labels in LGE space.

The neural network training was performed on the co-registered three sequence MR images and used the registered label as the ground truth. Actually, this label was a kind of 'pseudo-ground truth' due to the registration error, and the network training processing can be also referred as potential calibration processing. In other word, the training processing was not expected to have perfect similarity with original ground truth, and the registration error is promising to be reduced during learning processing. Some regularization techniques were applied in our work to strengthen this effect.

3   Stage3: Fine Tune and Post-processing

With the trained network in stage2, we fine-tuned the model with the provided 5 true labels of LGE data for more accurate cardiac segmentation in LGE space. The remaining LGE test data were predicted via the final model.

Finally, some post-processing techniques were applied for further accurateness and robustness of our segmentation model. The threshold of output probability segmentation maps was set according to the accuracy in validation set. Meanwhile a network of whole label was also trained, which means the right and left ventricular, and ventricular myocardium label formed a whole label as the ground truth of the neural network. It was found that the segmented boundary of the cardiac based on whole label training was more reliable than the composition of separate segmentation of three sub-labels, hence the segmentation of whole label can be regarded as a constraint of our segmentation scenario of RV, LV and LV myo, which means the part of positive segmentation results in separate RV, LV and LV myo segmentation processing outside the whole label region will be removed.

4 Experimental Setting and Results

4.1 Dataset

In this study, the proposed model was trained and evaluated on the dataset of multi-sequence cardiac MR image segmentation competition in MICCAI 2019. The dataset comprised 45 patients with T2 CMR, bSSFP CMR, and LGE CMR. The RV, LV and myo labels of T2 CMR, bSSFP CMR in first 35 patients were provided [9, 13], while for LGE CMR, only the labels of the first 5 patients was available, and the remain LGE CMR data was regarded as the test set.

4.2 Image Processing and Training Setting

The registration processing was based on Normalized Mutual Information criterion. For the image data, the interpolation method was 4th degree B-spline, while nearest neighborhood interpolation algorithm was chosen for label data. All the registration processing was performed in MATLAB SPM12.

The segmentation was performed on RV, LV and LV myo, and the whole label, respectively. All the input images were normalized using z-score (zero mean and unit std), and data augmentation was applied using axis flip, elastic transformation and rotation. The structure of the neural network was based on U-net framework, while the 'valid padding' was replaced by 'same padding', and L2 norm regularization was applied on the convolutional kernel parameters with a weight of $1e^{-5}$. Furthermore, a batch normalization layer was added after each convolution layer. The loss function was the common soft Dice loss. Our networks were implemented in Keras, Adaptive Moment Estimation (Adam) was used in the training, with initial learning rate $1e^{-4}$, batch size 10 and maximum epoch 200. Training was implemented on an NVIDIA Volta V100 32 GB GPU.

5 Results

Figure 2 shows the segmentation result of RV, LV and myo and whole label respectively for a case in the test set. The first line is the co-registered C0, T2 and LGE images input into the network, and the second line is the segmentation results of LV (red), LV myo (blue) and RV (green), while the results of whole label (yellow) and the integrated label of RV, LV and LV myo are shown in the third line.

We evaluated the purposed segmentation model on the test dataset of the competition, the evaluation metrics included Dice score, average surface distance and Hausdorff distance. Our model achieves Dice score of 0.8541 ± 0.0581, 0.7131 ± 0.1001

268   R. Zheng et al.

and 0.7924 ± 0.0871 for left ventricular, ventricular myocardium and right ventricular, respectively. The detailed performance is shown in Table 1 and Fig. 3, and we don't compared our results with other represented methods limited to the test set which don't released.

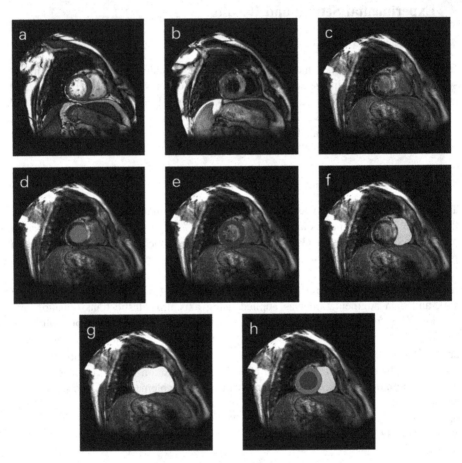

Fig. 2. Segmentation results of a case in the testing dataset. (a) (b) (c): co-registered C0, T2 and LGE CMR images, (d) (e) (f) separate segmentation results of LV, myo and RV, (g) segmentation result of the whole label, (h) the integrated label of separate segmentation (Color figure online)

Table 1. Detailed performance of the proposed segmentation model in test dataset

Dice			Average surface distance (mm)			Hausdorff distance (mm)		
LV	LV myo	RV	LV end	LV epi	RV end	LV end	LV end	RV end
0.8541 ± 0.0581	0.7131 ± 0.1001	0.7924 ± 0.0871	3.1939 ± 1.3595	3.0312 ± 1.1450	3.5774 ± 1.2711	14.9099 ± 6.4417	17.2826 ± 5.5731	16.9357 ± 5.5100

LV: left ventricular, RV: right ventricular, myo: myocardium, end: endocardium, epi: epicardium.

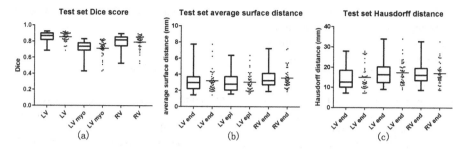

Fig. 3. Performance of the proposed model in test set, (a) Dice score, (b) Average surface distance, (c) Hausdorff distance

6 Discussion and Conclusion

In this work, we described a deep learning based registration and segmentation framework for multi-sequence MR segmentation. T2 CMR, bSSFP CMR and LGE CMR were effectively combined for cardiac segmentation in LGE space. The registration in our model was based on Normalized Mutual Information criterion and various interpolation algorithms were applied for image data and label. The segmentation processing was a cascaded U-Net framework, followed by some post-processing techniques. All the MR sequences were covered in our work for a better segmentation performance, however, the provided labels for C0, T2 and LGE were not fully utilized. A more effective strategy of label fusion for better utilization would be studied in the future work. Otherwise, some other modeling methods (e.g. learning based method) for motion correction between C0, T2 and LGE sequences in addition to simply using criterion based registration algorithm should be explored for this challenge for further better segmentation performance. As of now, the label of the test set and the performance rank has not been published, hence we cannot compare the performance of the proposed method with other works well, and this part will be improved later. The proposed method finally achieves average Dice scores of 0.8541, 0.7131 and 0.7924 for LV, LV myo and RV respectively in test set of MS-CMR Challenge 2019.

References

1. Alwan, A.: Global status report on noncommunicable diseases 2010. World Health Organization (2011)
2. Kim, H.W., Farzaneh-Far, A., Kim, R.J.: Cardiovascular magnetic resonance in patients with myocardial infarction: current and emerging applications. J. Am. Coll. Cardiol. **55**(1), 1–16 (2009)
3. Hu, H., et al.: Hybrid segmentation of left ventricle in cardiac MRI using gaussian-mixture model and region restricted dynamic programming. Magn. Reson. Imaging **31**(4), 575–584 (2013)
4. Qian, X., et al.: Segmentation of myocardium from cardiac MR images using a novel dynamic programming based segmentation method. Med. Phys. **42**(3), 1424–1435 (2015)

5. Petitjean, C., et al.: Right ventricle segmentation from cardiac MRI: a collation study. Med. Image Anal. **19**(1), 187–202 (2015)
6. Lorenzo-Valdes, M., et al.: Segmentation of 4D cardiac MR images using a probabilistic atlas and the EM algorithm. Med. Image Anal. **8**(3), 255–265 (2004)
7. Tran, P.V.: A fully convolutional neural network for cardiac segmentation in short-axis MRI (2016)
8. Charmchi, S., Punithakumar, K., Boulanger, P.: Optimizing U-Net to segment left ventricle from magnetic resonance imaging. In: Proceedings 2018 IEEE International Conference on Bioinformatics and Biomedicine (Bibm), pp. 327–332 (2018)
9. Zhuang, X.: Multivariate mixture model for myocardial segmentation combining multi-source images (2018)
10. Liu, J., et al.: Multi-sequence myocardium segmentation with cross-constrained shape and neural network-based initialization. Comput. Med. Imaging Graph. **71**, 49–57 (2019)
11. Estévez, P.A., et al.: Normalized mutual information feature selection. IEEE Trans. Neural Netw. **20**(2), 189–201 (2009)
12. Ronneberger, O., Fischer, P., Brox, T.: U-Net: convolutional networks for biomedical image segmentation. In: Navab, N., Hornegger, J., Wells, W.M., Frangi, A.F. (eds.) MICCAI 2015. LNCS, vol. 9351, pp. 234–241. Springer, Cham (2015). https://doi.org/10.1007/978-3-319-24574-4_28
13. Zhuang, X.: Multivariate mixture model for cardiac segmentation from multi-sequence MRI. In: Ourselin, S., Joskowicz, L., Sabuncu, M.R., Unal, G., Wells, W. (eds.) MICCAI 2016. LNCS, vol. 9901, pp. 581–588. Springer, Cham (2016). https://doi.org/10.1007/978-3-319-46723-8_67

Segmentation of Multimodal Myocardial Images Using Shape-Transfer GAN

Xumin Tao[1,2], Hongrong Wei[1,2], Wufeng Xue[1,2(✉)], and Dong Ni[1,2]

[1] The National-Regional Key Technology Engineering Ultrasound,
Guangdong Key Laboratory for Biomedical Measurements and Ultrasound Imaging,
School of Biomedical Engineering, Health Science Center, Shenzhen University,
Shenzhen, China
xwolfs@hotmail.com
[2] Medical Ultrasound Image Computing (MUSIC) Lab, Shenzhen, China

Abstract. Myocardium segmentation of late gadolinium enhancement
(LGE) Cardiac MR images is important for evaluation of infarction
regions in clinical practice. The pathological myocardium in LGE images
presents distinctive brightness and textures compared with the healthy
tissues, making it much more challenging to be segment. Instead, the
balanced-Steady State Free Precession (bSSFP) cine images show clearly
boundaries and can be easily segmented. Given this fact, we propose a
novel shape-transfer GAN for LGE images, which can (1) learn to generate realistic LGE images from bSSFP with the anatomical shape preserved, and (2) learn to segment the myocardium of LGE images from
these generated images. It's worth to note that no segmentation label
of the LGE images is used during this procedure. We test our model on
dataset from the Multi-sequence Cardiac MR Segmentation Challenge.
The results show that the proposed Shape-Transfer GAN can achieve
accurate myocardium masks of LGE images.

Keywords: Segmentation · LGE · Cross-modality · Shape transfer

1   Introduction

Late gadolinium enhancement (LGE) MRI technology can accurately identify
myocardial infarction (MI), myocardial fibrosis and cardiac amyloid and other
diseases. Its good spatial resolution and tissue specificity have unique advantages in the diagnosis of various types of myocardial lesions. To this end, correct
segmentation of LGE CMR images is a prerequisite of quantitative evaluation.

While recent advancements in deep neural network have results in many accurate models of automatic segmentation of cardiac left/right ventricle (LV/RV)
from bSSFP cine images, only a few efforts have been given to segmentation of
cardiac structures from LGE images. Contrary to bSSFP cine image where the
myocardium and the background blood pool have different intensity distributions
and can be well discriminated, the intensity of LGE images is heterogeneous for
the myocardium and the boundary of the pathological part is even invisible.

© Springer Nature Switzerland AG 2020
M. Pop et al. (Eds.): STACOM 2019, LNCS 12009, pp. 271–279, 2020.
https://doi.org/10.1007/978-3-030-39074-7_29

Recently proposed methods of LGE segmentation include model-based [1] and learning-based ones [2,3]. Zhuang et al. (2018) used multivariate mixture model to describe the likelihood of multi-source images in a common space and model the motion shift of different slices with a rigid transformation. After iteratively registration and segmentation, the model achieved good myocardial segmentation. However, the complexity of the model may hinder it from effective application in practice [2]. Xiong et al. (2019) proposed a dual fully convolutional neural network to extract global and local structures from MRI slices of different resolutions for 3D left atrium segmentation from LGE images. The network was trained with a dataset of 154 subjects and achieved accurate segmentation results [3]. Yue et al. (2019) used a deep neural network SRSCN, which incorporated shape prior and slice spatial information as regularization for LGE cardiac segmentation [1]. After being trained with LGE images of 25 patients, it can segment the LV, myocardium, and RV well. A drawback of these learning-based methods is that they require large manually labeled LGE images for model training, which is not always available and more prone to errors or an accurate registration between the cine MRI and LGE MRI.

The MS-CMRSeg 2019 challenge that held in conjunction with STACOM at MICCAI 2019 provides an open and fair platform for the multi-sequence ventricle and myocardium segmentation. However, there are only LGE images of 5 patients with ground truth label for training. This adds more difficulty during the development of learning-based model besides the above-mentioned ones. To relieve the problems of insufficient training labels, we proposed to generate plenty of image-label pairs by generative adversarial network (GAN). Goodfellow et al. (2016) first proposed GAN and achieved impressive results in generating realistic images from noisy input vectors [4]. Various strategies have been devoted to the development of GAN to improve the quality of the generated fake images [6–8] or to learn the disentangled representations that are aware of high-level semantic context. For our work, high quality of generated image-label pair is of critical importance to the final performance. To this end, we make use of the recently proposed CycleGAN [5], which employed a cycled reconstruction loss to ensure the consistency between the input and output domains.

We propose a novel method, shape-transfer GAN, for the segmentation of LGE cardiac images, without ground truth labels. Specifically, we introduce a shape preservation term to make the generated LGE images share the same myocardium shape with that of the input bSSFP image. In such a way, the proposed shape-transfer GAN is capable of generating realistic LGE images, and in the meantime learning how to segment these generated images. Without labels of real LGE images for finetuning, the obtained segmentor can be directly applied for segmentation of real LGE images. The method obtains good performance on LGE images of 40 patients, with dice metric of 0.847, 0.776, 0.686 for LV, RV and myocardium, respectively.

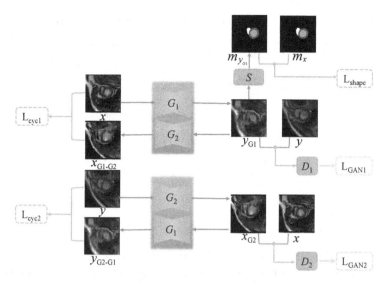

Fig. 1. Building block of shape-transfer GAN, whose loss includes three parts: adversarial learning loss (L_{gan}), cycle-reconstruction loss (L_{cyc}) and shape preservation loss (L_{shape}). G, D and S represent generator, discriminator and segmentation network respectively. And x, y represent bSSFP and LGE images respectively.

2 Method

The proposed Shape-Transfer GAN can learn a mapping functions between two domains bSSFP and LGE, with the anatomical shape of myocardium in the bSSFP preserved while the intensity distribution being changed into the style of LGE image. To obtain the myocardium shape and enforce the shape preservation loss, a segmentation module is also embedded in the generator. Once the adversarial learning is completed, the segmentation module can be directly applied to novel LGE images for myocardium segmentation. Figure 1 gives the building block of shape-transfer GAN, which contains three blocks: (1) adversarial learning (L_{gan}), where two generators and two discriminators are learned to generate realistic LGE images from bSSFP images, and also the inverse mapping; (2) Cycle-reconstruction learning (L_{cyc}), where the quality of the generated images are improved by the constraint of re-generating the original input image [5]; and (3) shape-preservation learning (L_{shape}), where the generated LGE images are constrained to preserve the anatomic shape of the input bSSFP image, and a segmentation model is embedded in the generator and learned in the meantime.

2.1 Adversarial Learning

We introduce two generators G_1, G_2, and two adversarial discriminators D_1 and D_2, where D_1 aims to distinguish between real LGE images $\{y\}$ and the generated ones by $\{G_1(x)\}$ from bSSFP images and D_2 to distinguish between real bSSFP images $\{x\}$ the and generated ones by $\{G_2(y)\}$ from LGE images. In such a way, a bidirectional mapping function can be learned for the two image domains. The objective function of adversarial learning is:

$$L_{GAN1} = \mathbb{E}_{y \sim P_{LGE(y)}}[\log D_1(y)] + \mathbb{E}_{x \sim P_{bSSFP(x)}}[\log(1 - D_1(G_1(x)))] \quad (1)$$

$$L_{GAN2} = \mathbb{E}_{x \sim P_{bSSFP(x)}}[\log D_2(x)] + \mathbb{E}_{y \sim P_{LGE(y)}}[\log(1 - D_2(G_2(y)))] \quad (2)$$

$$L_{GAN}(G_1, G_2, D_1, D_2) = \frac{1}{2}(L_{GAN1} + L_{GAN2}) \quad (3)$$

where $P_{bSSFP}(x)$ and $P_{LGE}(y)$ are the data distributions of the bSSFP and LGE images, respectively.

2.2 Cycle-Reconstruction Learning

To ensure meaningful information can be well kept during the domain mapping of the adversarial learning procedure, we introduce the cycle-reconstruction learning block. Only the previous generator and discriminator cannot necessarily lead to a good domain mapping, due to the oscillation learning procedure. The discriminator only makes global image-level decision of whether an image is fake or real, while the detailed local information cannot be guaranteed. Given this consideration, the cycle-reconstruction learning block is introduced, which re-generated the original image of source domain from the generated images in the target domain. A good mapping should keep well structure information of the source domain during this cycle-reconstruction procedure. We express the objective of cycle-reconstruction learning as:

$$L_{cyc1} = \mathbb{E}_{x \sim P_{bSSFP(x)}}[\|G_2(G_1(x)) - x\|_1] \quad (4)$$

$$L_{cyc2} = \mathbb{E}_{y \sim P_{LGE(y)}}[\|G_1(G_2(y)) - y\|_1] \quad (5)$$

$$L_{cyc}(G_1, G_2) = \frac{1}{2}(L_{cyc1} + L_{cyc2}) \quad (6)$$

2.3 Shape Preservation Learning

To make sure the generated LGE images $\{y_{G1}\}$ have clear and correct boundary, we make use of the available myocardium shape masks $\{m_x\}$ of the bSSFP images and introduce the shape preservation learning block, where the myocardium shape of the generated fake LGE image is constraint to be identical to that of the input bSSFP image. To achieve this, a segmentation network S is embedded into the generator G_1 to obtain the myocardium shape of the generated images. Shape preservation is described by the cross-entropy (CE) loss between the shape $\mathbf{m_x}$ of the of real bSSFP image and the output of the segmentation network:

$$L_{shape}(S, G_1) = \mathbb{E}_{x \sim P_{bSSFP(x)}}[CE(m_x, S(G_1(x)))] \quad (7)$$

2.4   Overall Objective

The overall objective of our shape-transfer GAN is:

$$L_{total}(G_1, G_2, D_1, D_2, S) = L_{GAN} + \lambda_1 L_{cyc} + \lambda_2 L_{shape} \tag{8}$$

where λ_1 and λ_2 adjust the balance of the three terms. After the shape-transfer GAN is learned, the segmentation network S can be directly applied to any novel LGE images.

3   Experiment

We validate our method with the dataset provided by the MS-CMRSeg 2019 challenge. In this section, we first describe the experiment configurations, which include details of the dataset, our experimental setup and the evaluation criterion. Then we report the performance of our method and compare it with existing state-of-art methods.

3.1   Experimental Configuration

Dataset. The Multimodal CMR data (includes bSSFP, LGE and T2 images) used in the paper were collected from 45 patients, where ground truth (GT) of myocardium (Myo), left ventricle (LV) and right ventricle (RV) in 35 patients were provided for bSSFP and T2 images, while for 5 patients GT of LGE images were provided for validation. The rest 40 patients are used for test. For each patient, the bSSFP images consist of 8–12 slices, with in-plane resolution of 1.25×1.25 mm and slice thickness of 8 to 13 mm. The T2 images have 3–7 slices, with in-plane resolution of 1.35×1.35 mm and slice thickness of 12 to 20 mm. The LGE images have 10–18 slices with in-plane resolution of 0.75×0.75 mm and slice thickness of 5 mm. The size of the images range from 256×256 to 512×512 and were resized and crop to 128×128 for Shape-Transfer GAN.

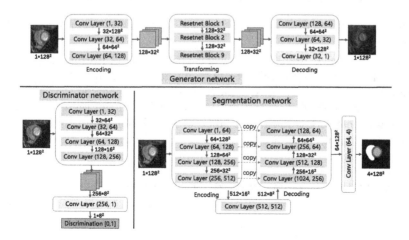

Fig. 2. The network details of generator, discriminator and segmentor.

Experiment Setup. Figure 2 shows the network details. We used AdamOpti-mizer with learning rate of 1e-4 for Shape-Transfer GAN and 1e-5 for segmen-tation network. The input of Shape-Transfer GAN were 2D slices from bSSFP images of 35 patients and LGE images of 45 patients. Note that the segmenta-tion network was pretrained with bSSFP image-label pairs and then the Shape-Transfer GAN was trained for 200 epochs.

Evaluation Metrics. To evaluate the segmentation performance, Dice score, Jaccard score, average surface distance (ASD) and Hausdorff Distance (HD) were used. Let V_{Seg} and V_{GT} be the segmentation and the ground truth volume, and B_{Seg}, B_{GT} their boundaries. They are computed as:

$$Dice(V_{Seg}, V_{GT}) = \frac{2|V_{Seg} \cap V_{GT}|}{|V_{Seg} + V_{GT}|}, \quad Jaccard(V_{Seg}, V_{GT}) = \frac{2|V_{Seg} \cap V_{GT}|}{|V_{Seg} \cup V_{GT}|} \quad (9)$$

$$ASD(B_{Seg}, B_{GT}) = \frac{1}{|B_{Seg}| + |B_{GT}|} \times \left(\sum_{p \in B_{Seg}} d(p, B_{GT}) + \sum_{q \in B_{GT}} d(q, B_{Seg}) \right) \quad (10)$$

$$HD(B_{Seg}, B_{GT}) = \max \left\{ \sup_{p \in B_{Seg}} \inf_{q \in B_{GT}} d(p, q), \sup_{p \in B_{GT}} \inf_{q \in B_{Seg}} d(p, q) \right\} \quad (11)$$

3.2 Performance Evaluation and Analysis

Ablation Study. We first conduct ablation study and validate the effectiveness of our shape-transfer GAN using the LGE images of the 5 patients for validation. The proposed shape-transfer GAN was compared with U-net and GAN with no shape preservation (no-shape GAN). We train the U-net directly with bSSFP images or the generated LGE images, and the provided labels in bSSFP domain.

As can be drawn from Table 1, when no adversarial learning is employed, U-net cannot be applied directly to LGE images due to the different intensity distributions. For no-shape GAN, the adversarial learning transfers this distri-bution from the bSSFP domain to the target LGE domain, therefore make the segmentation network trained with labels of bSSFP domain ready for the LGE domain. But the performance is still far from satisfaction. With the proposed shape preservation learning block, the performance can be clearly improved. Shape-Transfer GAN can keep the myocardium shape accurately in the generated LGE images, thus leads to better synthetic image-label pairs for learning.

Table 1. Ablation study of our method on validation dataset of 5 patients LGE images. Dice score ($Mean \pm std$) is presented.

Method	LV	RV	Myo
U-Net	0.249 ± 0.197	0.286 ± 0.069	0.043 ± 0.035
No-Shape GAN	0.589 ± 0.190	0.638 ± 0.092	0.303 ± 0.190
Shape-Transfer GAN	0.764 ± 0.125	0.738 ± 0.090	0.607 ± 0.117

Figure 3 shows the visualization results from three different slices for these methods. As can be obviously drawn, when no LGE labels were used for training, U-net cannot capture the shape of myocardium at all. It even makes false positive regions in distant background regions. With adversarial learning, No-shape GAN can well capture the shape of LV, RV and myocardium. However, there are still some regions that are not captured or boundaries that are not well aligned. With the shape-preservation learning, Shape-Transfer GAN can deliver accurate segmentation results. An interest observation from the first row is that a part of RV is missing in the ground truth label, while our method can fill it.

Table 2 shows the performance of our method on the test dataset, which has LGE images of 40 patients (three failure cases were excluded). Without true label information for model training, our method is still capable of segmentation well the LV, RV and myocardium of LEG images. Especially, our method achieves for LV segmentation Dice score of 0.847, ASD of 3.110 mm, HD of 17.986 mm.

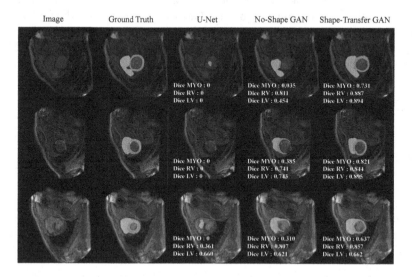

Fig. 3. Segmentation results of different methods for ablation study. Each row represents different slice from LGE images. The proposed Shape-Transfer GAN gives the best segmentation results.

278   X. Tao et al.

Table 2. Segmentation performance of Shape-Transfer GAN on test dataset of LGE images from 40 patients with three failure cases excluded.

Metrics	LV	RV	Myo
Dice	0.847 ± 0.054	0.776 ± 0.048	0.686 ± 0.078
Jaccard	0.738 ± 0.079	0.636 ± 0.063	0.527 ± 0.087
Metrics	LV endo	LV epi	RV endo
ASD (mm)	3.110 ± 1.039	3.022 ± 0.736	3.953 ± 0.908
HD (mm)	17.986 ± 4.028	17.453 ± 5.902	21.974 ± 10.026

Table 3. Performance comparison of our method and existing state-of-art methods on the same dataset.

Dice score	Shape-Transfer GAN	GMM+bSSFP	MvMM	SRSCN
LV	0.847 ± 0.054	0.836 ± 0.071	0.866 ± 0.063	0.915 ± 0.052
RV	0.776 ± 0.048	–	–	0.882 ± 0.084
Myo	0.686 ± 0.078	0.635 ± 0.120	0.717 ± 0.076	0.812 ± 0.105

Performance Comparison. Table 3 compares our method with existing state-of-art methods, including two GMM-based methods (GMM+bSSFP, MvGMM) [2], and one deep neural network based method (SRSCN) [1]. When compared with the GMM-based methods, our method can deliver comparable performance, but with less application complexity. The iterative optimization procedure adds the complexity of the GMM-based methods during practice application. When compared with SRSCN, our method fails to show better or comparable performance. This is due to the fact that SRSCN was trained with ground truth labels of 25 patients' LGE images.

4   Conclusion

We propose the Shape-Transfer GAN for cardiac segmentation of LGE MRI images, which can learn the procedure of generating realistic LGE images with the anatomical shape information well kept, and thus obtain an LGE segmentation network. Our method avoided the use of LGE label during the learning of the segmentation. We validated the effectiveness of the proposed shape-transfer technique and tested the final performance on a dataset of 40 patients. The good segmentation results prove that our method has a great potential in cases of medical image segmentation tasks with insufficient labeled data.

Acknowledgement. The paper is partially supported by the Natural Science Foundation of China under Grants 61801296, the Overseas High-Caliber Personnel Peacock Plan of Shenzhen, and the start-up funding of Shenzhen University.

References

1. Zhuang, X.: Multivariate mixture model for myocardial segmentation combining multi-source images. IEEE Trans. Pattern Anal. Mach. Intell. **41**, 2933–2946 (2018). https://doi.org/10.1109/TPAMI.2018.2869576
2. Xiong, Z., Fedorov, V.V., Fu, X., Cheng, E., Macleod, R., Zhao, J.: Fully automatic left atrium segmentation from late gadolinium enhanced magnetic resonance imaging using a dual fully convolutional neural network. IEEE Trans. Med. Imaging **38**(2), 515–524 (2019)
3. Yue, Q., Luo, X., Ye, Q., Xu, L., Zhuang, X.: Cardiac segmentation from LGE MRI using deep neural network incorporating shape and spatial priors. In: Shen, D., et al. (eds.) MICCAI 2019. LNCS, vol. 11765, pp. 559–567. Springer, Cham (2019). https://doi.org/10.1007/978-3-030-32245-8_62
4. Goodfellow, I., et al.: Generative adversarial nets. In: Advances in Neural Information Processing Systems (2014)
5. Zhu, J.-Y., et al.: Unpaired image-to-image translation using cycle-consistent adversarial networks. In: Proceedings of the IEEE International Conference on Computer Vision (2017)
6. Isola, P., Zhu, J.Y., Zhou, T., et al.: Image-to-image translation with conditional adversarial networks. In: Proceedings of the IEEE Conference on Computer Vision and Pattern Recognition, pp. 1125–1134 (2017)
7. Radford, A., Metz, L., Chintala, S.: Unsupervised representation learning with deep convolutional generative adversarial networks. arXiv preprint arXiv:1511.06434 (2015)
8. Mao, X., Li, Q., Xie, H., et al.: Least squares generative adversarial networks. In: Proceedings of the IEEE International Conference on Computer Vision, pp. 2794–2802 (2017)

Knowledge-Based Multi-sequence MR Segmentation via Deep Learning with a Hybrid U-Net++ Model

Jinchang Ren[1(✉)], He Sun[1], Yumin Huang[1], and Hao Gao[2]

[1] Department of Electronic and Electrical Engineering, University of Strathclyde, Glasgow, UK
{jinchang.ren,h.sun}@strath.ac.uk, yumin.huang.2016@uni.strath.ac.uk
[2] School of Mathematics and Statistics, University of Glasgow, Glasgow, UK
Hao.Gao@glasgow.ac.uk

Abstract. The accurate segmentation, analysis and modelling of ventricles and myocardium plays a significant role in the diagnosis and treatment of patients with myocardial infarction (MI). Magnetic resonance imaging (MRI) is specifically employed to collect imaging anatomical and functional information about the cardiac. In this paper, we have proposed a segmentation framework for the MS-CMRSeg Multi-sequence Cardiac MR Segmentation Challenge, which can extract the desired regions and boundaries. In our framework, we have designed a binary classifier to improve the accuracy of the left ventricles (LVs). Extensive experiments on both validation dataset and testing dataset demonstrate the effectiveness of this strategy and give an insight towards the future work.

Keywords: Cardiac image segmentation · Binary classifier · U-Net++

1 Introduction

Recent advances in the MRI technology have led to an effective way to manage the treatment plan for patients. Since the MR can provide a better enhancement in the infected area and highlight the illness part with special brightness, a variety of applications have been developed, such as the Carotid arterial plaque stress analysis [1], the tracking of myocardial deformation [2], etc. Among these tasks, the accurate segmentation of the MR image can help to extract the desired regions of interest (ROIs), which plays a key role in the clinical analysis. However, there are many challenging issues towards the performance of segmentation in MRI. Firstly, unlike the segmentation work in natural images, a more precise segmentation result is required in the MR image, even tiny errors may damage the result of further diagnose. Secondly, the manual segmentation of the desired boundaries is very time-consuming and error prone, which is not accessible in the practical applications. Several challenging examples are shown in the Fig. 1. What is more, it is crucial to fully utilize the provided multiple modalities of MR

© Springer Nature Switzerland AG 2020
M. Pop et al. (Eds.): STACOM 2019, LNCS 12009, pp. 280–289, 2020.
https://doi.org/10.1007/978-3-030-39074-7_30

images, which may improve the segmentation accuracy. Therefore, an effective and robust segmentation strategy is required, especially for the MS-CMRSeg Multi-sequence Cardiac MR Segmentation Challenge [3,4].

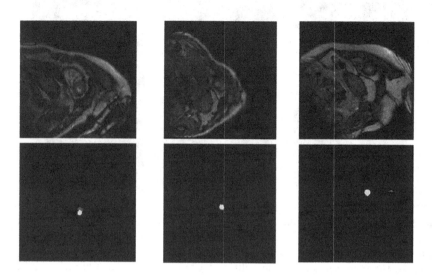

Fig. 1. Several examples of the challenging images.

In this paper, we propose an effective segmentation framework for the provided CMR images. To figure out the given task, we have analyzed the dataset and chosen a suitable deep learning framework first, i.e. the U-Net++ [4]. After that, some preprocessing techniques are considered before the U-Net++ to reduce the potential noise and improve the final performance. As the left vertical usually has a fixed shape in most of slices, we have designed a binary classifier module in the U-Net++ framework, which can significantly improve the accuracy of left ventricle.

The rest of this paper is organized as follows. In Sect. 2, the utilized dataset is introduced, along with a brief summary of the Multi-sequence Cardiac MR Segmentation Challenge. The motivation and implementation of our designed framework is detailed in Sect. 3. In Sect. 4, the experimental results and analysis are presented and discussed. Finally, some concluding remarks are drawn in Sect. 5.

2   Dataset

In this paper, we have conducted experiments on the dataset from MS-CMRSeg 2019 Multi-sequence Cardiac MR (CMR) Segmentation Challenge [3,4]. The whole CMR data are come from 45 patients where each patient has been scanned by three CMR sequences, including the late gadolinium enhancement (LGE),

282   J. Ren et al.

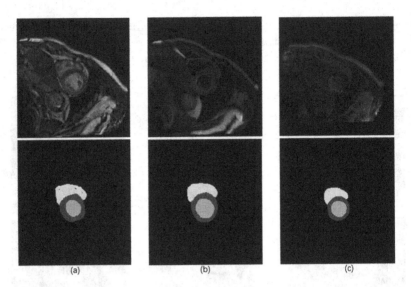

Fig. 2. Example of three different sequences from the same patient, the first row are the original images with false color and the second are the corresponding ground truth with false color, where the green, the cyan and the yellow pixels represents the left ventricle, the myocardium and the right ventricle, respectively: (a) bSSFP. (b) T2. (c) LGE (Color figure online)

T2 and balanced-Steady State Free Precession (bSSFP). In this challenge, the dataset is separated as training set and testing set. Four classes are labelled in the ground truth data, including the left ventricle, the right ventricle (RV), the myocardium and the background. The training set includes the LGE CMR images with ground truth of the first to the fifth patient, i.e. the validation dataset, the T2-weighted and bSSFP CMR image with corresponding ground truth for the first to the thirty-fifth patient. And for the last ten patients, only the T2-weighted and bSSFP CMR images are provided. For the testing dataset, the rest LGE CMR images are utilized for the final evaluation. For those three different sequences, each LGE CMR image usually consists of 10 to 18 slices, covering the main body of the ventricles, and the BSSFP image consist of 8 to 12 sequential slices which have been scanned at the diastolic end. Different from the other two sequences, T2 CMR image only has a small number of slices (3, 5, 6, 7 or 8 slices), which implies the constituted testing dataset has a relatively smaller size than the training set. In total, the number of slices from three sequences in the training dataset is less than 500 and the size of slices from these three sequences is inconsistent. Some examples from the training dataset are illustrated in Fig. 2.

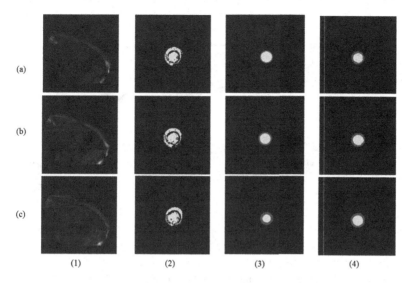

Fig. 3. Three classes segmentation results (a)–(c) by using K-means++ with Hough transform. (1) original images. (2) Results from K-means with Hough transform. (3) Results from further Hough transform. (5) Ground truth. The segmentation accuracy for left ventricle and myocardium after further Hough transform are 0.7443, 0.8677 and 0.5053, respectively.

3 The Proposed Framework

3.1 Motivation

In this section, our designed model will be discussed, which includes our motivation and implementation. Currently, numerous methods have been proposed for the segmentation problem, which can be classified as traditional methods and deep learning-based methods. To design a more robust framework, we have investigated both above methods and tried to combine them together.

First, some traditional image segmentation algorithms have been considered, including the Hough transform [5], the watershed [6], the active contours [7], the level set [8], and the K-means++ [9], etc. The Hough transform can achieve a better performance in left ventricle and myocardium, but it heavily relies on the chosen parameter. The watershed also suffers this dilemma and some redundant boundaries could be generated if parameters are not selected appropriately. For both active contours and the level set methods, they require some initial set of points to evolve the final boundary, which is not efficient in dealing with the given task. Although most of the traditional methods are not favorable, we have found out that the fusion of the binary K-means++ and Hough transform might be useful for the segmentation of left ventricles and myocardium, some results from a three classes (background, left ventricle and myocardium) classifier based on K-means++ and Hough transform are shown in the Fig. 3. What is more,

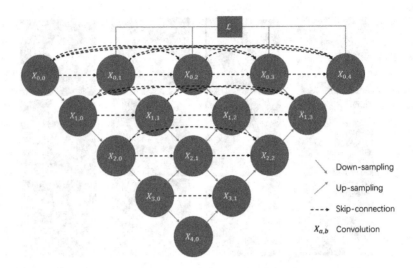

Fig. 4. The structure of U-Net++.

the binary classification demonstrates its superiority in the segmentation of left vertical, which can increase the accuracy.

In the last few years, the U-Net [10] framework has drawn great attention in the medical image segmentation area due to its efficiency and simple framework. With its skip connection architecture, the U-Net can better capture both local and global features, which fulfils the requirement of the medical imaging segmentation. According to the nested and dense skip connection, the U-Net++ is proposed to promote the performance and it has been proved to be a robust model. Compared to the U-Net, the U-Net++ can increase the accuracy from 1% to 5% in the validation dataset. Furthermore, the U-Net++ does not suffer from the heavy computational burden, which gives us a better option to investigate more. The structure of U-Net++ is shown in the Fig. 4. For increasing the segmentation accuracy, we have attempted to exploit some popular techniques, like data augmentation, etc. However, these techniques could not improve the accuracy significantly with less computational burden, which is not supportive for this challenge. For the data augmentation problem, the details are discussed in the experimental results.

3.2   Implementation

After the introduction of background of this challenge, the implementation of our proposed framework is presented in this subsection. Since the desired ROIs are located at the center of the slice and the size of each slice is inconsistent, we have employed a pre-processing step to deal with such inconsistency. We have resized all slices from the training dataset into the same size as both of their height and width are set to be 256. To remove the potential noise from the background, we have cropped the resized slices and keep the central part of each slice, where the final height and width are set as 128. After the pre-processing step, we have trained two classifiers simultaneously with the training set. As discussed above, the binary classifier aiming to distinguish the left ventricle and the rest classes are advantageous, we have trained one binary classifier to find the left ventricle. Another four-classes segmentation model has been trained to classify all four classes in each slice. In the final, we combine the results from these two classifiers simply by considering the classification map from the binary model as the priority. The classification map generated from the four class classifier is filtered by the classification map generated from the binary classifier. The diagram of our framework is presented in the Fig. 5.

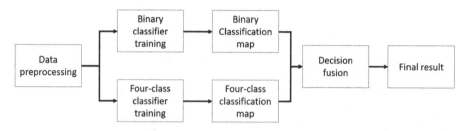

Fig. 5. The flowchart of our proposed framework.

Table 1. The mean and standard deviation of the Dice score on three classes.

	Left ventricle	Myocardium	Right ventricle
Dice	0.757 ± 0.127	0.470 ± 0.117	0.539 ± 0.151

4 Results

4.1 Parameter Settings

In this part, the utilized parameters in our proposed framework will be given in detail. The optimal parameters are chosen through the performance on validation dataset. For the training epochs, it is set to 600, and the batch size equals to 16. We have used the Adam optimizer with a learning rate of 1e-6. For achieving better performance, we have initialized the weight of loss of both classifiers, the binary model is set to be 1:6 for the background and the left ventricle and the four classes model is 1:6:6:6 where the background is set to be 1 and the rest are 6. Generally, we have only utilized the training dataset to train our model and the validation dataset to prove the efficiency of our approach. However, for the purpose of achieving better performance on the challenge, we have utilized the validation dataset to train the model in the last submission. For the hardware requirement, all our experiments and the training process of our proposed framework are conducted on the Google Colab with TESLA K80 (12 GB).

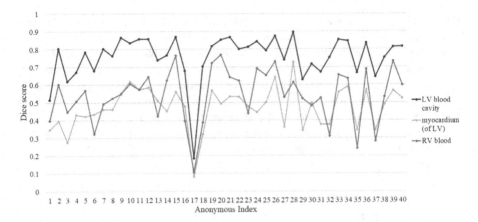

Fig. 6. The Dice score from the organizers.

4.2 Performance of Test Dataset

To evaluate the performance our proposed framework, we have tested our proposed framework on the challenge test dataset and received the feedback from organizers, including the Dice score, the Jaccard index, the Surface and Hausdorff distance. The result about the Dice score is shown in Fig. 6 and corresponding mean and standard derivation are depicted in the Table 1. From the result, it can be clearly seen that the accuracy of the left ventricles is much better than the rest, which proves that the binary classifier is suitable for the segmentation of left ventricles.

4.3 Experimental Analysis

In this part, we will present the related experiments to discuss some interesting issues and give some further comparison about our framework.

In our model, we have defined a pre-processing step and designed a binary classifier. Therefore, it is crucial to prove the significance of these two ideas. Therefore, we have done a comparison between our proposed methods and one four classes classifier framework on the validation dataset, which is depicted as 'Binary+Four' and 'Only Four'. Besides, we have also implemented the data augmentation step to inspect its function. The rest parameters are kept the same as above. The performance is shown in the Table 2, which includes the 'ROI'accuracy, the total accuracy and the training time. The 'ROI' accuracy is calculated only from the left ventricle, myocardium and right ventricle pixels, which is interpreted in Fig. 8. It can be recognized that after the combination of binary and four-class classifiers, the accuracy can be improved by 2%. As seen in Table 2, the effect of data augmentation can be noticed, where the accuracy is increased by 9% with more training samples from the data augmentation. Although data augmentation can generate more training samples and improve the accuracy, its huge computational burden seems impractical, especially for the limited time challenge or real-time applications (Fig. 7).

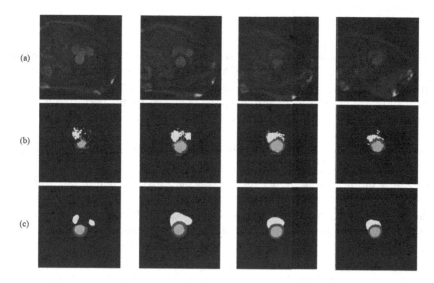

Fig. 7. Some results from the validation dataset. (a) original images. (b) segmented mask. (c) Ground truth.

Table 2. The mean and standard deviation of the Dice score on three classes.

Model	Augmentation	ROI accuracy	Total accuracy	Training time (h)
Binary+Four	Yes	0.6789	0.9803	18
Binary+Four	No	0.5893	0.9764	1.8
Only Four	Yes	0.6572	0.9802	9
Only Four	No	0.5707	0.9762	0.9

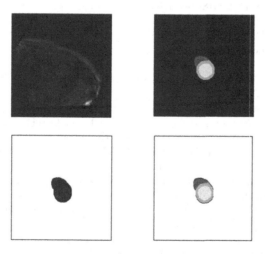

Fig. 8. The example of defined 'ROI'. Left top: the original image. Right top: ground truth of original image. Left bottom: cropped 'ROI'. Right bottom: ground truth of cropped 'ROI'.

5 Conclusion

In this paper, we have proposed a U-Net++ based framework for the MRI segmentation, especially for the MS-CMRSeg Multi-sequence Cardiac MR Segmentation Challenge. Although the performance on the right ventricle and myocardium are not good enough, we have obtained better performance on the left ventricle with the binary classifier module, which can give an insight about the Cardiac segmentation task.

Due to the time limitation of this challenge, there are still some unsolvable issues about the Cardiac MR segmentation. In the future, we will focus on the design of a more flexible model for the Cardiac MR segmentation, which can fully utilize the multiple sequence data and capture more 3D information. What is more, some multi-stage methods will also be investigated [11–16] and more reliable features will be extracted [17–20] to remove the noise and further improve the accuracy.

References

1. Gao, H., et al.: Carotid arterial plaque stress analysis using fluid-structure interactive simulation based onin-vivomagnetic resonance images of four patients. J. Biomech. **42**, 1416–1423 (2009)
2. Schuster, A., et al.: Cardiovascular magnetic resonance myocardial feature tracking concepts and clinical applications. Circ. Cardiovasc. Imaging **9**(4), e004077 (2016)
3. Zhuang, X.: Multivariate mixture model for cardiac segmentation from multi-sequence MRI. In: International Conference on Medical Image Computing and Computer-Assisted Intervention, Athens Greece, pp. 581–588 (2016)
4. Zhuang, X.: Multivariate mixture model for myocardial segmentation combining multi-source images. IEEE Trans. Pattern Anal. Mach. Intell. (2018). https://doi.org/10.1109/TPAMI.2018.2869576
5. Ballard, D.H.: Generalizing the Hough transform to detect arbitrary shapes. Pattern Recogn. **13**(2), 111–122 (1981)
6. Meyer, F.: Topographic distance and watershed lines. Signal Process. **38**(1), 113–125 (1994)
7. Chan, T.F., Vese, L.A.: Active contours without edges. IEEE Trans. Image Process. **10**(2), 266–277 (2001)
8. Sussman, M., Smereka, P., Osher, S.: A level set approach for computing solutions to incompressible two-phase flow. J. Comput. Phys. **114**(1), 146–159 (1994)
9. Arthur, D., Vassilvitskii, S.: K-means++: the advantages of careful seeding. In: Proceedings of the Eighteenth Annual ACM-SIAM Symposium on Discrete Algorithms, pp. 1027–1035. Society for Industrial and Applied Mathematics (2007)
10. Ronneberger, O., Fischer, P., Brox, T.: U-Net: convolutional networks for biomedical image segmentation. In: Navab, N., Hornegger, J., Wells, W.M., Frangi, A.F. (eds.) MICCAI 2015. LNCS, vol. 9351, pp. 234–241. Springer, Cham (2015). https://doi.org/10.1007/978-3-319-24574-4_28
11. Ijitona, T.B., et al.: SAR sea ice image segmentation using watershed with intensity-based region merging. In: 2014 IEEE International Conference on Computer and Information Technology, Xi'an, pp. 168–172 (2014)

12. Ren, J., et al.: Effective SAR sea ice image segmentation and touch floe separation using a combined multi-stage approach. In: 2015 IEEE International Geoscience and Remote Sensing Symposium (IGARSS), Milan, pp. 1040–1043 (2015)
13. Xie, X., et al.: Automatic image segmentation with superpixels and image-level labels. IEEE Access **7**, 10999–11009 (2019)
14. Huang, H., et al.: Combined multiscale segmentation convolutional neural network for rapid damage mapping from postearthquake very high-resolution images. J. Appl. Remote Sens. **13**(2), 022007 (2019)
15. Sun, G., et al.: Dynamic post-earthquake image segmentation with an adaptive spectral-spatial descriptor. Remote Sens. **9**(9), 899 (2017)
16. Hwang, B., et al.: A practical algorithm for the retrieval of floe size distribution of Arctic sea ice from high-resolution satellite Synthetic Aperture Radar imagery. Elem. Sci. Anth. **5**, 38 (2017)
17. Han, J., et al.: Background prior-based salient object detection via deep reconstruction residual. IEEE Trans. Circuits Syst. Video Technol. **25**(8), 1309–1321 (2015)
18. Han, J., et al.: Object detection in optical remote sensing images based on weakly supervised learning and high-level feature learning. IEEE Trans. Geosci. Remote Sens. **53**(6), 3325–3337 (2015)
19. Cheng, G., et al.: Effective and efficient midlevel visual elements-oriented land-use classification using VHR remote sensing images. IEEE Trans. Geosci. Remote Sens. **53**(8), 4238–4249 (2015)
20. Fang, L., et al.: Classification of hyperspectral images by exploiting spectral-spatial information of superpixel via multiple kernels. IEEE Trans. Geosci. Remote Sens. **53**(12), 6663–6673 (2015)

Combining Multi-Sequence and Synthetic Images for Improved Segmentation of Late Gadolinium Enhancement Cardiac MRI

Víctor M. Campello[1]([✉]), Carlos Martín-Isla[1], Cristian Izquierdo[1],
Steffen E. Petersen[3,4], Miguel A. González Ballester[2,5], and Karim Lekadir[1]

[1] Dept. Matemàtiques i Informàtica, Universitat de Barcelona, Barcelona, Spain
victor.campello@ub.edu
[2] BCN-MedTech, DTIC, Universitat Pompeu Fabra, Barcelona, Spain
[3] Barts Heart Centre, Barts Health NHS Trust, London, UK
[4] William Harvey Research Institute, NIHR Barts Biomedical Research Centre,
Queen Mary University of London, London, UK
[5] ICREA, Barcelona, Spain

Abstract. Accurate segmentation of the cardiac boundaries in late gadolinium enhancement magnetic resonance images (LGE-MRI) is a fundamental step for accurate quantification of scar tissue. However, while there are many solutions for automatic cardiac segmentation of cine images, the presence of scar tissue can make the correct delineation of the myocardium in LGE-MRI challenging even for human experts. As part of the Multi-Sequence Cardiac MR Segmentation Challenge, we propose a solution for LGE-MRI segmentation based on two components. First, a generative adversarial network is trained for the task of modality-to-modality translation between cine and LGE-MRI sequences to obtain extra synthetic images for both modalities. Second, a deep learning model is trained for segmentation with different combinations of original, augmented and synthetic sequences. Our results based on three magnetic resonance sequences (LGE, bSSFP and T2) from 45 different patients show that the multi-sequence model training integrating synthetic images and data augmentation improves in the segmentation over conventional training with real datasets. In conclusion, the accuracy of the segmentation of LGE-MRI images can be improved by using complementary information provided by non-contrast MRI sequences.

Keywords: Multi-sequence cardiac MRI · Late gadolinium enhancement MRI · Image segmentation · Image synthesis · Deep learning

1 Introduction

Late gadolinium enhancement magnetic resonance imaging (LGE-MRI) is widely used to assess presence, location and extent of regional scar or fibrotic tissue in

© Springer Nature Switzerland AG 2020
M. Pop et al. (Eds.): STACOM 2019, LNCS 12009, pp. 290–299, 2020.
https://doi.org/10.1007/978-3-030-39074-7_31

the myocardium. Whilst LGE-MRI is a well-established technique and key to many cardiovascular magnetic resonance (CMR) examinations there are challenges in quantification and interpretation due to a number of factors. Image analysis depends on image quality which can be affected by suboptimal CMR acquisition. Correct inversion times (TI) need to be identified and then TI require appropriate adjustments to allow good 'nulling' of remote, unaffected myocardium. This ensures optimal contrast between scar/fibrosis (bright) and normal, remote myocardium (dark). Timing after contrast administration is important to allow not only sufficient wash-out of contrast agent (gadolinium chelate) from the remote myocardium but also from the blood pool. Images acquired too early will leave the blood pool bright which makes differentiating subendocardial infarct from blood pool challenging.

In the existing literature, two main families of techniques have been proposed to automatically segment LGE-MRI data. The first one segments directly the LGE-MRI images by using different techniques such as graph-cuts [1], atlas-based registration [2], or more recently Convolutional Neural Networks (CNNs) [3]. However, these techniques generally lack robustness due to the limited availability of LGE-MRI datasets for training. As a result, the second family of techniques has considered exploiting other cardiac MRI sequences to provide additional signals for guiding more robustly the segmentation process. For instance, some researchers [4,5] proposed to segment first cine-MRI images and to propagate the obtained contours into the LGE-MRI images through image registration. Similarly but by using additional sequences, the authors in [6] implemented an atlas-based segmentation approach combining information from balanced-Steady State Free Processing (bSSFP), LGE and T2 sequences. However, these techniques are highly dependent on the image registration step, which is challenging due to the inherent differences between the cardiac MRI sequences.

In addition, in order to improve segmentation and increase the model robustness over unseen data, image synthesis has been proposed recently. The most common model combines generative adversarial networks (GANs) with a cycle-consistency constrain for image-to-image translation and two segmentation networks, one for each image domain, trained end-to-end in order to benefit from a combined loss function. This model has been applied for cross-modality segmentation improvement [7,8], domain adaptation across scanners [8] or across modalities [9] and segmentation of an unlabeled target modality using only the source ground truth [10,11]. Alternatively, a GAN can be trained to generate synthetic images from masks according to some conditional value, like the dataset style, as in the case of retinal fundus images for vessel segmentation [12].

In this paper, we propose an approach to circumvent the need for image registration, while addressing the lack of LGE-MRI images for training. Concretely, we implement a CNN-based approach that is capable of learning key properties of the cardiac structures simultaneously from multiple cardiac MRI sequences. Furthermore, image synthesis and data augmentation are used to generate new examples that take into account both the global appearance of LGE-MRI data and the local appearance of scar tissues. With this approach, direct deep learning based segmentation of LGE-MRI is enabled without the need for inter-sequence image registration and while exploiting the richness of multi-sequence cardiac MRI.

2   Method

2.1   Dataset

Data Description. The LGE-MRI dataset used in this paper was provided as part of the Multi-Sequence Cardiac Magnetic Resonance Segmentation Challenge (MS-CMRSeg). It consists of 45 patients from Shanghai Renji Hospital that were scanned using three MRI sequences: bSSFP, LGE and T2. Ground truth segmentations of the left ventricle (LV), right ventricle (RV) and myocardium (MYO) were provided for some of the cases according to the distribution in Table 1 (second row). Even though all sequences were acquired and selected for the end-diastolic cardiac phase, there were differences in the shape of the cardiac boundaries consistently between the three sequences for the same patient. Moreover, the slices were not aligned between the sequences in the direction of the ventricular axis, which further complicates the application of image registration. Note that all patients in the sample suffer from cardiomyopathies and that every LGE-MRI image presents a scar of variable size within the myocardial wall.

Table 1. MS-CMRSeg sequences details.

	bSSFP	LGE	T2
Number of patients	45	45	45
Segmented patients	35	5	35
Number of slices	8–12	10–18	3–7
Slice thickness (mm)	8–13	5	12–20
TR/TE (ms)	2.7/1.4	3.6/1.8	2000/90
In-plane resolution (mm)	1.25×1.25	0.75×0.75	1.35×1.35

Data Pre-processing. As a first step, intensity bias correction was applied to all sequences to correct for potential artifacts and the intensity histograms of all images were matched to a common one to obtain coherent appearances across images. Furthermore, before the training process, all images were interpolated and cropped so that they had a pixel size of 256×256 and the same resolution. They were also normalised such that the mean intensity and the standard deviation equal 0.5, thus ensuring most of the input values to be positive in between 0 and 1 for convenience in later representation of the images.

2.2 Increasing Training Sample

Before describing the CNN model implemented in this paper for LGE-MRI segmentation, this section presents two methods used to increase the number of training data and obtain higher LGE-MRI variability.

Data Augmentation. By using the provided segmentations, a set of 50 landmarks were evenly placed around the epicardium and endocardium. With these, the myocardium and left ventricle were rotated relative to the rest of the image, as shown in the examples in Fig. 1, in order to obtain an augmented dataset with varying locations of the scar tissues. Since the contour of the epicardium is not perfectly round in general, a Gaussian filter of size 3×3 was applied around the outer boundary to smooth the transition between the rotated and fixed regions, thus preventing image intensity discontinuities. A total of twenty 7.2 degrees rotations were applied. Thus, the LGE-MRI dataset was multiplied by a factor of 20 and the location of the scar in the myocardium ranged between the initial position and 144 degrees clockwise. This augmentation technique increases the variability in the scar locations within the myocardial wall that was otherwise very low due to the small number of patients available for training. Furthermore, further data augmentations were obtained by applying small rotations of the input images up to 15 degrees before training.

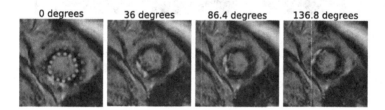

Fig. 1. Example of three rotations of the myocardial wall with respect to the whole image by using the landmarks provided in the leftmost image. This shows the changes in the location of the scar tissues

Image Synthesis. The rationale behind the proposed image synthesis is that there are many more segmented cine-MRI datasets available open-access or in clinical registries for training CNN models. Thus, to increase the number of annotated LGE-MRI cases for training, image synthesis from cine-MRI images sequences is proposed. To achieve this, the CycleGAN method [13] was implemented using the PyTorch library provided at this link[1].

This method translates images from one domain to another without the need for image registration or for the sequences to be from the same patients. It consists of a pair of generators G_{LGE}, G_{bSSFP} and a pair of discriminators D_{LGE},

---

[1] https://github.com/junyanz/pytorch-CycleGAN-and-pix2pix.

D_{bSSFP} that have opposed goals. The generator G_{LGE} (G_{bSSFP}) transforms the bSSFP (resp. LGE) sequence into a realistic LGE (bSSFP) image, while the discriminator D_{LGE} (D_{bSSFP}) attempts to distinguish between real and fake LGE (bSSFP) sequences. To achieve a good image translation between the two sequences, the loss function contains two terms: (1) an adversarial loss for each target domain that accounts for the similarity between the generated and real images, and (2) a cycle consistency loss that ensures that the transformed image $G_{LGE}(X)$ $(G_{bSSFP}(Y))$ is transformed back to X (Y) through G_{bSSFP} (G_{LGE}).

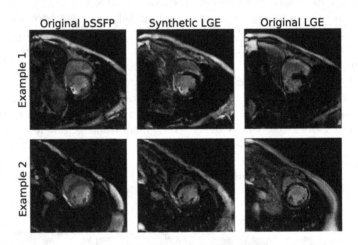

Fig. 2. Examples of synthetic LGE-MRI images. The leftmost column are the original cine images, the central column shows the transformed images to the LGE domain and the rightmost column is the most similar slice from the real LGE sequences, since they were not registered/aligned.

For the training of the CycleGAN model, all slices from the 45 patients for the LGE and bSSFP sequences were used during 200 epochs. The training took 12 h on a NVIDIA 1080 GPU with a batch size of 1. The Adam optimizer was used with learning rate of 2×10^{-4}, with first and second moment decay rates of 0.5 and 0.999, respectively. Some examples for the generated images are shown in Fig. 2.

In order to evaluate the quality of the generated images, two segmentation models (like the one described in the next subsection) were trained using the bSSFP images and the synthetic LGE images separately. The obtained results are presented in Table 2. In particular, the synthetic LGE images, that are anatomically similar to the original bSSFP, provide more information for the task of LGE segmentation.

2.3 CNN-based LGE Segmentation

Once a large set of training sample was obtained from the original, augmented and synthetic images, a modified U-Net architecture [14] was used for the image

Table 2. Average and standard deviation for the Dice score of segmentation results over the five labeled LGE volumes.

	LV		MYO		RV	
	avg.	std.	avg.	std.	avg.	std.
model trained w. bSSFP	0.503	0.406	0.370	0.301	0.515	0.434
model trained w. synthetic LGE	0.809	0.116	0.688	0.145	0.820	0.065

segmentation by integrating two techniques: (1) a deep supervision term in the upsampling path as proposed in [15] that will act as lower-resolution masks that are convolved to condition the final predictions; and (2) a reduction of the number of filters after each upsampling operation to match the number of labels as proposed by [16]. Each image in the dataset was provided as a single channel input, thus forcing the model to differentiate between sequences with a unique set of weights. Additionally, in order to avoid overfitting given the sample size, dropout was used after every max pooling and upsampling operations, except for the high level features in the architecture, as shown in Fig. 3.

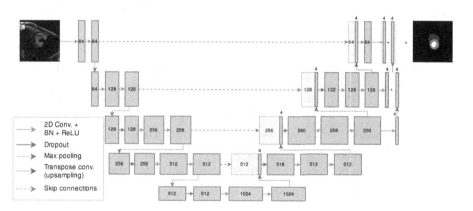

Fig. 3. Detailed architecture of the CNN model used for LGE segmentation. The numbers in the boxes correspond to the number of channels. Convolution operations have a kernel size of 3×3 and stride of 1, while transpose convolutions have a kernel size of 4×4 and stride of 2.

During training, 20% of the patients for each dataset was reserved for validation and early stopping. With a batch size of 8 images, this model took less than 36 h to achieve the best accuracy on the validation set after almost 90 epochs on a NVIDIA TITAN X GPU. The Adam optimizer was used with a learning rate of 10^{-4}, with first and second moment decay rates equal to 0.9 and 0.99, respectively.

3   Results

In order to define the best trained CNN model for LGE-MRI segmentation, various training sets were used by varying the input sequences and combinations of image synthesis and scar augmentation, as follows:

1. LGE sequences only;
2. LGE and bSSFP sequences;
3. All sequences (LGE, bSSFP and T2);
4. All sequences plus MYO and LV rotations in LGE sequences;
5. Number 1 plus synthetic LGE sequences;
6. Number 2 plus synthetic LGE sequences;
7. Number 3 plus synthetic LGE sequences;
8. Number 4 plus synthetic LGE sequences.

When evaluated on the validation set, the training set number 8 resulted in the best segmentations, showing the added value of image synthesis and data augmentation for LGE-MRI segmentation. Thus, we applied the corresponding CNN model to the test dataset composed of 40 LGE-MRI cases. The obtained segmentations were sent to the organizers of MS-CMRSeg Challenge for evaluation. The obtained results are summarized in Table 3, showing average dice scores of 90% (LV), 87% (MYO) and 81% (RV).

Table 3. Average and standard deviation for results over the test set.

	LV		MYO		RV	
	avg.	std.	avg.	std.	avg.	std.
Dice score	0.898	0.045	0.810	0.061	0.866	0.051
Jaccard index	0.817	0.072	0.685	0.084	0.768	0.078
Surface distance (mm)	2.0	0.8	1.8	0.5	2.3	0.9
Hausdorff distance (mm)	11	4	12	4	16	7

Two remarks are important to note regarding the results reported in Table 3: (1) Despite the high variability in the LGE-MRI datasets, especially in the presence, extent and location of the scar tissues, relatively consistent results are obtained with standard deviations for the dice scores around 5%. (2) Despite the availability of only 5 LGE-MRI volumes for training, the proposed approach was able to achieve comparable results to very recent deep learning techniques, which reported dice scores of 0.915 ± 0.052 (LV), 0.812 ± 0.105 (MYO) and 0.882 ± 0.084 (RV) based on 5 times more training cases (25 LGE-MRI images). [3]. This indicates the value of the proposed inter-sequence synthesis and scar augmentation for generating richer training samples.

Finally, for visual illustration, Fig. 4 shows three segmentation examples as obtained in this study. Model number 3 (second column) introduces errors that are corrected when adding synthetic images (model number 7 in the third column). The last column shows that the segmentation further improves when integrating the scar tissue augmentation as proposed in this paper (model 8).

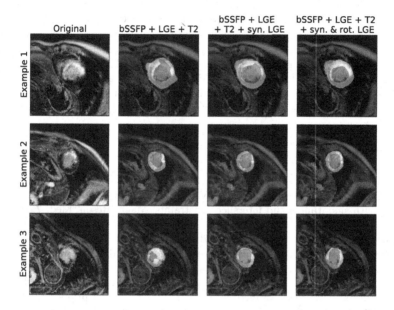

Fig. 4. Three segmentation examples as obtained by using different training combinations, showing the improvement achieved by integrating inter-sequence image synthesis (column 3) and scar tissue augmentation (column 4) during training.

4 Conclusions

This paper proposed to address the limited availability of training samples for LGE-MRI segmentation by enriching the CNN models using two complimentary methods. Firstly, since samples of annotated cine-MRI sequences are more commonly available, image synthesis of LGE-MRI images was implemented using a CycleGAN approach, thus obtaining a larger number of LGE-MRI cases during training. Secondly, we performed LGE-specific data augmentation through shape-guided rotations of the myocardium, which increases the variability related to the location of the scar tissues in the myocardium. The validation shows consistent results across the datasets, indicating the potential of this approach for enhancing the richness and generalization of LGE-specific CNNs.

Future work include the extension of the image synthesis to take into account local cardiac motion abnormality for synthesizing scar tissue, as well as the use of elastic deformations of the myocardium and scar to augment non-rigidly the LGE-MRI examples. Furthermore, extensive validation will be performed to assess in detail the relative importance of the different steps and sequences (bSSFP, T2) in enriching the CNN models for LGE segmentation.

Acknowledgements. This work was partly funded by the European Union's Horizon 2020 research and innovation programme under grant agreement No 825903 (euCan-SHare project). SEP acts as a paid consultant to Circle Cardiovascular Imaging Inc., Calgary, Canada and Servier. SEP acknowledges support from the National Institute for Health Research (NIHR) Cardiovascular Biomedical Research Centre at Barts, from the SmartHeart EPSRC programme grant (EP/P001009/1) and the London Medical Imaging and AI Centre for Value-Based Healthcare. SEP and KL acknowledge support from the CAP-AI programme, London's first AI enabling programme focused on stimulating growth in the capital's AI Sector.

References

1. Alba, X., Figueras i Ventura, R.M., Lekadir, K., Tobon-Gomez, C., Hoogendoorn, C., Frangi, A.F.: Automatic cardiac LV segmentation in MRI using modified graph cuts with smoothness and interslice constraints. Magn. Reson. Med. **72**(6), 1775–1784 (2014)
2. Kurzendorfer, T., Forman, C., Schmidt, M., Tillmanns, C., Maier, A., Brost, A.: Fully automatic segmentation of left ventricular anatomy in 3-D LGE-MRI. Comput. Med. Imaging Graph. **59**, 13–27 (2017)
3. Yue, Q., Luo, X., Ye, Q., Xu, L., Zhuang, X.: Cardiac segmentation from LGE MRI using deep neural network incorporating shape and spatial priors. arXiv preprint arXiv:1906.07347 (2019)
4. Wei, D., Sun, Y., Chai, P., Low, A., Ong, S.H.: Myocardial segmentation of late gadolinium enhanced MR images by propagation of contours from cine MR images. In: Fichtinger, G., Martel, A., Peters, T. (eds.) MICCAI 2011. LNCS, vol. 6893, pp. 428–435. Springer, Heidelberg (2011). https://doi.org/10.1007/978-3-642-23626-6_53
5. Tao, Q., Piers, S.R., Lamb, H.J., van der Geest, R.J.: Automated left ventricle segmentation in late gadolinium-enhanced MRI for objective myocardial scar assessment. J. Magn. Reson. Imaging **42**(2), 390–399 (2015)
6. Zhuang, X.: Multivariate mixture model for myocardial segmentation combining multi-source images. IEEE Trans. Pattern Anal. Mach. Intell. **41**(12), 2933–2946 (2018)
7. Zhang, Z., Yang, L., Zheng, Y.: Translating and segmenting multimodal medical volumes with cycle-and shape-consistency generative adversarial network. In: Proceedings of the IEEE Conference on Computer Vision and Pattern Recognition, pp. 9242–9251 (2018)
8. Cai, J., Zhang, Z., Cui, L., Zheng, Y., Yang, L.: Towards cross-modal organ translation and segmentation: a cycle-and shape-consistent generative adversarial network. Medical Image Anal. **52**, 174–184 (2019)
9. Chen, C., Dou, Q., Chen, H., Qin, J., Heng, P.A.: Synergistic image and feature adaptation: towards cross-modality domain adaptation for medical image segmentation. arXiv preprint arXiv:1901.08211 (2019)
10. Huo, Y., et al.: Synseg-net: synthetic segmentation without target modality ground truth. IEEE Trans. Med. Imaging **38**(4), 1016–1025 (2018)

11. Zhang, Y., Miao, S., Mansi, T., Liao, R.: Task driven generative modeling for unsupervised domain adaptation: application to X-ray image segmentation. In: Frangi, A.F., Schnabel, J.A., Davatzikos, C., Alberola-López, C., Fichtinger, G. (eds.) MICCAI 2018. LNCS, vol. 11071, pp. 599–607. Springer, Cham (2018). https://doi.org/10.1007/978-3-030-00934-2_67

12. Zhao, H., Li, H., Maurer-Stroh, S., Guo, Y., Deng, Q., Cheng, L.: Supervised segmentation of un-annotated retinal fundus images by synthesis. IEEE Trans. Med. Imaging **38**(1), 46–56 (2018)

13. Zhu, J.Y., Park, T., Isola, P., Efros, A.A.: Unpaired image-to-image translation using cycle-consistent adversarial networks. In: Proceedings of the IEEE international conference on computer vision, pp. 2223–2232 (2017)

14. Ronneberger, O., Fischer, P., Brox, T.: U-Net: convolutional networks for biomedical image segmentation. In: Navab, N., Hornegger, J., Wells, W.M., Frangi, A.F. (eds.) MICCAI 2015. LNCS, vol. 9351, pp. 234–241. Springer, Cham (2015). https://doi.org/10.1007/978-3-319-24574-4_28

15. Isensee, F., Jaeger, P.F., Full, P.M., Wolf, I., Engelhardt, S., Maier-Hein, K.H.: Automatic cardiac disease assessment on cine-MRI via time-series segmentation and domain specific features. In: Pop, M., et al. (eds.) STACOM 2017. LNCS, vol. 10663, pp. 120–129. Springer, Cham (2018). https://doi.org/10.1007/978-3-319-75541-0_13

16. Baumgartner, C.F., Koch, L.M., Pollefeys, M., Konukoglu, E.: An exploration of 2D and 3D deep learning techniques for cardiac MR image segmentation. In: Pop, M., et al. (eds.) STACOM 2017. LNCS, vol. 10663, pp. 111–119. Springer, Cham (2018). https://doi.org/10.1007/978-3-319-75541-0_12

Automated Multi-sequence Cardiac MRI Segmentation Using Supervised Domain Adaptation

Sulaiman Vesal[1]([✉]), Nishant Ravikumar[1,2], and Andreas Maier[1]

[1] Pattern Recognition Lab, Friedrich-Alexander-Universität Erlangen-Nürnberg,
Erlangen, Germany
sulaiman.vesal@fau.de
[2] CISTIB, Centre for Computational Imaging and Simulation Technologies in
Biomedicine, School of Computing, LICAMM Leeds Institute of Cardiovascular and
Metabolic Medicine, School of Medicine, University of Leeds, Leeds LS2 9JT, UK

Abstract. Left ventricle segmentation and morphological assessment are essential for improving diagnosis and our understanding of cardiomyopathy, which in turn is imperative for reducing risk of myocardial infarctions in patients. Convolutional neural network (CNN) based methods for cardiac magnetic resonance (CMR) image segmentation rely on supervision with pixel-level annotations, and may not generalize well to images from a different domain. These methods are typically sensitive to variations in imaging protocols and data acquisition. Since annotating multi-sequence CMR images is tedious and subject to inter- and intra-observer variations, developing methods that can automatically adapt from one domain to the target domain is of great interest. In this paper, we propose an approach for domain adaptation in multi-sequence CMR segmentation task using transfer learning that combines multi-source image information. We first train an encoder-decoder CNN on T2-weighted and balanced-Steady State Free Precession (bSSFP) MR images with pixel-level annotation and fine-tune the same network with a limited number of Late Gadolinium Enhanced-MR (LGE-MR) subjects, to adapt the domain features. The domain-adapted network was trained with just four LGE-MR training samples and obtained an average Dice score of ~85.0% on the test set comprises of 40 LGE-MR subjects. The proposed method significantly outperformed a network without adaptation trained from scratch on the same set of LGE-MR training data.

Keywords: Multi-sequence MRI · Deep learning · Domain adaptation · Myocardial infraction · MRI segmentation

1 Introduction

Myocardial infarction (MI) is the leading cause of mortality and morbidity worldwide [1,2]. Accurate analysis and modeling of the ventricles and myocardium

© Springer Nature Switzerland AG 2020
M. Pop et al. (Eds.): STACOM 2019, LNCS 12009, pp. 300–308, 2020.
https://doi.org/10.1007/978-3-030-39074-7_32

from medical images are essential steps for diagnosis and treatment of patients with MI [3]. MR imaging is used in the clinical workflow to provide anatomical and functional information of the heart. Different types of CMR sequences are acquired to provide complimentary information to each other, for example, T2-weighted images highlight the acute injury and ischemic regions, and the bSSFP cine sequence captures cardiac motion and presents clear boundaries. Moreover, LGE CMR can enhance the infarcted myocardium, appearing with distinctive brightness compared with healthy tissue [4]. It is widely used to study the presence, location, and extent of MI in clinical studies. Thus, segmenting ventricles and myocardium from LGE CMR images is important to predict risk of infarcts, identify the extent of infarcted tissue and for patient prognosis [5]. However, manual delineation is generally time-consuming, tedious and subject to inter- and intra-observer variations [6]. In the medical image domain, heterogeneous domain shift is a severe problem, given the diversity in imaging modalities. For example, as shown in Fig. 1, cardiac regions visually appear significantly different in images acquired using different MR sequences. Generally, deep learning models trained on one set of MR sequence images perform poorly when tested on another type of MR sequence. One approach to maintain model performance in such a setting is to employ domain adaptation e.g. image to image translation or transfer learning. Domain adaptation attempts to reduce the shift between the distribution of data within the source and target domain.

Related Work. Existing methods have approached multi-modal CMR segmentation using techniques such as cross-constrained shape [7], generative adversarial networks or 3D CNN. In [8,9], the authors first trained a CNN on the source domain and then transformed the target domain images into the appearance of source images, such that they could be analyzed using the network pre-trained on the source domain. However, these methods are based on generative adversarial networks and required substantial training data to achieve stable performance. On the other hand, there are limited works focusing on automatic LGE-CMR segmentation, which is a crucial prerequisite in a number of clinical applications of cardiology. Recently, few studies have attempted CMR multi-sequence segmentation. This type of method uses complementary information from multiple sequences to segment heart structures. [6] proposed an unsupervised method using a multivariate mixture model (MvMM) for multi-sequence segmentation. MvMM adopted to model the joint intensity distribution of the multi-sequence images. The performance of this method depends on the quality of registration.

Contributions. In this study, we develop a deep learning-based method to segment the ventricles and myocardium in LGE CMR, combined with two other sequences (T2 and bSSFP) from the same patients. T2 and bSSFP sequences are used to assist the LGE CMR segmentation. Our method introduces a feature adaptation mechanism using transfer learning which explicitly adapts the features from T2 and bSSFP sequences to LGE images with few target training data. We first train an encoder-decoder CNN on T2 and bSSFP images with pixel-level annotation and re-train the same network with a limited number of

LGE images, to adapt the learned features and imbue domain invariance between source and target domains.

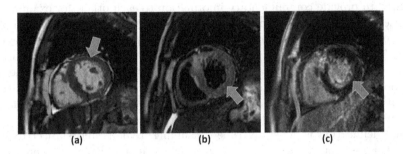

Fig. 1. Illustration of different CMR sequences: (a) bSSFP slice, (b) T2-weighted slice and (c) LGE slice. The red arrows point to left ventricle on different sequences. (Color figure online)

2   Method

2.1   Domain Adaptation

Deep learning methods are typically sensitive to domain shift and perform poorly on a new set of data with a different marginal probability distribution. However, annotating data for every new domain is a very expensive task, particularly in the medical area that requires clinical expertise. To segment LGE CMR images with very few annotated subjects, we attempted to get complementary information from other sequences with pixel-level annotations, and transfer the domain knowledge and initialize a second network with pre-trained weights. This is called as supervised domain adaptation [10].

Let's consider D_{tb} as the image domain for T2+bSSFP sequences and D_l for LGE sequences respectively. D_{tb} can be expressed with feature space S and associated probability distribution of $P(X)$ where $X = \{x_1, x_2, ..., x_n\} \in S$ [11, 12]. In a supervised learning task, domain $D_{tb} = \{S, P(X)\}$ consists of a model with associated objective function $\mathcal{F}_{tb}$, learning task of T_{tb} and a label space of Y. The objective function $\mathcal{F}_{tb}$ for task segmentation T_{tb} can be optimised using a pair of samples $\{x_i, y_i\}$ where $x_i \in X$ and $y_i \in Y$. After the training process, the learned model $\hat{\mathcal{F}}_{tb}$ can be used to predict on new samples of T2 and bSSFP images from D_{tb} domain. Now, if we consider D_l with LGE segmentation task T_l, we can transfer the learned weights from domain D_{tb} to improve objective function of F_l for segmenting LGE images in domain D_l where $D_{tb} \neq D_l$ and $T_{tb} \neq T_l$. In this way, domain D_l uses information from domain D_{tb} to segment LGE images. The final model trained on T2+bSSFP domain and adapted to target domain (LGE) can be denoted as $\mathcal{F}_{lge}$.

To construct the model $\mathcal{F}_{lge}$, we transferred the learned weights from $\mathcal{F}_{tb}$, then we retrain all the layers and fine-tuned the model on the limited training data from domain D_l. This is demonstrated in Fig. 2. All hyperparameters associated with the optimizer, the loss function, and the data augmentation scheme employed were kept the same for both models.

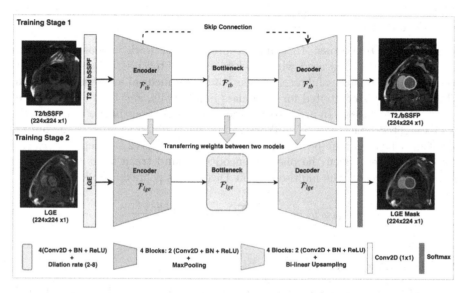

Fig. 2. Overview of our network architecture for feature transfer learning between different CMR sequences. The encoder-decoder first trained with T2+bSSFP images and in the second stage the network with learned weights retrained with LGE iamges.

2.2 Network Architecture

Our network architecture is a fully convolutional network inspired from [13] which comprises four encoder and decoder blocks, separated by a bottleneck block (refer to Fig. 2). The architecture includes skip connections between all encoder and decoder blocks at the same spatial resolution. Each encoder/decoder block consists of two 2D convolution layers, where, each convolution layer is followed by a batch-normalization and a Rectifier Linear Unit (ReLU) layer. In each encoder-convolution block, the input of the first convolution layer is concatenated with the output of the second convolution layer and zero-padded accordingly. The subsequent 2D max-pooling layer reduces the dimensions of the image by half. The use of residual connections [14] between convolution layers of each block in the encoder, help improve the flow of gradients in the backward pass of the network. The network utilizes a 1×1 convolution to aggregate the feature maps from the final decoder block. This operation improves discriminative power as feature maps with lower activations are more likely to be suppressed through the assignment of lower weights. Finally, a softmax activation function was used in the last layer of the first network to classify the background from the foreground classes. Compared to U-Net, we replace the bottleneck convolution layers of the network with dilated convolutions [15] of size 3 × 3, to enlarge the receptive field and enable the network to capture both local and global contextual information. The dilation rate of the four convolution layers is increased successively from 1 − 8, and subsequently, their feature maps are summed together, enabling the network to capture the entire image's field of view.

Multi-class Dice Loss: To train the proposed network, a modified version of the soft-Dice loss is used which is less sensitive to class imbalance. This is motivated by the successful recent works [13,16] for medical image segmentation. The Dice score is computed for each class individually, and then averaged over the number of classes. In order to segment an $N \times N$ input image (for example, a T1-weighted image with LV, RV, Myo and background as labels), the output of softmax layer is four probabilities for classes $k = 0, 1, 2, 3$ where, $\sum_c y_{n,k} = 1$ for each pixel. Given the one-hot encoded ground truth label $\hat{y}_{n,k}$ for that corresponding pixel, the multi-class soft Dice loss is defined as follows:

$$\zeta_{dc}(y, \hat{y}) = 1 - \frac{1}{K}\left(\sum_k \frac{\sum_n y_{nk}\hat{y}_{nk}}{\sum_n y_{nk} + \sum_n \hat{y}_{nk}}\right) \tag{1}$$

2.3   Data Acquisitions

We validated our proposed method on the STACOM MS-CMRSeg[1] 2019 challenge dataset with short-axis cardiac MR images of 45 patients diagnosed with cardiomyopathy. The dataset was collected in Shanghai Renji hospital with institutional ethics approval [6]. Each patient had been scanned using three CMR sequences: LGE, T2, and bSSFP. Ground truth masks of cardiac structures were provided for 35 training samples (T2 and bSSFP only) and 5 validation samples, including the Left ventricle cavity (LV), the right ventricle cavity (RV), and the myocardium of the left ventricle (Myo). The LGE CMR was a T1-weighted, inversion-recovery, gradient-echo sequence, consisting of 10 to 18 slices covering the main body of the ventricles. The acquisition matrix was 512 × 512, yielding an in-plane resolution of 0.75 × 0.75 mm and slice thickness of 5 mm. The bSSFP CMR images consist of 8 to 12 contiguous slices, covering the full ventricles from the apex to the basal plane of the mitral valve, with some cases having several slices beyond the ventricles. These sequences have a slice thickness of 8–13 mm and an image resolution of 1.25 × 1.25 mm. The T2-weighted CMR images consist of a small number of slices. Few cases have comprise just three slices, and the others have five (13 subjects), six (8 subjects) or seven (one subject) slices. The slice thickness is 12–20 mm and an in-plane resolution of 1.35 × 1.35 mm. Since T1 and bSSFP images have very few slices, we combined both sequences together for the training of our backbone network.

---

[1] http://www.sdspeople.fudan.edu.cn/zhuangxiahai/0/mscmrseg19/.

Preprocessing: There is a large degree of variance in contrast and brightness across the MS-CMRSeg 2019 challenge images. The variability results from different system settings, and data acquisition which makes it harder for neural networks to process the images. Due to low contrast, we enhanced the image contrast slice-by-slice, using contrast limited adaptive histogram equalization (CLAHE). We normalized each MR volume individually to have zero mean and unit variance and cropped all images to 224×224 to remove the black areas (background regions). Figure 1 shows MR slices of three different sequences of a patient after prepossessing. Furthermore, we use common training data augmentation strategies including random rotation, random scaling, random elastic deformations, random flips, and small shifts in intensity to increase training data. We employed the augmentation only on x and y axes and kept the volume depth the same. In this way, we do not degrade image quality.

2.4 Network Training

The organizers of the MS-CMRSeg challenge already split the data into training, validation and testing sets. In the first stage, we trained our model on 35 T2 and bSSFP sequences with pixel-level annotations and validated on 5 subjects using the adaptive moment estimation (ADAM) optimizer. For the second stage, we re-trained the model with five LGE subjects using 5-fold cross validation. The learning rate was fixed at 0.0001, and the exponential decay rates of the 1st and 2nd-moment estimates were set to 0.9 and 0.999, respectively. During training, segmentation accuracy was evaluated on the validation set after each epoch of the network. Networks were trained until the validation accuracy stopped increasing, and the best performing model was selected for evaluation on the test set. The batch size for training T2+bSSFP images was set to 16 and during fine-tuning for LGE-MRI, to 4. We employed connected component (CC) analysis as a post-processing step to remove the small miss-classified regions in the output of the softmax layer. For inference, we use the weights which achieved the best Dice score on the validation set of LGE-CMR data set. The network was developed in Keras and TensorFlow, an open-source deep learning library for Python, and was trained on an NVIDIA Titan X-Pascal GPU with 3840 CUDA cores, and 12 GB RAM.

2.5 Evaluation Criteria

To evaluate the accuracy of segmentation results, we used three different metrics to evaluate segmentation accuracy, namely, the Dice coefficient (Dice), Hausdorff distance (HD), and Average surface distance (ASD). The Dice metric measures the degree of overlap between the predicted and ground truth segmentation. It is the most widely used metric for evaluating segmentation quality in medical imaging. HD is defined as the maximum of the minimum voxel-wise distances between the ground truth and predicted object boundaries. ASD is the average of the minimum voxel-wise distances between the ground truth and predicted object boundaries. HD and ASD are evaluated using the shortest Euclidean distance of an arbitrary voxel v to a point P, defined as $\bar{d}(v, P) = \min_{p \in P} ||v-p||$.

3 Results and Discussion

The proposed model is evaluated on the task of LGE-MRI segmentation. We compare our domain adapted network with three different training strategies including training without domain adaptation and predicting using the model trained on T2 and bSSFP only. Table 1 summarizes the comparison results, where we can see that our proposed method significantly improved the segmentation performance relative to networks tested without the adaptation strategy, in terms of Dice, HD, and ASD metrics. The model without domain adaptation and trained from scratch only on 5 LGE MR samples achieved an average Dice of 66.9% on the validation set. Remarkably, for our proposed network with data augmentation, the average Dice improved to 80.9% and HD and ASD was reduced to 13.6 and 1.0 mm respectively. We achieved over 87.1% Dice score for the LV structure and over 80.2% Dice score for the RV. To illustrate the domain shift problem, we directly feed LGE-MR images to the first encoder-decoder after supervised training on T2+bSSFP domain. The result in Table 1 indicates that the source model completely failed on LGE-MR images with an average Dice score of 31.3%, HD score of 37.37 mm and ASD value of 11.06 mm. Notably, compared with testing using model trained on T2+bSSFP, our method achieved superior performance especially for the LV and Myo structures, which are difficult to segment due to the presence of scars and blood pool within the cavity. Figure 3 illustrates segmentation results produced with different methods. Our method demonstrated robust segmentation performance on 40 LGE CMR sequences in the test dataset, summarized in Table 2. We have achieved an average Dice score of 84.5% and HD, ASD score of 13.6 and 2.2 mm respectively. The proposed model is able to reach a Dice score of 0.788 in terms of myocardium segmentation. These results help to highlight the generalization capacity of our approach to segmenting cardiac structures in LGE-MRI. Adapting the features between two domains results to a better model weight initialization and consequently improved the discrimination power of the second model.

Table 1. Performance comparison between our proposed method and other segmentation methods for LGE-MR image segmentation on the validation data set.

Methods	Dice ↑				HD [mm] ↓				ASD [mm] ↓			
	Myo	LV	RV	Avg	Myo	LV	RV	Avg	Myo	LV	RV	Avg
W/o adaptation	0.527	0.775	0.705	0.669	57.23	129.67	124.13	103.68	2.96	1.37	1.35	1.89
T2+bSSFP	0.169	0.386	0.383	0.313	42.62	30.37	39.13	37.37	14.6	7.04	11.53	11.06
W-adaptation	0.671	0.862	0.766	0.766	17.6	13.25	22.78	17.88	2.77	**0.75**	3.81	2.44
W-adaptation+Aug	**0.749**	**0.871**	**0.802**	**0.807**	**11.35**	**15.66**	**14.05**	**13.69**	**1.06**	0.81	**1.18**	**1.02**

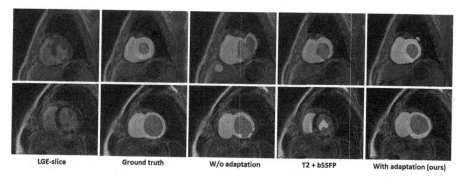

LGE-slice   Ground truth   W/o adaptation   T2 + bSSFP   With adaptation (ours)

Fig. 3. Visual comparison of segmentation results produced by different methods. From left to right are the raw LGE-MR images, ground truth, W/o Adaptation output trained from scratch on LGE-MR images only, output from model trained on T2+bSSFP images, and proposed network. The cardiac structures of LV, RV, and Myo are indicated in purple, blue and withe color respectively. Each row corresponds to one subject. (Color figure online)

Table 2. The Dice, Jaccard, HD and ASD score of domain-adapted method on the LGE CMR test dataset.

Structure	Test-set results ($m \pm sd$)			
	Dice ↑	Jaccard ↑	ASD [mm] ↓	HD [mm]↓
Myo	0.788 ± 0.073	0.656 ± 0.096	2.036 ± 0.616	12.53 ± 3.37
LV	0.912 ± 0.033	0.840 ± 0.056	1.806 ± 0.615	11.29 ± 4.55
RV	0.832 ± 0.084	0.721 ± 0.117	2.804 ± 1.376	17.11 ± 6.14
Average	$\mathbf{0.844 \pm 0.063}$	$\mathbf{0.740 \pm 0.090}$	$\mathbf{2.215 \pm 0.869}$	$\mathbf{13.64 \pm 4.68}$

4 Conclusion

In this study, we developed a robust deep learning approach for multi-sequence CMR image segmentation based on feature/domain-adaptation. Our network was first trained on T2-weighted and bSSFP sequences, and subsequently, the learned model weights were used to initialize the second network, and fine-tuned to segment LGE-MR images with a limited number of samples. The transfer leaning mechanism drastically reduces the domain shift during the training process. We validated our method on multi-sequence CMR images by comparing it with networks trained without domain adaptation. We employ our network on 2D slices as 3D models did not perform well on the MS-CMRSeg challenge 2019 dataset, given the limited number of axial slices. Experimental results highlight the advantage afforded by our approach, with regards to segmentation accuracy in LGE-MRI. Future work will aim to extend the framework using techniques for joint unsupervised image and feature adaptation using generative adversarial networks.

Acknowledgments. This work described in this paper was partially supported by the project EFI-BIG-THERA: Integrative 'BigData Modeling' for the development of novel therapeutic approaches for breast cancer. The authors would also like to thank NVIDIA for donating a Titan X-Pascal GPU.

References

1. Kim, H.W., Farzaneh-Far, A., Kim, R.J.: Cardiovascular magnetic resonance in patients with myocardial infarction: current and emerging applications. J. Am. Coll. Cardiol. **55**(1), 1–16 (2009)
2. ESD Group, et al.: European society of cardiology: cardiovascular disease statistics 2017. Eur. Heart J. **39**(7), 508–579 (2017)
3. Zhuang, X.: Multivariate mixture model for myocardial segmentation combining multi-source images. IEEE Trans. Pattern Anal. Mach. Intell. **41**, 2933–2946 (2019)
4. Hammer-Hansen, S., et al.: Mechanisms for overestimating acute myocardial infarct size with gadolinium-enhanced cardiovascular magnetic resonance imaging in humans: a quantitative and kinetic study. Eur. Heart J. - Cardiovasc. Imag. **17**(1), 76–84 (2015)
5. Kurzendorfer, T., Forman, C., Schmidt, M., Tillmanns, C., Maier, A., Brost, A.: Fully automatic segmentation of left ventricular anatomy in 3-DLGE-MRI. Comput. Med. Imaging Graph. **59**, 13–27 (2017)
6. Zhuang, X.: Multivariate mixture model for cardiac segmentation from multi-sequence MRI. MICCA I, 581–588 (2016)
7. Liu, J., Xie, H., Zhang, S., Gu, L.: Multi-sequence myocardium segmentation with cross-constrained shape and neural network-based initialization. Comput. Med. Imag. Graph. **71**, 49–57 (2019)
8. Chen, C., Dou, Q., Chen, H., Heng, P.-A.: Semantic-aware generative adversarial nets for unsupervised domain adaptation in chest x-ray segmentation. In: Shi, Y., Suk, H.-I., Liu, M. (eds.) MLMI 2018. LNCS, vol. 11046, pp. 143–151. Springer, Cham (2018). https://doi.org/10.1007/978-3-030-00919-9_17
9. Russo, P., Carlucci, F.M., Tommasi, T., Caputo, B.: From source to target and back: symmetric bi-directional adaptive GAN. In: CVPR, June 2018
10. Motiian, S., Piccirilli, M., Adjeroh, D.A., Doretto, G.: Unified deep supervised domain adaptation and generalization. In: 2017 IEEE International Conference on Computer Vision (ICCV), pp. 5716–5726, October 2017
11. Pan, S.J., Yang, Q.: A survey on transfer learning. IEEE Trans. Knowl. Data Eng. **22**(10), 1345–1359 (2010)
12. Ghafoorian, M., et al.: Transfer learning for domain adaptation in MRI: application in brain lesion segmentation. MICCAI **2017**, 516–524 (2017)
13. Vesal, S., Ravikumar, N., Maier, A.: Dilated convolutions in neural networks for left atrial segmentation in 3D gadolinium enhanced-MRI. In: Pop, M., et al. (eds.) STACOM 2018. LNCS, vol. 11395, pp. 319–328. Springer, Cham (2019). https://doi.org/10.1007/978-3-030-12029-0_35
14. He, K., Zhang, X., Ren, S., Sun, J.: Deep residual learning for image recognition. In: CVPR, pp. 770–778, June 2016
15. Yu, F., Koltun, V.: Multi-scale context aggregation by dilated convolutions. In: ICLR (2016)
16. Milletari, F., Navab, N., Ahmadi, S.: V-net: fully convolutional neural networks for volumetric medical image segmentation. In: 2016 Fourth International Conference on 3D Vision (3DV), pp. 565–571, October 2016

A Two-Stage Fully Automatic Segmentation Scheme Using Both 2D and 3D U-Net for Multi-sequence Cardiac MR

Haohao Xu[1,2,3], Zhuangwei Xu[3], Wenting Gu[3], and Qi Zhang[1,2,3]($\boxtimes$)

[1] Shanghai Institute for Advanced Communication and Data Science,
The SMART (Smart Medicine and AI-Based Radiology Technology) Lab,
Shanghai University, Shanghai, China
zhangq@t.shu.edu.cn
[2] Institute of Biomedical Engineering, Shanghai University, Shanghai, China
[3] School of Communication and Information Engineering, Shanghai University,
Shanghai, China

Abstract. Multi-sequence cardiac magnetic resonance (MR) segmentation is an important medical imaging technology that facilitates intelligent interpretation of clinical MR images. However, fully automatic segmentation of multi-sequence cardiac MR is a challenging task due to the complexity and variability of cardiac anatomy. In this study, we propose a two-stage deep learning scheme for automatic segmentation of volumetric multi-sequence MR images by leveraging both 2D and 3D U-Net. In the first stage, a 2D U-Net model coupled with the iterative randomized Hough transform is employed on the balanced-steady state free precession (bSSFP) MR sequences, so as to find the center coordinates of the left ventricles (LVs). The regions of interest (ROIs) are then localized around the center coordinates on the corresponding late gadolinium enhanced (LGE) MR sequences. In the second stage, a 3D probabilistic U-Net model is performed on the ROIs in the LGE data to segment the LV, right ventricle (RV) and left ventricular myocardium (MYO). Experimental results on the MICCAI 2019 Multi-Sequence Cardiac MR Segmentation (MS-CMRSeg) Challenge show that the proposed scheme performs well with average Dice similarity coefficients of LV, RV and MYO as 0.792, 0.697 and 0.611, respectively.

Keywords: Multi-sequence Cardiac MR · U-Net · Iterative randomized Hough transform · Image segmentation

1 Introduction

Accurate computing, analysis and modeling of the ventricles and myocardium from medical images is important in the computer-aided diagnosis and treatment management for patients suffering from myocardial infarction (MI) [1, 2].

Multi-sequence magnetic resonance (MR) imaging is used to provide anatomical and functional information of heart, such as the balanced-steady state free precession (bSSFP) cine sequence which captures cardiac motions and presents clear boundaries,

© Springer Nature Switzerland AG 2020
M. Pop et al. (Eds.): STACOM 2019, LNCS 12009, pp. 309–316, 2020.
https://doi.org/10.1007/978-3-030-39074-7_33

and the T2-weighted cardiac MR (CMR) which images the acute injury and ischemic regions [3]. Specifically, the late gadolinium enhanced (LGE) CMR can enhance the infarcted myocardium, appearing with distinctive brightness compared with the healthy tissues. The LGE is widely used to study the presence, location, and extent of MI in clinical studies. Thus, delineating ventricles and myocardium from LGE CMR images is of great importance.

However, fully automatic segmentation of multi-sequence cardiac MR is a challenging task, mainly due to the large anatomical variability in heart shape among subjects, the artifacts and intensity inhomogeneity generated during the acquisition procedures, and the blurry and indistinctive boundaries between substructures [4]. To objectively compare the approaches to multi-sequence ventricle and myocardium segmentation, the MICCAI 2019 has launched the Multi-Sequence Cardiac MR Segmentation (MS-CMRSeg) Challenge for accelerating future applications of automatic CMR segmentation methods in clinical practice.

In this work, we propose a two-stage deep learning scheme for fully automatic segmentation of volumetric multi-sequence CMR images by leveraging both 2D and 3D U-Net. In the first stage, we present a 2D U-Net model coupled with the iterative randomized Hough transform (IRHT) on the bSSFP sequences to search for the center coordinates of the left ventricles (LVs); we then localize the regions of interest (ROIs) around the center coordinates on the corresponding LGE sequences. In the second stage, we perform a 3D probabilistic U-Net model on the ROIs of LGE to segment the LV, right ventricle (RV) and left ventricular myocardium (MYO). We evaluate our proposed approach on the MS-CMRSeg Challenge datasets.

2   Methods

We perform fully automatic LV, RV and MYO segmentation by using two CMR sequences, consisting of the LGE and bSSFP [5, 6]. The MS-CMRSeg Challenge also provides a third sequence namely T2, but we do not use it in our study due to the fact that T2 images only have a small number of slices, typically three or five, and their inplane resolution is also the lowest (1.35×1.35 mm) among three sequences.

In the paper, we propose a two-stage scheme that first localizes the LV center coordinates and the ROIs in the bSSFP images, followed by obtaining the final segmentation in the LGE CMR data. This pipeline is shown in Fig. 1.

2.1   2D U-Net and IRHT for ROI Detection

The data provided by the organizer include 45 bSSFP CMR cases from patients with 35 manually labeled. We use the labeled and unlabeled data in a semi-supervised fashion. In other words, we firstly use the 35 labeled bSSFP cases to train a 2D U-Net network and then use the network to predict the labels of the remaining 10 bSSFP cases; all the 45 cases are utilized for determination of the ROIs. Here, we only train the model for LV segmentation and thus only the LV labels are used.

At the training step, firstly, the 3D images are transformed into 2D slices, which are then normalized and histogram equalized. Multi-scale information is extracted from the

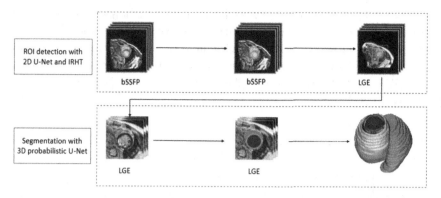

Fig. 1. Overview of our fully automatic two-stage scheme for CMR segmentation with double networks. The first network combines a 2D U-Net with the iterative randomized Hough transform (IRHT) to localize the center coordinates of left ventricles and thus obtain the regions of interest (ROIs) on bSSFP images. The second network is a 3D probabilistic U-Net, which performs refined segmentation on ROIs of LGE data.

2D slices by using the 2D U-Net. The gradient explosion problem in a deep network is prevented by jumping links, which makes the final recovered feature map fuse more low-level features. An adaptive moment (Adam) optimizer based on categorical cross-entropy loss function is used to optimize the segmentation model, and its adaptive learning rate controls the weight updating ratio and makes the model more convergent. Finally, the labels of bSSFP data in the test set are predicted by the trained 2D U-Net.

Because the coronal view of the LVs is in a circular shape, we first use the Canny edge detector to detect the pixels in the circles of LV boundaries. Then, we employ the IRHT algorithm to fit the discrete boundary pixels of the LV in an ellipse and link them to form a continuous circle. Therefore, the center coordinates of the LVs can be calculated. According to the center coordinates, we crop a region around the LV center on the LGE images as the ROI, and then we interpolate the ROI to a size of $256 \times 256 \times 20$. Afterwards, we feed the resized ROI to the second-stage U-Net.

It should be noted that it is essential to generate more training samples with data augmentation to improve the robustness of image segmentation [7]. We use the geometric transformation as the augmentation method, including flipping, shifting, rotation and sheer operations.

2.2   3D Probabilistic U-Net for Refined Segmentation

Figure 2 illustrates the second stage of our proposed segmentation method, i.e., the 3D probabilistic U-Net [8–10]. The network combines a 3D U-Net and a conditional variational auto-encoder (CVAE) [11–13], which can model complex distributions and deliver more accurate segmentation for ambiguous images. Furthermore, a low-dimensional latent space encodes the possible segmentation variants. From this space, we can obtain a random sample which is injected into the 3D U-Net to generate the corresponding segmentation map. There are a prior net and a posterior net in the 3D probabilistic U-Net. The prior net calculates the probability of the segmentation variants for an input image X. The prior probability distribution is modelled as an axis-aligned Gaussian with a mean of μ_{prior} and a variance of σ_{prior}. The posterior net learns to recognize a segmentation variant and to map it to a position μ_{post} with some uncertainty σ_{post} (Fig. 2).

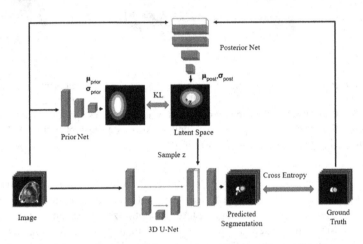

Fig. 2. The 3D probabilistic U-Net for refined segmentation. Arrows: operation flows; blue blocks: feature maps; white blocks: N-channel feature maps from broadcasting sample z; blue double-headed arrows: loss functions. The number of feature map blocks shown here is reduced for clarity of presentation. (Color figure online)

One key characteristic of the 3D probabilistic U-Net is its ability to model the joint probability of all pixels in the segmentation map. It leads to multiple segmentation maps, each of which provides a consistent interpretation of the entire image. The 3D probabilistic U-Net accounts for multiple plausible semantic segmentation hypotheses to resolve the present ambiguities, and hence it is able to learn hypotheses that have a low probability and to predict them with the corresponding frequency. Due to its merits, we adopt the 3D probabilistic U-Net on the segmentation tasks of LV, RV and MYO for ambiguous multi-sequence CMR images.

The network is trained with the standard training procedure for CVAEs by minimizing the loss function, given the raw image X and the ground truth segmentation Y. Finally, we use the connected-component labeling to select the largest connected-component for postprocessing of the segmentation results obtained with the 3D probabilistic U-Net.

Loss Function. In this study, the loss function combines a cross-entropy loss and Kullback-Leibler divergence with a weighting factor α. A cross-entropy loss penalizes difference between network output S and Y. The cross-entropy loss arises from treating the output S as the parameterization of a pixel-wise categorical distribution P_c. The

Kullback-Leibler divergence penalizes differences between the posterior distribution Q and the prior distribution P [14].

$$L(Y, X) = -\log P_c(Y|S) + \alpha \cdot D_{KL}(Q||P) \qquad (1)$$

Optimization. To optimize the network parameters, we also utilize the ADAM estimation algorithm, which is straightforward to implement and computationally efficient [15]. The training is performed in batches of 16 images with a learning rate of 0.001, and the maximum number of epochs is set to 100.

Data Augmentation. The data augmentation method is similar to that used in Sect. 2.1 and it includes geometric transformation.

3 Experiments

3.1 Datasets

This study made use of the CMR data provided by the Challenge organizer. The multi-sequence CMR data from 45 patients with cardiomyopathy had been collected from Shanghai Renji Hospital with institutional ethics approval and had been anonymized. Each patient had been scanned using three sequences including the LGE, T2 and bSSFP. The three sequences were all breath-hold, multi-slice, acquired in the ventricular short-axis views.

We only used two sequences namely LGE and bSSFP for LV, RV and MYO segmentation. We used the training sets of the Challenge, including Patient 1–5 with LGE images and their manual labels, Patient 1–35 with bSSFP images and their manual labels, and also Patient 36–45 with only bSSFP images but no labels. The LGE images of Patient 6–45 were used to test our proposed segmentation model according to the instructions of the Challenge.

3.2 Experimental Settings

The proposed two-stage segmentation scheme was implemented with Python 3.6 based on TensorFlow framework. The experiments were conducted on an Ubuntu 16.04 system with 2 CPUs (Intel Xeon), 2 GPUs (NVIDIA GTX 1080ti 11 Gb), and 256 Gb RAM.

3.3 Results

We tested and evaluated our proposed approach on LGE CMR of MS-CMRSeg Challenge. The Challenge uses the Dice similarity coefficient (or Dice score), Jaccard score, average surface distance (ASD) and Hausdorff distance (HD) as the evaluation metrics. In the experiment, we also compared our proposed hybrid U-Net consisting of both 2D U-Net and 3D probabilistic U-Net (denoted as 2D+3Dprob-U-Net) with the hybrid U-Net using 2D U-Net and classic 3D U-Net (denoted as 2D+3D-U-Net). The experimental results of the four metrics are enumerated in Tables 1 and 2.

Table 1. Dice score and Jaccard score on the LGE test sets

	2D+3D-U-Net		2D+3Dprob-U-Net	
	Dice	Jaccard	Dice	Jaccard
LV blood cavity	0.759	0.630	0.792	0.665
LV myocardium	0.573	0.412	0.611	0.445
RV blood cavity	0.622	0.467	0.697	0.546
Average	0.651	0.503	0.700	0.552

Table 2. Surface distance and Hausdorff distance on the LGE test sets

	2D+3D-U-Net		2D+3Dprob-U-Net	
	ASD	HD	ASD	HD
LV endocardium	5.619	41.914	4.159	36.129
LV epicardium	7.235	49.540	6.021	44.133
RV endocardium	8.768	53.837	8.327	55.152
Average	7.207	48.430	6.169	45.138

The results show that our proposed approach performs well in terms of the Dice score, especially for the LV blood cavity. With the help from the 3D probabilistic U-Net, our method gets improvements in terms of all four metrics. Table 3 shows the five patients whose average Dice scores of the LV, RV and MYO were the highest among 40 patients. As can be seen from Table 3, the scores of LVs were generally higher than those of RVs, and the scores of right ventricle were generally higher than those of myocardium. This is partly because the shape of LV is relatively regular and thus easier to predict. The cardiac structure near the LV myocardium is complex, and thus the Dice score of the MYO was usually the lowest.

Hausdorff distances of LV endocardium, LV epicardium and RV endocardium shown in Table 2 seem large. It may imply that some areas of endo- or epi-cardium were wrongly detected because of noisy data and ambigious boundaries. In future studies, more training samples need to be accumulated into the database to further improve the segmentation performance.

Table 3. Dice scores on the LGE test sets for five patients, ranked by the highest average Dice scores.

Patient index	LV blood cavity	LV myocardium	RV blood cavity	Average
28	0.898	0.751	0.875	0.875
24	0.906	0.760	0.749	0.805
40	0.896	0.713	0.802	0.804
35	0.883	0.666	0.857	0.802
39	0.888	0.652	0.854	0.798

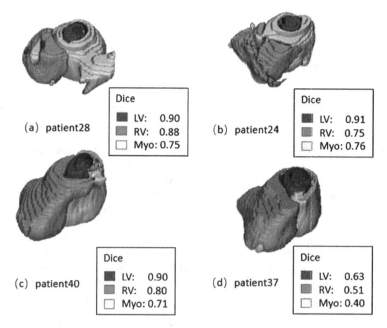

Fig. 3. Segmentation results of volumes with good (a) (b) (c) and bad (d) Dice scores for LGE CMR images for four typical patients.

Figure 3 shows the 3D rendering of three patients (a–c) with high Dice scores and one patient (d) with a low Dice score. For LV segmentation, the three good cases achieved high Dice scores around 0.90; and for RV and MYO segmentation, the Dice scores exceeded 0.7. These results indicate satisfactory volumetric segmentation of the three cardiac structures. However, for Patient37 (Fig. 3d), the Dice scores were between 0.40–0.65, indicating a relatively poor performance. It should be noted that for patient 24 (Fig. 3b), though our method performed well in overall evaluation, it also falsely detected some debris of RV, which was consistent with relatively high Hausdorff distances of 66.710 mm for RV endocardium.

The center coordinates of LV localized in bSSFP images at the first stage may not exactly coincide with those in LGE images, which is also one of the factors that induce differences between the predicted segmentations at the second stage and the truth grounds. Better localization of the center coordinates through accurate registration of the two sequences could benefit following refined segmentation, and it deserves further investigation in future studies.

4 Conclusion

In this paper, we have proposed a two-stage method for fully automatic segmentation of LV, RV and MYO in multi-sequence CMR by using a pipeline combining both 2D U-Net and 3D probabilistic U-Net. Results on the MS-CMRSeg Challenge show the good performance of our proposed method.

References

1. Kim, H., Farzaneh-Far, A., Kim, R.: Cardiovascular magnetic resonance in patients with myocardial infarction: current and emerging applications. J. Am. Coll. Cardiol. **55**(1), 1–16 (2009)
2. Kolipaka, A., Chatzimavroudis, G., White, R.: Segmentation of non-viable myocardium in delayed enhancement magnetic resonance images. Int. J. Cardiovasc. Imaging **21**(2–3), 303–311 (2005)
3. Wright, J., Adriaenssens, T., Dymarkowski, S.: Quantification of myocardial area at risk with T2-weighted CMR: comparison with contrast-enhanced CMR and coronary angiography. J. Am. Coll. Cardiol. Imaging **2**(7), 825–831 (2009)
4. Payer, C., Štern, D., Bischof, H., Urschler, M.: Multi-label whole heart segmentation using CNNs and anatomical label configurations. In: Pop, M., et al. (eds.) STACOM 2017. LNCS, vol. 10663, pp. 190–198. Springer, Cham (2018). https://doi.org/10.1007/978-3-319-75541-0_20
5. Zhuang, X.: Multivariate mixture model for myocardial segmentation combining multi-source images. IEEE Trans. Pattern Anal. Mach. Intell. **41**, 2933–2946 (2018)
6. Zhuang, X.: Multivariate mixture model for cardiac segmentation from multi-sequence MRI. In: Ourselin, S., Joskowicz, L., Sabuncu, Mert R., Unal, G., Wells, W. (eds.) MICCAI 2016. LNCS, vol. 9901, pp. 581–588. Springer, Cham (2016). https://doi.org/10.1007/978-3-319-46723-8_67
7. Yap, M., Pons, G., Martí, J.: Automated breast ultrasound lesions detection using convolutional neural networks. IEEE J. Biomed. Health Inform. **22**(4), 1218–1226 (2017)
8. Çiçek, Ö., Abdulkadir, A., Lienkamp, Soeren S., Brox, T., Ronneberger, O.: 3D U-Net: learning dense volumetric segmentation from sparse annotation. In: Ourselin, S., Joskowicz, L., Sabuncu, Mert R., Unal, G., Wells, W. (eds.) MICCAI 2016. LNCS, vol. 9901, pp. 424–432. Springer, Cham (2016). https://doi.org/10.1007/978-3-319-46723-8_49
9. Tran, D., Bourdev, L., Fergus, R.: Deep end2end voxel2voxel prediction. In: Proceedings of Computer Vision and Pattern Recognition, pp. 17–24. Springer, Heidelberg (2016). https://doi.org/10.1109/CVPRW.2016.57
10. Kohl, S., Romera-Paredes, B., Meyer, C.: A probabilistic U-Net for segmentation of ambiguous images. In: Proceedings of Neural Information Processing Systems, pp. 6965–6975. Springer, Heidelberg (2018). https://arxiv.org/abs/1806.05034
11. Kingma, D., Welling, M.: Auto-encoding variational bayes. arXiv:1312.6114 (2013)
12. Rezende, D., Mohamed, S., Wierstra, D.: Stochastic backpropagation and approximate inference in deep generative models. arXiv:1401.4082 (2014)
13. Sohn, K., Lee, H., Yan, X.: Learning structured output representation using deep conditional generative models. In: Proceedings of Neural Information Processing Systems, pp. 3483–3491 (2015)
14. Higgins, I., et al.: beta-VAE: learning basic visual concepts with a constrained variational framework. In: International Conference on Learning Representation, pp. 6–18 (2017)
15. Dong, H., Yang, G., Liu, F., Mo, Y., Guo, Y.: Automatic brain tumor detection and segmentation using U-Net based fully convolutional networks. In: Valdés Hernández, M., González-Castro, V. (eds.) MIUA 2017. CCIS, vol. 723, pp. 506–517. Springer, Cham (2017). https://doi.org/10.1007/978-3-319-60964-5_44

Adversarial Convolutional Networks with Weak Domain-Transfer for Multi-sequence Cardiac MR Images Segmentation

Jingkun Chen[1,4], Hongwei Li[2], Jianguo Zhang[1,3,4(✉)], and Bjoern Menze[2]

[1] Southern University of Science and Technology, Shenzhen, China
chenjk@mail.sustech.edu.cn, zhangjg@sustech.edu.cn
[2] Technical University of Munich, Munich, Germany
hongwei.li@tum.de
[3] Shenzhen Institute of Artificial Intelligence and Robotics for Society,
Shenzhen, China
[4] University of Dundee, Dundee, UK

Abstract. Analysis and modeling of the ventricles and myocardium are important in the diagnostic and treatment of heart diseases. Manual delineation of those tissues in cardiac MR (CMR) scans is laborious and time-consuming. The ambiguity of the boundaries makes the segmentation task rather challenging. Furthermore, the annotations on some modalities such as Late Gadolinium Enhancement (LGE) MRI, are often not available. We propose an end-to-end segmentation framework based on convolutional neural network (CNN) and adversarial learning. A dilated residual U-shape network is used as a segmentor to generate the prediction mask; meanwhile, a CNN is utilized as a discriminator model to judge the segmentation quality. To leverage the available annotations across modalities per patient, a new loss function named *weak domain-transfer loss* is introduced to the pipeline. The proposed model is evaluated on the public dataset released by the challenge organizer in MICCAI 2019, which consists of 45 sets of multi-sequence CMR images. We demonstrate that the proposed adversarial pipeline outperforms baseline deep-learning methods.

Keywords: Adversarial convolutional network · Multi-sequence cardiac segmentation

1 Introduction

Automatic segmentation of the tissues in cardiac magnetic resonance (CMR) images can provide the initial geometric information for surgical guidance [5]. However, manual delineation of heart structures in CMR scans is laborious and time-consuming. Late Gadolinium Enhancement (LGE) MR imaging is one of the most effective imaging modalities that can predict heart failure and sudden

© Springer Nature Switzerland AG 2020
M. Pop et al. (Eds.): STACOM 2019, LNCS 12009, pp. 317–325, 2020.
https://doi.org/10.1007/978-3-030-39074-7_34

death [16]. It enables doctors to visually exam the changes in the myocardium (myo) and confirm the existence of 'cardiomyopathy' and the degree of fibrosis.

There are three main challenges in CMR image segmentation: (1) the large anatomy variations between individuals, and the big diversity of imaging quality in the LGE. For example, due to microvascular occlusion, the contrast agent cannot reach certain areas of the heart, resulting in different enhancements; (2) the ambiguities of boundaries between different cardiac tissues, i.e., the intensity range of the myocardium in LGE CMR overlaps with the surrounding muscle tissue [4]; (3) Despite its clinical importance, LGE slice is much more difficult to annotate than both T2-weight and bSSFP, thus the annotations of LGE CMR are often not accurate or not available. In contrast, the annotations of T2-weight and bSSFP are easier and often available. To tackle these challenges, various methods have been proposed for whole-heart segmentation [8], ventricles segmentation [9,10], etc.

In recent years, deep convolutional neural networks (CNNs) [11] have achieved remarkable success in various computer vision tasks [12,13] as well as medical image segmentation [1]. Generative adversarial networks [2] as a recent machine learning technique, offers a promising avenue in image synthesis [6] as well as image segmentation [7].

We propose a framework to segment ventricles and myocardium from LGE CMR images based on CNNs and adversarial learning, when the annotations of LGE images are rather limited for training. Our contributions in this work are three folds: (1) we proposed an adversarial segmentation network containing two tailored modules: a segmentation model and a discriminator model, trained and optimized in an end-to-end fashion. The segmentation network generates the predicted masks, and the discriminator network aims to identify the segmentation mask and the ground-truth mask. The segmentation quality is improved in the min-max game. (2) since different modalities share structure information, we introduced a loss function named *weak domain-transfer loss* to leverage information from available modalities with rich annotations; (3) results show that the proposed method outperforms traditional CNN-based method.

2   Method

Our adversarial segmentation framework consists of a segmentation network and discrimination network. A dilated residual U-shape networks [14] is used as a segmentor (i.e. mask generator) G and a CNN classifier as a discriminator D. D is used to ensure that a generated mask being close to its ground truth mask conditioned on the same raw image; the segmentor and the discriminator are updated to improve the performance in an adversarial manner. We also leverage information from other common modalities using a *weak domain-transfer loss*. Figure 1 shows the framework of the proposed method.

Data and Preprocessing. The dataset is provided by the challenge organizers [3] and [4]. It consists of 45 patients, each with three MRI modalities

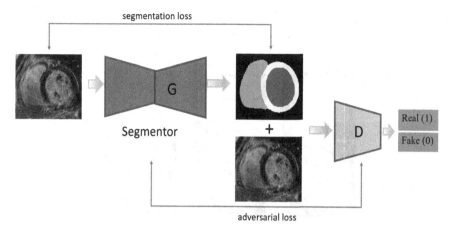

Fig. 1. Adversarial segmentation network architecture. It consists of a generator based on a dilated residual U-shape network and a CNN discriminator. The two networks are simultaneously optimized during the process of supervised learning and adversarial learning. Segmentation loss is a combination of individual-domain and domain-transfer loss, while the adversarial loss is a combination of the segmentation loss and the discriminator loss.

(LGE, T2-weight and bSSFP). It is noted that not all of the modalities come with the annotations of three heart regions (i.e., left ventricles, myocardium, and right ventricles). Annotations of all the three modalities are provided for patients 1–5; while patients 6–35 have manual annotations of T2-weight and bSSFP. Patients 36–45 have the raw MR scans of three modalities but without any annotations. When constructing the training set, only those MR scans with manual annotations are included. The test data contains the MR scans of LGE from patients 6 to 45, tasked to predict the masks of the three heart regions. Data augmentation is used for robust training. Three geometrical transformations (rotation, shear, zooming) are applied to all of the images and their corresponding masks. For each slice, we also crop a region with a fixed bounding box (224 * 224), enclosing all the annotated regions but at different locations to capture the shift invariance, resulting in 5 groups of cropped regions of interests. Before training the networks, the intensities of each 2D slice from three modalities are normalized using *z-scores* normalization to calibrate the range of intensities.

Weak Domain Transfer. Figure 2 shows some sample images with annotation masks of different modalities from the same patient. In Fig. 2, we can further observe from the annotations that the *bSSFP, T2* and *LGE* share some anatomical and structure information; For example, the right ventricle is always surrounded by myocardium, left ventricle is next to myocardium. The annotation masks of the corresponding slices from the three modalities have a certain level of overlap. Based on those observations, we hypothesize that the information from bSSFP and T2 can facilitate the segmentation of LGE. Hence we propose

to use the annotation masks on bSSFP and T2 modalities as the *pseudo* masks
for the unlabelled LGE modalities.

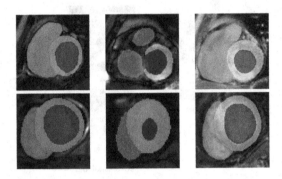

Fig. 2. From left to right are the images of the bSSFP, T2, LGE modalities from the
same patient, with ground truth masks imposed (best viewed in color). (Color figure
online)

The masks of bSSFP and T2 scans are transferred to LGE by using a normalized index which identifies the correspondence between axial slices from different
modalities. These masks from bSSFP or T2 are directly used as the *pseudo* masks
for the corresponding LGE. Specifically, for an axial slice i in bSSFP (or T2)
with annotations, its corresponding slice index j in LGE is computed as below:

$$j = \lfloor i * \frac{n}{m} \rfloor \tag{1}$$

where $\lfloor \cdot \rfloor$ is the floor function. n denotes the number of axial slices of LGE; while
m is the number of axial slice in bSSFP (or T2) respectively. Therefore the mask
of slice i in bSSFP (or T2) is treated as the pseudo mask of the slice j in LGE.

Notably, those masks are *pseudo*, therefore, the domain-transfer loss should
be set as a *weaker* one when combined with loss defined on ground truth annotations from expert. We will discuss this further in next section.

It is worth noting that our **transfer** is different from the *conventional transfer*, which often used a pre-trained model (e.g. on ImageNet), or a knowledge dis-
tillation framework of teacher-student learning [15]. Instead, our *transfer* is built
as part of the whole model, specifically tailored for the cross-domain annotation-
transfer problem.

Generator. Figure 3 shows the overview of the generator model, where a dilated
residual U-shape network is tailored and used for the segmentation network.
Residual blocks in downsampling and upsampling parts are connected through
skip connections. In total the entire network consists of only 0.16 million trainable parameters.

In training a segmentation model, it is aware that cross-entropy loss focuses
on individual pixels while Dice loss focuses on the overlap of regions. Thus, a

combination of cross-entropy loss and Dice loss is chosen to optimize the network. Images and ground truth masks from the three sequences as well as the transferred masks mentioned above are used. Therefore, the training loss includes two parts: individual-domain loss and domain-transfer loss. Individual-domain loss, denoted as $\mathcal{L}_{ID}$, is the difference between the ground truth mask and prediction while *domain-transfer loss* denoted as $\mathcal{L}_{DT}$, is the difference between transferred masks (pseudo masks) and predicted ones.

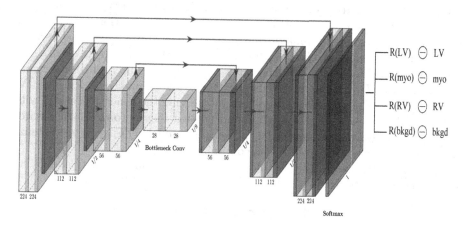

Fig. 3. Generator network architecture, composed of a downsampling tower and an upsampling tower.

Both of $\mathcal{L}_{ID}$ and $\mathcal{L}_{DT}$ consist of a linear combination of the multi-class cross-entropy loss $\mathcal{L}_{ce}$ and the Dice loss $\mathcal{L}_{Dice}$, formulated as:

$$\mathcal{L}_{ID} = \beta_1 \cdot \mathcal{L}_{ce} + (1 - \beta_1) \cdot \mathcal{L}_{Dice} \tag{2}$$

$$\mathcal{L}_{DT} = \beta_2 \cdot \mathcal{L}_{ce} + (1 - \beta_2) \cdot \mathcal{L}_{Dice} \tag{3}$$

The total loss function $\mathcal{L}_G$ is formulated as:

$$\mathcal{L}_G = \lambda \cdot \mathcal{L}_{ID} + (1 - \lambda) \cdot \mathcal{L}_{DT} \tag{4}$$

Notably, the domain-transfer loss leverages the information from bSSFP and T2 modalities. It is worth noting that λ in Eq. (4) is used to control the balance of the transfer; and it is set to 0.9, thus giving a much lower weight of the transfer loss 0.1 which is weak. In our experiments, β_1, β_2 are set to 0.9 after observing the segmentation performance on a validation set.

Mask Discriminator. We use a CNN as a discriminator to drive the generator to generate good-quality masks similar to the ground truth ones. The architecture contains several residual blocks with max-pooling layers. The raw images and the masks are spatially concatenated as a multi-channel input to the CNN. A (negative) binary cross-entropy loss $\mathcal{L}_D$ is used to train the model, defined as:

$$\mathcal{L}_D(\mathcal{S}, \mathcal{T}, D, G) = \mathbb{E}_{(x,y)\sim\mathcal{S}}[\log D(y|x)] + \mathbb{E}_{(x',y')\sim\mathcal{T}}[\log D(y'|x')] +$$
$$\mathbb{E}_{(x,y)\sim\mathcal{S}}[\log(1 - D(G(x,y)|x))] + \quad (5)$$
$$\mathbb{E}_{(x',y')\sim\mathcal{T}}[\log(1 - D(G(x',y')|x'))]$$

where $\mathcal{S}$ is the set of training data x with ground truth masks y, and $\mathcal{T}$ is the set of LGE data x' without masks, but with pseudo masks y'.

Adversarial Training of Generator and Discriminator. The objective of the proposed system is to produce appropriate segmentation masks on the target class during the min-max game of the two networks. Firstly we perform a supervised training on G using the MR scans with ground truth masks, the objective of G is to generate a good mask to deceive the discriminator network D. The goal of D is to identify the generated masks from the real masks. We aim to improve the segmentation quality by merging the generated masks with the original images as condition labels and putting them into the discriminator for adversarial learning training. The adversarial model is designed to minimize the adversarial loss which will reverse optimize the generator loss.

Equation 6 represents the total loss in the adversarial model. G and D are simultaneously optimized.

$$\min_G \max_D \mathcal{L}_{adv} = \mathcal{L}_D + \mathcal{L}_G \quad (6)$$

Algorithm 1. Training procedure of the adversarial model

Input: training images X, training masks Y, iteration j and k, batch size n
Output: Models: Segmentation model G, Discriminator D
---
i = 0
while $i \mathbf{\textit{j}} j$ do
| update G by $\mathcal{L}_{IN}$
| i = i+1
end
while $i \mathbf{\textit{j}} k$ do
| update D by maximizing $\mathcal{L}_{adv}$ using a mini-batch while keep G fixed
| update G by minimizing $\mathcal{L}_{adv}$ using a mini-batch while keep D fixed.
| i = i+1
end
return G

---

3   Experiment

Implementation. The proposed method is implemented using *Keras* library. The codes are available at https://github.com/jingkunchen/MS-CMR_miccai_2019. α is set as 0.9 thus, giving the weight of 0.9 for the categorical cross-entropy loss and 0.1 for Dice loss. Learning rate is set to 2×10^{-4}, and the learning decay is 1×10^{-8}. We use a batch size of 16. For the transfer loss L_{DT}, we use the ground truth (whenever available) masks of T2-weight and bSSFP, as the *pseudo* ground truth masks for the corresponding LGE slices. The correspondence between the LGE slices and the T2-weight (or the bSSFP) slices are established based on the simple index normalization along the z-axis of the 3D MRI scans[1]. We use Adam optimizer.

3.1   Results

It is noted that only 5 patients have LGE annotations available, thus we performe a very preliminary experiment to test the proposed method. We held out patients 4 and 5 for testing and the rest for training. Results are reported in Table 1 in terms of Dice score and Hausdorff distance (LV, myo, RV). We further compare three methods: dilated residual U-shape networks with Dice loss (U+D), adversarial model with Dice coefficient loss (U+A+D), adversarial model with Dice coefficient loss and transfer loss (U+A+D+T). The U-shape networks are specifically designed to segment biomedical images and perform well in myocardial segmentation of bSSFP CMR images [3]. Here we use dilated residual U-shape networks with Dice loss (U+D) as our baseline for a comparison. It could be observed that adding adversarial training improves the segmentation performance on both the myocardium and right ventricles, but performs worse on left ventricles. The proposed method with transfer loss outperforms both of them with only one exception of the lower Dice score the right ventricle.

Table 1. Average Dice and Hausdorff distance on patients 4 and 5

Method	Dice LV, myo, RV	Hausdorff Dist. LV, myo, RV
U-shape network (U+D)	70.5%, 50.0%, 70.0%	13.2, 12.0, 24.6
Adversarial model (U+A+D)	65.1%, 53.9%, **74.7%**	38.0, 16.1, 19.4
Adversarial transfer (U+A+D+T)	**76.0%, 59.6%**, 71.7%	**10.2, 12.1, 12.9**

Results on Challenge Test Set. We submitted the results of the methods of (U+A+D) and (U+A+D+T) on the testing set containing patients 6 to 45 LGE. Tables 2 and 3 summarize the average and median values of the results returned by the organizers. It could be seen that overall the approach of (U+A+D+T) outperforms (U+A+D), which confirms that promise of the proposed method.

---

[1] In practice, we find this works well. Ideally, registration could be performed to find the correspondence, which will be investigated further.

Table 2. Average Dice, Jaccard, Surface Distance and Hausdorff distance on patients 6 to 45

Method	Dice	Jaccard	Surface Dist	Hausdorff Dist.
	LV, myo, RV	LV, myo, RV	LV, myo, RV	LV, myo, RV
U+A+D	76.6%, 42.0%, 69.5%	0.62, 0.27, 0.54	5.5, 4.7, 5.5	22.1, 42.0, 32.7
U+A+D+T	**82.4%, 61.0%, 71.0%**	**0.71, 0.45, 0.57**	**3.9, 4.0, 5.0**	23.7, **24.6, 23.5**

Table 3. Median of Dice, Jaccard, Surface Distance and Hausdorff distance on patients 6 to 45

Method	Dice	Jaccard	Surface Dist	Hausdorff Dist.
	LV,myo,RV	LV,myo,RV	LV,myo,RV	LV,myo,RV
U+A+D	77.8%, 42.7%, 71.1%	0.63, 0.27, 0.55	5.3, 4.3, 5.0	18.5, 41.2, 28.5
U+A+D+T	**82.1%, 60.8%, 72.8%**	**0.70, 0.44, 0.57**	**3.8, 3.9, 4.6**	**15.4, 19.6, 22.8**

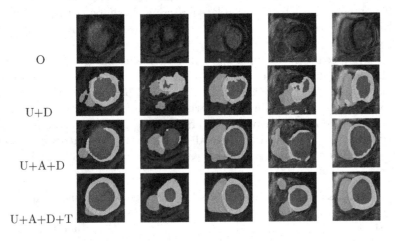

O

U+D

U+A+D

U+A+D+T

Fig. 4. The results of the segmentation. Rows from top to bottom: original images (O), dilated residual networks (U+D), adversarial model (U+A+D), adversarial model with Dice coefficient loss and transfer loss (U+A+D+T) (best viewed in color). (Color figure online)

Visualisation. Figure 4 shows some predicted masks of the LGE slices of four patients. It could be seen that adversarial learning improves the results of only using the dilated residual network, and the cross-modality transfer further refine the segmentation masks, especially for the left ventricles. Those observations are consistent with the results shown in Tables 1, 2 and 3.

4   Conclusions

We propose an automated method for heart segmentation based on multi-modality MRI images, which is trained in an adversarial manner. Specifically, our architecture consists of two modules, a multi-channel mask generator and a discriminator. In particular, we further introduce a domain-transfer loss function to leverage the information across different modalities for the same patients. Results show that such an idea is effective, and the overall framework performs better than the baseline methods.

References

1. Ronneberger, O., Fischer, P., Brox, T.: U-Net: convolutional networks for biomedical image segmentation. In: Navab, N., Hornegger, J., Wells, W., Frangi, A. (eds.) Medical Image Computing and Computer-Assisted Intervention–MICCAI 2015. Lecture Notes in Computer Science, vol. 9351, pp. 234–241. Springer, Cham (2015). https://doi.org/10.1007/978-3-319-24574-4_28
2. Goodfellow, I., et al.: Generative adversarial nets. In: NIPS, pp. 2672–2680 (2014)
3. Zhuang, X.: Multivariate mixture model for myocardial segmentation combining multi-source images. In: TPAMI (2018)
4. Zhuang, X.: Multivariate mixture model for cardiac segmentation from multi-sequence MRI. In: Ourselin, S., Joskowicz, L., Sabuncu, M.R., Unal, G., Wells, W. (eds.) MICCAI 2016. LNCS, vol. 9901, pp. 581–588. Springer, Cham (2016). https://doi.org/10.1007/978-3-319-46723-8_67
5. Zhuang, X., Shen, J.: Multi-scale patch and multi-modality atlases for whole heart segmentation of MRI. Med. Image Anal. **31**, 77–87 (2016)
6. Isola, P., Zhu, J.Y., Zhou, T., Efros, A.A.: Image-to-image translation with conditional adversarial networks. In: CVPR, pp. 1125–1134 (2017)
7. Luc, P., Couprie, C., Chintala, S., Verbeek, J.: Semantic segmentation using adversarial networks. arXiv preprint arXiv:1611.08408 (2016)
8. Zhuang, X., et al.: Evaluation of algorithms for multi-modality whole heart segmentation: an open-access grand challenge. arXiv preprint arXiv:1902.07880 (2019)
9. Petitjean, C., et al.: Right ventricle segmentation from cardiac MRI: a collation study. Med. Image Anal. **19**(1), 187–202 (2015)
10. Avendi, M.R., Kheradvar, A., Jafarkhani, H.: A combined deep-learning and deformable-model approach to fully automatic segmentation of the left ventricle in cardiac MRI. Med. Image Anal. **30**, 108–119 (2016)
11. LeCun, Y., Bengio, Y., Hinton, G.: Deep learning. Nature **521**(7553), 436 (2015)
12. He, K., Zhang, X., Ren, S., Sun, J.: Deep residual learning for image recognition. In: CVPR, pp. 770–778 (2016)
13. Long, J., Shelhamer, E., Darrell, T.: Fully convolutional networks for semantic segmentation. In: CVPR, pp. 3431–3440 (2015)
14. Li, H., Zhygallo, A., Menze, B.: Automatic brain structures segmentation using deep residual dilated U-Net. In: Crimi, A., Bakas, S., Kuijf, H., Keyvan, F., Reyes, M., van Walsum, T. (eds.) BrainLes 2018. LNCS, vol. 11383, pp. 385–393. Springer, Cham (2019). https://doi.org/10.1007/978-3-030-11723-8_39
15. Hinton, G., Vinyals, O., Dean, J.: Distilling the knowledge in a neural network. arXiv preprint arXiv:1503.02531 (2015)
16. Moon, J.C.: What is late gadolinium enhancement in hypertrophic cardiomyopathy? In: Revista Española de Cardiología (2007)

CRT-EPiggy19 Challenge

Best (and Worst) Practices for Organizing a Challenge on Cardiac Biophysical Models During AI Summer: The CRT-EPiggy19 Challenge

Oscar Camara[(✉)]

Physense, BCN MedTech, Department of Information and Communication
Technologies, Universitat Pompeu Fabra, Barcelona, Spain
oscar.camara@upf.edu

Abstract. During the last years tens of challenges have been organized
to benchmark computational techniques with shared data. Historically,
most challenges in conferences such as MICCAI have been devoted to
medical image processing, especially on object recognition or segmentation tasks. Due to the increasing popularity and easy access to machine
(deep) learning methods, as part of our current Artificial Intellingence
(AI) summer, the number of AI-related challenges has exploded. In parallel, the community of biophysical models also has a valuable history
of organizing challenges, including synthetic and experimental data, to
assess the accuracy of the resulting simulations. In this paper, the similarities and differences in computational challenges organized by these
communities are reviewed, suggesting best practices and what to avoid
when organizing a challenge on biophysical models. Specifically, details
will be given about the preparation of the CRT-EPiggy19 challenge.

Keywords: Reproducible research · Computational challenge ·
Electrophysiological modelling · Cardiac Resynchronization Therapy ·
Animal data

1 Introduction

Computational models in biomedicine have evolved during the last years to the
point of beginning to have an impact in some steps of clinical workflows [16].
A clear example is the success history of the Heartflow company[1] with the
simulation-based computation of Fractional Flow Reserve for coronary artery
disease. Nevertheless, initiatives promoting reproducible research and verifica-
tion/validation of the existing models on common data are still needed to make
further steps on their realism and prediction abilities. The cardiac modelling

---

[1] http://www.heartflow.com/.

M. Pop et al. (Eds.): STACOM 2019, LNCS 12009, pp. 329–341, 2020.
https://doi.org/10.1007/978-3-030-39074-7_35

community has a long-standing track record of collective efforts on this direction, including: model repositories such as CellML[2]; Open Access softwares such as OpenCMISS[3] [4], Chaste[4] [21], Continuity[5], SOFA[6] or CARP[7], among others; and benchmark studies with synthetic data such as the ones summarized in Niederer et al. [22] on cardiac electrophysiology and in Land et al. [18] on cardiac mechanics. Other than using analytical data for verification purposes, a usual practice in computational modelling is to test computational models with high-resolution data acquired in animal experiments (e.g. [5,28]). However, reproducibility, processing and management of these data are not easy, being also difficult to acquire large databases.

In parallel, the last years have seen an explosion of challenges in medical image and signal processing communities, mainly fostered at international conferences such as Medical Image Computing and Computer Assisted Intervention (MICCAI, mainly through its workshops)[8] or Computing in Cardiology (CinC)[9], among others. The Grand Challenge in Biomedical Image Analysis website[10] is a very useful repository listing most of medical image-related challenges whereas Physionet[11] [14] is a comprehensive resource, hosting some of the most used databases in challenges involving complex physiological signals.

Several factors have contributed to the recent increase of computational challenges such as having easier protocols to acquire and share large amounts of medical data with associated ground-truth, high scientific visibility for challenge organizers/participants as well as easy access to Open Source data science softwares and hardware infrastructure for fast processing (e.g. Graphical Processing Units and High Performance Computing). Obviously, the disruptive developments in Machine Learning (ML) in the past years (a new Artificial Intelligence, AI, summer), in particular with Deep Learning (DL) algorithms, has also had a major impact, promoting the participation in these challenges of non-experts in the biomedical engineering field, often agnostic to the targeted applications.

The substantial progress made in both biophysical modelling and biomedical data science communities towards algorithm reproducibility, facilitating open access to data and codes to all researchers, has been independent from each other. There is a lack of communication and joint initiatives between these scientific communities that would be very beneficial to both of them, e.g. to use common clinical data to set up benchmarks and to train machine learning techniques as well as for validation of cardiovascular multi-physics simulations. In this manuscript, a brief review of current benchmarks and reproducible research

---

[2] https://www.cellml.org/.
[3] https://opencmiss.org/.
[4] https://chaste.cs.ox.ac.uk/trac.
[5] https://continuity.ucsd.edu/.
[6] https://sofa-framework.org.
[7] https://carpentry.medunigraz.at/carputils/index.html.
[8] http://www.miccai.org.
[9] http://www.cinc.org.
[10] https://grand-challenge.org.
[11] https://physionet.org.

initiatives in medical data science and biophysical modelling is given, listing some good and bad practices learnt from the experience of organizing the CRT-EPiggy19 challenge on electrophysiological modelling.

2 Brief Review of Computational Challenges and Reproducible Research in Biophysical Modelling and Medical Data Science

2.1 Biophysical Modelling

Historically, the biophysical modelling community has been one of the pioneering scientific fields on Open Science, mainly due to the vision and resilience of several leaders of the field, with numerous initiatives shaping its research and helping thousands of investigators. Some examples with an important presence of cardiovascular applications include the definition of standards and creation of curated model repositories (e.g. cellML, FieldML, Physiome Model Repository[12], the new Physiome journal[13]), Open Source softwares (see list above), international networking forum (e.g. Physiome[14], Virtual Physiological Institute[15], COMBINE[16]) and derived conferences (Cardiac Physiome[17], VPH[18] or the Barcelona VPH Summer School[19], among others). In addition, substantial steps are recently being made towards promoting reproducible research from key healthcare players such as the National Institute of Health (e.g. Centre for Reproducible Biomedical Modeling[20]), the Food and Drug Administration (e.g. definition of best practices for verification, validation and uncertainty of computational models [24–26]), the Medical Device Innovation Consortium (MDIC; program on Computational Modeling and Simulation[21]) or the American Society of Mechanical Engineers (ASME; definition of standards for Verification and Validation in several computational modelling scenarios such as fluid dynamics and heat transfer, V&V 20 Subcommittee [2], or modeling of medical devices, V&V 40 Subcommittee [3]).

As for benchmarks and challenges, the complexity, high-level and multi-scale nature of the questions usually asked to biophysical models makes the generation of realistic ground-truth data very difficult (in contrast to low-level tasks in image processing such as object recognition), either analytically on synthetic data or with experiments on animal or human data. This is particularly true in

---

12 https://models.physiomeproject.org.
13 https://journal.physiomeproject.org.
14 http://physiomeproject.org/.
15 https://www.vph-institute.org.
16 https://co.mbine.org.
17 https://www.cardiacphysiome.org/meetings.
18 https://vph-conference.org.
19 https://eventum.upf.edu/28646/detail/4th-barcelona-vph-summer-school.html.
20 https://reproduciblebiomodels.org/.
21 https://mdic.org/program/computational-modeling-and-simulation-cms/.

cardiovascular applications since they involve the heart, one of the most sophisticated human organs, with multiple strongly-coupled physical phenomena such as electrophysiology, mechanics and haemodynamics. In addition, the real systemic functioning of the human body is not considered, isolating the cardiovascular system from the remaining organs and systems.

Some pioneering benchmarks have been proposed on synthetic data for the verification of cardiac electrophysiology [22] and mechanics [18], which have been very useful to the modelling community for comparing the different solver performance on common, even if simple, data. More sophisticated approaches to build ground-truth data include the building or use of (printed) phantoms connected to flow pumps in in vitro experiments to validate fluid simulations [31]. Ex vivo or in vivo experiments with animals allow the acquisition of high resolution medical data, and subsequent generation of ground-truth, which usually characterize the human cardiovascular system better than in vitro experiments. Over the years, several cardiovascular modelling challenges have been based on experimental models such as the ones taking place at the MICCAI-STACOM workshop[22]), from the initial electrophysiological simulation challenges (CESC'10 [5], 2011 [28]), to fluid simulation challenges for aortic coarctation (2012[23], 2013[24]) and a left ventricle mechanics challenge in 2014[25]. However, acquiring and processing experimental data is not straightforward and a previous detailed analysis on the usefulness of a given experiment is required, considering intra-species differences, ethical issues and associated costs.

2.2   Medical Image Processing

Open Science has also been promoted in the medical imaging community since its initial developments in the 90's, especially in some domains such as neuroimaging. The leading role of researchers such as Pr K.J. Friston (Institute of Neurology, University College London, United Kingdom) and other contributors to the Open Source Statistical Parameter Mapping (SPM) software [1,12][26] hugely influenced the neuroimaging community so that the main brain data processing softwares are currently freely available. Examples of these softwares besides SPM, some being routinely used by clinicians worldwide, include FreeSurfer [10][27], AFNI [6][28], FSL [17][29], or Brainvisa [13][30], among others.

Neuroimaging researchers have also been at the vanguard of data sharing. Just to name a couple of landmark projects that have helped thousands of researchers, one could mention the multiple brain atlases and templates released

---

[22] http://stacom.cardiacatlas.org/.
[23] http://www.vascularmodel.org/miccai2012.
[24] http://www.vascularmodel.org/miccai2013.
[25] http://stacom.cardiacatlas.org/stacom2014.
[26] https://www.fil.ion.ucl.ac.uk/spm.
[27] https://surfer.nmr.mgh.harvard.edu.
[28] https://afni.nimh.nih.gov.
[29] https://fsl.fmrib.ox.ac.uk/fsl.
[30] http://brainvisa.info.

by the Montreal Neurological Institute (MNI) [9][31] and the Alzheimer's Disease Neuroimaging Initiative (ADNI) [9][32] with thousands of multiple cross-sectional and longitudinal data of controls and AD patients that have been used in more than 1700 scientific papers (up to 2018). The historic involvement of the neuroimaging community in Open Science has been strengthened in recent times with several initiatives on standardization of data structures/processing pipelines and reproducible research such as the Brain Imaging Data Structure (BIDS) [15][33] that is based on OpenNeuro platform[34] for sharing data, the Clinica software[35] for reproducible and objective classification experiments [30] or the Stanford Centre for Reproducible Neuroscience[36].

Cardiovascular imaging has required more time to embrace data sharing policies, arguably due to a higher difficulty to obtain good quality data than in the brain, despite pioneering efforts such as the early open release of the Auckland Dog Heart data [23] and the Cardiac Atlas Project [11][37], both led by the University of Auckland. Fortunately, this trend is changing and large datasets of complete cardiovascular data are becoming available to the scientific community such as the colossal UK Biobank database[38], interestingly including brain and heart data that allows for holistic studies including both organs [7].

The fast growth (in short time) and diversity of computational challenges did prevent the common definition of standards and good practices for their organization, decisions being ultimately made based on each challenge organizer's own judgement. Recently, Maier-Hein et al. [20] thoroughly studied more than 150 biomedical image analysis competitions that represent a landmark step forward in their scientific quality and standardization. The authors identified some typical issues in challenges such as (lack of) reproducibility, (correct) result interpretation and (impossibility of) cross-comparison in most challenges. These issues are particularly critical in the current era of massive use of ML/DL algorithms, most of them used as black boxes independent of the final application, and with the only objective of being a couple of decimals better in accuracy metrics such as the Dice coefficient. These metrics are often too optimistic and far from reality in a clinical environment, hampering its real impact, which needs randomized clinical trials to be properly evaluated. Another critical point is the generation of ground-truth data to compare algorithms since its uncertainty and intra-observer variability are rarely considered. Nevertheless, the long-standing efforts of the medical imaging community, as summarized in [20], have led to the creation of best practice forms to organize challenges, which are currently used in conferences such as MICCAI. Unfortunately they are mainly focused on image segmentation techniques.

---

[31] https://mcgill.ca/bic/resources/brain-atlases.
[32] http://adni.loni.usc.edu/.
[33] http://bids.neuroimaging.io.
[34] https://openneuro.org.
[35] http://www.clinica.run.
[36] http://reproducibility.stanford.edu.
[37] https://www.cardiacatlas.org.
[38] https://www.ukbiobank.ac.uk.

2.3   Medical Signal Processing

Physionet [14][39] is the reference resource for data, software, challenges and tutorials related to complex physiological signals, clearly demonstrating the long history of medical signal processing, as well as the easiness to acquire large databases of signals rather than with images. On the other hand, it is still an open problem to find the required resources for labelling the vast amount of samples available in these databases, i.e. generating the ground-truth or training data for validation of computational models or training of machine learning algorithms. However, in conjunction with the CinC conference[40], Physionet has continuously organized annual challenges on available labelled data since 2000, targeting clinically interesting and varied problems from sleep apnea to Intensive Care Unit data or several arrhythmia applications.

As part of the scientific community around the CinC conference, it is worthy to mention the Consortium for ECG Imaging (CEI)[41] since it is an exemplary initiative gathering most world-wide research groups specialized on this field, working together to advance it and providing a repository of datasets for the validation of the developed techniques.

3   CRT-EPiggy19 Challenge: CESC'10

3.1   Cradle of the Challenge

In 2010, at the first edition of the STACOM workshop during the MICCAI conference held in Beijing, China, the Cardiac Electrophysiological Simulation Challenge (CESC'10) took place. Different modelling approaches were tested against optical mapping data of a perfused ex-vivo porcine heart [27], acquired at the Sunnybrook Health Sciences Centre, Toronto, Canada. Additionally, a modelling pipeline integrating the different approaches was developed, providing the best prediction power of depolarization isochrones in different pacing conditions [5]. It seemed more than appropriate to organize a new EP modelling challenge for the STACOM-MICCAI 2019 edition, to be held again in China (Shenzen). Coinciding with the Chinese Year of the Pig, multimodal Pig (kind of Big) Data was released to modelling researchers willing to participate in the Cardiac Resynchronization Therapy Electrophysiological challenge 2019 (CRT-EPiggy19) challenge[42].

3.2   Swine Model of Left Bundle Branch Block and Cardiac Resynchronization Therapy

Cardiac Resynchronization Therapy (CRT) is a successful electrical treatment for Heart Failure (HF), but still more than 30% of patients fulfilling the criteria for implantation do not respond to the therapy. A better patient selection

---

[39] https://www.cardiacatlas.org.
[40] http://www.cinc.org.
[41] http://www.ecg-imaging.org.
[42] http://crt-epiggy19.surge.sh/.

and stratification based on more sophisticated indices (i.e. beyond QRS duration and ejection fraction) and optimization of therapy settings such as lead configuration (e.g. number and positioning, biventricular vs. His-bundle pacing) and ventricular delays (inter-ventricular and atrio-ventricular) could reduce the rate of non-responders. Computational models are ideal tools for better understand pacing-based therapies such as CRT, providing additional information to the clinician on its optimal parameters for a given patient. Lee et al. [19] recently published a comprehensive review of computational models for CRT, showing the large variety of options in the different steps of the modelling pipeline.

Nevertheless, as for most clinical modelling applications, computational models for CRT suffer from the lack of shared rich data to compare the different options. This is especially complicated in CRT modelling due to the impossibility of acquiring human data at different stages of the disease (e.g. baseline, disease, after treatment). Some years ago, researchers at Hospital Clínic de Barcelona and Universitat Pompeu Fabra developed a swine model of left bundle branch block (LBBB) for experimental studies of CRT [29]. Radiofrequency applications were performed to induce LBBB. Half of the animals presented a myocardial infarction located at the septal wall. Imaging data and electro-anatomical maps (EAM) were acquired at baseline, with the induced LBBB and after implantation of a CRT device. This rich data is well suited for evaluating some features of the different cardiac computational models available nowadays, and was the basis of the CRT-EPiggy19 challenge.

3.3   Organization of the Challenge

The spirit of CRT-EPiggy19 was to collectively review the current state-of-the-art for computational cardiology models and their ability to predict pacing-based therapy outcomes, as well as the identification of the most critical phases and more promising solutions in the personalization modelling pipeline. More specifically, participants were asked to predict the electrical response of CRT and to propose the optimal device configuration in a swine model of left bundle branch block, given fully controlled data. All challenge participants were invited to contribute to the preparation of a journal article summarizing the main findings from the CRT-EPiggy19 challenge, similarly to the CESC'10 challenge [5]. The challenge will remain open to new participants for some months after the MICCAI-STACOM19 workshop.

3.4   Training and Testing Datasets

The training data included the LBBB and after CRT data of two complete infarcted and two non-infarcted datasets (total of 4 cases), while the test data (only LBBB) was composed of seven cases (3 infarcted and 4 non-infarcted). Unlike LBBB and CRT activation maps, baseline maps were not released, since they did not necessarily contribute to the prediction of CRT from LBBB. The electrical activation patterns of the training datasets have already been detailed in Soto-Iglesias et al. [32]. Figure 1 shows an overview of the EAM maps of the test data cases (after a LBBB), where the electrical dyssynchrony between the right and left ventricles can be easily observed (e.g. right ventricle activated way earlier than the left one due to the malfunctioning of the left bundle branch of the conduction system). The training and test data sets were uploaded onto the Zenodo portal[43], which is a catch-all repository founded by CERN and the OpenAIRE European Commission project to promote Open Science.

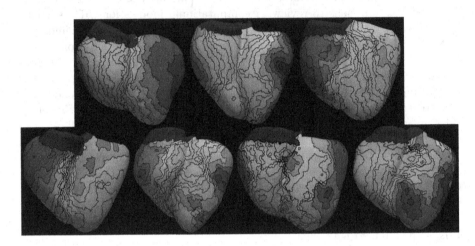

Fig. 1. Electro-anatomical maps of the seven cases composing the test data. All cases have a left bundle branch block that induced electrical dyssynchrony between the two ventricles. Red and blue areas indicate the earliest and the latest activation sites. (Color figure online)

Some of the main sources of variability in model personalization come from the extraction of anatomical data from medical images and the creation of the geometrical domain where models are run. In order to reduce this variability, biventricular finite element meshes were provided to each participant, built from the segmentation of magnetic resonance imaging (cine-MRI) data. These meshes included cardiomyocyte orientation (obtained with rule-based models; see Doste et al. [8] for details), several regional labels (AHA regions, endo- and epi-cardial walls, different ventricles) and the local activation times projected from EAM data. Additionally, the affected AHA segments and its transmurality were given for infarcted cases. Furthermore, for visualization and analysis purposes, 2D bi-ventricular representations were also provided.

3.5   Evaluation Metrics

Global and regional differences between simulated and measured CRT activation maps will be used to evaluate the prediction accuracy of each proposed model.

---

[43] https://zenodo.org/record/3249511#.XWKfu5MzZpg.

As global metric, we will use the difference in Total Activation Time (TAT, whole heart fully activated). The TAT will also individually be assessed for the LV, the RV, as well as for each AHA segment. TAT differences will be separately analyzed between simulations and measurements for infarcted vs. non-infarcted cases. Histograms of isochrones of electrical activation will be derived from simulations to estimate inter- and intra-ventricular electrical dyssynchrony (Soto-Iglesias et al. [32]). Each participant was asked to report the used hardware infrastructure, computational times and details about the implementation and a self-reported analysis for model integration onto a clinical workflow.

4 Dos and Don'ts When Organizing a Challenge on Biophysical Modelling

Don't Call It a 'Challenge' but Do Call It a 'Working Group': Nobody wants to be a loser and some researchers, including from companies, associate a Challenge with a high risk of damaging their reputation rather than an opportunity for dissemination. As the concept of a single winner do not help, the spirit of the event should be towards a collaborative Working Group (e.g. similar to the ECGI Consortium). In the case of the CRT-EPiggy19 event, after clarifying this aspect, which was risen by several researchers, more participants were willing to play with the data.

Don't Initiate the Challenge Without Having All (Ground-Truth) Data Curated Well in Advance and Do Be Flexible to Include More: Preparing and curating the data for a biophysical modelling challenge can take months and still not be fully complete, due to the large amount of multi-modal raw and processed data available. Participants may ask for additional data that might benefit everyone (e.g. the raw EGM signals to check possible LAT mistakes in the CRT-EPiggy19 challenge) and the organizers must be flexible enough to allow sub-studies not originally planned.

Don't Associate the Challenge to (the Deadlines Of) a Conference Workshop and Do Allow Enough Time for Participants: Even for research groups with long-standing experience on CRT modelling, it is not obvious to find resources (e.g. time of people) to participate in an "unexpected" project such as the CRT-EPiggy19 challenge, in particular if there are hard deadlines due to the presentation of results in a conference. Obtaining satisfactory simulation results from cardiac models on several datasets is more difficult than just running multiple iterations of machine learning algorithms with different hyper-parameters, for instance to set up the right boundary conditions for every case.

Don't Blindly Believe in Ground-Truth Data and Do Consider Its Uncertainty: Raw and ground-truth data are intrinsically associated with acquisition and experiment inaccuracies as well as intra-observer bias and labelling variability that might misjudge a given outcome of a cardiac simulation. It can even happen that the model is better than the data in some cases! Therefore, uncertainty needs to be considered at different levels, both from observational and modelling points of view. For doing so, it is necessary to have knowledge about data acquisition system principles and physiology to be modelled, preventing the agnosticism to these aspects.

Don't Bother About Tiny Differences in Accuracy Indices and Do Use Multiple Evaluation Metrics, Including Related to Potential Clinical Translation: It is absurd to rank challenge results based on a single accuracy metric for biophysical modelling high-level tasks. As brilliantly shown by Maier-Hain et al. [20], computational techniques will be ranked differently depending on the metric of choice, thus it is more fair to use multiple indices to better characterize the pros and cons of every algorithm according to different criteria. If possible, it would be positive to consider indices related to potential clinical translation or to the parameters used by clinicians to make clinical decisions.

Don't Extrapolate Results Obtained on Experimental Models to Human Data but Do Recognize Inter- and Intra-species Variability and Differences with Real-World Clinical Data: The experimental data used in the CRT-EPiggy19 challenge is practically impossible to obtain in humans (e.g. at different longitudinal healthy, diseased and treated stages), representing a unique dataset for the study of heart electromechanics abnormalities and the effect of different pacing therapy settings. In addition, it is an ideal dataset for calibrating and tuning cardiac computational models. However, organizers and participants need to be cautious on the conclusions drawn from cardiac modelling results on the swine model, especially on (over-)promising similar outcomes with human data. For instance, the fast conduction system (e.g. Purkinje network) is different in pigs than in humans (i.e. more transmural and endocardial, respectively), which makes the whole electrical and mechanical interaction of the heart different in the two species. Moreover, even with human data, similar caution is advisable from results obtained in the typically well-curated and complete databases used in challenges, which usually are quite different from noisy and incomplete real-world clinical data.

Don't Underestimate the Amount of Resources Required to Organize and Participate in a Challenge and Do Acknowledge All Contributors: The amount of time to organize and participate in a biophysical modelling challenge can easily be underestimated; the work of several people is needed for the acquisition of the data, the generation of ground-truth labels, selection of the cases to be analyzed, pre-processing of the data, challenge dissemination (e.g. web preparation), participant hunting, and post-processing of results, among multiple other tasks. It is important that all contributors are appropriately acknowledged.

5 Conclusions

Can the medical data scientists and machine learning communities learn something from biophysical modelling? And viceversa? The obvious answer to both directions of the same question is affirmative. For high-level predictive tasks, AI-based or biophysics-related models face similar issues (e.g. reproducibility, labelling and curation of large databases, generalization, clinical translation, etc.) that will benefit from joint solutions. On the one hand, data scientists cannot be agnostic to data to have a real impact in relevant clinical decisions and should be inspired by biophysical modelling that is intrinsically related to physiology and understanding of the studied phenomena. Adding prior knowledge on the targeted clinical application (e.g. through the training of ML algorithms on virtual populations generated with biophysical models) to the powerful performance of ML algorithms will improve its generalization and robustness, bringing them closer to be used on real-world data. On the other hand, biophysical modelling community should learn from the research, development and infrastructure decisions that have made the explosion of data science possible, including Open Science frameworks such as Tensorflow, standard release of developed codes as Open Source and a successful communication with clinicians, lot of them already adopting ML tools in a way that biophysical modellers have rarely achieved. Finally, the joint development of common standards and ontologies, publishing protocols (e.g. involving journals asking for code/data requirements) and education of early researchers on the overall benefits of reproducible research and Open Science will be beneficial for both scientific communities.

Acknowledgments. Most of the organization of the CRT-EPiggy19 challenge has occurred during an academic visit of the author to the University of Auckland, which was partially funded by a Salvador de Madariaga fellowship by the Spanish Ministry of Science, Innovation and Universities and an expert visit grant from the European Union's Horizon 2020 project EPIC (grant agreement No 687794). The CRT-EPiggy19 challenge is also partially funded by the Maria de Maeztu Units of Excellence Program (MDM-2015-0502) from the Spanish Ministry of Economy and Competitiveness of the Department of Information and Communication Technologies at the Universitat Pompeu Fabra, which is focused on data-driven knowledge extraction and promotes reproducible research and open science initiatives (https://www.upf.edu/web/mdm-dtic/reproducibility-in-research). I would like to thank all researchers participating in the challenge but also those who kindly explained me their justifiable reasons for not doing it. Special acknowledgments are given to all contributors of the CRT-EPiggy19 challenge, notably data collectors and clinical researchers (M. Sitges, A. Berruezo, M. Rigol, N. Solanes, A. Doltra, J. Fernández-Armenta), data curators (D. Soto, E. Silva, D. Andreu, C. Albors), data processors and scientific researchers (T. Mansi, E. Castañeda, B. Bijnens, G. Jiménez, N. Duchateau, J. Mill) and IT support (C. Yagüe) from Hospital Clínic de Barcelona, Siemens Healthineers and Universitat Pompeu Fabra. Finally, I would like to thank the anonymous reviewer of this paper for his fruitful comments and desire to initially reject it, which highly contributed to improve the manuscript.

References

1. Ashburner, J.: SPM: a history. NeuroImage **62**(2), 791–800 (2012)
2. ASME: ASME V&V 20–2009: Standard for Verification and Validation in Computational Fluid Dynamics and Heat Transfer. American Society of Mechanical Engineers, New York, NY (2009)
3. ASME: ASME V&V 40–2018: Assessing Credibility of Computational Modeling through Verification and Validation: Application to Medical Devices. American Society of Mechanical Engineers, New York, NY (2018)
4. Bradley, C., Bowery, A., Britten, R., Budelmann, V., Camara, O., et al.: OpenCMISS: a multi-physics & multi-scale computational infrastructure for the VPH/Physiome project. Prog. Biophys. Mol. Biol. **107**(1), 32–47 (2011)
5. Camara, O., et al.: Inter-model consistency and complementarity: learning from ex-vivo imaging and electrophysiological data towards an integrated understanding of cardiac physiology. Prog. Biophys. Mol. Biol. **107**(1), 122–133 (2011)
6. Cox, R.W.: AFNI: what a long strange trip it's been. NeuroImage **62**(2), 743–747 (2012)
7. Cox, S.R., Lyall, D.M., Ritchie, S.J., Bastin, M.E., et al.: Associations between vascular risk factors and brain MRI indices in UK Biobank. Eur. Heart J. **40**(28), 2290–2300 (2019)
8. Doste, R., Soto-Iglesias, D., Bernardino, G., Alcaine, A., Sebastian, R., et al.: A rule-based method to model myocardial fiber orientation in cardiac biventricular geometries with outflow tracts. Int. J. Numer. Meth. Biomed. Eng. **35**(4), e3185 (2019)
9. Evans, A.C., Janke, A.L., Collins, D.L., Baillet, S.: Brain templates and atlases. NeuroImage **62**(2), 911–922 (2012)
10. Fischl, B.: FreeSurfer. NeuroImage **62**(2), 774–781 (2012)
11. Fonseca, C.G., Backhaus, M., Bluemke, D.A., Britten, R.D., et al.: The Cardiac Atlas Project-an imaging database for computational modeling and statistical atlases of the heart. Bioinformatics **27**(16), 2288–2295 (2011)
12. Friston, K., Ashburner, J., Kiebel, S., Nichols, T., Penny, W.: Statistical Parametric Mapping: The Analysis of Functional Brain Images. Elsevier Academic Press, Amsterdam (2007)
13. Geffroy, D., Rivire, D., Denghien, I., Souedet, N., Laguitton, S., Cointepas, Y.: BrainVISA: a complete software platform for neuroimaging. In: Python in Neuroscience workshop, Paris, August 2011
14. Goldberger, A.L., Amaral, L.A.N., Glass, L., Hausdorff, J.M., et al.: PhysioBank, PhysioToolkit, and PhysioNet: components of a new research resource for complex physiologic signals. Circulation **101**(23), e215–e220 (2000)
15. Gorgolewski, K.J., Auer, T., Calhoun, V.D., Craddock, R.C., Das, S., et al.: The brain imaging data structure, a format for organizing and describing outputs of neuroimaging experiments. Sci. Data **3**, 160044 EP (2016)
16. Gray, R.A., Pathmanathan, P.: Patient-specific cardiovascular computational modeling: diversity of personalization and challenges. J. Cardiovasc. Transl. Res. **11**(2), 80–88 (2018)
17. Jenkinson, M., Beckmann, C.F., Behrens, T.E., Woolrich, M.W., Smith, S.M.: FSL. NeuroImage **62**(2), 782–790 (2012)
18. Land, S., et al.: Verification of cardiac mechanics software: benchmark problems and solutions for testing active and passive material behaviour. Proc. Roy. Soc. London A: Math. Phys. Eng. Sci. **471**(2184), 20150641 (2015)

19. Lee, A.W.C., Costa, C.M., Strocchi, M., Rinaldi, C.A., Niederer, S.A.: Computational modeling for cardiac resynchronization therapy. J. Cardiovasc. Transl. Res. **11**(2), 92–108 (2018)
20. Maier-Hein, L., Eisenmann, M., Reinke, A., Onogur, S., Stankovic, M., et al.: Why rankings of biomedical image analysis competitions should be interpreted with care. Nat. Commun. **9**(1), 5217 (2018)
21. Mirams, G.R., Arthurs, C.J., Bernabeu, M.O., Bordas, R., Cooper, J., et al.: Chaste: an open source C++ library for computational physiology and biology. PLOS Comput. Biol. **9**(3), 1–8 (2013)
22. Niederer, S.A., Kerfoot, E., Benson, A.P., Bernabeu, M.O., Bernus, O., et al.: Verification of cardiac tissue electrophysiology simulators using an n-version benchmark. Philos. Trans. Ser. A Math. Phys. Eng. Sci. **369**(1954), 4331–4351 (2011)
23. Nielsen, P.M., Le Grice, I.J., Smaill, B.H., Hunter, P.J.: Mathematical model of geometry and fibrous structure of the heart. Am. J. Physiol.-Heart C. Physiol. **260**(4), H1365–H1378 (1991)
24. Parvinian, B., Pathmanathan, P., Daluwatte, C., Yaghouby, F., et al.: Credibility evidence for computational patient models used in the development of physiological closed-loop controlled devices for critical care medicine. Front. Physiol. **10**, 220 (2019)
25. Pathmanathan, P., Cordeiro, J.M., Gray, R.A.: Comprehensive uncertainty quantification and sensitivity analysis for cardiac action potential models. Front. Physiol. **10**, 721 (2019)
26. Pathmanathan, P., Gray, R.A.: Validation and trustworthiness of multiscale models of cardiac electrophysiology. Front. Physiol. **9**, 106 (2018)
27. Pop, M., et al.: Fusion of optical imaging and MRI for the evaluation and adjustment of macroscopic models of cardiac electrophysiology: a feasibility study. Med. Image Anal. **13**(2), 370–380 (2009)
28. Pop, M., et al.: Construction of 3D MR image-based computer models of pathologic hearts, augmented with histology and optical fluorescence imaging to characterize action potential propagation. Med. Image Anal. **16**(2), 505–523 (2012)
29. Rigol, M., Solanes, N., Fernandez-Armenta, J., Silva, E., Doltra, A., et al.: Development of a swine model of left bundle branch block for experimental studies of cardiac resynchronization therapy. J. Cardiovasc. Transl. Res. **6**(4), 616–622 (2013)
30. Samper-González, J., Burgos, N., Bottani, S., Fontanella, S., Lu, P., et al.: Reproducible evaluation of classification methods in Alzheimer's disease: framework and application to mri and pet data. NeuroImage **183**, 504–521 (2018)
31. Shepard, L.M., Sommer, K.N., Angel, E., Iyer, V., Wilson, M.F., et al.: Initial evaluation of three-dimensionally printed patient-specific coronary phantoms for CT-FFR software validation. J. Med. Imaging **6**(2), 1–10 (2019)
32. Soto-Iglesias, D., Duchateau, N., Butakov, C.B.K., Andreu, D., et al.: Quantitative analysis of electro-anatomical maps: application to an experimental model of left bundle branch block/cardiac resynchronization therapy. IEEE J. Transl. Eng. Health Med. **5**, 1–15 (2017)

Prediction of CRT Activation Sequence by Personalization of Biventricular Models from Electroanatomical Maps

Juan Francisco Gomez[1,3], Beatriz Trenor[1], and Rafael Sebastian[2(✉)]

[1] Centre for Research and Innovation in Bioengineering (Ci2B),
Universitat Politecnica de Valencia, Valencia, Spain
[2] Computational Multiscale Simulation Lab (CoMMLab),
Department of Computer Science, Universitat de Valencia, Valencia, Spain
rafael.sebastian@uv.es
[3] International University of Valencia (VIU), Valencia, Spain

Abstract. Optimization of lead placement and interventricular delay settings in patients under cardiac resynchronization therapy is a complex task that might benefit from prior information based on models. Biophysical models can be used to predict the sequence of electrical heart activation in a patient given a set of parameters which should be personalized to the patient. In this paper, we use electroanatomical maps to personalize the endocardial activation of the right ventricle, and the different tissue conductivities in a pig model with left bundle branch block, to reproduce personalized biventricular activations. Following, we tested the personalized heart model by virtually simulating cardiac resynchronization therapy.

Keywords: Cardiac resynchronization therapy · Tissue properties personalization · Biophysical modeling

1 Introduction

Patients with a complete left bundle branch block (LBBB), show a significant delay between activation of the interventricular septum and activation of the left ventricular (LV) free wall. Therefore, decreasing the delay by pacing may restore mechanical contraction. Cardiac Resynchronization Therapy (CRT) is a successful electrical treatment for patients with ventricular dyssynchrony. During CRT, two synchronized electrical stimuli are usually delivered to reduce ventricular dyssynchrony. One stimulation lead is usually placed on the apex of the right ventricle (RV), and the other one on the epicardium of the LV lateral wall. Large randomized clinical trials [2,8] have led to the widespread adoption of CRT in patients with a prolonged QRS duration ≥120 ms. A significant intraventricular conduction delay reflected by a prolonged QRS duration (≥150 ms) with LBBB morphology remained the main indication to CRT. Nevertheless, a significant

M. Pop et al. (Eds.): STACOM 2019, LNCS 12009, pp. 342–351, 2020.
https://doi.org/10.1007/978-3-030-39074-7_36

proportion of implanted patients fails to respond sufficiently or in a predictable manner. There are a number of critical factors that have to be considered for CRT to be effective.

Since ECG criteria may be imperfect, there is increasing interest in advanced multimodality imaging to improve patients selection, guide LV catheter delivery and identify patients at risk for poor outcomes and serious ventricular arrhythmias [4].

Computational models for biophysical simulation are valuable tools for better understanding pacing-based therapies such as CRT [7], providing additional information to the clinician on its optimal parameters for a given patient [3,10]. In this study, we show a pipeline to personalize a computational model of a pig heart, using electro-anatomical maps (EAMs) acquired in LBBB, which is subsequently used to predict the sequence of activation under CRT.

2   Materials and Methods

2.1   Construction of Anatomical Models

For this study, we used two datasets from the CRT-EPiggy19 Challenge publicly available. The anatomical models used were segmented in a previous work by Soto-Iglesias et al. [9], and were afterwards improved by including a more realistic fiber orientation description [5]. The first dataset corresponded to a pig heart labeled as Neus, a non-infarcted case with a LBBB activation pattern, which was considered a CRT non-responder. The second model, labeled as Kira, was an infarcted case with a large scar located in the antero-septal and septo-apical areas, and a clear LBBB pattern and electrical dyssynchrony, who was considered a CRT responder.

The biophysical finite element models provided for each case were enhanced to obtain the required properties for simulation. First, models were remeshed with hexahedra to meet the requirements of our biophysical solver (ELVIRA) and to reduce the degrees of freedom. Second, all the properties of the original model were transfer to the new volumetric model and extra information related to endocardial, mid-myocardial and endocardial regions were added. For each case, we calculated the conduction velocities from the mesh at each segment of the AHA, for both the endocardium and the epicardium (we divided each AHA segment in two subregions). We observed high conduction velocities in the endocardium and the LV lateral wall at basal areas. We assumed that the effect was due to the Purkinje system, which was functional and allowed retrograde activation. Figure 1 shows the clear effect of the fast endocardial layer in the EAM of the case Neus in LBBB, where the isochrones are much wider (faster conduction velocity) in the LV endocardium and the LV epicardium. For instance in the models Kira and Neus, the average conduction velocities measured in all the endocardial AHA segments were 1.29 ± 0.69 m/s and 1.52 ± 0.97 m/s, respectively. Therefore, we added a fast endocardial conduction layer that was one element thick, to the RV and LV. We are aware that pig hearts present a

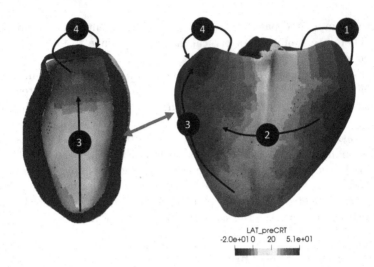

Fig. 1. Analysis of electrical propagation in ground-truth data. LBBB cases show a sequence of activation that can be summarized in four steps: (1) activation from RV endocardium tu RB epicardium and septal wall, (2) transmural propagation from RV to LV, (3) propagation from LV apex to base, with fast activation of the endocardium and slow in the epicardium, (4) transmural propagation from fast endocardium to epicardium in the LV lateral wall.

transmural Purkinje system, but since we do not have additional data, we opted only for the fast endocardial layer.

2.2 Biophysical Simulation

Detailed multiscale simulations were carried out for each ventricular model. Cellular electrophysiology was simulated by the ten Tusscher model considering transmural cellular heterogeneity, and electrical propagation by monodomain model.

2.3 Personalization of LBBB Activation Sequence

In order to obtain a personalized activation sequence for the LBBB patterns we developed the following methodology, summarized in Fig. 2. First, from the EAM, the LAT maps for the RV epicardium and the septal region of the LV endocardium are selected. In LBBB, those regions are expected to be activated by the RV endocardial sequence, since they are the closest ones. From the selected regions an inverse propagation to the RV endocardium is performed to obtain the original pattern of activation and the activation times in the RV endocardium. Once the RV stimulation sequence is obtained, it is used to activate the RV, obtaining the expected LBBB pattern. Following, the simulated LAT map is compared to the EAM to adjust the longitudinal and traversal conductivities.

Since the model includes a fast endocardial layer that functionally mimic the Purkinje system, those conductivities have to be set. Myocardial conductivities are obtained by looking at the epicardium isochrones, while Purkinje ones are derived from the endocardium. In models including scar, the elements were properly labeled, and the conductivity was set as 25% of the normal myocardium.

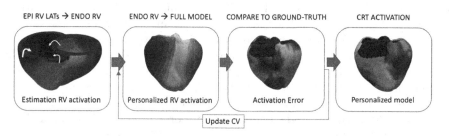

Fig. 2. Pipeline for personalization of the model parameters and simulation of CRT. EPI = Epicardium; ENDO = Endocardium

3   Results

3.1   LBBB Activation Sequences

For each of the models we followed the methodology developed to obtain the activation sequence of the RV endocardium. Conductivities were optimized in all the models iteratively by performing simulations and comparing the differences with the EAM data. Final conduction velocities are summarized in Table 1, together with mean square errors and total activation times. Note that we aim to reduce the average difference between LAT maps and not the final total activation time (TAT).

Figure 3 shows the results for the non-ischemic case Neus. As can be observed for the model Neus, the activation sequence is very similar at both the endocardium and the epicardium. Since the EAMs do not include the endocardium of the RV, the colormaps have been adjusted to be comparable, using the same scale, by shifting to the initial times (depolarization of the RV epicardium). The effect of the fast activated layer at the endocardium was key to obtain similar maps at the LV lateral wall. The TATs match between EAM and simulation, which is 71 ms. In the simulations, the isochrones are smoother, and do not reproduce the changes in the depolarization wavefront curvature observed in EAMs (Fig. 3(a) and (c)), which are probably due to the sampling and interpolation of the data. Even with the fast activation layer, the endocardium in the EAM is slightly faster (wider isochrones), than the simulation (Fig. 3(b) and (d)).

For the infarcted case, the model Kira, we simulated the activation sequences by personalizing the model as in Neus model. The real shape of the scar was not provided, but only which AHA regions were affected, and therefore, we simply reduced 25% the conduction velocities on those regions. As can be observed in Fig. 4(a), the epicardial RV activation was well reproduced, introducing the fast endocardial layer in the RV. However, we observed in the EAM a very slow conduction velocity (CV) in some regions of the LV endocardium (Fig. 4(c) top), compared to the LV epicardium (Fig. 4(c) down). That was unexpected since the scar in Kira model extends to the epicardium, but not the endocardium, and therefore we expected exactly the opposite result, which matches simulations (results not shown). Therefore, we updated the model to extend the scar to the endocardium. With the updated conductivities, we simulated properly the isochrones in LBBB in Kira model, with exception of the epicardium of the anterior wall and the apical region of the lateral wall Fig. 4(b) and (d). Those regions showed an abnormal fast CV (2,06 2,29 m/s) compared to the rest of the model (Fig. 4(b) top vs down), which was very remarkable considering that there is a large epicardial scar right under the anterior wall. The fast epicardial CV in the anterior versus posterior wall was present in both Kira and Neus models, although in the last was less marked.

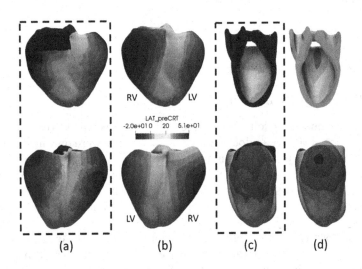

Fig. 3. Personalized LBBB sequence of activation for model Neus. (a) and (c) are anterior an posterior views of the model showing local activation times in the epicardium of the model (left) and the ground-truth data (right). (b) and (d) show endocardial and epicardial views of the LV lateral wall, respectively, where left subfigures correspond to simulations and right subfigures to ground-truth.

3.2   CRT Activation Sequences

Once the conductivities were estimated for the LBBB sequences, they were used for the CRT simulations. A priori, the fast endocardial layer was kept as it was functional for the LBBB sequences, and was expected to activate as well from

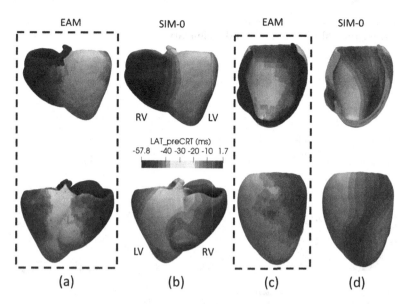

Fig. 4. Personalized LBBB sequence of activation for model Kira. (a) and (c) are anterior an posterior views of the model showing local activation times in the epicardium of the model (left) and the ground-truth data (right). (b) and (d) show endocardial and epicardial views of the LV lateral wall, respectively, where left subfigures correspond to simulations and right subfigures to ground-truth.

the CRT leads, or remote depolarization wavefronts travelling across the ventricles. Note that the fast endocardial layer can be personalized independently for the RV and LV. In the model Neus (see Fig. 5) the CRT leads were placed in the earliest activation sites, which were the RV endocardium (mirroring the earliest epicardial activation) and the apex of the LV epicardium (see Fig. 5(b)). The activation of the RV epicardium in the EAM was finished in less than 30 ms, which could be only explained if a fast RV endocardial layer spreads quickly the initial CRT lead impulse over the endocardium. After 10 ms of the RV epicardial breackthrough the wavefront reached the LV endocardium at the lower-septum (see Fig. 5(e)), coinciding with the activation of the LV lead, which was probably set 20 ms after the RV lead. On the LV endocardium the depolarization wavefront advanced slower than in the LBBB scenario, showing a much slower CV, or a poor access to the Purkinje system (see Fig. 5(d)). The simulation, reproduced well the activation pattern of the RV epicardium, with some differences at the basal region, and also the anterior and posterior walls. At the LV endocardium, in contrast to the EAM, the model showed much faster conduction velocities than the EAMs, and an activation sequence from endocardium to epicardium in the LV lateral wall due to the fast layer (see Fig. 5(e)). That was the largest difference, since in the EAM the activation: (i) follow a epicardium to endocardium activation sequence, with a large delay transmurally; and (ii) early activated regions in the base of the lateral wall, which coincided with the latest

Table 1. Estimation of CV parameters for computational models. CV = Conduction velocity (longitudinal/transmural); SIM = simulation;

Model		Tissue (m/s)		PKN (m/s)		TAT (ms)	
Name	Seq	CV_L	CV_T	CV_L	CV_T	SIM	EAM
Neus	LBBB	0.5	0.25	2.6	0.54	71	71
Kira	LBBB	1.78	0.58	1.4	1.3	68	59.5
Neus	CRT	0.9	0.5	1.0	0.9	65	58
Kira	CRT	1.78	0.58	1.4	1.3	49	40

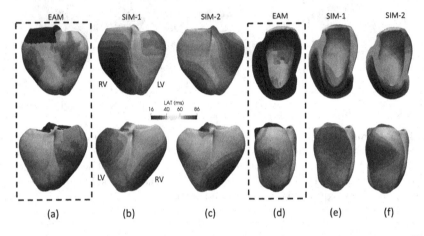

Fig. 5. Personalized simulations for prediction of CRT sequence of activation in Neus Model. (a) and (d) show anterior and posterior views of the EAM, and endocardial and epicardial views of the LV lateral wall, respectively. (b) and (e) show the simulations results using the personalized values obtained from the LBBB model. (c) and (f) show the simulations using personalized values obtained from the data post CRT implantation.

activated region in LBBB. Therefore, the model could not reproduce properly the activation sequence in the LV, which is very difficult to explain unless the LV lead would have been placed in the latest activated region in LBBB, that is the basal region of the LV lateral wall. Therefore, we updated the CRT lead locations to have a lead in the RV endocardium, and a lead in the LV epicardium lateral wall. In addition, we adjusted the fast conduction layer of the LV to an intermediate CV between Purkinje and myocardium. The results improved significantly (see Fig. 5(c) and (f)) and the sequence of activation matched properly between simulations and EAMs, i.e., there was a epicardial to endocardial activation sequence in the LV, and a delayed activation of the basal region of the LV endocardium.

In the case of Kira model, using the same set of conductivities obtained from the LBBB model did not obtain good agreement between EAM and simulations.

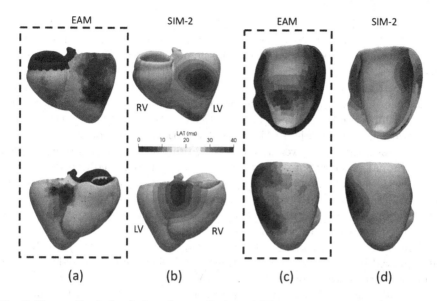

Fig. 6. Personalized simulations for prediction of CRT sequence of activation in Kira Model. (a) and (c) show anterior and posterior views of the EAM, and endocardial and epicardial views of the LV lateral wall, respectively. (b) and (d) show the simulations using personalized values obtained from the data post CRT implantation.

Kira model activates completely in 35 ms, which can only be accomplished if the conduction velocities all over the model are really high. If one considers a transmural Purkinje system, with a very fast access from the lead, such CVs could have been obtained. Average conduction velocities all over the model were 2.22 ± 1.17 m/s. Figure 6 shows the isochrones of Kira model obtained from EAM and from simulations. After recalculating all the conductivities, not based on LBBB but on CRT EAM, we could obtain similar results except in the anterior wall that showed a very large initial activated area.

4   Discussion and Conclusions

The accurate reproduction of activation patterns from real patient data using computational models is a complex task due to the large number of unknowns, variability and heterogeneity in the heart. Comparing simulations with EAMs introduces additional errors since the mapping is done sequentially and the activation of the heart may vary from beat to beat. In addition, it is very tricky to annotate the local activation times and hence to have a meaningful and faithful activation sequence of the patient that is spatio-temporally coherent. Therefore, differences are expected a priori, sometimes large, between simulations and EAMs.

An important feature added to our pipeline to obtain more accurate results was the fast conduction endocardial layer, which was independent for LV and

350   J. F. Gomez et al.

RV. Since the LBBB was artificially induced by blocking the LBB at the His Bundle level, the remaining structure of the Purkinje system was still functional, and could be activated retrogradely. This hypothesis was clearly confirmed in cases such as Neus, where the wavefront coming from the RV speeds up in the LV endocardium, advancing the LV epicardial wavefront and producing much wider isochrones. In addition, once the effect of the fast endocardium reaches the epicardium transmurally, it can be noticed a fast apex to base activation in the LV lateral wall, see Fig. 1. All these observations were properly reproduced once the fast conduction layer was included in the LBBB computational model. In the original paper by Soto-Iglesias et al. [9], authors reported that in the Neus model the fast conduction by Purkinje was not active in LBBB or under CRT, which does not agree with our observations, where this effect in LBBB is very clear (see Fig. 1), and was validated by the model who reproduced much more accurately the EAMs once the layer was included.

Under CRT in Neus model, the late activated basal regions of the LV initially differed from that of the simulations. Analysing the EAMs under CRT, it could be observed that the LATs at the LV basal region show large gradients transmurally, i.e., the epicardium was activated around 40 ms earlier than the corresponding endocardium. That effect was not observed during LBBB. We performed simulations with and without a fast endocardial conduction layer on the LV, and we concluded that there was a fast endocardial layer in the LV, but it was slower than in the case of LBBB, probably due to a different access of the Purkinje system. The activation of the LV epicardium under CRT was surprisingly high, almost as fast as the fast endocardial layer, which could be only explained by the presence of the Purkinje system in the epicardium of pig hearts, where the system if fully transmural [6]. The effect was also observed in Kira model, and remarkably in both cases the anterior wall showed much higher CVs than the posterior. We hypothesized that the anterior branch of the Purkinje system could have been functional whereas the posterior branch might be damaged. Auricchio et al. [1], found using concact and non-contact mapping that around 32% of LBBB patients, had ≥20 ms between the beginning of activation in the RV endocardium versus the LV endocardium, which was considered as incomplete LBBB. Complete LBBB patients show interventricular delays >40 ms. We consider that this could also be a case of incomplete LBBB, since the delay between the RV breackthroughs and the LV breacktrough was around 20 ms. In addition, as described in [6] for pig hearts the density of PMJs in the epicardium is larger and particularly in the anterior region compared to the posterior.

In conclusion, we have developed a pipeline to personalize globally, computational models of the heart from EAMs, to predict the electrical activation sequence of a given patient under CRT. Results show that a much detailed personalization of CVs is required to reproduce properly the activation sequence.

Acknowledgements. This work was supported by the "Plan Estatal de Investigación Científica y Técnica y de Innovación 2013–2016" from the Ministerio de Economía, Industria y Competitividad of Spain and Fondo Europeo de Desarrollo Regional

(FEDER) DPI2016-75799-R (AEI/FEDER, UE), and by the Dirección General de Política Científica de la Generalitat Valenciana (PROMETEU 2016/088).

References

1. Auricchio, A., et al.: Characterization of left ventricular activation in patients with heart failure and left bundle-branch block. Circulation **109**(9), 1133–9 (2004). https://doi.org/10.1161/01.CIR.0000118502.91105.F6
2. Bristow, M.R., et al.: Comparison of medical therapy, pacing, and defibrillation in heart failure (COMPANION) investigators: cardiac-resynchronization therapy with or without an implantable defibrillator in advanced chronic heart failure. N. Engl. J. Med. **350**(21), 2140–50 (2004). https://doi.org/10.1056/NEJMoa032423
3. Carpio, E.F., et al.: Optimization of lead placement in the right ventricle during cardiac resynchronization therapy. A simulation study. Front. Physiol. **10**, 74 (2019). https://doi.org/10.3389/fphys.2019.00074
4. Dawoud, F., et al.: Non-invasive electromechanical activation imaging as a tool to study left ventricular dyssynchronous patients: implication for crt therapy. J. Electrocardiol. **49**(3), 375–82 (2016). https://doi.org/10.1016/j.jelectrocard.2016.02.011
5. Doste, R., et al.: A rule-based method to model myocardial fiber orientation in cardiac biventricular geometries with outflow tracts. Int. J. Numer. Method Biomed. Eng. **35**(4), e3185 (2019). https://doi.org/10.1002/cnm.3185
6. Garcia-Bustos, V., Sebastian, R., Izquierdo, M., Molina, P., Chorro, F.J., Ruiz-Sauri, A.: A quantitative structural and morphometric analysis of the purkinje network and the purkinje-myocardial junctions in pig hearts. J. Anat. **230**(5), 664–678 (2017). https://doi.org/10.1111/joa.12594
7. Lopez-Perez, A., Sebastian, R., Ferrero, J.M.: Three-dimensional cardiac computational modelling: methods, features and applications. Biomed. Eng. Online **14**, 35 (2015). https://doi.org/10.1186/s12938-015-0033-5
8. Moss, A.J., et al.: MADIT-CRT trial investigators:cardiac-resynchronization therapy for the prevention of heart-failure events. N. Engl. J. Med. **361**(14), 1329–38 (2009). https://doi.org/10.1056/NEJMoa0906431
9. Soto Iglesias, D., et al.: Quantitative analysis of electro-anatomical maps: application to an experimental model of left bundle branch block/cardiac resynchronization therapy. IEEE J. Transl. Eng. Health Med. **5**, 1900215 (2017). https://doi.org/10.1109/JTEHM.2016.2634006
10. Tobon-Gomez, C., et al.: Understanding the mechanisms amenable to crt response: from pre-operative multimodal image data to patient-specific computational models. Med. Biol. Eng. Comput. **51**(11), 1235–50 (2013). https://doi.org/10.1007/s11517-013-1044-7

Prediction of CRT Response on Personalized Computer Models

Svyatoslav Khamzin[1,2](✉) iD, Arsenii Dokuchaev[1] iD, and Olga Solovyova[1,2]

[1] Institute of immunology and physiology UB RAS, Pervomayskaya 106,
620049 Ekaterinburg, Russia
s.khamzin@iip.uran.ru
[2] Ural Federal University, Mira 19, 620002 Ekaterinburg, Russia

Abstract. Congestive heart failure (CHF) is one of the leading causes of death worldwide, despite the optimal treatment. Cardiac resynchronization therapy (CRT) is one of the established methods for treating severe CHF with conduction disorders, in particular, complete left bundle branch block (LBBB). However, to the date, up to 30% of patients do not respond to CRT. This study is focused on the developing model-based approaches allowing one to predict consequences of ventricular pacing after installing a CRT device based on computational cardiac models.

In this work, we used experimental data from the STACOM 2019 "CRT-EPiggy" Challenge containing a training dataset of EAM data recorded in ventricles of 4 pig hearts. To simulate local activation time (LAT) in the model we used the Eikonal equation based model, which parameters were identified based on the experimental data. Solving an optimisation problem over the conductivity parameters of this model, we were able to achieve a good quality of LAT simulations before and after bi-ventricular pacing with a mean error of about 3 ms.

We found essential changes in the local conduction velocity (CV) in the ventricles at bi-ventricular pacing after CRT both in experimental data and simulations. To predict these changes and post-operational LAT from the pre-operational data, we used a population based approach to simulate effects of conductivity modulation due to pacing. This approach allowed us to predict an activation pattern at ventricular pacing based on the optimised model of LAT before pacing with an average error of 7 ms. Despite the promising overall results of our pilot study, the presence of rather big local errors in the model predictions requires further algorithm improvement.

Keywords: Computational models · Cardiac resynchronization therapy · Cardiac electrophysiology · Patient-specific simulations

1 Introduction

Heart failure is the leading cause of morbidity and mortality worldwide. In patients with chronic heart failure (CHR), the contractile dyssynchrony is an

M. Pop et al. (Eds.): STACOM 2019, LNCS 12009, pp. 352–363, 2020.
https://doi.org/10.1007/978-3-030-39074-7_37

often adverse factor, which reduces the systolic function of the heart. Cardiac resynchronization therapy (CRT) is the recommended treatment for advanced CHF patients with conduction system disorders, particularly complete left bundle branch block (LBBB) [1]. Implanted CRT devise delivers bi-ventricular (bi-V) stimulation to re-coordinate the contraction of the heart by reducing the ventricular dyssynchrony. However, in more than 30% of patients the procedure has no clinical effect and does not induce reverse remodeling response in the left ventricle (LV) [2].

The personalization of computational models in cardiology is a key step toward making models useful in clinical practice and cardiac surgery. A computational model, once properly calibrated, has the potential to forecast cardiac function and disease, and can help in planning treatments and therapies. In this paper, the main task of optimization was to personalize the activation pattern of LV excitation according to electro-anatomical mapping (EAM) data.

This work is our contribution to a big challenge aimed to develop an approach allowing one to predict a change in cardiac dyssynchrony after installing a CRT device based on personalized mathematical models able to reproduce individual activation pattern of cardiac excitation according to electro-anatomical mapping (EAM) data.

2 Methods

2.1 Experimental Data

In this work, we used experimental data recorded in pig hearts collected for the STACOM 2019 "CRT-EPiggy" Challenge [3]. The data includes a training data set on cardiac EAM recorded *in-vivo* on the epicardial (EPI) and endocardial (ENDO) surfaces of the LV and EPI surface of the right ventricle (RV) in 2 cases of the pig heart with myocardial infarction and 2 cases of no infarction. Each training data set contains recordings performed with LBBB on the sinus rhythm before operation and at bi-ventricular pacing after installing the CRT device. A decrease in ventricular dyssynchrony is estimated as a decrease in the total activation time (TAT) in the ventricles due to ventricular pacing. Note, the only in-operation data recorded instantaneously after the device installation were available for CRT results. No time delayed data suggesting myocardial remodeling due to ventricular pacing were provided for the Challenge. A testing data set contains 7 cases of LBBB data only. For each case, the anatomical geometry of the LV and RV was provided.

2.2 Electrophysiology Model

In the most of the cardiac modeling applications, simulations of the electrical activity in the heart at the organ level are based on a system of partial differential equations (PDE) describing electrical excitation propagation in the continuum tissue medium, where local electrical activity in cardiomyocytes is described by ordinary differential equations (ODE). Solution of such PDE/ODEs is computationally very demanding, due to the spatial scale of the wave front propagation is much smaller than the size of the ventricles and the temporal characteristics of different phases of the action potential generation in the cells require rather small time and space steps for the correct PDE/ODE numerical solution in the coupled electrophysiology problem. Therefore in this study, we used the Eikonal equation approach [4,5], allowing one to find the wave-front motion during the excitation process much faster than the calculation of PDE.

In the Eikonal model, the arrival times of the wave front t_a in the myocardial area Ω are described based on the spatially inhomogeneous orthotropic velocity function, encoded as $D(x)$, and the certain initial activation area Γ at time t_0. The Eikonal equation has the form:

$$\sqrt{\nabla t_a D \nabla t_a} = 1 \quad in \ \Omega$$
$$t_a = t_0 \quad in \ \Gamma \tag{1}$$

where t_a is a positive function describing the wavefront arrival time at location x and D symmetric positive definite 3×3 tensor which is determined by the myocardial fiber direction field and myocardial tissue conductivity along:across set here as 9:1.

The problem was solved on the spatial mesh built for a certain geometry model of the RV and LV with myocardial fiber direction defined from rule-based approach [6]. For calculations, we used the finite element method; the model was implemented using the FENICS library on Python.

2.3 Data Preparation

For each heart tested, the initial 3D finite-element mesh for two ventricles contained around 300k nodes and 1.5M cells. Using operations of decimation and remeshing we constructed new low-poly mesh of around 4k points and 12k cells which allowed us to perform much faster computing.

In the next step, we transferred the initial data on the electrode location to the low-poly mesh. The radial basis function (RBF) were used as in [7]. Based on the EAM data available for the EPI and ENDO surfaces of the LV, we performed approximation by RBF of the local activation time (LAT) in the all points in two ventricles.

2.4 Personalization of Cardiac Models

Developing a feasible method for personalization of a mathematical model, we attempted to use several approaches.

First, early activated points in the LV were found in the input EAM data set and set as an activation region in the Eikonal model. After that, we tried to solve an optimization problem to minimize the difference between the model solution and the interpolated input data over the components of the tensor D at each point in the computational domain. The distance between the simulated and input data was calculated as the following function:

$$J = \sqrt{\sum_{i=1}^{n}(t_i - \tau_i)^2}, \tag{2}$$

where t_i and τ_i denote the computed model output and interpolated LAT in i point, respectively.

The solving of the optimization problem over the entire tensor D with all varied parameters is computationally demanding and hardly being fulfilled even for the optimized mesh of 3000 to 4000 nodes we rebuilt for each model.

To decrease the complexity of the task, we tested two different approaches. In the first approach, we used an assumption of a discreet distribution of the regional conductivity in the ventricles with constant conductivity throughout each of chosen regions. Here, we split the grid-points into 50 groups based on their distance from each other using the Voronoi diagram. Then we solved the above minimization problem over the 50 regional conductivity parameters. However, using this splitting algorithm we were not able to achieve rather low error level (see Result section) and model solutions demonstrated visually inappropriate activation maps as compared to the experimental data.

In the second approach, we used an assumption of a continuous distribution of the regional conductivity within the entire ventricular volume gradually changing between a number of reference grid-points where the conductivity values are set. Later on we refer to this approach as to a surrogate model of regional conductivity distribution in the ventricles. Here, by computing the gradients of the interpolated LAT on the grid derived from experimental data, we computed a conduction velocity (CV) at each grid-point and found its local minimum and maximum in the domain for each LV model tested. In our training dataset, the CV maps have 30–40 extreme points in every case. Then, we used conductivity values at such grid-points of local extremes as the variables for the optimization problem; while the conductivity parameters in the rest of the grid-points were interpolated using RBF method. Using this surrogate model of regional conductivity, we found appropriate model solutions of the minimization problem as described in the Section Results.

The optimization problem was solved for both the pre- and post-operation EAM data for each heart of the training set. This allows us to compare conductivity distribution in the LV predicted by the model before and after CRT. The predicted conductivity values were shown to be significantly different in some LV regions suggesting that the electrical activity in the paced heart after installation of the CRT devise is not determined by the activation sequence only, but depends on some other unknown factors.

To solve the optimization problem, we tried a large number of methods, including genetic algorithms, particle swarm optimization, L-BFGS, SLSQP, Nelder-Mead and others. The genetic algorithm showed the best results, however, calculations for one case took about 2 days. Slightly worse results were obtained using the L-BFGS method, where calculations for one case took only about 2 h, so this method was used further for this work.

2.5   Prediction of CRT

At first, to check if the difference in the conductivity we found for the post- and pre-operation models is significant for the electrical activity of the paced LV, we used the conductivity values was computed for a model of the LBBB case to run a CRT simulation with activation points located at the position of electrodes in the RV and LV. However, we found completely mismatched activation patterns and total activation time (TAT) between the simulations and experimental data.

To find out why the model with pre-operational conductivity map failed to simulate CRT consequences, we carefully compared the CV patterns derived from the interpolated experimental EAM data recorded in the LV before and after implantation of the CRT device. We found some LV regions with significantly different values of the CV before and right after ventricular pacing. Moreover, these regions were unpredictably different among the heart cases we tested. The limited available experimental data did not allow us to define reasonable rules to determine specific location of the regions with post-operative conduction change and direction of the change in the LV.

Based on the assumption on possible instantaneous change in the conductivity in the LV after CRT, we proposed the following approach. Conductivity values for the model at bi-ventricular pacing (simulating consequences of CRT installation) were defined as follows:

$$C_{CRT} = W \cdot C_{LBBB}, \qquad (3)$$

where C_{XX} - conductivity values before and after CRT in a certain LV region, and W - unknown ratio of the conductivity.

To find the W factor for each of the heart cases from the training dataset, we divided the LV into the 17 anatomical segments according to the LV model used in AHA recommendations [8] and computed the ratio W between the conductivity predicted for the models after and before pacing in each of the LV segments, based on the solution of optimization problem. Thus, for an individual LV case from the training dataset, the distribution of the conductivity ratio in the LV was characterised by 17-element vector of the mean and standard deviation of the parameter W in the 17 LV segments. Using such approach for the entire training dataset, we computed an average vector of $\overline{W}$ values for the conductivity ratio with corresponding standard deviations σ for the 17 LV segments among the training heart cases. These factors derived from the training dataset were then used as a reference to generate local conductivity parameters in further CRT simulations. Based on the $\overline{W} \pm \sigma$ values, 1000 Monte-Carlo random samples of the W coefficients were generated and tested in a series of model simulations of ventricular pacing for each of the heart cases from training dataset. The sampled W values were used in the Eq. 3 to assign conductivity in the paced models for the centres of the 17 LV segments, while the conductivity in the remaining grid-points was interpolated via RBF.

In this way, for each case of the heart models we computed 1000 different activation patterns in the paced model based on the conductivity values predicted from the LBBB data (as a solution of optimization problem (2) for a particular LV model) and coefficients of the conductivity modulation based on the expected data from the training dataset. Then the average values of LAT for the case model were found and used as predictions of the heart response to pacing.

3   Results

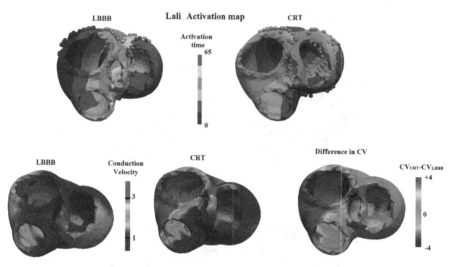

Fig. 1. Interpolation of the experimental electro-anatomical map data (shown as small spheres) on the ventricular mesh. Local activation times (LAT) and conduction velocity (CV) before (LBBB) and after (CRT) bi-ventricular pacing are compared for Lali 19 heart case.

3.1   LAT Interpolation Based on the EAM Data

The first step of the pre-processing of the input experimental data is interpolation of the EAM data recorded in a number of discreet points on the ENDO and EPI surfaces the LV and the EPI surface of the RV in each of the cases included in the training dataset. The results of RBF interpolation of the LAT map computed throughout the entire geometry mesh of the two ventricles are shown in Fig. 1 for one of the heart cases on the sinus rhythm before operation (labeled in the Figs as LBBB) and at pacing after CRT installation (labeled as CRT).

Owing to the LAT interpolation withing the entire volume of the ventricles, we were able to evaluate local conduction velocity (CV) in every grid-point of the ventricular mesh and to compare the velocity before and after operation

(Fig. 1, low panels). While in most of the ventricular volume the difference was not big, some regions demonstrated visible difference, which was not obviously associated with anatomical features or localization of the infarct scar or pacing electrodes in the ventricles. For example, we observed a significant increase in the CV in the apex of the right ventricle after CRT pacing for one heart case with infarction and one case with no infarction. In the two other cases analysed, the CV difference pattern was totally different, and other regions of high CV difference were revealed. Classification of such observations is also a subject for further analysis with need of more data available.

3.2 Personalization of the Ventricular Activation Model

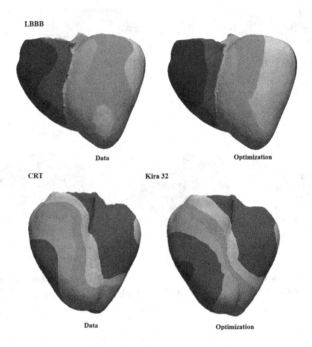

Fig. 2. Example of the model personification. Local activation times (LATs) are built on the input data (on the left) and predicted as a solution of the optimization problem with the surrogate model of regional conductivity (on the right) for the LBBB and CRT cases of Kira heart, respectively.

The interpolated LAT data based on the experimental EAM data were then used as an input data for the model parameter identification (model personalization, optimisation problem). Two approaches for choosing variable parameters of conductivity for the optimization problem (2) were tested (see Sect. 2)). Table 1 shows the mean error computed as the average difference between the predicted and input LAT values in all grid-points of the ventricular domain using these two approaches. Using the discreet conductivity approach based on the split of the grid into regions of the constant conductivity, the mean error is ranged from 7 to 15% for the model cases from the training dataset, which we considered as insufficient for reproducing the activation pattern.

Table 1. Mean LAT error (ME) of the optimization problem solution for algorithms based on the region splitting approach and on the surrogate model of the conductivity distribution

Pig name	Conductivity split		Conductivity surrogate model	
	LBBB ME, ms	CRT ME, ms	LBBB ME, ms	CRT ME, ms
Lali	11.05 ± 4.65	5.95 ± 2.12	3.55 ± 1.45	3.6 ± 1.6
Kira	5.1 ± 2.3	3.2 ± 1.1	4.1 ± 1.38	2.7 ± 0.8
Aksak	7.6 ± 3.47	3.5 ± 1.46	3.2 ± 1.49	2.75 ± 0.74
Neus	5.7 ± 2.21	6.36 ± 1.74	2.8 ± 0.96	4.4 ± 2.58

The algorithm based on the surrogate model of regional conductivity showed better results than splitting approach as shown in Table 1. Here, the mean error is 3–4.5%, but still far from perfect result of model personalization. Figure 2 shows an example of LAT simulated at the model parameters found as the solution of optimization problem (2) with the surrogate model of conductivity distribution. While there is some mismatch in the activation patterns between predicted and input data, we can consider this result as a good starting point for future improvement of the optimization algorithms.

3.3 Prediction of CRT

Figure 3 demonstrates an example of inappropriate mismatch between input LAT data at bi-ventricular pacing and model predictions computed with the optimal parameters of regional conductivity found for the LBBB model simulating LAT before pacing. This negative result demonstrates impossibility of the model to reproduce experimental LAT data in paced ventricles without modification of the conductivity parameters.

We evaluated the ratio between the conductivity parameters after and before pacing found as the solutions of the optimization problem for the LBBB and CRT models based on the experimental data from the training dataset. Figure 4 shows the distributions of the conductivity parameters in the training LBBB and CRT models together with their ratio computed in 17 AHA LV segments. The distributions of conductivity in the LBBB and CRT models have statistically different means (despite the regions 3 and 6 with label *), demonstrating an increase in the conductivity parameters in most of the LV segments in the CRT model at ventricular pacing.

The mean values of the segmental conductivity ratio were used to generate random samples of the multipliers in the formula (3) used to modify the LBBB

conductivity in the paced ventricular model (see Methods for details). The final
LAT prediction was computed as the average of LAT simulations generated in the
virtual trial on 1000 model samples with randomly modified LBBB parameters
(see Fig. 3, panel C for an example).

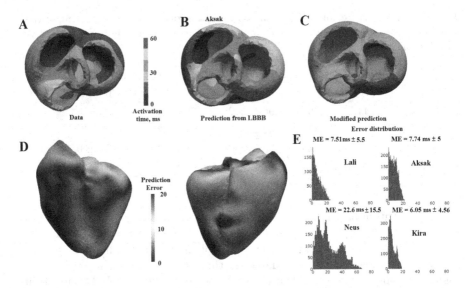

Fig. 3. Results of model prediction of local activation times (LAT) at bi-ventricular
pacing. LAT maps are built using the interpolated experimental data (panel A), simulations with conductivity parameters from the LBBB model optimization (panel B),
simulation with modified conductivity parameters for the Aksak data from the training
dataset (panel C). Error map of the LAT prediction for the Aksak data is shown on the
panel D. Distributions of the LAT prediction errors in every model from the training
dataset are shown on the panel E.

While the mean error in the entire ventricular domain is not as big, the
regional error in the model prediction can be essential. For Aksak heart example
shown in Fig. 3, the large difference between the model prediction and experimental CRT data is seen for the anterior wall, which can be explained as the
underestimated modification of the conductivity in this region due to CRT pacing. Figure 3, panel E shows the LAT error distribution observed in the ventricular grid-points for each case from the training set. In the 3 of 4 heart cases,
mean error is about 7–8 ms, but in some regional values the errors are bigger
than 20 ms. For Neus heart case, the prediction cannot be qualified as successful
as the average error is of 22.6 ms. This fail in LAT prediction in paced ventricles
can be explained by the presence of a large region of infarct scar which structural
details were not accounted in the presented preliminary data.

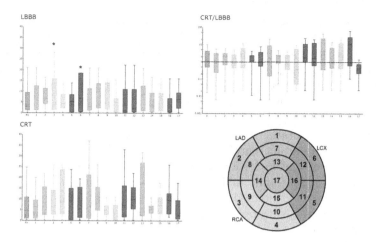

Fig. 4. Boxplots for the distributions of the conductivity parameters (mS/cm) in each of the 17 anatomical LV segments (according to the scheme on the right bottom panel) of 4 training LBBB and CRT LV models optimized on the experimental data (left panels) and the ratio (in the Log10 scale) between the parameters (right panel log scale).

4   Discussion

4.1   Interpolation of the Experimental EAM Data

In this study, we used RBF interpolation to compute LAT values in the entire ventricular walls from limited data experimentally recorded in discreet points on the ENDO/EPI surfaces of the LV and the EPI surface of the RV. Though the approach cannot overcome a lot of uncertainty related to the experimental data, we believe it helps to limit model simulations with the conductivity found as a solution of the optimization problem around the interpolated data and to avoid unphysiological values of the conductivity parameters in the ventricles.

Later on, we are going to compare results we obtained with using RBF interpolation with Gaussian Markov Random Fields approach [9] and other effective methods decreasing uncertainty. It is clear that evaluation of the quality of either approach needs much more input data available.

4.2   Model Personalization

The approach we suggested for the model fitting to the personal experimental data is based on the solving the optimisation problem with a number of variable conductivity parameters. Criteria for the choice of the variable parameters can be more or less grounded. Here, we tried two possibilities based on either the regional splitting of the conductivity or accounting for the peaks in the regional conduction velocity assessed from the input data.

The second approach we proposed showed much better results of model personification (see Table 1, and Fig. 2). However, there is still room for improvement. First, we did not test different metrics for the distance between the input data and predicted model output. This might help to produce better predictions. Another point of possible improvements is the choice of the amount of variable parameters for the optimization problem. Here, we used about 30 parameters, but the amount should be further optimised. Additionally, we are going to improve the computational costs of model personalization with using a surrogate model of cardiac anatomy with small amount of parameters defined from individual ventricular geometry. Parametrization of the heart geometry is shown to be a valuable approach in combination with computational models of cardiac function. Once created, the model allows one much faster computations. Similar approaches were used to test drugs [10] and to search for parameters of the bio-mechanical model [11].

4.3 Model Prediction

The global goal of the "CRT-EPiggy" Challenge we took part is predicting the outcome of CRT. As we revealed in this study, the main problem is the change in the local conduction velocity suggesting a modulation of the effective conductivity in the myocardial tissue right after CRT devise installation (see Fig. 4). One of the hypothesis on such conductivity change is the retrograde activation of Purkinje system [12,13] but the underlying mechanism of these changes still unknown.

Here, we used a population based approach to simulate effects of conductivity modulation due to pacing. We computed a large number of models with modified LBBB conductivity parameters from the range of possible changes in the conductivity shown in the optimized training models under ventricular pacing (see Fig. 4). The average LAT model output was then used to predict CRT. It showed much less error than in the model predictions based on the parameters found for the LBBB model before pacing (see Fig. 3). The results we achieved show rather good mean quality of the LAT prediction in the paced ventricles. However, the presence of big local errors requires further algorithm improvement.

5   Conclusion

In this paper we demonstrated promising preliminary data of using computational models to predict CRT response based on the pre-operation electrophysiological data. The use of proposed surrogate models to solve the optimisation problem for the LBBB and CRT training dataset and the population based approach allowed us to achieve rather good quality of model personification and prediction of the CRT response to ventricular pacing. The global problem of the challenge is still far away from the final decision and still requires further collaborative efforts in this way.

Acknowledgements. The work was supported by RSF grant No. 19-14-00134. Super-computer URAN of IMM UrB RAS was used for model calculations.

References

1. Abraham, W.T., Fisher, W.G., Smith, A.L., et al.: Cardiac resynchronization in chronic heart failure. N. Engl. J. Med. **346**, 1845–1853 (2002)
2. Chung, E.S., Leon, A.R., Tavazzi, L., et al.: Results of the predictors of response to CRT (PROSPECT) trial. Circulation **117**, 2608–2616 (2008)
3. Soto Iglesias, D., et al.: Quantitative analysis of electro-anatomical maps: application to an experimental model of left bundle branch block/cardiac resynchronization therapy. IEEE J. Transl. Eng. Helth Med. **5**, 1–15 (2017)
4. Franzone, P.C., Guerri, L., Pennacchio, M., Taccardi, B.: Spread of excitation in 3-D models of the anisotropic cardiac tissue. II. Effects of fiber architecture and ventricular geometry. Math. Biosci. **147**(2), 131–171 (1998)
5. Keener, J.P.: An eikonal-curvature equation for action potential propagation in myocardium. J. Math. Biol. **29**(7), 629–651 (1991)
6. Doste, R., Soto-Iglesias, D., Bernardino, G., et al.: A rule-based method to model myocardial fiber orientation in cardiac biventricular geometries with outflow tracts. Int. J. Numer. Meth. Biomed. Eng. **35**, e3185 (2019)
7. Mase, M., Ravelli, F.: Automatic reconstruction of activation and velocity maps from electro-anatomic data by radial basis functions. In: 2010 Annual International Conference of the IEEE Engineering in Medicine and Biology Society, EMBC 2010, pp. 2608–2611 (2010)
8. Cerqueira, M.D., Weissman, N.J., Dilsizian, V., et al.: Standardized myocardial segmentation and nomenclature for tomographic imaging of the heart: a statement for healthcare professionals from the Cardiac Imaging Committee of the Council on Clinical Cardiology of the American Heart Association. Circulation **105**, 539–542 (2002)
9. Coveney, S., et al.: Probabilistic interpolation of uncertain local activation times on human atrial manifolds. IEEE Trans. Bio-Med. Eng. **67**(1), 99–109 (2019)
10. Costabal, F.S., Matsuno, K., Yao, J., et al.: Machine learning in drug development: characterizing the effect of 30 drugs on the qt interval using gaussian process regression, sensitivity analysis, and uncertainty quantification. Comput. Methods Appl. Mech. Eng. **348**, 313–333 (2019)
11. Di Achille, P., Harouni, A., Khamzin, S., et al.: Gaussian process regressions for inverse problems and parameter searches in models of ventricular mechanics. Front. Physiol. **9**, 1–17 (2018)
12. Hyde, E.R., Behar, J.M., Claridge, S., et al.: Beneficial effect on cardiac resynchronization from left ventricular endocardial pacing is mediated by early access to high conduction velocity tissue: electrophysiological simulation study. Circ Arrhythm Electrophysiol. **8**, 1164–1172 (2015)
13. Romero, D., Sebastian, R., Bijnens, B.H., et al.: Effects of the purkinje system and cardiac geometry on biventricular pacing: a model study. Ann. Biomed. Eng. **38**, 1388 (2010)

Eikonal Model Personalisation Using Invasive Data to Predict Cardiac Resynchronisation Therapy Electrophysiological Response

Nicolas Cedilnik[1,2,3(✉)] and Maxime Sermesant[1,2,3]

[1] Université Côte d'Azur, Nice, France
[2] Inria Sophia Antipolis - Mediterranée Research Centre, Biot, France
nicolas.cedilnik@inria.fr
[3] IHU Liryc, Bordeaux, France

Abstract. In this manuscript, we personalise an Eikonal model of cardiac wave front propagation using data acquired during an invasive electrophysiological study. To this end, we use a genetic algorithm to determine the parameters that provide the best fit between simulated and recorded activation maps during sinus rhythm. We propose a way to parameterise the Eikonal simulations that take into account the Purkinje network and the septomarginal trabecula influences while keeping the computational cost low. We then re-use these parameters to predict the cardiac resynchronisation therapy electrophysiological response by adapting the simulation initialisation to the pacing locations. We experiment different divisions of the myocardium on which the propagation velocities have to be optimised. We conclude that separating both ventricles and both endocardia seems to provide a reasonable personalisation framework in terms of accuracy and predictive power.

Keywords: Electrophysiology · Computer model · Personalisation · Cardiac resynchronisation therapy

1 Introduction

For our participation in the STACOM piggyCRT challenge, we decided to use the Eikonal model of cardiac electrophysiology (EP). Using the fast marching method, simulations using this model are very fast to solve, which makes them both particularly suited to a clinical workflow [1] and easy to personalise. Moreover, as we are only interested in local activation times, the Eikonal model is relevant.

We determined the optimal parameters for this model, *i.e.*, the parameters that minimise the discrepancy between the recorded and the simulated pre-cardiac resynchronisation therapy (CRT) activation maps, for each pig. This model personalisation was then used to predict the post-CRT activation maps using the same parameters (except for the initialisation of the propagation).

© Springer Nature Switzerland AG 2020
M. Pop et al. (Eds.): STACOM 2019, LNCS 12009, pp. 364–372, 2020.
https://doi.org/10.1007/978-3-030-39074-7_38

2   Model Personalisation: General Framework

2.1   Eikonal Model

The Eikonal model of cardiac electrophysiology outputs an activation map, *i.e.*, local activation times (LATs) and is defined as follows:

$$v\sqrt{\nabla T^t D \nabla T} = 1 \tag{1}$$

where T is the local activation time, v is the local conduction velocity and D the anisotropic tensor to account for the fibre orientation. We experimented both with fibre orientations generated using the classic Streeter model and the provided OTRBM model.

To make it possible to use multiple onset locations with different delays, we ran one simulation T_i for each onset i. We then added the desired onset delay d_i to the whole activation map and combined them into a final activation map by choosing the minimal LAT for each element X of the domain Ω:

$$T_{\text{final}} = \min_{\forall X \in \Omega} (T_1(X) + d_1, T_2(X) + d_2, ...) \tag{2}$$

Instead of solving the equation on the unstructured grid provided by the challenge, we decided to voxelise them, *i.e.*, to define the domain on a regular lattice of 1 cubic millimetre resolution. Two reasons motivated this choice:

– morphological information on an individual heart is generally obtained from the segmentation of imaging data, which is naturally of this form,
– the fast marching method is faster on Cartesian grids.

As for the implementation, we used open-source fast marching routines available online [2].

2.2   Parameter Fitting with CMA-ES

We used the covariance matrix adaptation - evolution strategy (CMA-ES) [3] genetic algorithm to fit our model parameters to the recorded EP maps. This approach has been used before for a similar challenge [4], and is well suited for multi-parameters, non-convex optimisation problems.

We chose to minimise the root median square difference between the recorded data and the simulation output. This choice is justified by the noise on the training data probably due to the acquisition itself and to its registration on the image-derived myocardial geometry. This could lead to outliers driving the root mean square error.

3   Velocities and Domain Division

Given this framework, the main parameter that we tried to personalise was the local conduction velocity. But what is the optimal domain decomposition to define the number of local parameters to estimate?

Using different velocities for each voxel would both be impractical (too many parameters to optimise) and does not make sense from a physiological standpoint. Moreover, it would probably result in massive over-fitting to the pre-CRT maps with lower predictive power.

Keeping this in mind, we first tried to optimise a global speed for the whole domain, but also tried by individualising:

- both endocardia to capture both the Purkinje network (PN) and the left bundle branch block influences,
- both ventricle walls, for the same reason,
- the septum, for the same reason and because propagation through the septum could be much slower due to fibre orientation,
- the scar if present,
- the 17 AHA segments of the left ventricle (LV), to determine if this would be beneficial for the personalisation.

Fig. 1. An example of domain division. Yellow: wall, red: RV endocardium, green: RV endocardium, purple: connective tissue (outside the domain) (Color figure online)

As the optimisation process is reasonably fast with our framework, we decided to test several combinations of these "velocity zones", as shown in Fig. 5.

4   Onsets

Besides the local propagation velocity, the Eikonal model requires to specify starting points for the wave front propagation. Choosing such points for the pre-CRT sinus rhythm maps is not trivial at all.

4.1   Locations

Ideally, the simulated pre-CRT maps should use the atrio-ventricular (AV) node as unique onset. We first tried to parameterise our model in such a way, but this approach rapidly proved very inefficient due to the massive influence of the septomarginal trabecula (ST) in the activation of the right ventricle (RV). As a consequence, it seemed more reasonable to use two different onsets, both in the RV endocardial layer. Unfortunately, the pre-CRT maps did not include any EP study of the RV endocardial surface.

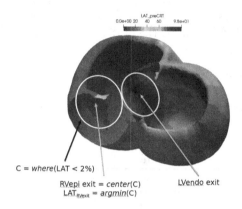

Fig. 2. Determination of onset locations for pre-CRT maps

To overcome this limitation of the personalisation data, we chose the centre of gravity of all the points whose pre-CRT LATs were below the second percentile of a given area and picked the closest RV endocardium point. Picking up the point with the smallest LAT may sound more relevant, but because of the propagation spread, likely due to the PN, the simulations fit better using the "percentile" way (more on this in Subsect. 4.3) This was done for both the LV area, approximately locating the LV onset and the RV area, approximately locating the ST epicardial exit point, as illustrated in Fig. 2.

4.2   Delays

To determine the delays associated to these onsets (see Eq. 2) we proceeded as follows:

1. Run an Eikonal simulation (Eq. 1) for each onset location.
2. Choose the delay such that the lowest LAT of the simulation match the data, respectively for the LV endocardium (LV onset) and the RV epicardium (ST epicardial breakthrough).

4.3 Radii

Picking unique points for the onsets caused the optimisation to converge on unrealistically fast velocities to compensate for the spreading of the early activation due to the PN. It seemed logical to overcome this difficulty by "dilating" our onsets. To chose the radius of these dilations, we conducted the following study:

1. We fixed the endocardial velocity as 3 m/s and scar velocity at 0.1 m/s.
2. We experimented a wide array of velocities for the rest of the domain, between 0.5 and 4 m/s.
3. For each velocity, we tested different onset radii, between 0 and 30 mm.
4. We looked for the optimal myocardial velocity/onset radius combination, *i.e.*, to combination that minimised the median square root error between the EP data and simulations.

The results of this study are shown on Fig. 3.

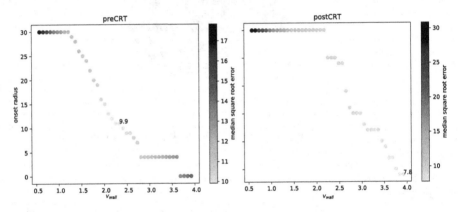

Fig. 3. Combinations of onset radius and wall speed that result in the best match between simulation and EP data. Endocardial speed was here set to 3 m/s, scar speed to 0.1 m/s.

Empirically, we could determine that an onset radius of 10 mm for the preCRT simulations and 2 mm for the post-CRT simulations allowed physiology-compatible velocities.

5 Constraints

We had to define parameter bounds for the optimisation process. We experimented with 3 types of regional constraints:

1. "Physiological": $v_{scar} \in [0, 0.5]$, $v_{wall} \in [0.5, 1]$, $v_{endo} \in [1, 4]$
2. "Loose": $v_{scar} \in [0, 1]$, $v_{wall} \in [0.5, 2]$, $v_{endo} \in [1, 6]$, to take into account the fact that the scar might be coarsely located
3. "No constraints": $v \in [0.1, 4]$

To add a confidence estimation and to evaluate to the relevance of the fibre orientation, the anisotropy ratio, defined as the ratio between the velocity in the transverse plane and the velocity in the fibre direction was also optimised: $r \in [0.2, 1]$.

6 Results

An example of fitting and prediction is shown on Fig. 4.

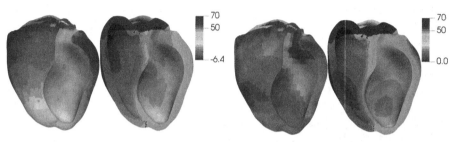

Fig. 4. From left to right: recorded pre-CRT activation map, our model with fitted parameters, recorded post-CRT activation map, our model's prediction. Colours indicate LATs in ms. (Color figure online)

6.1 Performance

The preCRT fit and CRT response prediction performances of the different constraints and domain divisions are shown in Fig. 5. Pre-CRT fit ranged from 9 to 17 ms of median square root difference, while post-CRT prediction performance ranged from 7 to 22 ms.

As expected, a very good preCRT fit is not correlated with a better postCRT prediction, but seems to rather be a sign of over-fitting.

The best approach in terms of prediction performance seems to be using OTRBM fibres and different speeds for both ventricles and both endocardia.

6.2 Parameter Fitting

Taking a closer look at the optimal parameters, we realised that "physiological" constraints were too strict: best parameters were virtually always 4 m/s for both endocardia and 1 m/s for both walls.

In these conditions, personalisation did not seem to be really interesting and this is what motivated our experiments with "loose" constraints. As can be seen in Figs. 6 and 7, this approach made proper personalisation possible.

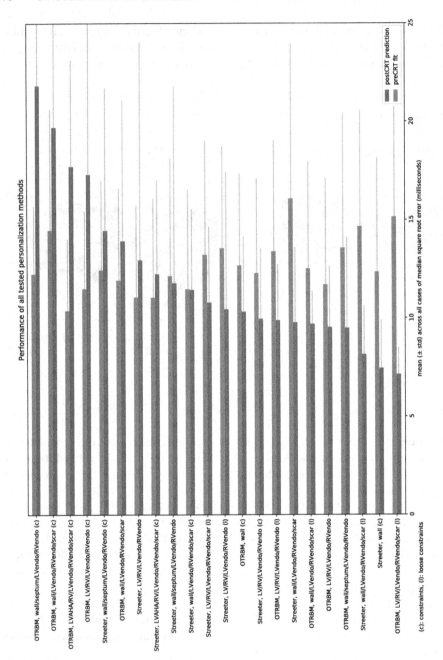

Fig. 5. Fitting and prediction performance of the different domain divisions we experimented

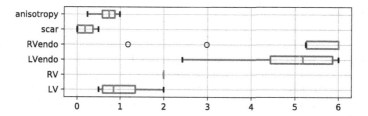

Fig. 6. Distribution of parameters obtained with the "best" domain division and constraints combination.

7   Discussion

As we were given a very small dataset (3 post-CRT maps) to evaluate the prediction performance, it is really difficult to draw conclusions as to which approach really provides the best personalisation. However it seems clear that dividing the domain in small zones, *e.g.* the LV AHA segments is both detrimental to the prediction performance and the personalisation duration. We lacked time to explore other parameters combination, for instance, different anisotropy ratios by domain division or even looser constraints.

Our main contribution probably lies in the way we defined the onsets for the pre-CRT simulations and the fast framework proposed. In a clinical setting, personalisation could probably be enhanced with imaging data [5,6] and possibly ECGI data, and CRT response has to be evaluated with mechanical simulations [7].

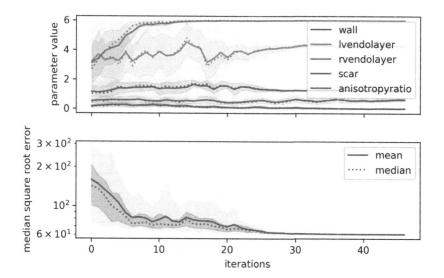

Fig. 7. Evolution of the parameters' values (top) and loss function (bottom) using "loose" constraints for the pig "lali19" during the optimization process. The coloured surfaces represent the [5–95] (light) and [25–75] (darker) percentiles of the parameters (resp. the loss). (Color figure online)

References

1. Cedilnik, N., et al.: Fast personalized electrophysiological models from CT images for ventricular tachycardia ablation planning. EP-Europace **20**, iii94–iii101 (2018)
2. Mirebeau, J.-M.: Riemannian fast-marching on cartesian grids using Voronoi's first reduction of quadratic forms (2017). https://hal.archives-ouvertes.fr/hal-01507334
3. Hansen, N., Akimoto, Y., Baudis, P.: CMA-ES/pycma on Github (2019). https://doi.org/10.5281/zenodo.2559634
4. Giffard-Roisin, S., et al.: Estimation of Purkinje activation from ECG: an intermittent left bundle branch block study. In: Mansi, T., McLeod, K., Pop, M., Rhode, K., Sermesant, M., Young, A. (eds.) STACOM 2016. LNCS, vol. 10124, pp. 135–142. Springer, Cham (2017). https://doi.org/10.1007/978-3-319-52718-5_15
5. Camara, O., et al.: Inter-model consistency and complementarity: learning from ex-vivo imaging and electrophysiological data towards an integrated understanding of cardiac physiology. Prog. Biophys. Mol. Biol. **107**(1), 122–133 (2011)
6. Chen, Z., et al.: Biophysical modeling predicts ventricular tachycardia inducibility and circuit morphology: a combined clinical validation and computer modeling approach. J. Cardiovasc. Electrophysiol. **27**, 851–860 (2016)
7. Sermesant, M., et al.: Patient-specific electromechanical models of the heart for prediction of the acute effects of pacing in CRT: a first validation. Med. Image Anal. **16**(1), 201–215 (2012)

LV-Full Quantification Challenge

Left Ventricle Quantification Using Direct Regression with Segmentation Regularization and Ensembles of Pretrained 2D and 3D CNNs

Nils Gessert[(✉)] and Alexander Schlaefer

Institute of Medical Technology, Hamburg University of Technology,
Hamburg, Germany
nils.gessert@tuhh.de

Abstract. Cardiac left ventricle (LV) quantification provides a tool for diagnosing cardiac diseases. Automatic calculation of all relevant LV indices from cardiac MR images is an intricate task due to large variations among patients and deformation during the cardiac cycle. Typical methods are based on segmentation of the myocardium or direct regression from MR images. To consider cardiac motion and deformation, recurrent neural networks and spatio-temporal convolutional neural networks (CNNs) have been proposed. We study an approach combining state-of-the-art models and emphasizing transfer learning to account for the small dataset provided for the LVQuan19 challenge. We compare 2D spatial and 3D spatio-temporal CNNs for LV indices regression and cardiac phase classification. To incorporate segmentation information, we propose an architecture-independent segmentation-based regularization. To improve the robustness further, we employ a search scheme that identifies the optimal ensemble from a set of architecture variants. Evaluating on the LVQuan19 Challenge training dataset with 5-fold cross-validation, we achieve mean absolute errors of $111 \pm 76 \, \text{mm}^2$, $1.84 \pm 0.90 \, \text{mm}$ and $1.22 \pm 0.60 \, \text{mm}$ for area, dimension and regional wall thickness regression, respectively. The error rate for cardiac phase classification is $6.7\,\%$.

Keywords: Left ventricle quantification · Transfer learning · Regression · Regularization

1 Introduction

Left ventricle (LV) quantification from cardiac magnetic resonance imaging (MRI) data is often employed for assessment of cardiac function and for diagnosing diseases [7]. The relevant LV indices include the myocardium and cavity area, three LV cavity dimensions, six regional wall thickness (RWT) parameters and the cardiac phase (systole and diastole). In practice, LV indices are usually obtained by manual segmentation of the myocardium which is time-consuming and associated with a high intra- and inter-observer variability [12].

© Springer Nature Switzerland AG 2020
M. Pop et al. (Eds.): STACOM 2019, LNCS 12009, pp. 375–383, 2020.
https://doi.org/10.1007/978-3-030-39074-7_39

In recent years, a lot of work has gone into automatic LV indices estimation which is challenging due to high variability of cardiac structure between patients and deformation during the cardiac cycle. To overcome these problems, deep learning methods have been employed as they have shown success for a variety of image-based learning problems. One approach is to segment the myocardium with a convolutional neural network (CNN) and calculate relevant metrics afterwards [1,10]. Alternatively, LV indices can be regressed directly from the images [8,16,17]. Other methods have combined segmentation and regression, e.g., by regressing indices from a segmentation with an end-to-end model [13] or by adding a regression path to a segmentation model [15].

Besides incorporating segmentation and direct estimation, handling temporal dependencies is important as well. Often, temporal dependencies are modeled using recurrent neural networks which have also been employed for LV quantification [16]. Another approach is to utilize spatio-temporal 3D CNNs to capture the relation between temporal slices [6].

In this work, we describe a new approach for LV quantification in the context of the LVQuan19 Challenge. In contrast to a majority of previous work, the associated dataset is significantly smaller (56 patients) and the MRI images are hardly preprocessed with a high spatial resolution but without any region of interest (ROI) cropping. Thus, an algorithm needs to deal with small dataset size and make use of the high image resolution while focusing on the relevant region in the image.

To address these challenges, we take previous approaches into account while putting a strong focus on using pretrained CNNs. Using transfer learning from ImageNet has been successful for a lot of medical imaging modalities, particularly when data is as scarce as in our case [9,11]. Models trained for the common problem of image classification can be adapted for regression by replacing the output layer. Thus, we perform direct LV indices regression using various pretrained CNNs. For temporal processing, we employ spatio-temporal 3D CNNs. We enable effective training of these parameter-intensive 3D CNNs with an initialization strategy where we assign pretrained 2D weights to 3D kernels. We address high spatial image resolution paired with uncertain ROIs by using a multi-crop evaluation strategy that covers the entire image. To incorporate segmentation information into predefined models, we propose an architecture-independent regularization by adding a decoder to the model. Finally, we integrate all our models with a new ensembling approach where we automatically select the best performing ensemble for each regression and classification task.

2 Methods

2.1 Dataset and Preprocessing

The LVQuan19 training dataset consists of short-axis MRI data from 56 patients. For each patient 20 slices representing one cardiac cycle are provided. The resolution of the MRI slices is either 256×256 or 512×512 with a pixel spacing between $0.6836 \frac{mm}{pixel}$ and $1.7188 \frac{mm}{pixel}$. For each slice, segmentation masks of the myocardium and cavity area, all 11 LV indices and the cardiac phase are provided. The LVQuan19 Challenge goal is the estimation of all 11 indices and the cardiac phase, the segmentation masks can be optionally used.

First, we resize all images to have a pixel spacing of $1 \frac{\text{mm}}{\text{pixel}}$. Second, we take a center crop of size 300×300 which is the smallest image size of all resized slices. We clip intensities between the 1st and 99th percentile. Afterwards, we perform image normalization by subtracting the mean and dividing by the standard deviation for each slice. Then, the intensities are scaled between 0 and 1. We convert the target indices to mm. Then, we scale all regression targets to a range of 0–1 for training. For evaluation, the targets are scaled back to their original range. We split the dataset into 5 cross-validation (CV) folds.

2.2 Models

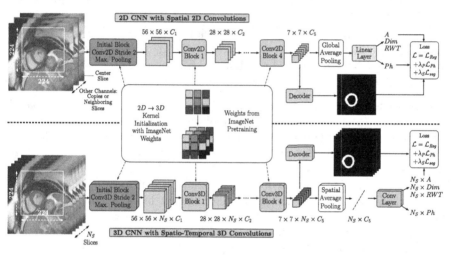

Fig. 1. Overview of our approach. We use both 2D CNNs with 2D slices (top) and 3D CNNs with temporally stacked slices (bottom). Both are initialized with pretrained weights from ImageNet. The initial and Conv2D/Conv3D blocks have a different structure based on the respective architecture.

2D CNN Approaches. The key idea of our approach is to use pretrained architectures for indices regression. Thus, we consider a pool of pretrained architectures including Densenet (DN) [5], Resnet (RN) [3], Resnext (RX) [14] and Squeeze-and-Excitation Networks (SE) [4]. The overall approach is shown in Fig. 1.

Each CNN was pretrained on ImageNet for classification of natural images into 1000 classes. We replace the model's output layer to match the number of outputs for our problem. We consider regression only with 11 outputs, classification (cardiac phase) with 2 softmaxed outputs or both simultaneously with 13 outputs. The pretrained model expects a 3-channel input image which we handle with two approaches. Either, we use a single slice, copied to all three channels or we include the two neighboring slices.

3D CNN Approaches. We also consider spatio-temporal 3D CNN approaches. We hypothesize that temporal context might improve indices regression. Furthermore, cardiac phase classification requires temporal context and including more slices might be helpful. The 3D CNN input is of size $H \times W \times N_S$ where H and W are the spatial slice dimensions and $N_S \in [1, 20]$ is the number of selected slices. We also employ pretrained models to tackle small dataset size. Thus, we reuse the same pool of 2D CNNs and extend them to 3D by replacing all 2D operations by their 3D counterpart. The 3D convolutional kernels are initialized by copying the 2D kernels pretrained on ImageNet of size $h_c \times w_c$ several times into the new kernel of size $h_c \times w_c \times d_c$. To ensure consistent value ranges, the new kernels' weights are multiplied by $1/d_c$. Throughout the entire network, we do not change the slice dimension, i.e., we produce N_S predictions for N_S input slices in a single forward pass. For this purpose, we replace the linear output layer by a convolutional layer with kernel size 1 which is able to handle arbitrarily-sized inputs. Due to increase in memory requirements, we only consider 3D variants of the smaller CNNs in our pool which includes Densenet121, Densenet161, and SE-Resnet101.

Segmentation Regularization. In addition, we propose a segmentation-based regularization (SR). Here, we add an additional decoder to the architecture, before its global average pooling (GAP) layer. The decoder upsamples the spatial dimension of the feature maps in several steps until the original input image size is reached. At each step, we apply a convolution with kernel size 1 which halves the current feature map dimension, followed by nearest neighbor upsampling with a factor of 2. Then, a standard Resnet block is applied. In total, there are 5 upsampling stages. At the output, we predict a softmaxed probability map which is used to calculate a cross-entropy loss with the ground-truth masks. During training, the loss is propagated through the entire network, forcing the core architecture to learn features for segmentation and indices regression simultaneously. We do not use the predicted segmentation explicitly for indices calculation, it only serves as a regularizer for the network. We employ this regularization strategy both for 2D and 3D CNNs.

Data Augmentation. Due to the small dataset size, we employ extensive data augmentation. We use random rotation with $\theta \in [0°, 360°]$ which we found more effective than simple $90°$ rotations. Furthermore, we employ random scaling by resizing the slices by a factor of $s_c \in [0.8, 1.2]$ with appropriate cropping and zero padding, if required. The targets are scaled accordingly (quadratic for areas). We chose a small batch size of $b = 8$ to induce more variation during training. We did not see any improvement for dropout, $L1$ or $L2$ regularization.

Model Input Strategy. The pretrained models' standard input size is 224×224 while our preprocessed images are of size 300×300. Therefore, we crop patches from random image locations during training. This should have a regularizing effect as the CNN gets more robust towards different relative LV locations in the images. For 2D CNNs, we randomly select a cropped slice from b different patients to construct a batch of size b. For 3D CNNs, we randomly select a sequence of N_S slices from b patients for each batch. For evaluation, we follow a multi-crop evaluation approach to cover the entire image [2]. We crop from 4 predefined locations in each slice and average the result. For 2D CNNs, this is repeated for every slice for each patient. For 3D CNNs, we crop sequences of N_S slices from every possible location $n_s \in [1, 20]$. Then, we average over all overlapping regions to obtain a final prediction for each slice. To handle the start and end of the sequence, we use cyclic repetition.

Training. In total, our loss function consists of the mean squared error (MSE) for regression, the cross-entropy (CE) loss for phase classification and the CE loss for segmentation. The two CE losses are not present in every model. If they are included, phase classification is weighted by $\lambda_P = 0.05$ and the segmentation loss is weighted by $\lambda_S = 0.1$. The final loss is the sum of all individual loss functions. For optimization we employ Adam with a learning rate of $l_r = 1 \times 10^{-4}$. We train each CV model for 150 epochs where a single epoch consists of 10 random crops from each patient in the training set. Overall, we train multiple models with different configurations s_i. The configuration options include the network architecture (e.g. Densenet121), the input dimension (2D or 3D), $N_S \in \{3, 5, 7, 10\}$ for 3D CNNs, weight initialization (random or ImageNet), segmentation-based regularization (on or off) and prediction targets (areas, dimensions, RWTs, phase).

Ensembling. Instead of deciding for a single model we search for the optimal ensemble. Let $S = \{s_1, \ldots, s_n\}$ be the set of all configurations we consider, and let $V = \{v_1, \ldots, v_m\}$ be the set of all CV splits. Then we obtain predictions $\hat{y}_{ij} = f(s_i, v_j)$ for all combinations of i and j after training configuration s_i on $V \setminus v_j$. We obtain the predictions per configuration through concatenation as $\hat{y}_i = \cup_j \hat{y}_{ij}$. Subsequently we perform an exhaustive search to identify the set $S* \subseteq S$ such that $\hat{y}* = \frac{1}{|S*|} \sum_{k \in S*} \hat{y}_k$ minimizes the error between $\hat{y}*$ and ground-truth y. For the challenge test set we obtain predictions with all models in the optimal subset $S*$ which are subsequently averaged into a final prediction. We search for the optimal subset for each task (areas, dimensions, RWTs, phase) individually to maximize performance. To keep the search time bounded, S only includes our top 20 configurations, ranked by individual CV performance.

Our proposed strategy potentially leads to implicit overfitting of the subset choice to the CV sets. Therefore, results reported for the CV sets might overestimate the performance gain of our ensembling strategy. We overcome this problem by introducing an additional test split for ensemble evaluation only. Here, we split each CV fold into two folds. We use the first portion of these new sets to find the optimal subset with our strategy. Then, we use the second portion of sets to evaluate the strategy.

Table 1. All results for different configurations. We consider the mean absolute error (MAE) with standard deviation in mm (mm² for areas) and Pearson correlation coefficient (PCC) for regression and the error rate (ER) for classification. Configurations include no pretraining (nopre), segmentation regularization (SR), joint indices regression and phase classification (Joint) and phase classification only (Class.). For ensembling, we consider taking the average over all models (Average) and our new strategy (Optimal). Results marked with a star (*) are evaluated on a different test split, see Sect. 2.2. We use models based on Densenet (DN), Resnet (RN) and Resnext (RX).

Configuration	Areas		Dimensions		RWTs		Phase
	MAE	PCC	MAE	PCC	MAE	PCC	ER
DN121 2D nopre	199 ± 129	0.935	2.98 ± 1.8	0.945	1.55 ± 0.9	0.770	–
DN121 2D	139 ± 74	0.972	2.38 ± 1.3	0.967	1.33 ± 0.7	0.835	–
DN121 2D SR	**133 ± 76**	**0.974**	2.08 ± 1.2	**0.975**	**1.30 ± 0.7**	**0.847**	–
DN121 2D Joint	161 ± 89	0.960	2.54 ± 1.3	0.963	1.39 ± 0.7	0.823	9.0
DN121 2D Class.	–	–	–	–	–	–	**8.4**
DN121 3D nopre	180 ± 165	0.940	2.77 ± 2.4	0.943	1.48 ± 0.8	0.798	–
DN121 3D	133 ± 82	0.971	2.26 ± 1.3	0.968	1.32 ± 0.7	0.838	–
DN121 3D SR	**126 ± 71**	**0.975**	**2.14 ± 1.2**	**0.972**	**1.30 ± 0.8**	**0.844**	–
DN121 3D Joint	146 ± 74	0.966	2.33 ± 1.2	0.969	1.43 ± 0.8	0.812	7.9
DN121 3D Class.	–	–	–	–	–	–	**7.5**
DN169 2D SR	122 ± 72	0.976	1.99 ± 1.2	0.976	1.27 ± 0.7	0.853	–
DN161 2D SR	127 ± 81	0.971	2.00 ± 1.1	0.978	1.30 ± 0.7	0.843	–
SE-RN101 2D SR	126 ± 70	0.974	2.01 ± 1.1	0.977	1.32 ± 0.8	0.844	–
SE-RN152 2D SR	124 ± 81	0.974	2.07 ± 1.2	0.975	1.29 ± 0.7	0.849	–
RX101-64d 2D SR	**118 ± 72**	**0.976**	**1.99 ± 1.0**	**0.978**	**1.25 ± 0.7**	**0.859**	–
SE-RX101 2D SR	135 ± 80	0.971	2.23 ± 1.2	0.973	1.33 ± 0.8	0.839	–
SENet154 2D SR	129 ± 81	0.973	2.12 ± 1.3	0.973	1.31 ± 0.8	0.846	–
Ensemble average	118 ± 76	0.977	1.96 ± 1.1	0.978	1.26 ± 0.6	0.856	7.7
Ensemble optimal	**111 ± 76**	**0.979**	**1.84 ± 0.9**	**0.980**	**1.22 ± 0.6**	**0.864**	**6.7**
Ensemble average*	117 ± 75	0.978	1.96 ± 1.0	0.978	1.23 ± 0.6	0.860	8.3
Ensemble optimal*	111 ± 75	0.979	1.85 ± 1.0	0.980	1.19 ± 0.6	0.871	7.0
Ensemble testset	371	0.925	3.02	0.957	2.53	0.826	11.5
DMTRL [16]	180 ± 118	0.945	2.51 ± 1.6	0.925	1.39 ± 0.7	0.768	8.2

3 Results

All results are shown in Table 1. For Densenet121 (DN121) with 2D slice inputs, the pretrained model with segmentation regularization performs best. The difference in the median of the absolute errors of DN121 2D and DN121 2D SR is significant for areas and dimensions (Wilcoxon signed-rank test, $\alpha = 5\%$ significance level). Combining regression and classification leads to a lower performance than training separate models. For DN121 in its 3D version ($N_S = 5$), the overall performance improves slightly with respect to its 2D counterparts. Again, the difference in the median of the absolute errors of the 2D and 3D model is significant for areas and dimensions.

Considering different architectures, improved performance can be observed for larger models. The best performing model is RX101-64d. With respect to ensembling, taking the average over all our models does not perform better than the best single model. Using our optimal subset strategy, performance is improved. When evaluating on a different test split (*), the performce difference is still large between averaging and our strategy. The difference in the median of the absolute errors for averging and our ensembling strategy is statically significant for all three indices. Our final ensembles mostly contain the models RX101-64d 2D SR, DN 2D SR variants, and DN121 3D SR. On the test set of the LVQuan19 Challenge, the performance of the ensemble is substantially lower. For reference, we include the results from DMTRL [16]. Note that these results are not directly comparable, as a different number of patients and different image resolutions were used.

4   Discussion

We address LV quantification from cardiac MR images with a focus on utilizing pretrained models. We consider a variety of deep learning models that have been successful for classification of 2D images. We adopt these models by replacing the output layer and performing direct LV indices regression from 2D MRI slices. We find a substantial increase in performance with pretrained weights, e.g., the MAE for area estimation improves from $199\,mm^2$ to $134\,mm^2$. This is likely tied to the new and small dataset which contains only roughly a third of the number of patients compared to most previous studies [13,16]. At the same time, the MRI images have a higher resolution which is closer to the standard input resolution of models trained on ImageNet. Both likely lead to a substantial advantage of utilizing pretrained models.

To incorporate previous segmentation-based approaches, we propose a segmentation regularization by adding an architecture-independent decoder close to the model output. The additional segmentation loss forces the model core to learn both features for direct indices regression and myocardium segmentation. Our results indicate that including the segmentation is advantageous as we observe a statisticially significant increase in performance both for areas and dimensions. This matches insights from previous work where using both a segmentation mask and LV indices lead to improved results [13,15].

Furthermore, we address temporal dependencies by extending the existing 2D CNN models to 3D. To enable 3D CNN usage with very limited data, we use an initialization strategy where we copy pretrained 2D weights to 3D kernels. Again, we find a substantial increase in performance by relying on pretraining, see Table 1. There is a significant improvement for dimension and area regression for 3D CNNs over 2D CNNs with an MAE of $139\,mm^2$ compared to $133\,mm^2$

for the areas. For the cardiac phase it is notable that the 2D approach with neighboring slices performs reasonably well and only slightly worse than 3D CNNs. Overall, enabled by our initialization strategy, spatio-temporal 3D CNNs improve performance over spatial 2D CNNs for LV quantification.

Next, we consider different baseline architectures for our approach. Using larger architectures with more layers and/or more feature maps tends to improve performance over the DN121 baseline. In particular, it is notable that the highest performance increase among different models is substantially larger than the performance increase of moving from 2D to 3D. RX101-64d 2D improves the MAE by $16\,\mathrm{mm}^2$ over DN121 compared to a $6\,\mathrm{mm}^2$ decrease caused by using 3D convolutions. In the best case, one would extend the best 2D model to 3D for performance maximization, however, this is limited by GPU memory and not feasible for the larger, higher performing 2D models. Summarized, using high-performing 2D architectures can be very beneficial for LV quantification.

Last, we combine all our models with a new ensembling technique where the best performing models were automatically selected based on cross-validation performance. The method improves performance over simply averaging predictions across all models. Also, we used separate test splits to ensure that the optimal subset selection does not implicitly overfit to the CV sets. Even for this evaluation scenario our ensembling method performs better than averaging with statistically significant performance differences. Interestingly, the selection method included both 2D and 3D CNNs, which indicates that both spatial and spatio-temporal information is important for LV indices regression. On the LVQuan19 test set, our method performs substantially worse than in our CV experiments. This indicates that the test set is very challenging and potentially differs from the training set. Similar observations were made for the last year's challenge [15]. Thus, generalizable LV quantification remains a challenging task.

5   Conclusion

We address left ventricle quantification from cardiac MR images using CNNs for direct indices regression and phase classification. To overcome the small dataset size we emphasize transfer learning with state-of-the-art architectures which we find to be very effective. Also, we incorporate temporal information in our models by extending pretrained 2D CNNs to 3D. We observe improved performance for temporal processing and our extension strategy for pretrained 2D CNNs appears to be useful. Moreover, we propose a segmentation regularization that forces our models to learn features both for myocardium segmentation and indices regression. Last, we demonstrate that a search for the optimal ensemble can further improve our method's performance. Future work could incorporate our proposed approach into other frameworks, for example, by considering multi-task relationship learning or recurrent models for temporal processing. Also, our approach could be compared to methods that estimate indices from a segmentation map instead of directly regressing the values.

References

1. Avendi, M., Kheradvar, A., Jafarkhani, H.: A combined deep-learning and deformable-model approach to fully automatic segmentation of the left ventricle in cardiac MRI. Med. Image Anal. **30**, 108–119 (2016)
2. Gessert, N., et al.: Skin Lesion classification using CNNs with patch-based attention and diagnosis-guided loss weighting. IEEE Trans. Biomed. Eng. (2019, early access). https://doi.org/10.1109/TBME.2019.2915839
3. He, K., Zhang, X., Ren, S., Sun, J.: Deep residual learning for image recognition. In: CVPR, pp. 770–778 (2016)
4. Hu, J., Shen, L., Sun, G.: Squeeze-and-excitation networks. In: CVPR, pp. 7132–7141 (2018)
5. Huang, G., Liu, Z., Van Der Maaten, L., Weinberger, K.Q.: Densely connected convolutional networks. In: CVPR, pp. 4700–4708 (2017)
6. Jang, Y., Kim, S., Shim, H., Chang, H.-J.: Full quantification of left ventricle using deep multitask network with combination of 2D and 3D convolution on 2D + t cine MRI. In: Pop, M., et al. (eds.) STACOM 2018. LNCS, vol. 11395, pp. 476–483. Springer, Cham (2019). https://doi.org/10.1007/978-3-030-12029-0_51
7. Karamitsos, T.D., Francis, J.M., Myerson, S., Selvanayagam, J.B., Neubauer, S.: The role of cardiovascular magnetic resonance imaging in heart failure. J. Am. Coll. Cardiol. **54**(15), 1407–1424 (2009)
8. Li, J., Hu, Z.: Left ventricle full quantification using deep layer aggregation based multitask relationship learning. In: Pop, M., et al. (eds.) STACOM 2018. LNCS, vol. 11395, pp. 381–388. Springer, Cham (2019). https://doi.org/10.1007/978-3-030-12029-0_41
9. Gessert, N., et al.: Automatic plaque detection in IVOCT pullbacks using convolutional neural networks. IEEE Trans. Med. Imaging **38**(2), 426–434 (2019)
10. Ngo, T.A., Lu, Z., Carneiro, G.: Combining deep learning and level set for the automated segmentation of the left ventricle of the heart from cardiac cine magnetic resonance. Med. Image Anal. **35**, 159–171 (2017)
11. Shin, H.C., et al.: Deep convolutional neural networks for computer-aided detection: CNN architectures, dataset characteristics and transfer learning. IEEE Trans. Med. Imaging **35**(5), 1285–1298 (2016)
12. Suinesiaputra, A., et al.: Quantification of LV function and mass by cardiovascular magnetic resonance: multi-center variability and consensus contours. J. Cardiovasc. Magn. Reson. **17**(1), 63 (2015)
13. Wang, W., Wanga, Y., Wu, Y., Lin, T., Li, S., Chen, B.: Quantification of full left ventricular metrics via deep regression learning with contour-guidance. IEEE Access **7**, 47918–47928 (2019)
14. Xie, S., Girshick, R., Dollár, P., Tu, Z., He, K.: Aggregated residual transformations for deep neural networks. In: CVPR, pp. 1492–1500 (2017)
15. Xu, H., Schneider, J.E., Grau, V.: Calculation of anatomical and functional metrics using deep learning in cardiac MRI: comparison between direct and segmentation-based estimation. In: Pop, M., et al. (eds.) STACOM 2018. LNCS, vol. 11395, pp. 402–411. Springer, Cham (2019). https://doi.org/10.1007/978-3-030-12029-0_43
16. Xue, W., Brahm, G., Pandey, S., Leung, S., Li, S.: Full left ventricle quantification via deep multitask relationships learning. Med. Image Anal. **43**, 54–65 (2018)
17. Xue, W., Lum, A., Mercado, A., Landis, M., Warrington, J., Li, S.: Full quantification of left ventricle via deep multitask learning network respecting intra- and inter-task relatedness. In: Descoteaux, M., Maier-Hein, L., Franz, A., Jannin, P., Collins, D.L., Duchesne, S. (eds.) MICCAI 2017. LNCS, vol. 10435, pp. 276–284. Springer, Cham (2017). https://doi.org/10.1007/978-3-319-66179-7_32

Left Ventricle Quantification with Cardiac MRI: Deep Learning Meets Statistical Models of Deformation

Jorge Corral Acero[1(✉)], Hao Xu[1], Ernesto Zacur[1],
Jurgen E. Schneider[2], Pablo Lamata[3], Alfonso Bueno-Orovio[4],
and Vicente Grau[1]

[1] Institute of Biomedical Engineering, Department of Engineering Science,
University of Oxford, Oxford, UK
{jor.corral,hao.xu}@eng.ox.ac.uk
[2] Leeds Institute of Cardiovascular and Metabolic Medicine,
University of Leeds, Leeds, UK
[3] Department of Biomedical Engineering,
King's College of London, London, UK
[4] Department of Computer Science, University of Oxford, Oxford, UK

Abstract. Deep learning has been widely applied for left ventricle (LV) analysis, obtaining state of the art results in quantification through image segmentation. When the training datasets are limited, data augmentation becomes critical, but standard augmentation methods do not usually incorporate the natural variation of anatomy. In this paper we propose a pipeline for LV quantification applying our data augmentation methodology based on statistical models of deformations (SMOD) to quantify LV based on segmentation of cardiac MR (CMR) images, and present an in-depth analysis of the effects of deformation parameters in SMOD performance. We trained and evaluated our pipeline on the MICCAI 2019 Left Ventricle Full Quantification Challenge dataset, and achieved average mean absolute error (MAE) for areas, dimensions, regional wall thickness and phase of 106 mm^2, 1.52 mm, 1.01 mm and 8.0% respectively in a 3-fold cross-validation experiment.

Keywords: Deep learning · Data augmentation · LV quantification

1 Introduction

Automatic quantification of the left ventricle (LV) has been greatly enhanced by the development of deep learning algorithms in the past few years. Convolutional neural networks have shown great accuracy and flexibility for LV quantification. Recently, the MICCAI 2018 Left Ventricle Full Quantification Challenge made possible to compare a wide range of deep learning algorithms performing on the same benchmark dataset with both direct regression [1] and segmentation based [2–4] approaches. Direct

---

Jorge Corral Acero and Hao Xu contributed equally.

© Springer Nature Switzerland AG 2020
M. Pop et al. (Eds.): STACOM 2019, LNCS 12009, pp. 384–394, 2020.
https://doi.org/10.1007/978-3-030-39074-7_40

regression approaches have shown promising results, while segmentation-based approaches were in general, at the time of the challenge, more accurate.

With the development of big databases such as UK Biobank [5], applying deep learning algorithms on big data has become possible in biomedical applications [6, 7], influencing the choice and design of neural networks. With more training data, deeper networks with more parameters can be trained, which usually results in better performance. However, in clinical practice, especially for pathological cases, it is difficult to acquire such big dataset, and data augmentation becomes important. In this regard, our recently developed augmentation method based on statistical models of deformation has shown promising results on a variety of datasets for segmentation task [8].

The MICCAI 2019 Left Ventricle Full Quantification Challenge has provided a benchmark dataset which, compared to the corresponding 2018 dataset, is closer to real-life clinical conditions, with no pre-processing applied to the images. We propose a segmentation-based quantification pipeline enhanced with statistical models of deformation, developed and evaluated on this dataset.

2   Methods

We propose a complete pipeline for quantifying the LV from cardiac MR (CMR) images, consisting of the following steps. We first build a population-specific atlas, and train an initial neural network to locate the centre of the heart in all the images. We then rigidly register each image to the atlas previously calculated. We build the statistical models of deformation, which we use to augment the images using different strategies. Finally, we train a second neural network to perform the fine segmentation and retrieve the LV metrics from the segmentation results.

2.1   Data

We developed and evaluated our pipeline using the MICCAI 2019 Left Ventricle Full Quantification Challenge dataset, which consists of 56 training subjects and 30 testing subjects. For each subject in the training data, a single short-axis (SAX) CMR sequence consisting of 20 frames was provided together with a set of clinically significant LV indices including regional wall thicknesses, cavity dimensions, cavity areas and myocardium and cardiac phase for each frame. Endocardial and epicardial segmentation binary masks were also made available as reference, and pixel-spacing values were also given for metrics evaluation. For subjects in the testing dataset, only CMR image sequences and pixel-spacing values were provided.

Comparing to MICCAI 2018 Left Ventricle Full Quantification Challenge, which had 145 training subjects and 30 testing subjects, the size of training dataset reduced by 61.4% and the testing dataset remained the same size [10].

2.2   Rigid Registration

Our rigid registration method was based on the maximization of cross-correlation of image intensities. In order to avoid converging to a local minimum, the algorithm was initialized to different transformations distributed in the space of possible transformations. Diffeomorphic Log Demons [11] was applied for non-rigid registration ($\sigma_{fluid} = 2, \sigma_{diff} = 1.8$ and $\sigma_i/\sigma_x = 0.82$).

2.3 Atlas

In order to build the atlas, the set of images, I, was first rigidly aligned, using only the first frame, and then non-rigidly registered.

For rigid alignment, the atlas was initialized to a randomly selected instance among the training set, which we denote as A_0, and cropped to completely contain the heart. The rest of the instances were first centred, assuming the mass centre of the epicardium reference segmentation as the centre of the LV, and then rigidly registered to A_0, constraining the transformation to rotations only. The obtained transformations for each of the first frames were extended to the other frames to obtain the registered set IT_0. The intensity average of the images in the IT_0 set was calculated to obtain the first iteration of the atlas, A_1.

For non-rigid alignment, the segmentations of IT_0 were non-rigidly registered to the segmentation of A_1, obtaining the transformation set T_1. The transformations T_1 were then applied to IT_0 and the average of intensities calculated to obtain the atlas, A. Since the segmentation masks were used, convergence was achieved in one single step.

2.4 Initial Segmentation and Rigid Registration

To initialize the rigid alignment, we trained a variation of U-Net [9] for epicardial segmentation. We first down-sampled all the images to 256 × 256 and normalized them by clipping the smallest and largest 5% intensity values. More details of the network are described in Sect. 2.6. Based on the initial epicardium segmentation of the first frames, we centred and oriented the set of images, I, to the atlas, A, as described in Sect. 2.2.

2.5 Statistical Models of Deformation

We implemented the statistical models of deformation following the SMOD+ method in [8]. Once the rigid registration was completed, the set of segmentations of the images, S, is non-rigidly registered to the atlas segmentation, A_s, obtaining the set of velocity fields, $\{v_i\}$, to diffeomorphically bring each image to the atlas space.

This set $\{v_i\}$ intrinsically encodes the shape variability of the set of images, I, with respect to the reference A. Thus, the distribution of $\{v_i\}$ can be sampled to obtain new velocity fields that implicitly lead to anatomically meaningful deformations within the space of plausible shapes, and we built a statistical model of deformations that can be exploited to generate new images.

In order to generate random deformations, v_g, we first reduced the dimensionality of the distribution of velocity fields by applying principal component analysis (PCA) on the residuals. Then, we sampled the relative weights of the main modes of variation with a multivariate Gaussian distribution, centred at 0 and with standard deviation σ. Finally, each of the images, i, was brought to the atlas space applying v_i and transformed back to the image space applying the inverse of the random velocity field, v_g. Thus, a new image with the appearance of image i but a random shape within the space of variability of the original images was obtained.

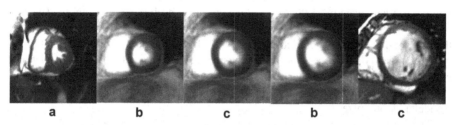

Fig. 1. Atlas and extreme cases of LV shape. The images were input images of the neural networks with the size of 128×128 and pixel-spacing of 1.1 mm. (*a*) and (*e*) are the smallest and largest LVs from the original dataset, respectively; (*b*) to (*d*) are generated by PCA mode 1 with $\sigma = -3$, $\sigma = 0$ and $\sigma = +3$.

2.6   Augmentation Strategies

We implemented two augmentations strategies: (1) standard augmentation based on random flipping, rotations (0–360°) and translations (±11 mm in x and y); and (2) augmentation based on SMOD+, which we combined with standard augmentation samples due to the large variability of LV sizes shown in Fig. 1.

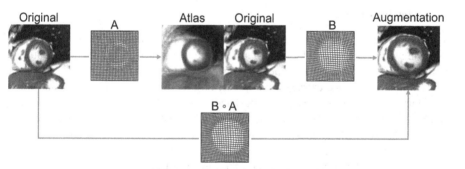

Fig. 2. Combined transformation stages.

The different transformations needed to generate a new image were mathematically combined by convolution as shown in Fig. 2, and therefore the images were interpolated and resized only once at the end of the process. The final resolution used as the neural network input was 128×128, with a pixel-spacing of 1.1 mm.

2.7   Neural Network

We compared two neural networks for the final segmentation task, which were a variation of U-Net [9] and a segmentation network based on VGG-16 [6]. For both networks, there were four 2×2 max-pooling stages with the stride of 2×2, and the number of filters were 64, 128, 256, 512 and 1024 for each stage accordingly. The size of all kernels was 3×3 and the activation functions were ReLU for all layers other than the output layer, which was sigmoid. The key difference between the networks was the up-sampling process, with step-by-step up-sampling stages for the U-Net and concatenated up-samples from each scale for VGG-16. This difference is shown in Fig. 3. We implemented the training with cross-entropy as the loss function and Adadelta as optimizer.

The initial segmentation network introduced in Sect. 2.3 shared the same U-Net architecture, while the input size was 256×256 and the number of filters were decreased to 16, 32, 64, 128 and 256 for efficiency.

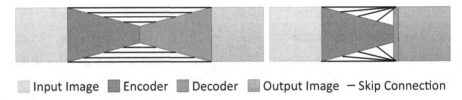

☐ Input Image ■ Encoder ■ Decoder ■ Output Image − Skip Connection

Fig. 3. Schematics of the two neural networks compared in this paper.

2.8   Metrics Evaluation

In the absence of a detailed description of metrics calculation in the challenge, the following approach was adopted. Metrics were calculated from our segmentation results by first converting the neural network outputs to binary masks and then thresholding at 0.5. We extracted the largest object from the binary masks and filled any existing holes. The areas were calculated by multiplying the pixel area times the number of pixels of the region. The dimensions were calculated by averaging the distances between the endocardial contour points and the cavity centroid within the corresponding section. To calculate the regional wall thickness, we first calculated the middle contour of the myocardium and then averaged the closest point-to-point distances between both endocardial and epicardial contours to the middle contour for each middle contour point. The phase estimation was calculated by first defining the frames with maximum and minimum cavity areas to be end-diastolic (ED) and end-systolic (ES) frames, and then assigning linearly interpolated labels to the other frames.

Applying our metrics estimation method to the reference segmentations provided by challenge organisers led to a bias when compared to the set of reference metric values also provided by challenge organisers. Such differences with respect to the provided dataset introduced unnecessary complexity when designing the pipeline and could have been at least partly (and for the areas fully) eliminated with the provision of detailed descriptions of metrics calculation by the organisers. To minimize possible errors that could be introduced within this stage, we calculated a correction factor λ using the reference area metrics (Ar) and the segmentation estimated areas (As), which was the only metric independent of LV orientation, by minimizing the error of (Ar − λAs). The square-root of λ was then multiplied to 1D metrics estimated from the segmentation.

3 Experiments and Results

We performed 3-fold cross-validation experiments on the training dataset, with the size of each fold being 18, 19 and 19. The subjects were randomly assigned to one-fold, and for each cross-validation experiment we used 4 subjects as validation set and kept the rest as training set.

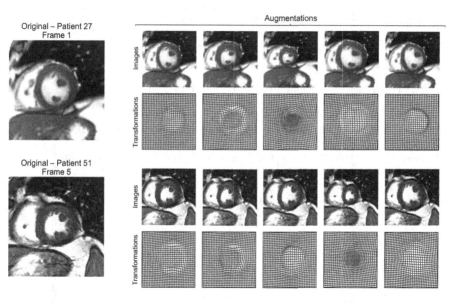

Fig. 4. Example of generated augmentations. Five randomly generated augmentations are shown for each of the two images. The augmented cases varied in size, shape and myocardium thickness of LV.

A model of deformation (described in Sect. 2.4) was learnt for each fold, and the metrics correction factors (described in Sect. 2.7) were also calculated for each fold independently. The network parameters were updated using the training set and model selection was performed using the validation set with early stop. For each training epoch, new instances of training images were randomly generated and used to update the network parameters. Examples of resultant augmented images were shown in Fig. 4, along with the combined transformations.

Table 1. Mean absolute error results.

	Base-line	U-Net Std.	U-Net σ = 1	U-Net σ = 2	U-Net σ = 3	VGG Std.	VGG σ = 1	VGG σ = 2	VGG σ = 3	Test
Dice Endo	1 ±0	0.950 ±0.02	0.949 ±0.033	**0.953** ±0.023	0.950 ±0.026	0.938 ±0.045	0.941 ±0.031	0.943 ±0.032	0.941 ±0.031	N/A
Dice Epi	1 ±0	0.966 ±0.01	0.965 ±0.019	**0.967** ±0.014	0.965 ±0.013	0.957 ±0.026	0.958 ±0.020	0.959 ±0.021	0.959 ±0.020	N/A
A1 (mm^2)	24 ±19	102 ±87	107 ±111	92 ±83	100 ±83	101 ±121	95 ±77	90 ±79	101 ±84	184
A2 (mm^2)	25 ±19	132 ±105	142 ±105	121 ±98	135 ±105	140 ±121	155 ±131	126 ±110	140 ±112	525
Areas (mm^2)	25 ±19	117 ±97	125 ±109	**106** ±91	118 ±96	121 ±122	125 ±111	108 ±97	120 ±101	355
Dim1 (mm)	0.64 ±0.72	1.59 ±1.53	1.73 ±2.30	1.46 ±1.28	1.58 ±1.45	1.40 ±1.78	1.40 ±1.16	1.32 ±1.08	1.51 ±1.23	2.59
Dim2 (mm)	0.68 ±0.74	1.70 ±1.39	1.81 ± 2.18	1.53 ± 1.31	1.60 ± 1.38	2.17 ± 3.01	1.72 ± 1.48	1.89 ± 1.65	1.96 ±1.77	2.33
Dim3 (mm)	0.77 ±0.87	1.65 ± 1.32	1.63 ± 1.59	1.56 ± 1.28	1.64 ± 1.26	2.01 ± 2.54	1.76 ± 1.55	1.83 ± 1.62	1.81 ±1.48	2.40
Dims (mm)	0.69 ±0.78	1.65 ±1.42	1.72 ±2.05	**1.52** ±1.29	1.60 ±1.36	1.86 ±2.52	1.63 ±1.42	1.68 ±1.49	1.76 ±1.52	2.44
RWT1 (mm)	0.35 ±0.45	1.01 ±1.03	0.98 ±0.89	0.85 ±0.68	0.89 ±0.68	0.89 ±0.75	1.01 ±0.89	0.91 ±0.80	0.91 ±0.84	2.40
RWT2 (mm)	0.41 ±0.37	1.23 ±0.85	1.23 ±0.92	1.05 ±0.78	1.18 ±0.86	1.19 ±0.90	1.19 ±0.94	1.15 ±0.84	1.22 ±0.87	2.39
RWT3 (mm)	0.33 ±0.27	1.27 ±0.97	1.22 ±0.95	1.06 ±0.87	1.26 ±1.03	1.21 ±0.97	1.21 ±0.97	1.15 ±0.92	1.26 ±1.00	2.20
RWT4 (mm)	0.36 ±0.45	1.20 ±0.90	1.27 ±0.97	1.21 ±1.02	1.23 ±1.00	1.22 ±0.99	1.16 ±0.93	1.13 ±0.91	1.29 ±1.10	1.91
RWT5 (mm)	0.41 ±0.37	0.91 ±0.75	1.02 ±0.79	1.00 ±0.74	0.97 ±0.78	1.10 ±1.30	0.93 ±0.78	0.99 ±0.89	1.14 ±0.97	1.98
RWT6 (mm)	0.45 ±0.43	0.91 ±0.76	0.85 ±0.72	0.84 ±0.66	0.88 ±0.67	1.08 ±1.31	1.02 ±0.78	0.99 ±0.92	0.93 ±0.74	2.21
RWT (mm)	0.38 ±0.40	1.09 ±0.9	1.10 ±0.89	**1.01** ±0.81	1.07 ±0.86	1.12 ±1.06	1.09 ±0.89	1.06 ±0.89	1.12 ±0.94	2.18
Phase (%)	2.0	7.9	8.3	8.0	8.1	8.2	**7.8**	8.4	8.2	9.5

Results of the experiments are shown in Table 1. Errors in LV metrics obtained from ideal segmentations are reported in the baseline experiment, which used the reference segmentation provided by challenge organizers after applying the correction factor. For area metrics, after applying the correction factor there was still a mean absolute error (MAE) of 25 mm^2, which is around 25% of the MAE with our best segmentation results. Such an error might have been removed shall we had an accurate description of metric calculations. We could also see a 2% phase estimation error, which is purely dependent on cavity areas and introduced during resampling the images, suggesting the reference phase was sensitive to small noise.

Comparing the two networks, the performance of the U-Net was better than VGG-16 based segmentation network for Dice score, area, dimension and regional wall thickness values. Despite a more accurate estimation of the endocardium using the U-Net, VGG-16 achieved a more accurate phase estimation. This could be caused by the effect of noise we detected in the baseline experiments. From the results we could see that there was a negative effect on the segmentation task by removing multiple stage up-sampling, even though VGG-16 is deeper in the down-sampling stages.

Comparing the two augmentation strategies, our modified SMOD+ approach with $\sigma = 2$ produced the best results. The performance of $\sigma = 1$ and $\sigma = 3$ were limited because the variation of the deformation was either too close to the atlas or far enough to become unrealistic, and for both cases the generalization of the network was disrupted with either unbalanced data or unexpected data. By calculating the p-values, we found significant differences between the two augmentation strategies.

Bland-Altman plots were produced to show the agreement between our best performing network with the reference metrics in Fig. 5. The vast majority of the data points lies within $mean \pm 1.96 \times std$ suggesting a good agreement between the two measurements.

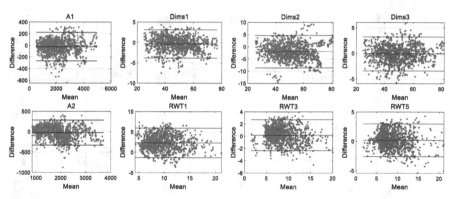

Fig. 5. Bland-Altman plots for U-Net with $\sigma = 2$. Areas, dimensions and three regional wall thickness metrics are shown.

We also evaluated qualitatively the segmentation results of our best performing network. Three examples with Dice score from high to low (including the worst case) are shown in Fig. 6. Our segmentation results from neural networks appeared to be consistent with image features, however, the manual reference segmentation contours were comparatively independent from image features. The values of Dice score showed similarity between our segmentation results and the provided references, and larger Dice score represented better similarity between the two.

For the testing dataset we used the entire training dataset to get the model of deformation and the correction factor for better generalization. We used all three networks of U-Net with $\sigma = 2$ and embedded the neural network predictions by averaging before calculating the metrics. The performance of our pipeline on the testing dataset is shown in Table 1. Comparing to the cross-validation experiment results using

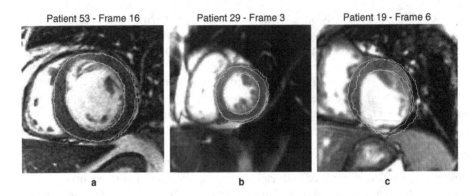

Patient 53 - Frame 16   Patient 29 - Frame 3   Patient 19 - Frame 6

a   b   c

Fig. 6. Segmentation results of training dataset. (*a*) to (*c*) correspond to Dice scores from high to low. The yellow contour is the reference segmentation, and the cyan contour is our proposed U-Net result based on SMOD+ augmentation. (Color figure online)

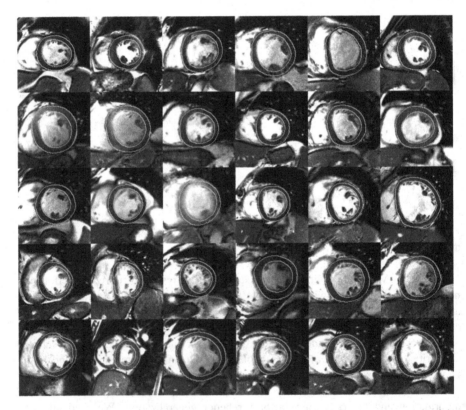

Fig. 7. Segmentation results of the testing dataset. We presented the segmentation result of the first frame of all subjects within the testing dataset. Different from the training dataset, there were no reference segmentation provided, and therefore only the segmentation results from our proposed neural networks are shown.

the training dataset, the testing dataset errors are comparatively larger. For metric A2 (representing myocardium area), the testing result mean absolute error is more than 4 times bigger and reaches 525 mm^2, which is larger than a square with the side of 2 cm.

In order to further investigate this difference between training dataset and testing dataset results, we produced the segmentation result of all the subjects in the testing data for qualitative analysis. Results for the first frame of each subject are shown in Fig. 7. From the visual inspection, the segmentation results of the testing dataset were comparable with the training dataset, and there was no clear evidence suggesting why would the metric evaluation of the testing dataset performed worse than in the training dataset based on the segmentation results.

4   Conclusion

In this paper, we have proposed a full quantification pipeline of the LV using CMR mages, developed and applied to the MICCAI 2019 Left Ventricle Full Quantification Challenge. We performed 3-fold cross-validation experiments on the training dataset, and for all the combinations of network structure and augmentation strategies, U-Net with our modified SMOD+ augmentation achieved the best results within our pipeline, showing the benefits of using multi-stage up-sampling and advanced augmentation strategies.

Compared to MICCAI 2018 Left Ventricle Full Quantification Challenge, the dataset was closer to real-life clinical conditions by removing the pre-processing of the images. At the same time, the size of the training dataset was reduced from 145 to 56 subjects. Both changes made the task significantly more challenging, which steered our focus towards the pre-processing and metrics evaluation stages, as well as the implementation of an anatomically meaningful augmentation method to enhance the neural network performance. Despite the more challenging task, our method achieved comparable results to last year's participants for both cross-validation on the training dataset and the final testing dataset.

The performance of our pipeline on the testing dataset did not reach the level of our cross-validation experiments, and based on the provided qualitative evaluation of the segmentation results the reason of such big differences between the mean absolute errors remains unclear to us. Similar performance drops in testing datasets were also identified in all the best ranking methods in MICCAI 2018 Left Ventricle Full Quantification Challenge [1–4]. It appears to us that this phenomenon is less dependent on the candidate methods, but rather closely related to the distribution of subjects in the training and testing dataset. Additional details on the testing dataset, and an explicit description of metrics calculation, would facilitate the interpretability of these results and improve future challenges.

Acknowledgments. This work was supported by the European Unions Horizon 2020 research and innovation program under the Marie Sklodowska-Curie (g.a. 764738) and by the British Heart Foundation (PG/16/75/32383). Authors are financially supported by a Wellcome Trust Senior Research Fellowship (to PL, 209450/Z/17/Z) and a BHF Intermediate Basic Science Research Fellowship (to ABO, FS/17/22/32644).

References

1. Li, J., Hu, Z.: Left ventricle full quantification using deep layer aggregation based multitask relationship learning. In: Pop, M., et al. (eds.) STACOM 2018. LNCS, vol. 11395, pp. 381–388. Springer, Cham (2019). https://doi.org/10.1007/978-3-030-12029-0_41
2. Kerfoot, E., Clough, J., Oksuz, I., Lee, J., King, A.P., Schnabel, J.A.: Left-ventricle quantification using residual U-Net. In: Pop, M., et al. (eds.) STACOM 2018. LNCS, vol. 11395, pp. 371–380. Springer, Cham (2019). https://doi.org/10.1007/978-3-030-12029-0_40
3. Xu, H., Schneider, J.E., Grau, V.: Calculation of anatomical and functional metrics using deep learning in cardiac MRI: comparison between direct and segmentation-based estimation. In: Pop, M., et al. (eds.) STACOM 2018. LNCS, vol. 11395, pp. 402–411. Springer, Cham (2019). https://doi.org/10.1007/978-3-030-12029-0_43
4. Guo, F., Ng, M., Wright, G.: Cardiac MRI left ventricle segmentation and quantification: a framework combining U-Net and continuous max-flow. In: Pop, M. (ed.) STACOM 2018. LNCS, vol. 11395, pp. 450–458. Springer, Cham (2019). https://doi.org/10.1007/978-3-030-12029-0_48
5. UK Biobank. https://www.ukbiobank.ac.uk/
6. Bai, W., et al.: Automated cardiovascular magnetic resonance image analysis with fully convolutional networks. J. Cardiovasc. Magn. Reson. 20(1), 65 (2018)
7. Petersen, S.E., et al.: The impact of cardiovascular risk factors on cardiac structure and function: Insights from the UK Biobank imaging enhancement study. PLoS ONE 12(10), e0185114 (2017)
8. Corral Acero, J., et al.: SMOD - data augmentation based on statistical models of deformation to enhance segmentation in 2D cine cardiac MRI. In: Coudière, Y., Ozenne, V., Vigmond, E., Zemzemi, N. (eds.) FIMH 2019. LNCS, vol. 11504, pp. 361–369. Springer, Cham (2019). https://doi.org/10.1007/978-3-030-21949-9_39
9. Ronneberger, O., Fischer, P., Brox, T.: U-Net: convolutional networks for biomedical image segmentation. In: Navab, N., Hornegger, J., Wells, W.M., Frangi, A.F. (eds.) MICCAI 2015. LNCS, vol. 9351, pp. 234–241. Springer, Cham (2015). https://doi.org/10.1007/978-3-319-24574-4_28
10. Xue, W., Brahm, G., Pandey, S., Leung, S., Li, S.: Full left ventricle quantification via deep multitask relationships learning. Med. Image Anal. 43, 54–65 (2018)
11. Orbes-Arteaga, M., et al.: PADDIT: probabilistic augmentation of data using diffeomorphic image transformation. In: Medical Imaging 2019: Image Processing, vol. 10949, p. 109490S. International Society for Optics and Photonics, March 2019

Left Ventricular Parameter Regression from Deep Feature Maps of a Jointly Trained Segmentation CNN

Sofie Tilborghs[1,2]([✉]) and Frederik Maes[1,2]

[1] Department of Electrical Engineering, ESAT/PSI, KU Leuven, Leuven, Belgium
sofie.tilborghs@kuleuven.be
[2] Medical Imaging Research Center, UZ Leuven, Leuven, Belgium

Abstract. Quantification of left ventricular (LV) parameters from cardiac MRI is important to assess cardiac condition and help in the diagnosis of certain pathologies. We present a CNN-based approach for automatic quantification of 11 LV indices: LV and myocardial area, 3 LV dimensions and 6 regional wall thicknesses (RWT). We use an encoder-decoder segmentation architecture and hypothesize that deep feature maps contain important shape information suitable to start an additional network branch for LV index regression. The CNN is simultaneously trained on regression and segmentation losses. We validated our approach on the LVQuan19 training dataset and found that our proposed CNN significantly outperforms a standard encoder regression CNN. The mean absolute error and Pearson correlation coefficient obtained for the different indices are respectively $190 \, mm^2$ (96%), $214 \, mm^2$ (0.90%), $2.99 \, mm$ (95%) and $1.82 \, mm$ (71%) for LV area, myocardial area, LV dimensions and RWT on a three-fold cross validation and $186 \, mm^2$ (97%), $222 \, mm^2$ (0.88%), $3.03 \, mm$ (0.95%) and $1.67 \, mm$ (73%) on a five-fold cross validation.

Keywords: Cardiac MRI · Automatic LV quantification · Convolutional Neural Networks

1 Introduction

Quantification of left ventricular (LV) parameters from cardiac MRI is important to assess cardiac condition and help in the diagnosis of certain pathologies. Relevant measurements include LV volume and myocardial thickness. Furthermore, also functional measures, e.g. ejection fraction, can be calculated from cine acquisitions. Quantification of LV indices can be performed completely manually, from a prior automatic segmentation of LV and myocardium or via direct regression. In 2018, the Left Ventricle Full Quantification Challenge MICCAI 2018 (LVQuan18) [1] had been organized to compare different approaches for automatic full LV quantification. In agreement with the current trend in medical image analysis, 10 out of 12 teams used convolutional neural networks (CNNs)

© Springer Nature Switzerland AG 2020
M. Pop et al. (Eds.): STACOM 2019, LNCS 12009, pp. 395–404, 2020.
https://doi.org/10.1007/978-3-030-39074-7_41

for either direct regression of LV indices [2–7], a prior segmentation of LV and myocardium [8,9] or a combination of the two [10–12].

In this paper, we propose a CNN-based approach for the regression of 11 LV indices: LV and myocardial area, 3 LV dimensions and 6 regional wall thicknesses (RWT) [2]. Simultaneously, we segment LV and myocardium using an encoder-decoder architecture. Different from the contributions in LVQuan18 who combined regression and segmentation by incorporating separate regression and segmentation branches at the end of their CNNs [10,11], we hypothesize that the innermost feature maps (FMs) of the segmentation CNN contain important shape information and use them to start an additional network branch for LV index regression. A similar approach, with a U-net backbone, is used in [13] for simultaneous hippocampus segmentation and clinical score regression from brain MR images. Furthermore, in contrast with LVQuan18 where images normalized for position, orientation and scale were used, our approach is developed for real clinical data variable in image size, cardiac orientation and position and image contrast.

2 Method

We propose an encoder-decoder CNN architecture for simultaneous segmentation and LV index regression. LV and myocardial areas, LV dimensions (3) and RWT (6) are directly predicted by the CNN for every time point in a cine scan separately. LV dimensions and RWT are defined according to the 17-segment model [14], i.e. inferoseptal (IS), inferior (I), inferolateral (IL), anterolateral (AL), anterior (A) and anteroseptal (AS) RWT and IS-AL, I-A and IL-AS LV dimensions. Cardiac phase estimation is performed automatically from the predicted LV areas: the maximal LV area of a subject characterizes the end of diastole while the minimal LV area represents the end of systole.

2.1 Preprocessing

Since image size and pixel spacing are not standardized in clinical practice, all images are resampled, using linear interpolation, to have an equal image size of 476×476 and a pixel spacing of $1\,\text{mm} \times 1\,\text{mm}$. Ground truth segmentations and LV indices are modified accordingly. Furthermore, we equalize the image histograms between patients by matching them with a reference histogram. This intensity transformation is performed with a piecewise linear function that was obtained by matching the 1% quantiles of the cumulative histogram of the patient's data with those of the reference dataset. Finally, each image is also normalized to have zero mean and unit variance. All LV index values are also normalized to have a mean of zero and a standard deviation of 1 over the training set.

2.2 Architecture

A schematic representation of the architecture can be found in Fig. 1. Three pathways can be distinguished: encoder (E), decoder (D) and regression (R)

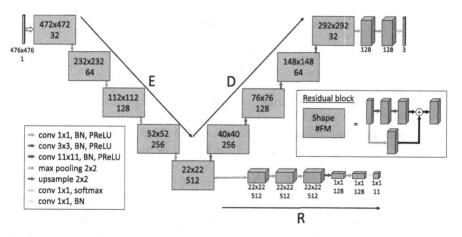

Fig. 1. Proposed network architecture with encoder (E), decoder (D) and regression (R) pathways. A detail of the residual block is given at the right. For every FM, the shape and number is given. For each residual block, 'Shape' indicates the output shape and '#FM' the number of FMs used in every conv layer in that block.

Table 1. Architecture variations.

Name	ED-RS	E-R	U-RS	ED-S	U-S
Pathways	E-D-R	E-R	E-D-R	E-D	E-D
Skip connections	No	-	Yes	No	Yes

pathways. The E-D framework is build with residual blocks that each have two 3×3 convolutional (conv) layers and a parallel pathway with a 1×1 conv layer. These two pathways are summed at the end of the block. The residual blocks are connected with 2×2 max pooling layers in E and with 2×2 upsampling layers in D. At the innermost FMs, we start the regression pathway which consists of 1×1 conv layers and one 22×22 conv layer to remove the spatial dimensions. All conv layers use valid padding and are followed by batch normalization (BN) [15] and a parametric rectifying linear unit (PReLU) [16] activation function. Softmax activation is used for the segmentation output and at the regression output, an additional BN layer is added. We perform LV index regression with three variations on this architecture: (1) proposed CNN (ED-RS), (2) encoder regression CNN (E-R) without simultaneous segmentation and (3) U-Net variant [17] (U-RS) where skip connections have been added. Additionally, we omit the regression pathway in variants (1) and (3), resulting in two new variants ED-S and U-S for segmentation only. An overview of all variants is given in Table 1.

2.3 Training

The loss function L is a weighted sum of the segmentation loss L_1 and the regression loss L_2:

$$L = L_1 + w \cdot L_2. \tag{1}$$

For the segmentation loss, the categorical Dice loss is used:

$$L_1 = 1 - \frac{1}{n} \sum_k \frac{2 \cdot \sum_v t_k(v) \cdot p_k(v)}{\sum_v t_k(v) + \sum_v p_k(v)} \tag{2}$$

where $t_k(v)$ is the true probability that voxel v belongs to class k, which is either 1 or 0, $p_k(v)$ is the class probability predicted by the network and n is the number of classes. We only use two classes, LV bloodpool and myocardium, and omit background. Mean squared error is used as regression loss:

$$L_2 = \sum_i (x(i) - y(i))^2 \tag{3}$$

with $x(i)$ the ground truth for index i and $y(i)$ the estimated value. The network is trained end-to-end over 80 epochs with Adam optimizer [18] and an adaptive learning rate (lr) which is halved every 8 epochs (max lr $= 1.6e{-}3$, min lr $= 1e{-}4$). The network weights are initialized according to [19] and a weight w of 1 is used in Eq. 1. We use online data augmentation to artificially enlarge the dataset: for all training images and every epoch, a new rotation factor is randomly sampled from a Gaussian distribution with a mean of 0 rad and a standard deviation of 2 rad. Furthermore, Gaussian noise with standard deviation between 0 and 0.3 was added every epoch to make the network robust to noise.

2.4 Postprocessing

After training, a linear regression between ground truth and predicted values of the training data is performed for every index separately. The obtained slopes and biases are used to adapt the CNN regression output values.

3 Experiments

The models were developed and validated on the LVQuan19 dataset. The training and test dataset contain cine MR images of respectively 56 and 30 subjects. For each subject, a mid-cavity short-axis 2D image is available for 20 time frames. The images of different subjects vary in pixel size (min $= 0.68$ mm, max $= 1.72$ mm), field of view (FOV, min $= 300 \times 300\,mm^2$, max $= 480 \times 480\,mm^2$), image contrast and cardiac position and orientation. For the training dataset, ground truth segmentations of LV and myocardium and ground truth values for LV indices are also available. LV index prediction is evaluated with the mean absolute error (MAE) and Pearson correlation coefficient (ρ), calculated for every index separately. Additionally, an error rate (ER) for cardiac phase identification is defined as the percentage of wrongly classified images. Furthermore, we validate the segmentation performance by calculating the Dice Similarity Coefficient (DSC) between ground truth and predicted segmentations. To test the

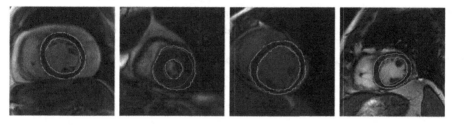

Fig. 2. Segmentation results of the ED-RS approach in the five-fold cross validation. Shown images have been corrected for pixel spacing, but not for contrast differences. Ground truth segmentation is shown in green and CNN result in red. (Color figure online)

initial stability of our results, both a three- and five-fold cross validation are performed on the training set. The statistical significance of the results is assessed using the two-sided Wilcoxon signed rank test with a significance level of 5%. Additionally, we validate the LV index regression performance of our proposed method (ED-RS) with a five-fold cross validation on the LVQuan18 training dataset. This dataset contains 80×80 images of 145 subjects for 20 time points which are corrected for position and orientation. To make the CNN suited to these smaller images, the CNN input and output shapes are changed to 80×80 and same padding instead of valid padding is used.

4   Results

In Table 2, the results of three approaches for LV index regression (Table 1) are compared. The results of the variant without joint segmentation (E-R) are significantly worse than the results of the variants with joint segmentation (U-RS and ED-RS). On areas and LV dimensions, ED-RS outperforms U-RS while for RWT, U-RS has lower MAE and higher ρ in the three-fold and ED-RS in the five-fold cross validation. Table 2 also shows the results on the test dataset and the results of the five-fold cross validation on the LVQuan18 training dataset. In Fig. 2, examples of endo- and epicardium segmentation are shown. Table 3 compares the segmentation results for four different approaches. Although no major differences in performance are observed, the encoder-decoder segmentation architecture (ED-S) without simultaneous regression tends to perform best. On the LVQuan18 dataset, we obtained a DSC of 95.7±2.4% for LV and of 88.9±4.2% for myocardium.

5   Discussion

In agreement with [10], we find that a joint segmentation of LV and myocardium significantly improves LV index regression. In contrast with the methods in LVQuan18 that included a segmentation loss and started a regression branch

Table 2. MAE, ρ and ER for three and five-fold cross validation on the training dataset, for the test dataset and for five-fold cross-validation on the LVQuan18 training dataset. Best values are shown in bold. For MAE, the values that did not show a statistically significant difference of absolute errors with the best value are also indicated in bold.

	3-fold			5-fold			Test	LVQuan18
	E-R	U-RS	ED-RS	E-R	U-RS	ED-RS	ED-RS	ED-RS
MAE								
Area [mm^2]								
LV	489	247	**190**	395	231	**186**	230	154
Myo	369	**227**	**214**	346	237	**222**	523	218
Mean	429	237	**202**	371	234	**204**	377	186
Dim [mm]								
IS-AL	6.25	3.11	**2.82**	5.04	2.96	**2.70**	3.52	2.38
I-A	6.17	3.55	**2.94**	5.42	**3.52**	**3.35**	3.51	2.21
IL-AS	6.74	3.72	**3.21**	5.53	**3.28**	**3.04**	3.56	2.62
Mean	6.39	3.46	**2.99**	5.33	3.25	**3.03**	3.51	2.40
RWT [mm]								
IS	2.17	1.56	**1.54**	2.08	1.58	**1.46**	3.14	1.35
I	1.90	**1.79**	**1.81**	1.93	**1.70**	**1.64**	2.71	1.61
IL	**1.94**	**1.88**	2.02	2.01	**1.71**	**1.74**	2.92	1.78
AL	2.00	**1.71**	1.80	1.94	1.81	**1.73**	2.16	1.67
A	2.02	**1.81**	1.93	**1.87**	**1.87**	**1.86**	2.12	1.46
AS	2.00	**1.66**	1.83	1.94	**1.61**	**1.59**	2.55	1.38
Mean	2.00	**1.74**	1.82	1.96	1.71	**1.67**	2.60	1.54
ρ [%]								
Area								
LV	0.71	0.93	**0.96**	0.83	0.95	**0.97**	0.95	0.97
Myo	0.63	0.87	**0.90**	0.68	0.87	**0.88**	0.84	0.87
Mean	0.67	0.90	**0.93**	0.75	0.91	**0.92**	0.92	0.92
Dim								
IS-AL	0.70	0.93	**0.95**	0.82	0.94	**0.95**	0.92	0.95
I-A	0.76	0.93	**0.95**	0.82	0.93	**0.94**	0.94	0.96
IL-AS	0.67	0.91	**0.94**	0.80	0.93	**0.95**	0.93	0.95
Mean	0.71	0.92	**0.95**	0.81	0.93	**0.95**	0.93	0.95
RWT								
IS	0.62	0.80	**0.80**	0.65	0.80	**0.82**	0.80	0.84
I	0.66	**0.71**	0.69	0.65	0.73	**0.75**	0.76	0.71
IL	0.66	**0.70**	0.66	0.63	**0.73**	0.72	0.78	0.68
AL	0.64	**0.71**	0.69	0.64	0.65	**0.69**	0.78	0.72
A	0.64	**0.70**	0.66	**0.71**	0.65	0.63	0.76	0.76
AS	0.68	**0.78**	0.75	0.72	0.77	**0.78**	0.75	0.86
Mean	0.65	**0.73**	0.71	0.67	0.72	**0.73**	0.77	0.76
ER [%]	13.3	13.0	**12.6**	12.2	12.2	**10.7**	13.7	9.2

Table 3. Mean and std for DSC. Statistical significant difference between S and RS are shown in gray and between U and ED with *. Best values are shown in bold.

DSC %		U-S	U-RS	ED-S	ED-RS
3-fold	LV	88.7 ± 17.7*	91.1 ± **12.7**	**91.3 ± 14.5***	90.5 ± 14.1
	Myo	82.5 ± 12.7*	83.3 ± 11.2	**84.4 ± 10.9***	82.8 ± 11.1
5-fold	LV	90.6 ± 17.1	89.2 ± 18.4	**92.2 ± 11.9**	91.3 ± 12.1
	Myo	83.9 ± 13.0	82.8 ± 14.4	**84.5 ± 10.5**	83.4 ± 11.5

from full-scale FMs at the end of the network [10,11], we started the regression pathway from the innermost FMs. This approach is more elegant since at prediction time, only encoding and regression pathways are required for LV index estimation. Furthermore, it decreases the total size of FMs from which the regression branch starts. In our case, the full-scale FMs have 2.728.448 features while the innermost FMs only have 247.808, which is a reduction of 91%. A five-fold cross-validation on the LVQuan18 dataset with the regression pathway R connected to the last residual block in the decoder pathway D was used for comparison of the two branching approaches and achieved a MAE of 158 mm^2 for LV area, 243 mm^2 for myocardial area, 2.44 mm for LV dimensions and 1.72 mm for RWT, indicating that our more efficient approach does not compromise performance. Similar approaches, starting a regression branch at the innermost FMs, have been presented in [20] for midpoint regression of LV, in [13] for clinical score regression from brain MR images and in [21] for determining cardiac position, orientation and scale. In these approaches, the presence of all relevant information for accurate segmentation in the innermost FMs is not enforced since additional pathways bypassing the innermost FMs are used in GridNet [20] or U-net [13,21] architectures. To evaluate the influence of such bypassing pathways, we compared our proposed approach (ED-RS) with its U-net variant (U-RS) and found that ED-RS performs better on area and LV dimension regression. For RWT regression, results of ED-RS and U-RS are similar. The results on area and LV dimensions are in accordance with our hypothesis that all relevant shape parameters should be contained in the innermost FMs of a encoder-decoder framework, but more research is needed to investigate the exact meaning of these features. We also compared the segmentation results of architectures with and without skip connections and found that skip connections did not improve the segmentation in this application.

Furthermore, since we observed a linear deviation between ground truth and predicted values of LV indices on the training set (Fig. 3), a postprocessing step that performs a linear regression was used. Intuitively, adding a separate 1×1 conv layer with a bias term to every regression output should be able to capture this mismatch. However, in some initial experiments with this extended architecture, we observed no improvement. Further experiments are thus required to identify the origin of and possible solutions to such deviations, aiming at an end-to-end trainable network not requiring postprocessing.

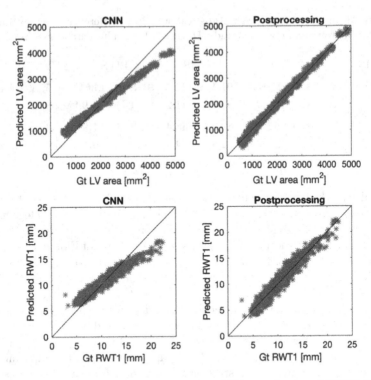

Fig. 3. Scatter plot of ground truth and predicted LV area (top) and RWT1 (bottom) of the training set before (left) and after (right) postprocessing when training on the full training set. Unity line (black) and linear regression (green) are shown. (Color figure online)

Finally, we performed a five-fold cross validation on the LVQuan18 training dataset. Our results are in line with the values reported by the LVQuan18 participants, but not reaching the performance of the top-scoring contributions [3]. However, we selected our network and training parameters using the LVQuan19 dataset and did not make any changes, except for adapting the input and output size of the CNN and changing the padding method.

The major drawback of our current approach is that LV indices are predicted for every time point separately. Because LV indices at different time points are highly correlated, it is expected that including multiple time points of one subject using a recurrent neural network (RNN) [2,4–6,11] or 3D network [7] will further improve the results.

6   Conclusion

We presented an encoder-decoder segmentation network with simultaneous LV index regression from the innermost feature maps and showed that this approach outperforms a standard encoder regression network.

Acknowledgement. Sofie Tilborghs is supported by a Ph.D fellowship of the Research Foundation - Flanders (FWO).

References

1. Li and Xue, LV Full Quantification Challenge. https://lvquan18.github.io/
2. Xue, W., et al.: Full left ventricle quantification via deep multitask relationships learning. Med. Image Anal. **43**, 54–65 (2018)
3. Li, J., Hu, Z.: Left ventricle full quantification using deep layer aggregation based multitask relationship learning. In: Pop, M., et al. (eds.) STACOM 2018. LNCS, vol. 11395, pp. 381–388. Springer, Cham (2019). https://doi.org/10.1007/978-3-030-12029-0_41
4. Liu, L., Ma, J., Wang, J., Xiao, J.: Automated full quantification of left ventricle with deep neural networks. In: Pop, M., et al. (eds.) STACOM 2018. LNCS, vol. 11395, pp. 412–420. Springer, Cham (2019). https://doi.org/10.1007/978-3-030-12029-0_44
5. Yang, G., et al.: Left ventricle full quantification via hierarchical quantification network. In: Pop, M., et al. (eds.) STACOM 2018. LNCS, vol. 11395, pp. 429–438. Springer, Cham (2019). https://doi.org/10.1007/978-3-030-12029-0_46
6. Debus, A., Ferrante, E.: Left ventricle quantification through spatio-temporal CNNs. In: Pop, M., et al. (eds.) STACOM 2018. LNCS, vol. 11395, pp. 466–475. Springer, Cham (2019). https://doi.org/10.1007/978-3-030-12029-0_50
7. Jang, Y., Kim, S., Shim, H., Chang, H.-J.: Full quantification of left ventricle using deep multitask network with combination of 2D and 3D convolution on 2D+t Cine MRI. In: Pop, M., et al. (eds.) STACOM 2018. LNCS, vol. 11395, pp. 476–483. Springer, Cham (2019). https://doi.org/10.1007/978-3-030-12029-0_51
8. Kerfoot, E., Clough, J., Oksuz, I., Lee, J., King, A.P., Schnabel, J.A.: Left-ventricle quantification using residual U-Net. In: Pop, M., et al. (eds.) STACOM 2018. LNCS, vol. 11395, pp. 371–380. Springer, Cham (2019). https://doi.org/10.1007/978-3-030-12029-0_40
9. Guo, F., Ng, M., Wright, G.: Cardiac MRI left ventricle segmentation and quantification: a framework combining U-Net and continuous max-flow. In: Pop, M., et al. (eds.) STACOM 2018. LNCS, vol. 11395, pp. 450–458. Springer, Cham (2019). https://doi.org/10.1007/978-3-030-12029-0_48
10. Xu, H., Schneider, J.E., Grau, V.: Calculation of anatomical and functional metrics using deep learning in cardiac MRI: comparison between direct and segmentation-based estimation. In: Pop, M., et al. (eds.) STACOM 2018. LNCS, vol. 11395, pp. 402–411. Springer, Cham (2019). https://doi.org/10.1007/978-3-030-12029-0_43
11. Yan, W., Wang, Y., Chen, S., van der Geest, R.J., Tao, Q.: ESU-P-net: cascading network for full quantification of left ventricle from cine MRI. In: Pop, M., et al. (eds.) STACOM 2018. LNCS, vol. 11395, pp. 421–428. Springer, Cham (2019). https://doi.org/10.1007/978-3-030-12029-0_45
12. Liu, J., Li, X., Ren, H., Li, Q.: Multi-estimator full left ventricle quantification through ensemble learning. In: Pop, M., et al. (eds.) STACOM 2018. LNCS, vol. 11395, pp. 459–465. Springer, Cham (2019). https://doi.org/10.1007/978-3-030-12029-0_49
13. Cao, L., et al.: Multi-task neural networks for joint hippocampus segmentation and clinical score regression. Multimed. Tools Appl. **77**, 29669–29686 (2018)

14. Cerqueir, M.D., et al.: Standardized myocardial segmentation and nomenclature for tomographic images of the heart. J. Am. Soc. Echocardiogr. **15**(5), 463–476 (2002)
15. Ioffe, S., Szegedy, C.: Batch normalization: accelerating deep network training by reducing internal covariate shift. In: ICML 2015 (2015)
16. Maas A.L., et al.: Rectifier nonlinearities improve neural network acoustic models. In: ICML 2013 (2013)
17. Ronneberger, O., Fischer, P., Brox, T.: U-Net: convolutional networks for biomedical image segmentation. In: Navab, N., Hornegger, J., Wells, W.M., Frangi, A.F. (eds.) MICCAI 2015. LNCS, vol. 9351, pp. 234–241. Springer, Cham (2015). https://doi.org/10.1007/978-3-319-24574-4_28
18. Kingma, D.P., Ba, J.: Adam: a method for stochastic optimization. In: Proceedings of the 3rd International Conference on Learning Representations (ICLR) (2014)
19. He, K., et al.: Delving deep into rectifiers: surpassing human-level performance on imagenet classification. In: Proceedings of the IEEE International Conference on Computer Vision 2015, pp. 1026–1034 (2015)
20. Zotti, C., et al.: Convolutional neural network with shape prior applied to cardiac MRI segmentation. IEEE J. Biomed. Health Inform. **23**(3), 1119–1128 (2019)
21. Ω-net: fully automatic: multi-view cardiac MR detection, orientation, and segmentation with deep neural networks. Med. Image Anal. **48**, 95–106 (2019)

A Two-Stage Temporal-Like Fully Convolutional Network Framework for Left Ventricle Segmentation and Quantification on MR Images

Zhou Zhao, Nicolas Boutry, Élodie Puybareau$^{(\boxtimes)}$, and Thierry Géraud

EPITA Research and Development Laboratory (LRDE), Le Kremlin-Bicêtre, France
elodie.puybareau@lrde.epita.fr

Abstract. Automatic segmentation of the left ventricle (LV) of a living human heart in a magnetic resonance (MR) image (2D+t) allows to measure some clinical significant indices like the regional wall thicknesses (RWT), cavity dimensions, cavity and myocardium areas, and cardiac phase. Here, we propose a novel framework made of a sequence of two fully convolutional networks (FCN). The first is a modified temporal-like VGG16 (the "localization network") and is used to localize roughly the LV (filled-in) epicardium position in each MR volume. The second FCN is a modified temporal-like VGG16 too, but devoted to segment the LV myocardium and cavity (the "segmentation network"). We evaluate the proposed method with 5-fold-cross-validation on the MICCAI 2019 LV Full Quantification Challenge dataset. For the network used to localize the epicardium, we obtain an average dice index of 0.8953 on validation set. For the segmentation network, we obtain an average dice index of 0.8664 on validation set (there, data augmentation is used). The mean absolute error (MAE) of average cavity and myocardium areas, dimensions, RWT are 114.77 mm^2; 0.9220 mm; 0.9185 mm respectively. The computation time of the pipeline is less than 2 s for an entire 3D volume. The error rate of phase classification is 7.6364%, which indicates that the proposed approach has a promising performance to estimate all these parameters.

Keywords: Deep learning · VGG · Left ventricle quantification · Segmentation · Fully convolutional network

1 Introduction

Left ventricle (LV) full quantification is critical to evaluate cardiac functionality and diagnose cardiac diseases. Full quantification aims to simultaneously quantify all LV indices, including the two areas of the LV (the area of its cavity and the area of its myocardium), six RWT's (along different directions and at different positions), three LV dimensions (along different directions), and the cardiac

© Springer Nature Switzerland AG 2020
M. Pop et al. (Eds.): STACOM 2019, LNCS 12009, pp. 405–413, 2020.
https://doi.org/10.1007/978-3-030-39074-7_42

phase (diastole or systole) [1,2], as shown in Fig. 1. However, the LV full quantification is challenging: LV samples are variable, not only because the samples can be obtained from different hospital, but also because some of them are not concerned by cardiac diseases. It is also challenging because there are complex correlations between the LV indices. For example, the cavity area has a direct influence on the three LV dimensions and the cardiac phase. The MICCAI 2019 Challenge on Left Ventricle Full Quantification[1] (LVQuan19) is an extension of the one of 2018 [2] with the difference that now the original data is given without preprocessing for training and testing phases, to be closer to clinical reality.

We propose then in this paper a two-stage temporal-like FCN framework that segments and estimates the parameters of interest in 2D+t sequences of the MR image of a LV. First, in each temporal frame, we localize the greatest connected component detected by the localization network, we dilate it using a size equal to 10 pixels, and we compute the corresponding bounding box. This results in a sequence of cropped LV's (that we will abusively call cropped volume). Second, we use these cropped volumes to train the LV segmentation network. The procedure is depicted in Fig. 2. Finally, the segmentation results are used for the LV full quantification.

The pipeline is based on our previous works [3,4] but with a new step: we added one localization network before the segmentation network. Compared with [5], our localization precision is higher, because we localize the entire LV region (the filled-in epicardium) instead of the center of the bounding box containing the LV structure. Compared with [6], our method is quicker and do not have memory limit problems. To take advantages of time information, we use 3 successive 2D frames $(n-1, n, n+1)$ at time n as inputs in the localization and in the segmentation networks, yielding to better results than the traditional approach which used only the information at time n for the nth slice.

We evaluated the proposed method using the dataset provided by LVQuan19 with 5-fold-cross-validation. Experiments with (very) limited training data have shown that our model has a stable performance. We added pre-processing and post-processing steps to enhance and refine our results.

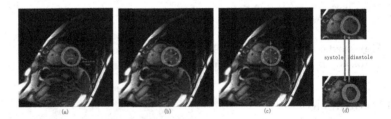

Fig. 1. Illustration of LV indices, including (a) the cavity area and the myocardium area, (b) three LV dimensions, (c) six regional wall thicknesses and (d) the cardiac phase (diastole or systole).

---

[1] https://lvquan19.github.io.

[2] https://lvquan18.github.io.

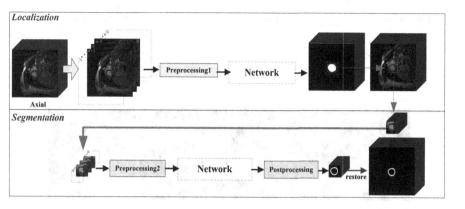

Fig. 2. Global overview of the proposed method.

The plan is the following: we detail our methodology in Sect. 2, we detail our experiments in Sect. 3, and then Sect. 4 concludes.

2 Methodology

2.1 Dataset Description

LV dataset used for this work was provided by the LVQuan19 challenge. It contains 56 patients processed SAX MR sequences. For each patient, 20 temporal frames are given and correspond to a whole cardiac cycle. All ground truth (GT) values of the LV indices are provided for every single frame. The pixel spacings of the MR images range from 0.6836 mm/pixel to 1.5625 mm/pixel, with mean values of 1.1809 mm/pixel. LV dataset includes two different image sizes: 256×256 or 512×512 pixels.

2.2 Preprocessings

Let us recall what we call *Gauss normalization*: for the $(2D + t)$-image I corresponding to a given patient, we compute $I := \frac{I-\mu}{\sigma}$ where μ is the mean of I and σ its standard deviation (σ is assumed not to be equal to zero). There are then two different pre-processing steps as depicted in Fig. 2.

– The first pre-processing (see preprocessing1 in Fig. 2) begins with a Gauss normalization. When we treat training data, we crop the initial slices into a 256×256 image to optimize the dice of the network (we do not do this for test datasets). Then we concatenate them for each n into a $256 \times 256 \times 3$ pseudo-color image where R, G, B correspond respectively to $n - 1, n, n + 1$ (we do not detail the cases $n = 1$ and $n = 20$ because of a lack of space).

– The second pre-processing (preprocessing2 in Fig. 2) is in four steps: (1) data augmentation using rotations and flips, (2) resizing with a fixed inter-pixel spacing ($0.65\,mm$), (3) Gauss normalization, and (4) we concatenate into a pseudo-color image like above.

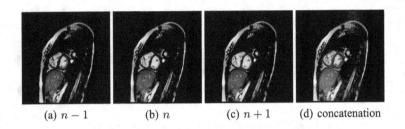

(a) $n-1$ (b) n (c) $n+1$ (d) concatenation

Fig. 3. Illustration of our "temporal-like" procedure. (Color figure online)

Because the VGG-16 network's input is an RGB image, we propose to take advantage of the temporal information by stacking 3 successive 2D frames: to segment the nth slice, we use the nth slice of the MR volume, and its neighboring $(n-1)^{th}$ and $(n+1)^{th}$ slices, as green, red and blue channels, respectively. This new image, named "temporal-like" image, enhances the area of motions, here the heart, as shown in Fig. 3.

2.3 Network Architecture

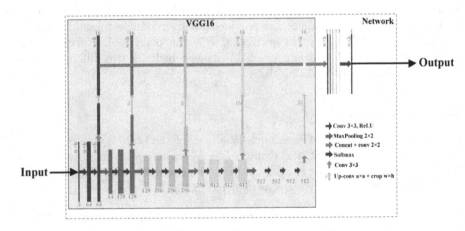

Fig. 4. Architecture of our networks.

The localization and the segmentation networks have the same architecture (see Fig. 4). First we downloaded the pre-trained original VGG16 [7] network architecture. We recall that this network has been pre-trained on millions of natural images of ImageNet for image classification [8]. Second, we discard its fully connected layers and this way we keep only the sub-network made of five convolution-based "stages" (the base network). Each stage is made of two convolutional layers, a ReLU activation function, and a max-pooling layer. Since the max-pooling layers decrease the resolution of the input image, we obtain a set of fine to coarse feature maps (with 5 levels of features). Inspired by the work in [9,10], we added *specialized* convolutional layers (with a 3 × 3 kernel size) with K (*e.g.* $K = 16$) feature maps after the up-convolutional layers placed at the end of each stage. The outputs of the specialized layers have then the same resolution as the input image, and are then concatenated together. We add a 1 × 1 convolutional layer at the output of the concatenation layer to linearly combine the fine to coarse feature maps. This complete network provides the final segmentation result.[3]

2.4 Postprocessing

Let us assume that we input the 20 cropped temporal slices of a patient into an image of size $20 \times width \times height$ (where the crop is due to the localization procedure) in preprocessing2 to obtain a $20 \times width \times height \times 3$ image. We filter then the ouput of size $20 \times width \times height$ by keeping only the greatest connected component in the segmented $(2D + t)$-image, and we compute the inverse interpolation on the x and y axes to get back the initial inter-pixel spacing. Finally, we add a zero-valued border to get back a $20 \times 256 \times 256$ or a $20 \times 512 \times 512$ image (depending on the shape of the input).

2.5 Evaluation Methods

The LV quantification as defined in LVquan19 relies on 11 parameters: the areas of the LV cavity and the myocardium, 3 dimensions of the cavity and 6 measurements of the wall thickness. We measure the areas (see Fig. 1 (a)) by computing the number of pixels in the segmented regions corresponding to the LV cavity and the myocardium. To measure the three cavity dimension values (dim1, dim2, dim3) (see Fig. 1 (b)), we proceed this way: because our final segmentation results is the LV myocardium, we first extracted the LV cavity from the segmentation results. We then compute the boundary of the LV cavity and calculate the distances between the points of the boundary and the centroid of the LV cavity along the integral angles $\theta \in [-30, 30[$ (in degrees). Finally, we average these distances. We do this for the six separated regions of the wall. Finally, we compute the mean dimensions for each pair of opposite regions and we obtain $(dim1, dim2, dim3)$. To measure the RWT's values, we first find the boundaries of epicardium and endocardium respectively, and we compute the distances between the points on the boundary of epicardium and the points on the boundary of endocardium along the same integral angles as before where

---

[3] Note that we designed our network's architecture to work with any input shape.

zero corresponds to the normal. Finally, we compute the mean among 60 distance values for each region. To classify the phase as systolic or diastolic, we use a simple method: we detect the time n_{max} when the cavity is maximal, and n_{min} when the cavity is minimal. Assuming that we have the case $n_{min} > n_{max}$, then for each time $n \in [n_{max}, n_{min}]$, we label the image as systolic phase, and otherwise it is a diastolic phase. We do the converse when we have $n_{max} < n_{min}$.

3   Experiments

We implemented our experiments on Keras/TensorFlow using a NVidia Quadro P6000 GPU. We used the multinomial logistic loss function for a one-of-many classification task, passing real-valued predictions through a softmax to get a probability distribution over classes. For the localization network, we used an Adam optimizer (batchsize=4, $\beta1$=0.9, $\beta2$=0.999, epsilon=0.001, lr = 0.002) and we did not use learning rate decay. We trained the network during 10 epochs. We recall that we used the filled-in epicardium connected component given in the GT as the "ones" of the output of our network. For the segmentation network, we used the same optimizer and the same parameters but we changed the batchsize to 1. Also, we considered three different classes[4] in the given GT: the background (0), the myocardium (1), the cavity (2) (we merge then 0 and 2 after the segmentation). This way, we obtained better results than using only the wall of the LV.

3.1   Results

We tested our method with 3- and 5-fold-cross-validations on the challenge dataset. An example of bounding box is depicted in red (we did not do any dilation here) in Fig. 5. We obtain an average dice index of 0.8953 on validation set. In practice, we extend next the box by a size equal to 10 pixels to ensure that the whole LV is included into the bounding box.

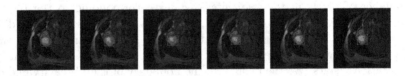

Fig. 5. Some localizations (in red) of the LV (in blue) of the 9th patient. (Color figure online)

For the segmentation, we compared ResNet50 with VGG16 as feature extraction on 3-fold-cross-validation (18, 19, 19) (see Fig. 6). VGG16 is then more efficient to detect boundaries than ResNet50 in our application.

---

[4] From a technical point of view, we proceeded to a classification more than to a segmentation.

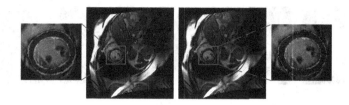

Fig. 6. Segmentation results (ResNet50-FCN on the left side vs. VGG16-FCN on the right side) for one same patient. The yellow color shows the false negatives. (Color figure online)

Table 1. Average results of compared methods on 3-fold-cross-validation. Values are shown as mean absolute error.

Dataset	Method	Cavity Areas(mm²)	Myocardium Areas(mm²)	Dims(mm)				RWT(mm)							Phase Error(%)	Dice (%)
				dim1	dim2	dim3	average	IS	I	IL	AL	A	AS	average		
Validating data	ResNet50-FCN	279.32	284.84	1.8359	1.6320	1.7767	1.7482	1.2106	1.3059	1.7157	1.6225	1.3303	1.2437	1.4048	15.1267	79.20
	VGG16-FCN (our method)	88.84	157.01	0.9799	1.0691	0.9443	0.9978	0.8320	0.9173	1.1190	1.1124	0.8895	0.8408	0.9518	8.0311	86.04

Table 1 presents the average results for the two compared methods. The 11 indices of LV full quantification and dice using the VGG16-FCN are better than when we use the ResNet50-FCN. For these reasons, we used the VGG16-FCN for the segmentation of the LV.

To verify the stability of our algorithm, we evaluated the proposed method with 5-fold-cross-validation (11, 11, 11, 11, 12). In Table 2, the average results are showed. Compared with 3-fold-cross-validation, the average areas error is improved from $122.93\,mm^2$ to $114.77\,mm^2$, the average dims error is improved from $0.9978\,mm$ to $0.9220\,mm$, the average RWT error is improved from $0.9518\,mm$ to $0.9185\,mm$, the average phase error is improved from 8.0311% to 7.6364% and the dice is improved from 86.04% to 86.64%.

Table 2. Average results on 5-fold-cross-validation. Values are shown as mean absolute error.

Dataset	Cavity Areas(mm²)	Myocardium Areas(mm²)	Dims(mm)				RWT(mm)							Phase Error(%)	Dice (%)
			dim1	dim2	dim3	average	IS	I	IL	AL	A	AS	average		
Validating data	94.31	135.23	0.9067	0.9792	0.8801	0.9220	0.8362	0.9147	1.0798	1.0560	0.8270	0.7973	0.9185	7.6364	86.64
Testing data	226.80	577.50	6.4934	3.8814	3.9835	4.7861	4.2693	1.8585	2.0570	1.9129	1.6441	3.6039	2.5576	9.83	-

In Table 2, we also reported the results on test dataset given by the organizers of LVQuan19. The test dataset was composed of processed SAX MR sequences of 30 patients. For each patient, only the SAX image sequences of 20 frames were provided (no GT).

In Fig. 7, the segmentation results on fifth patient of test dataset are showed, the yellow ring denotes the segmentation results.

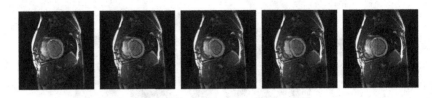

Fig. 7. Some segmentation results on the 5th patient of test dataset. (Color figure online)

4   Conclusion

In this paper, we propose to use a modified VGG16 to proceed to pixelwise image segmentation, in particular to segment the wall of the heart LV in temporal MR images. The proposed method provides promising results at the same time in matter of localization and segmentation, and leads to realistic physical measures of clinical values relative to the human heart. Our perspective is to try to better segment the boundary of the wall of the LV, either by increasing the weights relative to the boundary regions in the loss function, or by separating the boundary and the interior of the wall into two classes during the classification procedure.

Acknowledgements. We thank the organizers of the MICCAI 2019 LV Full Quantification Challenge for providing the LV dataset, NVidia for giving us a Quadro P6000 GPU for this research, and the financial support from China Scholarship Council (CSC, File No.201806290010)

References

1. Xue, W.F., Brahm, G., Pandey, S., Leung, S., Li, S.: Full left ventricle quantification via deep multitask relationships learning. Med. Image Anal. **43**, 54–65 (2018)
2. Xue, W., Lum, A., Mercado, A., Landis, M., Warrington, J., Li, S.: Full quantification of left ventricle via deep multitask learning network respecting intra- and inter-task relatedness. In: Descoteaux, M., Maier-Hein, L., Franz, A., Jannin, P., Collins, D.L., Duchesne, S. (eds.) MICCAI 2017. LNCS, vol. 10435, pp. 276–284. Springer, Cham (2017). https://doi.org/10.1007/978-3-319-66179-7_32
3. Xu, Y., Géraud, T., Bloch, I.: From neonatal to adult brain MR image segmentation in a few seconds using 3D-like fully convolutional network and transfer learning. In: Proceedings of ICIP, pp. 4417–4421. IEEE, Beijing (2017). https://doi.org/10.1109/ICIP.2017.8297117
4. Puybareau, É., et al.: Left atrial segmentation in a few seconds using fully convolutional network and transfer learning. In: Pop, M., et al. (eds.) STACOM 2018. LNCS, vol. 11395, pp. 339–347. Springer, Cham (2019). https://doi.org/10.1007/978-3-030-12029-0_37
5. Payer, C., Štern, D., Bischof, H., Urschler, M.: Multi-label whole heart segmentation using CNNs and anatomical label configurations. STACOM 2017. LNCS, vol. 10663, pp. 190–198. Springer, Cham (2018). https://doi.org/10.1007/978-3-319-75541-0_20

6. Wang, C.J., MacGillivray, T., Macnaught, G., Yang, G., Newby, D.: A two-stage 3D Unet framework for multi-class segmentation on full resolution image. CoRR abs/1804.04341 (2018)
7. Simonyan, K., Zisserman A.: Very deep convolutional networks for large-scale image recognition. CoRR abs/1409.1556 (2014)
8. Krizhevsky, A., Sutskever, I., Hinton G.E.: ImageNet classification with deep convolutional neural networks. In: Advances in Neural Information Processing Systems, pp. 1097–1105 (2012)
9. Long J., Shelhamer E., Darrell T.: Fully convolutional networks for semantic segmentation. In: Proceedings of CVPR, pp. 3431–3440. IEEE, Boston (2015)
10. Maninis, K.-K., Pont-Tuset, J., Arbeláez, P., Van Gool, L.: Deep retinal image understanding. In: Ourselin, S., Joskowicz, L., Sabuncu, M.R., Unal, G., Wells, W. (eds.) MICCAI 2016. LNCS, vol. 9901, pp. 140–148. Springer, Cham (2016). https://doi.org/10.1007/978-3-319-46723-8_17

Author Index

Printed in the United States
By Bookmasters